Peace Is a Shy Thing

Peace Is a Shy Thing

THE LIFE AND ART OF
TIM O'BRIEN

ALEX VERNON

ST. MARTIN'S
PRESS
NEW YORK

First published in the United States by St. Martin's Press,
an imprint of St. Martin's Publishing Group

www.stmartins.com

Designed by Steven Seighman

Map copyright © 2025 by Rhys Davies

The Library of Congress Cataloging-in-Publication Data
is available upon request.

ISBN 978-1-250-35849-3 (hardcover)
ISBN 978-1-250-35850-9 (ebook)

First Edition: 2025

10 9 8 7 6 5 4 3 2 1

For Quinn

and in loving memory of Barbara Vernon,
Ray Kaemmerling, and Ernie Harper

I'm young and happy. I'll never die. I'm skimming across the surface of my own history, moving fast, riding the melt beneath the blades, doing loops and spins, and when I take a high leap into the dark and come down thirty years later, I realize it is as Tim trying to save Timmy's life with a story.

Tim O'Brien
"The Lives of the Dead"
The Things They Carried

CONTENTS

PROLOGUE

March 14, 2020. York, Pennsylvania. Bob Wolf is reading *Dad's Maybe Book*, Tim O'Brien's latest, while his wife watches television in the other room.

"Bob, come look at this."

She replays the scene. A short, lean American soldier with glasses, high on drugs pilfered from a medic's kit, rows a Vietnamese boy out to fish by hand grenade. But he fumbles one, losing it in the water pooled at the bottom of the boat. His frenzied yelling fails to get the confused kid to jump out. What else can he do? He dives into the river to save himself. The explosion shatters the boat. Unlike the fish bodies, the boy's body never surfaces.

Bob has Renay go back to the opening credits. *Written by Kevin Falls & Tim O'Brien.*[1]

"Hey, isn't that your friend?" she asks.

Then: "What's wrong?"

"I was there," Bob answers. There and writing her a letter.

July 8, 1969. Quảng Ngãi Province, central Việt Nam. That morning, while Pfc. O'Brien sat radio watch in a sandbagged bunker about twenty meters from the South China Sea, the red-haired, mustached Sgt. Wolf, nicknamed "BuddyWolf," sat nearby writing Renay. It was a beautiful spot of earth, about a mile and a half of beach nestled between the sea's blues and the jungle's greens. Three bored American soldiers clambered into one of the shallow half-shell skiffs floating just off the beach to go fishing with hand grenades.

O'Brien and Wolf heard the exploding pop and raced to help. "Peterson's stomach area was a mess," O'Brien recalls. "I remember all the blood and seawater sloshing around at the bottom of the boat. I helped pull the boat in the last fifteen feet or so." Just after ten o'clock, he radioed battalion to request a helicopter dust-off for the casualties. Calling Peterson a KIA, killed-in-action, "was stretching it. Didn't know what else to say." The battalion daily log, referring to the American infantrymen as *packs*, recorded it thusly: "A Co called for urgent D/O at grid 775859 for 3 US packs with hand grenade frag wounds with 3 VN civ with frag wounds. Resulting from friendly handgrenade. D/O complete at 1030, taken to 27th Surg. Results: 1 US KIA, DOA, 2 US wounded, 3 VN wounded."[2]

Specialist Fourth Class Robert Walker Peterson, from Jacksonville, Florida, was twenty-one years old. He had been in Việt Nam for eight months. Wolf remembers that Peterson had only a week earlier returned from a Hawaii R&R with his girlfriend.[3] The military characterized his death as NON-HOSTILE, GROUND CASUALTY ACCIDENTAL SELF-DESTRUCTION. The other two Americans received fragmentation wounds to multiple parts of their bodies.

◊　◊　◊

Tim O'Brien has become the preeminent American writer of the war in Việt Nam. *The Things They Carried* is a staple of high school and higher education classrooms, appearing on more college and university course reading lists globally than any other U.S. novel or any other modern novel.[4] It became the most proposed individual book by local communities under the National Endowment of the Arts "Big Read" initiative; the general public chose it as one of forty titles for the Library of Congress's 2016 "America Reads" list of "books by American authors that had a profound effect on American life." The book's title story is the most anthologized American story of its era. It was the answer to a March 3, 2023, *Jeopardy!* question.

The Things They Carried is O'Brien's most widely beloved book, but *Going After Cacciato* and *In the Lake of the Woods* are equally significant. The first, which won the 1979 National Book Award, changed the course of the American literary response to the war. The second, from 1994, demanded that Americans never forget their own capacity for violent evil. O'Brien is the only writer of fiction to date to have won the prestigious Pritzker Award for Lifetime Achievement in Military Writing. He has supplanted Ernest Hemingway as the touchstone for the post-9/11 generation of literary-minded American veterans. In March 2022, O'Brien was elected to membership in the American Academy of Arts and Letters.

Nothing could have surprised Timmy O'Brien from Worthington, Minnesota, more. In his 1950s small-town childhood, O'Brien fantasized about becoming a writer but never spoke of his ambition because it seemed so remote a possibility. In high school and college, he steered toward graduate school, journalism, and politics. Then the war in Việt Nam "collided" with his life and "made" him a writer. He has said this time after time. O'Brien has devoted his career to exploring individual lives caught in the swirling onrush of events, people made by history and making their personal histories moment by moment.

While this literary biography covers O'Brien's entire life and career, at its heart is one writer's apparently unlikely beginnings on his way to being regarded as one of the best writers of his generation: "What he can do with language is what language can do."[5] This is the story of how the writer and the work, the individual works, came to be. At its heart of hearts is the war. Tim O'Brien's story is bigger than Tim O'Brien. Had he graduated from college in 1967 or 1969 instead of 1968, for example, he very well might not have ended up in Việt Nam. That's not O'Brien's story only, that's the country's story, too. His grandparents were born in the nineteenth century, his own children in the twenty-first; his maternal grandfather broke wild horses, his sons game on iPhones.

In his prime, O'Brien worked seven or more hours a day, six or seven days a week, often not breaking for birthdays or holidays. His peers at the annual Bread Loaf Writers' Conference recognized him as "one of the hardest-working writers in contemporary literature."[6] A fastidious writer, O'Brien would retype an entire page for a single correction rather than type over lines or mark up a draft page. He needed to see clean pages, as his reader would, to take in the length, shape, and rhythm of his sentences and paragraphs. He reworked each sentence to invest it with the immediacy of first utterance; rereading it, however many years later, should return him to the moment and emotion of its creation. A perfectionist, O'Brien revised published works for future printings. A feisty manager of his career, he early on fired off irritated letters to his publisher whenever he didn't see his books in stores. This was often the case in airports because he traveled a lot to give talks, do readings and interviews, and sell books. A friend once ran into him at a Harvard Square bookstore rearranging the shelves so that his books' covers faced out to catch a browser's eye.[7]

He's disarmingly short, five-seven on a good day. "Small, dark and elfin," one interviewer described O'Brien, fresh off his win for the NBA, with "a handshake that could cripple a wrestler and a smile that slides at you sideways."[8] He talks out of the side of his mouth, and as a younger man he spoke rather quickly (a debate team habit). His piercing movie star eyes peer at you past the pronounced nose. He's often restlessly energetic, at other times quite unassuming, shy even, and laid-back. An introvert who can stand on the sidelines or be the life of the party.

The writer Stanley Elkin once said of him, "Tim O'Brien is so humble, it's arrogant."[9] The small-town boy has owned very few suits over his adult life. He might hesitate to accept a speaking engagement because he genuinely feels he has nothing to say, although he'll do it if the price is right; he knows to check his inner hotshot because he's smarter and more articulate than most and knows it:

> And that's probably why I still wear a baseball cap and dress in blue jeans and not try to, you know, look fancy and so on. It's to remind myself of that. That you can achieve a lot but in the end we're all more or less in the same human boat. You know. Do the best we can through life making our mistakes and suffering our injuries and enjoying our joys. But as my dad once said, Tim, you gotta, you gotta avoid looking like you think you're a hotshot. I thought that word, *hotshot*, still hurts to this day, I think of that word.[10]

That's one reason for the steadfast caps, which he started wearing pre-fame in 1977 to cover his balding head.[11] It took decades for O'Brien to outgrow (mostly) the compensatory superiority of the bookish, insecure teen. His success baffles him, even though he believes it is utterly deserved. He's a retiring soul and an aggressive self-promoter, a homebody who has spent decades constantly leaving home for various events and gigs.

O'Brien is affable, warm, loyal, and funny. But he pounces on perceived intellectual faults. An illogical position affronts him; he can't say *It doesn't make any sense!* without the exclamation mark. He can be prickly to the point of being a prick. Quick-tempered since youth, especially over perceived wrongs and injustices. When riled up, he spits out go-to words, *rectitude, hypocrisy, evil*, for offenses grand and venial, often with an accompanying finger jab. When his computer glitches, he shouts to everyone in hearing range—in full pissed-off infantryman mode—that the machine has it out for him. For all his indignation about hypocrisies and betrayals, however, he didn't always conduct his personal life above reproach. He had trouble trusting; he had trouble being trustworthy.

O'Brien's good humor stands on a foundation of anxiety and rage. Toward the father he adored but could never seem to please—oldest son and namesake and all—the father he worried about becoming. Toward the magnanimous nation and the polite hometown that sent him to a repugnant war. Toward himself for letting them send him, the great moral failure of his life. Toward death for being itself, the hole that laughs at us all.

"The war and my person seemed like twins as I went around the town's lake," he wrote in his first book, the 1973 war memoir *If I Die in a Combat Zone, Box Me Up and Ship Me Home*, about the summer he let himself be drafted. "Twins grafted together and forever together, as if separation would kill them both.

"The thought made me angry."[12]

O'Brien resents being known as a war writer. The label misleadingly reduces the range and depth of his artistic expressions. He believes it diminishes his craft and belittles his accomplishments. The label also belies his struggle with being a combatant in the first place. Soldiering lives far outside his nature—that's what his books are about, the anti-soldier, not the warrior. Of the many honors he has accumulated, he most treasures the Dayton Literary Peace Prize's Richard C. Holbrooke Distinguished Achievement Award, the only one that recognizes the spirit of *why* he writes, *what* he writes, *how* he writes:

> I think that most good literature about war has to do not with war itself, it has to do with a reminder to all of us of all the things that are lost to human beings through wars. Not just lives but civility

and decency and politeness. Acts of generosity and kindness. Human concord. . . . How much you love your mom and your dad, and how much you love the feeling of a Sunday afternoon and walking down the street and seeing the sun is shining and the clouds are up there and there's a lawn mower buzzing down the street and there's a water sprinkler going.

Peace is a shy thing. It does not brag about itself the way wars are loud and noisy and you know you're in it. But you don't think at this instant "I'm at peace" 'til the word *peace* is said and you shut up for a second and . . . there's the peace.[13]

There it is.

O'Brien's peace came with his 2001 marriage to Meredith Baker and the arrival of their two children, Timmy—later Tim—and Tad. In his early seventies, O'Brien wrote *Dad's Maybe Book* as an epistolary memoir to his sons. But he also saw it, and Aaron Matthews's documentary film *The War and Peace of Tim O'Brien*, largely about the writing of the book, as offerings to their audiences. Maybe "they'll learn something about a man's journey, and maybe be able to use some of what they've learned for their own journey throughout their time on the planet." Maybe they will recognize something of their own pain and struggles and "be slightly emboldened or encouraged or at least have a sense of company that somebody else has taken this journey, too."[14]

Which is also why (isn't it?) we read—and write—biographies.

PART I

1

COLLISION

In 1964, the year Tim O'Brien started at Macalester College in St. Paul, Minnesota, Americans killed in Southeast Asia numbered a publicly invisible 216.[1] Congress had recently passed the Gulf of Tonkin resolution authorizing military force, but President Lyndon Johnson hadn't acted upon it. For many of O'Brien's generation, Việt Nam was little more than the fantastical setting for the 1963 debut of Marvel Comics' Iron Man, where deep "in a South Vietnam Jungle" millionaire inventor and playboy Tony Stark dons the high-tech suit to battle the menacing "WONG-CHU, THE RED GUERILLA TYRANT!"[2]

O'Brien turned eighteen on October 1 and dutifully registered for the draft from campus.[3] By the end of his first semester, he received his II-S Selective Service classification, the college deferment.[4] He couldn't be drafted.

Instead of the escalating military conflict half a world away, civil rights commanded student attention. Two years earlier, white mob violence protesting the integration of the University of Mississippi by James Meredith left 160 wounded marshals and two dead citizens. At the end of that academic year—O'Brien's high school junior year—officials in Birmingham, Alabama, countered a peaceful march by blasting Black children and youth with fire hoses and setting German shepherds upon them. More violence and confrontation followed. A month later, the Black civil rights activist and World War II combat veteran Medgar Evers was assassinated in Jackson, Mississippi.

Police brutality led to Black unrest in northern cities such as New York and Philadelphia the summer before O'Brien started college. During the white backlash against the Freedom Summer voter registration drive in Mississippi, "1,062 people were arrested, 80 Freedom Summer workers were beaten, 37 churches were bombed or burned, 30 Black homes or businesses were bombed or burned, four civil rights workers were killed, and at least three Mississippi African Americans were murdered because of their involvement in this movement."[5] The search for three disappeared activists—James Chaney, Andrew Goodman, and Michael Schwerner— riveted the nation for forty-four days until the FBI found their bodies. The monumental Civil Rights Act passed that summer.

Over the January interim term, the freshman O'Brien joined the debaters who piled into cars to tour throughout the Midwest, South, and East Coast. Since Yankees and college students had energized the early 1960s Freedom Rides and the Freedom Summer and suffered for it, driving to the University of Southern Mississippi was nerve-racking for O'Brien's carload. They drove fast, kept their debate trophies out of sight, and half joked about muddying their station wagon's license plate to disguise their northern origin.[6] There was a Freedom Rally in the spring at the student union welcoming home the sixteen students who had traveled to Montgomery and Selma to witness the national movement firsthand.[7]

Students mostly just hit the books, however. For many colleges, "a high dropout rate showed outsiders that a college was rigorous."[8] O'Brien was studious even for a studious campus. He recalls little social life over his four years. He lacked a car and money. His close friends were on the debate team and in student government. A date meant hanging out on campus, typically at the student union, or maybe seeing a movie. O'Brien remembers only one concert, the Lettermen. Chances are he could be found in his dorm room or in the library studying, or at the campus daytime coffeehouse and evening club venue No Exit his junior and senior years, strategizing on how to manage the student body issue of the day.

He'd always been an excellent student. His second-grade teacher's end-of-year write-up is typical of his elementary years:

> Timmy has made very good progress in reading and phonetic skills. He has become quite independent in word recognition. He has

a good understanding of a number of meanings and is accurate in number facts.

Timmy's work habits are excellent. He works well with a group. He has a nice attitude toward his work, and toward the other children. He is conscientious, courteous, and dependable.

Timmy contributes many worthwhile ideas. He expresses himself well. He enjoys dramatic activities. He participates in physical activities with enthusiasm.

Timmy has been an outstanding second grader. It has been a joy to work with him.[9]

Studious from the get-go.

In high school, O'Brien earned a fully funded spot on the annual United Nations Pilgrimage for Youth by winning an essay contest on the topic "What Has the United Nations Done to Preserve Peace?" The Odd Fellows fraternal organization's local chapter sponsored his trip. He left on June 15, 1963, for New York City to observe the UN before traveling down to Washington, D.C., where the Minnesota delegates rode in the Fourth of July parade and saw the sights—his postcard home mentions the Washington Monument and the Marine Corps War Memorial (the Iwo Jima statue, at the time not quite ten years old). The trip made stops at Gettysburg, Valley Forge, and Mount Vernon.[10] His leaders and the itinerary aside, O'Brien felt he was venturing into the world for the very first time. Those were giddy, liberating days.

Macalester awarded O'Brien one of five George F. Baker scholarships, covering all school expenses including his dorm housing and meal plan. Over the next four years, he often bummed dimes from people to get a soda and caught rides or hitchhiked between St. Paul and Worthington, his small hometown in the southern part of the state.

The nation underwent a sea change during O'Brien's time at Macalester. The war's numbers tell part of that story: from 216 U.S. personnel killed in 1964 to 16,899 in 1968, the deadliest year for Americans, the year O'Brien graduated.[11]

◊   ◊   ◊

In O'Brien's senior year he flubbed the interview for a Rhodes Scholarship to study at the University of Oxford after graduation, but it was an accomplishment to have made it to the interview stage. The conclusion of his application essay foretells the cogency, honesty, and vulnerability that will become the hallmark of his best writing. Here, the mix of confidence and humility touches on the insecurity that often afflicts the young and bookish:

> Finally, I need to say something about what I intend to do with my education; about what motivates me to continue academic inquiry.
>
> I am governed to a frightening degree by day to day needs and instinct; I constantly hover five or ten pounds overweight; I am always ready to drop what I am doing, no matter how important it is, to do what excites me at the moment; it is nearly impossible for me to organize my time and energies effectively. I take pleasure in my own excellence, in my own achievements, and in furthering my own self-image. These are irrational needs and acts, and I recognize them as real problems. Try as I may, however, their solution escapes me, leaving me stranded and spending my time forever plotting against this side of myself.
>
> My college years have been spent, by and large, trying to resolve some of these problems. Academia has helped but not remedied the problem of disorganization. A measure of academic success has only intensified the pleasure I have taken in my personal achievements, and I do not expect to ever find a remedy for that flaw. The major problem, the crucial one, revolves around my self-esteem. I want to respect myself, and when I look at my life, I want to say that it is good.
>
> Academic life has helped in this respect. I value knowledge, and when I am learning, I feel that a worthwhile process is occurring. Wisdom is largely a function of knowledge, and my self-respect is largely a function of how I assess my wisdom. Academic life has also taught me that a large part of my self-respect hinges on my *acting* in accordance with my knowledge and conscience.[12]

O'Brien's conscience would be tested soon enough.

He still had high hopes for admission into graduate school at Harvard's

Kennedy School of Government. "We're going to get you into Harvard, boy!" Dr. Theodore Mitau regularly boomed. Mitau, O'Brien's political science mentor, had fled Nazi Germany in the 1930s, the only member of his family to survive the Holocaust. He wrote the book on state politics, *Politics in Minnesota*, published in 1960, then three more political science books during O'Brien's Macalester years, while also consulting and working for governmental and nongovernmental public service agencies and offices. Suffice it to say, he was well connected.

The war helped motivate O'Brien's run for president of the Community Council—Macalester's student government—to organize what small antiwar gestures he could.[13] Under his leadership, the CC supported a nine-day "Vietnam Days" slate of activities and protests. It tried to pass a resolution on a letter to President Johnson condemning the war. It gave one hundred dollars to the Vietnam Relief Fund to support an orphanage in Cần Thơ, the largest city south of Sài Gòn. It endorsed the Macalester Committee for Peace in Vietnam's call to teachers either to cancel Friday afternoon classes or to conduct a "teach-in" on the war.[14]

O'Brien lacked the time and inclination for more personal anti-war activism. He did not make the fifteen-hundred-mile trip to D.C. with twelve other Macites to join the legendary march on the Pentagon in October 1967,[15] the subject of Norman Mailer's *Armies of the Night*. He did not join the peaceful protest outside Applebaum's grocery store three blocks north of campus, where three students were arrested for trespassing when passing out flyers encouraging people to boycott Dow products such as plastic wraps because Dow made napalm.[16] O'Brien did not participate in the next weekend's similar action by twenty-four students outside a Kroger grocery store.[17] He did not take a turn fasting for a day in an organized continuous collective protest.[18] The young O'Brien believed in institutions. He believed in working within the system. Protests, especially at that level, seemed pointless. Besides, he'd never been much of a joiner.

In January 1968, Macalester inaugurated the International Distinguished Service Award for twenty-somethings who could inspire Mac students. As CC president, O'Brien had a hand in extending the invitations. One of the five recipients that first year was David Gitelson, a Californian then in the International Voluntary Service stationed in Việt Nam's Mê Kông Delta. The gangly twenty-six-year-old cut a Johnny Appleseed figure, "roaming the Delta backwaters in blue jeans and flipflops, his voluminous sack filled with seed samples and mimeographed tips for farmers that he had painstakingly typed in Vietnamese on scraps of notebook paper."[19] Gitelson initially declined, writing with characteristic humility and cynicism to O'Brien that he rejected the "phony publicity" his work had received from people who had no idea if he did any good. He relented after his Washington, D.C., supervisor and O'Brien cabled pleas.[20] Another IVS worker went to Macalester to accept the award on Gitelson's behalf.[21] On the very day of the award, January 26, Gitelson's friends in Việt Nam learned that he had been killed under murky circumstances.[22]

Despite O'Brien's role in the award process, he remembers nothing about it. It's possible he simply signed messages to Gitelson written by Macalester's International Center. The significant event for O'Brien that interim term, perhaps distracting him from most everything else, was a girl.

A pretty blonde, Gayle Roby was a sophomore English major from St. Olaf College in Northfield, just south of the Twin Cities, taking an interim course on existentialism at Mac. According to Roby, they went to a bar at the top of a building in St. Paul with another couple for their first date; O'Brien had gotten an ID she could use, although she felt uncomfortable about it. On their second date they saw *Bonnie and Clyde* at the old Uptown Theater. He put his hand on her knee, only to jerk it away after she looked at him with surprise—just as Lt. Jimmy Cross pulls his hand from Martha's knee during the same movie's final scene in O'Brien's story "The Things They Carried."

That was it. They lived on different campuses and neither had a car. As Big Man on Campus, O'Brien was incredibly busy. He and Roby never really had a chance to know one another. Still, he became intensely smitten with the *idea* of her.

In February, he resumed dating Jane Reister, also a pretty blonde, whom he'd met a year earlier. O'Brien had agreed to participate in a debate event's extemporaneous speaking competition. The coach told a teammate he hadn't met yet—Reister—to help prepare him, as his time and energies had been elsewhere that year. A day or two after they met, O'Brien called to ask her if she would work on his campaign to become the junior class president.

"Maybe you could organize the freshman girls."

"But I'm not a freshman."

Thus began the "wonderful spring," Reister says, when she fell in love with Tim O'Brien. Jane was a sophomore from Oscaloosa, Iowa. The youngest of three girls by several years, the only one born after World War II, she was the indulged one, and at five foot four the tallest one. Like O'Brien, Reister came under debate's spell in high school. To Jane, Tim was smart, cute, and attentive, a campus busybody and newspaper headliner who knew a lot of people and appeared to be outgoing. She wouldn't discover his introspective nature until later. O'Brien went abroad to Europe that summer, and they took a break in the fall. She was always more in love with him than he was with her.

Meanwhile, on January 30, the military forces of North Việt Nam and the National Liberation Front had launched their massive joint operation in the south known as the Tết Offensive. It was the largest operation by either side to date, leading to the largest death toll and delivering the most disheartening images of the war—of Việt Cộng guerrillas fleetingly occupying the U.S. embassy in Sài Gòn and of General Nguyễn Ngọc Loan executing Nguyễn Văn Lém in the middle of a Sài Gòn street, Eddie Adams having snapped the famous photo the instant the revolver bullet burst through Lém's head. After several weeks South Việt Nam and the United States legitimately claimed military success, but Americans' support for the war would never be the same.

On Friday, February 16, O'Brien returned to Dupre Hall. Walking down the fifth-floor east-wing hallway through a cluster of other guys, he overheard the news of the end of graduate school deferments. He retreated into his dorm room and plunked into his desk chair. He stepped back out to make sure he'd heard right: no more graduate school deferments. Back at his desk, staring at the greenish cinder-block walls, he felt physically ill. He was an intellectual who knew nothing about guns, next to nothing about the outdoors, destined, he thought, for Harvard. His smugness about his value to the world, his confidence in his future, dissipated. Whenever Tim O'Brien recounts that afternoon, the bottom drops out all over again.

Within the week, O'Brien learned that he was one of eight seniors from Macalester, and one of 1,124 seniors throughout North America, designated as Woodrow Wilson Fellows worthy of graduate school financial support for their promise as future college instructors.[23] What bittersweet news.

He considered the navy as a way to avoid the combat infantry. It had been his parents' branch of service in World War II.[24] Ava Eleanor Schultz had enlisted in the U.S Naval Reserves in 1943 under the WAVES program (Women Accepted for Volunteer Emergency Service) and within a month received orders for active duty. After training in New York City and Milledgeville, Georgia, Ava served at the Norfolk Operating Base in Norfolk, Virginia, from February 1944 to September 1945. For three months she worked at the base movie theater before being transferred to an assignment as a store cashier and stock clerk.[25] That's when she met and fell in love with Bill (William Timothy) O'Brien.

Bill O'Brien enlisted in the navy reserves one month to the day after the Japanese attack on Pearl Harbor, entering active duty a week later. On January 13, 1942, he was assigned to the Office of the Commander, North Atlantic Naval Coastal Frontier, located in Manhattan, which a month later became the Eastern Sea Frontier, with responsibilities for the waters off the East Coast.[26] After stints preparing warships in New Orleans and in Long Beach, New York, Bill reported to Norfolk, Virginia, on September 5, 1943, to undergo training on his way to duty aboard a brand-new destroyer, the USS *McGowan*. In November, Bill transferred to the Brooklyn Navy Yard to join the *McGowan*'s crew, probably in time for its November 14 launch, only to come down with pneumonia; he transferred ten days later to the USS *St. Albans* Naval Hospital Ship docked at Long Island. During Bill's recuperation, the *McGowan* was commissioned for service and got underway, bound for the Pacific. Bill's illness resulted in reassignment to office work back at Norfolk beginning January 8, 1944, while awaiting a new ship posting. A month later, Ava arrived at Norfolk.

It was a head-over-heels wartime courtship of only a few months. The USS *John W. Weeks* was commissioned at the Brooklyn Navy Yard on July 21, the same day Bill's records indicate he reported on board.[27] On November 10, the *Weeks* departed New York along with three battleships and two escort carriers. A month earlier, and five days after his promotion to chief yeoman, Bill managed a quick trip to Norfolk to get married, in the David Adams Memorial Chapel, on October 6, 1944.[28] According to an announcement in a Minneapolis paper, the newlyweds "went to New York on a wedding trip," really to see Bill back to the *Weeks*.[29]

The *Weeks* linked up with the Third Fleet at Ulithi Atoll on December 27 and participated in four major operations. On April 7, during the Battle of Okinawa, the *Weeks* was pulling alongside the USS *Hancock* to pass over reconnaissance photographs when a kamikaze crashed into the *Hancock's* flight deck, hurling men and debris into the sea. The *Weeks* rescued twenty-three survivors from the water. The *Weeks* often formed picket or screen lines with other destroyers, acting as early warning for the main fleet from enemy planes and ships. Its final operation of the war included two days in July sweeping the vicinity of Tokyo Bay and fighting off four flights of kamikaze planes the afternoon of August 9—just a few short hours after the atomic bomb Fat Man devastated Nagasaki, three days after Little Boy had destroyed Hiroshima. The war in the Pacific over, Bill's and Ava's military careers promptly ended.

Timmy, his sister, Kathy, and their much younger brother, Greg, grew up hearing the stories of their parents' whirlwind romance and their father's life at sea. Bill's published articles about his service were one source of O'Brien's boyhood dream of writing.[30]

The navy as an escape from the draft made sense. It would be far safer than in his dad's day. It made sense, except that signing up with any branch struck O'Brien as acceptance and moral compromise. He wasn't willing to do it. Joining the National Guard could have resulted in being ordered to point a loaded rifle at fellow citizens, at friends even, on the streets of Minneapolis or St. Paul.

Then, on the *CBS Evening News* of February 27, Walter Cronkite, one of the most trusted figures in America, having just returned from Việt Nam, declared the war all but lost.[31] When the anchorman of anchormen spoke, Middle America heeded.

O'Brien hoped to make his way home to Worthington to caucus for Eugene McCarthy.[32] His Minnesota senator was the only major candidate running to end the war. In the evening's two-precinct straw poll, President Johnson won 39–13 over McCarthy,[33] although McCarthy fared better than expected. He finished a close second in New Hampshire a week later.

On March 14, the Minnesota press reported that Dr. Mitau had been

appointed the chancellor of the state college system. While Mitau's last semester on campus was O'Brien's as well, the news must have added to the
semester's gloom.

Meanwhile:

On March 16, in Quảng Ngãi Province, central Việt Nam, an infantry
platoon marched into a sub-hamlet and slaughtered some four hundred
civilians. Old men, women, and children. Babies. Many of the victims were
beaten, many of the women raped, before being murdered. The crimes at
the place the perpetrators called Mỹ Lai 4 would not come to light for the
American public for another eighteen months.

That same day, Robert Kennedy declared his candidacy for the U.S.
presidency.

"Here at Macalester College," O'Brien later remarked, "the world began
to heat up, you could smell the smoke you could feel the beginnings of a
sizzle in your blood."[34]

On March 19, sixteen-year-old high school student Ronald Brazee set himself on fire in Syracuse, New York: "If giving my life will shorten the war by
even one day, it will not have been in vain." He died in the hospital almost
six weeks later.[35]

On Wednesday, March 20, a Macalester chaplain, Rev. Alvin Currier, led a
program to increase awareness of alternatives to the draft, such as "conscientious objectorship, alternative service, and non-cooperation."[36] None of
which felt like real options for O'Brien.

The weekend of March 23 and 24, O'Brien and Reister joined the Macalester bus to neighboring Wisconsin on behalf of McCarthy's campaign, in
advance of the state's April 2 primary.[37] McCarthy supporters from other
Minnesota colleges did the same.[38] The students had to *get clean for Gene*,
had to make themselves look as upstanding as possible—O'Brien almost
missed the bus getting dressed and ready. Tim and Jane trooped around
Superior, Wisconsin. The trip felt a little pointless, as they mostly knocked
on doors in decidedly Republican blue-collar neighborhoods.

The Nobles County Democratic-Farmer-Labor convention was held on Saturday, March 30, in the county library in Worthington. O'Brien remembers caucusing for McCarthy in that basement DFL assembly. Johnson's fifty-one votes that evening easily beat McCarthy's twelve and Kennedy's four.[39]

During his television broadcast the next evening, President Johnson announced the beginning of the end: "Tonight, in the hope that this action will lead to early talks, I am taking the first step to de-escalate the conflict [. . .] unilaterally and at once." Operation Rolling Thunder, the bombing that had been ongoing since February 1965, would be significantly curtailed and eventually ceased as the president declared his intention to pursue "genuine peace."[40] Thereafter, every American serving in Việt Nam and every American still to serve in Việt Nam ran the risk of becoming, in the words of navy lieutenant John Kerry three years later, "the last man to die in Vietnam," the "last man to die for a mistake."[41]

Johnson finished his speech with the shocking news that he would not stand for reelection to the presidency. Cheering erupted in the Macalester dorms. Students whooped their way outside to celebrate. O'Brien stayed behind.

On the morning of April 2, two Macalester students, Charles Dingman and David Fisher, ceremonially refused to participate in the draft. About forty supporters attended the event. The students handed their draft cards to Dr. Lloyd Gaston, who "received them in the name of the church" to return to the respective draft boards, placing himself in violation of the Selective Service Act as well, subject to the same potential penalties.[42]

On April 4, James Earl Ray shot and killed the Rev. Martin Luther King, Jr., in Memphis, Tennessee. Cities across America erupted. In some cities, including the nation's capital, the local police, the National Guard, and the U.S. Army struggled to quell the civil disorder.

On April 11, Worthington's hometown army reserve unit was ordered to active duty, its soldiers among the 24,500 reservists called up that day by the U.S. secretary of defense, of whom about 10,000 would deploy to Southeast

Asia.[43] Until now, President Johnson had declined to send reservists and National Guardsmen because he needed to maintain the image of a limited war and to mitigate opposition among the "better connected, better educated, more affluent, and whiter" families whose sons joined their local units rather than risk being drafted.[44] The spring 1968 call-up responded to the growing criticism that the draft disproportionally put minorities and the working class into harm's way. It sent a message to those who suddenly no longer qualified for graduate school deferments, to college seniors like Tim O'Brien.

On Friday, May 10, delegates from the United States and North Việt Nam met in Paris to begin negotiating for peace, while over at the Sorbonne students clashed with police on the streets. According to the headlines, the same week set a new U.S. casualty record for soldiers killed in action, at 562.[45]

On May 17, Father Daniel Berrigan, his brother Father Philip Berrigan, and seven other Catholics against the war removed hundreds of files from the Catonsville, Maryland, Selective Service office and destroyed them in the yard with homemade napalm. "Our apologies, good friends, for the fracture of good order, the burning of paper instead of children, the angering of the orderlies in the front parlor of the charnel house. We could not, so help us God, do otherwise."[46]

On May 27, Tim O'Brien and 363 classmates graduated from Macalester College "into a world in which the moral and spiritual furniture ha[d] been rearranged," he would much later remark.[47]

During graduation week, O'Brien told Reister his life goals. One of them, she recalls, was "to write the great American novel by the time he was thirty." She met his parents and little brother.

He packed up his belongings and headed home to Worthington to wait.

2

BUSY TIMMY

After their war, Ava and Bill O'Brien settled in southern Minnesota just west of her hometown of Harmony. Austin, the Mower County seat, was a growing town of about twenty-three thousand when Tim O'Brien was born there on October 1, 1946, at eight thirty in the morning at St. Olaf's Hospital.[1] Why had Bill conceded to move to rural Minnesota? To be sure, he adored Ava. Over fifteen years later, during his second two-month institutionalization for alcoholism, Bill would write home about his "'what might have been' torment."[2]

Born and raised in Brooklyn, New York, to an Irish Catholic family surrounded by Irish Catholic families one or two generations removed from Ireland—if not recent arrivals—Bill loved Brooklyn to his core. Everyone called him Willie. The family lived in his mother's parents' house on Madison Street along with her sister, one of her uncles, and a boarder.[3] His children heard the stories. Stickball in the Bedford-Stuyvesant neighborhood streets, trips to Coney Island, pickup games of baseball and football at Prospect Park's Parade Grounds, five-cent ice cream, and the Dodgers over at Ebbets Field back when major-league baseball felt like a hometown affair. The subway was still a novelty for adults and an adventure for children. During the Great War, energy emanated from the Brooklyn Navy Yard from the men and money pouring in to build the country's battleships. World history was on the cusp of the American century. In the side streets, the din and thrum from Flatbush Avenue mixed with the sweet warm smells of neighborhood bakeries and the colors of apartment-window flower boxes.[4]

On Bill's eleventh birthday, February 28, 1925, his forty-five-year-old father, the first William Timothy O'Brien, died of a heart attack. Tim O'Brien was about the same age when Bill told him about it. O'Brien sympathetically imagined the loss of his own father as "the greatest horror that could visit me." He wondered how his dad had kept going. Bill's mom never remarried. When Bill became a father, he had only vague memories of how a father might love a son.

Bill dropped out of high school after three years. He had been working to contribute since he was twelve, but the Great Depression, which hit when he was fifteen, forced him to give up formal book learning for office training and clerical work.[5] It's impossible to know if he resented or relished his role as the family's oldest male. He loved books and learning his entire life. His children remember him as one of the most well-read adults of their Minnesota childhood. One didn't need a college degree to write, which he dreamed of doing, but it certainly helped. One obviously needed a college degree to earn a doctorate, which may have been a later fantasy.[6]

Nevertheless, Bill O'Brien came into his own in the late thirties. He was a smart, hardworking, personable young man. He could write and tell great stories. In 1936, he landed a job in the Printing Department of the New York World's Fair; by the time the fair opened, in 1939, he had taken the top post in the department, supervising thirty others.[7] The fair finished, Bill moved into hotel management at the plush Royal Victoria Hotel in Nassau, the Bahamas. After one month at the front desk, he was promoted to front office manager, and ten weeks later to second assistant manager. The same company ran the New Prospect Hotel in Shelter Island Heights on the eastern end of Long Island, to which he transferred when the Victoria wrapped up its winter season. Back in New York, Bill handled all reservations, supervised the front office staff, and worked with travel agents. He also finally scratched his itch to write, assisting the editor of the *Shelter Island News*.

These had been Bill's golden years. The World's Fair and the hotels, especially the Royal Victoria—dubbed the Grande Dame of the Bahamas—gave him a taste of cosmopolitanism and glamour. Although the Eighteenth Amendment was repealed in 1933, places like Nassau and Havana were still coasting on their Prohibition-era good-time-getaway reputations. Bill was eager to return to Nassau when the world delivered its infamous insistence, on December 7, 1941, that the United States could no longer sit out the war.

The small towns of the southern Minnesota plains were Ava Eleanor Shultz's world. Born in 1916 in Le Roy, she grew up on a horse-powered farm outside Harmony, the third of five daughters (counting an older sister, born a year earlier, who died in infancy). Tim O'Brien and his younger-by-one-year sister, Kathy, remember milk cows lumbering about, chickens always underfoot, their grandparents Paul and Myrtle canning everything, and a creepy bare-earth cellar beneath the house accessed by a slanted exterior door. Corn and soybeans were the area's major crops. Ava's dad traveled to the Dakotas once a year to bring back wild horses to break, some to keep, the rest to sell. Ava could behead a chicken if she needed to.

After high school, Ava worked at the Wesley Temple Drug Company in Minneapolis for a year before returning home to teach in a nearby rural one-room county schoolhouse. It was a hard five years, waking up before dawn to get to the building ready for the day; feeding and stoking the coal furnace; managing children from first to eighth grades all at once; helping the younger ones with clothes and shoes and food; and staying late to straighten the room, take care of minor maintenance, and prepare for the next day. She spent her summers back at the drugstore in the city. After a two-year course at Winona State Teachers College in elementary education, in 1941 she started teaching third grade in Preston, ten miles from Harmony.[8] Ava enlisted out of the patriotic fervor sweeping the country, for the adventure and independence rarely available to young women from the rural Midwest, and to tend a broken heart after her fiancé started up with another local girl (the mahogany hope chest he gave her survived the breakup to live at the foot of her marriage bed with Bill). After the war, she did what her upbringing trained her to do by returning home, new husband in tow.

Bill took a job as a car salesman. Southern Minnesota was flat farm country ripe for tornadoes, flooding, and accidents: car accidents, hunting accidents, boating and swimming accidents. Conformity and boredom were its other killers.

The young family lived in Austin for O'Brien's first seven years. Baby Timmy held his head up at two weeks; sat up at four and a half months; started to creep at five and a half months, stand at eight months, and walk at eleven months. His first tooth poked through at nine months. At ten months he spoke his first words—"Daddy, Hi!"—followed not long thereafter by *Judy, doggie, dirty, good, sure,* and *see.*[9]

Kathy came along fourteen months later.[10] Growing up, brother and sister were thick as thieves. Their costumes, always homemade, almost always matched: cowboy and cowgirl, Peter Pan and Tinker Bell. He teased her with a ditty that began "Stupid brainless no-good Kath—she's a dope, she needs a bath." She got even by calling him "Tubby T-Bone." Even in their junior high school years, when they drifted apart to make their individual ways in the world, they came up with pet names for one another, "Dub" and "Timothy-Wimothy."

Bill pulled the toddlers about in a red wagon and on a sled. He tossed balls for Timmy to catch or clumsily swing a bat at. Although not an outdoorsy family, they took some trips to nearby lakes and tried their hands at fishing. Despite their navy years, Bill and Ava weren't swimmers. They didn't teach their kids to swim.

For several weeks each summer, the working parents dropped the pair off each morning at Roy and Gladys Fickbohm's farm. Bill and Roy worked together as service managers for Park Motor Company, although by 1950 Bill had taken his first insurance sales job, with Equitable Life Assurance Society.[11] O'Brien and his sister adored the Fickbohms, who gave them the run of the farm under the care of their son Jimmy, ten years older than little Timmy. Those were blissful days of tractor rides and horses.

When O'Brien was three or four, he waded into a pond and sat in water over his head. He very nearly drowned in that stinky, filthy farm pond, but he wasn't frightened. A mysterious fish "like a barber's razor" passed in front of his face. Jimmy pulled O'Brien out. O'Brien returned the favor by naming a character after him in "The Things They Carried"—it's Jimmy Fickbohm's face that O'Brien sees when he pictures 1st Lt. Jimmy Cross. O'Brien also fired a weapon for the first time at the farm, a .22 shotgun. He practiced on a nest he thought was empty, only to watch dead hatchlings tumble to the ground. In his seventies, he still feels remorse.

Timmy the first grader and Kathy the kindergartner were too young to take stock of their mom's mental health crisis. Ava's mother had died the year before. O'Brien began dreading his own mother's death.[12]

Bill drove Ava to the Mayo Clinic in Rochester, an hour from Austin, in late November 1952 for two days. Her records describe physical ailments. She returned a few days later as an emergency referral from her local physician for mental and emotional health issues he could not manage. She went home that day, her troubles hardly behind her. Ava stayed at the Mayo in February 1953 for fifteen days, for a single day in June, and then for eight days in August. Upon discharge, the doctors recommended a regimen of "deep insulin comas" at Rochester State Hospital. Also known as insulin shock therapy, the treatment required hospitalization (institutionalization) for a diagnosis of acute schizophrenia. According to the Mayo doctors, Ava suffered depression, severe insecurity, paranoia, and faulty percepts and object relations leading to disturbing imaginings.[13] To fantasies and terrors.

Ava checked into the state hospital that very day, August 13, for a five-month stay.[14] Less than three miles apart, the Mayo Clinic and the Rochester State Hospital had a deep working relationship with a pipeline from the private clinic to the state institution. The clinic drove the hospital's early adoption of aggressive procedures such as shock therapies and lobotomies, beginning in 1941 and continuing well into the 1950s. Ninety-one Rochester patients underwent prefrontal lobotomies during the two-year period ending June 30, 1954. Mayo personnel performed procedures, provided consultations, and conducted research at Rochester. Although a reform movement was underway, Rochester still faced some of the overpopulation, understaffing, and facility dilapidation chronic in the 1940s.[15]

The new buildings were reasonably comfortable. The old buildings—seventy-five years old—were in horrible shape. Iron rods held crumbling exteriors together, and falling bricks posed a hazard to patients. One ward had three toilets, a single bath, and zero showers for "67 disturbed women."[16] The hospital's biennial reports tallied the number of escapees.

O'Brien always understood his dad to be talking about electroshock therapy. It is possible that Ava received electroshock therapy in addition to her insulin shock therapy, the one sometimes a gateway modality to the other. It's also possible she only received electroshock therapy. Official hospital reports document 17,817 "electrotonic treatments" from July

1952 through June 1954 but make no mention of insulin shock treatment. The superintendent was quite proud of the electroshock results.[17] A 1954 survey indicates that nursing students received experience with "electric shock" but not "insulin shock" treatments.[18] Given the close ties between the Mayo and Rochester, the doctors who referred Ava for insulin comas probably would have known if she were really destined for electroshock.[19]

The dates of Ava's shock therapy, late 1953 to early 1954, coincide with those of the American poet Sylvia Plath. In the mid-century United States, women were disproportionately subjected to shock therapies and lobotomies. The burdens and expectations for housewives contributed to their unhappiness and distress, and the predominately male profession was more likely to diagnose women than men as schizophrenic and to prescribe aggressive therapies accordingly. Schizophrenia had become the new hysteria. An outcome of "improvement" may have meant increased docility.[20]

A 1949 report indicates 62.6 percent of Rochester State Hospital's patients diagnosed with schizophrenia were women; in addition to those 337 women, an additional 106 were diagnosed with "involutional psychoses," a condition no longer recognized yet at the time associated with the onset of midlife, particularly menopause (the hospital had only eight such male patients). These two categories accounted for half of the female population.[21] From July 1952 to June 1954, women constituted over 60 percent of the hospital's onsite patients.[22] Ava was a smart, hardworking, attractive woman whose interests and accomplishments in school and her work ethic suggest where ambition and talent might have taken her in a later era of increased possibilities for women in the United States. In school she was involved with glee club, dramatics, and public speaking; outside school, with the church choir and the Parent-Teacher Association. Swimming and tennis were her athletic pursuits. Perhaps small-town rural Minnesota life proved as deleterious to her as to her husband.

Ava the "housewife" was discharged on January 23, 1954, as "improved."[23] Bill used to tell his son that Ava's treatment had changed her, had dulled her, as if with the quelling of demons came the quelling of spirits. The children never noticed. For them, Ava was always a smart, resourceful, steadfast, and loving mother who kept the family functioning. During his institutionalization for alcoholism several years later, Bill confessed in a letter to Ava that his worsening problem must have aggravated her condition.[24]

When Ava checked into Rochester in the late summer of 1953, Bill and the children moved in with her dad, Paul, and younger sister Nina across town.[25] The kids switched schools from Sumner to Neveln Elementary for O'Brien's second- and third-grade years.[26] He and Kathy only understood that their mom was sick. According to hospital records, Ava went home on weekends, lessening the impact on her children, who as adults were surprised to learn her hospital treatment lasted as long as it did.

The O'Briens crowded into the single upstairs bedroom. Grandpa Paul and Aunt Nina each had a small bedroom on the main floor. O'Brien bore a striking resemblance to Paul as a young man, a fact that perhaps engendered Paul's special affection toward his grandson, whom he sometimes took to see the matinees. The movies aside, O'Brien remembers him as a decrepit, pitiable old man who sat around the house wearing slippers. A farmer who regarded animals as objects, he once kicked Kathy's beloved dog Muggs down the basement stairs.

Aunt Nina rivaled Bill O'Brien for personality. Nina's master's in social work made her the most educated family member; her career at the local Department of Social Work, which she eventually headed, made her the most professionally accomplished. For little Kathy, unmarried Aunt Nina was the height of sophistication. She was the family's other great story-teller.

Nina's trademark stories were murder-mystery puzzles of the *who-done-it* or *how'd-they-do-it* variety. Tim and Kathy could ask yes-or-no questions to figure them out. *A man commits suicide by hanging himself. There's no furniture in the room. There is a pool of water on the floor underneath him. How'd he do it?* Answer: He stood on a block of melting ice. *A one-legged circus midget who walks with a cane is found dead with wood shavings scattered around his bed. What happened?* Answer: Circus mates pranked him by shaving his cane at night. Since he thought he was growing taller and thus might lose his livelihood, he killed himself. As an adult, O'Brien would always enjoy a good mystery novel and true-crime television.

After her discharge in January 1954, Ava moved into Nina's with the rest of her family, where they lived for another year and a half. To the best of O'Brien's recollection, his dad remained sober. Father and son played baseball with neighborhood kids on the field behind the house. They were living at Aunt Nina's during O'Brien's Indian Guides phase, with its head-bands and father-son camping trip, Big Bear and Little Bear, "pals forever," as he will write in *Going After Cacciato*. The novel's passage is straight memoir: canoe and gunnysack races, then the son's losing his dad and get-ting lost in the woods until another camper ran across him.[27]

Bill O'Brien's promotion from insurance salesman and field agent to district manager meant the family would be moving again. It gave Timmy serious butterflies to think of starting at a new school so soon after the last time, in a town he'd never heard of, with no friends at all.

◊ ◊ ◊

In 1960, the population of Worthington, in southwestern Minnesota, would reach 9,015, less than half of Austin's.[28] The O'Briens moved to Worthington in the summer of 1955. Greg was born a year later.[29] Bill O'Brien's drinking grew into a serious problem in the smaller town. At forty-two, with a wife and three children, he was undeniably middle-aged. Any dreams about moving back to New York City, or having a more per-sonally fulfilling career, were rapidly withering. The aftereffects of Ava's hospitalization might also have contributed. A letter from Bill to Ava in 1962 describes her as "unable to function as a wife and mother" before, during, and "for some time after" her time in Rochester.[30]

For Bill's ambitious, book-smart son, with no aptitude for or interest in the practical arts and local vocations, Worthington was insufferably pro-vincial, the very model of small-town high-horse small-mindedness. He was also a fresh teen asserting himself in the world by dismissing the adult world he knew. Yet siblings and peers shared his assessment.

In the late nineteenth century, a railroad established a crossing station to draw on Lake Okabena for its steam locomotives. Worthington was founded and incorporated at the site as an organized colony for a "homog-enous class" of temperance-observing, American-born Protestant evan-gelicals. It advertised its alcohol ban to prospective newcomers.[31] Children of those settlers were still presences in the middle of the twentieth century. The town's first liquor store opened in 1947, taking over part of the city hall garage.[32] Postwar demand won the day.

The town's conservatism is illustrated with a front-page *Worthington*

Daily Globe editorial cartoon from 1969. The image took advantage of Worthington's moniker as the Turkey Capital of the World. Every September, Worthington's Turkey Day celebration included a parade with a massive gaggle of turkeys bringing up the rear. The day before Thanksgiving 1969, in response to unprecedented recent nationwide anti-war protests, the *Daily Globe*'s cartoon shows turkeys marching down the main street bearing their own protest signs: FROM "TURKEY DAY" TO THIS? STOP THIS ANNUAL SLAUGHTER! Actual protesters huddle in the background, down a side street, their signs unreadable.[33] The first national draft lottery was conducted five days later.

Whether Republican or Democrat, the townspeople were all mainstream traditionalists whose country had won World War II. They supported their country, the president, and the war because, well, they just did. Often, in O'Brien's view, out of willful ignorance. The *Daily Globe* delivered an impressive dose of national and global news; if anything, it leaned slightly left—the Vance family that owned and ran it were Democrats and friends with Hubert Humphrey, a Democratic senator and the vice president under Lyndon Johnson. The biggest controversy O'Brien's classmate Apryl Vance can remember was the deluge of complaints and threats to end subscriptions caused by a cigarette advertisement.

Lake Okabena dominated the geography. People congregated at the beaches and shoreline parks and went boating. The waterside Centennial and Chautauqua Parks were walking distance from the O'Briens' home, the former a favorite teen hangout spot, the latter closer to downtown, with a bandshell and regular evening concerts. An older O'Brien very occasionally walked the lake's seven-mile circumference. More often he drove around it alone or with friends. After football games he and his friends—mostly the debate team set—"burned our eyeballs staring into the fires" they had made beside the lake while they "sang like bloody bluebirds" the social justice folk songs of the era: "Where Have All the Flowers Gone," "What Have They Done to the Rain," "Blowin' in the Wind," "If I Had a Hammer"— Pete Seeger; the Searchers; Peter, Paul and Mary; Bob Dylan.[34] A few times Kathy took off for the Hollyhock Ballroom in Hatfield, a sketchy place for underage drinking an hour's drive away. Her brother never went. Playing Ping-Pong or practicing his golf swing at the YMCA was his style.

When the O'Briens first arrived, the older kids were still in elementary school. Life rolled along and they enjoyed a happy mid-century childhood. All three O'Brien children use the word *idyllic*. They had the run of the neighborhood until nightfall or the evening curfew siren. They rode their bikes. Kathy liked to make the easy bike ride to the farm just outside town where it cost a quarter to ride a pony for an hour. O'Brien and his friends played soldier with gear from the military surplus store and their dads' closets, sometimes sneaking onto the country club golf course across the street after hours, often reenacting one of the 1950s war movies in all its heroic American-exceptionalist glory.

The O'Briens rented a small corner house at 1018 Elmwood, on the last block before the lake. Between the lake and their house were the town's two fish-rearing ponds. During the winter kids flocked there, using one iced-over pond for hockey, the other for skating. A warming shed stood on the stretch of land between them for breaks. Kathy believes her brother took more pleasure in skating than hockey. The two of them designed ice-dancing routines to perform for an audience of just themselves. O'Brien's was the driving spirit, doing the take-charge older-brother thing despite their nearness in age. He also choreographed an annual Christmas *Nutcracker* show that he and Kathy performed in the privacy of their home until they outgrew it.

The O'Brien home's proximity to the ponds made it the neighborhood's default base, warmer than the shed, with a Ping-Pong table in the basement and filled with the welcoming presences of kind Ava and gregarious Bill. Bill O'Brien loved kids, and they loved him right back. "He treated children as friends and as human beings, not just as children," O'Brien would write in his father's eulogy. "Neighborhood kids would ring the doorbell and ask if Bill could come out to play—not with us, but with our dad." He was famous for his stories, the funnier the better. Once he pretended to be on the phone with the Man in the Moon in front of a pair of thrilled neighborhood girls. He made up answers to their questions.

"The Man in the Moon says it's lonely up there," Dad told them. "He wants you to come visit."

"Well, how do we get there?" the girls asked, and Dad relayed the question, waited a moment, and said, "The Man in the Moon says you have to visit him in your dreams. You have to dream your way there."[35]

Another time he convinced Kathy that all the supermarket's eggs came from Rhoda the Rhode Island Hen. "Rhoda just squats there and lays egg after egg after egg after egg, one egg every two or three seconds, like a machine, all day long, all night long, week after week. Right now, the whole store is full of eggs—you can barely squeeze inside." Kathy called up a friend and they raced on their bikes to see for themselves.

More than one of O'Brien's friends wished Bill were their dad.

Bill coached Little League baseball teams with or without his sons on them, ensuring his players received equal field time and as much individual attention as he could give them, including those from Worthington's first Black families. He loved to play catch with Timmy and help him with his fielding and hitting. On weekends Bill sometimes relieved Ava in the kitchen to cook meat dishes, and for Christmas Eve he always served lobster tail in honor of his New England roots. Bill loved musicals and managed to gather a modest album collection. *Oklahoma!*, *South Pacific*, *Guys and Dolls*, *The Music Man*, *White Christmas*, and *Brigadoon* constituted the soundtrack of O'Brien's childhood. Thirty, forty years later, Tim O'Brien the accomplished writer often listened to show tunes to rev up before a public reading or lecture.

One neighborhood girl was Timmy O'Brien's first love. Kathy remembers hazel-eyed Lorna Lou Moeller as "ethereal," with "beautiful features" and a "pure soul." O'Brien ached with the full pang of new love. His mother called her mother to arrange a movie date. "She was so excited when I told her," her mom wrote O'Brien decades later. Bill and Ava took them to see *The Man Who Never Was*, a World War II film that plays with the reality of fictions in ways different from but also resonant with O'Brien's novels. The movie date features in "The Lives of the Dead," the final story in *The Things They Carried*, with Lorna Lou renamed Linda.

O'Brien had no idea Lorna Lou had recently developed an inoperable brain tumor. Just before Christmas, she had trouble staying on her feet while ice-skating.[36] The diagnosis came soon thereafter. She was too sick to go out, but her mom also knew she was so profoundly sick that a first date, maybe the only date of her life, couldn't be denied. What young O'Brien perceived on that date as her "poise and great dignity" was her holding herself together for the evening as well as her way of respecting its preciousness. It was a lovely spring night.[37]

A few weeks later, a miscreant pulled off her cap in the middle of class. A collective gasp registered the sight of stitches and hair tufts. O'Brien made a bouquet from flowers pulled from his yard, mostly tulips, and walked them to Lorna Lou's house. She met him on the front steps, he thinks at her mom's insistence. O'Brien didn't see Lorna Lou again before viewing her in the casket. She died in September, a month after her tenth birthday, a few weeks before his.

O'Brien didn't know Lorna Lou's symptoms had first announced themselves while she was ice-skating when he wrote the final paragraph of "The Lives of the Dead," in which he imagines the two of them immortalized in his book, the real people and their fictional counterparts shading together, "Timmy skating with Linda under the yellow floodlights," forever "young and happy [. . .] doing loops and spins" before leaping high "into the dark."[38] It must have shivered his soul to read about the ice-skating in her mom's letter.

The goon who knocked off her cap, Mike Tracy, lived in Cherry Point, an area less than a mile from the O'Brien house on the other side of the golf course. For the most part, Worthington kids didn't pay much attention to class differences. The O'Brien siblings played with the children of doctors, dentists, and bankers with the lakefront homes. The town's least fortunate lived in Cherry Point. As close as it was, Timmy and Kathy only went there to dash into a convenience store, the nearest one to their home.

O'Brien's other childhood nemesis, a freckled boy he got into a scrape with when the kid pushed his way into the bus line, lived in Cherry Point. O'Brien tells the story in his war memoir to show his lack of interest in proofs of physical courage. The fight came about because of the moral affront—the boy had disrespected the rules of the social order. It wasn't much of a bout. Somehow his bigger opponent ended up on the ground twice even though O'Brien never landed a blow. The scene replayed itself shortly after Pfc. O'Brien arrived in Việt Nam. During a chopper resupply, O'Brien the newbie stood at the end of the line. The large, gruff soldier in front of him, with months of field time under his belt, snatched the last beers. "What the fuck, asshole?!" O'Brien punched him in the face, landed atop him on the ground, and struck him a few more times. It was characteristic rage over an unfairness, if an uncharacteristic act of violence. He worried the man would have his revenge and never forgot that anxiety. The event became the basis for the "Friends" and "Enemies" chapters of *The Things They Carried*.

O'Brien loathed bullies. Mike Tracy's older brother Tom played the opposite role by protecting others—his intimidating size and unfazed calm usually sufficed to back the belligerents down. Sometimes Tom watched the O'Brien children when their parents were out, tossing them up in the air to their glee. The O'Briens were on Tom's morning newspaper delivery route, and knowing what Tom lacked at home in terms of good food and kind company, Bill would invite him in for a bite to eat, coffee, and pleasantness. When O'Brien was home on break from college, Bill sometimes invited Tom along for the family dinner at Perkins.

There were, however, two Bill O'Briens. Tim's aversion toward Worthington has always been tied up with his father's alcoholism. He blamed the town for his dad's despondence. The small-town judgmental gaze joined forces with his father's emotional cruelty to humiliate him during his vulnerable teenage years. Peers and friends were unaware. Their parents probably knew more, but Bill remained a well-respected community member. He wasn't the town's only afflicted adult. As one older lifelong resident noted, "Liquor was a taboo subject long after teetotalism was abolished in the city." Young Timmy certainly didn't talk about his father's affliction.

At times the episodes were harmless if bizarre. Bill once came home at two in the morning after being kicked out of the country club. With him, also drunk, were Dick Siebert, a former professional baseball player then coaching the University of Minnesota's team, and an assistant coach. Siebert was a legendary coach. Minnesota royalty. After they crashed through the front door, father pulled son out of bed, threw his mitt at him, and started rolling balls to him in the living room to show off his kid's backhand fielding moves. It wasn't until the next day that O'Brien heard the name "Dick Siebert." He knew who that was.

Another time, after running an errand, Bill left O'Brien in the car while he stopped in at the VFW hall, saying he'd be right back. Three hours later, hot, miserable, and upset, the boy got out of the car and walked home. His dad came home infuriated.[39] More than once Bill traveled to Minneapolis for a business meeting only to disappear into a binge for a day, two days, three days. One of O'Brien's cousins describes some of his dad's behavior as "batshit crazy."

The firstborn son received the brunt of their dad's meanness. "Tuck in your tummy, Timmy," Bill teased Tim during his stocky years. Nothing the namesake did satisfied the father. Bill never succumbed to lashing out with physical violence, but it seemed he might. O'Brien hid kitchen knives under his mattress. He rigged up a bedroom door alarm system with string and little bells. He lined up books end to end from the door to the opposite wall, imagining they would block the door from opening.[40]

Bill's little girl received none of the ill-treatment. Kathy believes their dad targeted her brother as a route to their mom. By coming to her son's defense, Ava gave Bill an opening to direct his emotional abuse at her.

Already inclined to spending time alone with his imagination, O'Brien sought refuge from the household ugliness even more. He burrowed himself in the basement or his bedroom, studying for school, reading books, writing his first short stories, and teaching himself magic. From the library he checked out how-to books such as Bruce Elliott's popular titles, several at a time, his favored ones over and over again. Worthington didn't have a bookstore, not that the family could have afforded to buy books anyway. O'Brien's tricks used common items—cards, coin, plate, sand, thread, handkerchief.

The new hobby rekindled the performative streak of those choreographed skating routines and *Nutcracker* dances. They were all a kind of storytelling. The practice and art of magic set the stage for O'Brien's writing career, a blueprint for his interactions of self with self and self with the world: hours upon hours, day after day, of working alone, crafting and honing, reflecting and perfecting, toward the end goal of captivating an audience. A magician's stage persona extends the person but is not the person, a fiction in which real blood pulses. For the adult O'Brien, Lance Burton's famous dove act stands apart. It's not a story per se, but a string of illusions without mechanical assists, all sleight of hand, for O'Brien the height of "fluidity, grace, and elegance." It mesmerizes by virtue of its quietness.

Beyond the solitude and refuge, O'Brien enjoyed the secrecy and creative power. Magic offered explanation and control. Magic explores the poetry of possibility. O'Brien the teacher would tell his students "that the measure of an artist is that artist's deletion of ugliness from the world."[41] He meant both the ugliness of poor craftsmanship and of life's indignities. Magic was O'Brien's first devoted foray into the momentary deletion of ugliness from his world.

His hobby wasn't wholly solo or dramatic. It was harmless and showy fun. Sometimes he recruited his sister and neighborhood kids as audience or assistants for shows put on in the basement. At thirteen, O'Brien was doing magic shows around town for birthday parties and the like. He rode his bike up and down the streets, stuffing homemade flyers into mailboxes: "My magic is modern and up-to-date with programs for young and old alike."[42] In the end, he did a handful of gigs, no more.

The home situation plunged from bad to unbearable. One time when Bill was drinking, Ava, crying in her bed, called for Kathy to bring her aspirin. Kathy brought two pills. Ava told her to go get the whole bottle.

In 1961, the summer before Tim started high school, Ava called the police. The kids watched the living room scene unfold, Ava crying, the two policemen urging her husband to come along as he hunkered in his reading chair shouting invectives at the cops, at Ava, at the universe. Ava's phone call was her vanishing trick. The family didn't see Bill for two months. Bill O'Brien checked into Willmar State Hospital on June 19, 1961, apparently involuntarily.[43]

The treatment didn't take. A year later Bill referred to that time as "those wasted two months in 1961."[44] He resented being there. He didn't take the therapy seriously. At the end of his residency, August 17, Ava and the kids picked him up and drove to Lake Miltona for a family-reunion vacation. Practically as soon as they set foot in their cabin, he had a bottle to his lips, a walloping *screw you* to his wife. The entire situation, the pressure to reacquaint and normalize, drove Tim to take out a motorboat for hours at a time on the lake despite his fear about water because he couldn't swim.

A few weeks later, he started high school.

◊ ◊ ◊

O'Brien put away magic, creative writing, and childhood sports. No more organized baseball or football for him.[45] Schoolwork, extracurricular activities, and his modest social life took over. He was Tim now, not Timmy. He wore the black-framed eyeglasses of the era in about half his casual photos but never in portrait shots.

During the 1961–1962 school year, O'Brien's first at the three-year Worthington High School, the family moved a few blocks, to 230 Eleventh Avenue. They had rented the Elmwood house, and Ava desperately wanted to own a home. She had scrimped and saved. Even then, the fourteen-thousand-dollar price tag and having to make monthly payments made her anxious. Built in 1957, the house wasn't any larger than the family's first Worthington home. As a visiting college girlfriend later described it, the O'Brien house on Eleventh Avenue "was conventionally bland in the suburb of a town that seemed [. . .] too small to have suburbs. Their rambler was cramped and plainly furnished and seemed inadequate to contain their lives or even to hold back the sharp prairie winds."[46]

O'Brien moved into the brown-tiled basement, his room part cinder block, part (fake?) pine panels. The washer and dryer and the house's only shower were also in the basement. As often as he could, O'Brien avoided the shower with its slimy concrete floor, grabbing a quick one at the YMCA or elsewhere. He slept in a bunk bed. At some point Greg moved into the basement with him.

Vodka was Bill's liquor of choice. Sometimes O'Brien dumped out or partially dumped out bottles he found hidden around the house and in the garage, as Greg would do after his older brother left home. A few times O'Brien diluted a bottle with water. Bill stashed his empties in the basement rafters until he could sneak them out of the house.

In the fall of O'Brien's junior year, his mom sat down with him in his basement room to explain that she had kicked his dad out and was filing for divorce. The expulsion took place on a Saturday evening; Ava's rage that night worried Bill for its "violence."[47] That Ava decided upon divorce in mid-century traditional America bespeaks the severity of her husband's illness. Betty Friedan's seminal book on the plight of American women, *The Feminine Mystique*, came out in February 1963, four months after Ava O'Brien's conversation with her son.

Bill O'Brien briefly stayed at the squat redbrick Thompson Hotel downtown. Under pressure from Ava, he checked back into Willmar State Hospital the first week of October 1962. Bill's second institutionalization coincided with the Cuban Missile Crisis, the closest the United States and the Soviet Union had come to nuclear war. The O'Briens and the world were on the brink.

In addition to "Alcoholism," Bill's patient-card diagnosis notes a "passive-aggressive type" of "Personality Trait Disturbance."[48] He cared about his treatment this time around. Bill started as a cottage janitor and after his first month switched to become the Alcoholics Anonymous chairman. His therapy consisted of sessions with the doctors, AA meetings, psycho-dramas, and conversations with Rev. Gordon Grimm, a Lutheran minister. The language of Bill's letters home suggests that he spent most of his time on AA's step 4, the "searching and fearless moral inventory" of himself.[49]

Ava and the children visited Bill once, toward the end of his eight-week stay. O'Brien found it extremely awkward to meet with his dad, both life-long intimate and complete stranger, in this institutional environment.

Bill successfully pleaded with Ava to let him come home. They never divorced. The second time at Willmar didn't take either. His AA meetings in Worthington turned into a ruse to placate Ava. After the meeting, he'd often go out for a drink before heading home. He barely held on to his insurance job, bringing in little income. Ava kept the family afloat with her meager schoolteacher salary. Selling her share of her parents' house in Austin to Nina when Paul Shultz died in 1958 helped. Whenever the family spent time at her sister Marion's, Marion sent Ava on her way home with a handful of cash and some of her own clothes. O'Brien recalls potato pancakes for dinner most nights. His father never hit or shoved anyone, or threw anything. He knew his grown son had a short temper and would fight back.

Whatever temporary dysfunction Ava experienced back in the 1950s, she sustained the family. For Kathy, the insistent truth-seeking in her brother's writing comes from their mother. If Bill was the storyteller, Ava was the "truth teller." It's a lovely way to frame the marriage of invention and truth in O'Brien's work as the conjoined inheritance from his parents. Most moms did not work outside the home. Ava earned a reputation as a wonderful teacher whose classroom Worthington parents sought for their children. Ava struck one of Kathy's friends as more cerebral than jolly Bill O'Brien, as the parent who, in her quiet, sweet way, pushed their three kids

to attain academic success. Ava avoided family games because the competitiveness was too much.

One of the most significant experiences of O'Brien's intellectual development was participating in the high school debate team. He joined in his
last year of junior high school, going to tournaments with high schoolers
as partners. The debate topics expanded his curiosity about and knowledge
of the body politic and international affairs. Debate meshed with O'Brien's
predisposition to appreciate different perspectives and resist closed-minded
positions.

The coach, David Kanellis, called O'Brien "the spark of our debate team
during his last two years."[50] O'Brien won or placed in numerous tournaments over the four years. Debate was his passion. He immersed himself in
it, researching and preparing day and night. He fit everything else around
debate. Like O'Brien's dad, Kanellis had served in the navy aboard a ship
during the war, the destroyer escort USS *Roy O. Hale*. Unlike O'Brien's
dad, he encouraged Tim's interests and talents. O'Brien perceived his father as not caring about either the debate topics—which was surprising
given Bill's wide reading and interests—or his son's success. The hurt of
feeling he was a disappointment never went away.

Kanellis "validated" O'Brien's liberal ideas; he helped make them "intellectually defensible." Armed with a mandolin, Kanellis sang Woody Guthrie
songs and other songs from the labor-movement era, including "I Dreamed
I Saw Joe Hill Last Night," the 1930 poem-turned-anthem about the labor
leader and songwriter executed in 1915. O'Brien and his friends sang along
(he could sing it from memory sixty-some years later). Those sessions took
place in Kanellis's basement. One teammate and friend, Gary Melom, recalls Kanellis as a steel trap of learning with an unassuming intellect, a
large man with a "wonderful presence" who "looked like a dockworker"
and once walked into a debate tournament session claiming to be the clueless bus driver. For Melom, Kanellis "convinced us we had brains." When
O'Brien became a writer, Kanellis's would be one of the distinct faces in the
quasi-amorphous audience to whom he imagined writing.

Kanellis practiced rigorous, blunt intellectual honesty, and had no
qualms in joining his students in politely criticizing other teachers. Whether
influenced by his coach's example or acting from his own pluck, O'Brien
profiled his junior-year English teacher for her assignment to write an essay

on someone they knew. Concluding that she was a lousy educator, he failed
the paper. "You'll never amount to anything," she wrote on it. In his senior
year, O'Brien took a course from Kanellis that combined psychology and
sociology, with readings from Freud and Adler. Such a course would have
been rare and innovative in any school setting in those days.

Maybe a half dozen times in the summers, O'Brien drove with Melom
or another debate-set friend to hang out with their coach at Lake Okoboji,
a resort area on the other side of the Iowa border with a Coney Island–
style lakefront amusement park, where Kanellis worked as a seasonal security officer. O'Brien thought of it as a "wild place." O'Brien saw the Everly
Brothers in concert at Lake Okoboji for what was perhaps the biggest cultural event—in terms of rock and roll's emergence with his generation—of
his young life.

The summer before O'Brien's senior year, Malcolm Browne's photograph
of Thích Quảng Đức's self-immolation in Sài Gòn hit the front pages of
newspapers everywhere. The monk martyred himself to protest the South
Vietnamese government's violent suppression of Buddhism. He ended
up changing history. Six other self-immolations followed in the months
ahead.[51] With the Buddhist crisis, the United States made the precipitous
turn toward supporting the coup, on November 2, 1963, that killed President Ngô Đình Diệm and his brother and chief adviser Ngô Đình Nhu, shot
in the back of an M113 personnel carrier.

Twenty days later, President Kennedy was shot while riding in the back
of a Lincoln Continental convertible limousine. "It was then that I understood that the fine and beautiful fictions I lived by had little power against
the stark facts of reality and biology," O'Brien wrote for *The Washington
Post* on the ten-year anniversary of Kennedy's assassination. In class the
afternoon it happened, Kanellis told his students, "*Sic semper tyrannis.*
Thus always to tyrants." Thus history happens and even the mighty fall. "For
Pete's sake," Kanellis said. "He was only human."[52]

O'Brien had just turned seventeen. For the next decade, his generation
campaigned for rightness and justice: "We were outraged that the world
did not abide by the purity of the idealism we had learned from our first
teacher."[53] If Worthington's moral compass pointed in a different direction
than O'Brien's, he had nevertheless absorbed its moral rootedness.

Kanellis's class excepted, high school wasn't particularly rousing. O'Brien earned good grades but not straight A's.[54] His best friend their senior year, Steve Goff, jokes that O'Brien became an accomplished writer despite their English classes. Yet O'Brien's analytical brain appreciated the endless-seeming diagramming of sentences. O'Brien the writing teacher would not suffer grammatical gaffes lightly. A writer who can't master the rules can't possibly achieve the "linguistic felicity" on which a story rides. Achieving that felicity sustained the long, frustrating days at typewriter and computer.[55]

Kanellis identified O'Brien's "greatest strengths" as "intellectual curiosity, complete honesty, perseverance, and an ability to relate well to people." Still, what the teenage O'Brien experienced as self-doubt and shyness translated to some as aloofness. In both classroom and social settings, he was sometimes "combative," as one classmate recalled. His quick wit could be off-putting. To his set he was an endearing, vulnerable, empathetic, and loyal friend, to other high schoolers a quirky brainiac who marched to his own drum. What he internalized as his father's intractable disregard amplified the normal adolescent anxieties. He was achingly sensitive and supremely clever with a hair-trigger contentiousness.

O'Brien served on the student council and in the International Relations Club. The IRC hosted an annual United Nations Assembly for students from about twenty schools. He was also involved with the Biology Club, the German Club, the *Worthington High Star* newspaper (which he doesn't recall), and the Thespian Club. He took the stage in the school's fall play junior and senior years, *The State Versus Maxine Lowe* and *The Curious Savage*.[56] In the first, in a bit of typecasting, O'Brien the star debater played a trial lawyer. His character in the second, Hannibal, a resident of an insane asylum, believes he's a violinist. Little Greg O'Brien had a small part as John Thomas Williams, the doll whom another resident believes is her son. In the last scene, Hannibal plays a violin beautifully and John Thomas is a real boy. How apt for a future writer dedicated to dramatizing the role of imagination in our lives.

Outside school, O'Brien worked for the *Worthington Daily Globe*. The *Daily Globe* published in the afternoon, allowing it to run news from that very day, much of it off the wire services. After school O'Brien walked to the paper's printing facility from which he drove a company car to distribute the paper to outlying communities. The young man's seriousness impressed the editor in chief. James Vance, married but without children, was rumored to be gay. A rumor like that made him joke fodder, especially for teenage boys. O'Brien avoided situations where the two would be alone—in the photographic darkroom, for example. Vance later became one of the emerging writer's staunchest fans and advocates.

On Friday and Saturday nights, coaches and others phoned in to O'Brien bare-boned game updates that he transformed into stories. He received information and spun away, drawing from a premade list of verbs at the ready. Johnny didn't score, he *bulldozed* to the basket or *hurled* himself into the end zone. This larking was the first time in print that he did what he and his characters would famously do in *The Things They Carried* and other works: heat up the truth.

In May 1968, when O'Brien went home after college with crossed fingers, the Selective Service Administration ran the draft through local boards, not yet the national lottery. The Department of Defense informed the SSA of its manpower needs; the SSA divvied up the request among the states; the state offices divvied up the requirement to local boards. The local draft board was a discretionary body that could consider the individual case as well as community needs. Community members comprised each board. O'Brien's neighbors.

3

SWEETHEART OF THE SÔNG KRÔNG NÔ

One of the most memorable stories in *The Things They Carried* tells the outlandish tale of a young soldier who manages to fly his girl-friend from the United States to his small medical compound along the Trà Bồng River—the Sông Trà Bồng. She arrives by helicopter. Tall and leggy, blond-haired and blue-eyed, all of seventeen, with "a complexion like strawberry ice cream."[1] The war changes her. She eventually disappears into the Vietnamese landscape in a story as much about storytelling and the male imagination as about her. A drafted follow-up story, "The Real Mary Anne," begins, "Nobody believes me, of course, but of all the stories in this book, 'Sweetheart of the Song Tra Bong' comes most directly from actual events"—at which point this unpublished piece turns nearly as fanciful as "Sweetheart."

Many readers reject the very premise. Fly a civilian to an outpost deep in-country? It couldn't have happened; it didn't happen. Yet O'Brien based it on a rumor that he heard soon after joining his combat infantry platoon, a rumor grounded in truth. Not only could it happen, it *did* happen. At least once, O'Brien's senior year of high school.

Ken Hruby graduated and received his commission from the U.S. Military Academy at West Point in May 1961. After the Infantry Officer Basic Course and Ranger School at Fort Benning, Georgia, 2nd Lt. Hruby headed to the Defense Language Institute at the Presidio in Monterey, California, to study Vietnamese. In the fall of 1963, he met the soon-to-be Billie (Jensen) Hruby. They married six weeks later. Then on to Việt Nam for the now first lieutenant.

Hruby began his assignment as an adviser to a battalion in the 23rd Infantry Division of the Army of the Republic of Vietnam (ARVN), based out of Ban Mê Thuột, in the central highlands close to Cambodia. In April 1964, the unit relocated a little to the south, to an abandoned French outpost on the Krông Nô River—the Sông Krông Nô—between Ban Mê Thuột and Da Lat, the former French colonials' mountain retreat. Some highland "Montagnard" ethnic Mnong Gar tribes made their homes in the neighboring villages along the river. The seminomadic Mnong Gar (also called Mnungar or M'Nông), meaning the people of the forest, practiced slash-and-burn rice cultivation across the rugged landscape.

Upon learning that Lt. Hruby was a newlywed, his commander gave him three weeks' leave. Ken and Billie spent a week in Hong Kong before traveling on Air Vietnam to visit Sài Gòn and then on to the beach city of Nha Trang. This early in the war, the military allowed family members to live in Việt Nam, nearly all of whom stayed in Sài Gòn. The couple spent nights socializing at the Nautique Hotel in Nha Trang, where they hung out with some pilots. The alcohol-infused conversation eventually took up the challenge of getting Billie to Ban Mê Thuột. One of the guys, a warrant officer, told them to show up at the airfield the next morning. They did, whereupon he whisked them onto a cargo plane. By way of explanation, he turned to Ken and said, "She's an army nurse, right?"

At Ban Mê Thuột they transferred to a helicopter for the hop down to the ARVN battalion base camp on the Sông Krông Nô. On the way into camp, a member of the helicopter crew announced over the radio that they were returning the long-lost lieutenant and his "round-eyed baggage" (or something equally slangy). The entire visit lasted only a few hours. They lunched with Vietnamese officers and walked about the villages. Photographs show brunette Billie in a long-sleeve belted dress so pale a pink it appears white, with sunglasses and headscarf, posing beside M'Nông villagers. Then it was back to the helicopter for the return trip to Ban Mê Thuột.

On the approach, at about eight thousand feet, the door gunners kicked open the doors and began letting loose with the mounted M60s. The large bullet shells leapt out of the guns, bouncing all around the metallic compartment while the machine guns thud-thud-thudded away. It made a shocking racket. The pilot, Capt. Vic Webber, radioed that they were just showing off for a lieutenant's "round-eyed" wife. He had one more trick for her. He shut off the engine to stick an autorotation landing. The air pressure change of the quick drop permanently damaged her hearing; a childhood bout of diphtheria had probably made her eardrums more vulnerable.

The radio calls from the helicopter flights about Billie would have been picked up by army air traffic controllers in central Việt Nam. From there the story (if not its particulars) became a jungle legend.

This retelling makes no claims about how widely the legend spread, or whether any other couples pulled off a similar tryst that could have served as grist for the army's rumor mill. It can't prove Ken and Billie Hruby's as the source story of young love and chutzpah O'Brien heard in Việt Nam that inspired his tall tale of high school love, chutzpah, and innocence lost, "Sweetheart of the Song Tra Bong." O'Brien's is finally a story about soldiers relaying the story, daring one another (and themselves) to imagine it and, on some level, believe. One can easily imagine the legend's passing from grunt to grunt, base to base, road march to road march, year by year, until reaching a highly imaginative private first class, a combat infantryman, enduring a war he hated in Quảng Ngãi province, 1969:

—*You know a guy once choppered his girl all the way from stateside to some Montagnard ville in the middle of fucking nowhere.*
—*For real?*
—*No shit.*
—*I wonder how he pulled that off.*
—*Guess it can't be too hard. Just balls and brains. Balls and brains.*
—*I guess it could be done. Hunh.*

4

SOAPBOX

Tim O'Brien's first publication was a letter to the editor in the *Worthington Daily Globe* on Wednesday, August 16, 1961. He was fourteen. The topic was the Berlin crisis, the Soviet Union's effort to push the United States, United Kingdom, and France out of West Berlin (under joint occupation since the end of World War II). In early August, the Soviet Union cut off all access and began constructing the Berlin Wall. President Kennedy jumpstarted military readiness at home while bolstering European forces "with 40,000 ground troops and several Tactical Air Force fighter squadrons."[1] At the peak of the crisis, ten Soviet T-54 tanks squared off against four American M48 tanks one hundred yards apart at a Berlin crossing point.[2]

"Young Reader Urges Firm American Stand," the only hawkish thing O'Brien ever published, fulfills its title's exhortation. It opens with warranted apocalyptic drama over the potential for nuclear war. Then comes the call to arms:

> In Laos, Viet Nam, Japan, Korea, Formosa, Tibet, Cuba, and even in our own United States we can witness the communists industriously chipping away at the human race, holding boldly aloft their banner of world domination. They can and inevitably will achieve this goal unless we, the last great Allied power remaining, act now. . . .
>
> "Try to get us out" must be our battle cry as we prepare for a Berlin-sparked war. We must dig in, getting ready for the worst, hoping for the best, praying for peace.[3]

The command of current events aside, one could hardly expect a message any less conventional from a young Worthingtonian. Nevertheless, the letter shows O'Brien reaching for adulthood by claiming his voice and engaging the world.

◊ ◊ ◊

It must have been extra exciting. O'Brien and his fellow freshmen arrived at Macalester College in 1964 during a period of tremendous expansion. The new fine arts center was completed the year before. Two new dormitories, a new dining hall, a new humanities building, and a new football stadium had just opened. By the end of the academic year, the college would dedicate its new science building. Each of O'Brien's four years at the college brought in new faculty members, increasingly with doctoral degrees.[4] O'Brien's entering class brought the college's total enrollment to 1,683, the largest student body since the immediate post–World War II years—a number topped in successive years.[5] The majority of his classmates came from small towns in the upper Midwest. They welcomed the heady novelty of studying at an academically rigorous place committed to international engagement.

The campus's World Press Institute annually hosted fifteen international journalists to study at Macalester and to spend time with news organizations around the country. The school offered a wealth of opportunities for travel abroad. According to O'Brien's classmate Charley Underwood, Western Europe in the summers "was infested" with Macites. And not just Europe—Underwood spent his sophomore year in the Congo. Every fall, Macalester organized an International Week, and every year Mac students gathered with Canadian counterparts for the Canada-U.S. Conference. Several prominent faculty members came from outside the United States. Evening events, required convocation lectures, and student-organized affairs frequently had a global focus. The student paper was as likely to run an article about Iran or Africa as about breakfast hours in the cafeteria. Underwood recalls about one hundred African students studying at Mac, and students came from such far-flung places as Iceland, Israel, Lebanon, and Việt Nam—this on a campus of under two thousand students. Starting in 1950 through O'Brien's four years and beyond, Macalester flew the UN flag with the U.S. flag outside the library.

Joining him on campus that first fall were National Merit Scholars from around the country supported by scholarships from DeWitt Wallace, the founder of *Reader's Digest*. O'Brien found himself among smart, talented peers in a serious place. Academic work became a passion. O'Brien blossomed at Macalester. His photograph and name appear far more than any of his classmates in the student newspaper over the next four years.

The Young Republicans—the YGOP—may well have been the largest organization at Macalester in the early and mid-1960s. Students typically brought their parents' hometown values to a college with a conservative nature rooted in its Presbyterian heritage. But it was also the mid-1960s. "Dope hit the campus in 1967," remembered Rev. Al Currier, LSD "the following spring."[6] Psychedelic artwork made inroads on the pages of the student newspaper. As one of O'Brien's classmates later reflected, those four years at Macalester "catapulted me from a preacher's kid, teetotaler, Girl Scout life into one of guerrilla theater, Petula Clark, 3 a.m. existential exegesis, and Estée Lauder."[7]

The American military's presence in Southeast Asia garnered occasional lectures on campus and articles in the student paper during O'Brien's first two years. Toward the end of his freshman year, BOMB HANOI campus sidewalk graffiti led to a back-and-forth as an anti-war crew revised it to BOMB THE WORLD IN THE NAME OF DEMOCRACY and BOMB THE WORLD—YOU CAN DO IT. A counter-revision, BOMB THE SPU (the Student Peace Union), was accompanied by a new message, BLOCKADE NORTH VIETNAM.[8]

In O'Brien's sophomore year, the campus Young Democratic-Farmer-Labor party (YDFL) drafted and circulated a petition supporting the war. In short order, they and the Young Republicans passed the same motion "to endorse President Johnson's policy in Viet Nam." O'Brien then offered a motion for his liberal peers' consideration, affirming the "fundamental right" of "peaceful and lawful" protest and criticism. Unlike the president's war strategy, the right to dissent "engendered considerable debate before it was given the club's endorsement."[9] Although he disagreed with the war, either O'Brien had not yet concluded that the United States should pull out of Việt Nam or, more likely, he didn't want to upset the consensus of both political camps.

A spirit of moderation often brought the two parties together. This moderation was born of a culture of propriety, postwar unity, and a common information stream. Most everyone watched the evening news from the same three television networks and read the same nationally distributed wire-service news articles. A habituated decorousness ruled the day. Professors never discussed in class the events roiling the nation, whether foreign entanglements or civil rights, due to an allegiance to content instruction and an ingrained sensibility that such discussions simply didn't belong in a classroom. O'Brien might scoff at hypocritical deference to respectability, but he didn't care to ruffle feathers either. He preferred achieving consensus, working politely within systems, and being liked by both authority figures and peers.

Being class president as a junior and then student body president as a senior left O'Brien no spare time for the debate team.[10] He missed the yearlong immersion in a contemporary issue, the drive to expertise, the preparation, the performance, the competition. In the Community Council, though, he could make a difference. O'Brien's CC agenda focused on the chief concern of students, the in loco parentis issue. Students objected to the many ways the college parented them outside the classroom rather than respecting their autonomy as adults. The student-power movement was sweeping across the nation's campuses. At Mac, student leaders struggled to organize their peers for much beyond grousing.

In his senior year's first issue of *Mac Weekly*, the new president called on the student body to rally behind five goals: abolishing dorm curfews for women at least twenty-one years old or with parental permission (which were de facto curfews for the men); studying the requirement to leave dorm room doors open with an opposite-sexed guest; exploring the possibilities for alcohol consumption by those of age; increasing student participation and leadership in curricular decisions; and establishing a "Student Dormitory University" to "stimulate more intellectual growth outside the classroom" geared to student interests.[11]

O'Brien worked within the system by strategizing with administrators and facilitating conversations among students, faculty, and those in power. He did not believe that all extracurricular life should be under student control.[12] Mary Ackerman, two years younger and the first woman to chair a major CC committee, describes O'Brien as a "logical, caring, strategic, empathetic student leader," never showy, and "tightly wound in a good way." His CC peers recognized their president's intelligence. Their respect for it, according to Ackerman, "undergirded his leadership." At meetings, other students studied his reactions, learning as much from his silences as his comments.

O'Brien's presidency fell short of his expectations. Students did not receive formal representation at faculty meetings, dorm hours did not change, and doors had to remain open with a guest in the room. But he managed to increase library hours, secure funds to start dorm hall libraries and a new literary journal, and keep the Dorm University idea on the table. O'Brien's most lasting achievement was the creation of the student course evaluation informational booklet intended to make teaching talent matter for a professor's career at least as much as publications and crony reputation. He had spearheaded the resolution to passage his junior year, with the details hashed out during his last fall on campus.[13] His CC approved the creation of the Black Liberation Affairs Committee.[14]

O'Brien's frustration when the faculty voted to preserve the open-door policy drove him to lead a boycott his last weeks on campus, encouraging dorm residents to ignore the rule and close their doors if they wished. The students wouldn't let the issue go. Most of what failed to change regarding student power was changed the year after he graduated. If O'Brien could have worked with the innovative and responsive new president who would replace the set-in-his-ways president of O'Brien's senior year, the small revolution could very well have transpired under his leadership.[15] At least he'd managed to get the CC to support anti-war initiatives.

In O'Brien's final semester on campus, he wrote a piece for *Mac Weekly* reflecting on his disappointing tenure as Community Council president:

> So you begin to lose confidence in yourself when you are CC President. Not a psychological breakdown. Instead, it is a discovery that you are not the Savior; that you (or your beliefs or your arguments) will not have much or any impact. You discover that you are really not very effective in doing, in accomplishing, in persuading, in motivating or inspiring.
>
> ... And in those conflict situations you begin to learn that you have to change; that you have to give in at crucial points; that you have to conciliate. So you do that, and you learn again the lesson that you aren't always right; you may never know if and when you are right. And with that realization, you are personally enriched.

... You have packed into one year the experience that must ac-
cumulate over five or ten or twenty years for other students. And you
thank everyone for letting you do that.[16]

The mix of confidence and humility was characteristic.

The primary record of O'Brien's college writing is his articles in *Mac Weekly*.
"Survey Finds Republicans at Mac More Authoritarian" appeared in February of his sophomore year and analyzed a survey using Theodor Adorno's
theory of the authoritarian personality. The article reads like the classroom
assignment that it was, with one conversational touch, a lighthearted self-
referential disclaimer explaining the methodology's rationale for sampling
every ninth name on an alphabetized list. "Too many O'Briens, for example, would not be representative of the Macalester student body, and the
Irish background might result in political inclinations not representative of
most Macites."[17]

The fall semester of his junior year, O'Brien wrote a political column
titled Soapbox. The first, looking at Minnesota gubernatorial politics, was
an outlier.[18] The second, arguing for the significance of public scrutiny of
foreign policy, set the stage for a series about Việt Nam.[19] O'Brien's third
Soapbox contended that all nations possess the same right to sovereignty
free of military intrusion: "Military aggression against any nation, then,
ought to be rigorously opposed by the United States." O'Brien was hardly
subtle in leading his readers to apply his ideas to the war in Việt Nam. The
column's last section showed O'Brien struggling between Kennedy-esque
Cold War global idealism and anti-war isolationism, the problem that has
persistently confounded American foreign policy. In this last section, the
incipient creative writer wisped:

[T]he United States ought to have a larger and, I think, more sublime objective in mind when formulating its foreign policy. While
remaining realistically cautious in its conduct, America should take
a positive role in establishing a lasting harmony among nations under conditions of peace, economic security, and intellectual honesty.

Obviously, the objective now is an idealist one. And yet the "image" is what counts. The vision of a fraternal world society, if kept in the minds of policy-molders and diplomats, can have a salutary effect on the spirit of the conduct of international politics if nothing else. And if that image is maintained and is made the ultimate goal of foreign policy, the world and the United States has [sic] not lost a last remaining hope for the harmonious interaction of people.[20]

The eventual artist's dedication to the imagination shines through. Without the image, without the vision, the United States and the world cannot achieve the peace and security they so desire. Nor can individuals. People can't realize in their lives, can't make happen, what they don't (or can't) imagine. Yet as O'Brien will write in *Going After Cacciato*, watching his protagonist Paul Berlin fail to imagine himself imagining deserting the war, "Imagination, like reality, has its limits."[21]

O'Brien's next Soapbox objected to the United States' imposition of its values on other nations as morally indefensible: "America stands for diversity and for the freedom to be diverse" at home and abroad.[22] Three weeks later, "Viet Nam Perspective" finally brought O'Brien to the pressing issue of the day. The essay begins by asking whether one should prefer "to live under totalitarianism or not to live at all." Is the fight to live more freely worth losing one's life or taking another's? Decidedly not, he answers. To enjoy life, one needs to be alive. People can enjoy life in other systems of government and social organizations. By what right can Americans say otherwise? By what right can we deprive others of their life's joys by killing them? A nonviolent if more gradual process of increasing freedoms and securing stability does not risk losing or taking the fundamental condition of life's potential, that of being alive. The columnist anticipated the novelist in evoking the sensory pleasures of existence: "Men can enjoy scents, colors, tastes, art, and a whole gamut of other joys," he writes, "without being politically free."

The final Soapbox column appeared in the last issue before holiday break. Titled "Christmas," it argues that the Christmas and the "corresponding Southeast Asian holiday" truces of 1965 and 1966—not military escalation—encouraged political negotiations from both sides. Why can't American policy treat every day like Christmas by adopting "an attitude of peace, love, hope, and humanism"?[23]

O'Brien's attention to the war his junior year spoke to the swelling U.S. military involvement in Việt Nam. Combat units first deployed with the landing of marines on the coast of Da Nang in March 1965, O'Brien's second semester on campus. During a televised news conference on July 28, 1965, President Johnson had announced the doubling of the monthly draft intake to increase troop levels in Việt Nam from 75,000 to 125,000. "We do not want an expanding struggle with consequences that no one can foresee, nor will we bluster or bully or flaunt our power. But we will not surrender, and we will not retreat."[24] The war's "jeopardy became personal" for O'Brien with Johnson's line-in-the-sand posturing. By the fall of 1966, the comfortable bubble of the war's abstraction was rapidly thinning. American fatalities jumped from 6,350 in 1966 to 11,363 in 1967.[25] Enlistment due to the draft peaked in 1966 at 382,010.

"I wrote those columns because I was trying to save my own life," O'Brien said a decade later at a symposium on the war at Macalester. "I didn't want to get drafted."[26]

Some of O'Brien's male classmates took steps to avoid ending up as ground combatants, whether switching career paths from law school to medical school, joining the naval reserves, or even applying for conscientious objector status. Rev. Currier's work as a draft counselor boomed. In the fall of 1967, O'Brien's senior year, the campus YDFL changed its tune, passing a resolution that praised Senator Eugene McCarthy's efforts on behalf of free speech and that called on the White House to reconsider its escalation policy, halt the bombing of North Việt Nam, and enter peace negotiations.[27]

White student activists turned their efforts from civil rights to the war— because of the war and because (according to Underwood) the growing number of Black students on campus meant fewer leadership opportunities for whites in the fight for racial justice. In the fall of O'Brien's junior year, the Soapbox semester, other students and some faculty organized committees to address the war.[28] When other students traveled to anti-war assemblies in Washington, D.C., and New York City in the spring, O'Brien stuck to campus.[29] He was not among those students who politely challenged Senator Mondale to take a clear position on the war in Việt Nam by quietly holding up signs during his appearance on campus at Olin Hall on Veterans Day: SENATOR MONDALE, ARE YOU A HAWK, A DOVE, OR A FLYING SQUIRREL?

SENATOR MONDALE, COMMITMENT, THE ANSWER TO YOUR TWILIGHT ZONE. SENATOR MONDALE, YOUR FENCE IS MOVING. SENATOR MONDALE, PEOPLE ARE DYING FOR YOU TO DECIDE.[30]

Time magazine's Choice '68 nationwide poll of college campuses showed that 44.3 percent of Macalester students preferred the liberal Democratic presidential candidate, Eugene McCarthy. Only 9.19 percent would have voted for the Republican Richard Nixon. Just under 89 percent of Macites favored withdrawal or reduction of U.S. troops in Việt Nam, and just over 84 percent voted to cease or suspend bombing.[31]

It was a paranoid and divisive era in so many ways. In February 1967, the liberal National Student Association publicly acknowledged the CIA's role in its business, compelling Macalester's NSA coordinator to report to her Community Council peers—O'Brien included—that the college was "in no way implicated" and that she was "not a CIA agent."[32] Six months later, the radical Students for a Democratic Society disaffiliated with the NSA despite the political kinship between the two organizations.[33] A few weeks after that, Minnesota's YDFL separated from the Young Democratic Clubs of America, citing the national organization's support for President Johnson's war.[34]

A January 1968 *Mac Weekly* commentary wondered if the installation of civil defense sirens atop the football stadium "portends future intimate relationships and contracts between the college administration and various governmental units."[35] Even if facetious, the article still testifies to the mood.

One gargantuan factor fueling students' cynicism, outrage, and activism during the late 1960s was their disenfranchisement. Most college-age Americans, most draft-eligible Americans, could not vote. Until the ratification of the Twenty-Sixth Amendment in 1971 extending the minimum voting age from twenty-one down to eighteen, their only means of political agency were voter registration and turnout drives, grunt-level campaign work, and protest. Their country could decide to send them to kill and maim and be killed and be maimed overseas, but they had no say. Country and campus treated them like children while expecting them to sacrifice like adults.

No wonder they were pissed.

5

ADVENTURES IN AMITY
AND MELANCHOLY

Việt Nam would not be Tim O'Brien's first experience overseas. The Minnesota-wide Student Projects for Amity among Nations was the most distinguished summer overseas program available to Macalester students. Since 1960, DeWitt Wallace had provided scholarships to cover expenses and lost summer wages to male SPANners.[1] Mike Frederickson, a SPAN student a year ahead, sat on the selection committee when O'Brien nailed the interview with a brilliant analysis of Hans Morgenthau's approach to international relations. Morgenthau had advised President Kennedy but turned against President Johnson's foreign policy, most visibly in a televised debate over Việt Nam with Johnson's hawkish adviser McGeorge Bundy in June 1965. After O'Brien left the room, the committee voted instantly and unanimously.

O'Brien was one of fifteen students assigned to Prague, Czechoslovakia, the largest SPAN contingent for 1967.[2] It was the summer before the Prague Spring's promise of democratization and the resulting Soviet invasion. O'Brien's cohort had spent Saturday mornings during the school year at the University of Minnesota taking a crash course on Czech language and culture. O'Brien's aunt Catherine, who had worked in naval counterintelligence, called her brother Bill quite aghast. Communist Czechoslovakia? *No nephew of mine will turn out Red!*

Once in Paris, SPANners were on their own. O'Brien stayed one or two nights at the Hotel Angleterre near Les Halles market before traveling by train to Stuttgart. From there, he and Robin Kleffman hitchhiked south to Reutlingen, where Kleffman bought a 1952 250cc BMW motorcycle and the inexperienced O'Brien a Vespa. Then O'Brien suggested they hit the public pool. Maybe there'd be girls. Kleffman, a competitive swimmer, dove in. What Minnesotan didn't know how to swim? Kleffman was out of the pool when he saw O'Brien's nose and lips just peeking out of the water. O'Brien wasn't thrashing. He was starting to drown. Kleffman, the trained lifeguard—also a weight lifter, shot-putter, and discus thrower—leapt as far as he could toward O'Brien, swam up underneath him, held him out of the water, and walked underwater to the side of the pool. Both men recognize that Kleffman saved O'Brien's life. Another close call: On the way to New York during the high school Odd Fellows trip, O'Brien had managed to pull himself out after mistakenly jumping into the deep end of a motel pool.

The two spent a week together before making their way separately to Prague. Since O'Brien had never driven a motorcycle and was mechanically disinclined, even the little Vespa intimidated him. As O'Brien exited Hersbruck, where the cobblestones turned to asphalt on the way out of town, the motorcycle reared, flipping all the way over, landing him on his back, and smashing into his shoulder. He had fractured his clavicle.

O'Brien shared a hospital common room with three farmers, older men with broken limbs who swigged beer much of the time. O'Brien's limited high school German could not keep up. Elfrieda Meyer, an inexperienced X-ray technician, visited him in the common room more than duty required. She spoke some English. Whenever she left, the farmers chortled. When the hospital discharged O'Brien, Elfrieda invited him to stay with her family. He slept in a closet of a room for a few nights, sneaking downstairs to her room while her parents slept. One early morning he was returning upstairs and passed her father on the way down. "Guten Tag," the flushing O'Brien greeted him. Herr Meyer, who spoke no English, scowled. At dinner one night he gobsmacked O'Brien by saying, "Hitler war nicht so schlecht." *Hitler wasn't so bad.*

A gas station mechanic fixed the Vespa at no charge. O'Brien took two weeks to trek around Germany and Czechoslovakia. It rained every day.[3] He often slept outside. He would never get over the discomfort and displeasure of camping and outdoor life.

In Prague, he boarded at a house of recent design but shoddy construction on the edge of the city. The paint was peeling, the place already rickety. He soon settled into a routine, working during the day and eating cheap Czech *biftek* (beefsteak) at the same dining hall most nights, sometimes just bread to save cash. On rare occasions, he met up with other SPAN students. Mostly he spent the summer alone.

Although O'Brien had traveled to do an economics project, Europe rekindled his childhood ambition. He decided to write a novel instead. "A Man of Melancholy Disposition" appears to be lost, much to O'Brien's relief. He sometimes belittles it as the project he did simply to fulfill the SPAN requirement. Evidence of the lost novel's youthfulness survives in one preserved fragment, a few paragraphs captured by a reporter for the *St. Paul Pioneer Press*:

> It was a grotesque day, the kind of day that made kings build castles, thick walls, warm fires, the kind of day that fostered ale and strong beer, fortitude, the sort of limpid, languid, rainy, quiet, thundering green-dark day that made men build Prague and live there, safe.
>
> A good day for serpents and snakes, salamanders and bats, gypsies and giants, not meant for men.
>
> But for those who understood it.

The reporter described it as "a 225 page psychological novel." He faithfully conveyed O'Brien's confidence: "Featuring common themes of suicide and betrayal he's cut deep into the contemplative Czech character."[4] O'Brien was under the influence of Graham Greene at the time. The novel had a Cold War thriller plot, with a Czech political reformer trying to escape the country to avoid arrest by the communist authorities. At one point he rides in a car's secret trunk compartment. Gypsies were involved.

Part of the novel's inspiration derived from encounters with two people in Prague. For his forgone economics project, O'Brien interviewed George Wheeler, an American economist who had worked in the Roosevelt administration and then, in April 1950, abandoned the United States for Czechoslovakia. Wheeler preferred the word *emigrate* to *defect*: "I had the courage to use my rational faculties." The move resulted from his conclusion that Czech-style communism, not American-style capitalism, offered "real prospects for human development and fulfillment." The current economic reforms, he answered, did not disrupt his adopted country's communist core.

O'Brien asked Wheeler if Czechoslovakia was "a nation people will be happy living in." Wheeler's response conveys the heart of "A Man of Melancholy Disposition":

> "Are people ever happy?" he said flatly. "I don't think so. People wander their way through life in a permanent state of dissatisfaction, restlessness, and despair. Wasn't it Thoreau who said that men 'lead lives of quiet desperation.' [sic] Well, that's right.
>
> "But, as I said before, men must be rational. They must use their human capacity of thought in order to cope with desperation, restlessness, and dissatisfaction. Men must at least try to wrestle with their problems even if they lose."[5]

A few years later, after the war and while drafting a different novel with the working title "A Man of Melancholy Disposition"—published as *Northern Lights*—O'Brien defined such a man as "naturally a man; meaning man is naturally melancholy; or, put another way, naturally discontent—out of key with his time, any time, as Ezra [Pound] said it; or, put another way, naturally happiness-seeking. To be a happiness-seeker one must of course be unhappy."[6]

If George Wheeler fed the novel's theme, O'Brien's fellow boarders Eric and Irene Meier, East Germans on vacation, fed its plot. Two days after interviewing Wheeler, O'Brien, Eric, and a Czech friend, Lubos Manytek, were drinking late at night when Eric started crying. He and Irene were attempting to flee Eastern Europe for the freedoms of the West, but his uncle hadn't shown up. O'Brien feared "a trap for unsuspecting and stupid Americans" until a panicky Eric phoned his uncle in front of him and Lubos, pleading, "Bitte kommen, bitte kommen!" *Please come, please come!* The uncle agreed to come the next day, "driving a car with a space under the back seat where Eric and his wife could hide."[7] O'Brien never learned the Meiers' fate.

O'Brien did not toss the novel aside after returning from Europe. Dorm neighbors remember the tap-tap-tapping of the upperclassman's typewriter as he poured himself into the novel, often to the accompaniment of Eva Pilarová's "Rekviem" in Czech. (The song had played everywhere in Prague, having become an anthem for political liberalization.) Professor Harley Henry's initial reaction is lost, but he wrote a year later with feedback on a new draft:

> I am still a bit confused about the *locus* of the narrator's telling of the story and the attitude [. . .] from which he tells the story. [. . . A] firmer grip on the point of view, and the narrator's shortcomings and inconsistencies seems necessary. [. . .] As it now stands, this can best be accomplished by involving yourself more with the narrator, not as expert story teller and organizer of events, etc., but as faulty, confused human being. This will tend to diminish the importance of the other characters *per se* and make them foils for the narrator-protagonist through his attitude toward them.[8]

Or, Henry suggested, O'Brien could rewrite the book in third person. O'Brien thought well enough of the book at the time to submit it to at least one major publisher in New York City.[9]

The writer's relationship with his fictional narrators would become an ongoing aesthetic concern. The betrayal theme would also recur. One observation O'Brien made to the *Pioneer Press* reporter expressed a challenge that he would face throughout his career: "You can't use strict academic techniques to appreciate a culture; the problem is breaking down abstractions. To really have a [rapport] or empathy with the country you must combine the academic with the creative."[10] Or, as he'd describe it in his early seventies with most of his career behind him, "Your intellect and your emotions are in constant contest. They're always competing. The intellect wants to explain the world," but "emotions want to be emotions."[11] Something of that dualism informed O'Brien's profiles of Wheeler and Meier, in the one's rationality and the other's desperation.

Fifty years later, Professor Henry remembered only salamanders. The image came from O'Brien's childhood. For brief periods in the fall and spring, depending on rainfall and snowmelt, salamanders in search of temporary ponds for breeding swarmed the neighborhood, and as boys will be boys, O'Brien and his buddy Mike Bjerkesett amused themselves by crushing them under their bike wheels, leaving a great stench in their squishy wake. Bjerkesett was the main friend with whom O'Brien would play war on the golf course. The very summer O'Brien was writing about those sala-manders, a car wreck left Bjerkesett paraplegic.[12]

O'Brien had met Lubos Manytek at the long table in the *hostinec* where O'Brien ate dinner. Manytek was just a few years older. In late May or early June, he took O'Brien to his residence hall to meet his roommate, a twenty-six-year-old North Vietnamese student "on call with the NVN regular army if needed." Several compatriots lived in the dorms, too, as communist countries such as Czechoslovakia had replaced France, Indo-china's former colonial overlord, as the Vietnamese education destination. O'Brien's notes spell what he heard as the man's name, "Le Ledoc," the son of an important party functionary.[13] Even in the theoretically classless communist North Việt Nam, whether one fought in the war was often a matter of privilege. Le believed he could serve his country better with his economics expertise than with a rifle.

In that skinny dorm room, the three muddled along in French, Czech, German, and English. Le's conviction rattled O'Brien, who asked ques-tions without disputing. The North was winning, Le insisted. It controlled three-quarters of the land, 80 percent of the Southerners supported the Việt Cộng, and "the strength of the VC is increased with each bomb dropped." The "evil Americans" stood between his country and peace; they must leave so that a real political solution could ensue.[14] He hoped he and the army-eligible American "would not meet again."[15]

O'Brien wrote to Jim Vance offering to turn the meeting into an ar-ticle for the *Worthington Daily Globe*. Vance was interested in it and two others, one on "the American defector"—George Wheeler—and one on Czechoslovakian president Antonín Novotný. Vance was already courting O'Brien to work for the paper after graduation.[16] The articles didn't appear until the next summer. Vance certainly had his hands full as racial un-rest and urban violence pitted Black America against police departments and the National Guard. Newspapers sometimes described the violence in terms of hours-long pitched battles as soldiers deployed tanks and ma-chine guns against civilians.[17]

One solo excursion outside Prague took O'Brien to Lidice, a small town that Hitler had ordered eradicated in June 1942. SS agents murdered the men, sent the women and most of the children to concentration camps, and selected a small number of children for Germanization. "I expected to be horrified to reach the place where so many bodies had perished, so many souls terrified and strangled, so many hearts beating wildly in the night," he told the *Pioneer Press* reporter. "I listened for empty voices; I listened for sobs and screams—'Goddamned we've been betrayed, Goddamned we die now!' I looked for torches blinking at me like serpent's eyes."[18]

O'Brien's Worthington pal Steve Goff caught up with him in Prague in late July.[19] Goff had spent his junior year of high school in Crailsheim, Germany. He had traveled back this summer to see friends and as a kind of therapy. During Goff's sophomore year at Carleton College, his father had succumbed to colon cancer. Six months later his mother was diagnosed with pancreatic cancer. She died in September.

O'Brien on his Vespa and Goff on a used motorcycle, the two headed south toward Athens. Goff's sidecar was perfect for carrying knapsacks and sleeping bags. Still in Czechoslovakia, the Vespa's handle grips for the throttle were stolen. O'Brien struggled riding through Austria and over the Alps, the tail of his duster coat constantly working its way out from under his seat, his hands freezing and slipping on the exposed, icy-wet metal of the handles.

Two years later, a foot soldier in Việt Nam, O'Brien would fantasize about setting himself up in a cottage in Freistadt, Austria, after the war, where the "mountains were formidable, the air was clear, the town had a dry moat around it, the beer was the best in the world, the girls were not communists, and they had blue eyes and blond hair and big bosoms."[20] O'Brien and Goff slept outdoors several times. One morning the clop-clopping of horses and the churning of wagon wheels woke O'Brien. The site of the horse-drawn wagons, the men driving them, and the women in headscarves transported O'Brien to an earlier century. In Yugoslavia, the two travelers pulled into a hostel during a downpour. The young woman who checked them in said to O'Brien, "Du bist schön." In their room, Goff told him she had called him beautiful. It irked O'Brien that Goff hadn't told him earlier, while it irked Goff that O'Brien, not nearly as fluent in German, drew her attention.

In Athens, they saw the Parthenon, the Acropolis, the typical sites. They stayed somewhere cheap and made a daily stop at the Hilton so O'Brien could enjoy a strawberry daiquiri. They also spent several days on Paros to avoid the more tourist-infested islands. They shared the ferry ride to and from with locals and their chickens. They hiked, lounged about, people-watched, and slept on the beach.

Goff's motorcycle needed major repairs, plus their summer was running short on days. They sold their rides and bought train tickets. O'Brien is sure the two of them traveled together to Hersbruck, where he introduced Goff to Elfrieda before parting ways; Goff is sure they parted in Athens and he never met her. Whichever happened, O'Brien left by train for Paris in something of a hurry to catch his flight home.

If O'Brien's Odd Fellows' high school summer trip to the East Coast four years earlier had given him a euphoric taste of independence from home, his SPAN summer proved formative in a different way. He often felt lost and lonely. Middle-class America "gives you ways and means of getting through life" as you grow up; it provides solutions and safety nets. But during that European experience all risks, all solutions, all opportunities, were his own. It was a great "life lesson" in flying by the seat of his pants. The spirit of that summer, with its two long road trips, found its way into the soldiers' road trip to Paris—including a weeklong stop in Athens—in *Going After Cacciato*. In a letter during the late stages of writing the novel, O'Brien answers the *Why Paris?* question by reflecting on how it represents for his character Paul Berlin in Việt Nam the same vision of a place "where life is calm and happy, where nature is kind, where people do the right things, where there is harmony and peace and tranquility" that O'Brien daydreamed about in Việt Nam, places such as Freistadt, Austria; northern Minnesota; and Paros, Greece.[21]

6

GREETING

On May 27, 1968, Tim O'Brien and 363 classmates graduated from Macalester College. The same day, the Supreme Court handed down its decision in *United States v. O'Brien*—David Paul O'Brien—ruling that prohibiting the burning of draft cards did not violate the First Amendment's guarantee of free speech.

Home in Worthington, O'Brien had just finished a round of golf on the course about five minutes away. He pulled the letter from the mailbox, took it inside, and dropped it on the kitchen table in front of his parents, who were having lunch. No one spoke. The O'Brien family's future changed in an instant, as the *if* that had dominated their lives became *when*.

O'Brien has retold and written the moment when he opened his draft notice as an early June day, with the yellow paper cawing at him all summer long from his billfold. It's more likely, however, that upon returning home he received not the draft notice, but instructions to report for the armed forces physical examination. On June 7, O'Brien reported to St. Paul for his physical and was classified I-A: AVAILABLE FOR MILITARY SERVICE.[1] As O'Brien had no expectation of failing the exam, no plans to lie, the instructions were tantamount to the draft notice itself, the order to report for induction. Now the *if* really was *when*.

It felt like the Nobles County draft board had been biding its time until graduation renewed his eligibility. The O'Briens had moved to town nearly twenty years before, but Bill still felt like an outsider, his family less valued. Gary Melom believes he and O'Brien were marked for the draft because of their politics. Someone in the community told Melom that "the draft board was keeping a close eye on" the liberal debate crew. In high school, they had done "things from time to time that irritated the establishment," such as going to meetings to challenge Republican candidates "with really basic questions we were pretty sure they couldn't answer." O'Brien's memoir reports doing just that at a League of Women Voters meeting.[2] One drunken night in 1966 after failing out of Macalester, Melom volunteered for the army in order to have enough control over his enlistment to avoid combat.[3] He was certain that he'd be drafted otherwise. As for his buddy Tim's getting drafted two years later: "He got screwed."

O'Brien doubts any such prejudice played much of a role in his selection. At its inception, as continued after World War II, the Selective Service System envisioned exemptions not as an out from military service but as a mechanism for shunting young adults into productive careers and family life. The system drafted citizens during peacetime, too. One typically imagines the white-collar class, but local boards also acted out of local interests:

> Farmers often convinced draft boards that their sons were essential
> to the continued operation of the family farm. Plumbers, electricians,
> and other craftsmen lobbied local boards for automatic deferments
> for union apprentices. [. . .] Rural draft boards regularly granted
> deferments to truck drivers, laborers, and others whose employers
> were close friends of board members.[4]

Preferential treatment wasn't out of the question. Delinquents could be given the choice between the justice system or military service. By the time O'Brien faced selection in the late 1960s, with the military's manpower requirement reaching its peak and the courts cracking down on the unfair disparities, local boards had tightened up their practices.[5]

Of course Tim O'Brien took being drafted personally. The bitterness of betrayal saturates his accounts of that summer. The very community he did not care to disappoint, the very community he loved as home, was the very community sending him to war. The hometown board—his neighbors—"did the dirty work" before "scurry[ing] off to Wednesday-night bingo or Friday-night church suppers or Saturday-night square dancing." Why not *their* sons? "And if you're so hot for war, what the fuck are you doing in Worthington,

Minnesota? What the fuck are you doing choosing other people's kids to fight a war you're unwilling to go fight yourself? I used to yell these things, and many similar things, as I drove around Lake Okabena."[6]

June was a rough month in Việt Nam. The first week set yet another record for casualties, at 438 killed and 3,870 wounded, having increased from the prior week by 12 and 1,183 respectively.[7] The *Worthington Daily Globe* printed information about local casualties: "TEN GIS FROM REGION KILLED IN VIETNAM"—"SECOND SHELDON SOLDIER KILLED IN VIET WAR"—"EIGHT STATE GIS DIE IN VIETNAM."[8]

Robert Kennedy's murder on June 5 plunged a nation already in the middle of a chaotic presidential campaign deeper into grief and chaos. On June 14, the beloved child psychologist Dr. Benjamin Spock, Rev. William Sloane Coffin, Jr., and two others were convicted for "conspiracy to counsel young men to avoid the draft."[9] By the end of the month, news broke that the military was abandoning the base at Khe Sanh, where only a few months earlier more than twenty-three hundred marines had been killed or wounded during a brutal, headline-commanding seventy-seven-day siege.[10] Khe Sanh, a massive deception operation by the North Vietnamese to misdirect attention away from their Tết Offensive buildup, had been a heralded place of heroic resistance for Americans.

Not even the weather gave O'Brien a break. A tornado ripped through nearby Tracy, Minnesota, on June 13, then a summer "hurricane" tore through the region a week later, with winds up to one hundred miles per hour that tore down farm buildings. The storm brought down Worthington's radio tower and shattered storefront windows.[11]

Across the country, racial tensions erupted in the Watts and Cleveland riots and elsewhere, including St. Paul. Norman Mailer described it at the time as "a year when the Republic hovered on the edge of revolution, nihilism, and lines of police on file to the horizon, visions of future Vietnams in our own cities upon us."[12] Now in its second year, planning for the nation's 1976 bicentennial must have looked like a rather lame antidote to the body politic's ills.

The first half of the summer, O'Brien worked as a de-clotter on the pork assembly line in Worthington's Armour meatpacking plant. It wasn't his first manual labor job. During the summer between his sophomore and junior years at Macalester, he worked at a furniture store in Cicero, Illinois. He and a high school friend studying at the University of Chicago crashed at a frat house. O'Brien enjoyed stock boy duties. He took pleasure in sore muscles. O'Brien and the other stock boy fancied the business must have been a front. They moved furniture around all day in a dilapidated store that never seemed to sell anything. O'Brien needed the money, but he mostly wanted to spend the summer in Chicago.

The job at the Armour plant was more foul than strenuous. It involved maneuvering and firing a specialized water gun suspended from the ceiling to blast out the blood clots from each pig corpse's upper body. "Goggles were a necessity, and a rubber apron, but even so it was like standing for eight hours a day under a lukewarm blood-shower. At night I'd go home smelling of pig. I couldn't wash it out."[13] The story "On the Rainy River" uses the graphic imagery of rows of slaughtered pigs, and the persistent stench, to summon the war. O'Brien quit after a few weeks, angering his father, who had gotten him the job.

In early June, O'Brien visited Jane Reister at her home in Oskaloosa, Iowa, and golfed with her dad. At some point—according to Reister—O'Brien mentioned to her a plan to start on another novel that summer, although he doesn't recall any such plan.[14] Working at the plant and worrying about his fate left little time or energy. When not at the plant, O'Brien played golf and pool, hung out with friends, and agonized over what to do. Should he acquiesce to the draft and probably end up in Việt Nam, or remove himself to Canada, perhaps never to return home? "On the Rainy River" is memoir until the moment the narrator named Tim O'Brien decides to tell "the full truth" of the fictional rest of the story as he walks out of the pork plant, goes home to pack a suitcase, and drives to the Rainy River, on the Canadian border, where he'll finally decide.[15]

Tim O'Brien believed in country, community, the American dream, obligation, loyalty, respect, responsibility, and civic service. He clung to the civil, the orderly, and the proper, behind which pulses the human hunger to belong. Tim O'Brien equally believed the American war in Việt Nam wrong as a matter of foreign policy and an irresponsible, morally repugnant betrayal of ideals. He saw evil in Hà Nội's communism, evil in Washington's neo-imperialism, and unconscionable evil in the human suffering of the armed conflict between them. How could he compound the evils? That summer right-minded principles and instincts locked horns.

This defining psychomachia would become fundamental to O'Brien's understanding of good fiction, as repeated in innumerable lectures, classes, and workshops. "It is the intersection of specific human circumstances with abstract value which is the *moral aboutness* of a book." He rejects the presumption that the artist necessarily knows "at least in some sense, *which* values to assert and which not to assert." Because how can we know? For O'Brien, meaningful fiction hinges not on resolution, not on the challenge to do the right thing, but on quandary. "It is rather a question, both in art and in life, of struggling with uncertainty."[16] When O'Brien credits the war with making him a writer, he doesn't only mean the thirteen months he spent in Southeast Asia. Despite his conviction in the wrongness of the war, O'Brien had the intellectual maturity to remain open to doubt, for "who really knew, anyway?"[17]

That summer he imagined living in Canada in hiding, literally on the run from authorities. He'd lie awake at night half dreaming nearly cinematic sequences of pursuit by Mounties. To reject the army would be to turn his back on home as well as all the futures he'd imagined for himself in America. To reject the war would be to embarrass his parents. His father would feel even more of a town outcast. Worthington would take it personally. But for O'Brien to defy his conscience by entering the military would be to involve himself in sanctioned homicide. The back-and-forth with himself and with friends all summer was fiercely discursive, with "plenty of references to the philosophers and academicians of war" that overlaid gut terrors.[18]

And where did love fit in? Love of country and neighbor, but also love of humanity, integrity, and life? The need to be loved?

O'Brien aired his turmoil to friends from high school and college. His family understood; he did not inflict his predicament any further on them. Jim Vance, the *Daily Globe* editor, advised O'Brien to answer the call to service.[19] To one or two friends, he fantasized about showing up for the bus at the appointed hour to proclaim his decision with placards of utmost economy: FUCK LBJ! and FUCK THE WAR! The conversations took place in cafés, in tavern and drugstore and bowling alley, on the golf course, and in a car coursing the seven-mile route around Lake Okabena.

O'Brien had to get out of Worthington. Everyone expected him to do his duty; their looks were too much to handle. He needed privacy and headspace. He repaired to a house on Vernon Street less than a block from

Macalester in St. Paul, rented by three guys he knew at Mac.[20] He slept on
a cot by the furnace in the bare basement.

Jane Reister was in Europe with Macalester's Student Work Abroad
Project (SWAP), sending O'Brien postcards from her travels. She had no
idea what to write about his plight. In an early letter, she told him that "you
need this summer to yourself" but never mentioned the situation again except to invite him to Europe before he had to report, whenever that might
be.[21] On Tuesday, July 2, she received a dozen red roses from him, neatly
arranged in blue paper and wrapped with cellophane and a large pink bow.
They arrived at the office and created a scene among her co-workers. Her
letter of thanks the next day expressed mild if flirty confusion about his
reason for the delivery.[22] Only later did she wonder if the roses bade her
farewell in signaling his intent to flee to Canada.

In the Twin Cities, O'Brien went to see the new John Wayne film *The
Green Berets*, which opened at the Lyric on Hennepin Avenue in Minneapolis on Friday, June 28.[23] What a bizarre experience. Whereas Hollywood
had rushed to get World War II movies into theaters during World War
II, the war in Việt Nam had resisted the screen for years. Wayne made the
film to drum up support for the flailing war effort. On its release, one journalist wrote, "The kindest of the reviews have suggested that 'Green Berets'
is a World War II type propaganda picture, made a quarter of a century too
late."[24] The new film's risible jingoism and cringy acting outdid most of its
World War II predecessors.

Why on earth did Tim O'Brien want to see *The Green Berets* weeks before entering the army? Perhaps to glimpse his future, however inaccurate.
Perhaps to add the film's argument to his internal debate about what he
should do. Perhaps to be a kid again watching a war flick or a western. Was
he able to laugh at its inanity?

GREETING: YOU ARE HEREBY ORDERED FOR INDUCTION INTO THE ARMED
FORCES OF THE UNITED STATES.

In the second six months of 1968, the United States inducted 90,200 young
men into the armed services. O'Brien was one of the 1,809 from Minnesota.[25]
The letter must have come in mid-July. He and everyone else once headed

to graduate school couldn't be called up until July 1, and most enlistment
orders were cut two to four weeks before the induction date, which for
O'Brien was August 14. For all the family's hypothesizing and consterna-
tion, the board appears to have followed the rules by selecting those eligible
"in the order of their dates of birth with the oldest being selected first."[26]
Four years of college deferment jumped O'Brien to the head of the line.

It's possible the kitchen moment happened then, in July, with O'Brien
returning from St. Paul for a round or two of golf. Something fateful did
arrive in early summer. It's impossible to untangle the memories and facts.
O'Brien didn't dally in contacting Harvard to request delayed entry. The
letter guaranteeing future admittance, dated July 24, closes with strained
office-speak sympathy that almost reads as deadpan sarcasm: "I am sorry
that your education has had to be interrupted and offer you my best wishes
for your coming endeavor."[27]

He also did not dally in exploring his options within the army, corresponding with a Mac friend currently a private first class at Fort Knox, Tennessee. If "your prime concern is (like mine and that of so many college
grads) staying alive and getting out of the Army as soon as possible, be an
enlisted man, take your two years of underpaid monotony, and get out,"
the friend wrote. In terms of a desk job, "A college degree used to be a
virtual guarantee of a good job, but with so many college grads now being
drafted, that might no longer be true."[28]

Possibly the very week he received his draft notice, O'Brien landed his
first professional publications, three paid articles in the July 16, 17, and 19
editions of the *Worthington Daily Globe*. They were the articles from his
Prague summer: the interview with the North Vietnamese junior officer
studying economics, the one on democratic hopes after President Antonín
Novotný left office, and the one on George Wheeler and Eric Meier, the
American and East German seeking better lives and societies outside their
birth countries. Articles about Czechoslovakia had become much more urgent by midsummer as it faced off with the Soviet Union. Vance was grateful to have the articles. On June 28, he had written O'Brien that he would
take the interview, asked him to write the other two, and offered forty-five
dollars for the series.[29]

It must have been strange for O'Brien, in June 1968, to reconstruct
the interview with the North Vietnamese lieutenant. The piece portrays

O'Brien as playing devil's advocate to Le Ledoc, challenging the man's pro–Hà Nội ideas and praising America's government and society even as O'Brien engaged this debate inside himself, engaged it urgently and personally. The Tim O'Brien of June 1968 briefly eclipses the Tim O'Brien of June 1967 in the description of walking to meet Le: "I was about to talk with a man I might kill on the battlefield next year. Or a man who might kill me."[30] The final words of the Wheeler-Meier article acutely reflected O'Brien's crisis as he mulled over giving up the United States for Canada:

> One man, George Wheeler, escaped an "oppressive" political system in the West to seek refuge and happiness in Czechoslovakia, a communist state. Another man, Eric Meier, escaped the "horrible" politics of communism so that he might make a new life in the West.
>
> It is strange that men can see things so differently, and it is frightening to see men risk their social position, life and liberty for the sake of "escape."
>
> But it is also encouraging. It heartened me to meet, there in the heart of East Europe in 1967, two men willing to live out their convictions; to make a try at achieving their dreams.[31]

Vance's printing the articles in July 1968 proved a kindness. It gave O'Brien a postwar life to anticipate.

Ten days later Mike Tracy, the bully of O'Brien's youth, was killed in St. Paul while hanging out with friends from his motorcycle club, El Forasteros. The "most unusual funeral in the history of Worthington" took place on Wednesday, July 31. More than a hundred members of Tracy's motorcycle club attended. The procession from the Westminster Presbyterian Church, quite near O'Brien's house, to the cemetery stretched two miles; at the grave site, the bikers stood arranged like "Legionnaires or VFW men at a military funeral."[32] O'Brien, in St. Paul, missed it.

In the end O'Brien did not deliberately follow Socrates's example in *choosing* to defer to the society to which he owed his fortunes, allegiance, and moral code. O'Brien has described his boarding the bus for the army at the end of the summer as resulting from a state of indecisive paralysis. He "submitted" to "gravity," to "a sort of sleepwalking default."[33] Other draftees have vouched that O'Brien's story, as told in his war memoir and "On the

Rainy River," is their story. O'Brien has also understood his moment of indecision to be a decision. It has racked him ever since. "I was a coward," he famously has his fictional avatar declare at the end of the short story. "I went to the war."[34]

His sleepwalking body went kicking and screaming. Up until a few weeks before boarding the plane for Việt Nam, O'Brien harbored the hope, almost an expectation, that the military would find a better use for a young man of his proven book smarts—not to mention his outdoorsman and mechanical ineptitudes—than jungle combat. O'Brien didn't fully appreciate it, but his friend from Fort Knox was right. The percentage of draftees with college degrees more than tripled from July through October, from less than 5 percent to 16 percent.[35] With recent graduates being inducted either through the draft or by enlisting to avoid combat, O'Brien confronted stiff competition for those precious noncombat assignments.[36]

O'Brien returned home from St. Paul for the final days before reporting. On August 12, after an early dinner, the family assembled in the kitchen for goodbyes before his dad was to drive him to the bus station. As O'Brien gathered himself to walk out the door, Bill made a final check of his son's papers and stopped him. They'd gotten the date wrong. He had another twenty-four hours to kill.

O'Brien took a solo car trip around the lake, then retreated to the basement to make some of the signs he had fantasized about, signs he tore into pieces, took outside, and stuffed into the garbage can.

O'Brien stepped up into the appointed bus the next afternoon. That very day Jane Reister dashed him a postcard from Norway. "I've been thinking of you today—what a miserable day this must be for you. But the worst (I hope) will be over in two months, and I hope it will go quickly."

7

IN THE MILL

A photograph in the *Worthington Daily Globe* the next day carried this caption: "Four young men left Worthington by bus at 7 p.m. Tuesday to report to the induction center at Sioux Falls," South Dakota, sixty miles due west. O'Brien didn't know the other three, all two years behind him in high school. The four stand behind a belly-high chain fence. O'Brien wears jeans, a tee, and black-framed glasses. He's the smallest of the four. None of them knows where to look, how to position hands, whether to smile. "They are (left to right) Donald J. Ult de Flesch, Raymond Dickey, Tom O'Brien, and Michael W. Kleve. The four Nobles County youths have had physical examinations and were to be sworn into the armed forces today. The most likely station for first duty is Ft. Lewis, Wash."

Someone tore out that corner of the paper to save. O'Brien years later circled "Tom," drew an arrow to the margin, and wrote, "Wrong guy got drafted!"[1]

It was the thirteenth of August. The bus stopped at other small towns to pick up other young men. Those whom the introspective O'Brien in his memoir scorns as "the tough guys" spent the short ride "drinking beer and howling in the back seats, brandishing their empty cans and calling one another 'scum' and 'trainee' and 'GI Joe.'"[2] The new inductees spent the night at the Sioux Falls YMCA on South Minnesota Avenue, five short blocks down Eleventh Avenue from the Military Entrance Processing Station. O'Brien "went out alone for a beer, drank in a corner booth, then [. . .] bought a book" to read in his room.[3]

Late the next morning, they headed to the processing station for induction. O'Brien remembers the room as brightly lit with fake "blondish" wood paneling and an American flag, "sort of like a conference room in a Holiday Inn, a room in which the Rotary Club is scheduled to meet after we kids got dispatched to a war." After several legs by jet, they arrived at McChord Air Force Base outside Tacoma, Washington, next door to the army's Fort Lewis.

Recently emptied of the Fourth Infantry Division, which had deployed to Việt Nam, Fort Lewis in 1966 became a personnel center for processing soldiers going to and returning from the Pacific theater as well as a basic training center. Because the center assigned bodies to units as they arrived, O'Brien's training platoon consisted mostly of new soldiers from the upper Midwest, including the busload he traveled with. All the platoon's thirty-seven eventual graduates were white except for two or three, and these were probably Dakota and Lakota Sioux.[4]

One of those young men was another small-town Minnesotan, Erik Hansen. O'Brien had noticed him either at the YMCA or Sioux Falls airport in Sioux Falls. Hansen was older than the others and carried himself accordingly even as he paced nervously. At twenty-four, he was a slight, brown-haired man with cigarette in hand. The day it arrived, the platoon trudged into its quarters, the second floor of one of the double-decker barracks among the rows of identical white-clapboard barracks. On the lower bunk in one of the two rows of double-decker beds, Hansen saw a German-language dictionary. He supposed its owner hoped for a job other than the infantry and a posting other than Việt Nam, someone curious about the world. Sensing a kindred soul, Hansen claimed the top bunk. The dictionary belonged to O'Brien.

They did not remain bunkmates for long, but it didn't matter. "I made a friend, Erik," O'Brien writes in the war memoir, "and together he and I stumbled like galley slaves through the first months of army life."[5] A few years later Hansen would be the best man at O'Brien's wedding. He would also become O'Brien's first reader, artistic confidant, and closest lifelong friend.

Hansen grew up in Tyler, sixty-five miles north of Worthington. His and O'Brien's paths probably crossed at interschool events or on Turkey Day in Worthington, for which Hansen's family sometimes traveled down. Tyler began as a Danish settlement; Hansen's grandfather, one of the first to plow the lands there in the 1880s, came to the United States to serve as a story-teller in an immigrant folk school (*folkehøjskole*). Hansen had received a football scholarship offer from Macalester. The team was horrible, and having no desire for four years of pummeling, the skinny 140-pounder chose Grand View College, a two-year junior college in Des Moines, Iowa, with deep ties to the Danish community.

Like O'Brien, Hansen thrived in college and became student body president. Then he headed to Europe to explore his roots, spending a year at a folk school in Snoghøj, Denmark. He returned to Minnesota to finish his bachelor's degree in American studies at the state university. After a year in the doctoral program for Scandinavian studies, he left school for good to get back to Europe—where he received his draft notice, forwarded from home. Hansen could have easily stayed abroad. He very nearly did. He did not believe in the military intervention in Việt Nam. But as he wrote in "Sisters," an autobiographical short story published in 1979, he felt guilty about the person who would be sent in his place. He worried that if "opposition [to the war] was to have a marked effect, it had to come from inside the country, inside the military, if necessary."[6] He also fretted about his family, because to resist the draft by staying abroad would have meant *staying* abroad, exiling himself and severing ties indefinitely. He didn't want to embarrass or hurt his parents, and he was scared.

Kindred souls.

To O'Brien, the rest of their platoon mates were tykes who read *Hot Rod* magazine and ate up the army's rhetoric of man-making adventure. O'Brien's father was sending him issues of *The American Scholar*.[7] Hansen also aspired to write. In the early sixties, he worked at a gas station on Highway 14 and fantasized about meeting Ernest Hemingway en route between the Mayo Clinic at Rochester and Idaho. For O'Brien to find someone like Hansen in that place, at that time—the eclectic education, the maturity, the cosmopolitanism, the shared politics and writing dream—what were the odds?

Their first week of basic training consisted of the rudiments: learning military ranks, structure, and lingo; beginning to learn to march and perform manual of arms; and learning how to salute, wear the uniform, make the bed, shine shoes, clean the barracks, and respond when addressed by a superior.

One Worthington recruit, Mike Kleve, became the platoon guide, the ranking trainee who operated as a middleman between the drill sergeants and the recruits. The top drill sergeant, a man named Guyton (the memoir's Blyton), had called Kleve to the upstairs barracks where he waited with two other sergeants and a small man in jeans looking like another new private, but probably another instructor. Sgt. Guyton ordered Kleve to shove the man into a wall locker and lock it. He did. Guyton told Kleve to drag the locker to the window. Kleve obeyed, figuring the scene for a test; Guyton wouldn't order the defenestration. Guyton had Kleve lift the wall locker onto the windowsill when one of the other sergeants reminded Guyton they had somewhere to be. The three NCOs skedaddled, leaving Kleve to free the man. The next day Guyton affixed the platoon guide stripes to Kleve's uniform. Sgt. Guyton probably chose to test Kleve because he was a big man who seemed on board with the program. In Việt Nam, Kleve would carry the machine gun. O'Brien and Hansen found Kleve too enthusiastic. Kleve thought of himself as a mother hen who sought to ease life for his fellows by contenting their instructors.

On August 21, a drill sergeant ordered O'Brien's platoon to join the other platoon downstairs to hear about the Warsaw Pact's invasion of Czechoslovakia, concluding with words to the effect of "All you bastards are going to die in World War III." Soon thereafter, the company assembled to hear about their commitment options. *You think you have a two-year commitment*, the sergeant pitched. *You really have a six-year commitment: two years of active duty, two years of active reserve—so weekend drills and summer training—and two years of inactive reserve, which is your name on a list in case there really is a world war. Or you can sign up now for three years of active duty, then three years of inactive reserve, and you get to pick your advance training post, which could influence your branch assignment*—whether a combat arms branch such as infantry or artillery, or a support service branch such as transportation or the signal corps. Trainees interested in the three-three option stayed to learn more. The rest were excused.

O'Brien and Hansen sat on opposite sides of the room. They made eye contact. O'Brien's look said, *This is bullshit*. He left. He detested the army and refused to sign up for one more day. He felt "lucky" on "that fateful day in August" as he gambled that the military would find a better use for him than combat infantry in Việt Nam.[8] Hansen stayed. Even though the three-

three option meant an extra year of active duty, it meant relative freedom after three years, whereas the two-two-two option most likely would have trapped him stateside after Việt Nam, so four years instead of three before he could get back to Europe and the woman he had fallen in love with right before flying home to enter the army. He chose Fort Eustace, Virginia, for advanced training, the home of the army's transportation corps. Had the friends sat next to each other, they probably would have stayed together or left together.

In the second or third week of training, Hansen naïvely took up Sgt. Guyton's offer to talk privately. When Hansen shared his objections to the war, Guyton erupted. He ordered him up against the wall and kept him there, nose to the wall, for what felt like an hour, ranting, raging, calling him every name in the book. *Commie! Traitor! Hippie! Faggot! Coward! Pussy!* He stopped only after Hansen retorted that the one protest he ever joined was against the assassination of Martin Luther King, Jr.—Sgt. Guyton was Black. Hansen laid low for a spell, playing obedient, but Guyton harassed him for the rest of training. Guyton told Kleve to put Hansen on as many details as possible: KP (kitchen patrol), fire guard, trash call, et cetera. Such extra work sucked up what little spare time a trainee had. Guyton once pressed Kleve for O'Brien's politics and war stance. Kleve shrugged him off. He knew but didn't know, not from O'Brien anyway. Except to Hansen, O'Brien kept his thoughts to himself. As far as Guyton was concerned, O'Brien remained guilty by association.

The rest of the two-month training program gradually added knowledge and skills. The new soldiers received instruction on chemical, biological, and nuclear warfare; first aid for combat; close-quarters (hand-to-hand) combat; rifle marksmanship; map reading and land navigation with a compass; bayonet assault; hand grenades, rifle grenades, and land mines. Toward the end of basic training, the platoon bivouacked for a week to practice living in the field and to work on squad-level tactics such as coordinating fields of fire. Some of this training occurred at a mock Vietnamese village.

O'Brien made for a mediocre trainee. He performed his tasks without enthusiasm but also without grumbling. According to Kleve, O'Brien was a respectable soldier, more competent than he self-reports. O'Brien did lack the outdoorsman background that Hansen enjoyed as a Boy Scout, camper, and hunter. At the end of one firing range session, O'Brien cocked his M14's operating rod to pull the bolt back while popping off with "Clear, Drill Sergeant!" only to send a round that shouldn't have been there spinning out of the chamber through the air, gleaming as it caught the light in its torturously slow descent.

"We march to the night infiltration course. They use machine guns on us, firing overhead while Erik and Harry and White and Kline crawl alongside me, under barbed wire, red tracers everywhere, down into ditches, across the finish line. Then in dead night we march back to the barracks."[9] They marched everywhere, and everywhere they marched, they sang. The memoir's title comes from one of their cadences:

If I die in a combat zone,
Box me up and ship me home.
An' if I die on the Russian front,
Bury me with a Russian cunt.

Sound Off!

The misogyny and racism of their training offended O'Brien.[10]

Those eight weeks were a hallucinatory blur, especially in memory. Relating the experience, O'Brien is prone to descriptors such as *savage*, *petty*, *barbaric*, *hellish*, even *evil*. The new soldiers weren't led, they were browbeaten. Cleaning and polishing consumed supposed free time. The soldiers grabbed a few hours' sleep on nights they didn't have pointless guard duty. It was not uncommon for them to make their beds, tightened to inspection standards, and then sleep on top of the covers, in full or partial uniform for the first formation, to save time in the morning. Four months after returning from Việt Nam, O'Brien wrote Hansen about fighting "to stay awake" during the training lectures at Lewis, "eyes numb, ears deaf, the future bleak, the mind unbelieving: really—simply unbelieving."[11]

The platoon experienced all the clichés: the push-ups for screwing up; the collective punishment for one trainee's folly, such as having the entire platoon hold their rifles overhead while marching. Looking back, Hansen has cited the brutality of the 1987 film *Full Metal Jacket* for its accuracy, not hyperbole. One day one of the Sioux hurled a boot through a window, shattering the glass. O'Brien's friend Blair GreyBull, a Hunkpapa Lakota and volunteer recruit from Standing Rock Reservation, walked away—in shame, Hansen imagined, for the other man's failure to uphold a stoic dignity.[12] Guyton had it in for a soldier named Kline, an overweight, whimpering oaf. Kline grinned stupidly; he blubbered. His incompetence and imbecility astonished.[13] When Mike Kleve saw the film *Full Metal Jacket* over twenty years later, he couldn't shake the sense that he was watching the real Kline, not the film's Pvt. Pyle (played by Vincent D'Onofrio). O'Brien and Hansen shared that sense. Whereas the film's platoon tried to help its buffoon along, their platoon let Kline fail. He later washed out and started over in the next cycle.[14] A decade later, he would serve as a prototype for the title character of *Going After Cacciato*.

Basic training demeaned by design. Despite the introduction to warfighting skills, by 1966 basic training's focus had shifted from field training to the discipline of garrison soldiering, meaning drill and ceremony—the parade ground skills—and the associated sundry cleaning, shining, and polishing, and their attendant inspections. The obsession with spotless floors and trashless grounds. Division commanders in Việt Nam pressured basic training leadership to increase the program's rigor while creating in-country refresher courses for soldiers fresh off the planes.[15] Moreover, by 1968, the training cadre was anxious about the anti-war sentiment sweeping the nation's youth, the college-educated in particular, and about the growing resistance movement within the ranks—including at Fort Lewis.[16]

The weather conspired with the drill instructors to dole out misery. It rained most days; the wet-weather anoraks barely sufficed. Although O'Brien's class began training in mid-August, the season turned cold soon enough and the old barracks had no heating. "Above us the sixty-mile-distant mountain stood to the sky, white and shivering cold," O'Brien wrote. "The mountain was named Rainier, and it stood for freedom."[17] On the precious few days the trainees could see it through the rain and clouds. On the days they didn't forget to look up.

O'Brien's mother and sister wrote several times about his relationship with Jane Reister, like Kathy a Macalester senior. After two years at a junior college, because as a young woman from Worthington Kathy didn't imagine other possibilities, she had joined her brother at Macalester. Kathy and Ava chastised O'Brien for what they saw as his unfair treatment of Jane. "[S]he's been doing the giving and you've been doing the taking," Kathy wrote after Jane visited with her in her dorm room until two thirty in the morning.[18] Kathy's birthday letter to O'Brien continued to try to set him straight. "I don't think it was right for you to ask her to spend all that money to fly out if you just think of her as a nice kid, like you said in your last letter. If it's Gayle Roby you like so much, ask her to come."[19]

Roby is the memoir's anonymous girl to whom he wrote so besottedly during basic.[20] In the draft of the memoir, O'Brien wrote about both: "I thought about two girls. After thinking, they became women, only months too late." The published memoir revises Reister away, as the "two girls" and "women" become "a girl" and "a woman."[21] The published book omits naming Roby while curtailing the draft passage's youthful reverie about her:

> I insisted she had a special religiosity. Did she deny that it was the discovery of the goddess inside her that made up my love? I thought about this argument, realizing it was perfectly true and perfectly futile. Perhaps we are not allowed to see the goddess except for a moment, and perhaps that vision, catching them stark and unclothed and too utterly perfect, is sufficient every time to drive them away.[22]

Then the draft finally turns to Reister, whom it does not name:

> I spent time thinking about another girl as well, wishing I could trust her and doing a lot of remembering about our times together in college. [. . .] I thought I knew her. But it always ended with the feeling she could not be trusted. She signed her letters, love. She hinted she loved me, a little afraid of being bullied out of it. Still, she was willing to fly two thousand miles for my first pass, whenever it would come; she was willing to take a chance on me, willing to wait.[23]

The trust problem was O'Brien's. It came from an abiding insecurity. He did not believe she could love him in the way and to the degree that she did because, deep down, he didn't believe he could be so loved. The insecurity would hound his relationships for a long time to come.

In addition to reporting on his golf game, O'Brien's father updated his son on local sports news. Ten years O'Brien's junior, Greg the middle-schooler had demonstrated a lot of talent on the football field. Bill O'Brien also wrote about local army reservists "fighting shipment to Vietnam." Seventy-five soldiers from the 452nd General Support Company were join-ing a national trend to file suit against deployment to what they posited as an illegal war. The trend gained momentum in September, after Supreme Court Justice William Douglas began staying the army from sending re-servists and Guardsmen to Việt Nam. The full court reversed those stays on October 7. O'Brien couldn't have known it, but a unit from Burbank, California, stationed at Fort Lewis, sued for nondeployment the day after the Supreme Court's decision.[24]

O'Brien kept his personal resistance under the radar. "I mouthed the words, shaping my lips and tongue just so, perfect deception. But no noise came out. Failure to bellow 'Yes, Drill Sergeant!' was a fist in the bastard's face. A point for the soul." He kept to himself and "maintained silence."[25] O'Brien's defensive mechanism was the familiar adolescent one of respond-ing to the hurt of not fitting in by owning it, clinging to his sense of superi-ority, retreating alone or sticking with the other bookish kids. He allowed himself a camaraderie with Hansen based on what they regarded as sav-ing their souls. They feigned submission and sometimes even enthusiasm, shouting *hoo-ah* as loud as the rest. "Simply to think and talk and try to understand was evidence that we were not cattle or machines."[26]

The pair discussed literature, philosophy, politics, the war, the world, women. *What would Socrates do? When is invention legitimate in non-fiction storytelling?* Hansen had begun planning a novel, "The Inviolate House," which he would work on for decades but never publish. Much of the rare time they could steal from the army they spent on an enormous log in a seating area beside the barracks. Hansen introduced O'Brien to Ezra Pound's "Hugh Selwyn Mauberley," a poem O'Brien would reflect on throughout his tour in Việt Nam. He also taught O'Brien to smoke, which O'Brien considered another dimension of his resistance, a personal plea-sure the army couldn't deny and a much-needed posturing.[27]

Their platoon mates recognized O'Brien and Hansen as different from themselves. Guyton hazed them in explicitly homophobic ways: "You two college pussies out there hidin' and sneakin' a little pussy. Maybe I'll just stick you two pussies in the same bunk tonight, let you get plenty of pussy so tomorrow you can't piss."[28]

At Fort Lewis, there was a third member of the coterie: T. E. Lawrence. Hansen brought to training his two bibles, Lawrence's *The Seven Pillars of Wisdom*, his epic memoir of guerrilla warfare in Arabia during the Great War, and *The Mint*. "With *The Mint*," O'Brien "gave in to soldiering."[29] O'Brien did not have time to read it. He gleaned his understanding of it by listening to Hansen and in snatching passages when he could. While it's impossible to know what exactly Hansen said or O'Brien read, it's not difficult to see why O'Brien took to the book.

In August of 1922, Lawrence of Arabia, until quite recently a colonel and an adviser to Winston Churchill, joined the Royal Air Force under the pseudonym John Hume Ross as a new recruit. He wanted "to write a real book," and with the RAF as the perfect subject, he decided he needed the perspective of the lowest ranks.[30] Lawrence's experiences in the RAF's version of basic training, which his book dubs *the mill*, resembled O'Brien's. Garrison tasks and drill:

> So far we get only the curses, defencelessly. [. . .] We are tossed through the day, haphazardly, from hand to hand. [. . .]
>
> I think the barking of sergeants and sergeant majors on parade always denotes a miscarriage of authority, wanting to spread blind terror. They have transformed us fifty civilians into very frightened troops in a few days.[31]

One young man killed himself. Although Lawrence discovered some measure of solidarity with the others, he regarded himself as different, apart: above. He could hardly stand the vulgarity—the farting, fighting, and joshing. The obscenities and the masturbation. Theirs was a shallow and thoughtless existence, his a deep and thoughtful nature.[32] At Fort Lewis, O'Brien felt the same, felt far above "the unconscious, genuflecting herd."[33]

O'Brien wanted to be a great writer. Lawrence was an incredibly success-ful writer, a prominent soldier-scholar. *The Mint* relishes language, from "whispered adjurations" and "appellant moon" to "silly twat."[34] It even includes a vulgar cadence like the ones in O'Brien's memoir. Episodic, thematic, reflective, and not strictly chronological, *The Mint* suggests itself as a precursor to *If I Die in a Combat Zone, Box Me Up and Ship Me Home.*

O'Brien spent his rare free time at the post library, where he read *The Quiet American*, Graham Greene's 1955 novel about the French war to hold on to colonial Việt Nam. In one scene, the British Thomas Fowler and the American Alden Pyle spend the night in a watchtower manned by two South Vietnamese. Fowler sympathized with the Vietnamese for having to suffer a war they didn't care about and foreigners they resented. The Anglo pair also pass the night fearing whatever approaching dangers the darkness enabled. O'Brien never reread the novel, but fifty years later remembered it as evoking the spooky dread of nighttime soldiering in Việt Nam.

O'Brien had discovered Hansen and Lawrence early. "I seemed to detect in your last letter a bit of bending to the inevitable, and that's good!" O'Brien's father wrote on September 8.[35] A couple of weeks later, O'Brien's letters expressed further pride. "This is great," Bill O'Brien wrote, "you'll return a better man for accepting your inevitable military rape and, if not purely enjoying it, at least wriggling a little to let the Army think you may be."[36] O'Brien had been able to leave post for dinner with his aunt Helen and her husband, Eddie, who lived in the area and who reported to his mother that—as she wrote to her son—"you were looking very well and seem to have accepted your fate with good grace and adapted well to army life."[37]

O'Brien's letters home from this period are lost, but it's reasonable to speculate that they were efforts toward self-convincing, as acts of the imagination, rather than reliable expressions of actual acceptance. O'Brien still struggled to make a restless peace; his final surrender was still to come. And he had lost his gamble. The news "blared" from "that hideous loudspeaker" on graduation day, October 15—he would remain at Fort Lewis for Advanced Infantry Training.[38] Some of the privates, including Erik Hansen, were headed to different branches and posts. To the rest Sgt. Guyton barked, "Every one of you swinging dicks is going to Việt Nam."

8

RUBICON DAYS

On the eve of his Advanced Infantry Training course, O'Brien wrote to Gayle Roby. The decree of his AIT assignment two days earlier gave him a stark choice: become a combat infantryman or a deserter. He offered her Robert Frost's "The Road Not Taken" in its entirety, only slightly misquoting a single line.

Then he turned to Joseph Heller: "I know how Orr felt in *Catch-22*. I'm downing my own plane now, time after time, practicing. Do you understand, Gayle. Pick that book up tonight. Steal it or something. And read thru. Please don't stop, even (especially) when you're laughing. And concentrate on Orr. He's the important one. Put it all aside—all your school work—and read it." In Heller's dark farce of World War II, the other airmen in the squadron wonder why Orr crashes into the sea so often. Readers eventually learn that he's been practicing for the time he'll down his plane, clamber into his lifeboat, and row to Sweden to freedom, out of the army, out of the war.

O'Brien liked the idea of Ireland. It felt like "home." The letter closes by attempting to enlist Roby to his cause, pleading for her to write the "longest" and "truest" letter of her life, hoping she'll "love me some."

In *The Things They Carried*, the invented Tim O'Brien character invents a story about killing a Vietnamese soldier with a grenade. He imagines both men bookish youths very much like himself. In that letter to Roby, the real Tim O'Brien describes having dreamed "about walking through a jungle, yanking the pin out of a grenade and throwing it at a man; it frightened, and I ran back through the green, bullets following. I wonder about dreams and prophecy."[1]

O'Brien reported to his AIT unit, Echo Company of the 4th Battalion, 3rd Recruit Training Brigade, on Friday, October 18, 1968.[2] After helping his new platoon straighten up the barracks, O'Brien headed into Tacoma, where he spent the rest of the day researching how to desert. He consulted magazines, he called the bus depot, the Seattle airport, and Air Canada, convincing himself that he could do it. He wrote his parents to ask them to send his passport and immunization records because, he fibbed, he would need them for R&R trips out of Việt Nam.[3]

That night O'Brien took in the main streets' collection of "bars and twenty or thirty pawn shops, old hotels and some wretched looking people." It was dark, cold, and wet. He longed for the company of a sympathizing young woman. He checked into a hotel, showered, and went back downstairs to the bar, where he watched a waitress flirt with a sergeant for a good tip only to sit with a civilian man whom she let touch her under the table. With shorn head and a blank slate of a uniform, O'Brien felt small. Pathetic. Unmanly. "I sulked at my round little table, and when I realized how obvious and repelling a greenhorn is, I paid for the beer and left without tipping anyone." He returned to his room to watch TV before sleeping. The rest of the weekend passed more pleasantly alone in his room and in his head.[4]

Bill O'Brien maintained more optimism than his son, encouraged by a film about AIT on television that reported at least some of its graduates would head to Germany, Korea, or Panama. "Hope springs eter.," he wrote his son. The news of "some kind of a breakthrough in cease fire negotiations" also "heartened" Bill.[5]

Toward the end of AIT, O'Brien described the experience in a letter to Erik Hansen as not much different from their rain-filled basic training. It was much colder, it sometimes snowed, and the chapel loudspeaker's Christmas music "hurts, of course." There was more running.[6] The privates received more weapons training, with the major difference from the basic course being the addition of collective training. The hours devoted to Information and Indoctrination, as well as to Drill and Ceremony, were mostly replaced by Squad Tactics and Patrolling.[7] Along with the near certainty of deployment came the absence of camaraderie. As much as O'Brien had felt distinct from his fellow recruits in basic training, he felt the solidarity of getting through it with them, with other Minnesotans. He missed that feeling in AIT. He missed Erik Hansen. O'Brien was as lonely as he'd ever been.

When not training, O'Brien did the common things, such as ogling Jane Fonda as Barbarella and grabbing doughnuts, but he mostly spent his time in the usually empty post library. He read. He planned. He made a quick study of Swedish history and culture to better acquaint himself with the final destination he'd decided upon. He wrote to his family—probably just to his father—"a teacher," Jane Reister, and Gayle Roby, explaining his decision to desert, explaining how hard it was "to embarrass people you love." He decided to mail the letters from Canada.

With each letter he included a passage from *The Quiet American*.[8] Greene's novel depicts the end of the French era in Việt Nam and the quiet rise of the American era—of which the death of the title character would prove chillingly prophetic. O'Brien's memoir's description of the passage points to this one, spoken from a French military pilot to the narrator, a British journalist:

> You know better than I do that we can't win. You know the road to Hanoi is cut and mined every night. You know we lose one class of St. Cyr every year. We were nearly beaten in '50. De Lattre has given us two years of grace—that's all. But we are professionals: we have to go on fighting till the politicians tell us to stop. Probably they will get together and agree to the same peace that we could have had at the beginning, making nonsense of all these years.[9]

The Paris peace talks were well underway when O'Brien copied out this passage. Its inclusion riposted his father's optimism.

There are two versions of this next episode, perhaps the most crucial of Tim O'Brien's life. The first version emerges from extant documents, including and especially the 1973 memoir. It does not, however, match O'Brien's clinging memory.

Key evidence is a letter to Erik Hansen written the weekend beginning Friday, December 6, 1968, in which O'Brien catches Hansen up on life since parting ways. The shared knowledge driving the letter is the possibility of Tim's desertion:

> [P]lugged through first 3 weeks of AIT, waiting for an initial pass before doing anything; got sick the day of the departure and ended up in the hospital (Madigan) with pneumonia—2 weeks of sleep and thought; decided to hold out until Christmas, when I could perhaps see you and, certainly talk to Al Currier—an interested Mac chaplain [—] & the woman of my thoughts[. . . .] So, two more weeks in AIT, then home to Minneapolis-St. Paul via Northwest's aircraft—arrival Dec 20th at 12 in the nighttime.[10]

O'Brien's illness might have resulted from a pneumonia-influenza epidemic, dubbed the "Hong Kong flu," which killed 703 Americans the week ending December 14.[11] The woman he hoped to see in Minnesota was Roby.

Three weeks into AIT, the weekend of Friday, November 8, the weekend of his first pass, Jane Reister had planned to visit. She put off the trip and stayed at Macalester after O'Brien called on the sixth to tell her his pass had been canceled. She hoped to visit the next weekend when she wouldn't have a paper to write.[12] It was perhaps the next day when he called Jane back to tell her he had his weekend pass after all. She went straight to Kathy O'Brien's dorm room, "so torn between wanting to go [. . .] so badly and knowing she shouldn't because of all her work, that she was practically in tears," as Kathy reported. Her letter berated O'Brien for wanting Reister to spend money to fly to see him and invest herself emotionally "if you are really stuck on this Gayle Roby like you said." Jane decided to stay at Mac.[13] The Friday of his pass, his illness hit.

Reister did not visit the next weekend, because O'Brien was in the hospital. She did manage to visit two weeks later, after his release from the hospital, for the weekend before Thanksgiving—she could not visit over the holiday break, because he did not have time off then. She had a debate exhibition against a team from Strathclyde, Scotland, on Friday, November 22, that she couldn't skip.[14] She woke before dawn the next morning to catch the earliest flight. The couple stayed in a hotel room off post, where O'Brien demonstrated some of his training as a way of messing around. He asked her to push him, for example, and when she did, he spun her around and flipped her onto the floor.

That Saturday, Reister realized how profoundly troubled O'Brien was. He asked her to talk to Rev. Currier and put the two men in touch. Besides the letter to "a teacher" that might have been Currier, it doesn't appear that they successfully communicated. Back at Macalester, Reister did speak with Currier. He wished O'Brien had approached him before being inducted. He did not know how to be helpful in a case of desertion.[15] Reister had arrived midday Saturday and left Sunday afternoon. She had Monday classes; he had Monday training. They spent less than twenty-four hours together.

"It was nice that Jane could go to Washington to see you," Ava wrote to her son the Sunday just after Thanksgiving before chastising him on his too-casual affection and treatment of Reister. Ava's letter also revealed that her husband had withheld their son's plans to desert.[16] Between Reister's visit and Thanksgiving Day, O'Brien gained audiences with the battalion chaplain and then the battalion commander to express his disillusionment with the war. His memoir is almost comical in depicting the officers' patriotic dismissiveness. Oddly enough, the chaplain's callousness and shield-beating seem to have been typical.[17]

By the end of the following week—the first week of December—O'Brien received his orders for the Republic of Việt Nam. He read them right before opening a letter from Hansen, and then wrote his friend the letter about deferring his decision about Canada until going home for Christmas on the twentieth. "I'm pretty sure I won't go to Nam, but that remains to be finally determined."[18] On Friday, December 6, perhaps the very day O'Brien received his orders to Việt Nam and wrote Hansen, he was assigned to a different AIT company.[19] It's possible that the army reorganized training for the Việt Nam–bound soldiers, though it's more likely that the brigade moved O'Brien to a company that started after his first one to make up for the two weeks he had spent in the hospital.

The next weekend, on Friday the thirteenth, O'Brien boarded a bus on a Seattle pass, fully intent on leaving the army and the country behind.

The story of that life-defining weekend O'Brien tells in *If I Die in a Combat Zone, Box Me Up and Ship Me Home*: "A week or two before Christmas I had enough money, the right documents, and final plan."[20] On the bus, he sat beside a lieutenant forty-eight hours from departing for Việt Nam. A light snow fell. Once in Seattle, he rented a room, grabbed clam chowder at a diner across from the hotel, and took a cab to the university, where he strolled into a sorority looking for a blind date. The tactic didn't work, the girl who came to the door using as her excuse her big upcoming exam, presumably an end-of-term final.

He headed downtown to wander. Both films recorded in the memoir as playing at theaters that he walked by, *Finian's Rainbow* and *The Graduate*, appear in Seattle movie listings for that night (and that weekend, but not in late January 1969, the approximate time of O'Brien's remembered version—although the memoir might have conflated two weekend passes into one, intentionally or not).[21] The last person he describes seeing was a prostitute near the harbor. He declined her invitation and her plea for a few dollars. Back at the hotel, O'Brien vomited, then crashed. He woke, then vomited more. He had been feeling physically unwell from the moment he got on the bus. He burned the letters he had written to family and friends about deserting. He spent all the next day sick, too, and on Sunday he took a bus back to Fort Lewis.

O'Brien wrote the hotel-room regurgitation scene as a bodily rejection of his plans. The spirit was very nearly willing; the flesh not at all. Imagination has its limits. O'Brien was clearly suffering the vestiges of his earlier pneumonia—in the version that fits the documentation.

In the remembered version that flits through interviews, profiles, and conversations in the decades to come, the aborted desertion weekend occurred about two weeks before he actually flew out for Việt Nam—which wasn't until February 1969—and it preceded his hospitalization. He could barely function that weekend and passed the Sunday bus ride back to Fort Lewis in an agonizing, hellish daze. He did not spend the rest of that day in the library, the doughnut shop, and the barracks, as per the memoir. In this version, he headed straight for medical care upon his return. In these retellings, the memoir's references to December and to Christmas get it wrong. This version fits the letter's decision to wait until he could meet with trusted souls over his Christmas leave home.

Either way, Currier was right. O'Brien should have sought his advice before reporting for service. In historical context, he was more likely to resist the draft by scooting into Canada the summer before induction than desert the army after.[22] Yet a decision against Việt Nam would have been just as consequential. The Ken Burns and Lynn Novick film *The Vietnam War* includes the story of a young marine who fled to Canada, forever exiling himself from kith and kin: "Many years later, Robin Harrison, still adrift, got caught up in the world of drugs and died, ten thousand miles from home in a hotel room in Hong Kong, another casualty, his brother Matt came to believe, of the war in Vietnam."[23]

On December 20, O'Brien flew home to Minnesota for the Christmas holiday. Family photographs show him smiling and hamming it up with Kathy and Greg, grateful and relieved to be home.

Hypothesis: Had Tim O'Brien been born a year later, had he graduated from Macalester a year later, in 1969, he might not have let himself wind up in Việt Nam.

Data bear out the hypothesis. The army's desertion-rate increase from 1968 to 1969 nearly doubled the prior year's increase. The 1969 raw numbers had doubled from 1967, from 21.4 per thousand to 42.4 per thousand. Other evidence, such as the numbers of AWOL soldiers and in-service conscientious objection applications, support the fact of a rise in soldiers resisting Việt Nam between 1968 and 1969.[24]

More deserting soldiers meant the act became more plausible for others. Had O'Brien graduated in May 1969, his path would have been eased by the Canadian government's decision, on May 22, 1969, to accept U.S. military deserters.[25] A Pfc. Tim O'Brien still undergoing emotional contortion at Fort Lewis would no longer have to fear life in Canada as a life on the lam.

The increased number of desertions was aided by the GI Movement, a decentered activism campaign that brought together soldiers, veterans, and civilians to abet individual resistance to combat assignments. The first GI "coffeehouse" opened its doors in late 1967 outside Fort Jackson, South Carolina, a relaxed watering hole for soldiers and trainees that also fostered anti-war interests.[26] The coffeehouse outside Fort Lewis opened in the first week of October 1968 during O'Brien's training days. Its organizers called it the Shelter Half, after the half of a tent carried by an individual soldier—just as it takes two soldiers to construct a small tent, it takes both soldiers and civilians to shelter struggling GIs. Staffed by veterans and concerned citizens, the coffeehouse provided Fort Lewis soldiers with cheap food, free leisure activities, and a place to talk openly. By the end of October—the month O'Brien graduated from basic training—the local GI-Civilian Alliance for Peace (GI-CAP) group used the Shelter Half to put out the first issue of *Counterpoint*, the area's first underground anti-war publication for soldiers, distributed around Tacoma and, when possible, on post.[27] The army had too thoroughly insulated its recruits for O'Brien to learn about these incipient efforts.

Soon GI-CAP's weekly meetings saw upward of fifty uniformed attendees, and on February 16, 1969, when O'Brien was already in Việt Nam, GI-CAP "sponsored a peace rally in downtown Seattle, with two hundred active-duty people leading a crowd of several thousand."[28] The local GI Movement would go on to conduct such activities as an amphibious assault of Fort Lewis, on July 13, 1969, with a flotilla consisting of "[s]ix rowboats, two canoes, three rubber rafts, and a motorboat"—

> The Free the Army frogman wore long johns "painted with peace signs" while the rest of the invasion force dressed in a uniform of "khaki shirts with the pink and black FTA insignias." One of their banners read, "You are Surrounded LAY DOWN Your Guns."[29]

By the early summer of 1969, the army promulgated a "Guidance on Dissent" letter for base and unit commanders.[30] Would O'Brien as a new recruit have checked out the October 20, 1969, movement organizational meeting held in a post facility that the military police disrupted?[31] Would the solidarity and support have persuaded him to desert?

It's also possible that had O'Brien graduated from Macalester in 1969, he would never have entered the army in the first place. The tumultuous spring and summer of 1968 unmoored the vulnerable student body. O'Brien was at Fort Lewis when the college's new president, Arthur S. Flemming, spoke at a fall symposium. He wanted the war to end, promoted the cause of Black Americans, and believed in a publicly engaged political life. Flemming, a

Republican, embodied the era's pragmatic porousness between the two major political parties. To an audience of over three hundred, he chided Mac students for not being activist enough on several issues, Việt Nam and the draft among them.[32]

On Sunday, October 27, 1968, the Macalester Draft Information Center opened in the former Plymouth Church Center, just west of campus. Twenty trained draft counselors, all Mac students, staffed the office. Aiming to provide essential information about the Selective Service System, the office did not hide its anti-conscription politics. In this vein, "violation of the Selective Service law will be encouraged only to the extent that when a counsellee [sic] himself determines that resistance must be his course of action, he will be supported to the hilt in acting upon this decision. Counsellors [sic] will, in all cases, defend the right of young men to follow their consciences, whether or not this leads to illegal acts."[33] The Macalester center walked a fine line.

One can easily imagine Tim O'Brien on that very Sunday afternoon at the Fort Lewis library studying his desertion options on his own, entirely alone. As close as he came to crossing into Canada in the fall of 1968, one can almost as easily imagine his completing the journey a year later under the influence of the new campus mood and an office dedicated to helping him live his conscience. Not necessarily through expatriation, either. O'Brien would never have stooped to the dishonesty of faking anything: physical or mental unfitness, homosexuality, conscientious objector status, membership in a radical organization, or a calling to seminary. But there were other ways, such as administrative challenges to his local board that could have either exempted him or delayed the process until he could have taken his chance with the lottery system. Could an exit strategy have been found? According to Lawrence M. Baskir and William A. Strauss's 1978 book *Chance and Circumstance: The Draft, the War, and the Vietnam Generation*, "From the earliest days, counselors were enormously successful. Through newsletters and word of mouth, they learned each other's tactics. It was rare for a counselor to have a success rate of under 90 percent."[34]

Unlucky timing, unforgiving circumstances. The lottery system randomness that O'Brien did not experience is pivotal to the season 3 Việt Nam storyline of the series *This Is Us* in 2018 that O'Brien helped write. Had

Nick "Nicky" Pearson been born a day later—had he been born *two minutes* later, on October 19, rather than October 18 at 11:58 p.m.—he would not have gone into the army and on to Việt Nam.[35] Had O'Brien been born one year later, in October 1947 rather than October 1946 . . .

◊   ◊   ◊

Right before deploying to Việt Nam, Erik Hansen visited O'Brien in Worthington during his Christmas leave. Jane Reister traveled by Greyhound bus and stayed a few days. O'Brien accompanied her to St. Paul the Saturday before interim term began. It was a bitter Minnesota January weekend. The mood was "grim" because of his impending departure for Việt Nam. They didn't talk much, although she let him know she would wait for him to come home. She moved into her dorm room on Sunday evening after their goodbyes and believes he flew out to Washington the next day, the sixth of January.

At Fort Lewis on January 31, 1969, he was assigned to a "casual" company, an administrative unit for managing and quartering transient soldiers between postings with nothing to do but wait[36] (and apparently named after the casual wards providing bare-bones overnight lodging for vagrants in nineteenth-century England). The period between the sixth and the thirty-first would have been the window for O'Brien's remembered version of his aborted desertion.

Over his holiday leave, O'Brien would have kept up with the world. Apollo 8 launched on December 21 for its boomerang trip around the moon and back, "soaring higher and faster than man has ever flown," in preparation for the later Apollo flight to land on the moon.[37] The *Worthington Daily Globe* featured Việt Nam in several stories, some on orphanages and one on the military's Chiêu Hồi "Open Arms" program, whereby former Việt Cộng worked as informants, scouts, and interpreters for the Americans.[38]

In an end-of-year piece, O'Brien would have read about how 1968 saw more war casualties than ever from the area—seventeen killed, with three from Worthington: Randall Young, Joel Anders, and Jerome Jansen.[39] O'Brien probably read about military operations in an area where unbeknownst to him he would soon be fighting, the Batangan Peninsula: "The area is honey-combed on higher ground with tunnel systems, some three layers deep."[40] Men in that campaign would soon become comrades and friends. On January 16, O'Brien would have read about the recommencement of the Paris peace talks now that the parties had finally agreed upon the shape of the negotiating table—round, not square.[41] Dispatches from the peace talks and the possibility of the beginning of an American withdrawal occupied the news cycle until the end of the month. O'Brien was on his way to a war that was supposed to be ending.

Returned to Fort Lewis, O'Brien spent a few days in the casual company's transient barracks, hanging out with a couple of young men destined for Việt Nam. The trio had no military responsibilities beyond waiting. On or about February 4, a bus carried O'Brien on the short trip to the McChord Air Force Base airfield.[42] Walking to the jet, he reached down to sweep his fingers along the tarmac, more reflexively than sentimentally, a *might-as-well* gesture. He was dejected that neither of his two new buddies accompanied him on the over-twenty-hour flight to the "tropical killer-dreamscape," as he would one day call the war in Việt Nam.[43]

9

INTO THE COMBAT ZONE

Deplaning at Cam Rahn Bay on February 4, 1969, Private First Class Tim O'Brien was not one of the chatty fellows favored with a flight attendant's godspeed peck.[1] The dusking mountains to the west at day's end formed eerie, shaggy silhouettes. The soldiers lined up to fly home looked exactly how he expected ragged veterans to look.

Next stop, Chu Lai, the American Division's coastal base on the South China Sea. The division operated at the southern end of the military sector adjacent to the DMZ dividing Việt Nam. Chu Lai sprawled with head-quarters and logistics structures, a training center, hospitals, detention center, Graves Registration, press offices, and artillery units, plus American lifestyle support: a PX shopping center, recreational beach, miniature-golf course, food shacks, bars with floor shows, and more. It was a small, weirdly indulgent city in the middle of a brutal war. *Going After Cacciato* cites the tooth-to-tail ratio of combat-to-support personnel as one to twelve. Assignment to a combat infantry battalion was "statistically improbable,"[2] the bad hand dealt to Pfc. O'Brien.

On February 7, O'Brien began the combat course at the division's Combat Center. The training consisted of basic skills review for such equipment as the claymore mine and the M79 grenade launcher while acclimating the soldiers to the natural and tactical environment. At the mine and booby trap confidence course, an instructor warned the newbies, as O'Brien reported to Hansen, that "90% of the casualties (including wounded) were from mines and booby traps!"[3]

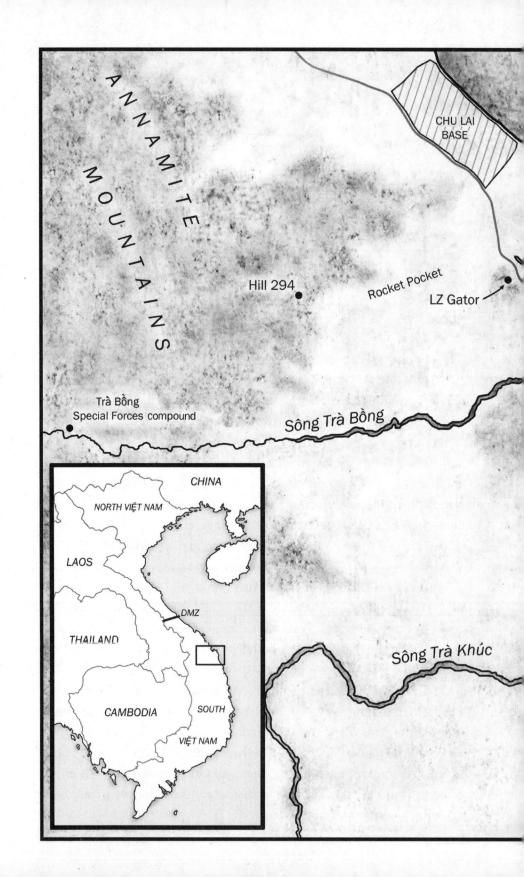

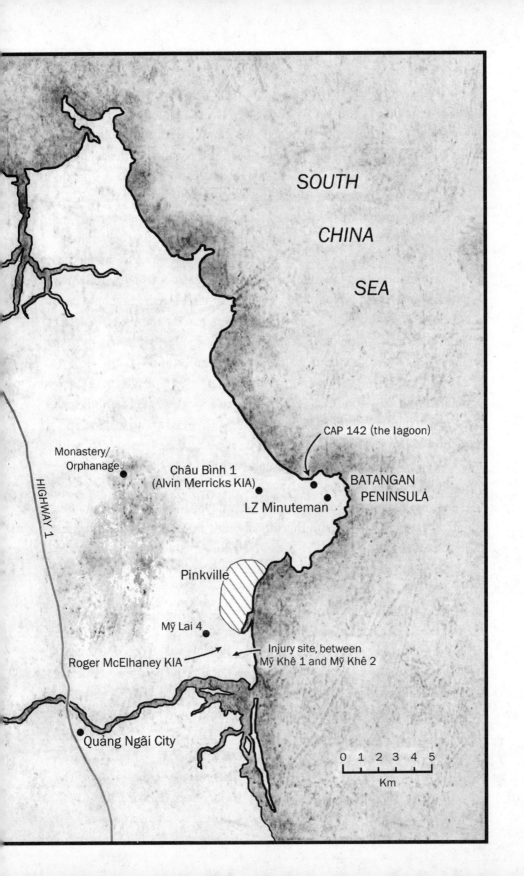

SOUTH

CHINA

SEA

CAP 142 (the lagoon)

Monastery/
Orphanage

Châu Bình 1
(Alvin Merricks KIA)

BATANGAN
PENINSULA

LZ Minuteman

HIGHWAY 1

Pinkville

Mỹ Lai 4

Injury site, between
Mỹ Khê 1 and Mỹ Khê 2

Roger McElhaney KIA

Quảng Ngãi City

0 1 2 3 4 5
Km

Pfc. Hansen had been at his duty station for several weeks in a relatively safe rear-echelon job at Long Bình. O'Brien wrote that letter the night before leaving Chu Lai for his assigned battalion. The training was repetitive and boring, and gave him time for beer and reading in the evenings. The nights offered a show of spectacular flashes and streaks beyond the Chu Lai perimeter. On base everything seemed to pulse with hidden significance, everyone's eyes shooting imagined messages—"pity" from the chaplain, "concealed anger" from the Vietnamese girls selling cold drinks.[4] That can of Coke could be the last one to touch O'Brien's lips, handed to him by someone whose brother or sister or lover could be his killer, by someone whose sibling or parent or beloved another American could have killed. That can could eventually house a homemade explosive. The letter to Hansen sounded a lifelong refrain: "I refuse to believe what's happened, yet I also do believe it, both at the same time. Unpleasant."[5]

On February 18, 1969, a truck delivered O'Brien and five other new soldiers to Landing Zone Gator, the home base for the 5th Battalion, 46th Light Infantry Regiment[6]—written "5–46" (or "5–46 Infantry") and spoken "fifth of the forty-sixth," *regiment* being a historic legacy term with no corresponding organizational structure (brigade being the next higher command).

The drive had not taken long. LZ Gator occupied a hilltop less than four kilometers from Chu Lai's southernmost entrance. One of the 5th of the 46th's missions was to protect the skinny piedmont's southern approach to Chu Lai. Rising between the Trì Bình and the Nam Bình hamlets, the hill abutted Highway 1 and overlooked the lowlands east across the highway toward the sea and south several kilometers deep. Immediately to the west loomed the tailing edge of the Annamite Mountains, to which Gator's hilltop belonged, a jutting orphaned runt.

O'Brien's new unit, Alpha Company, was out in the field that day, leaving O'Brien to twiddle his thumbs and pull mundane duties. The battalion compressed its operations, quarters, and landing zone into an area about 200 meters wide and 250 meters long. Bulldozers had scooped out the hilltop to create the living and working space. Sandbagged bunkers turreted the outward-facing forward slope—the *military crest*—around the protective rim. Below the bunker ring, belts of concertina wire, trip flares, and claymore mines supplanted the vegetation. The enemy sappers who crawled at a snail's pace to create lanes for their attacking comrades by snipping wires and defusing mines, and by exploding bunkers when they gained tossing distance, had nothing to hide their movements but night's darkness.

Needs not met by Gator were met by Nuoc Mau, the closest clutch of civilian shacks and hooches: laundry, marijuana—the "Nuoc Mau 100" fat joint—and prostitutes. Nuoc Mau was so small the military maps did not put a name to its cluster of tiny squares right beside the highway. Soldiers called it "the Ville," with context distinguishing it from all the other villes.

Biding time, O'Brien watched the Swedish art-house film *Elvira Madigan*. He'd seen it in college. What an odd film for LZ Gator. Based on a true story, the film involves a nineteenth-century Danish count who deserts the army, his wife, and his children for the love of a famous tightrope walker, Elvira, who deserts her family circus for her love of him. Both are too famous to stop running and settle down. In the final scene, these penniless, starving lovers, who look as robust and glowingly beautiful as at the beginning of the film, commit a double suicide.

The film appalled O'Brien. Gorgeous society-defying young lovers frolicking in a sun-kissed pastoral European forest, tenderly groping, picnicking, and chasing butterflies—what a painfully far cry from his circumstances. The Elvira actor, the very blond Pia Degermark, epitomized O'Brien's ideal of female beauty. For someone who had very recently nearly deserted the army himself but surrendered to society's rules—would such a companion have been what he needed to cross over?—the lovers' choice to kill themselves in some crazed notion of romantic self-fulfillment rather than "hold a menial job" disgusted him.[7]

O'Brien's new Alpha comrades returned early in the evening on February 22, having been outside Gator's wire for the last ten days.[8] They were filthy and raucous, ready for beer, pot, sleep, and little else, especially not for O'Brien the FNG, the *fucking new guy*.

At 0115 in the morning, incoming mortar rounds woke O'Brien. The company first sergeant ordered everyone out of the barracks. O'Brien grabbed his gear and scurried clunkily out. He took cover behind the metal conex where the battalion stored its beer. Other men took their time dragging themselves out. "They sat on some sandbags in their underwear, drinking the beer and laughing, pointing out at the paddies and watching our mortar rounds land." Eventually, the platoon trooped out to check the perimeter, minus three soldiers who returned to their cots.[9]

Gator received about thirty mortar rounds as well as some small-arms fire and rocket-propelled grenades (RPGs) that night. A Vietnamese sapper team penetrated the perimeter near the main gate. The attack lasted an hour, leaving one American and seven enemy dead, and eighteen Americans wounded.[10] It was O'Brien's first encounter with the Việt Cộng, the southerners allied with the communist North Vietnamese Army. More properly known as the National Liberation Front, or NLF, the VC consisted of a political structure—a shadow government—and a guerrilla military organization. Forever after, the "deadness of death" for O'Brien thrums with that early-morning corpse collection inside the perimeter. The stun and ugliness of Vietnamese bodies tossed into a truck bed, limbs and heads flopping and lolling to stillness. They were summarily dumped on the ground in Nuoc Mau as a practical matter—the Vietnamese could deal with their own dead—and a warning.

A tracker dog following a blood trail led O'Brien's company to the Nam Bình 3 sub-hamlet. In his memoir, O'Brien remembers encountering only women and children in the place; the battalion log reports that the company rounded up about twenty Vietnamese, then called the National Police to finish searching the village and assist them with the "suspects." None were detained. O'Brien's squad returned to Gator at two in the afternoon.[11] They ate a late lunch and passed the rest of the day filling sandbags and debating the severity of the night's attack, using O'Brien's ignorance to entertain themselves. That night the platoon set up an ambush 2.5 kilometers north of Gator, right outside Đông Bình 1.[12] It was O'Brien's first night truly in the field, in the Quảng Ngãi countryside.

On his return to Việt Nam and his old area of operations twenty-five years later, O'Brien took Jonathan Schell's *The Real War*, which included Schell's two major works of war correspondence from the 1960s, *The Village of Ben Suc* and—more significant for O'Brien's purposes—*The Military Half: An Account of Destruction in Quang Ngai and Quang Tin*.[13]

Quảng Ngãi province, where the 5th of the 46th Infantry operated, had a centuries-long history of resistance, rebellion, and revolution. After World War II, Schell writes, "French troops never succeeded in entering the province in force." After the end of French occupation in 1954, enough "Vietminh soldiers and political organizers" remained in the area that by "the early nineteen-sixties, a whole generation of young people [in the area] had known no government other than that of the Vietminh and the National Liberation Front." The U.S. military conducted its campaign to separate civilians from militants through forced relocation and resettlement with "particular vigor" in Quảng Ngãi. From 1965 to 1967, the United States and its allies destroyed "approximately seventy per cent" of the area's homes, displacing "about forty per cent" of the population into refugee camps.[14] This in a culture where people lived in profound connection to their family's ancestral lands.

Most of the devastation came from aircraft, but the ground war delivered intimate cruelties. Brian De Palma's 1989 film *Casualties of War* used the Americal's shoulder patch because of the division's and Quảng Ngãi's reputations, even though the atrocity on which De Palma based the film was committed by soldiers of the 1st Cavalry Division in Bình Định province.[15] One can validly object to an overemphasis on American cruelties as overlooking Vietnamese cruelties and as naïvely misunderstanding the nature of the war. But that's beside the point. Any destruction, maiming, or killing attributable to the American presence contributed to the stares of fear and hatred that Pfc. O'Brien perceived over the next thirteen months. Moreover, the enemy forces were formidable. One of O'Brien's company commanders, an experienced Special Forces officer, believed their Area of Operations to be "the ultimate VC combat environment. I have read some stats that helped convince me of that. I will go on record saying, there was not another VC combat AO as trying as ours. They were well led and equipped, and motivated for VC."[16]

None of which Pfc. O'Brien knew. He had been told a little by his Chu Lai Combat Center instructors about Bold Mariner and Russell Beach, the joint operations begun in January whose major phases his new brigade had recently completed in conjunction with the U.S. Marines, other U.S. Army units, and the Army of the Republic of Vietnam, or ARVN (pronounced "Arvin"). The operations involved removing civilians from the Batangan Peninsula and attempting to eradicate the enemy, with the marines assaulting

the peninsula's beaches and moving inward (Bold Mariner) as the inland
army units moved beachward (Russell Beach). The Batangan was the hub
of VC activity. "I'm operating near Chu Lai," O'Brien told Hansen in that
first letter, "on the peninsula that the marines attacked with 5000 troops
last month—'only' 46 were killed sweeping the place, even though 2 regi-
ments of NVA are supposedly still there."[17] This was the mission that saw
90 percent of the marines' casualties from mines and booby traps. It was a
failure despite claims of success. David Taylor's history of O'Brien's unit in
Việt Nam, *Our War: The History and Sacrifices of an Infantry Battalion in
the Vietnam War, 1968–1971*, confirms the impact of mines on the marines
and the extent of the VC's successful evasion. He reports different U.S. casualty numbers: thirty-one American Division soldiers killed, seventy-seven
wounded; twenty-five marines killed, seventy-seven wounded.[18]

"A charming place to spend a year," O'Brien concluded to Hansen.

The American's primary function was *pacification*—debilitating the enemy while protecting civilians to win hearts and minds. Determining who
was which was no small challenge. When O'Brien joined Third Platoon,
Alpha Company, Operation Russell Beach had entered its *extensive pacification* phase. As Taylor notes, new operational phases meant nothing to
the grunts, even if they heard such higher-level terms: "Their daily routine
remained the same, killing, interdicting, wounding and capturing the enemy and discovering more caches and tunnels, detaining more refugees
and suffering more casualties from mines."[19]

O'Brien's first night ambush passed uneventfully except for the fact that it
was night, perhaps the night described in the "Ambush" chapter of *If I Die
in a Combat Zone* (although in its aim to represent all night ambushes, the
chapter takes some creative license).[20] The platoon leader, Lt. Mark White,
led it himself with O'Brien's first squad and with second squad. Night missions were the worst. O'Brien was tortured by his own imagination:

> There'd have to be a moon or some stars or it's just pitch black.
> And you're scared out of your mind. What's in the blackness? Are
> they creeping up on me now? And is there an attack imminent or not?

When we did these night guards in our foxholes we'd switch off every two hours. [. . .] Somewhere around the third watch of the night, it's now like 3:30 in the morning, something like that, the boogeymen come out in your brain—[. . .] And they're trying to kill you.[21]

The next night, two platoons (including O'Brien's) marched to an ambush site a little over a kilometer to the east, among Trung An's sub-hamlets. About an hour before midnight, while checking the area before hunkering down for the night, they "flushed" nine VC, but it was too dark to fire at them. The platoons scrapped the ambush plans and rejoined the rest of the company.[22] The black-clad Vietnamese, absorbed back into the black night, rejoined the ranks of the boogeymen, the haunts, the ghosts.

The next several weeks were blessedly dull. Alpha Company covered the coastal area south of the Chu Lai base and east of Gator between Highway 1 and the Trà Bồng River's outlet into the sea, all beaches, dunes, wetlands, paddies, hillocks, palm copses, and the hamlets that went with them. Patrols and ambushes ranged in size from a single squad to two platoons; movements rarely exceeded a couple of kilometers. A very rare and fleeting suspicious sight or sound resulted in weapons being fired or artillery being called in the general direction, subsequent searches finding no dead. With a full moon on March 4, sparse vegetation, and the light-reflecting sand and sea, the nights were the brightest of O'Brien's entire tour. Those weeks were "mostly a vacation" of "no VC, no mines, sunny days, warm water to swim in, daily resupplies of milk and beer." The people had no reason to upset the advantages of living beside Chu Lai. Women and children followed Alpha about, hawking sodas and smut, the women sometimes themselves. It cost little to pay a kid to clean your weapon or carry your gear. "Champion" was the Vietnamese boy who accompanied O'Brien.[23]

At some point in these first weeks, explosions just outside the platoon's night position sent everyone diving into their foxholes, but they turned out to be grenades tossed by bored soldiers who then shot their weapons and threw more grenades at a pretend enemy to prank everyone.[24] It maddened O'Brien. It wouldn't be the last time he experienced stupid shenanigans. Sometime in early March a GI pelted a blind old man with a milk carton while the man was helping the platoon bathe at a well.[25] O'Brien would come to understand the pelting not simply as a precursor to worse acts but as an act of evil in its own right.

In those first weeks, O'Brien got the job of radio-telephone operator, or RTO, carrying the radio for the platoon leader and often making and receiving calls in the lieutenant's stead.

Third Platoon returned to LZ Gator by truck on the morning of March 17.[26] The period hadn't been as quiet for the companies operating in the more dangerous areas to which Alpha would rotate. Or for the civilians. A mishap from friendly mortar fire resulted in the evacuation of eleven wounded soldiers from Delta Company on the seventeenth. This occurred the day after two Vietnamese girls, six and eight years old, stepped on a jury-rigged mine and were dusted off—evacuated by helicopter—with lower-extremity injuries. Before week's end, a five-year-old girl and a six-year-old boy were injured fiddling around with an M79 grenade launcher round.[27] Dutifully recorded in the battalion's daily log, civilian casualties did not appear in the end-of-day totals or in the battalion's daily "Plans and Summaries" submitted to the higher command. The uncounted didn't count.

O'Brien always believed that "for every dead Viet Cong or North Vietnamese soldier, there'd be two or three dead civilians." It seemed to him like "we were accomplishing exactly the reverse of what we were told we would be accomplishing" because dead civilians produced "more enemies."[28] A year and change later, a *Worthington Daily Globe* article estimated upward of 200,000 civilian casualties over the past year, with 50,000 to 60,000 killed, not including the civilians counted in the exaggerated enemy-combatant death toll of 138,982.[29]

So it goes. Within a few days, Seymour Lawrence, O'Brien's future publisher, would release *Slaughterhouse-Five*, Kurt Vonnegut's astonishing novel about the firebombing of Dresden in World War II: "It is so short and jumbled and jangled, Sam, because there is nothing intelligent to say about a massacre."[30] Vonnegut had been a prisoner of war in Dresden at the time. After the war, he imagined dashing off a book about the experience, a bestseller for sure, but it would take another twenty years and the war in Việt Nam to bring it into being.

Alpha Company left Gator by helicopter the morning of March 18, Third Platoon having enjoyed only one night's sleep in the barracks.[31] They landed eight kilometers to the southwest, in the vicinity of Đú'c An, Bình

Yên, and Nam Trung, smack in the middle of the so-called Rocket Pocket, the corridor where the Sông Trà Bồng flows out from the Annamite Mountains into the piedmont on its course to the sea. An absolute tangle of hills, streams, villages, footpaths, and jungle, the Rocket Pocket served the VC as a major infiltration avenue as well as a launching ground to hurl rockets over the last mountain spur into Chu Lai. Alpha spent two days working its way back on foot. Humping to Gator, in grunt-speak. The nights were as dark as they could get, with zero illumination on the company's moonless first night in the Rocket Pocket.

At six the morning of the nineteenth, an hour before sunrise, the company received small-arms and automatic-weapons fire, RPGs, and mortar rounds "from all sides of the perimeter." It was a hit and run—the enemy immediately beat feet to the east as Alpha called in artillery in that general direction. Two Alpha soldiers were evacuated with shrapnel wounds. That night at eleven, Alpha's main body received a little more of the same, while Third Platoon's third squad shot at some running VC. Neither side hit anybody.[32] Alpha evacuated a soldier for heatstroke before noon on the twentieth and reentered the wire at LZ Gator three hours later.[33] Alpha headed back to the Rocket Pocket on Sunday, March 23. In the next week the company saw two dust-offs, one for three heat casualties and one for a shrapnel wound.[34]

On the afternoon of March 31, choppers hopped Alpha from Gator to LZ Minuteman, in the heart of the Batangan's protuberance into the sea, and an hour later lifted Third Platoon over to a rice paddy to the west, just north of Phú Mỹ 2.[35] The company regathered to spend the night on the small hilltop between Nghiêm Quang 1 and Phú Mỹ 1 in the heart of Pinkville.

Pinkville's reputation was as bad as or worse than the Batangan's. Pinkville referred to a specific built-up area with a relatively dense population that military maps indicated with a pinkish color. Although some of Mỹ Lai's sub-hamlets and equally dangerous neighboring hamlets were outside the pink, for the soldiers of 5–46 Infantry, they belonged to Pinkville. O'Brien later wrote home about that day: "Choppers dumped us into *mined* rice paddies out here on the rough-tough Batangan Peninsula. We found tunnels, blew them with grenades. That night we were hit with AK-47 fire and grenades. Exciting, but fast: no one hurt, except my nerves!" The company fired back into the night with small arms and mortars.[36] Quiet settled in, although it was impossible for the grunts to shake the knowledge that the people who had just tried to kill them, whom they never saw, were still out there beyond the perimeter.

The next afternoon the company found itself dropped at LZ Gator and then immediately sent west back into the Rocket Pocket, where it spent the first week of April humping to Gator.[37]

◊ ◊ ◊

During O'Brien's first weeks of basic training, Gayle Roby had sent him "This Loved One," a W. H. Auden poem from 1929. Auden was twenty-two, the same age as O'Brien for most of his tour in Việt Nam. At Fort Lewis, O'Brien memorized it, reciting it to himself while "marching for shots and haircuts and clothing issue."[38] O'Brien carried the poem and the practice to Việt Nam. He took pleasure in the sound and pace of the poem walking the land with him. The next time the unit stopped, he would pull it out of his ruck to study the lines that had escaped him.

It was poetry as war's antithesis, as artifact of civilization, of what it means to be civilized, of human decency, and love, and peace, and art. It was also a puzzle. As he marched, as he sat bored at an LZ, as he pulled guard duty, he meditated on what Auden meant in writing the poem and what Roby meant in sending it. Is it a breakup poem, Pfc. O'Brien asked himself, a poem of indifference? He finally concluded that Roby meant to signal the absence of a romantic future, a fare-thee-well poem. Maybe, though, she simply liked its spell and wanted to share it. That thought pestered him, too.

O'Brien knew next to nothing about Auden, so he didn't understand the "neighborly shame" of the speaker's attraction to another young man. He would not have read the last lines as the speaker's guarding himself against a taboo love that could never be. As he tried to visualize Roby's face while imposing grandiose words upon her—"'mysterious,' 'Magdalen,' 'Eternal'"—he "was learning that no weight of letters and remembering and wishing and hoping is the same as a touch on temporary, mortgaged lands."[39]

"Touching is shaking hands / On mortgaged lands," O'Brien's favorite couplet of any poem, suggests mortality as well as the fleetingness of intimacy where touching becomes gesture, at once hello and goodbye, full of grace yet "no real meeting / But instinctive look / A backward love," a love in passing, already passed by.[40] The poem finally was and wasn't about Roby: "I didn't know her well enough to say that Gayle per se was on my mind. It was the possibility of Gayle that was on my mind. I only had two dates with her, three maybe, so I barely knew her. But the person who would send you that poem, you can see why you'd be interested. It's not about physical beauty, it's something else that was alluring to me."

The poem also resonated with his soldiering, the coins passed in "a cheaper house" reminding him of the Nuoc Mau whorehouse down the hill from Gator, and symbolically of the meaningless waste of time and bodies that was his war.

The poem kept O'Brien going: "All that weight, and the heat of the day, and the prospect that maybe my next step is my last. It was a way of getting through the days that felt meaningful to me." Fifty years after Việt Nam, Tim O'Brien could still recite it. Regardless of Roby, regardless of the war, he still finds it "a gorgeous piece of writing, just mysterious enough to beckon me."

Everything changed for O'Brien on April 3. The platoon leader led a squad-sized night patrol near Trì Bình 4 while O'Brien and the rest of the platoon stayed in its night defensive position. He heard the shooting start about an hour later, then received a radio call reporting that the patrol had "opened up on some VC smoking and talking by a well." The assault ended in ten minutes. One member of the patrol had been very lightly wounded. O'Brien relayed the lieutenant's report to the company, which passed it to the battalion: two killed Vietnamese and possibly five wounded.[41] O'Brien reported confiscated equipment but not the platoon leader's souvenir—an ear he had sliced off one of the dead. The lieutenant called in helicopter gunships to sweep the area, producing a scene O'Brien recounts in *If I Die*:

The sky and the trees and the hillsides were lighted up by spotlights and tracers and fires. From our position we could smell the smoke coming from Tri Binh 4. We heard cattle and chickens dying. At two in the morning we started to sleep, one man at a time. [. . .] Smoke continued to billow over to our position all night, however, and when

I awaked every hour, it was the first thing to sense and to remind me of the ear.

They searched the village in the morning, "then burned most of it down."[42] That morning the platoon leader, squatting, shirtless, and grinning, held up the ear again while someone snapped a photo. In the evening local officials confirmed the identity of one of the dead men. Lê Bia was twenty-six years old, a VC village security chief.[43]

In *If I Die in a Combat Zone*, O'Brien calls the platoon leader Mad Mark. Mark White was an extremely capable junior officer. He excelled at reading maps and moved deftly through the terrain. He would not dream of ordering his soldiers to do something he hadn't first done himself. More often than most platoon leaders, he led squad-sized operations rather than staying behind with the rest of the platoon. He carried a shotgun for its close-range potency and its shock and awe. He practiced tactical restraint, declining unnecessary risks. Everyone respected his energy and efficacy. He had a calming demeanor as he took care of business. After the war, one of O'Brien's platoon mates named a son after him. But with that martial edge came a certain savagery. Lê Bia's ear—there's a 50 percent chance it was his ear—was not the only souvenir, the burning of Trì Bình 4's homes not the only burning of homes.[44] The memoir depicts the night patrol as possessed of an almost childish glee when they unwrapped the ear to show it off to the others, as if they were little boys pouring salt on a slug to watch it writhe, playing at the evil of it. "Who's gonna eat a goddamn dink," Lt. White states in *If I Die*, responding to a question about what to do with the ear. "I eat women, not dead dinks."[45] He was two years younger than O'Brien.

Between the ear and the intense hour-long gunship assault on the sub-hamlet, the war's abstract, geopolitical immorality had taken a terrible new form.

U.S. military deaths in Việt Nam now exceeded the total from the Korean War, as American military manpower reached its peak later that month at 543,482.[46]

The platoon made the short walk back to LZ Gator on April 5. The next morning, Alpha Company flew by Chinook to assume the defense of LZ Minuteman on the Batangan Peninsula.[47] Most of Alpha had been to Batangan during Operation Russell Beach before O'Brien arrived at the battalion. The area trembled the nerves because of how heavily it was mined and booby-trapped, intensifying the feeling that the land itself stalked the Americans.

According to one contemporaneous American source, the locals sometimes understood Ba Làng An—literally simply Three Villages Called An, referring to Vân An, An Chuẩn, and An Hải—to mean the Three Villages of Peace.[48] *Peace*, however, is a poor approximation. The linguistic history of the region is extremely complex due to the number of cultures that laid forceful claim to it over the centuries, but "An" could be understood to mean *settled* or *pacified*[49]—a term, in other words, imposed by the settlers and pacifiers. What awful irony: As Alpha Company occupied Minuteman in April 1969, Operation Russell Beach was deep into its fourth and final phase: "Extensive Pacification." By operation's end in July, over twelve thousand civilians had been removed from the peninsula, nearly 80 percent of the population.[50] It was pacification through expulsion; *settled* or *pacified* meant *depopulated*. The Americans and South Vietnamese shunted the remainder to refugee villages protected by Combined Action Platoons (CAPs) composed of U.S. Marines and local militiamen.

Landing Zone Minuteman had been established toward the end of the massive cordon and clearing phases of Russell Beach. Whichever company rotated to occupy it and secure the area also spent time improving its defenses—digging, filling sandbags, building, clearing fields of fire, laying concertina wire and mines. To Bob Wolf, the site had no tactical merit and existed primarily as a show-and-tell stop for VIPs.

For all the fear of the Batangan, O'Brien welcomed the time on Minuteman. It mostly consisted of bunker duty on the LZ itself—no long marches, no going out looking for a fight. He couldn't step on a mine if he didn't leave the perimeter. Minuteman had at least some of the comforts of Gator, as he wrote his family: "showers, hot chow, cold pop, time to read and write." Moreover, by the fourth day at Minuteman, the company commander, Capt. Ben Anderson, took Pfc. O'Brien out of Third Platoon to serve as one of his own RTOs. O'Brien's enthusiastic letter home dated April 10 shared the news, adding that the new job meant even less time in the field because most missions were conducted by platoons and squads, not the entire company.[51] During its three weeks on Minuteman, Alpha set out squad-sized night ambushes and sent out small units for sundry daytime missions, including refugee protection, only rarely joined by the commander, only rarely with O'Brien.

The letter to his family included the bare bones of "a couple good war stories" because they now "bored" him. For stories that bored him, O'Brien used a lot of exclamation marks. First is the story of the "exciting" but "fast" mission to the Batangan of March 31 told above; second, a strange version of the night Lt. White made a trophy of an ear: "Few nights later, 6 of us raided a ville, caught 10 VC at a well and blasted them before they shot us. It was a slaughter—they only threw one grenade our way. That's enough war to last me till the apocalypse!!" The exclamation marks reflect the upbeat mood and relief of having left the platoon for a moderately safer assignment as well as the adrenaline memory of the actual event. They reflect his youth, too. He was also writing from a particular role to a particular audience, a son at war writing home. Of course he didn't mention the ear. More interesting is O'Brien's use of the first-person plural. He all but wrote himself into the action that he had heard over the radio and then learned about. Dramatic effect aside, that "us" conveys the profound responsibility O'Brien felt, and still feels, for just being there.

The first days at Minuteman, a resupply helicopter brought a letter from Hansen that either included or referenced Ezra Pound's poem "Hugh Selwyn Mauberley," a section of which Hansen had recited to O'Brien back at Fort Lewis. O'Brien's reply springboards off Pound's poem to this prose flight, at once romantic and dismaying, sure and baffled, the prose of an aspiring writer contending with the overwhelming:

> For we would be better men, more loving men, more virtuous, if we could somehow—through acts of powerful will—shed the lie at home, display no egotism at having killed or seen killing & not have gone insane; for, of course, we should go insane to do it & see it, since neither of us puts an ideological filter to the horror, we do not justify it; we recognize our complicity, in my case something worse than

that—in evil. Pound recognized the evil; as we do. He saw, moreover, how men, even *knowing* they do wrong, kill "for fear of censure, for fear of weakness." And he wasn't trapped, as we are trapped, in the killing, in the deed. And for us to *overcome* our flaw, our cowardice by being brave for society, our past (now, the nightmare).

The letter might be the earliest document in which O'Brien articulates the cowardice that he has attributed to letting himself be drafted and that has racked him for the rest of his life.

The April letter closes with a poem O'Brien wrote for the friend he met in sight of Mount Rainier, a poem fashioned after the "Fire Sermon" segment of T. S. Eliot's *The Waste Land.*

Dharma
    is the right of wrong—
    the wrong of being in khaki
    in winter;
    the goodness of a dream or an act,
    paid for by
Artha
    which is the price:
    spent in suffering.
Kàma
    is but playfulness
    and I will reject that, too,
    in the end;
    for it is the right of wrong,
    hence hurt,
    that comes first;
    truly
    brutally
    we are the mercenaries
    of a green and wet forest,
    while over us on the hill sixty miles distant,
    the snows the cold of Rainier
    stand proud and durable:

Moksa
    which is freedom.

Thinking of his friend in combat, Hansen's letter had quoted Eliot's poem's famous opening lines: "April is the cruellest month, breeding / Lilacs out of the dead land, mixing / Memory and desire, stirring / Dull roots with spring rain."[52]

O'Brien was right to look forward to the time on Minuteman. Patrols infrequently saw the enemy. The most unusual encounter came when a roving squad saw twenty-three lights and heard loudspeakers taunting Chiêu Hồi, the name for former VC working with the Americans as guides and interpreters.[53] Only three soldiers required dusting off for wounds, two resulting from a brief small-arms and mortar attack on LZ Minuteman and one from a squad ambushed the next day.[54] The same day as the ambush, Capt. Anderson boarded a helicopter for what the military called a visual reconnaissance (VR) and what he called "dink hunting." The Huey drew fire that slightly wounded Anderson in the butt cheek, then returned fire more effectively. It landed, picked up the injured VC, and returned to Minuteman.[55] Alpha accidentally shot and wounded one Vietnamese militiaman and three civilians when they fired at suspicious movement from Minuteman toward the neighboring refugee camp.[56]

But the battalion log can't be entirely trusted. Alpha's officers had no desire to put their soldiers at greater risk than necessary. The patrols and ambushes reported to battalion didn't always take place. Sometimes the hoax entailed calling actual artillery on random grid coordinates, the fire support officer even hazing the howitzer unit over the radio when the rounds missed the nonexistent target. "Phony ambushes were good for morale," O'Brien wrote, the "best game we played on LZ Minuteman."[57] They reminded him of the baseball action he invented for his *Worthington Daily Globe* sports reports.

Minuteman was a barren, stumpy plateau of red dirt with zero shade. The soldiers did what work and play that they could in the mornings, then lay about sweltering through the afternoons. By the twelfth, every day hit or topped ninety, with little cloud coverage and only a very few slight and short evening showers for relief. O'Brien enjoyed getting to know the commander better on the LZ, sometimes over a game of chess. Anderson declined to talk with his subordinate about the politics and morality of the war. He had graduated from the U.S. Naval Academy at Annapolis but arranged for an army commission. O'Brien felt his captain "was the best man around, and during the April afternoons it was sad he wore his bars."[58]

On Minuteman, O'Brien befriended Alvin "Chip" Merricks, a Black soldier from Orlando. The pair were routinely assigned bunker detail together. The race difference initially exacerbated the tension of two strangers forced together. Soon enough, the two young men were bantering simply as two young men. Merricks, older by a year, had been in Việt Nam three months longer. He was sharp and funny. They bitched about the army. They talked girls. Merricks introduced one woman after another as *the one*—it didn't take long for O'Brien to start busting his chops about it. Merricks was mischievous. He smoked pot, which O'Brien didn't mind when they were on a landing zone or other base. Merricks started exchanging letters with Kathy, and O'Brien with one of Merricks's sisters. They joked about the sensation they would cause double-dating back home. Although they usually hung out in segregated circles, they had become tight friends. Best friends.

Alpha returned by Chinook to Gator on April 25, and the next day headed by truck to Chu Lai for a stand-down.[59] Swimming, drinking, and horsing around. They ate well, bathed, and slept. O'Brien played Ping-Pong with a new sergeant, the soft-spoken Roy Arnold, beating him mercilessly. The tone of the memoir's description of Chu Lai's floor show is incongruity: a young Korean woman dancing for young American men in Việt Nam, finishing her act to "Hey Jude," a song by four British lads, a song O'Brien's unit sometimes murmur-sang as they marched. They were girls and boys forced into playing women and men. They were fodder to a war that, like all wars, trucked in the cheapness of the human body. Pathos, not eros.

The Timmy O'Brien from Worthington, Minnesota, who half believed the soldiers' canard that some Vietnamese prostitutes weaponized their vaginas with razor blades,[60] had to juxtapose the image of this alive female Korean with images of two dead female Vietnamese. The first one receives her own short chapter in *If I Die*, "Mori," where American men gather around the body of an Asian woman, probably an NVA nurse. But this one quavers and moans because she is dying, shot by an Alpha soldier.[61] The memories combine in the story "Style" from *The Things They Carried*, in which O'Brien dramatizes soldiers struggling to respond to a girl dancing after they have burned down her village.[62] The dead nurse from "Mori" subtly re-appears in "The Man I Killed," in which soldiers stand around a dead NVA soldier, a young man the narrator imagines as effeminate and as a version of himself. In the memoir, O'Brien uses the phrase "the man who shot her" five times; in the fiction, he uses the phrase "the man I killed" four times (title included). Both killers study the dead faces with shock, care, and guilt.

Due to the memoir's scrappy composition process and the workings of O'Brien's immediate postwar memory, the second Vietnamese girl Pfc. O'Brien saw does not appear in *If I Die in a Combat Zone*. Here he tells the story to filmmaker Aaron Matthews:

> There were a hundred of us, we were working as a company, and we were on one side of a rice paddy cross, going along the edge of the rice paddy and the other side of the rice paddy, maybe hundred and fifty yards away, there was a bunch of bamboo and banana trees—all this foliage, it just erupted. We swiveled toward it and just started shooting back, and it went on for eight or ten minutes.
>
> Afterward our company commander said listen, we have to go across the village toward where the enemy had been to see if any of them had been hurt or killed. And on the way across the paddy, almost directly ahead of me, just a little bit off to my right, there was a body lying in the rice paddy. It was a little girl maybe eleven or twelve years old, or ten, I mean, she was young. And she was dead and her face had been just shattered, blown away so that she didn't really have one side of her face.
>
> There's a friend of mine whose name I can't remember, I can see his face, like right now. Blond kid. We both stopped and looked down at her, and we looked at each other, and a thought came to me as our eyes locked after looking at this dead little girl. I mean, it haunts me and probably always will haunt me. It was the look of uselessness and waste to it all. That here were these two armies shooting at one an-other, and the only casualty was this little girl of maybe twelve years old. And so much of my war was that way. There were dead Ameri-cans, and dead Viet Cong and NVA. But there was a whole boatload of wounded and dead civilians. Who, probably, all they yearned for was a meal and peace and all the things I yearned for.

I remember thinking to myself as I was walking away from that little girl: Well, she's dead, so the world must now be a much better place. Because that's what wars are for, aren't they? One way or another they're to make the world a better place. More liberty and more freedom and whatever wars are fought for. We don't fight them to make the world a worse place, yet the world sure as hell didn't feel like a better place after that little girl's face blazed into my memory forever.

And I felt culpable. I remember thinking, Did my bullet hit that little girl? There's no way you'll ever, you'll never know. Everybody was shooting. You'll lie awake thirty or forty years later thinking, Dear Jesus, I hope it wasn't my bullet, I hope it wasn't mine. But the hope isn't enough. In the end, you know you were there and you pulled the trigger and you're responsible and you did it. Whether your bullet did it or somebody else's is in the end kind of irrelevant, except that it's not irrelevant to your dreams. And it's not irrelevant to how you live the rest of your life.[63]

Fifty years later, hers is the face that haunts O'Brien. To the people who say, "Forget it. Deal with it. Move on," he spits back, "Let them try doing it and see how it works for them."[64]

The Vietnamese soldier was killed during O'Brien's time with Third Platoon, before Minuteman and Chu Lai. The civilian girl was killed after the stand-down, during his time in the field with Capt. Anderson, probably in May. Neither one made it into the battalion log.

10

MAY WAS THE CRUELEST MONTH

At Chu Lai, the gung ho battalion commander dropped by to warn the company about its next operation. *Some of you will be injured. Some of you will die.* Soldiers hated Lt. Col. Alfred Barnes for his bluntness of tactics and manners. Helicopters lifted Alpha out of Chu Lai the morning of April 29, and by 10:30 a.m. landed the company in a clearing beside a large cemetery in Dông Xuân, halfway between the Batangan and Pinkville. The company spent the rest of the day preparing operations for the next three nights. By 3:55 a.m. on May 2, Alpha had moved three kilometers west to a piece of ground three kilometers due north of Pinkville.[1]

On the third of May, Alpha Company landed by combat assault at the southern edge of Mỹ Khê 1 just after three in the afternoon, in the heat of the day.[2] The company took fire from the southeast. They hit the ground and fired back until the enemy position fell silent. They cleared the position, finding three dead Vietnamese combatants and capturing two others.[3] Alpha left the sub-hamlet to continue patrolling. While O'Brien was thinking about "Coke and rest," the bushes on the far side of the rice paddy to the east burst open with fire.[4] Jerry Karr remembers the screams of two men after a grenade exploded on the other side of a dike, one yelling that he couldn't see. Bullets smashed into Karr's rucksack, knocking him off the top of the dike.[5]

Here is how O'Brien described what happened in a letter to Erik Hansen two weeks later:

> We CA'd into a hail of close-range gunfire! Good lord, it was unbelievable. It came out of a ville, we charged through an open paddy, men fell all over the place, and I (CO's RTO as I've mentioned before, I'm sure) fell next to the Capt., pinned down behind a dike so small it couldn't house the Brazilian grub ant (2" long, ½" wide, maybe with a height of ¾ centimeter—thus, SMALL SMALL SMALL). He rushed out, only 6 feet from the ville's hedge row. I didn't, of course, having retained a pinch of necessary sanity. Sadly, I ought to have followed. A grenade landed by me [and] another RTO [. . .]. Turning my head & muttering Gayle's name, I listened to the remarkably piddling explosion (gre. maybe 5 feet away) & only had to suck at a sore palm. The other guys took the force.[6]

Guarding the captured Vietnamese from earlier complicated the reaction. O'Brien remembers James Claussen staring at the homemade Chicom grenade, a red can with a fish on it, that had landed fizzling among them. Claussen took the brunt of the blast. O'Brien's radio protected his back from whizzing shrapnel. Wayne Streiff, the huge private first class they called "Water Buffalo," "Buffalo," or "Buff," huddled on the ground with him.

O'Brien managed to fire toward the tree line while talking on the radio with the battalion commander in his helicopter. Bullets missed him by inches, from enemy AK-47s to his front and friendly M16s from behind. Another RTO caught a round between his jugular and clavicle that has lodged there ever since.[7]

Sgt. Arnold took a squad and stormed toward a thicket of bamboo to lead a concealed charge around the enemy's flank when "a group of NVA opened fire on him, hitting him six times, the automatic weapons fire zipping up his body, starting at his right thigh above the knee with the last round entering the left shoulder." Capt. Anderson and two others raced to pull him back, not knowing he was already dead.[8] Lt. White carried Arnold out of the bushes and loaded him onto the helicopter.[9] Roy Arnold had undergone additional training after AIT to become an "instant NCO," a "Shake-and-Bake" sergeant with no field unit experience. He had been in-country a month less than O'Brien. The others called him Arizona because he was from Phoenix. Everyone liked him. Kind, laid-back, too sweet to be a soldier yet taking the fight to the enemy that day. "I wish I would have let him win at Ping-Pong back at Chu Lai," O'Brien says.

Pfc. O'Brien radioed for a helicopter dust-off at 5:08 p.m. for Arnold's body and the five wounded.[10] They had dismounted the helicopters only two hours before. A medic treated O'Brien in the field for minor shrapnel slivers in his hand, hip, and leg. Although he would receive a Purple Heart, the injury was not worth reporting in the moment. "Nothing hurt much."[11] The memoir covers the firefight in two different chapters and with different details, giving little reason to connect the two as the same—one passage entirely omits his wounding.[12] Hardly a wound at all. Years later, he would write his embarrassment over a silly wound into "The Ghost Soldiers." At the time, Pfc. O'Brien was livid about losing his eyeglasses: "[A] searing rage bubbled up inside me—my goddamn *glasses*—and it was those lost glasses, or my own incompetence, not just the endless gunfire, that made me truly and dearly want to kill and keep killing. I remember crabbing around in the ditch, full of fury, yelling at God and the war because I couldn't find my goddamned glasses."[13] Maybe that's what Karr heard.

The company headed north, deeper into Pinkville, as evening came on. At 6:10, they fired at three more VC, killing one, chasing off the others. The battalion attached the reconnaissance platoon from Echo Company to strengthen Alpha that night. The recon platoon set up an ambush south of Alpha and exchanged fire and grenades with a VC squad. Taylor's history reports that "During the night the men of Alpha could hear taunts from nearby VC & NVA regulars."[14]

The day's casualties prompted Nathan Riley, Alpha's first sergeant—the highest-ranking noncommissioned officer, who typically ran the show in the rear when the commander was conducting the missions—to leave LZ Gator and patrol with the company until replacements could arrive. Perhaps he fancied his presence would help morale.

Alpha humped all day on the fourth, a quiet but tense day. Anderson's questioning of locals yielded no information. Alpha and a South Vietnamese army (ARVN) company were either to cross the Diêm Điem River at a large bridge just beyond Mỹ Lai 5 and north into Giêm Diên 2, or to position themselves on the south side to block the enemy from crossing south.[15]

As Alpha approached the Diêm Điem bridge, sniper fire picked up. The company instead crossed a smaller bridge, over a tributary on the south side of the Diêm Điem under fire, one at a time, as fast as their awkwardly bouncing and clanking equipment allowed.[16] Seventy-five meters across. The captain went first. O'Brien, as an RTO, might have gone second. He remembers that run as "the one truly brave thing" he did in Việt Nam, the mustering of enough nerve to race double-time fully exposed to enemy fire from both sides of the river. As each soldier reached the far side, Anderson flashed him a V-sign, for victory or valor, but writing a few months later O'Brien added that it "came to mean vindictive—as in vengeance."[17]

At about six thirty, an Alpha soldier, Sgt. Patrick James "PJ" Kihl, was hit in the shoulder by shrapnel and quickly dusted off.[18] It happened soon after the company finished the crossing. Kihl had fired his M79 grenade launcher to suppress enemy fire but the round hit a nearby low branch, exploding slightly above and right in front of him.[19] O'Brien remembers the ARVN company of about one hundred soldiers sitting on the dikes surrounding a square rice paddy. He believed the ARVN, sitting casually in the open, invited what happened next.

By seven forty-five the mortars and small-arms fire began to rain in. "We crawled about in gullies and along paddy dikes, trying to evade. We saw the red quick flashes of their mortar tubes, but no one dared fire back, for it would do nothing but give away more precisely our position." The commander hollered that they were being bracketed—that the enemy was adjusting fire closer and closer. He had O'Brien call for gunship support and his fire support officer for artillery. They were crawling along with the other RTO, the fire support officer, and the first sergeant, trying to find a way through a thick hedgerow into a ville on the other side. The commander yelled at O'Brien to keep up, not realizing his radio antenna was alternately dragging through the paddy muck or snagging in the brambles. They found an opening and led about half of Alpha crouching through into the ruins of a sub-hamlet. O'Brien plopped himself on a wall near a collapsed stone pagoda, seething, mortar rounds still coming down. "Get down!" Anderson yelled. "Don't get yourself fucking killed because you are pissed at me!" O'Brien complied.

Half the company spent the night in the relative protection of the wrecked ville, the other half pinned down in the sloppy wet paddies with the ARVN company.[20] One Alpha soldier ended up with a bad case of ringworm.[21]

Early the next morning, 1st Sgt. Riley—"Top," as all first sergeants are called—marched near the commander and the RTOs at the front of the column. O'Brien heard a dull blast and looked over to see him crumple amid "dirt and a cloud of red smoke."[22] Both legs were injured, one foot mangled, from an American M79 grenade-launcher round. Some Alpha soldiers later accused the attached Echo recon platoon of accidental friendly fire.[23] Top was dusted off by seven thirty for the first leg of his trip home.[24]

Helicopters hopped Alpha over the Hầm Giang River that afternoon to land them a kilometer away, between An Thinh 1 and Dáp Mỹ 2. During the first night watch shift, O'Brien stayed up to keep a buddy company. The buddy told him another Black soldier in Alpha had fired the grenade at Top to warn him, not hurt him.[25] The Black soldiers resented the fact that Top seemed to give rear jobs only to whites. It was an amazing shot with a weapon few soldiers had an instinct for aiming accurately. The M79 functioned like a handheld, trigger-fired mortar to lob a fragmentation munition farther than hand grenades can be thrown—the stubby launcher pointed into the sky, not at the target. Yet the first sergeant was the only person hurt despite being only a few meters away from others, including O'Brien.

The company continued humping the next day, away from the Mỹ Lai sub-hamlets toward the northwest in the heat, over steep jungle hills, across streams and lowland marshes, and through paddies and sub-hamlets. "I remember that in Việt Nam the single greatest act of valor that I was capable of was simply to walk," O'Brien has reflected. "Because with every step there were land mines everywhere and legs lying everywhere, and dead people. [...] It's just an act of volition to make myself take one more step. And survival was like going into this very evil casino run by Satan."[26] For O'Brien, the Russian roulette scene in the film *The*

Deer Hunter perfectly captures "the emotional and spiritual experience" of a combat mission.[27]

In the late morning, an unseen sniper sniped at them only to be chased off by a single artillery blast. Two hours later the company ran across and detonated an errant artillery round.[28]

More walking the next two days, northeast toward the Batangan Peninsula, eventless days but for the heat and fear and whatever stayed unreported to the battalion.[29] O'Brien's wounded hand became infected, another detail he used for "The Ghost Soldiers." He caught a resupply chopper back to Gator for treatment and to pick up a new pair of glasses, returning within a day or two. It was around this time when, after discovering and blowing three tunnels with grenades—and blowing them again, for good measure, for the fun of it—the firefight ensued that opens *If I Die in a Combat Zone*. There were no casualties, and according to the memoir, Capt. Anderson told O'Brien not to bother reporting it to battalion, as he didn't "want to spend time playing with gunships, and that's what they'll make us do."[30]

The war memoir's chapter "My Lai in May" blurs the chronology. It suggests that during these couple of days, "it took little provocation for us to flick the flint of our Zippo lighters" on the thatched dwellings, "taking our revenge in fire" against "the phantom Forty-eighth Viet Cong Battalion," always there, rarely sighted.[31] The chapter is a revised version of an article written and published during his Việt Nam duty, the one after and about the Mỹ Lai massacre revelations where Capt. Anderson's "V" came to mean vengeance. (Later essays, "The Vietnam Veteran—Prisoner of Peace" (1974) and "Ambush" (1992), confuse and condense the chronology even more.) It's more likely, however, that the events precipitating the Zippo revenge were still to come.

By the dark early-morning hours of Friday, May 9, Alpha had established a cordon just west of Châu Bình 1 on the central road into the Batangan. The company encircled the village with the hopes of either catching VC unawares when they left for the day or flushing them out. Capt. Anderson, the artillery spotter, Pfc. O'Brien, and the other RTOs nestled against a paddy dike on the western edge of the ville. It didn't take long for the enemy to emerge. The platoons opened fire. Illumination rounds, floating down beneath dainty parachutes, lit the scene. The artillery officer made the call and the explosive rounds began to land. Then three figures trying to sneak away appeared to the command team's front. Anderson whispered to aim low. Their group stood up from behind the dike. O'Brien and Anderson both fired:

> It was the first and only time I would ever see the living enemy, the men intent on killing me. [...]
> I neither hated the man nor wanted him dead, but I feared him. [...]
> The figures disappeared in the flash of my muzzle. [Anderson] hollered at us to put our M-16s on automatic, and we sent hundreds of bullets out across the paddy. Someone threw a grenade.

When the sun rose a little higher, the captain and the artillery lieutenant investigated. They "found a dead man with a bullet hole in his head. There were no weapons. The dead man carried a pouch of papers, some rice, tobacco, canned fish, and he wore a blue-green uniform." O'Brien declined to look. He hoped it was not the man he had met in Prague.[32]

There was no way to know who had killed the man. O'Brien's fictional avatar in The Things They Carried expresses his guilt for the death of a fictional Vietnamese man, shot in the face, he didn't kill but might have: "I blamed myself. And rightly so, because I was present." The avatar admits he "was young" and "afraid to look. And now, twenty years later, I'm left with faceless responsibility and faceless grief."[33] O'Brien drew from this event for the three-story sequence whose central story, "Ambush," bears the same title as his war memoir's pertinent chapter.

It had been Alpha's most successful ambush, even though the low body count disappointed the officers. The battalion logs documented three enemies killed and another three captured of the fifteen or so the company spotted.[34] While the command group debriefed and radioed its reports, O'Brien's old platoon headed into the sub-hamlet to check and clear it.

Then came an explosion.

O'Brien looked up to see the plume. What no one yet knew: His best friend Chip Merricks had stepped on a rigged 105mm artillery round, blowing apart himself and a squad leader, Tom Markunas. Merricks and Markunas had moved along a hamlet trail apart from the others. The platoon RTO radioed O'Brien for an immediate dust-off in case someone had survived the blast. These calls were the worst part of the job. O'Brien had to derive the grid coordinates from the map and then encode them with the daily code book before sending. Any misstep could send the helicopter to the wrong spot, costing precious time, possibly costing a life. The pressure was agonizing.

O'Brien relayed the urgent dust-off request to battalion. A minute or two later, he and Anderson arrived on scene. The biggest piece of Merricks's body and a few other pieces hung off tree-tall bushes several feet from the ground. Most of Markunas's lay on the trail. Other pieces of both men clumped about on the ground. O'Brien radioed battalion to cancel the urgent dust-off.[35]

The platoon bagged the remains for pickup. O'Brien lent a hand. In his fictional reinventing of the awful memory, in "How to Tell a True War Story," a soldier sings Will Holt's folk-rock "Lemon Tree" as they pull down the pieces of Curt Lemon. The song is a cautionary tale about the loss of innocence that comes with romantic heartbreak, when the girl leaves the boy for someone else. "It *wasn't* a war story," O'Brien's narrator rejoins. "It was a *love* story." A grief story, as Rat Kiley, who'd "lost his best friend in the world" in a village on the Batangan, shoots a water buffalo calf into pieces. Later he'll write Lemon's sister, who won't write back.[36]

Alpha took close-quarters revenge. O'Brien lost himself, kicking a captured Vietnamese "around some, crying a little at the same time—crying and kicking, kicking that dink until maybe he'd turn into Chip."[37] O'Brien was hardly the only one:

When a booby-trapped artillery round blew two popular soldiers into a hedgerow, men put their fists into the faces of the nearest Vietnamese, two frightened women living in the guilty hamlet, and when the troops were through with them, they hacked off chunks of thick black hair. The men were crying, doing this. An officer used his pistol, hammering it against a prisoner's skull.[38]

"Mind your own business," another soldier recalls the pistol-wielding Lt. White telling him.[39] The company pulled out so the commander could call an air strike. The jets used napalm:

I heard screams in the burning black rubble. I heard the enemy's AK-47 rifles crack out like impotent popguns against the jets. There were Viet Cong in that hamlet. And there were babies and children and people who just didn't give a damn in there, too. But Chip and Tom were on their way to Graves Registration in Chu Lai, and they were dead, and it was hard to be filled with pity.[40]

The battalion log notes secondary explosions inside the sub-hamlet during the air strike, a strong indication of stored munitions. The company moved two kilometers to the southwest, on the other side of a small hill from Châu Bình 1, just outside Con Chiêu 2, where they spent the night.

The night before their deaths, Markunas had teased Merricks for fiddling with a lock of hair tied by a ribbon he had pulled from an envelope.[41] Neither Tim nor Kathy O'Brien remembers her sending a piece of her snipped hair to Chip, but "it sounds like something I might have done," she says. "He seemed so lonely."

O'Brien wrote Chip's sister. She never wrote back.

The unspoken casualty was a soldier devastated by Markunas's death. According to Carl Foley, Capt. Anderson had the troubled soldier removed from their combat company because of his father's illness. Foley believes otherwise: "But I saw him that day. I pray he recovered."[42] This might be the man O'Brien's memoir calls Philip, although the soldier Foley names does not look like the man O'Brien renamed "Philip" (perhaps there were two?):

If you are not overwhelmed by complete catatonia, you may react as Philip did on the day he was told to police up one of his friends, victim of an antipersonnel mine. Afterward, as dusk fell, Philip was swinging his entrenching tool like a madman, sweating and crying and hollering. He dug a foxhole four feet into the clay. He sat in it and sobbed.[43]

No one said a word. He left in the morning.

More mindless patrolling inland from the peninsula the next couple of days. The temperature stayed in the upper nineties. Two VC shot in the leg, captured, dusted off. A couple of incoming mortars, an artillery response, negative results. A light moving through the night, a jungle will-o'-the-wisp, an artillery response, negative results.[44] Life must have felt like it did for Conrad's Marlow in *Heart of Darkness*, watching a British man-of-war blindly firing its naval cannons into the African continent: "Pop, would go one of the six-inch guns; a small flame would dart and vanish, a little white smoke would disappear, a tiny projectile would give a feeble screech—and nothing happened. Nothing could happen."[45]

Elsewhere, the notoriously bloody ten-day battle at "Hamburger Hill" began.

Alpha settled atop another high, steep hill late in the day on May 11. From this position Lt. White, "perched on a rock, pushed his spectacles against his nose," took slow aim, and casually shot a Vietnamese in the leg. He was practicing with a sniper-scoped M14 carbine on a man working in the rice fields. O'Brien harbored serious doubts about the man's belligerent status but dutifully called the report to battalion as he had received it, identifying the victim as a VC. The ambiguity and guilt would have its fictional day in John Wade's shooting of the old man with a hoe in *In the Lake of the Woods*. The evening had otherwise been a welcome break, the soldiers cheered by a helicopter delivery of "hot food, mail, Coke, and beer."[46]

Just after midnight, in the opening hours of May 12, Alpha for once was grateful to be in the bush. The enemy launched a general offensive primarily targeting LZ Gator and its sister bases. O'Brien heard the panicky radio chatter. Gator survived the night but with major casualties, ten wounded and four dead.

Among the dead was the battalion commander, Lt. Col. Alfred Barnes. A satchel charge tossed into his quarters early during the assault strongly suggests his elimination to have been a primary objective. The VC detested him for his effectiveness. His soldiers disliked his spit-and-polish style and hated his aggressively taking the fight to the enemy. When the news reached Alpha, Lt. White and a cluster of soldiers followed O'Brien's lead in singing "Ding-Dong! The Witch Is Dead."[47]

The gratitude ended midmorning when, coming down the hill, Pfc. Charles Slocum stepped on a mine that blew off an arm and a leg. Hours later, another Alpha soldier dislocated a shoulder diving into his foxhole when a grenade and small-arms fire burst open the evening.[48] According to Taylor, Alpha's only kill that day was a water buffalo. The wounded buff charged out of a hamlet into a paddy surrounded by two Alpha platoons. They opened fire at it, fearful of a charge and very nearly hitting each other until a soldier "took the beast down with one shot."[49] This buffalo's death doesn't match the one O'Brien describes in *If I Die in a Combat Zone*:

> Some boys were herding cows in a free-fire zone. They were not sup-posed to be there: legal silhouettes for our machine guns and M-16's and M-79 grenade launchers. We fired at them, cows and boys to-gether, the whole company, or nearly all of it, like target practice at Fort Lewis. The boys escaped, but one cow stood its ground. Bullets struck its flanks, exploding globs of flesh, boring into its belly. The cow stood parallel to the soldiers, a wonderful profile. It looked away, in a single direction and it did not move. I did not shoot, but I did endure, without protest, except to ask the man in front of me why he was shooting and smiling.

O'Brien imagines an answer to that question in "How to Tell a War Story," when the grief-stricken fictional Rat Kiley slaughters a baby water buffalo: "It wasn't to kill; it was to hurt [. . .] it was a question of pain."[50]

Same-same for four more days, the company still covering the entrance area to the Batangan, more hunted than hunting. Incoming grenades and bullets the next morning; two wounded soldiers dusted off.[51] Alpha was sniped at twice that day before finally seeing and shooting at two VC, killing one; they received sniper fire again as they settled into their night defensive position.[52] Sniper fire the morning of the fourteenth sent three more GIs by helicopter to the hospital,[53] one of whom looked stone-dead to O'Brien, but all survived. In the evening Alpha set up south of Phú Nhiêu 5. After a brief exchange of fire with an enemy soldier poking out of a tunnel, the company reported another twenty to twenty-five VC from around the village attempting a flanking maneuver. The battalion log records the rest: "A Co set fire to the village, fire gets out of control so they moved away and suspect VC to be following." They spent the night only half a kilometer east of the burning sub-hamlet, a kilometer west of the sea.[54]

The next day was the quietest, with a couple of soldiers pinned down by sniper fire before finding their way back to the rest of the company for the night.[55] Late in the morning of the sixteenth, heavy small-arms fire wounded another Alpha soldier. The artillery response had no effect. An hour later the company spotted four enemy, fired on them, and called in artillery, also to no effect.[56]

Alpha had had enough. Battalion ordered all but one platoon to the relatively secure CAP 142, the lagoon site on the Batangan coast, before returning them to LZ Gator the next day. It was a ten-kilometer march. Along the way, they received sniper fire, O'Brien's pack came undone, and the bands that bundled the lengths of the radio antenna broke, releasing all six feet of it to drag along behind him. "We walked like madmen, canteens going dry, and nothing stopped us. Finally came the sand, pines, a stretch of miraculously white beach, a sheaf of blue and perfect water." They shed weapons and accoutrements and hurled themselves into the sea. "[I]f we'd had a raft and courage, that ocean could have carried us a thousand miles and more toward home."[57]

Alpha returned to LZ Gator in the late afternoon of May 17.[58] That evening, the first chance he had, O'Brien wrote to Hansen about experiencing "the hell promised all trainees in those classes back at Ft. Lewis. Tired—utterly exhausted to the fluid in my bone cells (what has not evaporated in this heat[)]—I wonder if this letter will even be finished." This is the letter in which he reports on the day he received his wound and Roy Arnold was killed. The rest of the letter summarizes the past weeks' horrors:

> 3 guys very dead—one a close buddy whose sister I write—25 wounded—5 w/out legs and/or arms, others with asundry [sic] hurts, some minor but, I could tell from the screams & aghast faces & red exposed meat that quickly gets dirty, what with the victims rolling in the red clay, scuffing the gore, fighting the medics, conscious of

nearly everything (which, I think is hideous!) that the fellows usually
suffer, suffer.

Immediately following this summary, without transition, he drops Hansen
into a poem:

Haunted
    not so much by the real sights
    (including—well, words don't give sights—
    bone through dirty red meat, frayed
    something like hamburger but not
    nearly so cellophane-neat-wrapped
    and hardly as salable—
    though a good, quick bullet
    through a leg, missing the bone,
    sending Tony home
    is worth 79¢ a pound)—
    but by the thought thought
      ought not for me
      to happen
      ought not for me
      to hurt;
      sought not this,
      wrought not this (myself, anyway, not alone)

Haunted
    Ever a day turns
    like earth by spade to night
    and never the pony to grow
    a camel to feed me
    Bay to deseed me—
    Funny (crooked step, an old man toppling by came over nightly
      dark cobblestones.)

Whether he wrote the poem on the spot or copied it from a field notebook,
perhaps with tweaks, isn't clear. O'Brien admits his depression and reiterates

his exhaustion. He resumed the letter the next day with a final note upon learning that he returns "to the boonies" that very night.[59]

That day's letter home neglects to share with family his wounding or the graphic portrayal of suffering. It instead emphasizes the repetitive nature of the war, the daily bullets from unseen snipers who promptly vanish into the jungle, and the "perpetual marching up hills & through brush, scraping your arms on thorns, hoping you miss the mines, guzzling gallons of foul well water, drinking cold coke when resupply bring it in, waiting for mail," all the while "hating the war and the lack of good reason behind it, living with the knowledge I'm a coward for being here rather than pitting myself against it, any way possible." The letter closes with a homey image of playing golf with father and brother: "That's the place to be!"[60]

Alpha stayed one more night on Gator, returning to the boonies early the next morning.[61] The last two weeks of May proved relatively peaceful. They patrolled around villages south of LZ Gator before moving into the southern Rocket Pocket, where the entirety of their reports to the battalion consisted of two enemy sightings, one captured suspected VC, an empty tunnel, a dud mortar round, a minefield, and one dust-off for a heat injury.[62]

Meanwhile, Kathy O'Brien and Jane Reister graduated from Macalester.

On the morning of the twenty-ninth, Alpha performed a helicopter combat assault to the base of Hill 294, then started the very steep ascent. The ride terrified O'Brien because the company was entering the territory of the professional, well-organized, well-equipped North Vietnamese Army (NVA), the area where a Hồ Chí Minh Trail tributary fed the guerrilla war being waged in Quảng Ngãi.

Hill 294, one of the small easternmost peaks of the Annamite Mountains, was the farthest west and highest point that O'Brien ever humped. Hill 294 was the place the future novelist would imagine as Cacciato's jumping-off point for his AWOL trek into Laos, destination Paris: "Leading to the mountains were four klicks of level paddy. The mountains jerked straight out of the rice; beyond those mountains and other mountains was Paris. The tops of the mountains could not be seen for the mist and clouds."[63]

It was a miserable climb for the soldiers, with all their gear, without any trails, straight up through thick brambles and over huge trees and boulders. O'Brien rarely felt less of a soldier than when struggling up that mountain. Officially, Alpha spent the next two days and nights searching and clearing the mountain, finding nothing. Enormous bomb craters pitted the landscape from B-52 interdiction missions against the inflow of combatants and material—they become the rain-filled craters of *Going After Cacciato*'s Lake Country. Alpha's soldiers sat atop the mountain bored, especially the command group. To pass the time they reread mail and counted leeches. O'Brien and Capt. Anderson played gin rummy.[64] The helicopter resupply delivered two packages from O'Brien's family that included walnut bars, raisin cookies, and canned citrus. He shared the bounty, which disappeared in "a flash."[65] The moon shone nearly full atop Hill 294, the forgotten memory of which resurfaces in Cacciato's moon-round face.

They left the area the last day of the month, walking and slip-sliding down the mountain, to make their way back east on foot to the southern Rocket Pocket.[66] In the Tây Phước 1 sub-hamlet,[67] they drank from what felt like the coldest well in the entire country. The villagers treated the soldiers well, doing whatever they could for army rations or money. They scrubbed backs, they sold cold drinks. The fan-armed young women flirted. The mood changed when Jim Rhodes—"Kid" to the other grunts—discovered an AK-47 in some bushes.

With night falling, the officers ordered the soldiers to round up three local men in part to prevent the enemy from attacking. All were old, one so old O'Brien thought he wasn't long for this life. Lt. White took the lead during the field-expedient interrogation as he tried to beat information out of the men. The Vietnamese owned O'Brien's sympathies:

> "Where are the rest of the weapons?" The old men couldn't even understand him. "We'll burn down the village if you don't show us more weapons!" The old men were worried about their cuts and blood. They might have known where some guns were. But then the VC would beat them. Might as well be the foreigners, the GIs, as their own people beating them. Tell or don't tell: how do they win?

It was one of the angriest moments of O'Brien's tour and White knew it. The GIs tied the Vietnamese men to skinny trees for the night, the oldest man sitting down, the other two upright, the American officers and their RTOs encircling them. During his early-morning guard shift, O'Brien removed the gags to give them water. He had to shake one of them into consciousness; as far as he remembers, only the oldest drank. O'Brien woke his replacement and snagged some shut-eye.[68] In the memoir's version, the company's Vietnamese scout shouted the questions at them in Vietnamese while whipping their legs with a stick.[69] They called him "Mike." He looked thirteen or fourteen, out of place in jungle fatigues.

Alpha returned to LZ Gator at midday on June 2 to assume the base's defenses for the month. They manned the bunkers, they set out listening posts for early warning, they provided security for nearby activities like roadwork, and they maintained and upgraded Gator's defensive perimeter. O'Brien monitored the radio six hours a day in the tower at the battalion headquarters, or TOC (Tactical Operations Center), and a few times joined Capt. Anderson for a platoon-sized sweep outside the wire or pulled bunker duty. It was blissfully boring. Hot food and showers, cold Cokes and beers, killing time at what passed for a club, trips down to Nuoc Mau, and for O'Brien time to read and write. He wrote home immediately, a cheerful and mundane letter that thanked his family for the two packages of goodies that had tumbled out of a helicopter at Hill 294; marked the end of his fourth month in-country; talked about money and a bill owed to Harvard Books; and wished he were there golfing with Greg and Dad. He asked about Mike Kleve, his fellow Worthington recruit and basic training platoon guide, whom he had learned "got wounded by a booby trap." He hoped the injury wasn't "too bad—the frag from booby traps isn't too bad if you aren't up on top of it."[70]

In fact, the wound was bad. Kleve carried a machine gun in the 9th Infantry Division out of Đồng Tâm Base Camp, south of Sài Gòn. On a mission in early June, his company came under fire while moving through a ravine. They were ordered up the bank to form a firing line. As they reached the top, the soldier ahead of him broke right, and Kleve took a few steps forward on the path. That's when he tripped the rigged explosive. The shrapnel shredded his posterior. He was a bloody mess. He survived with severed nerves to his right leg and permanent intestinal damage.

In the upcoming days or weeks, O'Brien wrote the articles that would become his first publications about the war. He mailed them home, where his father probably typed them before submitting them to the papers. O'Brien was still at Gator when the *Minneapolis Tribune* printed "Boredom Is Real Vietnam Enemy, State Soldier Says" on June 29 and the *Minneapolis Star* ran "Soldier Describes 1st Bloody Battle" on July 4. "Boredom" describes the time on Hill 294 and the pointless and cruel interrogation of the three old villagers. It's also the more political of the two. He commends the company-grade officers who "see it is futile to commit more lives to a war that's nearly ended; or, if not ended, to a war that will not be won," who camp out for a week or two instead of actively looking for a fight.[71] The soldiers O'Brien knew never talked about winning the war the way their fathers in uniform had talked about winning World War II. They could hardly conceptualize what winning would look like, what objectives could possibly be met. They spoke in terms of surviving.

"Bloody Battle" distills that awful week in May: Roy Arnold's death, the crossing of the bridge, the soldiers pinned down in the paddy by mortars, Chip Merricks's death, and O'Brien's kicking at a captive. The article omits O'Brien's wound and the first sergeant's injury. It anticipates O'Brien's memoir in being somewhat episodic—after the longer description of the day Arnold died, it gives each incident the single-paragraph treatment—and in scrambling the order of events and compressing them into a shorter time frame. Tim O'Brien's writing on LZ Gator foreshadows his fictional Spec. Paul Berlin remembering from his observation post: "The order of things—chronologies—that was the hard part. Long stretches of silence, dullness, long nights and endless days on the march, and sometimes the truly bad times: Pederson, Buff, Frenchie Tucker, Bernie Lynn. But what was the order? How did the pieces fit [. . .]?"[72] It was a common scene, soldiers sitting around trying to reconstruct the sequence of shared experiences.

The attack that killed Lt. Col. Barnes was a fresh memory; the repairs still underway served as constant reminder. Staring into the darkness from a lonely, primitive bunker, listening for a twig snap, played on the nerves and the imagination. Enemy mortars used the tower in the middle of the compound where O'Brien stood radio watch as an aiming stake.

For the relative relaxation of those weeks on Gator, Alpha suffered five casualties. One soldier's weapon discharged as he left the mess hall, shooting him in the foot.[73] A soldier on bunker duty heard something to his front. He pulled the pin on a grenade and began to throw it. But his hand hit a communications wire and the grenade dropped onto the bunker floor. The explosion sent fragments into his legs and torso.[74]

The other three casualties occurred at Chu Lai. A rocket attack struck a graduation ceremony for the Combat Center's reconnaissance course. It killed four battalion soldiers, including two from Alpha, and wounded two, including one from Alpha.[75] All had looked forward to two weeks out of the bush, two weeks of beach and bars. One of those killed from Alpha, Gordon MacMillan, had shared that first-day truck ride to Gator with O'Brien.

O'Brien might very well have read about Kathy and Jane's graduation ceremony in papers, clippings, or letters, around the time of the Chu Lai ceremony tragedy. Macalester's administration gave the class of 1969 free rein to design its own celebration. The class had demanded the right, among other reasons, in order to stave off the otherwise inevitable graduation speech by Hubert Humphrey—the former Minnesota senator, Johnson's vice president, the hawkish 1968 Democratic presidential nominee, and a controversial new faculty member.

Instead of a parade of middle-aged speakers out of step with the new generation, the class organized a three-screen audiovisual extravaganza with "slides of Vietnam destruction and of children in the war-ridden African nation of Biafra, recordings of protest songs, and a light show accompanied by loud music which drew shouts of 'Turn it down!'"[76]—according to Reister, Stravinsky's *The Rite of Spring* and a number of pop songs. Students didn't wear the traditional cap and gown. Some women wore muumuus. A lot of students brandished black armbands to signal their grievances with the war. Technical problems marred the event—the loud music at times drowned out the narration, already garbled by the inadequate sound system. Many parents booed; some walked out. Students applauded and raised clenched fists.

It amounted to a modest peep amid a fury of coast-to-coast campus protests that spring, the most widespread and violent of the war so far, with students killed and National Guardsmen ordered up, from the University of California at Berkeley to North Carolina A&T University in Greensboro.

The first week of June, U.S. military losses in Việt Nam surpassed total U.S. losses in World War I. President Nixon stepped up his plans to begin bringing troops home, a move met with both welcome and cynicism. The citizens of Nobles County, Minnesota, celebrated the announcement that its army reserve unit would soon be coming home.[77]

11

THE SUMMER OF '69

The most consequential event for Alpha Company on LZ Gator in June 1969 was the change of command from Capt. Anderson to Capt. Smith. Anderson became the battalion's supply officer. Smith was a battalion newcomer (this book preserves the pseudonym O'Brien gave him in *If I Die*). O'Brien devotes a chapter of his war memoir to Anderson in reflecting on courage and wisdom. When Alpha maneuvered as a company, Anderson took point, the first man in the long column, O'Brien just a few steps behind him. Anderson pre-plotted artillery targets on either side of their route not simply for a more rapid response, but (against standard operating procedures) also to be able to call artillery ahead of the column. It's not like the VC didn't already know the company's location and direction—a column of a hundred well-armed lumbering men can't hide. Anderson's random artillery rounds sometimes flushed the enemy out, and maybe sometimes chased them away. When he could get a helicopter, he liked to fly visual reconnaissance ahead or on the flanks of the marching company, or outside its perimeter when settled into a position. Fifty years later he still called it "dink hunting."

Anderson had plucked O'Brien from Third Platoon to be his RTO because he "wanted the best" talking for him to the higher command. He considered O'Brien the most important person in the company after himself: "Tim did everything I asked of him and more." They played chess and cards. They talked. O'Brien's education and smarts made an impression.

Theirs was the kind of friendship that a commander and subordinate by necessity held at bay.

Smith was a good man, a good staff officer, well-intentioned, caring, amiable. But his preparedness level did not suit him to command a combat infantry company at that time and place. The company soon lost trust in Smith's tactical instincts. It didn't help that his soldiers always compared him to Anderson.[1]

On the afternoon of July 5, Alpha Company returned to the Batangan, where for ten days they operated out of CAP 142—the lagoon—and CAP 143, screening the peninsula with patrols and ambushes to prevent VC infiltration from the northwest.[2] O'Brien and the rest of the command group camped at CAP 142. A week later, O'Brien wrote about the "hundred fishermen" in "a hundred bark skiffs" each "lighted by a single lantern, a hundred lights bobbing down behind waves." The description abruptly turns from the serene to the coarse:

> The fishermen will take their catch into the village. It is not a village Gauguin painted[. . . .] The place is made of army tin; the huts are long, metal barracks, one contiguous to the next, identical in squalor, crammed full of families, surrounded by rows of the new kind of army concertina wire, the wire with little razor blades replacing barbs. Two thousand people live here.[3]

Manufactured and jury-rigged mines cordoned off the village. Especially for those who never left the beach, time passed in relative relaxation. "It was fifty cents for anything and everything" from the displaced Vietnamese—soda, porn, back rubs, weapon cleaning—"except prostitutes, which cost five dollars."[4] The GIs feasted on fresh seafood, which they cooked on the beach.[5]

This was the mood that led the three soldiers to go fishing with hand grenades in a skiff the morning of July 8, resulting in Spec. Peterson's death. The sandbag bunker where O'Brien sat when he heard the grenade go off squatted more or less where the invented rickety guard tower stands in *Going After Cacciato*, the tower from which Paul Berlin imagines his squad chasing Cacciato from Quảng Ngãi to Paris. The horseplay spooks the game of chicken-with-smoke-grenade in *The Things They Carried* right before Curt Lemon steps on a rigged artillery round.

The patrols and ambushes never made contact with the enemy, although they discovered and destroyed a number of tunnels, usually by grenade, a couple of times by air strike, and once with engineer assistance. The morning of July 13, a patrol radioed O'Brien to request a dust-off after a soldier investigating tunnels triggered a planted 81mm mortar round that blew off a foot and the other leg and sent fragments into his face. Sgt. John Martin died in the air, which the company probably didn't learn until the next day. Within days, O'Brien included Martin's death in the article about the lagoon, following a classic tactic for war stories by shattering the serene scene established in the opening. The piece ends politically: "Certain blood for uncertain reasons. No lagoon monster ever terrorized like this."[6] The article omits Peterson's death.

Reports of an enemy attack against all the Batangan CAP sites and LZ Minuteman, by a mixed force of VC and NVA potentially a thousand strong, put Alpha on high alert the night of July 14.[7] The attack never came, and in the morning the company humped to Minuteman, where they boarded helicopters for a combat assault into Pinkville.

It was the first day of Operation Nantucket Beach. This operation had two major purposes. First, to renew the pacification effort of Russell Beach by extending the eradication and control efforts inland from the Batangan, particularly toward the southwest, from the coastal Mỹ Lai and Mỹ Khê hamlets of Pinkville to Quảng Ngãi City. Second, to begin the process of *Vietnamization*, the transferring of military operations from the Americans to the South Vietnamese. When Alpha Company disembarked the choppers on the south side of the hardball Route 521 and linked up with an American cavalry troop riding M113 armored personnel carriers (APCs), it was under the control of the 6th ARVN Regiment on paper but not in practice.[8] The company landed between Mỹ Lai 4 and Mỹ Khê 3. In conjunction with the cavalry troop, a Vietnamese provincial unit, and some national police, they spent the rest of the day sweeping through the Mỹ Khê sub-hamlets, uncovering a handful of explosive booby traps.[9] Alpha did the primary work while the cavalry's APC provided support by fire with their .50-caliber machine guns.

A distressing familiarity. They had trod this exact strip of earth those awful days in May. That night they set up their defensive position on practically the same spot where Roy Arnold was killed and O'Brien and five others were wounded. The APCs formed a circle perimeter within which Alpha camped along with Vietnamese women and children, living prophylactics against mortars and RPGs.[10]

The next day went from a bad morning to the second-worst day of the war for O'Brien, after the day Chip Merricks died. In *If I Die*, he relates the day in more detail over more pages than any other day of the war. By eight o'clock the company had injured a woman hiding in or near a bunker by Alpha's soldiers conducting a slapdash recon by fire, checking bunkers not by entering them but tossing grenades in and moving on. The battalion logs report her having concussion injuries; she was a civilian but also a suspected VC whom they evacuated to a field hospital.[11]

O'Brien has published two different accounts. As *If I Die* describes the episode,

> She was seventy years old and bleeding all over. The medics patched her as best they could. She was conscious. She watched them wrap bandages around her breasts. They jabbed her with morphine. Then we called a dust-off helicopter, and when it came the medics and the soldier who had hurt the woman tried to help her up. She scrambled like a wet fish. She was nearly dead, but she crawled, on all fours and whimpering, trying to get back into her hole. To get her into the helicopter, the medics had to carry her. She hollered all the way. The bandages were dangling, and blood was in her hair and eyes. She was screaming, but the bird roared and lifted and dipped its nose and flew away with her.[12]

In "Prisoners of Peace," someone found her in a bunker. He didn't bring her out because, he said, "She'll fall apart in my hands. How do you carry slush?" Other soldiers went in and pulled her out. "Fuckin' gook," another said. "You can't kill gooks." The old woman refused water. She bit one of the four men carrying her to the helicopter.[13]

By ten in the morning, Alpha had two soldiers wounded by a Bouncing Betty mine.[14] Within the hour, in spitting distance of Mỹ Khê 1 and Mỹ

Khê 3, the "shit hit [the] fan," as many years later O'Brien would write in his notes from the battalion log at the National Archives.[15] The day after the shit hit the fan, he wrote Hansen:

> Yesterday was a horror. Think of the Battles of Bull Run.
>
> We were on APCs, returning from a sweep of 3 villes. Out in an open paddy, water & mud 3 feet deep, foul as hell. RPGs and small arms came blasting out of a treeline to our front. We grunts jumped off to fight and to allow the carriers to fight. The APCs backed up under the fire, smashed our men and their heads and legs to pieces. 1 guy was drowned under a carrier. 1 had his foot cut off. Another had his leg broken, and all the while we were getting chopped up by the gooks. We tried to outrun our own carriers that were backing over us, but plenty of men weren't able to waddle fast enough & they went under. Everyone was throwing off packs and canteens & ammo & radios, trying to move faster. Finally we regrouped and dusted everyone off. So damn tired and nearly crying, it was so awful. Then we tried to crash into the tree line, and we were nearly there when a PF [South Vietnamese Popular Force militiaman] with us stepped on a booby-trapped mortar round, blowing to hell himself and four of us. Finally we retreated, I hope forever, from that place. 5 guys came into the company with me; 3 are dead and one is in the world nursing a bullet hole, grinning like a shriveled banana. A rear job can't be too far away.[16]

Pfc. Rodger McElhaney carried the additional weight of the radio as Second Platoon's RTO. He could not pull himself out of the muck. He was one of the five other newbies who had shared the first-day-in-the-bush truck ride with O'Brien from Chu Lai to LZ Gator.[17] The two companies searched for the body only after three back-to-back jet air strikes followed by a helicopter gunship run. The log attributed the day's casualties to enemy RPGs.[18] In addition to McElhaney and the unnamed dead Vietnamese soldier, ten GIs and two Vietnamese were evacuated for wounds. Another six Americans were treated in the field.[19]

The catastrophe resulted from poor leadership. O'Brien's memoir depicts Smith as a Tennessee bumpkin who constantly dithered with the cavalry troop commander about how to proceed. At one point Smith asked his soldiers what he should do. Someone remembered him crying. Pfc. O'Brien suggested they pull out of the sub-hamlets. "What the hell is the matter with that direction?" he asked, pointing to the way they had come. The two captains didn't heed that advice until after the Vietnamese scout stepped on the mine.[20]

The entire snafu O'Brien would fictionally resurrect for the "In the Field" chapter of *The Things They Carried* by having Kiowa drown in a village's common outdoor latrine area during a mortar attack. In the story, the confederation of failures and derelictions leading to Kiowa's death encompasses a much larger field of players, all the way from a young soldier who needed a flashlight to show off a picture of a girl, to "an old man in Omaha who forgot to vote."[21] O'Brien intends the young soldier to be read as the novel's Tim O'Brien character such that the story boosts the theme of guilt by presence. O'Brien didn't get McElhaney killed, but he was there. "Nobody's fault," one of the short story's other soldiers tells the kid. "Everybody's."[22]

Stateside, Americans were reading headlines about the weeks-long lull in combat and the first troop withdrawals. Worthington eagerly awaited the return of its army reservists.[23]

The battalion did not wait for Alpha to reach the planned pickup spot. It dispatched helicopters to hustle the shocked company back to the lagoon.[24] The next several days were blessedly quiet. Routine ambushes and patrols resulted in one mortar mission against a dozen VC with "negative results" after ineffectual machine gun fire from navy Swift boats; and a Viet Cong teenager who turned himself in to the platoon at CAP 143 as a Chiêu Hồi.[25]

While O'Brien and company rested by the South China Sea, Neil Armstrong and crew landed at the Sea of Tranquility. Over a few transistor radios, Alpha in its bunkers followed Apollo in its capsule. It was three hours and seventeen minutes after midnight on July 21, Quảng Ngãi time. Six hours and thirty-nine minutes later, Armstrong stepped on the moon. The instant pride that inundated the home front didn't win over the hearts and minds of Americans mired in Việt Nam. Many of them felt even more forgotten, even more dispensable. *They can send men to the moon, but they can't get our asses out of Việt Nam?* went the in-country refrain.

One morning later, choppers ferried Alpha to the western side of Tam

Hôi 1, a sub-hamlet about a third of the way back toward Gator that sat on one of the main roads into the Batangan. Delta Company landed on the eastern side. The battalion commander "ordered F-4 Jets to drop na-palm and two hundred fifty-pound bombs on the hamlet to soften it up."[26] O'Brien has written about that morning bombing at least twice. In *If I Die*, he describes it in a terse, almost reportorial paragraph. In an article pub-lished a year later, he abandons understatement:

> The jets were our magic wands. They came in out of the sun, swept in low. They passed over the village, and the village magically blew apart and disappeared. [. . .]
>
> There was more black smoke, blacker black smoke. The jets came in again and again and again.
>
> "Jesus," someone said. "They're not bombing a village. They're bombing smoke."[27]

O'Brien would use the language of magic in his 1994 novel *In the Lake of the Woods* as the narrator makes villages, memories, and people disappear.

The two companies and the accompanying police force entered the vil-lage. In the memoir (misremembering which battle), O'Brien says he saw "an old lady wander[ing] about, smiling," clearly in shock. According to David Taylor, she wouldn't take water. Delta's acting commander ordered a dust-off. She refused. The Americans left her and went on with their work.[28] The forty or so VC who had quartered there overnight had already beat feet to elsewhere.[29]

In its night defensive position, Alpha received a couple of hundred rounds of small-arms fire. It felt routine: incoming fire, no injuries, artil-lery called in the vicinity, negative results.[30]

More hopping by Huey the next few days as the battalion scrambled its companies over short distances to pounce on locations of reported enemy activity, all a part of Nantucket Beach's mission to control the lowlands area between Highway 1 and the Batangan Peninsula.[31] Most missions involved multiple companies. If the soldiers had had such language, they would have thought of it as war by whack-a-mole, only they wouldn't have said *mole*.

In the early morning of July 23, Alpha landed near the tiny Phú Nhiêu

3.[32] A few hours later they were picked up again and moved less than a klick south, to the high ground overlooking Liêm Quang 1 (while gunships raked Phú Nhiêu 3). The ville was on fire from napalm and it was a hot LZ—six soldiers were wounded almost immediately. O'Brien described the scene in a *Washington Post* article in advance of the 1973 memoir:

> Bullets slashed out of the bushes. One of them hit a GI in the leg; he dropped and began to bleed. A grenade sailed like a football into the clump of squirming American soldiers. It exploded and two GIs fell. "Jesus!" they screamed in unison. "Medic!" The bushes erupted again. A young lieutenant was shot in the groin. He crumpled, but did not scream. The GIs began to return fire, tentatively at first. Then the whole platoon turned their M-16s to the bushes, toward the invisible enemy, emptying all they had into a short stretch of Vietnam jungle. But they shot blindly, putting a bullet through a buddy's chest.[33]

At eleven o'clock, Pfc. O'Brien called for a dust-off.[34] He, Capt. Smith, and several others took cover in a gully. When O'Brien realized that the helicopter above them bore the battalion commander, he radioed him directly and asked that he land to help save a soldier's life.

The lieutenant colonel refused, barking, "My job is to direct the fight!"

That O'Brien insisted twice more, a private first class to a colonel, says a lot about the chaos and his frustration. Extra soldiers on the helicopter could have dismounted to make room for the casualties and join the fight. A radio or two could have been tossed overboard. The commander's refusal enraged O'Brien.[35] He begins that 1973 article criticizing the military's generosity with medals to officers with this episode, as the battalion commander would receive a Distinguished Flying Cross—in actuality, however, for a later event.[36]

An intense hour-long running battle fought at close range followed those opening minutes. Another company was fighting on the other side of Liêm Quang 1. Helicopter gunships firing away added to the din and smoke. For O'Brien the RTO, firefights involving several units and layers of command were especially harrowing because of all the radio traffic and the communications he had to pay attention to and relay, always with the added pressure of encoding coordinates. The helicopters evacuated six Alpha soldiers. Pfc. Myron K. Renne died at the hospital from a sucking chest wound—Renne was probably killed by friendly fire when his buddies reflexively let loose suppressive fire without aiming, as O'Brien would write in the article.[37] The lieutenant had his left testicle shot off by a round that went through his hip. His groin was a bloody mess. The soldier who waited with him for the dust-off remembered "how tight the Lt. held my hand I thought he was going to break my hand, his grip of pain was that bad. He kept saying over and over, 'What's my wife going to say?'"[38]

The battalion commander did not alight to recover Renne and the lieutenant until the platoon made a safe landing zone for him ten minutes after the firefight ended.[39] Alpha swept through the burned ville, discovering four dead VC.[40]

O'Brien's memoir doesn't attribute the KIA to friendly fire. O'Brien didn't witness it and couldn't confirm it. Before the company left the village, Renne's best friend told O'Brien the firing came from behind while the pair were charging up front. The buddy sounded sure and made a convincing case. Still, it was a long, messy firefight, with squads getting separated and turned around. There's no way to know. Besides, once bullets fly, does it really matter? It's interesting to speculate why O'Brien felt comfortable ascribing the fatal wound to fratricide for the article, which he wrote after the memoir but which he knew would be published first.

There's another difference. The article omits O'Brien's outraged effort to hasten the evacuation; the memoir fictionalizes it by having First Platoon's unnamed RTO rather than O'Brien hound the battalion commander. It was O'Brien, then, whom the commander ordered to "relay your damn requests through your CO," and who after a pause repeated the request, snarking that his company CO was now conveniently "unconscious and bleeding."[41]

That night the company set up in the sub-hamlet with Smith, O'Brien, and the command group in the middle of the ville and with the line platoons just inside the edge, out of sight:

The place had been smoked that day—I suppose by artillery, or gunships, or by both—and I remember there was wreckage and death-stink everywhere. The guys seemed spooked by the place. And by all that happened during the day. In the middle of the night, [Smith] suddenly opened up on full automatic, right in the center of the village, our own troops in a perimeter around us. A miracle no one was shot. Scared the shit [out] of everyone. Certainly it did me—I was sound asleep two or three feet away—my heart still ticks erratically from the damage. Turned out [Smith] had shot a pig.[42]

The company spent the morning checking out and blowing some twenty-five tunnels. At one point their Vietnamese scout called out to two military-aged males, who fled. Soldiers fired after them.[43] Around this time, O'Brien received a call for a dust-off from the soldiers performing the demolition. Capt. Smith told him to stay put as he checked it out. It felt like an hour later before Smith returned. He told O'Brien that the "idiot" practically blew off his own face heating his breakfast can with a C-4 explosive charge. Others repeated that version of the soldier's death to O'Brien later. The battalion log, however, only records that Pfc. Everett Brauburger suffered a "concussion from a block of wood from a demo charge" and "massive cerebral trauma."[44] In *If I Die*, O'Brien writes that a chunk of clay ripped off the man's nose "and he drowned to death in his own blood. He had been eating ham and eggs out of a can."[45] Because O'Brien did not witness the incident, the memoir keeps the cause ambiguous.[46]

The next day, Alpha made two more moves by helicopter. The early-morning trip landed them southeast of LZ Gator and the Sông Trà Bồng near the Tam Hôi hamlet, four kilometers from the sea. In response to a report of a possible enemy battalion, Alpha was picked up in the afternoon and dropped on a small mountaintop, the highest ground in the area conducive to a landing zone: "We landed next to a statue of the Buddha, and a monk strolled out to meet us. He brought watermelon and another fruit. So we went inside the gates and walked down perfectly swept paths, through gardens and small statues."[47] A flock of parentless children lived with him. The area had been thoroughly mined. Most civilians had left their homes for safer living. The monk pointed out the best places for foxholes. The soldiers gifted the monastery with C rations. The medics examined the kids.

The bald old man was quite forthcoming about recent enemy movement and periodic occupation of the very same fighting positions. He spoke with O'Brien in French, voicing what he knew the Americans must be wondering—that perhaps he worked for the Việt Cộng, that perhaps the monastery harbored an enemy base to which they would return after the GIs left. The monk smilingly suggested he might make an excellent character in a Graham Greene novel, the "revolutionary priest." Or maybe instead he shared his gentle peace with all.[48]

That night Third Platoon on the eastern slope spotted three VC and called for artillery. Ninety minutes later one of its squads tossed two grenades at three VC (who may or may not have been the same) and then pulled back inside the monastery perimeter.[49] When a position reported hearing movement, a possible VC probe, grenades and hundreds of pellets blasting out of a claymore mine silenced the dark. The only casualty was the lightly wounded Buddha statue. The expected battle never erupted.

The monastery encounter gifted O'Brien one of his precious few memories "of civility against the atrocity and murderousness of it all." Of grace, even. The next morning, July 26, Alpha made its way down the mountain, blowing some mines on the way.[50] They worked their way through the scattered sub-hamlet of Trường Thọ 3 and then the Duyen Lộc hamlet to a small valley, where helicopters met them beside the Sông Hâm Giang to extract them back to LZ Gator, whereupon they dumped their gear and boarded trucks for another Chu Lai stand-down.[51]

◊ ◊ ◊

Although O'Brien did not know it, the next five weeks would be his last humping the countryside with Alpha.

On July 29, the company trucked to Gator, geared up, and moved by Chinook back to the gateway area into the Batangan, landing between Route 523 and the hilltop where they had heard about Lt. Col. Barnes's death.[52] Alpha worked with Delta Company for the next several days. According to David Taylor, Alpha's insecure commander "deferred to Delta's commander whenever possible while Alpha's platoon leaders tried to make the best of his poor leadership."[53] That night they set up ambushes south of the road, in the middle of the Phú Nhiêu sub-hamlets, a long-standing VC stronghold.[54] The next day they rounded up thirty civilians, mostly women, for basic medical care and questioning by special teams. Four of the women were detained and flown away as "defendants," presumably for more serious interrogation.

Alpha also found and destroyed three tunnels in the area and received a large influx of sixteen new soldiers.[55]

Early the next morning, Delta fired on two VC, accidentally wounding two Alpha soldiers who were treated in the field. The enemy vanished into Phú Nhiêu 4. Later that day the companies parted as helicopters moved Alpha five kilometers farther inland, between Tam Hôi 2 and 5.[56] Atop the tall hill to their south sat the monastery where they had spent the night a week earlier. Not that many of the soldiers realized it. Plopped about by helicopter, blindly following their leaders as they humped, most grunts spent their time in the field feeling utterly lost. That was even so for Pfc. O'Brien, despite being a part of the command group as an RTO.

The first week of August saw more of the same: checking villes and conducting regular night ambushes; occasionally blowing tunnels, bunkers, and spider holes; occasionally receiving small-arms fire from an unseen enemy, sometimes responding with artillery, less often firing back; and a couple of times detaining civilians. "Rice denial" had always been a part of the mission. Sometimes Americans removed the rice, sometimes they destroyed it. At times rice denial became a convenient excuse for burning hooches. The days were tense. Everyone was on edge.

On August 1, the day the company searched Tam Hôi 1 and 2, Alpha forced women and children to check out tunnels before GIs tossed grenades to collapse them. That night three soldiers received light wounds from sniper fire. More sniper fire pestered them in the morning, and machine gun and automatic rifle fire and mortars that evening.[57]

On August 3, the company searched Tam Hôi 4, where they found several mines, including one bundled inside three beer cans that created a huge explosion when detonated. The entire sub-hamlet had been mined and booby-trapped. The company searched it anyway, finding nine hundred pounds of rice inside dwellings, and twenty-five pounds of corn, one hundred pounds of potatoes, three hundred more pounds of rice, and twenty-five pounds of salt inside two tunnels. They evacuated the food and blew the tunnels and a couple of 105mm howitzer rounds. The company received more small-arms fire that night and fired back with grenade launchers before calling in artillery.[58] The kind of day that would never make any history book, but the kind of day when nerves ran high as the soldiers sweated it out minute by minute.

At first light they marched a klick to the northeast, crossing over Route 523 before attacking Lạc Sơn 1. The day was uneventful until the afternoon. Fifteen more temporary civilian detainees, three more VC shot at but who got away, and two dust-offs for Alpha. One soldier stepped on a mine and another became a heat casualty. That night the company received a single incoming M79 grenade launcher round, to no effect.[59] The next afternoon, a team of three or four VC engaged an Alpha squad, shooting one American in the leg before disappearing. The American was dusted off by one thirty. First Platoon departed by helicopter for another mission as the company spent a second night in Lạc Sơn 1.[60] The company found and destroyed a mine the morning of August 6, which was otherwise a quiet day.[61]

Not so the next. In the morning, O'Brien and the command group were in a clearing encircled by the Lạc Sơn sub-hamlets when O'Brien heard the dull thud of a rigged artillery round. He looked up to see black smoke billowing skyward over the foliage. He radioed the patrol that had headed in that direction. No one answered. After an eternity of minutes, a survivor stumbled into the clearing, covered in blood, in a panic, shouting, "They're all dead! They're all dead!" A couple of medics sprinted to the spot, and Capt. Smith ordered a platoon to follow.

Two were dead, another three wounded. Pfc. Roosevelt Abraham, the patrol's RTO, had triggered the explosion. It blew apart both of his legs, killing him instantly and destroying the radio. Pfc. Charles Reefer did not live for the dust-off. He bled out, fragmentation wounds covering his entire body. Their bodies and two of the wounded were evacuated by the battalion commander, who happened to be in the area in his Huey. According to Taylor's history, the commander initially refused to land because of too much small-arms fire—but there was no enemy fire. One "incensed" Alpha grunt unloaded a magazine at the commander's Huey to give him a taste of his nonexistent danger. The dust-off chopper soon reached the scene to pull out the third wounded soldier. One of the soldiers who helped get Abraham's remains on the chopper reported "the bottom half of his body was like Jell-O."[62] O'Brien's memoir tells a slightly different story, in which this time the battalion commander touched down to pick up the casualties, an action for which he received a Distinguished Flying Cross, "an important medal for colonels," O'Brien wryly writes.[63]

The company stayed put for the rest of the day, with orders for a one-kilometer night march northeast to the outskirts of An Phước 2.[64] As the pandemonium waned, O'Brien wrote Erik Hansen:

I'm writing to you from under a poncho-liner hooch, on a hot mid-morn [sic], atop a red clay hill, where—45 minutes ago—we lost 5 men to a booby trapped 105 round, two dead, others less their legs and blood. I've finished calling in their dustoff. All the macabre details of name, extent of injuries, "how it happened"—all taken care of and now I'm trying like hell to ignore the red dirt all over me; and the flies, the dry heat, the depression that, for me, is always subsequent to the deaths. I'm not immune, and, careful as I am, there are too many mines for hope to keep you going—or a feeling for good luck.

Then a jarring subject change: "I received a picture & letter from Gayle yesterday, and for hours afterwards I'd reverted to my civilian consciousness: spirited, idealistic, futuristic happiness."[65]

Gayle Roby was kicking about Europe that summer with the boyfriend who would become her husband. She is the unnamed "girlfriend" in Europe with her boyfriend, a trip the war memoir implies O'Brien read about in a letter he received when the exhausted company reached the lagoon in mid-May.[66] Was O'Brien thinking of Roby forty-five minutes earlier when Abraham and Reefer were killed? In "The Things They Carried," Lt. Cross blames himself for Ted Lavender's death because he was daydreaming about a girl, Martha, instead of his platoon's security, when Lavender was shot. In one photograph of her he carried he could see "the shadow of the picture-taker." Like Roby, Martha was an English major who quoted poetry, who went with Jimmy to see *Bonnie and Clyde*, and who signed her letters "Love," not meaning "what he sometimes pretended it meant."[67] The unnamed Tim O'Brien character shines his flashlight to show a photo of a girl, perhaps drawing the mortars that kill Kiowa, in "In the Field."

Such fantasies are the emotional lifelines of any wartime soldier's inner life. For his 1978 novel *Going After Cacciato*, O'Brien would use an epigraph from the Great War poet Siegfried Sassoon: "Soldiers are dreamers." The novel also depicts a moment similar to Taylor's account of Abraham's and Reefer's death day. O'Brien does not write about or recall the soldier unleashing his weapon at the battalion commander's Huey, but in the novel Jim Pederson shoots after the Chinook pulling away from the battle whose crew had shoved him out the door and, seconds later, probably given him his fatal injury while wildly firing its machine guns.[68]

The plume of black smoke rising above the tall foliage will persist as one of O'Brien's starkest visual memories from the war. As with the hilltop monastery, he dearly wanted to revisit it during his 1994 return trip but failed to make it happen. He wanted to stand where he had stood and look toward the plume's ghost, aligning the memory-image within the frame of the real.

The letter's abrupt volte-face from the morning's casualties continued. After imagining traveling Europe with Roby, Hansen, and a companion for Hansen, O'Brien appealed to Hansen again to request a late October R&R to Sydney, Australia, so that they could enjoy each other's company as well as the city's offerings. The letter concluded as a "resupply bird" approached with "cold coke" to "be guzzled" and, Tim hoped, a letter from Gayle or Erik.[69]

When did Alpha hear?

That that very evening, on August 7, one of their own, Pfc. Leo Joe Adakai, was killed at Cam Ranh Bay when about thirty satchel charges exploded in the hospital complex where he was recovering from a wound received July 16 in the same swampy paddy where McElhaney died beneath the tracks of an American APC.[70] He was from the Shoshone-Bannock Tribes' Fort Hall Reservation in Idaho, his injury the day McElhaney drowned suggestive of the fictional Kiowa's death by drowning in a field of mud and shit in *The Things They Carried*.

Alpha conducted a night march to set up a blocking position to the west of An Phước 2, which Bravo would sweep the next day. Alpha found a 105mm round and a tunnel with five hundred pounds of rice on the eighth, then set up night ambushes south of An Phước 1. Helicopters flew them inland west of Tam Hội 1 by noon the next day, and that evening Alpha platoons received fire twice.[71]

On either the eighth or the ninth, Capt. Smith released O'Brien for three days at Chu Lai to look for a desk assignment.[72] He would have caught a resupply bird back to LZ Gator and probably a truck to Chu Lai. He missed the unannounced change of company command on the morning of August 10. That Capt. Paul Longgrear took over Alpha during ongoing field operations indicates the urgency of the need to remove Smith. Longgrear had already had a successful Special Forces command, winning a Silver Star at the Battle of Lang Vei, but he wanted a regular infantry company command.[73] It did not take long for Alpha to respect his soldiering and leadership.

Moments before Longgrear arrived, a soldier tripped a homemade mine. Pfc. Abelardo Rodriguez-Guzman was killed and five others were wounded. The dust-off was called at 7:45 a.m. and completed by 8:10; Capt. Longgrear took command at 8:00.[74] How sad for Capt. Smith to leave within minutes of the last man killed under his command. The next day, Longgrear discovered some of the soldiers had a hand grenade with Smith's name written on white tape.[75] This was news to O'Brien fifty years later: "I slept next to the guy every night!" Maybe O'Brien's proximity to Smith prevented the commander's being fragged. At the time, he was aware of some "half-serious talk" after the APC fiasco about the captain's "being a marked man."[76]

Failing to find a new job in the rear, O'Brien rejoined the company on the eleventh or twelfth of August. After a bit of sniper fire, Alpha moved by Huey helicopters the morning of the twelfth, the slicks landing on the west side of the steep hill overlooking the lowland entrance to the Batangan, where they found a twenty-five-hundred-pound stash of food and other material and a tunnel.[77] The next day they humped many kilometers to the northwest, toward Bình Sơn and CAP 137, on the east bank of the Sông Trà Bồng. The largest village in the area, Bình Sơn served as the district center for South Vietnamese military and political operations. Over the next week, Alpha Company patrolled and set ambushes to the east of the village. During the entire time—according to the battalion log—the only activity was one ineffective attack by small arms and grenade launchers, two youth who claimed to have escaped from the VC, a there-and-back combat assault to seize and investigate an unoccupied village, and two casualties, probably heat injuries.[78]

For American literature, the important event that August is the tale of Shorty and Smitty. Before Capt. Longgrear took command, Shorty and Smitty, two white guys from O'Brien's old platoon, walked away from the war. As Longgrear and O'Brien understood it, the two wandered about the countryside for three weeks, for a spell of that time shacking up with a couple of Vietnamese women in a small-hamlet hooch. Shorty and Smitty were not very capable soldiers, nor were they very bright. They had enough wits, gumption, and imagination, however, to walk away from Capt. Smith's perilous command. They do not appear in battalion documents as either AWOL or MIA. One of them had recently been at Chu Lai convalescing from wounds, so it is possible he signed out of the medical facility without signing back in to the battalion.

During that slow week at Bình Sơn and CAP 137, Alpha's soldiers shot the shit about Shorty and Smitty, what could have happened, what might have been, what still could be. Pfc. O'Brien joked that Shorty and Smitty might as well have hightailed it to Paris.[79] In *Going After Cacciato*, novelist O'Brien would make the City of Lights Cacciato's destination. His oafish characterization of Cacciato imparts a Tweedledum and Tweedledee vibe to Shorty and Smitty.

Meanwhile, some four hundred thousand people gathered in a New York field for the several-day, generation-defining concert known as Woodstock.

Alpha Company air assaulted first thing in the morning on August 21 to An Thơi 1, less than two klicks from the sea. Detained villagers told the company that VC had been there the day before but caught wind of the insertion and scattered into the bush in pairs, awaiting Alpha's departure to return. Parts for jury-rigged mines, a food stash, and a tunnel complex seemed to confirm the intelligence. On leaving for Vân Tường, the next hamlet to the north, Alpha received a sputtering of small-arms fire, perhaps from one of the evading enemy pairs. They returned fire and used search dogs, finding nothing.[80] Alpha settled for the night in the fields surrounded by the Vân Tường sub-hamlets.

This was the "stubby, flat hill" in the middle of "an old corn field" where O'Brien's memoir says the company spent "most of August," when in fact it served as Alpha's base of operations only for a week. The spot's elevation hardly appears on the military maps; it was indeed flat, only a smidge higher than the surrounding area. The soldiers had no shade to protect them from the sun and little vegetation to hold down the dust. The "soil was so chalky," O'Brien wrote, that they couldn't maintain a decent foxhole, settling instead for "narrow sleeping trenches." The memoir calls this period "not bad," a time of clockwork VC attacks such that the soldiers of Alpha timed their routine around them, including when they urinated.[81]

O'Brien has also described August's fear factor as exceeded only by May's and July's, however, and the battalion log indicates a period of constant enemy activity. The company perimeter received fire of varying munitions and magnitude daily and responded with varying combinations of small-arms fire, artillery, and gunships. Patrols engaged or were engaged by VC several times. On the twenty-fourth in An Cuòng 1, First Platoon discovered an unoccupied series of tunnels and bunkers with weapons, some food, mine-making gear, and documents. That night enemy mortars wounded one American and one Vietnamese soldier.[82] O'Brien's former platoon moved by helicopter to support a cavalry operation for a couple of days.

Incoming grenades, small-arms fire, mortar rounds, and even a couple of thrown satchel charges the night of August 25 was the worst barrage O'Brien experienced. He dove into his shallow sleeping trench only to land atop someone else, leaving O'Brien mostly exposed. "I dug it, you fucking lazy asshole! At least get out of the way so I can be on the bottom!" Capt. Longgrear watched incoming mortars walking across the company's position, each one nearer than the last, straight toward him. The one that should have killed him impacted fifteen to twenty feet on the other side of his foxhole. Five injured Vietnamese soldiers had to be dusted off. Gunships strafed the area from where the incoming had originated, causing serious secondary explosions.[83]

The commander led an element of the company early on August 27. They spied two Vietnamese running into Vân Tường 2 and disappearing into some kind of hooch-bunker hybrid. Longgrear and O'Brien left the middle of the column and went up. The captain bent over to peer into the entrance before tossing in the first grenade. Grenades and M16 rounds from others followed until the thing was a smoking wreck. The soldiers finally pulled out the two badly injured VC. One turned out to be a "VC honcho"— the language appears in both O'Brien's memoir and the battalion log (slang sometimes became semi-official terminology). According to *If I Die in a*

Combat Zone, one of the VC was a bullet-riddled boy, already dead, and the honcho an old man who died before the medevac chopper arrived: "We left him sprawled out there; chickens were pecking away at the dust around him when we went away." According to the battalion log, the first was a woman with a leg blown off, and she and the honcho were dusted off alive. Longgrear interrogated the man in the field. The log records his name as Vo Dan. Longgrear "was elated"; his enthusiasm soured O'Brien's opinion of him.[84] The stern faces of the onlooking villagers rattled O'Brien. He questioned the rectitude of the war for the umpteenth time.

Later in the day the company captured two nurses and a teenage boy and detained fifteen civilians. They received small-arms fire and mortar rounds and called in gunships and artillery.[85]

On the twenty-eighth of August, First Platoon fired at three VC, killing one and wounding one, the wounded one getting away. The platoon also detained two young women. Capt. Longgrear received permission for a change of location beginning the next day. And Shorty and Smitty showed back up. They probably arrived with the resupply helicopter. The next morning Alpha headed about a kilometer and a half to the northeast, to the beach outside Vân Tường 4, to provide security for the Vietnamese constructing a new refugee village. Not long after the company stepped off, just south of the sub-hamlet, Smitty stepped on a mine.

The squad loaded Smitty on a poncho with the foot that had been blown off. Against Longgrear's orders, Sgt. Bob Wolf hurriedly hacked a landing spot out of a bamboo thicket and had his RTO call a resupply bird overhead. When the helicopter landed, Wolf threw off the supplies and pulled off a soldier to make room for Smitty—presumably for Pfc. Hollis J. Watts as well, wounded by shrapnel in the face.[86] Wolf and the pulled-off soldier stood unmoving for forty-five minutes, waiting for the helicopter to return, because they were standing in a minefield.

The company made it to the beach that afternoon, many of the soldiers heading straight to the sea, flinging off their clothes. O'Brien recalls sniper fire driving the naked soldiers scampering out of the water. The next morning a sniper wounded a Vietnamese woman helping clear brush for the company's defenses. On the patrol's empty-handed return from searching for the sniper, either the tunnel dog or his handler tripped a mine, wounding the handler.[87]

The dust-offs for the civilian and the dog handler were the last of O'Brien's army career. Within a day or so, to his great surprise and delight, he finally got his desk job. There's a photograph of him the day before his departure, helmeted, shirtless, and grinning in a deep foxhole—he wasn't taking any chances that night—the South China Sea behind him. The army had dubbed the spit of land on the photo's horizon LZ Paradise. The next day O'Brien boarded a chopper and headed back to LZ Gator for the duration of his tour.

12

GATOR DAYS

One can imagine O'Brien boarding any routine resupply chopper bound for Gator, perhaps the helicopter transporting captured enemy documents and medical equipment on September 1.[1] Gator was now a forward support base, but few bothered to say *FSB*.

Pfc. O'Brien was promoted to specialist fourth class within days. At the promotion board, an NCO asked the same question asked of Pfc. Paul Berlin in *Going After Cacciato*: "What effect would the death of Ho Chi Minh have on the population of North Vietnam?" For Berlin, who fought in Quảng Ngãi a year before O'Brien, it was a random question. Not so for O'Brien. President Hồ Chí Minh died on Tuesday, September 2, 1969, but Hà Nội did not announce his death until Thursday. In between, the newspapers reported Hà Nội's official line from four in the morning on the third that he was gravely ill as well as Sài Gòn's interpretation that he was near death or already dead.[2] O'Brien's board must have occurred on Wednesday, September 3. O'Brien doesn't remember his answer, doubtless a dull mumbled thing not nearly as inspired as Paul Berlin's line, "Reduce it by one, sir."[3]

Hồ Chí Minh died exactly twenty-four years after his proclamation of Vietnamese independence at Hà Nội's Ba Đình Square by reading a document that invoked the United States' own Declaration of Independence. World War II just ended, Japan's occupation of Việt Nam was over. American OSS officers stood nearby, bearing witness.

By September 6, 1969, the U.S. military put all personnel in Việt Nam on alert for countrywide attacks in honor of Uncle Hồ and Independence Day. Da Nang, central Việt Nam's major port city, suffered fifty-two rockets and several sapper attacks that inflicted serious damage and knocked out about 75 percent of its electricity.[4] The United States ceased offensive operations for four days starting on the eighth to respect the leader's death and his followers' right to mourn.[5] The threat of armed disruptions to mid-September's local elections sustained the jitters, only to be followed by another countrywide alert in the week leading up to September 27, "the anniversary of the South Việt Nam resistance," according to the battalion log, likely referring to the Bắc Sơn Uprising of 1940 against France. From that unsuccessful uprising eventually emerged the Việt Minh as well as the National Liberation Front (the Việt Cộng).[6]

For all of that, the 5th Battalion of the 46th Infantry experienced no uptick in hostilities. Life on Gator treated Spec. 4 O'Brien kindly. He worked in the S-1 shop, the battalion office responsible for personnel matters and most administrative paperwork. His boss was the S-1, the adjutant, "a young and likable captain."[7] O'Brien so relished the sound of Capt. Richard Cacciato's last name that he used it for the title character of *Going After Cacciato*, although the man is nowise a model for the character. Five clerks shared office space with Cacciato. In the shack's adjoining rooms were the battalion commander's and the battalion executive officer's offices. Former Alpha officers now on staff sometimes stopped by to do business: Lt. White, Capt. Anderson, and Capt. Smith, who "comported himself like Santa Claus," says O'Brien.

Alpha arrived by helicopters and took over the defense of the FSB on September 20. O'Brien and his old company most likely had the pleasure of standing in formation the day in early October when the brigade commander pinned a Silver Star on Anderson for gallantry in action. The action had taken place on February 23, O'Brien's first night in the field, when Anderson assaulted and killed with hand grenades three North Vietnamese soldiers, was wounded in the thigh, and then killed two more with his M16.[8] O'Brien didn't witness the events and might not have even known who his company commander was. Still, the ceremony for the man he admired so much, the friend whose friendship he couldn't openly embrace, must have touched him.

Alpha would not return to the field until October 9.[9] His pool of friends had shrunk considerably after he left Third Platoon to become the commander's RTO way back in April, as the platoon had turned over a lot of soldiers since then. O'Brien made several trips to Alpha's quarters on Gator. His friends treated him warmly, but he mostly found himself listening to stories he had not been a part of. He felt as much outsider as insider with Alpha on Gator, an unease that would become the dominant mood of his story "The Ghost Soldiers."

Monsoon season was just beginning. The next few months would grow increasingly dreary and wet. O'Brien counted his blessings that he did not have to slog through the mud day after day in the countryside, but Gator's defoliated hillocks and hollows created a boot-sucking mess. O'Brien penned a public safety announcement in the battalion newsletter:

> Besides putting everyone into a pensive mood, turning our thoughts to past rainy days back in the States; besides those cozy nights on the bunker line, warmly tucked away in your leak-proof, gas heated bunker; besides the added adventure of picking your way to the NCO-EM club without slipping and drowning yourself in a gushing gully of mud and water; besides all those thrills and consolations, the monsoon season can be dangerous.[10]

Needless to say, the bunkers were hardly leak-proof, gas-heated, comfy places to spend the night.

Among his other duties, O'Brien edited the mimeographed newsletter, *The Professional*, a weekly or so enterprise of four to eight pages, typed in two columns, with limited hand art. The readership did not extend beyond the perimeter. O'Brien put together about a dozen issues, writing under his name and most everything that didn't carry a byline. The contents were announcements and puff pieces—summaries of each field company's activities, positive stories from the field, information about reenlisting, and R&R recommendations. He remembers writing "Hoffy Gets Hitched" about a senior NCO who married during his R&R in Sydney, Australia.

Only three issues from O'Brien's editorship have been located. At least a couple of his pieces were rerun by the brigade newsletter, *The Bayonet*. The very title of O'Brien's "Gallantry Nets the Silver Star" tells everything anyone needs to know about the spirit of unit newsletters.[11]

"Ghost Ship Runs Aground" appeared in *The Bayonet*'s November 17 issue. Soldiers from Charlie Company had discovered an abandoned "49-foot Chinese fishing junk" stuck and listing "on a sandbar 100-meters offshore." The battalion commander and operations officer grabbed a helicopter to investigate, eventually swimming out to the boat to find only empty crates aboard. A navy swift boat failed to tug it to shore when the towline snapped. End of story. The compelling aspect of the story is O'Brien's interest in the *mystery* of it. Here are the story's opening and closing:

> It floated in silent and unnoticed.
>
> Where it came from was a mystery. Where it was headed and why were just as perplexing. But one thing was for sure—the ghost ship wouldn't be going anywhere for a while. [...]
>
> With darkness rapidly approaching, the infantrymen had to abandon the effort until another time.
>
> Before "abandoning ship" [Maj.] Disney removed the inscribed Chinese identification plate, leaving the meandering junk, still homeless and now nameless, last seen aground on a shifting sandbar of the South China Sea.[12]

Mystery as a mainstay of O'Brien's understanding of character and as an element of his literary aesthetic would see its fullest expression in the 1994 novel *In the Lake of the Woods*, whose plot turns on the forever unsolved mystery of a veteran's disappeared wife and a disappeared boat.

The Professional of October 4 is the first located issue listing O'Brien as editor. For "A Reason for It All," the writer—O'Brien?—interviewed the battalion commander, Lt. Col. Julian F. Wagner, to summarize and sometimes quote his explanation of the battalion's and the individual soldier's roles in the war. The article ends with a quotation from Wagner that alludes to a type of American abroad—the ethnocentric, ignorant, self-important blowhard popularized by Eugene Burdick and William Lederer's 1958 novel *The Ugly American*, which was made into a film in 1963.

"We cannot win the hearts and minds of the Vietnamese by being Ugly Americans," Wagner said.[13]

The next issue attaches O'Brien's name to material: "Professional Thoughts: Editorial"; an untitled poem with a single-word first line, "Posted"; and an anecdotal story, "Trick or Treat."

"Professional Thoughts: Editorial" picks up where his *Mac Weekly* commentary left off, now from the middle of the war. It begins by referencing a Henry Kissinger essay in *Foreign Affairs* on its way to recognizing the difficulty for either side of outright military victory:

> As long as Vietnamese citizens remain sympathetic to or terrorized by the Viet Cong; as long as some Vietnamese nationals mutter to one another that GI's are intruders in a culture they don't understand and barely accept; as long as Vietnamese are compelled, by the necessity of survival, to speak a foreign language in their own country to GI's, who make no similar effort; as long as those conditions and attitudes fester, even within a small circle of Vietnamese, the core of Viet Cong manpower, support, and supply survives. And little more is needed for insurgency to continue effectively as the events in Cuba, Czechoslovakia, Vietnam, and in America's war protest movement testify.[14]

Since the Vietnamese people are the key, they must be treated with "dignity" and "respect"—words that Wagner had used. If the American grunt is the essential element in a war about people, his first weapon ought to be their language. The piece ends with some Vietnamese vocabulary. It's the second in a series of such lessons O'Brien provided.

The untitled poem appears at the end of the last column on the issue's last page:

Posted
   lucid
      in the desert of West Libya,
We, the soldiers of an awful white
      anchorage;
     wrote our battle in the
     sand.

1920

    Arabs cascaded to our foils,
       and, cavaliers, we met
       on the ivory to red
       to black bareness of
       empty sweeps of sand.

Years

       and my white skin covered
       one another; crouching dermis
       in the sun, layer over layer,
       charcoal over carbon;
       another and another page
       yellowed to a fragile end, turned,
       and

Now

       it is a book that is lost and
       frozen as a corpse in dead of desert

Nous avons gagné la guerre,	*[We won the war*
Mais ma maison à Paris	*But my house in Paris*
Est maintenant trés [sic] vieux.[15]	*Is now very old.]*

O'Brien's poem places his war within the history of European colonial wars abroad. The desert imagery and the theme of meaningless conquest evoke Percy Bysshe Shelley's "Ozymandias." If human triumphs amount to dust in the wind, why commit the evils of war?

"Trick or Treat" profiles the monk who joked about being a Graham Greene character.[16] "Am I intriguing?" the monk asks, rhetorically. "Perhaps I am merely a coward, trembling before the prospect of becoming a combatant. Afraid to assume a position. Do you think I am a coward?" The political disengagement echoes that of Greene's narrator in *The Quiet American*. In the article, O'Brien judges the monk "cowering." His mountaintop isolation is not holy, it is camouflage, pretense, hypocrisy; and "hypocrisy acknowledged is no less an evil." This story of a principled if lonely escape masking cowardice speaks to one of O'Brien's prewar anxieties about fleeing to Canada. "Trick or Treat" constitutes a spiritual first draft of "On the Rainy River." O'Brien impressively quotes a stanza from the classic

Buddhist poem *Cheng-Tao-Ko*, which he learned in a Hindu and Buddhist philosophy course he loved at Macalester. It was the same course that gave him the vocabulary of Hinduism's four life goals—*dharma, artha, kàma, moksa*—around which he wrote the poem sent to Erik Hansen in April.

Meanwhile, on Wednesday, October 15, hundreds of thousands of Americans across the country—"possibly millions," according to *The New York Times*; the largest protest of the war—participated in the Moratorium to End the War in Vietnam.[17] At Macalester, a rising Black politician, Georgia state legislator Julian Bond, joined Senator Walter Mondale on the field house stage to denounce the war and the Nixon administration's continuation of it to a "spirited and boisterous" crowd of well over five thousand.[18]

O'Brien traveled to Sydney, Australia, for a week of R&R beginning on or about October 25.[19] His hopes to coordinate his trip with Hansen did not pan out. As he wrote to his family:

> Visited the Australian Museum and gawked at kangaroos, wallabys [*sic*], and fossilized swagmen! Ate lobster, natural & fried oysters, lamb chops, roast duck, shrimp; drank the best red & white wine with every meal. Took out some interesting girls—spent a fortune to see Buddy Greco at Sydney's #1 hotel, The Chevron. Walked all over the heart of the place; a buddy & I went with two broads to Bondi Beach where we damn near froze in Baltic sea-like water, ice cubes & all. (The "all" includes 3 sharks which chased us out of the ice tray, horns blaring and kids bawling!). I made a lot of temporary friends, am aching to return [home], and am even laying plans to do just that.[20]

Much of this letter discusses his financial situation. Most days he spent alone.[21]

The dates were arranged by an R&R Center at the airport. Arriving soldiers walked off the plane and into lines in front of women with boxes of information cards on the young women who volunteered. The soldier in front of O'Brien passed along the received wisdom he had heard: "Ask for a swimmer, because then you'll know she can't be fat." When he made it to the table, O'Brien—who hated water, couldn't swim, and had almost drowned three times—told the woman he liked swimming. The woman dialed up a girl and handed the phone to O'Brien. She was a Scottish girl working as a nanny, and at dinner her questions appeared to confirm O'Brien's hunch that the women who signed up wanted a "love-ticket" to America. After a dinner that seemed interminable, he dropped her off at her home, feigning feeling ill.

Having tasted normal life, freedom, and a little glamour, O'Brien was devastated when he got back to Việt Nam. He received his three sergeant chevrons on October 31. The rank meant nothing in terms of responsibility or authority—a typist was a typist was a typist—but it increased his monthly pay by fifty dollars and lent his grousing more credence.[22]

Around this time, he received a Dear John letter from Gayle Roby. Her heart had never been fully in it, after all of two dates nineteen months earlier. In her letters to O'Brien overseas, she had deliberately withheld romantic affection. As he would represent them in his fiction, her "letters were mostly chatty, elusive on the matter of love."[23] When she saw the dorm note that she had missed his phone call from Australia, she realized how much the idea of her mattered to him. But she was in love with the man with whom she had traveled to Europe after their summer study abroad (an impromptu wedding would take place in January). O'Brien hung onto Auden's poem. It would become the stockings sent to *The Things They Carried*'s character Henry Dobbins, which he wore while he "plodded along" because they "gave access to a spiritual world, where things were soft and intimate" even after the girl "dumped him" in late October.[24]

On the night of November 8, a mortar foul-up killed thirteen civilians at the lagoon. O'Brien followed the developing tragedy over the radio in his office. A miscommunication had caused rounds from the battalion's medium mortars at LZ Minuteman to strike the CAP 142 village, about a kilometer away. Eleven civilians died in place. Two of the approximately thirty evacuated wounded died at the medical unit. Among the dead were eight children, ranging in age from two to fifteen, whom O'Brien's memoir names: the brothers Bi Thi Cu and Dao Van Cu; Le Xi; Dao Thi Thuong; Pham Thi Ku; Pham Khanh; Le Chuc; and Le Thi Tam.[25] The names and ages don't appear in the battalion logs. O'Brien must have copied them for himself, from the investigative reports he typed up, and carried them home.

O'Brien worried that the event would hit American newspapers. It didn't, but even if it had it would have been eclipsed by one of the biggest stories of the war. On November 13, someone in Connecticut would have read this

Hartford Courant headline about 2nd Lt. William Calley: "Boyish-Looking, but Army Accuses Him of Killing 109 Civilians," by Seymour Hersh. The next day, some papers reported three to four hundred victims, and by the seventeenth the number from some major news outlets reached 567.[26] On November 20, the Cleveland *Plain Dealer* published exclusive photographs taken by Ronald Haeberle accompanied by another Hersh article, "GIs Call Viet Killings 'Point Blank Murder,'" which quoted an eyewitness who heard the number ranged between 170 to over 700, with an "official" tally of around 300.[27]

What came to be known as the Mỹ Lai Massacre happened on March 16, 1968, O'Brien's senior spring at Macalester, in a ville—the Mỹ Lai 4 sub-hamlet that the locals called Tuan Yen—he knew intimately. Mỹ Lai and Mỹ Khê were two of the four hamlets comprising the Sơn Mỹ village, squarely in the 5th of the 46th's area of operations. It was all in Pinkville. Reading about the massacre, O'Brien instantly understood the mix of horror and hatred in the people's eyes, the feeling of deep and troubling disquiet he felt there. He'd been wounded outside Mỹ Khê 3. An early chapter in Hersh's book *Cover-Up* details the smaller atrocity committed by Charlie Company a few days earlier at Mỹ Khê 4. Hersh quotes a soldier talking about his comrades holding a shooting contest targeting a crawling baby.[28] "I won't sleep well tonight," O'Brien wrote Erik Hansen after reading the book in 1974. "I remember. I'm stunned by memory."[29]

Additional warnings of NVA and VC offensives raised the tension in the first half of November 1969. The American military command worried about attacks inspired by "'National Day' marking the anniversary of the overthrow of the Ngo Dinh Diem regime in 1963," three weeks before President Kennedy's assassination. The military command disseminated the text of a captured document indicating that the enemy planned "to accelerate the annihilation" of South Vietnamese forces and administrators "at hamlet and village level" in response to the first withdrawal of American soldiers and the growing anti-war movement in South Việt Nam, and "in support of the struggle campaign for peace which would be initiated by the American people on 14 & 15 November."[30] The document was referring to what would become the largest single-site protest in American history, when a half million anti-war protesters descended on Washington. The candlelit "March Against Death" paraded past the White House to the

Capitol, bearing twelve coffins carrying the names of the dead. Although some militants and revolutionaries tried to stir up trouble, the "Give Peace a Chance" message won the day. The mood was solemn and spirited.

Back at FSB Gator, the press descended upon Mỹ Lai 4 on the sixteenth and seventeenth. The battalion received the task of securing the area and establishing an LZ, although helicopters ferried the reporters back and forth from Chu Lai, bypassing Gator.[31] O'Brien's office was abuzz. He patiently listened to the anti-press rantings of a few staff officers.

The rest of the month and all of December were otherwise ho-hum. The *Playboy* Playmate and the *Dean Martin Show* dancer who toured the Americal area of Quảng Ngãi in November did not stop at Gator.[32] The weather sucked. Rain, wind, cold, rain, and more rain. O'Brien very nearly skipped Thanksgiving dinner in the mess hall because of the effort it took to heave his feet through the mud in the cold mist, and although he enjoyed the plentiful traditional fare, during the meal he dreaded the walk back to his cot.

Meanwhile, the United States conducted the first national draft lottery on the evening of December 1. Macalester students knew their close friends' birthdays and had lists of other people's birthdays. On campuses across the land, life stopped in front of television sets. Life stopped and lives reset before the unabashed randomness of history.

O'Brien was not one of the few field troops designated to see Bob Hope's USO show on Christmas Eve day at Chu Lai, yet he and another soldier sent on a liquor run "caught a glimpse of Bob Hope trying to be funny in the rain."[33] The fog obscured the sky on that seventy-degree day. A twenty-four-hour ceasefire began at 6:00 p.m. on the twenty-fourth. Loudspeakers played Christmas music. Soldiers got shit-faced. Another cheerless holiday for O'Brien.

On the morning of December 31, the battalion operations officer, Maj. Robert Disney, nabbed Sgt. O'Brien for a helicopter ride to the site of a just-concluded firefight between ARVN and VC forces. Disney wanted O'Brien to write about it for *The Professional*. Although American gunships and artillery saved the day for the South Vietnamese, O'Brien had no idea why he and Disney were there. The action hadn't involved the 5th of the 46th; there didn't appear to be any Americans around. He figured he must be somewhere in the battalion's area of operations, which they were, between Nam Yêm 3 and Lạc Sơn 1, two sub-hamlets practically on top of one another about two and a half klicks from the sea.

The ground still smoked. O'Brien watched Vietnamese soldiers pile Vietnamese bodies on trucks. Fourteen ARVN and twenty-one VC killed, another thirty-nine ARVN wounded. It was gruesome. It took O'Brien back ten months to his first night with Alpha, when the VC attacked LZ Gator and the next morning the company loaded bodies on trucks. That had been the first time O'Brien confronted the dead in Việt Nam. This would be the last.[34] When he transforms the December-morning memory into fiction, in the story "The Lives of the Dead," he imagines himself—via his first-person narrator—on the corpse detail:

> There were twenty-seven bodies altogether, and parts of several others. The dead were everywhere. Some lay in piles. Some lay alone. One, I remember, seemed to kneel. Another was bent from the waist over a small boulder, the top of his head on the ground, his arms rigid, the eyes squinting in concentration as if he were about to perform a handstand or somersault. It was my worst day of the war.[35]

If O'Brien ever wrote the article, that issue of *The Professional* has not yet turned up.

The military's full investigation of the massacre at Mỹ Lai 4 was underway. The battalion executive officer coordinated the security and activity at the site, his team dubbed Task Force Roman, the site dubbed Area of Operation Babylon, and the operation itself Operation Hammurabi.[36] It's a bizarre allusion to one of the world's oldest historical documents. On the one hand, the Code of Hammurabi established a legal system with fixed rules and punishments. The government, not individuals, dispenses justice; evidence of guilt must be established. On the other hand, the code is perhaps best known for its retributive justice of *an eye for an eye*. While the allusion could have suggested legal justice for the Vietnamese victims, it could just as well have suggested a defense of the American soldiers who violated and killed them, upholding their vision of retributive violence. The latter seems more likely if the executive officer did the naming. O'Brien's memoir captures the spirit of one of the XO's rants to a reporter:

> Jesus, what the hell do you think war is? Don't you think some civilians get killed? You ever been to Mỹ Lai? Well, I'll tell you, those *civilians—you* call them civilians—they kill American GI's. They plant mines and spy and snipe and kill us. Sure, you all print color pictures of dead little boys, but the live ones—take pictures of the live ones digging holes for mines.[37]

In *If I Die*, O'Brien calls the XO "Major Callicles," after the Greek figure in Plato's *Gorgias* who advocates might-makes-right in opposition to O'Brien's hero Socrates, who believed in ratiocination as the route to discovering the moral good. For Callicles's vision of natural law, it is worse to suffer wrongs than to commit wrongs.

Task Force Roman continued its mission until January 11, 1970. For nearly two weeks, it hosted various groups, including Lt. Gen. William Peers and members of the Peers Commission charged with investigating the events, and Lt. Calley's defense team. The press visits occurred toward the end of Operation Hammurabi. The XO resentfully handled security and, along with the battalion commander and operations officer, the briefings. The briefings presented cursory background information because the officers were not permitted to refer to the "alleged incident." Soldiers weren't permitted to speak to reporters.[38]

Yet on January 8, after O'Brien left the office on his way to chow, he saw a red-haired man in a motley of green fatigues, the kind of improvised uniform worn by reporters. The man stood up and approached O'Brien, who remembers him as working for Reuters. The conversation went something like this:

> —*I'm trying to find soldiers who work in the Sơn Mỹ AO. Do you?*
> —*Yeah. I used to anyway.*
> —*Did the news about Sơn Mỹ surprise you? Did you see anything else like it?*

—Well, nothing that big. I did see some illegal stuff.

—Like what?

—I'm not going to tell you.

—Why not?

—Because I'm going to write about it.

The reporter's look struck O'Brien as expressing disbelief, even disdain, that this grunt imagined himself the writer. The reporter waved dismissively as he turned away.[39] O'Brien might have already started writing about the things he'd seen in an article that would appear in the January 21 edition of the *Worthington Daily Globe*.

O'Brien justifiably disliked the title Jim Vance gave the article—"My Lai: 'They' Are Dinks and You Curse Their Lying Tongues." While doubtless it pulled some readers into the article, O'Brien fretted that "a quick look at the headline would, in the absence of a careful perusal of the article, link me forever in [a reader's] mind with hardboiled, dink-hating, jingoism."[40] The article directly addressed the massacre in ways the memoir's version will not. Its conclusion's condemnation of the racism is worth quoting:

> If the alleged incident at My Lai 4 in March, 1968, occurred as reported, it was a crime, and there is no justification to be culled from reference to the participants' brutal experiences in and around the My Lai's, just as [my] unit's actions are not assuaged by pointing to dead buddies, hostile civilians, and the omnipresent mines. GIs, growing up on the image of the American soldier as a khakied savior, generously giving of himself to fight for enslaved and grateful souls, has [*sic*] a difficult time understanding that this is not France, that My Lai is a far cry from Paris and its cheering, willing young chicks. The difference is that My Lai is not occupied nor enslaved by the enemy. The residents of Pinkville are the enemy—or his children or his wife or his bronzed old mother. And still GIs find it incomprehensible, their hostility. "Ungrateful, stupid dinks," we call them. Dinks, which is a word laden with all the contempt of World War II's "nip" and "kraut," the Korean War's "gook," Castro's "yankee."
>
> Pinkville is the enemy's home, that can be said as surely as one can say anything about what happens here. Given that fact, the outrage of

American troops at the sullen faces, mines, and unanswered questions reaches ludicrously. What more can be expected from the enemy and his family?

If outrage does not justify what might have happened in March of last year, neither does the fact that the slain women and children were hostile relatives and friends and sympathizers of the Viet Cong. If so, we could smile at our consciences and justify similar atrocities by past and present enemies: when, in retribution for the killing of [Reinhard] Heydrich, the Nazi occupiers of Prague traveled a few kilometeres [sic] to the west, cordoned off the village of Lidice and marched the inhabitants off to a nearby field where they were killed. The official explanation: Lidice was the suspected refuge of Heydrich's killers. Today, Lidice, Czechoslovakia, is a flowered memorial to that event. One wonders how the Vietnamese will commemorate My Lai 4 twenty years from today.

O'Brien's academic self emerges in the next three paragraphs as he reviews and summarily rejects theories from social psychology and Alan Watts's take on Freud's id. The article strikes a balance between head and heart to penetrating effect.

Whatever are the roots, the affliction seems to be manifested in war and particularly, most acutely, in the sort of events this unit experienced last May in Pinkville. It was a hard way to peek into your own soul, and the headlines may have been a shocking denouncement for the American public, but some soldiers here are hoping we can proceed from a new level of understanding, individually and as a nation. Some of us are convinced, with Alan Watts, that "the most intense darkness is itself the seed of light, and all explicit warfare is implicit love."[41]

Love, a word that will trouble much of O'Brien's future writing. Representative Ancher Nelsen read the article into the *Congressional Record* on February 5, 1970.[42] Vance submitted it for a Pulitzer Prize.[43] Both accolades would become part of the pitch to publishers for the 1973 memoir.

The war outside AO Babylon continued. The VC hit Gator hard ninety minutes after midnight on January 4 with a series of mortar salvos followed by satchel charges and additional mortar rounds, surely accompanied by grenades and maybe small-arms fire (battalion documents do not mention them). The two-hour attack ended when helicopter gunships came on station and emptied their guns. Two bunkers were destroyed, several buildings damaged, and a stock of U.S. mortar rounds exploded, wounding two GIs. Mike Hatfield had the top of his head sheared off by a satchel charge that landed behind him and never walked or talked again.[44] Miraculously, the night assault killed only one American. As soon as the incoming fire ceased, soldiers sweeping the perimeter found six dead Vietnamese and several blood trails.[45]

O'Brien has a dim memory of a night that might have been that night. When the attack started, he grabbed his weapon and headed into an unused pit lined with a few ragged, half-empty sandbags, about twenty meters from the office. He wasn't particularly scared, as the action sounded to be from a far perimeter—this memory accords with the damage done to the artillery battery's separate area on Gator, near a helipad. He remembers the illumination flares; he remembers the battalion operations officer, Maj. Disney, in the office the next morning talking about the perimeter sweep.

The January attack on Gator appears to have been O'Brien's last combat action, such as it was for him. As he wrote to Hansen, "we were hit hard a few nights ago. Sappers. It was, as you know, a long and light-bellied night. Numerically, we WON—one to six was the score—but more important, I won, zero to zero." He hadn't killed or been killed. O'Brien was feeling *short*, per army slang, excited by the countdown but also spooked by the stories of others killed or injured during their last days in Việt Nam. After he returns from an upcoming leave, he asserts, "I will hide under this typewriter for 49 days; it will be good!"[46] That casual crack to Hansen, to which O'Brien did not give a second thought, prophesied a writing career of refuge and salvation.

After Task Force Roman wrapped up, the XO unraveled. He resumed his moral crusade against prostitutes, pot, and anything and everything that smacked to him as undermining good order and discipline. Having spent the war basically behind a desk, one night probably in January he rustled O'Brien into a jeep, collected a Vietnamese scout at Nuoc Mau, dragooned another American soldier, and headed north of Gator to set up a four-person ambush outside Trì Bình 4. They took up a position near where Lt. White had showed off the ear. The drunken, cursing officer ditched the ambush after an hour and headed back to Gator, where their commander admonished him: "Things were tense, but afterward the major paced around his office, grinning and winking at everyone. 'All it takes is guts, right, O'Brien?'" A few nights later, he and a captain in the office burned down Nuoc Mau's brothel with gasoline, "and the next day he was given two hours to leave LZ Gator for good. It hurt him, leaving."[47]

The battalion's military situation eased for the rest of O'Brien's tour of duty. Monsoon rain and winds canceled more than one operation. Intelligence of intensified enemy actions around the Tết celebrations, late January through mid-February, never panned out.[48]

In the thirteen months of O'Brien's time in the battalion, his name appears only once in a daily staff journal, in the quartermaster's log of January 18. As with the *Daily Globe* photo from the day he boarded the bus into the army's clutch, the trivial entry gets his name wrong: "Rec'd call from SGT O'Brine Bn S-1 refer transport of three EM to Div. ED. CTR. for GED."[49]

A day or two later O'Brien took a week's leave. He had longed to return to Sydney but missed that flight and ended up in Manila. He quickly recovered from the bummer of not going to Australia as he succumbed to the Philippines' charms for a "poignant, very fulsome" week. "There was a boatload of humor, affection, sex, drunken numbness and other extravagant emotions to be finally enjoyed," he wrote Hansen. "I imbibed in excellent wine (Beaujeaulais [*sic*], Chablis, others) and ate lobster a la Chine, shrimp curry, lamb chops." He might have exaggerated the stories he told his mates back on Gator, especially his description of the young woman he "chummed" with. The flattering description—"charming," "slender," "cute"—was "all true, though, true enough."[50] He mostly recalls being alone, reading, sleeping, going to a USO show, visiting the beach, drinking, and one night awkwardly comforting the crying Filipino prostitute spending the week with a senior NCO in the hotel room next to O'Brien's.

Back on Gator he was more bored than before. O'Brien spent his last months thinking about life after Việt Nam. His initial Date of Estimated Return from Overseas—DEROS—fell in early February, twelve months from the date of his arrival. By November 9, from FSB Gator, O'Brien had

extended his tour thirty-nine days so as to separate from the military immediately upon return to the States rather than "spend 5 awful months as
a stateside grunt" in completion of his original two-year obligation. He'd
contacted three Australian newspapers, "aching" to write about the war
before starting Harvard the next September: "No way to write honestly
from within, partially because you're a culprit yourself and masochism is
no fun."[51]

He read a lot, among other books John Kenneth Galbraith's *The New
Industrial State* and John W. Spanier's *The Truman-MacArthur Controversy and the Korean War*, pursuing the interests that were leading him
to graduate school in political science, but he was thinking about Harvard Law School too.[52] He was also considering alternatives to Harvard—
especially if the money didn't work out. He sent out feelers to "Reader's
Digest in Sydney, to Macalester's International Studies Institute (for summer work abroad), and even wrote [Eugene] McCarthy, who's in turn writing the State Department for possible openings abroad." He might wind
up knocking about southern Europe—back to Greece—"on a low budget
jaunt."

Perhaps the most telling line from his last surviving letter from Việt
Nam falls in the passage about his hopes to travel: "Or at least to be all
alone, on my own schedule, for a while."[53] A straightforward and profound
desire to be in command of his own time, of his own body, for the first time
in years. When and where to wake up. What to wear, what to eat. Where to
go. To owe nothing to anyone, to avoid even the smallest acts of compromise and negotiation that life with others always entails.

He also spent his last months on Gator writing. In addition to the Mỹ
Lai article, O'Brien published four other pieces in the *Worthington Daily
Globe* from January to April, all written and sent from Việt Nam. Versions
of at least one, and perhaps all four, first appeared in *The Professional*. The
first one, "'And You Will Leave Tomorrow,' Said the Monk; 'I'll Be Happy,'"
is a revised version of "Trick or Treat." The second one, "'Go Down to Charlie Company and Saddle Up for the Field,'" shares the same anecdotal style
and approximate length. It's about a Vietnamese interpreter and scout from
the Chiêu Hồi "Open Arms" program for former enemy combatants who
requests a pass to go home and visit his sick baby. The episode occurred
during O'Brien's time in the S-1 office. The captain who rejected the request

was probably his boss, the adjutant. The story will land again in the memoir in a chapter ironically titled "Hearts and Minds" because of the officer's misstep in failing to secure the man's loyalty.

"From Vietnam: Some Thoughts on Mines, a War, and Bitterness" is a short reflective essay that O'Brien would publish again in *Playboy* a few months after his homecoming, then as a chapter of *If I Die*, both times under the title "Step Lightly." The final *Worthington Daily Globe* article, "'Some for Adventure, Some from Fear of Weakness,'" probably the last thing he wrote in Việt Nam, circles back to basic training. It would become the core section of the memoir's early chapter "Under the Mountain." The article features Erik Hansen; its title comes from Pound's "Hugh Selwyn Mauberley," which Hansen had introduced to O'Brien. The article's consideration of cowardice continues O'Brien's public introspection begun in "Trick or Treat."

O'Brien was beginning to think about how to write *true* war stories. "From Vietnam" confesses that it only tells "half-truths" in order to tell "another truth."[54] He was likely writing about the mine fiasco of August 7, and by "half-truth" he meant just that: the decision not to relay, even the impossibility of relaying, a full and exact account of what happened, not to mention how it was subjectively experienced. Factual minutiae distract and dilute. Moreover, a declaration of half-truth can gain more purchase on the reader's imagination, can yield the more powerful effect, than a drawn-out detailing. The *Daily Globe*'s version of the monk's tale appends an opening clause: "I enjoy telling true stories, and this one is about a monk who strolled with me through his gardens."[55] O'Brien recognized that the encounter sounded fabricated. The dialogue was especially clunky, and the literary references felt contrived. The memoir omits the weakest-written and therefore the most unconvincing part, the conversation with the monk.

Alpha returned to take over Gator's defense on February 12. At a hot LZ the night before, the helicopter crews had opened up with their machine guns at the wood line. Once all the flights away had been completed, the company realized it was missing a soldier. A search party found the body the next morning in an open rice paddy. The round had entered the back of his head and out his face, its size and the direction consistent with having been shot by an M60 machine gun from a helicopter behind him.[56] O'Brien has no recollection of learning about this death by friendly fire from his former company mates on Gator. The constant fear of such a death, the bodily memory of bullets from friendly helicopters zipping and ricocheting by, inspired Pederson's fate in *Going After Cacciato*, killed by an American helicopter door gunner.

Perhaps the last LZ Gator casualty of O'Brien's tour was the specialist who shot himself in the foot while on bunker duty the evening of March 4.[57] While the log recorded the mishap as an accident, some battalion staff—O'Brien included—believed it was deliberate.

Sergeant O'Brien closed out his time in Quảng Ngãi as the battalion closed down Gator. It was being moved elsewhere. Trucks and helicopters spent March transporting the stuff and the soldiers of the 5th Battalion, 46th Light Infantry Regiment back to Chu Lai. The second week of March, O'Brien caught a ride on one of those trucks to out-process from the division and Military Assistance Command, Vietnam (MAC-V). He flew out of Việt Nam around the fifteenth of March, 1970.[58] Did O'Brien learn before he left Việt Nam or at home about the combat death of his high school classmate Sgt. Jerry Russell on March 6? "Everyone liked him. He belonged on his farm," a mutual friend said. Not in the war. Russell had been married seven months to the day.

After deplaning at McChord Air Force Base in Washington, O'Brien leaned down to swipe the ground with his fingertips, more reflexively than patriotically. He had touched the same tarmac thirteen months earlier. He might as well do it again.

PART II

13

RETURNEE

A t Fort Lewis, O'Brien processed out of the army in no time:

"Got any problems we need to talk over?" The army shrink stares at you. "No, sir." Blink. "Good, good." "Thank you, sir." "Good luck." "Yes, sir." Next.

I'm maladjusted: no problem readjusting.

Soon, discharged, you shed your uniform and you fly home. It is a day, day and a half, between war and peace.[1]

Kathy O'Brien was living in St. Paul. Friends drove her to the airport to retrieve her brother. When she saw Tim, her heart sank. He looked pale. He didn't smile. He barely spoke. The war's personal cost hit her for the first time. She settled him on an apartment couch, where he slept the day away.

Soon thereafter, O'Brien made his way to Iowa City to see Jane Reister, who was in graduate school for history. He promised to come back over Easter weekend at the end of March. When he didn't, Reister phoned him. He had no explanation. *I don't have anything to say*, she says he said before hanging up.

The patriotic March for Victory brought ten to forty thousand middle-aged Americans to Washington on April 4. Nominally a gathering in support of the administration's Việt Nam policy, the culture war took center stage. The gathered waved their Bibles and their American and Confederate flags. The speakers extolled "prayer and Bible readings in school" and denounced "desegregation, sex education, abortion, and 'Godless Communism.'"[2]

In April, O'Brien took a job with the Metropolitan Council, an organization that conducted policy and planning work for the Twin Cities. Arranged by either the International Center or the World Press Institute at Macalester, it wasn't much of a job. O'Brien's boss hunkered him in a small room to read "arcane" books but never asked for a report. He did require O'Brien to play on his Saturday flag football team. The job was a courtesy. O'Brien lived in a house rented by a different trio of guys from Macalester, on Summit Avenue near the governor's house.[3] A latecomer and transient, he slept in the bleakest room in the house.

President Nixon spoke to the nation on Monday, April 20: "We can now say with confidence that pacification is succeeding," that "the South Vietnamese can develop the capability for their own defense," that "all American combat forces can and will be withdrawn."[4]

On April 27, Jerry Rubin of the radical Youth International Party—the Yippies—came to town to lead a protest at Honeywell, Inc.'s annual shareholder meeting against the corporation's arms sales. Rubin was fresh from the ludicrous trial of the Chicago Seven, the leaders of the protests at the 1968 Democratic National Convention. The *Minneapolis Tribune* described the gathering at Macalester's football stadium as a "big yippie-rad-pacifist pep rally."[5] O'Brien went. He felt like an absolute alien, or as if he had returned to a world gone more than a little mad and he had missed the maddening. Whereas in his day, student outreach fundraising involved coeds ironing men's shirts, that afternoon women sported muumuus and men and women both wore flared jeans and tie-dye. Girls cursed like sailors. A man traipsed around him in a wedding dress. Their plugged-in so-called music sounded like a chorus of banshees. Pot filled the air. LSD filled a few bodies. O'Brien couldn't identify with celebrity radicals or the spirit of irreverent abandon. The political theater seemed as unreal as the combat theater of Việt Nam.

Speaking to the nation on Thursday, April 30, the president admitted to ground operations underway against North Vietnamese bases in Cambodia.[6] Protests resurged. On Monday, May 4, National Guardsmen opened fire on demonstrators at Kent State, killing four white students. The war had come home. The murders activated many anti-war Việt Nam veterans. W. D. "Bill" Ehrhart, a former marine, "sobb[ed] uncontrollably"; John Musgrave, another former marine, thought, "My God, we're killing our own children."[7] O'Brien quit his pointless job that very day.

That evening, Macalester students closed off Grand Avenue, the main road through the middle of campus. Earlier in the day, several Mac students had blockaded Hubert Humphrey's faculty office with concertina wire and signs protesting the war and his presence on campus.[8]

On May 6, about three thousand area students marched on the state capitol seeking a special legislative session to stop Minnesotan bodies and money from going to the war. In Mankato, students from Minnesota State University burned effigies of President Nixon and Vice President Agnew in front of the post office.[9]

From the front page of the *Worthington Daily Globe*:

> At the University of New Mexico in Albuquerque, 11 persons were hospitalized with stab wounds after National Guardsmen with fixed bayonets advanced on 200 student peace protestors. [. . .]
>
> In New York City, about 70 persons were injured when a roving band of 1000 construction workers, some wielding clubs and crowbars, attacked peace demonstrators in the vicinity of City Hall.[10]

This was the "Hard Hat Riot" of May 8.

On May 9, Macalester became the assembly area for a second march on the state capitol in St. Paul. Thousands assembled at Mac to join up with the ten thousand marching from the University of Minnesota. It rained the first part of the day but cleared up as the march progressed.[11] O'Brien participated, marching now with sense and purpose and direction, "heading for that state capitol to say 'No.'"[12] On the Mac grounds before stepping off, he bumped into, of all people, Gayle Roby, up from St. Olaf College, in the final days of her senior year. She was with her husband. The newlyweds were off to India for Peace Corps service. She and O'Brien didn't talk long. Did he think about "This Loved One" as he humped toward the capitol?

Initial estimates sized the crowd anywhere between ten thousand and sixty-eight thousand, though some marchers swore it was more than eighty-six thousand. The Minnesota Vets for Peace in Vietnam led, bearing a prop coffin painted with an American flag accompanied by "a ghoulish figure robed in black, wearing a white mask and carrying a sign saying 'Death Wins All Wars'" and an amputee who did "the whole route in his wheel chair."[13] Somewhere far back in the two-mile column walked O'Brien.

Striking students or bold administrators shut down more than 450 campuses nationwide by May 10.[14] On May 14, police firing into dorms at Jackson State College killed two and wounded at least a dozen Black students. By the end of the month, protests touched almost one-third of American colleges and universities.[15] Student protesters went beyond core liberals. Moderates, independents, and plenty of Republicans were appalled by the violence. About half of Macalester's students were "working on one committee or another."[16]

In small teams, Mac students visited with groups in civic organizations, churches, neighborhood meetings, schools, and people's homes, to explain their anti-war position, conducting eighty such meetings in short order.[17] The effort was headquartered at the alumni affairs office. A few of O'Brien's friends from the dorm, a couple of years behind him, helped lead this work. They remember O'Brien speaking at a meeting held in a suburban home. "His presence was very powerful," recalls Peter Fenn. Here was this clean-cut, white, diminutive young man, extremely articulate, wearing a button-down shirt, the furthest cry from the "bums" label President Nixon had slapped on student protesters. Freshly home from the war, O'Brien looked like his audience. As he spoke, according to Guy Reynolds, "You could hear a pin drop."[18] O'Brien doesn't remember any of it.

O'Brien borrowed a family car and took off for Lake Superior's Madeline Island, accessible only by ferry, where Kathy had summered waiting tables. He stayed somewhere between ten days and two weeks. The car radio and beer kept him company. He slept on the beach in a sleeping bag, around which he dug a trench, an army habit. He didn't think much about his war, and when he did, it "seemed impossibly distant, almost unreal," its images "the property of another human being." His thoughts turned to girls and his future. Was Harvard in the fall the right path, or should he take some time to "husk corn in South Dakota"?[19]

At the end of May or early June, O'Brien called up Guy Reynolds to invite him on a road trip to Chicago, where he needed to do some paperwork for the "Step Lightly" essay forthcoming in *Playboy*. He probably could have handled the paperwork through the mail. But he didn't have anything else going on. A road trip sounded fun. Perhaps it would be good to meet editors in person. O'Brien and Reynolds teased each other about meeting Playmates. In Chicago, they took care of O'Brien's business on the fourth floor of the *Playboy* building, not a bunny-costumed hottie in sight. Instead, the super-handsome man they dealt with flirted with Reynolds.

The country had turned upside down. In April, Massachusetts prepared to file a suit challenging the federal government's sending citizens to war when Congress had not bothered to declare war.[20] Officials in other states, including Minnesota, made similar noise. In June, the U.S. Senate repealed the Tonkin Gulf Resolution of 1964, which had given two presidents the authority to prosecute the war. Congress took up several other bills targeting the war, on cutting off the military incursion into Cambodia, on ceasing to fund the war, on ending the draft.

The Paris Peace Talks entered their third year.

The White House dubbed that Fourth of July *Honor America Day*. Some took offense at the day's propaganda. "It's a disgraceful exploitation of religion by an administration using this kind of thing as a means to prop itself up," complained an anti-war organizer. "It's all there—folklore, sectarian politics, just like Nazi Germany. It's scary."[21]

On July 9, O'Brien wrote Erik Hansen, still in the army but stationed now in England. Having drafted two dozen versions of the letter, he finally resigned himself to sending something to his soul's dearest friend:

> Gayle is married, not to me. The country is shot it seems. Mankind is teetering, by bomb or by bad air, on self-destruction. Other souls, maybe not unlike mine in the way they shiver in first hand fright, are now in basic, or in AIT, or arriving in Vietnam, staring at the mountains as their plane goes from Cam Ranh to Pleiku or Da Nang or Chu Lai or wherever.

The knowledge Harvard promised him gave "no real comfort to those who bellow at betrayal or holler for help from a bloody paddy or fight back tears at the last letter from a figment of love." O'Brien had trouble sleeping,

"Hypertension of some variety combined with a documentary style nightly replay of Vietnam or basic or AIT, one episode smoothly and maddeningly running into another," disbelief that any of it had happened.

Days of listless dismay spent on tennis, a little swimming, the evening news, cigarettes, and such light reading as John Locke's *Two Treatises of Government*. He didn't visit Hansen in Europe, because he couldn't rouse the energy to get a new passport.

For a star student like O'Brien, Harvard graduate school offered a place and path of familiarity, comfort, mastery, achievement, and belonging, the exact opposite of the war. One would think he couldn't wait to get to Cambridge. But it didn't feel like that to O'Brien. "I sort of want to cop out of that, too. But copping out of Harvard takes effort, takes will."[22] He was drifting, superficially resuming the life that had been interrupted without having to make any decisions or exert himself, following the path of least resistance.

It is commonplace to lay-diagnose Tim O'Brien with PTSD and interpret his writing as symptomatic of trauma. O'Brien has flat-out resisted this diagnosis and such analysis.

When O'Brien stepped off the plane at McChord in 1970, it would be a full decade before the American Psychiatric Association's *Diagnostic and Statistical Manual of Mental Disorders* (*DSM-III*, 1980) added post-traumatic stress disorder as a subtype of anxiety disorders. In the 1970s, the guidelines of *DSM-II* (1968) considered such stress disorders temporary, resolved over time for a normally adaptive individual. If symptoms persisted, the diagnosis became one of neurosis or psychosis independent of the inducing trauma or stress—the problem was the abnormally adaptive *person*, not the trauma.

The national conversation about veterans followed suit by focusing on the word *readjustment*. America expected these children of the War World II generation to just get on with it, as their parents supposedly had. From 1966 until 1974, the U.S. Congress discussed and passed different versions of a Vietnam-Era Veterans' Readjustment Assistance Act, in essence an extension of GI Bill benefits for veterans of earlier wars to those who served in Việt Nam. The heart of this assistance was education, job training, and employment incentives, with special considerations for the disabled. *Readjustment* meant moving veterans into the workforce. The need for healing wasn't considered. The Vietnam Veterans' Psychological Readjustment Act, which would establish storefront Vet Centers for group counseling and basic psychological care, did not pass both houses and become law until 1979.

The connotation of *readjustment* began to shift around 1973, the year the war ended for the United States. Service members who had been POWs for years and won widespread sympathy returned home. The Vietnam Veterans Against the War had no choice but to repurpose itself, although it had started involving itself with mental health issues prior to the military withdrawal, creating the first veteran rap groups in December 1970. The two primary psychiatrists working with the rap groups called attention to what they were learning. Dr. Chaim Shatan published "Post-Vietnam Syndrome" in the May 6, 1972, *New York Times*, and Dr. Robert Jay Lifton would be nominated for a National Book Award for his 1973 *Home from the War: Vietnam Veterans, Neither Victims nor Executioners* (the last clause of Lifton's subtitle is the title of Albert Camus's important 1946 essay about the cost of perpetrating violence). Other books dared the darkness of some veterans' lives: Murray Polner's *No Victory Parades: The Return of the Vietnam Veteran* (1971), Charles J. Levy's *Spoils of War* (1973), and John Helmer's *Bringing the War Home: The American Soldier in Vietnam and After* (1974).

O'Brien's memoir, *If I Die in a Combat Zone, Box Me Up and Ship Me Home*, would come out in March 1973. Two months earlier, O'Brien received a call from *The Boston Phoenix* asking for a piece about the American intervention's imminent end from a veteran's perspective. The assignment tortured O'Brien with its futility. What could he possibly say? How could anyone give meaning to that decade of meaningless bloodshed?[23]

He took up the gauntlet of *readjustment*. The essay's subtitle says it all— "No Problems: That's My Problem." O'Brien announces his argument in the first paragraphs:

> If I'd lost an arm, I could say readjusting was difficult. Or if I'd been shell-shocked. Or if I were black and came home to find nothing

changed. If I were unemployed or hadn't been able to get back into school, or if I'd been blinded.

But none of this is true. I've had no problem readjusting.

Readjustment is the byword these days. Everyone talks about readjustment.

At the time, O'Brien was choosing among three enviable futures: finishing his Harvard PhD, converting his reporting for *The Washington Post* into a career, or having a go as a creative writer. The article recognizes others' homecoming struggles without dismissing them as readjustment failures. "But they're them and I'm me, and I can't talk authoritatively about them." The war caught him up, then released him:

> Readjustment. It's like forgetting a foreign language. Stop looking for mines in the pavement. Step on a crack, you'll break your bloody back. Stop saying *didi-mau* to your little brother. Stop asking girls for boom-boom. Stop whistling marching songs when you walk to the drugstore: *I wanna be an Airborne Ranger. I wanna live a life of danger, stand up, hook up, shuffle to the door, step right out and count to four, an' if that chute don't open wide, say your prayers and tell 'em you tried.* The old lingo fades. The terror fades, and it's just a word—terror—and all you can think is the word, not the feeling. The names of places, if you ever knew them, fade. Names of comrades and officers fade. Your anger fades, and so does your frustration and bitterness.[24]

O'Brien followed the pattern presumed by *DSM-I* and *DSM-II*. He resumed the path toward a career, and nothing about his inner life indicated neurosis or psychosis. Readjustment achieved.

The byword operates as a punch line in O'Brien's first published story, "Claudia Mae's Wedding Day," which appeared later that year in *Redbook*. Robert, a veteran, proposes to Claudia Mae by mail from Việt Nam. Right before the wedding his about-to-be father-in-law, like O'Brien's father a veteran of the Pacific War, attempts some bonding, to comic effect:

> "Well, I have to admit it's a little tough on you guys. I've read all about your problems in *Time* and *Newsweek*. Nobody wants to hire

a Viet vet. Drugs and everything. Psycho cases, all that. Sure, I know it's rough. It's not like World War Two—I'll tell you that much. After that war they couldn't wait to hire a vet. Get him back in the stream of things. Readjustment."

"What's there to readjust to?"

"You should know more about that than me. Aren't you a little messed up? Bad dreams? Blank moments?"

"I don't think so," Robert said. "I don't know. I don't remember . . ."

Claudia Mae's father stared at him. Finally he shook his head and stood up. "Well, if you have any problems—adjusting—let us know—okay?"

Robert nodded gravely.[25]

Besides the well-intended parents, the story mocks the liberal-hearted minister who carries a copy of *Winning the War Against War* (a title O'Brien invented) and hands Robert a business card: "Counseling for troubled minds in troubled times."[26]

In 1972, William Pelfrey, a Vietnam veteran whose war novel *The Big V* had just been published, contributed a piece to *The New York Times* about the challenges his generation faced in writing the great American novel of their war experiences. They couldn't rival the Great War writers such as Dos Passos, Hemingway, and Remarque in portraying disillusionment and "abhorrence," and the "'lessons' of Vietnam have saturated the public."[27] The alienation of Vietnam veterans was already a cliché of endless articles, studies, television shows, and politicians' stump rhetoric. There was nothing new to say. "Claudia Mae's Wedding Day" found originality by making the cliché and the cliché-making apparatus its very subject.

O'Brien's other story from 1973 was accepted for a veterans' anthology that was never published. "Our Fathers' War" is narrated by a childless World War II vet who never deployed overseas and befriends a young Vietnam vet who in high school lost both his parents to cancer (like O'Brien's friend Steve Goff). During the war, shrapnel blinded Gregory Caufield in one eye. He has returned to his small, rural southern Minnesota town, where he works at the library and plays golf and tennis with the narrator. Unlike "Claudia Mae's Wedding Day," this story shows sympathy for the older man's sympathy toward the young man: "It is just that a man who loses his parents and an eye and goes to war and comes back all before he is twenty-five is someone who deserves sympathy. There is no psychology involved. It is simple."[28]

Caufield resembles O'Brien in his hometown, in being short, and in being a golfer. But Caufield is a natural athlete who did not fuss over stance and swing. He did not go to college before the war, where he served as a lieutenant and platoon leader. He didn't much question or study the war beforehand and even after had little to say about its rightness or wrongness. Like Hemingway's Harold Krebs in "Soldier's Home," he starts learning about the war from books. "Novels?" the narrator asks. "Brrrr. Nope," Caufield answers. "Nonfiction mostly."[29]

As the story ends, this young man who is not morose about the war is headed to the University of Minnesota, to get on with it. It's a readjustment story with no mention of readjustment in it. "Everyone thinks a veteran is nuts or his soul is in turmoil, you know?"[30] O'Brien has imagined a version of himself at that biographical moment. The fictional one works at a library circulation desk in a holding pattern before pursuing his education; the real one was studying at Harvard in a holding pattern before pursuing his fiction.

O'Brien consistently maintained his lack of what was first called post-Vietnam syndrome and eventually PTSD.[31] Fifty years later, he acknowledges exhibiting some symptoms of PTSD after coming home, but only like someone infected with COVID-19 who suffers a runny nose. Yet the new returnee's anger and bitterness were only in temporary remission.

A better framework for the war's impact on O'Brien is *moral injury*. Jonathan Shay brought the term to wide consideration in his 1994 *Achilles in Vietnam: Combat Trauma and the Undoing of Character*. According to the Department of Veterans Affairs, "In order for moral injury to occur, the individual must feel like a transgression occurred and that they or someone else crossed a line with respect to their moral beliefs. Guilt, shame, disgust and anger are some of the hallmark reactions of moral injury," whose features and symptoms can resemble PTSD's.[32] For O'Brien, being complicit in killing and harming others for no discernible good was a moral failure of lifelong duration. What about the Vietnamese? As O'Brien has harped time and time again, "We had 59,000 American deaths. God knows how many wounded. But nothing comparable to what the Vietnamese suffered. I'm not talking just about the enemy soldiers. I'm talking about the babies, women, and teenagers."[33] Three million dead. "What about their burned-to-the-ground houses? What about their PTSD problems? What about their missing legs? What about their Gold Star Mothers?"[34]

The PTSD ascription is a moral convenience with ramifications, four capital letters that explain a soul away. For O'Brien, a writer must keep the wounds open so that the rest of us don't forget. To keep the rest of us reflecting and talking, the writer can't fall prey to cliché. It's at once a moral problem and an aesthetic problem. Affixing the PTSD label to a work of art, to its characters or their author, analyzing them in terms of trauma theory, reduces the work of art to that label, that subject, that theme. It diminishes the whole in the way categorizing any work or person insults, belittles, and dehumanizes. It overlooks artistry and the other vital matters at hand. It betrays the reader's intelligence, imagination, and curiosity. It ends conversation.

Lifton did not have the language of moral injury or PTSD when writing *Home from the War* in the early 1970s, and he resisted the terms *post-Vietnam syndrome* and *readjustment* as pernicious political tools that propagated the war machine. By locating the ills entirely in the individual, such terms exonerated society. Lifton, rather, advanced the notion of *animating guilt*, a framework for addressing dissatisfactions without as well as within. Lifton's vets sought new "forms" of living simultaneously responsible to themselves and to society—not readjusting themselves to fit back into a world order that had betrayed them but working to change both to achieve a new moral collaboration and balance.[35]

O'Brien's war writings have always undertaken that dual responsibility. The boy from 1950s small-town Minnesota still believes in being a good neighbor. He just wants to redefine what goodness means. He directs the urgency and import outward. He writes for others while seeking the self-knowledge gained, in Lifton's terms, by "illuminating one's guilt."[36]

One of Lifton's most instructive examples is a former sergeant who created a forty-minute color slideshow of photos from the war in Việt Nam accompanied by Woodstock-style rock that veterans and civilians found extraordinarily powerful. Toward the end of the sequence, he added a slide of himself in Việt Nam as a form of "penance." But, Lifton writes, "once gaining access to that kind of truth, the problem he and others faced was

holding on to it. They sensed that in each retelling—in each public presentation or performance—there was inevitable movement away from the
source, away from the truth." After a while the vet "had to give up showing
it because he found himself merely going through the motions, which he
felt to be unauthentic."[37]

O'Brien, too, has spoken of his war writing as a kind of penance. Lifton's sergeant's relationship with his single piece of communicative art
speaks to O'Brien's with his ongoing oeuvre. The guilt never goes away,
nor should it. "On the contrary," Lifton asserts, "the process of converting
static to animating guilt is continuous and continuously important."[38] To
express his experiences authentically, to animate his guilt continuously and
responsibly—for others—O'Brien couldn't allow his writing to stagnate on
the last successful piece. Moreover, Lifton says,

> But as an animating relationship to guilt comes to predominate,
> it is increasingly accompanied by play. Piaget has said that a child, in
> order to understand anything, must construct it himself or "re-invent
> it" through play. [. . .]
> Adult play may become tinged with sadness or tragedy, but it is
> deepened and even liberated by awareness of mortality.[39]

For O'Brien, the writing process very much involves childlike play as he
loses himself in the pretend and re-creates himself and his world. By writing a "Tim O'Brien" character into *The Things They Carried*, O'Brien authentically captures his ongoing relationship to himself and his experience
of war. The work needs to pulse with the uncertainty, anxiousness, and
vulnerability of the war. Every new work achieves its authenticity in its
animating originality of form; it preserves his relationship with his war by
playfully reinventing it.

Tim O'Brien spent thirteen months of his life in Quảng Ngãi, Việt Nam,
then six back in Minnesota before moving on. July's despondent letter to
Erik Hansen does not exclusively define O'Brien's state of mind. He was,
after all, heading from the physical and brutalizing to the intellectual and

civilized. If the war was America's swampy lowland, Harvard was "the high ground," its "pinnacle."[40]

In September 1970, he landed in Cambridge, where he would live until the end of the millennium. Though he couldn't know it, having no real sense of the contemporary literary scene, Boston was a propitious place for a young writer as well as for the mature writer he would become. There, he wrote his first books; there, he created his most enduring art.

14

LINES OF DEPARTURE (1)

O'Brien registered for graduate school classes on September 23, 1970. He had moved into Richards Hall a few days before. His letter to Erik Hansen about his first days in Cambridge referenced Thomas Wolfe and William Faulkner, called his response to the red brick and ivy "almost pre-memory," and prayed that the students and the place live up to their "potency"—if not, it will be "the height of perfidy," on par with "committing your life to the good, reading and obeying the laws, only to find Drill Sergeant Guyton in the throne of the Deity." This lower-middle-class kid from rural Minnesota had a lot of "tawdry glitterings" to take in those first days.[1] Kathy moved to Boston a few weeks later. She took a job with a publisher, Little, Brown and Company, and moved in with a friend who lived a ten-minute walk from the dorm.

O'Brien began making friends from the dorm, chiefly Robert Simpson, a biophysicist. O'Brien's inquisitiveness impressed Simpson. Whereas other students couldn't get beyond the first sentence of Simpson's research recapitulation, O'Brien concentrated, nodded earnestly, and asked good questions.

Early that first semester, O'Brien learned about Cambridge's place in the battles of Lexington and Concord during the Revolutionary War. Try as he might, he couldn't get new acquaintances interested. O'Brien approached the two-hundred-year-old battles through his own experiences, identifying with the well-outfitted British regulars habituated to orderly combat "blundering through unfamiliar terrain" fighting an enemy—the scrappy

American colonists—"that refused to fight conventional battles." O'Brien "had more in common with those long-dead redcoats than with the living men and women all around."[2]

O'Brien couldn't talk about his war directly. What would he, what could he, say? Who cared to listen? "[I]f you stand five minutes in front of the Harvard Coop," he wrote in October 1973, "you'll see maybe a dozen army jackets" worn mostly by "college kids," not veterans: "Pretenders." As his research verified. "In 1971–1972, Harvard College's 6,000 students included only 89 vets," whereas over half its students in 1947–1948 were veterans.[3]

The problem went deeper than an absence of other veterans. In his classic essay "What Did You Do in the Class War, Daddy?," James Fallows describes Harvard and MIT students' contempt for those who fought. One earned the right to opine on the war by having read the right things, not by being one of the "pigs" with firsthand knowledge.[4] O'Brien didn't face open hostility. Yet as Professor Samuel Popkin recalled of that time and place, "the worst thing in the world was to try to explain anything about the war if you'd been there," because the ideologues on both sides didn't listen but would cast aspersions without missing a beat.

The absence of other veterans proved a mixed blessing, as Harvard became an asylum from the war. But he couldn't not write about it, on sleepless nights, trying "to dump the terrible shit on pieces of paper."[5] That first year, Bob Simpson saw the notebook and scraps in O'Brien's dorm-room desk drawer. "What's that?"

O'Brien told him in so many words.

"You should turn it into a book."

O'Brien dated as often as he could, usually dinners and movies. He and Kathy occasionally hung out. His inherited fondness for baseball, still the national pastime, turned him into a Red Sox fan. O'Brien played in a regular basketball game and matched his Ping-Pong skills against Simpson's in the dorm's rec room. When a residence Ping-Pong tournament rolled around, the ever-competitive O'Brien entered the top division. He and Kathy or he and Simpson and maybe a third student took weekend trips out of Cambridge. They skied nearby slopes, mostly in New Hampshire, once in Vermont.

But for the first year and a half, coursework dominated. It felt like his undergraduate days, with sodas from the dorm vending machines getting him through the all-nighters. Sodas and now cigarettes—Simpson has a vivid image of a bucket full of butts and ashes by O'Brien's dorm room desk.

History, politics, reading, deep study, disputation. O'Brien's fortes. His professors were brilliant, fascinating, intellectual influencers. For Judith Shklar's History of Political Theory he learned from but did not enjoy Thucydides; he really enjoyed the slew of readings from Plato. Bernard Bailyn's history class The Emergence of the Liberal State was the most beneficial in curing him of his ignorance about Anglo-American history. The import of the Glorious Revolution and the resultant 1689 Bill of Rights "amazed" him. He complemented those courses with a more contemporaneous and local pair, Doris Kearns's The American Presidency and Robert Bowie's U.S. Foreign Policy Under Changing Conditions.[6] Second semester, O'Brien took Edward Banfield's Concepts in Political Theory, Arthur Maass's The Legislative-Executive Processes, John Montgomery's Problems in the Interpretation of U.S. Foreign Policy, and Bailyn's The Colonial Period of American History. His interests lay in political philosophy—the big questions—and in American politics, policy, and history. He thought about a dissertation on Plato until Professor Bailyn reminded him he would "of course" need to learn ancient Greek. The *of course* threw O'Brien for a loop. The necessity had not occurred to him.

In none of his three semesters of coursework did O'Brien enroll in Revolution and Politics in Vietnam; War; or History of Modern Vietnam.[7] Nor did he have a course with Michael Walzer, who was at work on *Just and Unjust Wars* (1977). Which is not to say that Harvard provided an impervious ivory-tower escape from the war. O'Brien's lack of interest in the courses was intellectually genuine, and he probably had zero taste for the campus brouhaha surrounding them. One of the professors, Samuel Huntington, was a target of wrath from leftists who blamed him for the pacification program in Vietnam. His class was interrupted at least once by haranguing students, and one day he arrived home to find A WAR CRIMINAL LIVES HERE "painted in big, black letters on our yellow door."[8]

At 1:02 a.m. on October 14, 1970, a bomb exploded in the offices of the Center for International Affairs, not far from O'Brien's dorm. Professor Bowie was the center's founding director, and for a long time Henry Kissinger had been the associate director. At the time of the bombing,

Kissinger served as President Nixon's national security adviser. The center's relationship with the government made it a target, with four preceding incidents dating back to September 1969. The Proud Eagle Tribe, the forerunner to Women's Brigade of the Weather Underground, took credit for the bombing.[9] O'Brien had slept through it, only to hear about it from another student, anticlimactically.

February brought a public and nondisruptive teach-in to campus, consisting of a lineup of professors, politicians, and journalists speaking from a lectern. The audience numbered twelve hundred packed into the one-thousand-seat Sanders Theater, and an overflow of another eight hundred or so in Memorial Hall and Lowell Lecture Hall. The event was also broadcast on WGBH radio.[10] O'Brien does not recall the event. He doesn't think he went. Harvard's anti-war activism lacked the fervor of the previous two years. O'Brien remembers a campus of industrious students going about their studies.

O'Brien followed news about the war, especially admiring his future *Washington Post* colleague Bill Greider's Mỹ Lai trial coverage. On March 29, 1971, at Fort Benning, the army jury convicted William Calley "of the murder of not less than 22 Vietnamese people."[11] Two days later he was sentenced to a lifetime of confinement and hard labor. Calls for clemency followed immediately.[12] The next day, April 1, President Nixon ordered Calley out of the stockade and into his quarters while the case underwent review. Greider's editorials defended the conviction. The jurors were themselves soldiers, after all, who understood that "there is killing and then there is killing." To the veteran complaining about the conviction by confessing that he killed civilians too, Greider wrote bluntly, "ask him if he herded people together, unarmed and unresisting, put them in a ditch, then stood over them and fired."[13]

In an April 13 letter to Hansen, O'Brien first mentions the idea of writing a war memoir:

The "Step-Lightly" piece has been reprinted in 2 college textbooks, composition books, I think. The editors have thus contributed to my dollar-status considerably, but, more important, have engendered a low flame—just an ember, really—that's been burning for a year &

more: to write a "book": A collection of "pieces" on the order of "Step Lightly," maybe taking as a core the Tribune, Star, & Daily Globe pieces. At any rate, I'm recently spending time on the idea.[14]

It's tempting to see the courts-martial and the public's response as stoking his low flame. O'Brien could provide what few could, the background of having soldiered in Pinkville in the late 1960s. O'Brien wraps *If I Die in a Combat Zone, Box Me Up and Ship Me Home* around the massacre, with passages offering it as his contribution to the national conversation.

By the time of the April 13 letter, Ben Bagdikian had interviewed O'Brien in a Boston hotel for a job as a summer "fill-in reporter" at *The Washington Post*. Bagdikian had not been at the paper very long and would not be there much longer, on his way to becoming a legendary print journalist. O'Brien's acceptance meant he couldn't hang out with Hansen in Europe as planned. O'Brien canceled his plane tickets. "Is it excessive flexibility, this failure to do the thing that's been calling me for years? Or is it excessive ambition?"[15]

The week after O'Brien's letter to Hansen, about fifteen hundred veterans descended upon Washington. The Vietnam Veterans Against the War (VVAW) called their occupation of the capital Operation Dewey Canyon III as a retort to the U.S. military's offenses into Laos, Dewey Canyon I (1969) and Dewey Canyon II (1971). The D.C. incursion famously culminated with veterans hurling their medals over a barrier onto the Capitol steps in an act of protest and, unexpectedly, of catharsis. Dewey Canyon III saw the navy veteran and future senator John Kerry testify before the Senate Foreign Relations Committee, where he uttered one of the most poignant lines of any anti-war movement: "How do you ask a man to be the last man to die in Vietnam? How do you ask a man to be the last man to die for a mistake?"

The Calley trial and Dewey Canyon III resulted in a substantial increase in veteran anti-war activism. VVAW's membership jumped to twenty-five thousand, with an untold number of mobilized fellow travelers. O'Brien was not among them. In the spring of 1971, he was deep into his coursework-heavy first year at Harvard. Besides, he'd never been much of a joiner. Rabbling wasn't his style. O'Brien soured on the strident, stringent rhetoric of organized movements whose ideas for effectiveness often did not tolerate divergence from their absolutist terms or acknowledge the good faith of those they demonized. O'Brien did not agree with the nation-building approach of some Harvard dons around him, but he trusted that they were good people trying to understand and bring order to a complexly awful situation.

The summer brought long hours working at the *Post* and drafting the memoir. While a part of O'Brien wished he had participated in those veterans' demonstrations, he didn't regret not going. "I really did want to get a book out about the realities of the war. [...] I wanted to write a book about the infantryman's experience through the eyes of a soldier who acknowledged the obvious: that we were killing civilians more than we were killing the enemy," that "the war was aimless in the most basic ways, that is, aimless in the sense of nothing to aim at, no enemy to shoot, no target to kill."[16] He was doing his part the best way he could.

O'Brien arrived at *The Washington Post* during its rise to a national stature on par with *The New York Times* and *The Wall Street Journal*. Before he published his first article, the Pentagon Papers story broke. In 1967, Secretary of Defense Robert McNamara had ordered a thorough study of American policy toward Việt Nam from 1940 to the present. Titled *Report of the Office of the Secretary of Defense Vietnam Task Force*, it became known as the Pentagon Papers after *The New York Times* reporter Neil Sheehan gained access to a large portion of the report from Daniel Ellsberg, an analyst who had worked on it.[17] Sheehan's first article appeared on June 13. It succinctly summarized the discoveries. First, the full extent of U.S. activities in Việt Nam was never made public. Second, the original "containment of Communism" mission had morphed into "the defense of the power, influence and prestige of the United States, in both stages irrespective of conditions in Vietnam." Third, the leaders pursuing the war were aware of its futility but continued spilling blood.[18]

When the White House obtained a court injunction to stop the *Times* from further publication, *The Washington Post* stepped in, publishing its first article drawn from the report on June 18. The person who acquired the papers for the *Post* was Ben Bagdikian, the assistant managing editor who had hired O'Brien. Bagdikian had flown back from Boston to Washington with the boxed-up photocopied papers on the seat beside him. He led the argument to publish the papers against the threat of legal action: "The only way to assert the right to publish is to publish."[19] The *Post* joined the *Times* in a lawsuit, and on June 30, in a watershed First Amendment case, the Supreme Court ruled that the press had a right to publish the material.[20]

O'Brien the summer intern played no role in the unfolding fight and can't be said to have enjoyed a ringside seat. But his wasn't a nosebleed seat. He wrote one article that mentions Mike Gravel's public reading from the Pentagon Papers during a subcommittee meeting during which the senator "had broken down and wept."[21]

The newsroom—the city, the nation—roiled. O'Brien had known the war was wrong and probably unwinnable. It turned out the White House had, too. In the memoir, O'Brien acknowledges that in objecting to the draft he didn't know everything, and some of what he didn't know was "hidden away [. . .] partly in the archives of government."[22] It is near certain O'Brien wrote these words in the wake of the Pentagon Papers revelations. In a letter sent in a *Post* envelope postmarked from D.C. on August 11, he reported that the book was up to around thirty-five thousand words, "slightly exceeding my original goal for the whole thing," with half still to go. The original plan for a short book of essays, "glimpses of combat life," had become "something more, an amorphous, not very well organized, rambling scream at the military."[23]

O'Brien's first *Post* article that summer announced the Democratic Party's choice of Miami Beach for its 1972 convention.[24] He sat at his desk without a clue how to proceed. No one had taught him what a lead was or how to structure a story. He typed his first two- or three-page draft and carried it over to Mary Lou Beatty, an editor at the national desk. Beatty read through it, didn't say a word, didn't look up, crumpled the pages, and tossed them into the trash can. O'Brien slunk away to try again. With his second draft, she gave some guidance but said "nothing complimentary." He returned to his desk. The clock was ticking. A half hour until the deadline. Beatty walked over, sat in his chair, and said, "Watch me." She wrote up the first half page and left O'Brien to finish the story. At the time he villainized her for the absence of coaching, but later came to appreciate it.

Of the thirty-seven articles O'Brien wrote that summer, nine dealt with the military or the war. Two reported on suspicions over the legitimacy of the upcoming presidential election in South Việt Nam. Two covered the POW issue. In the first, "POW Kin Clash at Session Here," relatives of imprisoned service members heatedly disagreed over the best approach for bringing loved ones home. Some supported John Kerry of the Vietnam Veterans Against the War in his plea to end the war immediately. Others thought Kerry was callously using the issue to further his political ambitions and misrepresenting those POW families who believed in the war.[25]

In late August, O'Brien covered a New York news conference in which members of the Families for Immediate Release "denounced White House backed plans for a $25 million advertising campaign to persuade Hanoi to give imprisoned American soldiers more humane treatment." The group that wanted to end the war saw this move as an empty political stunt.[26] Which it was. Focusing on POWs allowed President Nixon to show concern, turn attention away from the grunts still slogging it out, ignore the VVAW, highlight veterans who supported him, and further demonize the North Vietnamese.[27] O'Brien's article quoted Valerie Kushner, whose husband Hal had been a POW since November 30, 1967. Decades later, O'Brien and Hal Kushner spent hours together as program advisers for the 2017 series *The Vietnam War*.

The two Việt Nam stories that perhaps caused him some anguish were the results of the August 5 draft lottery and Attorney General John Mitchell's announcement that the federal government would not pursue a grand jury indictment for the May 1970 killing and wounding of the Kent State students. The descriptive detail suggests he attended the lottery in the Commerce Department auditorium.[28] That article made the front page, below the fold—one wonders if he thought back to the moon landing when he was in Việt Nam as he read the above-the-fold article about astronaut Alfred Worden's "surrealistic deep space ballet," the first ever space walk.[29]

In a related piece, O'Brien relayed the findings by a House committee that legislators had not kept up with the citizenry's increasing anti-war sentiment. The article allowed O'Brien to use his graduate school chops as he cites two political scientists on the constituency-legislator relationship.[30] O'Brien also reported on an outsized expenditure by the Pentagon for a public relations program that selected civilians to watch military training, ride in military vehicles, and even fire military weapons. Congressman Henry Reuss was less concerned about the cost overrun than "whether the Pentagon ought to be engaging in this kind of expensive show business in the first place."[31] O'Brien wanted to contribute "something on basic & AIT training—a sort of 'in-depth-interview-experiential-analytical' piece," but apparently failed to persuade his editors.[32] He wrote a version of it anyway, for the memoir.

O'Brien's first above-the-fold front-page story, "Women Organize for More Power," was one of three articles on the founding three-day convention of the National Women's Political Caucus, held in the Statler Hilton Hotel in D.C.[33] The leadership included Shirley Chisholm, Betty Friedan, Fannie Lou Hamer, and Gloria Steinem. "I remember Bella Abzug's hat," he says. "She always wore a big round-brimmed hat." O'Brien was in the conference room when caucus participants shouted down liberal icons Eugene McCarthy and Dr. Benjamin Spock for being sexist.[34] He also attended the East Wing ceremony for Nixon's certification of the Twenty-Sixth Amendment, which guaranteed the right to vote at eighteen years of age.[35]

O'Brien's other stories ranged from such issues as a deadly horse virus in Texas to favored-nation status for communist Romania, Ralph Nader's consumer advocacy, the tussle between the Pentagon and the Atomic Energy Commission over the nation's nuclear arsenal, the relationship between the labor unions and the White House, and whether the federal government should help pay for school busing. Papers nationwide frequently printed these articles off the wire.[36]

Each day brought a new adventure. He arrived in the morning, received an assignment, and went to work. First stop, the morgue, the vast holdings of clippings and miscellaneous material, for a crash course on subjects he knew little about. He often went in on Sundays to study up when the office was quiet and he didn't have a new assignment. Unlike with debate, he did not have the luxury of months on a single subject. National politics, he learned, is "not nearly so evil and corrupt as I'd imagined, the people are often as decent as any to be found in the universities—literate and concerned and trying like hell. I like history. This place is full of it."[37]

O'Brien thought well of his *Post* colleagues and had soured on graduate school. "God knows a PhD is no boon to the reporter."[38] Not that he was entirely sold on newspaper work. More and more, he itched to be a writer, not a journalist. He had a small apartment on Corcoran Street, north of the White House. Thursday and Friday were his days off. He spent them reading, going out with young women, or exploring on his own. He fantasized about traveling in Europe with Hansen *next* summer, even while he applied to return to the *Post*.[39]

O'Brien was back in Cambridge by September 11.[40] Over the upcoming academic year, he filed some stories for the paper about Harvard and New England, but mainly he turned his attention to surviving school, finishing the memoir, and finding a publisher.

◊   ◊   ◊

On or not long after his twenty-fifth birthday, in October 1971, O'Brien disparaged his "dispassionate" fellow academics: "Their professionalism—the professionalism I have to eat and drink daily, a prison diet—is mechanical. The important issues seem to have been lost. What is the just politics? What is a wise statesman?"[41] To be fair, O'Brien's classes that semester were quantitatively based, Models and Methods in Quantitative Political Analysis, and Empirical Political Theory. No wonder he likened the profession to "designing sewer systems." In contrast, the *Post*'s "reporters and editors care about these important matters—they seem committed to tearing away the superfluous trappings of national politics."[42] His professors and the other students did have a passion for the higher value of their subject. O'Brien just didn't share it.

That fall, O'Brien's Models and Methods professor, Samuel Popkin, received a subpoena to testify before a federal grand jury investigating Daniel Ellsberg and the Pentagon Papers leak. The two men were friends and academic colleagues. Every class period, someone asked Popkin what he planned to do—out of serious concern and to tease about whether they'd have a final exam if their teacher were in jail.

The harassment usurped Popkin's life. He appeared before the Boston grand jury several times. His refusal to answer questions on the grounds of academic freedom eventually landed him in jail. The FBI wanted him to name everyone he'd spoken with about Việt Nam. He declined. Among others whose privacy Popkin protected were military officers studying at Harvard on their way to their next assignment. The federal government released him in November 1972 after only a week, when it unexpectedly dropped the grand jury investigation.[43]

Not yet thirty years old, Popkin had traveled several times to Việt Nam since 1966, for months at a time, and when O'Brien knew him, he was working on his book *The Rational Peasant: The Political Economy of Rural Society in Vietnam* (1979). He co-taught with Samuel Huntington the Revolution and Politics in Vietnam course that O'Brien did not take. Popkin's association with Huntington and with his politically controversial adviser at MIT, Ithiel de Sola Pool, had made him a persona non grata to radical leftist academics like Noam Chomsky. With the Pentagon Papers business, those same firebrands instantaneously "lionized" him, transforming him in their eyes from a "fascist" collaborator with the Center for International Affairs into a hero of the resistance. In truth, Popkin was neither snookered by visions of a peace-loving, noble communist North Việt Nam nor persuaded by the domino theory. He considered the conflict a civil war the United States never should have entered, yet he "did not think we were on the wrong side." People such as Huntington and himself "were trying to stop the fucking violence" as practically as they knew how.

Popkin did not know that the tousled, waifish student was a veteran. He wishes O'Brien had reached out to him as other veterans had. He had stories to share. And he would have listened.

Other than the two courses, O'Brien spent his classroom time as a teaching assistant. Once a week the professor delivered a lecture to a few hundred students, then two or three times that week O'Brien met with sections of about twenty undergraduates. He wasn't much older than his students, most of the Harvard courses he had taken mixed graduate and undergraduate students, and he only had a few semesters of knowledge beyond Macalester. He worked hard to stay one step ahead of his charges. He drudged through preparation and grading. The joy of intellectual performance he had thrived on in debate did not translate to the daily obligations of the classroom.

O'Brien cared more about his book anyway. He had assembled the memoir quickly, mostly in D.C. That fall, Alfred A. Knopf rejected it because the publisher had already acquired Michael Herr's *Dispatches* and did not see a market for competing titles. Kathy O'Brien's colleagues at Little, Brown told him there was no appetite for Việt Nam but suggested that he send his memoir to the esteemed Boston-based publisher Seymour Lawrence. O'Brien submitted "Pop Smoke"—*If I Die*'s original title, a reference to smoke grenades—to Lawrence and to a New York agent by the end of the year, knowing he had another fifteen thousand words or so to write.[44]

The interested New York agent repeated the caution that "Vietnam stuff" doesn't sell. O'Brien was peeved. "Christ, how can a war produce apathy?"[45] Even before O'Brien entered the army, a *New York Times* book review had bemoaned the endless stream of books about Việt Nam.[46] One of the published memoir's reviews, a very positive one, began by labeling the war "a subject with which most of us are weary to death."[47] Writing in 1975, James Fallows observed, "Among the high-brow audience, it is scarcely possible to attract a minute's attention on the subject of Vietnam veterans," partly because of "the *kind* of war we fought, and our eagerness to forget it," but also because of "*who* the veterans are." That would be the lower class, the "proles," that "the intelligentsia has virtually willed out of existence."[48]

Other veterans trying to craft works of witness ran into this presumed public indifference: Bruce Weigl, Bill Ehrhart, James Webb, Wallace Terry.[49] The novel *Neverlight*, which Donald Pfarrer finished in 1970, did not find its way into print until 1982. Philip Caputo couldn't publish his memoir *A Rumor of War* until 1977.[50] Oliver Stone wrote the *Platoon* screenplay in 1976 and the first draft of his adaptation of Ron Kovic's *Born on the Fourth of July* by 1979. The cameras did not roll for him that decade. Stone concluded the war was a dead subject. That *Platoon* made it to the screen in 1986 he calls "a miracle."

A telling case is the story of 1st Casualty Press. In 1970 and 1971, three veterans assembled an anthology, *Winning Hearts and Minds: War Poems by Vietnam Veterans*, that forty-two publishers turned down.[51] Undeterred, the editors launched 1st Casualty Press and published the book in 1972. Its surprising success led McGraw-Hill to enter a joint contract to publish and distribute it and two follow-on anthologies. The first anthology of American creative writing from the war, *Winning Hearts and Minds*, is a landmark in the war's literary history. The press's second volume, a story collection titled *Free Fire Zone*, came out in 1973 but fared poorly, perhaps because of the recent permanent ceasefire between the United States and North Việt Nam. McGraw-Hill scrapped the final project, a mix of poetry and prose about homecoming called *Postmortem*—the book that would have included O'Brien's early story "Our Fathers' War."

O'Brien's frustration over the marketplace amounted to moral indignation. He was also worried about a real opportunity passing him by. Mỹ Lai was becoming old news. In 1971, despite the glut of nonfiction books on the war, there were next to no memoirs by American ground combatants.[52] By grunts. In the fall of 1972, O'Brien would read John Parrish's *12, 20 & 5: A Doctor's Year in Vietnam* (1972) and Ron Glasser's *365 Days* (1971), an army doctor's account from a hospital in Japan. A real urgency to produce a literary grunt memoir may have hastened O'Brien's process, contributing to *If I Die*'s form.

Seymour "Sam" Lawrence's first reaction to the manuscript and to O'Brien's potential is preserved in an interoffice memo dated February 29, 1972. Lawrence found the book "thoughtful" and "well-written," perfect for "a good college market." But it needed reworking. Reorganization, "more personalities, more local color (prostitution, dope peddling, corruption), more about his family, his girl, etc. The Platonic dialogues should be cut." As for the author, Lawrence already championed him and glimpsed the future: "If ever there was a case for taking on an articulate reporter at an early stage in his career, Tim O'Brien is a striking example. He will certainly go far in whatever he does—as a journalist, or government official, or possibly as a novelist."[53]

That same day, Lawrence wrote O'Brien a terse note that he was recommending the book as a paperback as well as a hardback to Dell. O'Brien was guardedly optimistic. He was also still sending new chapters.[54] O'Brien's relationship with Lawrence began, as O'Brien fondly tells the story, with an April phone call to his dorm room. At first O'Brien didn't connect the caller with the publisher. The caller's stutter didn't help. Then it hit. Sam Lawrence wanted to publish his book.

They met for lunch. They talked about literary stars of the day. They wound up at Lawrence's Beacon Street office. Sometimes when O'Brien tells the story, they were both sloshed; other times, Lawrence was considerably drunker, O'Brien not much for alcohol in those years. The matter of the New York agent came up. "What's he done for you?" Lawrence asked.

"Nothing," O'Brien answered. Lawrence called and fired him on the spot. A little rudely, O'Brien thought. But he didn't say anything, because he had just landed his book with the person who published Kurt Vonnegut, Katherine Anne Porter, Richard Yates, Tillie Olsen, and Dan Wakefield. They didn't discuss O'Brien's fiction ambition that day. O'Brien was shy about it, the possibility feeling so remote, cliché, and forward that it chagrined him.

Against the odds, Lawrence secured a contract by the end of the month.[55] Lawrence's double imprint meant a publishing house handled production and distribution for the talent that he discovered. Delacorte Press (a Dell imprint) downplayed the war in marketing and packaging the hardback because it ranked the war "somewhere between cancer and New Zealand lyric poetry in sales appeal."[56] Dell's publishing partner Delta Books opted to wait on reviews and sales of the hardback before committing to a trade edition because the war was a "super-saturated" subject.[57] Both *Esquire* and *The Atlantic Monthly* declined to run an excerpt because they were moving on from the war.[58]

O'Brien had other reasons to celebrate that spring. On May 18, 1972, he successfully completed his oral exams.[59] He was ready to start the dissertation: "The idea is to discern whatever patterns have emerged about the avowed ends for which we have gone to war or have almost gone to war" since World War II.[60] O'Brien sought to understand the language by which the nation's leaders justified, rationalized, or sold armed action. Rectitude was on his mind. As he wrote in the memoir, "I wondered how writers such as Hemingway and Pyle and Jack London could write so accurately and movingly about war without also writing about the rightness of their wars."[61]

He had also begun to fall in love. He'd had an active dating life from the moment he arrived at Cambridge. O'Brien's conservative small-town upbringing through the mid-1960s, and then being in the army, immersed him in a culture that conditioned teenage boys to talk about women as *broads*, *dolls*, even *dollies*. He wasn't above white lies while flirting. He also clung to his fantasy of a soulmate, of a connection "more sublime."[62] The people he dated were almost always more interested in him than he was in them. The timing of mutual romantic affection never synced. Until he met Ann Elizabeth Weller.

Weller worked with O'Brien's sister in Boston. She struck Kathy as quite reserved, even timid, and without much social life. Kathy asked her to lunch a few times, then invited her to celebrate St. Patrick's Day, which in 1972 fell on a Friday. O'Brien called to see what his sister was up to, having no plans himself, and she invited him to join them, no matchmaking in mind. At one point Kathy returned to the living room from her kitchen to find Tim and Ann getting acquainted on the couch, no words necessary. Tim's cozy display didn't surprise her. Ann's did.

Like Jane Reister and Gayle Roby, Ann was blond and slender. Her quietness lent her a mystery that attracted O'Brien. She had a very sharp mind. She came from Hagerstown, in north-central Maryland, wedged between West Virginia and Pennsylvania. She went to college in Westminster, Maryland, graduating a couple of years behind O'Brien. She lived in the South End of Boston, with a couple of other girls from western Maryland. Her parents were extremely religious though not zealous—comfortable, calm, dignified—and socially conservative. Ann was more liberal. She and her roommates' favorite pals were a couple of gay men. Like her parents and unlike most people his age, she was comfortable in her own skin. She was hopelessly kind and sweet, without a whiff of pretension. They were two homebodies who were curious about the world, and of a sudden about each other.

The *Post*'s assignments for O'Brien in the summer of 1972, thirty-five of them, again varied considerably. One drew from the Pentagon Papers to focus on the several attempts at peace in Việt Nam between 1964 and 1968, coincidentally his pre-army Macalester years[63]—surely O'Brien felt the sting of those failures. Another reported on an army study recommending that chemical defoliants remain an option for future wars despite the controversial use of Agent Orange in Southeast Asia.[64] He co-wrote it with Jack Fuller, who had been a plucky army reporter for *Stars and Stripes* in Việt Nam. Despite political differences, the two men got along. Both were born in October 1946. In addition to a journalism career capped by leading the *Chicago Tribune*, Fuller wrote seven novels, one, *Fragments* (1984), about the war. Fuller and O'Brien remained friendly throughout their lives.

Early that summer, O'Brien missed an opportunity to scoop Seymour Hersh, the reporter who had exposed the Mỹ Lai massacre and cover-up. O'Brien's principal source for veterans' issues was Stuart Feldman, a federal government attorney who would one day cofound the Council of Vietnam Veterans, the predecessor to the Vietnam Veterans of America. Feldman fed O'Brien contacts and position papers.[65] In June 1972, he gave the young reporter a lead about an exodus of officers among the faculty at the U.S. Military Academy who were leaving the army, many over the war. O'Brien didn't leap on it. A week later, he read Hersh's June 25 *New York Times* front-page headline: "33 Teachers at West Point Leave Army in 18 Months."

O'Brien developed a handful of other go-to sources: Forrest "Rusty" Lindley, an ex–Green Beret and VVAW member; Jim Mayer at the VA, the former head of the National Association of Collegiate Veterans; Arthur ("Art" or "Artie") Egendorf, a veteran and psychologist; and Bobby Muller, Vietnam Veterans of America's future founder. Every now and again, O'Brien called on friends from Alpha Company for a quote. Most of his sources were onetime interviews, usually over the phone, or sources drawn from studies, reports, or other news items.

O'Brien wrote about the global trafficking of narcotics from places such as Việt Nam. "Targets of Political Appeals" recognized that some efforts in the name of veterans (of all wars) amounted to little more than political posturing during a presidential campaign year. It was absurd: "Different wars, different memories. Veterans are not a homogenous group, not in terms of age, not in terms of re-entry into society, not in terms of their perceptions of the rightness or wrongness of their wars."[66] The contrast between the GI "optimism" at the Battle of St. Vith during World War II and the pessimism of the GI in Việt Nam O'Brien wrote into the memoir he was revising for publication that very summer. "What's this place called?" another soldier asks.

"Tell them St. Vith," O'Brien says he said.

"What? That's the name of this fucking place? [. . .] What's the difference, huh? You say St. Vith. I guess that's it. I'll never remember."[67]

O'Brien reported on the rift in VVAW between those committed to its original purpose and the new leadership, accused of allowing the organization to become another organ of staple leftist causes.[68] Several of O'Brien's 1972 *Post* stories focused on the presidential campaign. He wrote about turnout in the primaries by the newly enfranchised student voters as well as the Federal Communication Commission's decision to permit Georgia Senate candidate and white supremacist J. B. Stoner's racist language in television ads.[69] His biggest election assignment was the campaign of the Democratic vice presidential candidate, Sargent Shriver. The brother-in-law of the late John F. Kennedy, the progressive Shriver had been an influential and effective government official and ally but had never held elected office. O'Brien traveled with Shriver while the experienced Bill Greider, who had written about the Calley trial, followed McGovern.

On the campaign trail, Greider invited O'Brien to a poker game in another reporter's hotel room. The cards and alcohol made their rounds until three in the morning. The game probably took place late on August 21 in Austin, Texas, the night before McGovern and Shriver helicoptered to Lyndon Johnson's ranch to receive his endorsement. It was the only time the running mates appeared together during O'Brien's time on the trail. If so, it was O'Brien's first or second night with Shriver. After the meeting, Shriver flew to Dallas for an event O'Brien covered.[70]

That friendly, ruthless all-night poker game captured the journalists' relationship. Rivals and buddies (other than O'Brien the greenhorn), they competed for stories but also swapped yarns and information. They were similarly friendly partners with and suspicious antagonists toward the campaign staffers. As with much of O'Brien's time at the *Post*, he felt ridiculously young and ignorant. More than once he had to "gut it up" to ask of the reporter beside him who they were being briefed by. Frequently he couldn't work up the nerve to ask a question before someone else asked it or the conversation had moved on. Shriver's aide, Mike Barnicle, was good-humored and welcoming, yet O'Brien was too terrified to approach him.

After Dallas, O'Brien accompanied the Shriver campaign to Baton Rouge and Atlanta, then on by plane to Cincinnati and Cleveland before finishing at the Robert F. Kennedy Memorial Tennis Tournament in the Forest Hills neighborhood of Queens, New York City. He published three articles that week, although he sent regular one- or two-page memos to Greider to incorporate into his reporting. Shriver had just joined the ticket two weeks earlier. O'Brien's stories reveal a disorganized, hopeless campaign.[71]

The "plush and subtly aristocratic" Forest Hills tennis center, O'Brien's last stop, was another world for this kid from small-town Minnesota, "akin to an 18th century sporting tournament for kings and princes, sponsored for the benefit and pleasure of the world's elect and pretty people." O'Brien had never experienced such a display of moneyed, elegant insularity. There was a self-consciousness in it; it certainly made O'Brien self-conscious. The event's "fairy-tale array of famous people" included Shriver and his wife, Eunice; Ethel Kennedy; Senators Ted Kennedy, John Tunney, and Jacob Javits; the *Washington Post* columnist and humorist Art Buchwald; the comedian Alan King; and tennis stars Arthur Ashe and Rosemary Casals.[72] At some point O'Brien made the smallest of small talk with King and with Ashe.

The *Post* piece that ended at Forest Hills was O'Brien's last article for the summer. As with the year before, he contributed a couple of stories as a stringer after he returned to Cambridge. He did not have the chance to write about one of the biggest stories of the summer of 1972—one of the biggest stories of American presidential history—even though he was the *Post*'s first brush with it, namely, the break-in at the Watergate Office Building, orchestrated by the Committee to Re-elect the President, for the purpose of bugging the Democratic National Committee headquarters.

The security guard called the police just before 2:00 a.m. on Saturday, June 17. O'Brien, on call in the office, was dispatched to check out the break-in that no one suspected was anything more than a run-of-the-mill burglary. When O'Brien arrived, there were some police cars and a few reporters. He and the others stood around the lobby waiting for something to happen.

Eventually the police came down, carrying out the DNC office door that the crooks had jimmied open. The lollygagging reporters chased after it, the first lead they had. O'Brien sprinted for the lobby door, hands outstretched to push it open, only to crash through the identical plate glass window beside it—the security log suggests he smashed into an inward-swinging glass door. The glass cut up his hands and arms. A girl working in the building helped wipe the blood and put on Band-Aids. They went on a date that night.

O'Brien's immediate worry was whether the *Post* would have to pay for the damage. Once his editors fathomed the potential significance of the break-in, the big guns swept it. The byline went to Alfred Lewis. The long list of contributing reporters includes the two who picked up the story and took it all the way to the White House, Bob Woodward and Carl Bernstein. O'Brien's name falls last in the list.[73]

The day of the break-in, besides the guards and officers, O'Brien's is the only name to appear in the foundational document of the scandal that brought down a president and exacerbated a nation's political cynicism, the security guard's notes: "At 4:47 Tim OBrien [*sic*]. Reporter with the Wash. Post ID #413 walked in to [*sic*] lobby door breaking glass. He was not hurt. Reported it to maintenance."[74]

◊   ◊   ◊

O'Brien owed the final draft of "Pop Smoke" to his publisher two days earlier, on June 15, 1972. There's no evidence that he missed this deadline.

The last U.S. ground combat troops flew out of Da Nang on August 11. Nine days later, *The Washington Post* printed "The Enemy at My Khe," a version of the chapter that O'Brien's published memoir will call "July." The book had a new title, "Fire in the Hole."[75] The phrase is soldier-speak for warning others about an imminent explosion, commonly shouted when chucking a grenade into a tunnel. O'Brien mailed a complete copy of the draft to Erik Hansen for final feedback. Hansen's single-spaced three-page letter proved his worth as O'Brien's reader and editor. His insights ranged from word choice and prose sloppiness to conceptual reflections. Hansen's most consequential advice critiqued O'Brien's thinking of himself as *reporting* the war:

> I just don't think you can merely *report* about yourself. It goes deeper because all sorts of psychological dead-ends and doorways have to be tested in order to make any coherent progress. [. . .] When will yuz guys learn that when it comes down to the big "I" there are no facts! Precisely because it's there that you run up against the dialectic of the inner self and the outer order—and then you've got an angst that ain't no statistic.[76]

O'Brien replaced the verb "report" with "tell war stories" to solve his writer's problem that a grunt can't offer any profound lessons about war. "He can tell war stories," however.[77] Hansen's counsel was pivotal in O'Brien's thinking about making art from life.

Hansen didn't think the new title resonated over the course of the book. By September 11, O'Brien had incorporated nearly all of Hansen's suggestions into the galleys—the last version before publication—and added revisions of his own. To address Hansen's worry about the new title, he added the chapter "Nights." The production team considered the changes "extensive" and mostly "unnecessary," noting that O'Brien would be charged for "all costs above 10% of our composition expense."[78] O'Brien didn't care. The pattern for all his books was set, as his sense of perfectionism drove him to revise, revise, revise, until the very end—and then revise again, afterward, for future printings.

"It's done," O'Brien wrote in a letter postmarked on his twenty-sixth birthday. "I'd hoped," he confessed to Hansen, "to have the book do my remembering for me, get it out of my dreams, but it's not worked. The other night, Ann told me, I woke up next to her, having said in my sleep: 'The tracks, get off the tracks,'" meaning M113 armored personnel carriers, the vehicles that had crushed limbs and drowned Rodger McElhaney when they backed up under fire in three-foot-deep muddy water.[79] The book might not have instantly purged his dreams, but it did liberate him from the need to shackle his later fiction too closely to literal experience.

"Fire in the Hole" had to go because of its similarity to Frances Fitz-Gerald's *Fire in the Lake: The Vietnamese and the Americans in Vietnam.* FitzGerald's book came out the month after O'Brien had proposed his new title and was already on the *New York Times* bestseller list, on its way to a Pulitzer Prize and a National Book Award.[80] O'Brien proposed "The Spirit of the Bayonet," which would have misrepresented O'Brien's reluctant soldiering self. He also thought about returning to the original title, "Pop Smoke," or using the chapter title "Step Lightly," both having the advantage of brevity, a packed punch like *Bleak House* or *Moby-Dick.*[81] Lawrence had been pressing for an explanatory subtitle, and O'Brien toyed with nearly a dozen. The final title's length exploded the possibility of a subtitle. *If I Die in a Combat Zone, Box Me Up and Ship Me Home* was settled on by October 19.[82]

O'Brien sent Lawrence lists of people to whom to send advance and review copies. Beyond prominent names associated with the war, such as John Kerry, Joan Baez, Daniel Ellsberg, and Gloria Emerson, O'Brien asked that copies be sent to Norman Mailer and Tom Wolfe because they wrote "personalized journalism" similar to what O'Brien understood he was doing.[83] That O'Brien knew about these participant-observer creative works of new journalism is one testament to his postwar literary self-education. He also discovered George Orwell's essays, "gems of lucidity. Unsentimental backward looks. Vicious, to-the-heart-criticism. He's a master of the essay, a form I like because it is (a) short (b) true (c) not artificial (d) something like brilliant conversation, if done properly."[84] Although he discovered Orwell's essays after completing the bulk of *If I Die in a Combat Zone*, what he saw in them matched what he sought to accomplish in his essay-chapters.

In February 1973, O'Brien sent along a list of review copy destinations with introductory language for Lawrence to use with each, and he created a mailing list of between eight hundred and one thousand names.[85] He wrote and rewrote jacket copy and other promotional material. As fast as the reviews came in, he excitedly sent copies to Lawrence and mined them for blurbs for future printings, a practice he continued throughout his career. Inevitably, he sent more than the publisher could accommodate (he considerately prioritized them for Lawrence).[86] When he learned of a market whose bookstores didn't carry the memoir, he fired off a letter. He arranged for his own readings and coordinated with the Delacorte publicity team to blitz the Twin Cities and Sioux Falls region with TV, radio, and newspaper interviews.[87] In bookstore-less Worthington, O'Brien organized to have the *Daily Globe* offices sell the book. He wanted more Boston exposure.[88] He wanted copies sent to the Military History Book Club to consider selling it to club members. Back in Washington in August 1973, he pushed Lawrence for a *Post* ad buy and TV and radio appearances.[89]

"As you can see," O'Brien wrote Lawrence in April 1973, "I want very much to help in any way I can to make this book a healthy, if not block-busting, enterprise for you."[90] All this for a book that only moderately satisfied him. The accumulating positive notices could only have validated his calling to write. He was eager. His confidence and ambition were growing.

15

COMBAT CODA

If I Die in a Combat Zone,
Box Me Up and Ship Me Home

Tim O'Brien's war memoir, published three years after his return, ends with O'Brien on the flight home from Fort Lewis–McChord to Minneapolis–St. Paul.

It's a perfect ending, with O'Brien being hurtled into an unsure future, back to a place and to people now both familiar and strange, as he is to them, as he awkwardly changes out of his Class A uniform into civies in the tiny plastic bathroom. Except for the shoes. He'll need them, as he did his boots in the war, to just keep walking. The oddness of putting them on for the very first time in basic training lingers in the oddness of wearing them off the plane.

When O'Brien completed drafting the book in 1972, the war was itself still up in the air. It hadn't ended, not for Việt Nam, not even yet for the United States. The memoir couldn't carry inside it the knowledge of what later happened. For the published book's readers in 1973, images of POWs reuniting with their families on airfield tarmac; images two years later of the last American helicopter leaving the embassy rooftop in Sài Gòn, leaving people behind; images of soldiers and sailors pushing helicopters off ship decks to tilt and bob on the surface before sinking into the depths . . . these images could not stare out from the image of a young man changing clothes in a cramped airplane bathroom.

O'Brien explained his ending in a letter postmarked on his twenty-sixth birthday to Erik Hansen, the book's first reader and editor:

> I like it, one of the best pieces of evocative writing I've done. The plane, you'll remember, does not land. It ends up there, five hundred feet in the air, dawn-gray outside. Which, I guess, is how it did end—non-ending, for that is where I would be if I were to be anywhere when I die. Utter aloneness, Erik. Warmness against the Minnesota March chill, looking down and waiting, thinking back, sort of knowing I'm happy to have it done.[1]

The movement from certain uncertainty to literal mortality is unexpected. It acknowledges how he might have returned—in a body bag in a plain military casket in a cargo hold—while teasing with a metaphor that isn't quite a metaphor, on the verge of fantasizing about total finality beyond the simple and understandable desire to be left alone.

As the young Ernest Hemingway started writing at *The Kansas City Star* and the *Toronto Star*, the young Tim O'Brien learned writing dateline reportage for *The Washington Post*. Nonfiction reportage ipso facto tells its readers, *you weren't there*, whereas these budding artists strove for the *being there* effect. The harder a text locates and dates itself in the real world, the more it walls off its elsewhere, elsetime readers. To immerse the reader in its world and its characters' lives, the opening line of Hemingway's *A Farewell to Arms* defies the journalistic dictum of establishing who, what, when, and where: "In the late summer of that year we lived in a house in a village that looked across the river and the plain to the mountains."[2] *If I Die in a Combat Zone* similarly begins in medias res, inside dialogue to boot. The first reviews began the conversation about its fictionality based on its style and effect. *The Philadelphia Inquirer* saw it less as a "personal narrative" or account of the war than "a novel in the first person," while reviews from England called it an "autobiographical novel" and a "semi-fictionalized story."[3]

Nearly every chapter can stand alone and several of them did, as articles, before taking up permanent residence in the memoir. As essays, the chapters focus not on incidents or events chronologically arranged but on elements of and reflections on O'Brien's experiences. The chapter "Ambush," for example, encapsulates the dozens of ambushes he experienced with a representative few. Accounting for every day overseas didn't matter to O'Brien. Delivering a fair impression of his interior life did.

When O'Brien added "Nights" to help bring out the new title, "Fire in the Hole," he offered Hansen this explication:

Dante, the journey to hell and back (remember that Audie Murphy movie?); the negative expletive, watch out, destruction; the fires burning in men's bellies, millions of small fires across the land, GIs come home, bellies filled with lead and hates and guilt and bitterness and despair; the fires burning in our minds, the questions and thoughts and intellecting: go to war? desert? fight in a wrong war? who is brave and who is cowardly and does it matter?; the fires burning in men's memories, charring and ash-heavy, now that it is over and we are home, the foot soldiers, home "to old men's lies," having walked our mile, "eye-deep in hell," but not home innocent and the same, because, as you say, it is not possible to go home barefoot, not from a war like the one we went to, Erik. In practical terms, though, you are right again. The clues that would lead readers to murmur, ah, I get it, are not clear—though they mustn't be obvious. So I added a final chapter to the book, which will go not at the end, but in the first part of the work, breaking up the monotony of having to read straight through "Pro Patria" and "Beginning" and "Under the Mountain" and "Escape." The new chapter will be the fourth, picking up where the first left off ("Days"), using the same technique of lots of dialogue, making it real, and it's titled "Nights," and tries to make some of the fires a little more explicit.[4]

By the time Hansen could have read this letter, Lawrence had already scotched the title because it sounded too much like FitzGerald's *Fire in the Lake*. The new chapter stayed.

Yielding chronological care to aesthetic punch, the chapter "Mori," about the dying North Vietnamese female soldier, falls nearly in the exact middle of the memoir. With its central placement and no indication of when the man who shot her shot her, no mooring in time, the chapter floats among the others. Its spirit seeps into theirs. This complicated moment epitomizes the young men's emotional response to doing their job—killing the enemy. They were young men but still boys, struggling between necessary cruelty and sincere empathy, dealing with their still-adolescent and mid-century attitudes around gender and sex in a war with racist dimensions:

> "She's a pretty woman, pretty for a gook. You don't see many pretty gooks, that's for damn sure."
>
> "Yes. Trouble is, she's shot dead through the wrong place." A dozen GIs hovered over her. [. . .]
>
> "I wish I could help her." The man who shot her knelt down. "Didn't know she was a woman, she just looked like any dink. God, she must hurt. Get the damn flies off her, give her some peace."[5]

It should go without saying that dramatizing sexism and racism doesn't mean a text or its author subscribes to them. The man who shot her gives her Kool-Aid from his canteen and cools her forehead with water. O'Brien fabricated the flies, an overbearing craft decision he came to regret.

Other scenes appear with zero to minimal chronological indicators, such as the incident sometime "[i]n March" when a soldier pelted a blind elderly farmer with a milk carton for no reason. The vignette is its own chapter, with no before or after. The "Step Lightly" chapter, written as a stand-alone essay about the various kinds of mines, doesn't bother with dates. It does not link the breakdown of the man it renames Philip to the deaths of Tom Markunas and Chip Merricks. The events of those horrible two weeks of May in Pinkville, starting the day of O'Brien's wounding, O'Brien spreads throughout the memoir beyond the "My Lai in May" chapter. A 1974 essay for *Penthouse*, "Prisoners of Peace," condenses the time frame to a few days. The essay "Ambush" from 1993 moves the period to April and compresses much of it into a single day to better mirror events from the American Revolution.

All three works combine people into single characters. In *If I Die*, there's "Bates," for example, named after a sailor Bill O'Brien knew in the navy, who stands in for three different soldiers. Composite characters relax the reading experience, presenting fewer names to distinguish and track. They also defang potentially hurtful descriptions of actual people. "Prisoners of Peace" (1974) includes a nonexistent composite soldier named Kansas, "Ambush" (1993) a nonexistent character named Kiowa, a name O'Brien used for a fictional character in *The Things They Carried* three years earlier. The memoir sometimes changes names and details, or drops drafted scenes, to protect people and respect their privacy. O'Brien sometimes disguises his own role. In the first edition, he disguised his unit, calling it "the Fourth Battalion, Twentieth Infantry."[6] O'Brien's understanding of literary nonfiction accords closely with the documentary film tradition, emphasizing faithful expression and the reading experience over fussy and often impossible facticity.

Sometimes O'Brien's nonfiction diverges from chronological verity not for the sake of art and reading ease but from the fallibility of human memory. Writing the memoir in the early 1970s, the fresh veteran snatching bits of time to write late at night in his Harvard dorm room had the articles he had previously written but no access to military documents, sporadic contact with or consolation from his former war comrades, and next to no personal notes. Even during his time in Việt Nam, O'Brien couldn't keep sequences straight. Days and nights, firefights and ambushes and dust-offs, experienced in bleary-eyed exhaustion, blurred together. The articles he wrote in-country sometimes err in their chronicling. In *Going After Cacciato*, Spec. Paul Berlin, manning a guard tower at night, tries to sort out the order of what he's been through the past months. As platoon RTO, company RTO, and battalion clerk, O'Brien knew a mite more about his situation than most of the enlisted infantrymen around him, yet he remained basically a clueless grunt, dropped seemingly willy-nilly, hither and thither and yon, throughout Quảng Ngãi.

Thoroughness clogs. All memoirs are partial in both senses of the word. O'Brien wrote his in something of a rush and wasn't entirely satisfied with it, as he revealed to Hansen—

It is, looking at it now, better than my nightmares about it, worse than my splendid dreams. It is fairly honest, though not completely honest. It is not complete; more can be said about Tim O'Brien and the war; still, it isn't unmanageable. It has a title, now, and I find it acceptable, though not ideal: If I Die in a Combat Zone (Box Me Up and Ship Me Home). You remember the song, of course. This is the first time I've written it down; long, isn't it? If I were to start over, knowing it would be published—which I didn't know or even suspect when I started—I would do it more continuously, the writing; not in bits and pieces; I would try to integrate it more. But, as I say, it is done.[7]

O'Brien told Hansen he was "only one-half to three-quarters satisfied" with the published book, whose reviews he cared about "because I care about IF I DIE, and I care about IF I DIE because I care about writing a bigger, deeper, better book later on, and having it published."[8] At least in that letter, O'Brien regarded the memoir as practice and credential.

That O'Brien called it "fairly honest" does not mean dishonesty or absence of confession, only incompleteness. He had assembled the book hastily, overlooking things a different process might have included. He was also learning that to say one truth at times one must "let the half-truths stand." The fog of war is a milieu of half-truths—to stuff the memoir with everything he could remember, to present a book with the pretense of completeness, risked misrepresenting the swirl of it all. Some memories and details might distract, might spoil the whole. Here's a half-truth he let stand: The memoir doesn't mention that some of the guys grumbled "Philip" had faked the breakdown to get out of the field. Philip's reaction to his friend's death impressed O'Brien as genuine—why muddle his impression, his truth, why diffuse the prose's thrust, with other men's grumbling maybe-truth?

The most confessional part of If I Die in a Combat Zone probably presents to most readers as accusation. O'Brien wrestled with whether and how to depict Lt. White, the platoon leader he thought committed war crimes. But leaving out Mad Mark's misdeeds would have crossed into dishonesty in O'Brien's self-portrayal. If White's actions profoundly marked O'Brien's experiences, so did O'Brien's inactions. That's the confession. He did not report to his commanders or other authorities what he had witnessed. "Writing about it wasn't revenge. It was atonement. Just like writing about war is atonement for having gone to the war in the first place."

The girl with half of her face shot off, the only casualty of that intense firefight, didn't make the memoir despite her importance throughout O'Brien's life. Nor the evening when a monk carried a dead girl inside Alpha Company's perimeter straight up to Lt. White. O'Brien was about seventy-five meters away and couldn't hear the conversation. Later someone told him the monk struggled through the foreign language to make himself understood. *You did this. By being here. Here's what you did.* Perhaps it had happened in mid-May, after Lt. Col. Barnes's death, when Capt. Anderson had been called back to Gator. The monk turned and walked away.

When in late February, March, or early April, where in Việt Nam, did O'Brien ditch the German dictionary he had been hauling around in his rucksack? When did the suppressor-fitted sniper's M16 originally issued to O'Brien get swapped out for a standard M16?

The memoir doesn't include the two nights in March, while O'Brien was still with Third Platoon, when movement tripped the flare in front of his position. SOP required the soldier on guard to blast the claymore mine. The first time, O'Brien's partner couldn't get the safety off, and in no time Lt. White appeared, fixed the mine, and triggered it. Both nights they found a dead mongoose instead of the expected VC.

Does the memoir sufficiently capture the war with the natural world? Mongooses, leeches, mosquitos. The sapping heat and humidity, and the heat casualties. During an ambush in the rain, the poncho hood can't be worn, because the *thap-thap-thapping* blocks out the sounds one needs to hear.

The defoliation operations.

The sheer exhaustion that led to bad command decisions, poor judgment, inexcusable behavior. You aren't supposed to walk on paths, but if the guy you are following does, and you are worn ragged, you do.

The heat injuries, trench foot, and dysentery. In O'Brien's case, the hygiene challenges that years later required significant repairs to his teeth, including a partial denture.

Does the memoir capture the full context of the battalion's military missions? Freshly dug empty graves indicated the probability of imminent attack. *Rice denial, hunter-killer teams, snatch missions*—it certainly misses the disturbing richness of the jargon. Snatch missions sometimes had designated *snatch boxes* where helicopters could drop down and grab a suspicious-looking Vietnamese. A snatched *VCS* (Việt Cộng Suspect) was a *MAM* or *MAF*—military-aged male or female. Unit logs are full of lingo: *millionaires, blue ghosts, sabers.*

Yet rice denial often became food redistribution. Vietnamese received vaccinations and medical care for illnesses, injuries, and birth defects having nothing to do with the war. O'Brien's battalion collected donations to support a nearby orphanage. Plenty of soldiers didn't mind the war but hated the army. It pained BuddyWolf to have missed an Alpha nighttime combat assault to reinforce a CAP being overrun by the NVA. He had been reassigned to LZ Gator with O'Brien and had to follow "the best night of the war" over the radio, "and that pissed me off."[9] O'Brien heard it too, but he would not have shared Wolf's pining.

For every soldier in Capt. Anderson's column who routinely flicked a lighter on a hooch, or tossed furniture outside, there was a soldier who doused the fire and returned the furniture. For every Tim O'Brien from Worthington, Minnesota, with a lifetime of moral injury who detested the war and the army, there's a Mike Kleve from Worthington, Minnesota, with a lifetime of physical impairments who looks back with no complaints or regrets. For every veteran who sees something of their experience reflected in O'Brien's writing—he was hardly the only young man to submit to the war because he didn't discover the courage to say *no*—there's a veteran who finds his depictions unrelatable and deplorable, like the fellow Quảng Ngãi soldier who likened O'Brien to that other "stab-in-the-back" veteran, the filmmaker Oliver Stone. For him, O'Brien's and Stone's art pander to gross, pervasive misconceptions.

O'Brien has never held himself up as a typical soldier or his work as collectively representative. Had the memoir's title not been so long, perhaps it would have included one of the clarifying subtitles Lawrence encouraged him to add, *War Stories of a Young Liberal* or *War Stories of a Part-Time Pacifist*. Although most of O'Brien's Alpha Company veteran buddies disagree with his politics, there's consensus about the facts on the ground. And there's love.

Early on O'Brien recognized the "Tim O'Brien" narrating persona of

If I Die in a Combat Zone, Box Me Up and Ship Me Home as just that. A persona. About to transform a handful of stories about a character named Paul Berlin into the first draft of *Going After Cacciato*, O'Brien in a letter to Hansen called Berlin "largely the Tim O'Brien of *If I Die*."[10] The schism of one's paper selves will become part of the narrative fabric of *The Things They Carried*, a work of fiction O'Brien, ever the novelist, believes expresses his war far better than the only "fairly honest" memoir did or any nonfiction could.

What was it about Quảng Ngãi province, 1969–1970?

Tracy Kidder served as a junior intelligence officer at the brigade headquarters on LZ Bayonet. The end of his tour overlapped the beginning of O'Brien's. In *My Detachment*, Kidder writes about when his team located the Việt Cộng 48th Main Force Battalion at the beginning of Operation Russell Beach—his report steered the action on the Batangan Peninsula that O'Brien's battalion undertook the month before O'Brien's arrival. After the war, Kidder's nonfiction writing earned him a Pulitzer Prize and a National Book Award, among other honors.

Also stationed at Bayonet was Michael Casey, an enlisted military policeman who investigated Nuoc Mau's burned-down brothel. Casey won the Yale Younger Poets Prize for his 1972 book *Obscenities*, the first of several poetry collections. The book's most famous poem, and probably Casey's most famous poem, is "The LZ Gator Body Collector."

The poet Yusef Komunyakaa, then James Brown, served in the Americal Division, his tour of duty also overlapping with O'Brien's. Based at Chu Lai, he wrote articles for *American* magazine and the division's *Southern Cross* newspaper. *American* contains perhaps Komunyakaa's first published poem, a clunky glorification lyric straight out of the nineteenth century he'd doubtless obliviate if he could.[11] He too became a distinguished writer; his accolades include the Pulitzer Prize and the Wallace Stevens Award. His most famous war poem is the widely anthologized "Facing It," about a veteran's encounter with the Vietnam Veterans Memorial in the nation's capital. The story in "Re-Creating the Scene," another poem from his book of war poetry *Dien Cai Dau*, ends on LZ Gator, a place Komunyakaa might have visited, perhaps passing O'Brien between shacks. Another of the book's poems alludes to Gator as the firebase where "Satchel charges / blew away the commander's bunker."[12] Komunyakaa would have known about the death of Lt. Col. Barnes, a fellow Black GI.

There's also Adelaide "Lady" Borton, who served with the Quaker American Friends Service Committee at a hospital in Quảng Ngãi for two years beginning in 1969. Her well-regarded works include the book *After Sorrow: An American Among the Vietnamese* and *Sensing the Enemy: An American Woman Among the Boat People of Vietnam.*

What was it about Quảng Ngãi province, 1969–1970?

16

LINES OF DEPARTURE (2)

When O'Brien returned to Cambridge from Washington for the fall semester of 1972, he rented an apartment on South Russell Street in Beacon Hill. Ann moved in with him. It was a tiny place with sloped ceilings on an upper floor. For a desk, O'Brien placed an old door across two sawhorses.

He was a teaching assistant again, living mostly off income from Harvard and the GI Bill (about which he felt some guilt). Teaching remained unrewarding and scholarship had lost its sheen. Neither stacked up to the writing dream. On days O'Brien didn't have to be on campus, he sometimes succumbed to his new rocking chair and the television.[1] In the evenings the couple might stroll through a church graveyard, studying the inscriptions; on weekends, knock about Boston or head by rented car, bus, or train to Gloucester, western Massachusetts, or farther afield in New England. He sometimes worried he should be working on the dissertation or his writing, but he was in love, and it was good to get away from the desk.

Lyndon Johnson, the president who had escalated a war he detested, died on January 22, 1973. It troubled O'Brien that everyone seemed to have forgotten the old debates about the war. His article on readjustment for the *Boston Phoenix*, "Surviving in Vietnam and the U.S.A.," appeared the day after Johnson's death. That evening, he and other graduate students enjoyed dinner at Professor Karl Deutsch's home. O'Brien was an intimidated wreck. An émigré from Prague, Deutsch was one of the most prominent political scientists of the era. His *Nationalism and Social Communication*

(1953) had been instrumental in introducing quantitative methods to the field. The gathering unexpectedly ended up in front of the television set watching President Nixon:

> *A ceasefire, internationally supervised, will begin at seven p.m., this Saturday, January 27, Washington time.*
>
> *Within sixty days from this Saturday, all Americans held prisoners of war throughout Indochina will be released. There will be the fullest possible accounting for all of those who are missing in action.*
>
> *During the same sixty-day period, all American forces will be withdrawn from South Vietnam.*
>
> *The people of South Vietnam have been guaranteed the right to determine their own future, without outside interference.*[2]

The American war in Việt Nam was over.

O'Brien walked back alone that crisp Cambridge night. In high school, he had written a history paper about the situation in Việt Nam. He remembered the passage from *The Quiet American* that he had read at Fort Lewis and written about in the soon-to-be-published memoir:

> Greene depicted a French bomber pilot talking with [a British] jour-nalist over a beer. The pilot, responsible for killing faceless Viet-namese in the French war against the Viet Minh, says he is weary of carrying the personal burden of a war that was not right from the outset and which would be ended, sooner or later, on the same terms upon which it could have been terminated years before.[3]

Greene had published his novel eighteen years earlier, and now O'Brien carried with him the personal burden of a war he should never have en-dured. How could one sustain youthful idealism in the face of personal witness to man's unjust cruelty to man since time out of mind?

He thought about "all the fucking dead people." Scenes and faces from the war came back. He felt the "overness" as a kind of "emptiness." He looked for Bob Simpson in the dorms. When Simpson didn't answer O'Brien's knock, O'Brien made his way to his apartment.

O'Brien hadn't yet dropped out of school. His parents pressured him to stay, for the prestige and security of a Harvard PhD. Besides the money, he cherished the freedom to read what he wanted, to tangle over time with an intellectual challenge of his choosing, to write prose he could be proud of, and to set his own work conditions, schedule, and tasks. He loved the long summer break and shorter breaks throughout the academic year. It proved hard to relinquish the old ambition of his prewar self. Those thirteen months of combat aggrandized his sense of Harvard as war's antithesis, the civilized life of ratiocination, self-authorship, and peace.

Yet only literature seemed to him to engage the big questions and how they actually played out in people's lives. Neither academic political science nor journalism sated O'Brien's postwar dream to entwine his life, through words, with the permanent and universal. Heading into and throughout his third year in the graduate program—the first dissertation year—O'Brien did not have plans for another summer at *The Washington Post*. By early summer 1973, *If I Die* was published, he and Ann were engaged, he had landed his first major story publication in *Redbook*, and his first novel was all but under contract.[4]

A New York newspaper strike had delayed the memoir's publication until May. Lawrence didn't want O'Brien's book competing with the resulting review backlog or possibly being sidelined.[5] In Worthington, the *Daily Globe*'s Jim Vance hosted a party at his house following O'Brien's afternoon reading at his beloved Carnegie Library.[6] Erik Hansen drove down from St. Paul to join the celebration. O'Brien spent a couple of days doing interviews in the Twin Cities area.[7] He returned to Boston on the Fourth of July.[8]

Then Dick Harwood, managing editor at the *Washington Post*'s National Desk, called to invite O'Brien to work for a full year as a staff leave replacement. O'Brien suspected he'd be able to stay beyond that year. To Lawrence, he wrote about it as an exciting opportunity; to Hansen, as a joyless detour.[9] He'd be working on the dissertation as well as the novel, which was eventually published as *Northern Lights*. O'Brien signed the book contract on July 25, the day he wrote Lawrence about the *Post* offer.[10] He took the job.

Kathy O'Brien married her first husband the weekend of August 11. The groom fancied himself a rock musician, so they had what O'Brien calls a "hippie" wedding. *Blended* might be a better word. It took place in the historic colonial Old West Church on Cambridge Street in Boston's West End, a minister presided, and the organist played Pachelbel's "Canon" for the processional and "Ode to Joy" for the recessional—but during the ceremony two of the groom's bandmates, one a guitarist, switched things up by singing the Beatles' "In My Life." While the women in the wedding party wore simple floor-length cotton dresses, Kathy's mostly white with small colored flowers and her bridesmaids in matching gingham, the groomsmen wore loose kurtas, as if channeling the Beatles on their 1968 trip to an ashram in northern India. O'Brien "loathed" the shirt, but Kathy thought he "looked great in it."

O'Brien and Weller married the next weekend. Having moved out of their Cambridge apartment on the way to D.C., they lived for part of that in-between week with Ann's parents in Hagerstown.[11] O'Brien spent the Friday afternoon before the wedding signing copies of *If I Die* at a local bookstore.[12] They held their ceremony outdoors, at 2:00 p.m. on Sunday, August 19, at the Weller Farm outside Hagerstown. As the Worthington high school quarterback, young Greg O'Brien missed both weddings. Erik Hansen flew in from St. Paul to be the best man. Bob Simpson from Harvard was in the wedding party. Two editors from the *Post* attended. Several of the women organizing the food wore Mennonite bonnets.

Tim wore a white suit and dark tie, Ann, her hair down and parted in the middle, an unadorned powder-blue, scoop-necked, short-sleeve, floor-length dress with a sash. The couple stood at the edge of a footbridge over Beaver Creek, the minister on the bridge facing them.

"It is fitting that a marriage should begin on the edge of a bridge," began Rev. Bartow Harris, reading words written by O'Brien. The wedding homily turned the bridge ceremony into a predictable metaphor about joining lives, connecting past and future, sustaining husband and wife over waters sometimes troubled, sometimes calm, delivering communication, unity, intimacy. O'Brien asserted the physical truth about bridges: They bring together, but they "do not fuse. Two islands connected by even the strongest bridge do not make a single continent. The parties to this marriage will, even with their love, remain separate creatures, to be judged by what they do separately as well as what they do in concert." *Creatures* is such an O'Brien word.

Then the vows:

"I will be generous, Ann. I will share my time and my energy, which are my most valuable possessions."

"I will be kind, Tim. I will be forbearing and patient and I will ask that of you."

"I will be brave and temperate, as best I can be."

"I will be honest and fair and I will ask that of you."

"I will love you."

"I will love you."[13]

O'Brien's words are telling, in cherishing his writing time and in hedging his pledge to be brave and temperate. Ann outright promised kindness, forbearance, patience, honesty, and fairness. The separate-but-together spirit of O'Brien's commitment he'll spin into the language of Jimmy Cross and Martha's uncertain relationship in "The Things They Carried."

Local papers printed an article that devoted far more column inches to the young writer of a new war memoir than to the wedding, much less to the bride's separate self. The title one paper gave the article, while referring to World War II and the war in Việt Nam, unintentionally tainted the groom's journey from combat to matrimony: "Tim O'Brien: He 'Grew Out of One War into Another.'" This article preserved the ceremony quoted above. The article first appeared the day before the wedding, using the future tense: *will be read, will exchange*. In other words, O'Brien provided his sermon script in advance to the reporter who interviewed him. He'd gotten carried away with his eager book promotion.

Around the time O'Brien had asked Ann to marry him, he wrote the story "Claudia Mae's Wedding Day." He had sent the nuptial news to Hansen on April 26, 1973, and in the same letter mentioned working on stories, "a new and fun pastime."[14] This line records O'Brien's earliest postwar efforts at fiction. He had made the turn. On May 15, he passed along the acceptance news from *Redbook* for his "competent [. . .] tale about a rained-out wedding." O'Brien liked the story's humor and dialogue but asked Hansen not to judge him for this "literary doodling."[15]

"Claudia Mae's Wedding Day" appeared in the October 1973 issue, which arrived in mailboxes in September, a few weeks after the O'Brien wedding. In addition to its comic send-up of civilians' attempts to sympathize with the returned-from-the-war-yesterday groom, the story stays smartly open-ended about the veteran's and the couple's futures. The rain won't relent. Everyone agrees to move the ceremony indoors, in front of the fireplace, until Robert troops outside to the familiarity of rain and woods:

> He stood at attention, military style. His spit-shined shoes were in four inches of water. He smelled the forest. Water soaked into rotting, fallen timber, soaked into the forest floor. Little salamanders crawled about in the water. The rain was steady. Robert sang, "Here comes the bride. Dum-dum-dee-dum. Dum-dum-dee-dum. Dum-dum-dee-dum-da-da-dum-dum-dee-dum."[16]

The wedding party scrambles out to him. The couple marries in the downpour.

The story wraps up less than two hundred words later, the traditional music and dancing replaced by Claudia Mae's father playing his *Victory at Sea* album. She doesn't know the first thing about her husband's war. The true knot tied is between the marital and the martial. "Let's have three cheers for the groom! Three cheers for the U.S. Army," a man ejaculates beforehand, and afterward, as guests race to cottage and car, sings "As the Caissons Go Rolling Along," the old artillery march. All afternoon the man's wife helps herself, squeezing and kissing the uniformed Robert, his body at once cannon fodder and society fodder as it always had been. Robert was a sergeant in the 1st of the 46th, the sister battalion to Sgt. O'Brien's 5th of the 46th. The point wasn't to write a kind of alternative autobiography, but to have the language roll off the pen, no research required, the language unstilted.

From submission to acceptance happened quite fast. Anne Mollegen Smith picked the story up from the slush pile, a direct submission mailed in by an unknown writer. Titled "Dum-Dum-Dee-Dum," the story made her chuckle loud enough for another editor walking by in the hallway to hear and ask what she was reading. "I just knew that here was talent," Smith remembers. Smith passed the story on to her colleagues, who also liked it. Her boss thought it dragged slightly and asked for O'Brien to cut two pages. He obliged and they bought the story. The entire process took maybe two weeks. *Redbook* bought between twelve and sixteen stories annually from among the thirty-eight thousand to forty thousand unsolicited manuscripts they received by the unpublished and the unknown.

This was the era during which the top women's magazines were literary forces to be reckoned with. The editors believed their subscription-based readership cared about good writing: "*Redbook* began as an all-fiction magazine in 1903 and published five stories and one condensed novel in every issue until the 1970s."[17] Ironically, once women began entering the workplace and establishing themselves as serious professionals, women's magazines began catering to a vision of the stylish, empowered new woman with disposable income of her own. O'Brien's story arrived at the exact right moment. "We were looking for fresh voices to write about the experiences of their generation, to be the mark of distinction for the magazine," Smith recalls, people such as Anne Tyler, Joyce Carol Oates, Robert Olen Butler, Toni Cade Bambara, Leslie Marmon Silko, Ursula K. Le Guin, and Toni Morrison. In those years, the magazine twice won the American Society of Magazine Editors award in the Fiction and Belles Lettres category.

O'Brien's letter acknowledging acceptance was, Smith says, "perfect, humble, thrilled, excited." With his first story submitted to a major fiction outlet sold, his memoir forthcoming, and his marriage upcoming, O'Brien that spring of 1973 must have felt high as a kite.

Kirkus Reviews and the *Times Literary Supplement* called out *If I Die in a Combat Zone* for its youthful intellectual posturing but forgave it because it worked to establish the narrator's unfitness for war. It was a genuine book, both concluded, if not a great one.[18] Positive notices appeared in such national publications as *The New Yorker*, *Playboy*, *The New Republic*, *Publishers Weekly*, *Penthouse*, and *Newsday*, and in newspapers across the country. The *Sunday Times* in London judged the book "outstanding" and "superb."[19] Several reviewers praised the quick pace and readability afforded by the essayistic vignette approach.

In *The Washington Post*, Malcolm Browne compared the memoir to Orwell's *Homage to Catalonia* as a well-written book whose time would come after the present exhaustion with the subject, a "reassuring balm" for fears that America had lost its "good sense, humanity or even sanity."[20] O'Brien valued this praise because Browne had won a Pulitzer for reporting on the war. He had taken the photo of Thích Quảng Đức's self-immolation in Sài Gòn.

O'Brien underlined a couple of passages from Annie Gottlieb's review in *The New York Times*: "Tim O'Brien writes—without either pomposity or embarrassment—with the care and eloquence of someone for whom communication is still a vital and serious possibility, not a narcissistic vestige. It is a beautiful, painful book, arousing pity and fear for the daily realities of a modern disaster."[21] Gottlieb's insights were prescient. Although in his fiction O'Brien would always circle his own life, and would one day invent a fictional Tim O'Brien character, his motive was the deep hope of real communication.

By late May, *If I Die* required a third printing, a surprising, exciting feat.[22] *The New York Times* named it one of its Outstanding Books of the Year, and the American Library Association would choose it as one of thirty-four titles for its annual Best Books for Young Adults.[23] O'Brien's publishers nominated it for a Pulitzer Prize. He knew it wouldn't win but felt flattered and grateful nevertheless.[24]

After the wedding, Tim and Ann O'Brien settled into their Washington apartment on Connecticut Avenue near Chevy Chase, Maryland. She found an office job near the *Post*, so the newlyweds sometimes enjoyed lunch breaks together. His first day was Monday, August 27; his first article (co-written) landed on the front page on September 1.[25]

The pressure, the hours. He was a shy introvert who had to implore strangers for information. "Nor do I like having to write stories that are essentially wrong: wrong in their superficiality, in their unnamed sources, and newspaper like statements of staccato fact."[26] O'Brien cared fiercely about honesty. He couldn't brook the way news reporting achieved it—only as much as column inches allowed, always deferring to sources, and having to give unquestioning credence to all sides in the name of objectivity. Headlines often carried a tagline, *says so-and-so*. To O'Brien the apprentice, reporters were transcribers and quote collectors, not truth seekers. President Nixon's criticisms of the press made outlets like the *Post* extra cautious.

The oil and gas crisis that threatened to upend the economy, exposing the nation's energy dependence upon the Middle East, dominated the next twelve months of O'Brien's professional life. Half of the slightly over 160 articles he wrote dealt with the crisis and related issues. Despite his hard work to get it right, O'Brien felt like an impostor. He had no prior experience or expertise on an extremely complicated industry and its vast economic impact. He especially felt like an impostor discussing the subject on Sunday-morning talk shows.

The crisis reached its peak with the independent truckers' strike that started on February 1, 1974. Soon, as O'Brien would write, "Trying to 'persuade' company and unionized drivers to honor their shutdown, the independent truckers used guns and rocks and knives and threats." And dynamite, boulders, and Molotov cocktails. People were killed, bridges made unusable. A few states called up the National Guard to assist the police in providing armed escorts; "Nixon was on the verge of declaring martial law." Some truckers compared the violence to the guerrilla warfare they'd known in Việt Nam. The strike closed factories, reduced operations, and led to layoffs.[27] A "major food chain began airlifting meat from Chicago to Boston."[28]

After it was over, O'Brien met with some of the primary players among the truckers in D.C. bars and took a ride in a rig to research an article for *Penthouse*. This piece of long-form journalism allowed O'Brien to enliven and humanize the strike:

> He climbs into his big Ford truck, and there inside the cab he shows off his toys: eight different gauges and dials peer out from the dash. Four brake systems. Switches, lights, pedals. An air conditioner. Buttons and levers. A stereo tape recorder and headphones. A citizens-band radio.
>
> Robinson starts the truck and lets the pressure build; then he releases the brakes and the rig hisses and trembles, and he takes it to the road. It is midnight. The truck is primitive inertia. The road comes rolling along at you like hot lava. Speed combines with power, 70,000 pounds of gross weight.
>
> "Like riding a comet," Robinson shouts.
>
> A certain rhythm controls everything—the sway of the truck, fifty-five feet of truck swaying and rocking, rocking and swaying.
>
> "It's the open road," Robinson shouts. "Open road feels good." The

open road seems to explain it all—wagon trains, cowpokes on the Chisholm Trail, the Northwest Passage, the Seven Seas . . . "Feel it?"

Country-and-western music plays . . . "King of the Road" . . . Jim Croce singing about Ol' Speedball Tucker, *got a broom-stick on the throttle* . . . Johnny Cash . . . Del Reeves singing "Truckers' Paradise." And the road flows by, the engine whines like an animal. Robinson feeds it diesel fuel and controls with his arms and wrists.[29]

For O'Brien's fiction, movement is essential. Characters must move; people are bodies in the world. Motion counterpoints the writer's and reader's sitting, sitting, sitting.

O'Brien's boss gave him a belated honeymoon trip the first week of December, sending him to Puerto Rico to report on the National League of Cities' five-day gathering, although he spent more time with the three thousand attendees than with his wife. The few pieces he contributed on the Watergate scandal covered press briefings and the like. Nothing investigative. Once, reporting on Senator Barry Goldwater's comments for a Sunday-morning television talk show, O'Brien misheard Goldwater, resulting in a lead that cites Goldwater as calling Nixon "probably the best President we've had in this century" when Goldwater had given Truman that honor. The front-page article was titled "Goldwater Lauds Nixon as Leader":

> And the stuff hit the fan. The *Post* had to print a correction. [. . .] It was all very embarrassing. Then two or three days later, Ben Bradlee got a letter from Goldwater. He said he'd read the transcript and the syntax was so clouded that maybe he owed me an apology. That's sort of how it went for me in Washington.[30]

O'Brien wrote articles on consumer affairs and news out of the White House and Capitol. Several articles fell under the broad category of civil rights, such as charges of racial bias in employment practices and of a presidential administration that neglected Black Americans. In 1974, O'Brien wrote about the Atlanta murder of Martin Luther King, Jr.'s mother, Alberta Williams King, another front-page story. She was at the church organ when a twenty-three-year-old man opened fire with two handguns as he waged war against Christianity.[31]

In May, O'Brien traveled to Orono, Maine, to conduct interviews about the recent controversial convention of gay New Englanders at the University of Maine, hosted by the campus's new Wilde-Stein Club. The university's approval of the event rocked the state. "'It made the Vietnam and Kent State furor look like fun and games,' says university chancellor Donald R. McNeil. 'For Maine, the homosexual thing went deeper into people's guts . . . We never got as many letters on the Kent State protest as on this Wilde-Stein thing.'" According to O'Brien's article, it was an eventless event. No protests, confrontations, or orgies.[32] He felt slightly awkward only because, as a child of 1950s conservative middle America, he had never been around the openly gay. He didn't want to unintentionally offend. The Stonewall riots that launched the modern gay rights movement had occurred the summer he was in Việt Nam.

O'Brien wrote over a dozen articles for the *Post* about veterans' issues, chiefly the debate over educational benefits and the persistent troubles at the Veterans Administration. He also reported on veterans' planning for Independence Day, the fourth and final day of their July D.C. protest. Two separate groups had rallied in the capital, the Vietnam Veterans Against the War–Winter Soldier Organization (VVAW-WSO), and an upstart organization, the American Veterans Movement (AVM), led by Ron Kovic, the wheelchair-bound veteran who would go on to write the widely read 1976 memoir *Born on the Fourth of July*, later adapted for a 1989 Oliver Stone film of the same name. The VVAW had changed a great deal since its Washington incursion of 1971.

The real story of Dewey Canyon IV, the July 1974 action covered by O'Brien and other *Post* reporters, was the organizational schism. The war over, the VVAW found itself "in disarray," as one historian described it, "torn between the conflicting ambitions of a veterans' self-help group and a revolutionary cadre."[33] O'Brien reported on how Kovic and his supporters felt that the VVAW had abandoned "the veteran whose main concern is not imperialism but a decent job."[34] Kovic's AVM formed a coalition with the Chicano National American GI Forum and the Veterans Office of the National Puerto Rican Forum to stage a Second Bonus March, modeled on the 1932 Bonus March on Washington of homeless World War I veterans, and focused on government funding for veterans' assistance programs. The "bread-and-butter" issues.

O'Brien's article went beyond the groups' philosophical differences to point out the personality conflicts. The anti-war veterans' two former most effective public faces, John Kerry and Ron Kovic, generated a lot of resentment. The two could hardly be more different. Kerry, the Lincolnesque, staid Yalie, strove to work through legislative committees and within the system. Kovic preferred crashing the Republican National Convention in Miami Beach and from his wheelchair on the convention floor shouting down the renominated President Nixon.

O'Brien managed to cast his personal aversion to Kovic as reportage. He quoted an anonymous VVAW member's opinion about Kovic's "massive ego" and cited one of Kovic's comrades as balking a little about Kovic's "bull game." O'Brien's own language is generous in evoking the physicality of the man: "Kovic exudes power. He has a force of personality that strains from his chair." That sentence characterizes Kovic's presence while embodying O'Brien's straining to escape journalistic convention and to contain his dislike.

One exemplar of his craft was the *Post*'s Bill Greider, whom Timothy Crouse in *The Boys on the Bus* describes as the master of the "soft" lead, backing into his stories with a vignette or a piece of "color." His articles "read like letters."[35] Greider, who had written the Mỹ Lai trial coverage O'Brien had so admired, didn't have the time to actively mentor O'Brien. He did serve as a model, however. Here is O'Brien's soft lead into the Second Bonus March piece:

> "Hel, brother!" cries the kid in the bush hat.
>
> He rushes up, that fierce comradeship glowing. He has been drinking or smoking or popping, who knows, and he shakes hands in the new-fangled way, as men used to arm wrestle in taverns. Unspoken in the ritual and in his warm eyes: I know you, we've been through it together, we're alike.
>
> Others emerge from the room where they're planning the July 4 Bonus March. A barechested chap comes out, the well-tanned stump of an arm jutting from his torso. They all look tired, like generals

who have spent the night preparing for battle against a far superior force, having done all they could.

They congregate in the hallway. Unalike as men can be, sharing little more than a war, they go through complicated handshakes, pumping up enthusiasm, talking of coalition and togetherness. "Our army never disbanded," says Angel Almedina, a tough-talking product of his Spanish Harlem barrio.

The first word befuddles. A greeting, a nickname, a typo? The reader doesn't learn a single name until the end of the fourth paragraph. But not the person's role. Where does the scene take place? The writer speculates, admits to not knowing, and quotes the unsaid, the words contained in a gaze. The article dramatizes, not explicates, how the organizers spent more time and energy on their factional rivalry than on their strategy against their actual opponent, the government. That O'Brien's editors allowed him such a lengthy soft lead demonstrates how much he had earned their confidence. It also demonstrates his non-journalistic inclinations.

O'Brien's prose benefited enormously from the eighteen months spread over three years at *The Washington Post*. He learned the clarity, power, and grace gained by concision.[36] He discovered how to ask of each idea, sentence, phrase, word, *Is it essential? Does it enrich?* He let go of his ego about his natural talent; rigorous revision entered his habits. He trained himself to step into the reader's shoes. *Does the opening pull in or put off? How much of what can a reader tolerate? Where does the story needlessly try his or her patience?* The experience went a long way toward curing him of his youthful penchant for long-winded, clause-stuffed decorousness. Direct and parsimonious prose, however, would be a career-long challenge.

With the authority of a published book, O'Brien wrote a couple of non-reportage pieces for the *Post*. "'The Crumbling of Sand Castles'" was one of eight essays marking the tenth anniversary of President Kennedy's death. It appeared alongside essays by Greider and the paper's executive editor, Ben Bradlee. He also reviewed John Sack's *The Man-Eating Machine*. Its argument, O'Brien wrote, is that Americans are mindless cogs carrying out the will of the System, Sack's case studies being soldiers from his war, including William Calley. "Sack's flippant condemnations, cute generalizations, arrogant dismissals of reason—it all disgusts me," scathed O'Brien the pissed-off infantryman.[37] (One never wanted to be on the wrong side of O'Brien's moral line. His denunciations of certainty and absolutism only went so far.) In *The Boston Globe*, O'Brien called Herbert Tillema's *Appeal to Force* a "landmark" study of the United States' decisions on whether to intervene in military conflicts abroad—the book was uncomfortably close to O'Brien's dissertation topic.[38]

O'Brien's most significant freelance work during his year at the *Post* was his contribution to a *Penthouse* series, The Vietnam Veteran. The magazine's publisher, Bob Guccione, was infuriated by the country's mistreatment of Việt Nam veterans.[39] The series' editors worked with retired marine Lt. Col. William Corson. Corson had served in World War II, Korea, and Việt Nam, where he was the founding commander of the Combined Action Program, the "CAP" units of a few marines integrated into a local defense platoon to protect designated communities. The village by the lagoon where Peterson killed himself fishing with a grenade was CAP 142.

Guccione reached out to Corson because of his 1968 book about the war with a self-explanatory title: *The Betrayal*. Corson worked out of D.C. He and O'Brien met for drinks or dinner a few times. The series ran from March 1974 to August 1975, although Guccione's passion resulted in *Penthouse*'s continuing to print pieces about veterans, the war, the VA, and the military for several more years—such as the future National Book Award winner Larry Heinemann's story "Firefight" (October 1975), a version of which formed part of his quasi-autobiographical 1977 novel *Close Quarters*. The series was a 1975 finalist for a National Magazine Award (an "Ellie") in the Reporting Excellence category, losing out to Noël Mostert's reporting on supertankers in two issues of *The New Yorker*.[40]

O'Brien's three contributions to the series included the leadoff article, "Prisoners of Peace." He wrote it in October—two months after his wedding—and though it paid two thousand dollars and promoted his book, O'Brien was weary of writing about the war.[41] The plight of veterans and their causes consumed much of O'Brien's emotional energy at a critical juncture. In the army, O'Brien's identity as a soldier among soldiers perplexed him; out of the army, his identity as a veteran among veterans perplexed him. He did and didn't fit in. The nation and its leaders seemed not to want to be bothered, the whole war a giant fire-and-forget mission. *Are veterans important?* he asks in "Prisoners of Peace." *Do we matter?*[42]

"Prisoners of Peace" covers a lot of ground. It deliberately, angrily, deservedly rambles. Its first word, "We," begins a basic-training scene embodying all trainees at whatever fort during whichever cycle. The essay periodically returns to this collective voice. Other sections are first-person-singular autobiographical accounts dated May 3, 4, and 5, 1969, albeit with an inaccurate compression of time and characters standing in for multiple actual people. Still other sections call on O'Brien the journalist, citing statistics and quoting officials, psychoanalysts, studies, and veterans. O'Brien offers two stories of courage, both about good soldiers who turned against the war, one struggling with an undesirable discharge, a category of "bad paper," the other struggling with paraplegia from a spinal cord severed in combat. O'Brien names this man, Robert "Bobby" Muller, but cagily does not identify him as a VVAW national leader.

There's a montage or kaleidoscope effect achieved by recycling through these tonalities that keeps readers off-kilter, not knowing what's around the corner. Like being in the war:

> The war was a roller-coaster ride. Carnival noises in the background, blinking lights and animal smells, blinding speed, pure motion, carny hawkers screaming in the background, shrill voices, up and down, zoom, swoosh, hang on for dear life, hang on to your hat, hang on to your head. The war rattled us, bucked and squealed. It ran crazy on its track, well-oiled and in high gear. Somewhere off on the sidelines, down below in the crowd, were our families—blurred faces crying for us, cheering for us, taunting us, everyone holding his breath. Clenched fists held up to us. The tears of our mothers, the hard memories of our fathers. The roller coaster went wild and we hung on. Our girlfriends were watching us—fine curled hair, lithe thighs, warm eyes. Our hometowns, our friends, our neighbors. They wanted us to go.[43]

The passage anticipates the story "On the Rainy River," whose protagonist has a similar vision of family and townsfolk and cheerleaders. O'Brien lifted the flight home nearly verbatim from the *Boston Phoenix* essay. Plato shows up. O'Brien paraphrases himself from *If I Die*—"What war comes down to, now that it's over for us, is a batch of war stories." He brings numbers to bear: "In

1946, popular magazines printed over five hundred articles about veterans. In 1972, they printed less than fifty."[44] Kudos to *Penthouse*.

The article also draws on the stereotypes O'Brien had elsewhere decried. The unintegrated, potentially violent loner vets: "Like wolves. A capacity for fierceness. Naturally shy, unsocial. Stalking under the moon. Loners."[45] The worrisome unemployment and drug addiction statistics. His use of the first-person plural seemingly lumps him among those with post-Vietnam syndrome, whose lives he describes with *we*. He cites a VA study determining that 51.6 percent "of recently discharged vets"—"of us," he says—"have readjustment problems."[46]

Claudia Mae's father, O'Brien's fictional World War II veteran who at least tries to connect with his almost son-in-law fresh from Việt Nam, becomes in this article a judgmental, self-righteous jerk who calls Việt Nam veterans "candy-assed" and "softies." Stop whining! Readjust already![47] New knowledge might explain this shifted portrayal as O'Brien learned how the two mainstay veterans' organizations, the Veterans of Foreign Wars and the American Legion, lobbied against extending benefits to their sons and daughters for fear of losing their own slice of the VA pie.

A few printed letters to the editor did tell the veterans to shut up, grow up, and get on with life.[48] Most—to the degree that one can trust *Penthouse*'s curating—responded appreciatively. "I just want to thank *Penthouse* for the first honest article about Vietnam vets. It has helped me and I'll wager thousands like me," wrote one vet. Another: "It's about damn time somebody printed the truth." Yet another suggested the magazine send a gift subscription to President Nixon and the government scrap its next lunar mission in order to fund GI benefits. *Penthouse* published notes from the singer-songwriter and anti-war activist Country Joe McDonald and from Georgia state senator Max Cleland, a Việt Nam veteran, triple amputee, and future head of the VA.[49]

For O'Brien's second piece, *Penthouse* had him interview several veterans separately, its editors then excerpting and combining the transcripts to form a mash-up interview. O'Brien interviewed Corson, two ex-grunts who had lost both their legs, and a vet pursing a Harvard PhD in clinical psychology, Arthur Egendorf, Jr., the author of the same issue's article "The Unstrung Heroes."[50] O'Brien's final piece for the series, "The G.I. Bill: Less than Enough," expanded on his *Post* articles on the fight for benefits, pointing out that "those who need the Bill most—blacks, the educationally disadvantaged, married men with families—are not using it."[51]

Along with the money, visibility, and networking from the series came two new friends, fellow contributors William Crawford Woods and Corinne Browne.[52] Woods had previously worked at *The Washington Post* as a television and rock critic, and now as a freelancer he published reviews and commentary in the paper. His 1970 novel *The Killing Zone* juxtaposed the professional savagery of the American fighting man with a new kind of battlefield leadership driven by computers. A draftee, Spec. 4 Woods was stationed in Japan, working for the army radio station at the Far East Network headquarters (1966–1968). He did news reports and scripted some shows. He felt guilty for living a big-city life. The 249th general military hospital, which received the severely wounded, was next door.

Woods and Browne lived together. Her first book, *Body Shop: Recuperating from Vietnam*, had just come out (1973). *Body Shop* conveys the lives of the amputees at Letterman General Hospital, inside Presidio Park, within sight of the Golden Gate Bridge, as the men recover from their wounds and relearn to function. Browne gets out of the way, letting the veterans be themselves and tell their own stories. Browne took to her veteran friends wholeheartedly, becoming something of a den mother.

Woods and O'Brien hit it off immediately. O'Brien struck the somewhat older man as full of "Midwestern innocence. He's incredibly sweet-natured, forthcoming, and jovial"; O'Brien described Woods as "a full-bearded literati."[53] They must have met sometime between late October and mid-November 1973—on November 22, O'Brien wrote Hansen about *Body Shop*, a book presumably given to him by Woods. The letter discussed it in terms of what he wanted for his novel in progress, *Northern Lights*: "Very real stories: how they lost their legs, the action, the feeling, the memories of pain. [...] No brilliant writing, no gimmicks. But painfully honest, painfully real, and therefore lovely."[54] He almost cried reading Browne's gripping narrative.

Minnesota-born and twice-divorced, Browne fascinated O'Brien:

Corinne about 36. She looks 25; she even seems 25, except for that wise, end-of-innocence quality that sometimes actually flows like blood out of people. But she is full of life, willing to take enormous risks, a fine mother. I feel like an anachronism around her: as if my childhood sweetheart, young and lovely, aged and learned, while I struggled against some horrible straightjacket, never growing up, never able to float gently on time's current.[55]

He alludes to Tolstoy, Flaubert, and Fitzgerald's *The Great Gatsby*. He describes Browne's eyes as "'puddles of a well-aged wine, red,' a novelist might say." O'Brien was not yet mature enough an artist to write "a *bad* novelist might say." Although O'Brien never consciously had Browne in mind when creating any of his women characters, the letter's language of a sweetheart who surpasses the adoring boy-man in independence, vitality, worldliness, and emotional wisdom suggests she struck a chord in O'Brien's imagination. One can't deny the reverberation in some of his female characters.

When O'Brien met Browne, she had already begun researching her next book, *Casualty: A Memoir of Love and War* (1981). The two amputees O'Brien interviewed for the *Penthouse* mash-up, Tim "Woody" Woodville and Mike Tyson, he knew through her. *Body Shop* featured both. Woody, the book's most prominent character, served in O'Brien's battalion and received his wound in February 1971. They must have had a good deal to talk about.

Browne and Woods were O'Brien's connection to interviewees for the July 4, 1974, demonstrations. Kovic and other vets quartered at the Browne and Woods home on Military Road in advance of their occupation of the top floor of the Washington Monument. O'Brien visited the house more than once. Woods remembers weapons and "a real sense of potential violence in the air." Kovic "used to roll his wheelchair to the top of the stairs and launch off into space, sure somebody would catch him, and somebody always did. The vets were so painful and so good to be around. I tried to help one quadriplegic set his head differently . . . and dropped it. I thought I would die of shame but everybody laughed. They were very, very tough." Kovic's crew—including Woods—timed their action such that the photograph of two wheelchair-bound veterans at the monument hit the front page the morning of "Honor Vietnam Veterans Day."[56]

It was the first anniversary of the termination of the U.S. military mission in Việt Nam. Bill Greider's piece about the day brought together three events: President Nixon's appearance at a ceremony at Fort McNair; a poorly attended patriotic luncheon at the Washington Hotel; and, at the Capitol, "hundreds" of veterans "packed together in a Senate hearing room, choking together on their bitterness."[57] O'Brien probably fed information from one of the events to Greider. The opening of his *Penthouse* GI Bill article shortens and rearranges Greider's story. One can practically see O'Brien at the typewriter, looking at a marked-up copy of the *Post* original as he struggles for new language, just the sort of sharing and rewriting that journalists did.

O'Brien's long hours at the *Post* and his other writing aside, Tim and Ann enjoyed their honeymoon year in D.C. Soon after getting married, they bought a car, their first, a sporty red used two-door 1970 MGB GT, and household comforts: "a stereo and a radio and dishes and tons of food and flowers and all the other stuff." O'Brien wrote to Hansen about his "wonderful" wife. "Even-tempered, which I need; the balance of powers." Hansen had returned to Scandinavia, living on Vesterøy, a Norwegian island, where he hoped to finish his novel in a small seaside house. O'Brien envied his situation.[58]

With the luxury of a car, the O'Briens toured the Shenandoah Valley up and down Skyline Drive. They ventured into Appalachia, enjoying the Blue Ridge Mountains. They humored one another, Tim dragging her along as he studied Civil War battlefields and locales, Ann stopping at craft stores and workshops where he waited outside with his cigarettes. Although the MG was fun in the city, it had no power for the mountains and was prone to breakdowns. Those inconveniences added to the youthful romance. The weekend excursions were perfect getaways for O'Brien from the pressure of the newsroom, even as he felt some guilt at leaving his writing desk behind.

If I Die had unexpectedly good sales and more-than-solid reviews. He was making some money with freelance writing. As long as he stayed in school, O'Brien continued to receive GI Bill benefits. Soon Ann's employment would bring money into the household.

O'Brien had learned to leverage previous work and knowledge to create new work. His June 1972 *Washington Post* article on the student vote became the springboard for "The Youth Vote," published in *The New Republic* two months later, and his journalism on veterans and on the trucker strike led to the *Penthouse* articles. *Penthouse* planned to print his piece on the Pentagon's too-generous medal distribution in its November or December 1972 issue, "tentatively entitled 'The Military Medal Racket,'" but did not follow through.[59] Instead, the *Washington Post* ran "Medal Mania: Footnote to a Long War" in its Sunday Outlook section on February 25, 1973.

Playboy's rejection of "Our Fathers' War" was nevertheless encouraging. An assistant fiction editor had given it a "favorable" recommendation, and his boss called it "a well-written and affecting story" with a skillful "quiet handling of the theme" that in the end he found too "understated" and "subtle" for his readers.[60] Sounding much more the old hand than he was, O'Brien was already giving publishing advice to Erik Hansen.

Then there was the first novel. It had been under contract since July 1973, and he had written most of the draft in his off-hours during those twelve months at the *Post*. In April 1974, O'Brien was caught between the "braying donkey" of journalism and the "elusive, sometimes lovely, sometimes nagging woman" of fiction. He worried about where to commit his hours.[61] He still struggled to wrap his head around the possibility of life as a novelist, yet the braying donkey never had much chance.

Returning to Cambridge in September 1974, the O'Briens settled into an apartment at 243 Garden Street. They had sold the MG before leaving Washington. On October 9, O'Brien met the deadline for handing over the completed draft of *Northern Lights*. He and Ann surely celebrated that night, with a nice dinner perhaps. The next day he wrote Hansen:

> Yesterday, around midafternoon, I deposited it in the home of Seymour Lawrence, who of course was not there to utter congratulations, thanks, or words of consolation. As ever, it's the blank blink. A barking dog, two kids and his wife. "Here it is." "What?" "It. The book. *The* book." [...] I might say, now that it's turned in (not finished), that, even as it stands, it is a book I'm proud of.[62]

O'Brien thrilled in the accomplishment. Although he would loiter in the Harvard program a few years more, there was for him no other path forward than writing fiction. The dreaming child was becoming the father of the man.

17

JUVENILIA

During the January interim term of his sophomore year at Macalester, O'Brien dropped out of the debate team's annual tournament road trip after he caught pneumonia. He flew home from Kansas, a bit delirious, and went straight to the hospital, where one day his father thumped down a load of several hefty, time-filling library books. "I love you, Tim." *Did he just say that?* O'Brien thought. *How sick am I?*

> I was struck in that moment by the fact that my father had just done something very difficult and brave. The word "love" had never fit well in my dad's mouth—or mine for that matter. I wanted him to crawl into that hospital bed with me. I wanted him to say it all again. But he didn't and he never would. After a few minutes he gave me a cheery goodbye and moved out of the room.[1]

O'Brien recuperated at home, not returning to campus until after classes began. He passed the time reading those books: Gore Vidal's *Julian*, Margaret Mitchell's *Gone with the Wind*, Herman Wouk's *Marjorie Morningstar*, James Jones's *The Thin Red Line*, three or four others. Bill O'Brien preferred fiction rooted in history "but not historical fiction per se," a taste that influenced O'Brien's interest in novels about people caught up in their historical moment.

The next fall, the semester of his Soapbox column, O'Brien took Roy Swanson's class Modern Novel, the first of his only two literature courses (beyond freshman English), followed by Survey of American Literature the fall of his senior year.

So fortuitous. Swanson only taught at Macalester for two years, O'Brien's sophomore and junior years. He grounded his approach on his expertise in the classics, comparative literature, and philosophy—all of which appealed to O'Brien, who described himself as a political science and philosophy major.[2] As best as anyone remembers, the course covered five novels for sure: Kingsley Amis's *Lucky Jim*, Ernest Hemingway's *A Farewell to Arms*, James Joyce's *Ulysses*, F. Scott Fitzgerald's *The Great Gatsby*, and William Faulkner's *The Sound and the Fury*. In addition to interpretive questions, Swanson devoted attention to how the writers constructed their novels at the sentence level. *Why this turn of phrase? Why this length, pace, rhythm? Why this paragraph break? Why this word?* O'Brien came to understand a work of literature not only as a story in which to lose himself, but also as a built object. As something *he* could build. The word *work* in the term *a work of literature* took on a new dimension.

The course also imparted the necessity of critical discrimination. Swanson opined on works he found lesser than their reputations. He disparaged *The Great Gatsby* for what he considered its easy symbolism. Swanson was a colorful personality. He wore a watch on each wrist, had a clutch of pens sticking out of his pocket, and styled his hair after Elvis Presley even as he dressed conventionally, in suit and tie.

O'Brien; his sister, Kathy; her roommate; and Mike Frederickson formed a study group for the course. Frederickson was a senior. He had initially intended to study political science, but his classes motivated him to switch to English and dream of becoming a writer. The next semester he would win a Rhodes Scholarship; after Oxford, he lived in Canada for about ten years to avoid the war.[3] The study group's biggest challenge was making sense of *Ulysses*. O'Brien remembers relying on Frederickson's intuitive grasp of the novel; Frederickson demurs, attributing O'Brien's understanding of the novel to his persistence and work ethic.

O'Brien credits Swanson with teaching him the potential of fiction and language. Without that course, he might never have imagined his way into writing novels.

When asked about the origins of his writing life, O'Brien usually goes much further back. The Little Golden Book *Busy Timmy*, about all the things little Timmy could do by himself, enamored little Timmy O'Brien of Austin, Minnesota. The character was and wasn't him. It lent him a life outside himself inside the covers of a book.[4]

Around age nine or ten, O'Brien stumbled upon some of his father's articles from the navy, and from that stumbling emerged his conscious desire to become a writer.[5] Just like Dad.

He wrote his first "novel" when he was maybe eleven. On summer days after baseball practice, he often stopped at the old 1905 Carnegie library on the way home. He loved its personality, majestic on the outside, with a hexagonal dome and Ionic columns flanking the entrance, and homey on the inside, with its worn furniture, its ceiling fans, and its smells—the books, the leather, the floor wax, the mustiness. The books themselves were "almost superfluous" to the peacefulness of the place. The reading room for children was in the basement, with short tables surrounded by bookshelves, potted plants on the windowsills, an old springboard wagon in one corner, and an aquarium in the back of the room filled with weedy plants, large snails, and maybe fish.[6] "That old Carnegie library, since demolished, was probably the single seminal influence on my later career."[7] Not excelling at baseball and too small for football, O'Brien turned to reading in the stately bedraggled library.

One of O'Brien's favorite library books was *Larry of Little League*, by Curtis Bishop. Published in 1953 with a ten-year-old protagonist, more or less the time and age O'Brien discovered it, the book had much for him to identify with. Larry is short for his age, his family has no extra money, and he walks to and from afternoon practice. Even small-town Little League politics comes into play, as the boys worry whether coaches' or sponsors' sons have a better shot at making a team. Larry isn't a talented player. A little too determined, he can't relax into his swing (decades later, a golf partner of O'Brien's thought his swing slow and overly deliberate). But Larry is committed, hard-working, spirited, and above all smart. The team wins the league championship without his ever playing on the field. Instead, he spends the season as the third-base coach, reading the game, directing the players, and becoming instrumental in the team's success. The book values hard work, loyalty, sacrifice, and intelligence. The team's beloved coach might have resembled Bill O'Brien in his love of the sport and fondness for telling tall tales about himself, tales told taller and taller until his charges caught on.

O'Brien wrote "Timmy of the Little League" over thirty-some pages in a writing tablet. As with many children trying their hands at fiction, he wrote a pale imitation of a beloved book, a story about a version of himself—with a dose of one-upmanship over the fictional Larry and the real Timmy. Fictional Timmy had mean skills on the diamond that led his team to the league championship, the state championship, and on to Williamsport, Pennsylvania, where it trounced Taiwan to win the world championship.[8] Writing the story gave O'Brien immense pleasure. Making things up was fun, especially an almost-could-be version of himself or someone he could never be, could never have been, except in his imagination.

O'Brien loved sports and sports stories. Games have suspense, drama, and structure. Seasons have suspense, drama, and structure—their episodic continuity, their rhythms, became second nature for O'Brien the writer. He also watched serial films in those days and later commented on how their weekly chapters' double effect of resolution and enticement influenced his books' episodic structures.[9]

Bill O'Brien was at his best and most beloved when telling stories, stories like the one about the man in the moon that often invited the imagined into the known daily world. He gave his son *Busy Timmy* as a birthday present. A board member of that Carnegie library, he was always bringing books home for himself and the family. He was a voracious reader. Ava read a lot, too, but not as much, nor did reading appear to Tim to be as meaningful to her.

In *Dad's Maybe Book*, O'Brien describes watching his dad read, seeing his dad transported away from Worthington to a place of joy and calm—and, temporarily, sobriety. The son doubted even he gave his father such a feeling: "I am seized by a fierce and impossible desire to *become* that book. I want to *be* those words. I want to *be* those pieces of paper. I want my father to look at *me* that way." The downpour of italics here is startling in a book in which O'Brien elsewhere advises his sons against using "gim-micky" italics, except "sparsely and only when other possibilities failed."[10]

As with magic, books provided relief from the tense life of a family defined by the father's alcoholism. Huck Finn was an early hero, an exam-ple of a boy who escapes small-town life.[11] Huck is also a boy who escapes a habitually drunk dad. O'Brien admired his fellow Midwesterner Mark Twain's other famous boyhood tale, *The Adventures of Tom Sawyer*.

In the 1950s, books and the radio still held their own (and then some) with television and movies. O'Brien was "big on *Grimm's Fairy Tales* when [he] was very young."[12] There were always copies of *The Saturday Evening Post* around the O'Brien home, the stories in those pages the only models of contemporary fiction available. "Kiowa Moon," an Alan Le May story serialized in the *Post* in 1957, and later published as *The Unforgiven*, swept O'Brien into its world and inspired his dreams of making such worlds himself.[13] The Hardy Boys and Nancy Drew series and other mystery tales fed his incipient awareness of craft, as he couldn't help but notice their authors manipulating his reading experience. As a teenager, he appreciated the classic Whittaker Chambers translation of Felix Salten's *Bambi: A Life in the Woods.* Joseph Alexander Altsheler's eight-volume The Young Trailers series was formative—he reread it in the mid-1970s. Set in the late eighteenth century, the series tells the story of a teenage boy and his pioneer family during America's expansion into the Midwest.[14] Its coming-of-age story in a time of historical change fits O'Brien's postwar compulsion to write. He probably read his dad's old copies.

One summer Bill assigned him to read five stories of his choosing from a thick book of Ernest Hemingway's stories. Afterward, his dad said, we'll talk about them. O'Brien wasn't old enough—the emotional drama beneath the surface inaction of typical Hemingway stories requires adult maturity, and O'Brien was just a kid. He worried about what he might say to his father about stories in which nothing happened, nothing interesting and certainly nothing exciting, but it didn't matter. His father never came back to have that conversation.

Dad's Maybe Book dates the moment to the summer of 1957 or 1958, when he would have been eleven or twelve, but also to the summer the police showed up and his dad went to Willmar State Hospital, which didn't happen until 1961, when O'Brien was fourteen.[15] The latter seems a more imaginable age for a son to receive a Hemingway reading assignment from his father. That was also the summer of Hemingway's second and final extended hospitalization at the Mayo Clinic in Rochester, the very place that had diagnosed Ava. Minnesotan newspapers carried the news of Hemingway's April 1961 return to the Mayo, reporting the misleading public diagnosis of hypertension. One can't help but wonder if the Hemingway news led Bill O'Brien to introduce the author's work to his son. Bill was at Willmar when Mary Hemingway and a New York friend drove Hemingway away from Rochester on June 26, passing through Worthington that day on the way home to Ketchum, Idaho. "In the flat fields of southwest Minnesota the corn spread out about a foot high for miles," Mary Hemingway wrote in her memoir; "we had wild roses and kinnikinnick, which as children we thought to be Indian tobacco, among the grasses of the roadside and the perfume of new-mown hay sweeping into the car."[16] Perhaps they stopped for lunch at the Gobbler Café downtown. Bill O'Brien was still at Willmar when Ernest Hemingway killed himself on July 2.

O'Brien didn't see it back then, but one of the Hemingway stories he read for his dad, "Cat in the Rain," reflected the father-son relationship—the young husband on the bed, reading books, ignoring his new wife, who is left to stare in the mirror, brushing her hair while hoping for something that would love her back. A cat? A child? O'Brien titled his second memoir *Dad's Maybe Book* because he had dawdled on it for so long that the family took to calling it that, as in *maybe it will be a book someday*. But one can read *Dad's Maybe Book* by Tim O'Brien as *his* dad's maybe book, as if O'Brien has become the book in Bill's lap Timmy longed to be. Maybe all his books are his dad's maybe books. The audience in O'Brien's head while writing has always included his father, a "conspicuous presence" with a "front row seat" alongside dead writers O'Brien never met.

In middle school, O'Brien and a couple of friends produced a little news-paper. Apryl Vance's family owned and ran the *Worthington Daily Globe*, where Barb Griffith's dad oversaw the printing press operations. Jim Vance was Apryl's uncle; Mr. Griffith probably helped mimeograph the kids' pa-per. Did distribution get beyond three households? No copies have survived. O'Brien also wrote a sports column for his junior high paper, *The Gobbler*.[17] From a young age he cared not just about writing but about being read.

Six short stories are preserved with O'Brien's papers at the University of Texas's Ransom Center.

"The Peanut Man" was written for a school assignment—there's a man-uscript version that includes an explication of the story's "meaning" as well as a column-typed shorter, revised version clipped from a paginated source. The unnamed titular character is an old man who sells peanuts for a living in an unnamed metropolis. The handwritten version makes explicit that he knows death is upon him. The printed version adds the old man's resentment of his father for apprenticing him to the beggar's life. In both versions the sun beats mercilessly, expressing the "frustration after frustration of daily life—relentless, meaningless tasks." The old man finds consolation at life's end in this, that despite apparent differences in people's lives, "It's the same with everyone." In death, we are all peanut shells floating away down a stream.

"Let's Make That Water Fall!" is a clever fable set in 1770 in which three white boys, not yet twenty, struggle with a drought. Inspired by the made-up book *The Magic of the Pon-Pon Indians*, the youth costume themselves as Pon-Pons and try a rain dance. Their outfits and their bobbing and leaping are so ridiculous that animals of all sorts—including, in northern Minnesota, a hyena—fall into hysterical laughter. The laughter draws more animals to the scene and spreads to animals across the Minnesotan woods. They laugh so hard they cry. "As dusk fell the tears of over ten thousand animals engulfed all Minnesota. Indeed, even today, at the bottom of each of the state's lakes, lies an uncontrollable bundle of protoplasm attempting to wrestle back tears of laughter, the very tears that *The Magic of the Pon-Pon Indians* predicted so many years ago, the tears that allowed Minnesota to quench its thirst." It's a fascinating story about the absurdity of cultural appropriation that validates the indigenous culture in the very act of being appropriated. It's also a story about the power of books. "Let's Make That Water Fall!" earned O'Brien an A. Woods, water, and protoplasm would return in O'Brien's first novel.

Reminiscent of the beloved war films of his youth, films such as *To Hell and Back* and *Pork Chop Hill*, "A Soldier Can't Die Forever" is a two-page marvel for readers of O'Brien's Vietnam War fiction. Even though the action takes place in World War II, the "good war" of the "greatest generation," the mood foretells the purposelessness and betrayal associated with the war in Việt Nam. "I was lost in [the war], an insignificant, mud-spattered soldier, marching through the swamps of some obscure island," the narrator says. The story's tropical Pacific island locale foretells O'Brien's future of jungle warfare in Southeast Asia:

I didn't know where I was going, save for the presently focused objective. The link between myself and the outcome of the war was non-existent. [. . .]

I became more confused, more utterly lost in a nameless and senseless inertia of motion.

"Why?" I asked myself. "Why?"

Roughly twenty-five years later, in his famous story "The Things They Carried," the actual war veteran would write this:

They marched for the sake of the march. They plodded along slowly, dumbly, leaning forward against the heat, unthinking, all blood and bone, simple grunts, soldiering with their legs, toiling up the hills and down into the paddies and across the rivers and up again and down, just humping, one step and then the next and then another, but no volition, no will, because it was automatic, it was anatomy, and the war was entirely a matter of posture and carriage, the hump was everything, a kind of inertia, a kind of emptiness, a dullness of desire and intellect and conscience and hope and human sensibility.[18]

O'Brien the veteran would write and speak versions of this sentence over and over again. The resurfaced word *inertia* testifies to his younger self's empathetic imagination.

For a child born to the triumphant generation and raised on those 1950s war movies, the young O'Brien creates a narrator with a sharply ambiguous relationship to patriotism.

Yes, my country loved me, for death was wrought day after day by my gun or knife or hand. Oh, how my country loved me!

Here comes the state-paid nurse now. Well, back to my cell until next month.

Indeed, the country loves me. I am their's. [*sic*]

It's hard to read such a passage and not think about how love and country mesh and collide, about the way obligation slides into a kind of bondage, in O'Brien's adult writing. The closing language of the "state-paid nurse" and "cell" evokes not a military hospital but a mental ward, as if that has been the scene all along. Did O'Brien's parents' hospitalizations lurk here?

Written on the same paper, with the same hand and pen, the story "And He Painted a Picture" is another about the world war. It's the least interesting and least well-written of the six. A Minnesotan family of five has its Christmas dinner interrupted by a stranger. The man turns out to have been a Nazi soldier, a POW whom the narrator's father saved from despair. In gratitude to the American soldier and to God, the German painted the nativity scene that hangs in the Minnesotan home's den. He has tracked it down to add the missing element: a smile on Jesus's face. The story reads like it's trying to be a cliché of a Norman Rockwell painting.

O'Brien wrote the other two stories when he was fourteen, on his dad's Equitable Life Assurance Society stationery. "Two Minutes" channels Bill's difficulty adjusting to small-town Minnesota by reversing his and Ava's situation. In the story, Nancy kills herself in her New York apartment because of her failure to adapt to city life from the Indiana farm where she grew up. She moved to the city out of love for the narrator, a young man named Bill. The story changes perspectives rapidly among a third-person narrator describing Nancy's last moments, Bill's rushing to her apartment to save her, and Nancy's last words written in her diary.

The story dances around its true subject, Bill O'Brien, in Nancy's diary:

> I'm in love with a boy named—names. What in the world am I doing thinking about names. Five minutes from now I won't even be alive. Oh well, I still love him.
>
> Before I go I'd better get something straight. Bill (at second thought perhaps names are important) had nothing to do with this, it wasn't his fault at all. I'm just sick of living, sick of this city.

Does Nancy's self-consciousness about naming Bill reveal that O'Brien knew he was writing about his dad? On Bill O'Brien's office letterhead, to boot. Did O'Brien's fourteen-year-old soul suspect that his father contemplated suicide? The story also suggests young O'Brien's sorting out responsibility. The fictional Bill feels tremendous guilt for inducing the move and for arriving at the apartment two minutes too late. But he's not to blame,

Nancy assures the darkness. Whom to blame for Bill O'Brien's depression? Bill? Ava? Bill's disappointment of a son?

O'Brien wrote the story during the period his dad's drinking worsened. He also wrote it at that stage when he was discovering girls. The final archived story, "Tulips," is a lighthearted melodrama about self-consciousness in the face of young love. A high school boy named Tim crushes on a girl and finally brings himself to ask her to homecoming. On their way home from the dance, the car breaks down. It is Minnesota-cold outside. The couple strains to converse before resigning to do what they want to do. The story ends with the kiss, not by describing it, but by having a first-person narrator interrupt the third-person story to offer a doggerel:

> There are tulips in the garden
> Tulips in the park
> But the sweetest tulips of all
> Are the "two lips" that meet in the dark.

It's possible to see Lorna Lou Moeller, the girl who had died of cancer not long after a movie date with Timmy O'Brien, in Londa, the romantic interest in "Tulips." In this reading, Timmy's nervousness about Lorna Lou translates into Tim's about Londa. The Tim of "Tulips" carefully, properly opening the car door for Londa suggests Timmy's proper delivery of tulips to Lorna Lou's front door. *Tulip* will be one of those words from the past that never just means "tulip" for the narrator of *Tomcat in Love*.

The first-person narrator of "Tulips" has been popping into the story all along, in parenthetical commentary on something he's just written, such as when the main character "hops (well at least falls) out of bed and walks (sorry, crawls) to the bathroom." The narrator's intrusions don't bespeak a teen boy's self-consciousness. O'Brien's narrator is more assured. His revisiting his word choices becomes the adult O'Brien's slow writing process, the revising and revising again for the right words, the perfectionism.

The most interesting of the narrator's parentheticals, for readers of *The Things They Carried* with its fictional narrator-character named Tim O'Brien, is this one: "Tim (oh, yes, that's his name) gets out of bed after his mother's third call and his father's first." The first-person narrator nowhere else identifies himself as *Tim*. So *inside* the text the reader learns, from the fictional narrator also inside the text, that the protagonist shares the name of the writer *outside* the text. The impossibility is solvable only if the fictional narrator's comment means his own name is "Tim"—which just happens to be the writer's name.

"Tulips" suggests just how much Timmy O'Brien inhabits *The Things They Carried*. The 1990 book of fiction's narrative nesting reenacts, or replicates, or recovers, the narrative nesting of "Tulips," and in that process, the novelist approaches—at some level achieves—the headspace of the real fourteen-year-old Timmy O'Brien. Which is not so far, after all, from the Timmy O'Brien who wrote "Timmy of the Little League." It's the childhood pleasure of readerly identification with, even confusion with, a story's protagonist, as explored by the child writer. In the last lines of *The Things They Carried*, both forty-three-year-old writers, the one inside and the one outside the text, realize that writing the book has been "Tim trying to save Timmy's life with a story."[19] Tim O'Brien squirreling away to write becomes Timmy O'Brien retreating into himself, reimagining himself and his world, creating other worlds. Serious play. The stories become the basement mirror in front of which Timmy practiced magic.

In hindsight, that Tim O'Brien grew up to become a writer seems a foregone conclusion. He was a bookish kid who dreamed of writing and loved public performance, whether choreographing ice-skating routines, doing magic shows, starring on the debate team, or acting in the school play. As a child, he understood that performance required focused attention and preparation accomplished by virtue of hours upon hours in his own company for an imagined audience. The performance permitted him to do his own thing with other people. He demanded perfection while absorbing the art of impromptu, inventive storytelling, where fact and fiction mix and mingle and dance, from Aunt Nina, David Kanellis, and, mostly, his father.

Once, to a post-reading question about whether he would have become a writer if he hadn't gone to Việt Nam, he guessed so, citing his boyhood dream, the *Busy Timmy* and *Larry of Little League* spin-offs, as well as his college novel, "A Man of Melancholy Disposition." And he even gave Worthington backhanded gratitude—there's a reason, he said, why so many great American writers come out of the monotonous Midwest, where there's nothing to do but read and imagine.[20]

18

A MAN OF MYTHIC REALISM

Northern Lights

I 've been spending time, too much damn time, writing short stories. Back in my Vietnam days I gave story telling a try, and they were awful, really awful," O'Brien wrote Erik Hansen in May 1973. He blamed their "superficiality" on the short story form, restrictive and arbitrary as poetic form, "like a caterpillar that is so entranced at its form that it refuses to grow into anything else." Now he'd written seven or eight "pretty dismal" new stories in preparation for a novel.[1] He was impatient to give the real ambition a go. It was the spring *If I Die* hit the bookstores and he and Ann became engaged.

In addition to "Our Fathers' War" and "Claudia Mae's Wedding Day," that practice season yielded "A Perfect Communion," just over nine double-spaced typescript pages. "He was hungry," the story begins, "and he had been hungry for days, for as long as he remembered, and his friend Harvey Tillema lay under the snow, buried where he'd tumbled and died." The reader already knows how the story ends: "Perry had done all he could, and he ate."[2]

Cannibalism was in the news. In the fall of 1972, Uruguayan Air Force Flight 571 had crashed in the Andes Mountains. Its survivors, which included members of a rugby team, kept alive by eating the dead. Closer to home, Marten Hartwell crashed his bush plane in Canada's Northwest Territories above the Arctic Circle, two passengers dying that first day, the third three weeks later. Hartwell survived by eating off one of the dead. The story broke in early March.[3]

Snow, mountains, and frozen bodies. On May 15, 1973, O'Brien sent a draft of "A Perfect Communion" to Hansen. Paul Perry and Harvey Tillema are close friends, indoor office types seeking "a little communion with nature."[4] The premise of domesticated male ennui and insecurity leading to a disastrous nature survival tale drew from the same cultural well as James Dickey's sensational 1970 backwoods novel *Deliverance*. Dickey's characters even joke about cannibalism. The movie adaptation hit theaters in August 1972. O'Brien read *Deliverance* during his self-apprenticeship years; he had asked Lawrence to send Dickey a proof copy of *If I Die* for a blurb, and Lawrence would compare O'Brien's vision for his first novel to Dickey's book when arguing for an advance.[5] O'Brien's prose reflected his immersion in Hemingway and Faulkner. The story's aberrant May mountain snowstorm, and Perry's nicknaming his best friend (whom he eats) "Rabbit," perhaps nodded to *For Whom the Bell Tolls*—in Hemingway's novel, Robert Jordan falls for a woman he calls "Rabbit" who serves him rabbit stew.

O'Brien told Hansen that he for sure didn't "want to write a novel about cannibalism." Soon after O'Brien sent the story to Hansen, maybe the same day, Sam Lawrence called and asked if he wanted to write a novel.[6] Ten days later, O'Brien sent him "A Perfect Communion" as the climax of a planned novel, along with an outline and a twenty-six-page first chapter, "the best darn thing I've written." By early July it was under contract. Lawrence believed O'Brien was "a rising star."[7] O'Brien titled the proposed novel "A Man of Melancholy Disposition." Although he sometimes wrote pridefully about the work in progress, he approached it as a training exercise.

Thirty-something Paul Milton Perry is "ruthless" out of insecurity and indifference. He wants to be a better, more grateful man. He doesn't know if he loves his wife, but he appreciates her, "durable and lasting, like a good old house." Harvey is Perry's best friend and law partner at their Boston firm. An alcoholic, he has just finished a three-month stay at the Mayo

Clinic, having attempted suicide on his wedding night. Addie, Harvey's wife, has a "homely" face but "a pair of big boobs" and "fine long legs" on a "huge" body that is nevertheless graceful. In a cottage fireplace confession, her companions learn that she poses for nude photographs.

There's a darkly humorous early country-fair scene in which Harvey nearly throws himself off the Ferris wheel he rides with Addie. There's Perry's fascination, part attraction, part repulsion, with Pliney's Pond. There's a couple-swap golf game, which Perry and Addie win.

> Then—in a way I haven't figured out yet—it becomes sack time for Perry and Addie. It will be a long scene. His goal, more or less, is to do something so godawful that he will feel remorse, which is at least a more intense kind of feeling than his perpetual melancholia, his perpetual indifference. But he does not feel remorse. He feels animal pleasure: screwing his friend's huge homely wife is, for Perry, like taking a plunge in Pliney's Pond. Quieting, stilling, deep in primitive elements. But no remorse. The change he seeks just won't come.

The melancholy and betrayal themes have resurfaced from the Prague summer's "A Man of Melancholy Disposition."

Over the long winter the affair continues, while oblivious Harvey slips deeper into his sickness and alcohol. Come spring, Perry decides to help Harvey by taking him on a two-week hiking adventure, starting at the cottage and heading into the wilderness. Harvey gets "healthier, stronger, more certain."[8] But as in a naturalist plot from late-nineteenth-century America, the random and indifferent snowstorm sweeps the story to its grisly end.

O'Brien doesn't remember the cannibalism story at all. While fun to imagine, maybe the idea failed to satisfy O'Brien's abiding interest in moral choice and ambiguity. Maybe he realized that cannibalism was overtaking the 1970s B-movie industry. The realism-sensationalism balance would certainly be a challenge to pull off. Maybe he dashed off the proposal to get the advance money and never seriously considered writing the novel. But the long treatment and his enthusiasm for it seem genuine, and some of it survives in *Northern Lights*.

O'Brien married and started his year at *The Washington Post*. The long, "hectic" hours at the paper and his inexperience made it hard to gain traction on the novel.[9] Shortly after the wedding, the story underwent its first big shift, as he wrote his publisher in September. Paul Perry had become a preacher, the setting moved to northern Minnesota, and Paul and Harvey were now brothers.[10] From Hansen, O'Brien would learn about cross-country skiing and the remote cabin life of the Norwegian wind and wood, which "sounded primitive and fertile."[11]

The letter to Lawrence was the last to mention cannibalism. Over the next three weeks, Harvey becomes a veteran and O'Brien discovers the novel's thrust, the rivalry between "philosopher" and "warrior." Paul the introspective softie, contrary to his fundamental nature, yearns to live up to his brother's heroic outdoor manliness.[12] Harvey the veteran misdirects a biographical interpretation—it's Paul's hamstrung effort to master his body and become a wilderness warrior that reflects O'Brien's to be a soldier. Harvey's underdevelopment frustrated O'Brien. The writer hadn't found the person beneath the hard-drinking, foul-mouthed veteran cliché.[13]

A month later, O'Brien worried about the two-hundred-page draft's lack of emotional impact. He wanted depth and action, but he'd stumbled into the pitfalls of telling, not showing, and of writing characters who were little more than ventriloquist dolls. All pensiveness, no pace. At times the letters to Hansen displayed the pompous straining of a young writer: "Man neither battles unhappiness merely through philosophy or merely through grand action" but through both, "responding, searching, thinking and acting, battling blindly, flailing."

Finally, the two women emerge:

> The book has become monopolized by a [...] very aimless, directionless, confusing love story. Christ, I don't understand it myself, and that's very disturbing. Very bad, really. Perry is married. Comfortably. But that spark of love we all want is not there. Well, it is ignited by a girl named Addie. She is a creature of my imagination, but embodies both the rough and refined of a number of women I've

respected. A certain woman: clarity is the word for her. Thoughts linked on a chain. Predictable, but in an unusually decent way, and quite likeable as well as loveable.[14]

Addie, still the object of male rivalry, is now the fetching single girl of the published novel. Paul's wife is now named Grace, to honor Ann O'Brien's kindness, dignity, and patience.

One of O'Brien's New Year's resolutions was "diet and exercise" to steel him to finish the draft, and perhaps to channel Paul Perry's physical-training mindset.[15] By mid-February, the plot stalled even as pages kept coming.[16] The draft climbed to over three hundred pages by month's end with plenty of "malarkey." O'Brien "discovered" Flannery O'Connor: "What she does is what writing is all about."[17] Her example reenergized him.

Ten days later, Harvey was "finally coming into focus" and threatened to "dominate the novel" with the illness brought on by the blizzard— "(Bronchitis, my doctors called it in AIT.)" It wasn't looking good for either brother. Harvey will survive the woods only to "charge again" someday after the book's time frame, and "sooner or later, it will kill him, one way or the other." Paul "suffers doubly," suffers death's inevitable and the knowledge of its meaninglessness.[18]

O'Brien neared the end of the story and the hard business of revising what he'd written, "a lot of which is horseshit." In its meandering plod, O'Brien cared more about sounding good than respecting character and story. The revision ahead also involved "the matter of history and tradition." O'Brien's burst of reassessment had taken advantage of a twelve-day-old strike at the *Post* by reporters, editors, and advertisers. Alas, the strike ended four days later.[19]

One of the elements remaining from the cannibalism material is the forest fear established on the first page of the proposal's drafted first chapter: "Rising steam carried out of the forest tissue odors of growth and bacterial wastes, decaying plant life, dead and living animals, old pine needles." That chapter and the final novel combine scientific language—*photosynthesis, oxygenation, metabolism, protoplasm*—with an atavistic sense of the natural world. Invisible critters are at once "microorganisms" and "ancient animals." Salamanders by "the thousands" parade from their holes to nourish and mate, the salamanders recovered from his summer-abroad novel of the same working title. In *Northern Lights*, Pliney's Pond becomes the locus of Paul's fascination with and repulsion by the swirl of rot and fecundity at the core of biological perpetuation. To this general fear, *Northern Lights* adds O'Brien's memory of nearly drowning at the Fickbohm farm, as Paul nearly drowns at the pond during a sink-or-swim lesson presided over by his father, whom he can never please.

With their mother dead since before either son can remember, the pond functions as a trite symbol of the association of womanhood with Mother Nature and the life cycle, with the fundamental creatureliness of human existence. Paul burdens his wife, Grace, with his womanhood complex. His confusion over what she represents sexually paralyzes him. At the end of the novel, after Paul has faced death in the wilderness, he grows up, accepting domesticity, accepting morality, loving Grace for who she is, and wanting a baby. Paul makes love to the conjunction that is Grace and Pliney's Pond. The heavy-handed conjunction is one instance in which the novel undermines O'Brien's portrayal of real people. The threat of nuclear war symbolized by the dad's bomb shelter suggests the male threat of man-made annihilation that counterpoints the female threat of natural individual death symbolized by Pliney's Pond.

Back in Boston, his career at the *Post* finished, O'Brien handed the completed draft through a cracked-open screen door to Lawrence's wife, Merloyd, on October 9. He had written fifteen pages a day to meet the deadline. His workspace was a wreck, he told Hansen:

> A huge box at my feet is overflowing with mistakes, fury, jumbled phrases, new currents, disregarded brainstorms, a couple dozen coke bottles and at least enough obviously empty Lark packs to grind into bond and print a tobacco stained copy of Ullyses [*sic*]. And since finishing yesterday, I've been a zombie, sitting here staring at what's left of my finger nails, smoking cigarettes, fingering the typewriter, wanting to start over, try again, do better, do something.

O'Brien felt proud in delivering the intended themes and creating characters of "flesh and blood." He chiefly worried whether he had succeeded "in giving the adventure a soul."[20]

The novel had its new title now, taken from Robert W. Service's 1907

ballad "The Cremation of Sam McGee." O'Brien included the last two stan-
zas on the epigraph page up until the galleys, along with the biblical passage
from Revelation that stayed. Sam McGee's burning body keeps the narrator
warm:

> *The Northern Lights have seen queer sights,*
> *But the queerest they ever did see*
> *Was that night on the marge of Lake Lebarge*
> *I cremated Sam McGee.*

There's no documented or recalled reason why O'Brien scrapped his beloved title "A Man of Melancholy Disposition." The sales director probably
insisted. As with the late-arrived title of *If I Die*, O'Brien found it "a bit
difficult to think of the fucking book as titled."

Over the next few weeks, O'Brien met with Dan Wakefield, whom Lawrence had hired to edit the novel. O'Brien reworked it and submitted it for
copyediting in early November.[21] Wakefield received an Eames chair for
remuneration. Having his writers work as editors, with payment in trade,
was Lawrence's standard albeit unusual practice. Kurt Vonnegut had edited Wakefield's 1970 novel *Going All the Way*. Wakefield asked O'Brien to
consider reordering the plot "chronologically—a linear lay-out." O'Brien
obliged, compared the two versions, and agreed to the change for the sake
of character development and momentum.[22]

O'Brien does not recall a nonlinear draft; he doesn't believe it existed.
Letters between O'Brien and Wakefield suggest a structure like that of John
Hersey's 1959 *The War Lover*, which alternates between a B-17's final bombing mission—the Raid chapters—and the preceding five and half months
of its crews' lives—the Tour chapters. Hersey's protagonist, Bo, eventually
learns that romantic love yields to the life principle and embraces tamed domesticity, very much as Paul Perry does. The two novels' warrior characters,
O'Brien's Harvey and Hersey's Marrow, self-destruct.

Too much backstory delayed the dramatic action for over two hundred pages—that anyway was the judgment of Lawrence's sales officer, Ted
Maas.[23] Maas confirmed O'Brien's worry: The adventure story lacked soul,
and the effort to give it soul crippled the adventure story. On December
16, Lawrence told O'Brien to shorten the novel.[24] He then hired a freelance

editor, who passed along possible cuts amounting to 104 pages. That it only took him a week to ditch seventy-five pages conveys the extent of the bloat. "I'm learning I'm learning!" he wrote Lawrence.[25] He sent a gracious note of thanks to the freelancer.[26]

When, a month later, he received the galleys, he shared his joy with Hansen. But he knew the book needed more tightening.[27] *Northern Lights* to this day needs more tightening. In the decades after publication, O'Brien planned to revise away the verbiage and the drag. He eventually relinquished the idea. It wasn't worth the time he had left on earth. But the writing process taught him a great deal. The effort to capture the "starkly beautiful" and "terrifying" woods of northern Minnesota helped him when he set *In the Lake of the Woods* there.[28]

In the spring of 1975, his exuberance propelled him toward the next book. He couldn't wait to subject himself again to the "delicious masochism," the "delicious agony," of his craft.[29]

◊   ◊   ◊

Paul Milton Perry and his wife, Grace, live in Paul and Harvey Perry's childhood home, inherited from their father, the small Minnesota town of Sawmill Landing's fire-and-brimstone preacher of the apocalypse. Paul has a going-nowhere job processing farm loans for the Department of Agriculture. Grace's "vast womanly" and motherly soul "oozed like ripe mud."[30] He takes more pleasure ejaculating insecticide than being in bed with her. The closest husband and wife come to lovemaking is her masturbating him. The melancholic man-boy can't even do that for himself. Paul crushes on Addie, a slender, athletic, free-spirited young woman with "walnut-colored skin" described in animal similes: *like a deer, like a fish.*[31] He's something of a voyeur toward her. Addie flirts back anyway. There's not much else to do in town.

The novel begins on the day Harvey returns from Việt Nam minus one eye, a detail O'Brien reuses from "Our Fathers' War." The war holds zero meaning for the town; the politics and military situation receive no attention. Harvey's constant talk of being elsewhere, Alaska maybe, or Africa, or Boston, Miami, Berlin, or Australia, practically quotes O'Brien's letters to Hansen, the difference being Harvey's quest for action versus O'Brien's longing for solitude. Harvey and Addie become attached. The two couples travel to the Winter Carnival ski races at Grand Marais, where Addie falls hard for a good-looking young Olympic skier. The Perry brothers head home by way of the wilderness, on skis, through a snowstorm. They stay lost for over a hundred pages. Harvey very nearly dies; Paul strikes out alone to save them.

Back in Sawmill Landing, Harvey takes to drinking. Paul quits exercising, regains weight. Addie quits Harvey and lights out for Minneapolis. Paul reconciles himself to starting a family with Grace. They decide to move to Iowa. In six pages of undated typed notes from the novel's composition, O'Brien twice records "shelter" and "obligation" as the source of Paul's melancholic avoidance and eventual contented acceptance.[32] Paul Perry is the first of O'Brien's protagonists rent by the catch-22 that other people constitute both threat and shelter. Society infringes; society saves. In the beginning, Grace's very touch is charged with this dilemma. *Northern Lights* engages the terms of O'Brien's lifelong debate over his service in Việt Nam. The first novel resolves too conveniently, through Grace. In later works, O'Brien crafts more complicated stories of conflicting obligations and competing sanctuaries.

Harvey the veteran, meanwhile, has not changed. He continues to prattle about a life of globe-trotting and wilderness adventure, nothing but escapism and fun, Paul in tow.

"'Doesn't it sound great?' Harvey kept saying. 'Doesn't it?'"[33]

◊   ◊   ◊

In April 1974, still hard at the draft, O'Brien told Hansen about his recent reading: "Eudora Welty's *Losing Battles*, Joy Williams' *State of Grace*, and Hemingway's *The Nick Adams Stories*. Hemingway beat them cold, a one round knockout and he wasn't in good shape, either."[34] Erik Hansen likes to quip that while he wanted to live like Hemingway but write like Fitzgerald, O'Brien wanted to live like Fitzgerald but write like Hemingway.

Northern Light's last line rewrites the last line of *The Sun Also Rises*, "Isn't it pretty to think so?"[35] Paul Perry and Addie's relationship restages Jake Barnes and Brett Ashley's in Hemingway's novel. Jake's war wound precludes his consummating his passion for Brett; Paul's marriage precludes his for Addie. In an early scene, Paul watches Addie dance in a bar among boys from Silver Bay, just as in an early scene Jake watches Brett dance in a Paris bar among a group of gay men. The Olympic skier descends from the young bullfighter for whom Lady Brett Ashley falls—Brett calls herself a "bitch," Addie calls herself a "witch."[36]

What was O'Brien trying to accomplish? In some interviews and in conversation, he has called *Northern Lights* a "spoof" and "parody" of Hemingway.[37] To Hansen he expressed loftier goals. He wanted a novel with soul; he wanted real characters who suffer their own character; he wanted an epic. Yet parodies cast caricatures, not characters. The scene depicting Paul Perry making love to Grace and symbolically to Pliney's Pond, which resembles Hemingway's Robert Jordan making love to Maria and symbolically to the Spanish earth, is too thematically important to be parody (like Jordan, Paul also bears the burden of his father's suicide). No wonder some critics understood the Hemingway moments as ill-advised mimicry. How does a text parody texts it has so much in common with and still take itself seriously?

Enter the supreme high modernist novel, James Joyce's *Ulysses*. O'Brien gives Grace Perry a soliloquy toward the end of Part I that appears to pattern itself on Molly Bloom's famous one at the end of Joyce's grand book— O'Brien alluded to the soliloquy and father-son drama in a letter while working on the copyedited manuscript.[38] O'Brien had his marked-up copy of *Ulysses* from Macalester at his desk while working on *Northern Lights*. In Roy Swanson's class, O'Brien must have read or heard about T. S. Eliot's essay "*Ulysses*, Order, and Myth," the source of the term *mythic method*. For Eliot, by linking Leopold Bloom's story to *The Odyssey*, Joyce instituted a way of dignifying characters' small, contemporary lives by ensconcing them in a time-honored paradigm from mythology.

The 1960s were the heyday of mythic criticism. As the decade wore on, the orderliness of mythic criticism lost its hold to the era's turmoil and to literary theory, feminism, and postmodernism. Professor Swanson admired the poet, classicist, and mythologist Robert Graves, whom he invited to campus in November 1966.[39] Swanson was a trained classicist familiar with Carl Jung's idea of the collective unconscious, the "common psychic substrate of a suprapersonal nature which is present in every one of us."[40] Jung looked to mythology to identify cultural avatars of what he called the archetypal. In literary interpretation, the mythic method became bound up with Jungian archetypal criticism.

The mythic method and mythic criticism appeal to young adults of a literary bent by bringing their childhood interest in the fantastic and the heroic into their maturing lives. It lends a familiar framework to grown-ups' literature and aggrandizes their messy, stumbling, seemingly isolated emergent human journeys. Bringing mythology into their own fiction would elevate a story to collective experience. A shortcut to gravitas.

O'Brien does not remember Graves's lecture, although he took Swanson's Modern Novel class the very semester of Graves's visit. He recalls studying a few of Graves's poems his freshman year, and at one time read the novel *I, Claudius*, though he claims no memory of Graves the mythologist, of either *The White Goddess: A Historical Grammar of Poetic Myth* or the two-volume *Greek Mythology*. According to *Mac Weekly*, Graves's performance intermixed lecture and poetry, focusing on the theme of "woman as the Muse, and the bearer of the love-gift, poetry."[41] The *Mac Weekly* article announcing the talk quotes from *The White Goddess*—or more probably, it quotes Graves from Swanson's recent book, *Heart of Reason: Introductory Essays in Modern-World Humanities* (1963).[42] All this to say that O'Brien's influential English professor subscribed to mythic criticism, which must have seeped, however diluted, into O'Brien.

While O'Brien was working on *Northern Lights*, Hansen was working on "The Inviolate House," bouncing ideas off and soliciting feedback from O'Brien. Hansen had the idea for his novel as early as basic training, where he talked with his new friend about it "up in the second floor barracks of B51, one of those days at the start of it all."[43] Hansen had been struggling with the death of a close friend in a car accident, being drafted, and the chaos that was 1968. That era-changing year reminded him of the Norse gods' overthrow by Christianity a thousand years before. Instead of linking a contemporary human story to a mythic tale, "The Inviolate House" rewrote the myths into an allegory for the contemporary human world.

In one letter to Hansen, O'Brien called Harvey "a Thor figure."[44] But *Northern Lights* had other mythologies in mind. Set in northern Minnesota, where Scandinavian immigrants settled, O'Brien's novel turned to the *Kalevala*, the epic national poem of Finland compiled from oral sources and published by Elias Lönnrot in the nineteenth century. O'Brien borrowed an English translation from the Harvard library along with a more general book on Finnish culture and mythology. Whether O'Brien consulted John Martin Crawford's 1888 translation or W. F. Kirby's 1907 translation, he would have encountered descriptions of Finland as a land of thousands of lakes, marshes, and severe weather, which recalled northern Minnesota.

The poem begins with a creation myth. Ilmatar, the Daughter and Virgin of the Air, "descended into the sea, was tossed about by the winds and waves, modelled the earth, and brought forth the culture-hero Väinämöinen, who swims to shore."[45] O'Brien transplants the story to the Minnesota frontier, to where the brothers' grandfather had immigrated from "a fishing community north of Helsinki." Pehr Peri kicked about "in a dark succession of lumber camps and pine forests" before he "emerged at the age of twenty-two in a camp outside Sawmill Landing." His sudden arrival into this wilderness town resembles Thomas Sutpen's in Faulkner's *Absalom, Absalom!* His young son's existence is never explained, as if the wilderness itself were the boy's mother in a non-Christian patrilineal immaculate conception.[46]

In notes made while writing *Northern Lights*, O'Brien typed the following:

water-mother: unknown, marshy (like Perry's notion of Grace and his own mother and, wow, Pliney's Pond.) "sea of swamps" Water most significant element in Finnish Kalevala. Then fire.[47]

The novel describes Pliney's Pond as "Sea of swamps, mother marsh, womb of man."[48]

Much of Paul's confusion about Grace stems from having been raised without women around by a misogynist father. Their grandfather preached not a message of solace or hope but assured "that things would get worse" in an "apocalypse" of "forest fire, death in the snow, a new Ice Age." The sermons, "more pagan than Christian," played upon the fearful frontier mind. He preached "silent suffering, fortitude."[49] Despite his sermonizing, in 1919 Pehr Peri hanged himself in the church, leaving his son to take the pulpit to continue to preach endurance.

However much Grace represents the Mother Nature of Pliney's Pond, she also encapsulates succoring, civilized domesticity. When a heat storm (a rainless electrical storm) disrupts Harvey's birthday party, while Grace implores retreating indoors, Paul becomes enamored of Addie's elemental wildness. He views her with a racist, misogynist lens inherited from father and grandfather:

> Addie's eyes were black. She was barefoot. Her feet were under her, her legs were dark. The sky crashed. Grace was whispering. He watched Addie. Her cheekbones were high and shining, Asiatic, Indian, primitive, shining, upward looking, and the lighting flashed again, and her hair was long and back over her shoulders without knots or bows or curls.[50]

Besides its elemental elements, the novel gets after mythic timelessness by dodging historical markers. The unfolding contemporary world does not faze Sawmill Landing. The looming nuclear apocalypse is a ready-made for the religious and mythic apocalypse.

Paul Milton Perry's name proclaims the Christian dimension, from John Milton, the seventeenth-century poet of *Paradise Lost*, and St. Paul, blinded on the road to Damascus—the Perry patriarchs preside over Damascus Lutheran Church. The two religions tie the novel together: "In one way, the novel began in the Old Testament (Kalevian in many peculiar ways)," which Perry rejects, "and, in the last half, turned to the New Testament."[51]

That turning is the spiritual movement from only enduring to what another letter declares as "the possibility of change, and salvation, by the means of a backward tracing. To be found, we must be lost. To see, we must be blinded first. And, in our beginning is our ending, as is our end also our beginning."[52] O'Brien invokes the Christian spiritual "Amazing Grace" as well as "Little Gidding," the final poem of T. S. Eliot's *Four Quartets*, a religious sequence completed during World War II.

Psychologically for Paul Perry, the novel begins and ends at Pliney's Pond. "And the end of all our exploring," Eliot's poem declares in its last stanza, "Will be to arrive where we started / And know the place for the first time." *Northern Lights* also communicates the movement from the old gods to the new with the death of Jud Harmor, the novel's seer-like figure intended as a kind of host for the Perry brothers' father's lingering spirit.[53] But the old gods die hard, if at all. Jud's crazed prophecies prove true. Whatever New Testament salvation comes to pass for Paul, his solution appears to involve what Robert Graves, in *The White Goddess*, might describe as a rejection of the "escapism" of asexual, fraternal "Platonic" or "Socratic" love and an embrace of the ancients' understanding "that man's love was properly directed toward women," toward the tripartite goddess "who presided over all acts of generation whatsoever: physical, spiritual, or intellectual."[54] Toward steadfast Grace.

◊   ◊   ◊

Northern Lights was never meant to fit an archetypal pattern exactly but to nod to forces of psychology, biology, and culture coursing in everyone:

> I am writing it as realism. That is because I think it is real—not surface real, but real-real, as the public faces of people are, whatever they hide. We can only guess at what is hidden, and I think a writer is deviant if he maps out the psychology with such planned clarity that it all makes sense; the very idea is that for us humans it doesn't all make sense, try as we may, and our defenses against failure to understand are interesting to me, and important, I think.[55]

The question that dogs: How do you write inscrutability?

Kirkus Reviews' early notice predicted the mixed critical response upon publication: "The very earnestness and clapboard verisimilitude of this first novel, manifested in speech that marks time rather than bringing events and personality to the flood, rescues the heavy-handed symbolism. It's a long, slow trek, but worth going the distance."[56] Symbolism's relationship to verisimilitude was an ongoing concern for O'Brien and Hansen. In November 1973, a year before submitting his first full draft, O'Brien fretted over how to integrate the Paul-Saul story and theme, fearing "that such efforts are tricky, tenuous and easily lost on the reader, even good readers. But to make it unsubtle is to ruin a work of art—like making the Mona Lisa a Glamour Magazine cover girl."[57] O'Brien agreed that the novel's "symbols turn into cymbals that crash too often and too loud."[58] He subscribed to Hemingway's idea that symbols should not be imposed but rather found in realistic details. He was still learning how to do it.

O'Brien's predilection for realism was reinforced by his association with *Ploughshares*, a new literary journal started out of a Cambridge pub by DeWitt Henry and Peter O'Malley. The story "A Man of Melancholy Disposition," excerpted from the novel in progress, appeared in the fall 1974 issue. Henry edited this special issue on realism to demonstrate "how fictional works can sometimes be more truthful than real life,"[59] the idea at the heart of O'Brien's "How to Tell a True War Story." O'Brien wrote "A Man of Melancholy Disposition" in late summer or early fall of 1973. Paul the minister and Grace live in St. Paul. The main action is his witnessing a stillbirth to a woman intending to put the baby up for adoption, her anesthesia-free suffering competing against a severe toothache for his attention. There's no hint of anything mythic. The only remnant in the novel, besides Grace's wanting a baby, is Paul's toothache.[60]

Henry and O'Malley saw *Ploughshares* as spearheading a generational revolt against the establishment. For them, going against the grain meant promoting the realist fiction deemed outmoded by the ruling postmodern pooh-bahs, writers like Donald Barthelme, Thomas Pynchon, and Robert Coover, as well as the critics and academics who acted as gatekeepers. O'Brien joined James Alan McPherson, Richard Yates, Andre Dubus, and other realist writers in that 1974 issue. Sympatico writers guest-edited each issue of *Ploughshares* so that the artists themselves would be the arbiters and curators of value and quality. O'Brien co-edited three issues in the 1970s (spring 1976, fall 1977, winter 1978) and participated in events organized by the *Ploughshares* team. Thus, at the outset of his career, O'Brien found himself in spirited conversation with fellow talented practitioners who shared his dedication to the realist story.

Around the time the *Ploughshares* issue was available in the fall of 1974, O'Brien and Hansen had an exchange about contemporary fiction. A review of Joseph Heller's new novel, *Something Happened*, asserted that theirs was an era "when the most urgent awareness is of the undramatic nature of the individual."[61] O'Brien wasn't having it. He harangued against no-talent writers who've "gone off on some crazy acid trip, thinking that Hunter Thompsonesque foamings matter more than stories, people." Such writers cared more about dazzling with their cleverness than saying anything about, doing something for, real lives:

Absurdist literature—this is what really tees me off—is a pain in the butt. The writers of it are too dumb to know, or too freaked to know, or too plain cowardly to know that real suffering occurs in the world, inner suffering that relates to outer events, and physical suffering that relates to outer events. Drama is about suffering, I submit, and there are as many forms of it as there are human complexities.

O'Brien was hopeful. The writer's moral duty is "to propose solutions and to test them through our imaginations on the characters who suffer." Solutions didn't mean happy endings. "Life is too sad to be absurd," and absurdist literature throws up its hands and doesn't bother to try "to answer the problem of dramatic suffering."[62]

O'Brien listed the writers he thought did their job right: the John Barth of *The Floating Opera*, Joseph Heller, James Jones, Tillie Olsen, the Kurt Vonnegut of *Slaughterhouse-Five*, Bernard Malamud, Fyodor Dostoevsky, Graham Greene, James Joyce. O'Brien's letters talked about the absurdist, not the postmodernist, but those terms weren't clearly distinguished.[63] O'Brien didn't like *Something Happened*, because it committed the fallacy of imitative prose, expressing boredom by being boring. By contrast, O'Brien admired Olsen's story "I Stand Here Ironing" for being compelling despite nothing happening but a woman ironing. Earlier that year, O'Brien had read Olsen's *Yonnondio*, which Lawrence had just published and sent to him. O'Brien found it "magnificent," a "classic," written in "some of the finest prose I have ever read."[64] *Yonnondio* is confrontationally real in its depiction of the awful conditions of 1930s American capitalism even as it achieves the mythopoetic.

Olsen's anger must have touched O'Brien, whose next novel ventured into his war anger. That's one of the weaknesses of *Northern Lights*. It lacks the outrage of moral injury; it lacks O'Brien's personal turmoil and conviction. A month later, in a letter to his high school debate team buddy Gary Melom, he called *Northern Lights* "a traditional kind of novel, which is the kind of novel I believe in."[65] He told Melom about the recent spate of stories he'd written, the stories that would become *Going After Cacciato*—it's as if his war-induced rage and guilt drove him to the experimental nature of the next novel, a rage uncontainable by a "traditional" form. O'Brien never thought of *Going After Cacciato* as postmodern, certainly not if that term aligned with absurdist fiction, not if his understanding of it excluded it from the realist narrative tradition.

Real people, earnest suffering, genuine if imaginative reckoning. Not realism for realism's sake, but for insight's sake. O'Brien occasionally took exception to the term: "Personally, I don't know how any fiction can be labeled as 'real' or even 'realistic,' especially if it is very good fiction."[66] He rejected the term *realism* because some literati denigrated it and because he rejected the potential implication that such work never got below the surface of things.

O'Brien's goal, at least with *Northern Lights*, was to marry the surface real with the real-real. When Hansen suggested that Paul Perry's return to civilization proceeded too slowly, weakening the emotional impact, O'Brien contended that having him zip into town wouldn't be realistic; the pace fit the substance of "gradual epiphanies, no sudden epiphanies," which was his experience of emotional growth. The denouement has substance in "the selling of the house, for instance, which is the act of love and mercy that flows out of the survival of Paul Perry; it is the karma, the act, that finally actualizes, solidifies, his change."[67]

The husband of the couple from St. Paul interested in the Perry home is an artist who paints abstracts: "That abstract business is hard to swallow, I know. It doesn't mean I don't make use of nature. Actually, the idea is to expand on what you see in nature. Extend reality, if you see what I mean."[68] Is one to visualize the landscapes of Salvador Dalí or Yves Tanguy? The couple buys the house, the husband intending to turn the bomb shelter into his studio. Does the novel take the artist seriously for grounding his art in the apocalyptic reality haunting O'Brien's novel, for tethering his imagination to the real; or does it mock him for abstracting the real, for turning an actual, functional bomb shelter into a playpen for nonrepresentational doodling, however clever?

The challenge of expanding or extending reality without forgoing realism would continue throughout Tim O'Brien's career.

If not Dalí or Tanguy, perhaps Henry Breasley?

The later Breasley anyway, the Breasley whose 1963 move to wooded Brittany rejuvenated his art. Breasley's paintings from this period drew heavily on the new locale, one of the old forest's last holdouts, yet had a surrealist effect, too—a strange, impossible blend of the nineteenth-century romantic landscape painter Samuel Palmer with the twentieth-century modernist painter Marc Chagall. Breasley loved to quote the iconography of fifteenth-century Italians such as Pisanello and Uccello. His 1965 masterpiece *Moon-hunt* gained much of its power from the ambiguity of those blatant echoes, both homage and parody, the kind of power that perhaps O'Brien was after in *Northern Lights'* allusions to Hemingway, Joyce, and Faulkner. Breasley also had a soft spot for Arthurian and related legends, and the archetypal ideas of Carl Jung. His work had a suggestive mythic method all its own.

Hidden behind all that the imagery is the personal. A Breasley work from the early 1970s began with a sketch of an indistinct childhood memory that the painting progressively covered. Its erased presence nevertheless grounds the work in a felt human confrontation and imagined solution. Breasley trashed abstract visual art as meaningless, heartless play, an inexcusable, even malignant assault on the artistic tradition. His opinion was akin to O'Brien's opinion of literary absurdism. *Where are the people? Where is the suffering?* Breasley traduced everything he disliked about contemporary art with the phrase *the ebony tower.*

Which is also the title of John Fowles's novella about the fictional Henry Breasley.

In January 1975, O'Brien picked up a copy of *The Ebony Tower*, Fowles's latest book. The first and title story he characterized to Hansen as "a remarkable tale" that urged him "to keep writing short stories." He read it during the same time he was doing the last-minute trimming of *Northern Lights* at Lawrence's insistence; it wasn't an influence so much as an uncanny corroboration. Fowles's story was, he wrote, "a nice little answer to our dialogue over something v. nothing happening, abstraction v. life-reality, or whatever the fuck it was about." In March he wrote that it may be "the best story ever written."[69]

It's easy to see why the story appealed to O'Brien. The time is the present: early 1970s. Fowles's story opposes two ways of being artists and men. David Williams, the contemporary painter and art critic, has traveled to Coët to interview Henry Breasley, the irascible old titan of modernist art. The contest is between David's sterile intellect and Henry's pulsing soul. David

Williams and Paul Perry both flirt with becoming something else, the heroic artist or the wilderness hero, a becoming wrapped up in sexual adven-
turesomeness bucking against conventional marriage. David concludes that
he could never be a great artist because he could never be anything other
than a decent, respectful bloke. The same character that prevents him from
infidelity with one of the young women living with Breasley—"One might,
if one wasn't what one was"—is the same character that prevents him from
originality and immortality in art.[70] Character and imagination have their
limits. As with Paul Perry, David's awareness is the real tragedy.

"I survived," David tells his wife after emerging from the woods of
northern France.

"I'm okay," Paul tells his wife after emerging from the woods of northern Minnesota.[71]

Fowles's story is brilliantly ambiguous about how David and the young
woman decide *not* to fall into bed. It feels to David that the decision happened to him, despite his desire yet befitting and even resulting from his
character. O'Brien knew that feeling all too well from the summer of 1968,
the summer he was drafted. Like David Williams, Tim O'Brien dreaded
social censure. Breasley, a veteran of the Spanish Civil War, uses language
that must have struck a chord: "Too many people die for decency. Tolerance. Keeping their arses clean."[72]

Fowles's man of melancholic disposition resigns himself to a conventional,
unremarkable, emasculated life. O'Brien's, on the other hand, embraces his
domesticated future and discovers his masculinity within it. Just over a year
into his own marriage, O'Brien could hardly have concluded Paul's story
any other way. He dedicated the book to Ann. O'Brien's long letter to Gary
Melom ends with a paragraph about married life and his "terrific" wife. He
wants to buy a home nearly anywhere else—"New Hampshire, or northern
Minnesota, or Vermont, or Arizona, or New Mexico, or Montana, or Old
Mexico, or Ireland (southern, of course), or Idaho, or who knows?"—to buy
a home, to stop moving, to settle down.[73]

19

ENDINGS AND BEGINNINGS

The dissertation sputtered along. In the weeks prior to Christmas 1974, O'Brien flew to New York City to submit his copyedits of *Northern Lights* to Delacorte, attend a sales conference, and meet his agent, Lynn Nesbit. Ann had taken a job at *Sail* magazine.[1] The new year saw O'Brien apply in a rush for National Endowment for the Arts and Massachusetts Arts and Humanities Foundation fellowships to relieve him of the financial need to teach. As he wrote to Sam Lawrence while wrapping up his review of the *Northern Lights* galleys,

> It'll be nice to have the PhD—I don't know exactly why—but I'm pretty sure I don't want to teach politics at Harvard. The aim now is to spend full-time—once the thesis is finished—at pursuing excellence in writing fiction. High time I set myself to such standards, without also trying to be a reporter, article-writer, scholar, and everything else under God's sun.[2]

A few days later he wrote Gary Melom in a similar spirit that the dissertation distracted him from "the real thing." To Melom, another aspiring fiction writer, O'Brien dumped on journalism as a field in which no practitioner "cares about excellence."[3] It was an utterly unfair and immature remark by an amateur novelist for whom literature dwelt in the highest sphere.

By late February 1975, the dissertation had advanced to 115 pages.[4] In early March O'Brien botched an interview before his program's faculty selection committee in a replay of his Rhodes Scholarship interview.[5] He didn't want to teach. His performance was a matter of pride.

On the other side of the world, the Republic of Việt Nam was shattering into nonexistence. The North Vietnamese took the port city of Da Nang, less than ninety miles north of LZ Gator, on March 29. South Việt Nam's second largest city, Da Nang had been where the United States' full military involvement began with the marines' beach landing ten years earlier. Cam Rahn Bay, where Pfc. O'Brien had flown into Việt Nam and Sgt. O'Brien had flown out, fell on April 3. The artillery bombardment of Sài Gòn began on April 29. The next day, the United States abandoned its embassy and NVA tanks crashed over the iron fence into the Independence Palace grounds where the South Vietnamese president had resided and run the government since 1967.

None of O'Brien's surviving letters mention the end of the war. He recalls not feeling much of anything. Sài Gòn's fall had been coming for months. For years.

The very day of Sài Gòn's fall, O'Brien's former platoon leader ended his life in a hotel room outside Scranton, Pennsylvania. After a successful semester in college, drug and alcohol abuse and violence pounced. He appeared to improve after many sessions of inpatient and outpatient mental health treatment. He had taken a job as a cook at a small restaurant. It is easy to imagine him, alone in his room at the Spruce Hotel, following the news of South Việt Nam's dying days. Mad Mark's glory days, Mad Mark's sins, had all been for naught.[6]

As the North Vietnamese won their War of Liberation, the United States began the yearlong celebration of its own independence. On a Wednesday night in April, Tim and Ann joined a crowd of over five hundred at the Boston Public Library for what O'Brien called "an Archibald MacLeish poem-reading shindig," the inaugural event for the city's inaugural bicentennial exhibit *Literary Boston*. The eighty-two-year-old MacLeish was a former Librarian of Congress and one of the most decorated writers around, with three Pulitzers, a National Book Award, a Bollingen Prize, a Tony Award, and soon the Presidential Medal of Freedom. His performance mixed commentary with poetry.[7] O'Brien thought "Night Watch in the City" a "damn nice" poem.

That week he and Ann "took in the parades and music and speeches" in the warm weather, leaving him feeling "like an American, through and through." He didn't care for the "bigotry and violence" of contemporary Boston, but he imagined "it would have been a fine place, say, in the year 1776." He was nostalgic for "a cause to believe in." His faith in citizenship and the public square had slipped.[8]

Back home after a May trip with Ann to Worthington, O'Brien received advance reviews for *Northern Lights*. The *Publishers Weekly* write-up made him giddy. "[I]t was very fucking lovely," he wrote to Hansen. "I couldn't have ordered a more glowing judgment at gunpoint."[9]

Northern Lights came out on August 1.

On August 6, O'Brien traveled to D.C. to research his second *Penthouse* piece. Then, from August 12 to 24, he attended the legendary Bread Loaf Writers' Conference at Middlebury College for the first time, on the nomination of Anne Mollegen Smith at *Redbook*.[10] He had an amazing time thinking about writing and making friends: George Elliott, Seymour Epstein, Hilma Wolitzer, Elizabeth Goodenough, Linda Pastan. Both *If I Die* and *Northern Lights* sold out.[11] The novelist John Irving instantly recognized him as the "shining star" of the hopefuls, a student group that included Tess Gallagher, Marianne Ginger, and Askold Melnyczuk.[12] The Bread Loaf set discovered two sides of Tim O'Brien: the Midwestern middle-class youthful deference, what Irving remembers as an "explorative hesitancy," and the aggressive competitiveness on the tennis court.

O'Brien and Irving hit it off. In the mid-sixties, Irving had wanted to go to Việt Nam, but to his great disappointment, his senior spring he was dismissed from his college's ROTC program upon becoming an expectant father. By the time he met O'Brien, he had come to see this as his good fortune, as by 1968 several friends had died in the war.

O'Brien would return to Bread Loaf nearly every year for the next twenty years. The bucolic mountaintop setting became a homecoming of kindred spirits and a ritual carnival. His second time, a year later, sealed his passion for the conference. "People are important. Period," he wrote Erik Hansen a few days after it ended. It was a needed lesson and tonic for someone who spent his days in practical isolation:

> Two weeks of Bread Loaf, intense as it is, packs in more living, real life, than a year of days in most other settings. And its juxtaposition to the drib-drab of ordinary life makes it all the more wonderful. . . .
>
> You can't write at Bread Loaf, but you can't have true people experience at the typewriter. A classic thing, yes? . . .
>
> People. They're more important than art.[13]

While O'Brien was at Bread Loaf in 1975, Lawrence submitted *Northern Lights* for a new award for first novels.[14] Another Việt Nam veteran, Loyd Little, ended up winning the inaugural PEN/Hemingway award for *Parthian Shot*, his novel about the war.

One novel out in the world, a vision for the next one at hand, the welcome by fellow writers from Bread Loaf into their circle: O'Brien submitted to his calling, trying to catch the fictional Cacciato.

To hear him tell it, and to read some of his letters, he didn't leave the writing desk or reading chair much at all, even for weekends, birthdays, or holidays. He read voraciously—books he understood to be ones he should know; books he learned about in *The New York Review of Books*, *The New York Times Book Review*, *The Boston Globe*, *The Washington Post Book World*, *The Saturday Review*; books friends recommended; books that piqued his interest at bookstores. He copied out passages and sometimes whole stories and poems from writers he admired: F. Scott Fitzgerald, Ernest Hemingway, Irwin Shaw, Flannery O'Connor, Emily Dickinson, Joyce Carol Oates, Robert Frost, Ezra Pound, others. Tillie Olsen, maybe? He was teaching the rhythm of sentences and paragraphs to his fingers. In 1979, he cited Gertrude Stein as a big technical influence.[15] Starting in the 1970s and continuing through most of his career, he kept a book or two of poetry on his bedside table.

He took breaks for golf, a regular afternoon basketball game at Harvard, movies, and the Red Sox. On the golf course, Ann sometimes served as "caddie-advisor."[16] In the early spring of 1975, he readied himself for golf season by setting aside twenty minutes a day to pitching and putting a golf ball around the apartment "onto a make-believe green of bedclothes."[17]

He and Ann traveled about New England as their budget permitted.

They occasionally skied in Vermont, New Hampshire, or Maine, once or twice with Kathy and her husband, with his Harvard friend Bob Simpson and his wife, Kris, with Erik Hansen: "Blazing down out of the mountains, I swear, is as big a thrill as writing down ten pages of good prose, and a separate kind of thrill, one I ain't used to with such a sedentary life."[18] He remembers a trip to Montreal with the Simpsons. And there were trips to be with his family, for Worthington's Memorial Day and Labor Day golf tournaments, for Christmas (more often than to Ann's family in Maryland, at least according to evidence from his letters).

Professional and professional-social life got him out of the apartment for readings and events mostly in Boston, with the rare trip to New York or Washington.[19] These were the big years of his *Ploughshares* work. He also associated with the PEN/New England literary organization. There were occasional meetings followed by a party, often at the home of the writer Anne Bernays, one of the organization's founders. O'Brien remembers the parties she and her husband, the editor and celebrated biographer Justin "Joe" Kaplan, hosted in their Dutch colonial house in Cambridge on Francis Avenue, also known as professors' row. The economist John Kenneth Galbraith, the psychologist Henry Murray, and the cooking personality Julia Child were neighbors. "If there's a writers' community in Boston," the novelist James Carroll wrote after Kaplan's death, Anne and Joe "established it. There was a period of about 15 years when their house was the center of the writing life in Boston. Joe was the pillar, and Anne was the flame."[20]

Kurt Vonnegut, John Updike, and Bernard Malamud were among the attendees. These were mostly male affairs. The O'Briens' apartment at 56 Kirkland was around the corner, an easy walk. Tim never took Ann—for the most part, she didn't join his literary circles. According to Bernays, everyone loved O'Brien. They found him emotionally responsive, sincere, and "unfull of himself," the opposite of certain other writers. O'Brien played a lot of Ping-Pong in the sunroom, as competitive as ever. A few times people suspected he was high. They were probably right. From the seventies into the 1990s, O'Brien occasionally did cocaine, mostly with writer friends, at Bread Loaf and the Joiner Center, for example, once bingeing over three days with the novelist Robert Stone, sometimes but rarely alone. "Everybody around me was doing it." It made him feel "so fucking smart. It makes you a genius!"

For the money and to increase the chance the magazine would consider his fiction, O'Brien wrote a piece on tennis for the men's magazine *Gallery*. The piece started with the autobiographical story from the Forest Hills tennis club during the Shriver campaign before morphing into a punny fictional parody of his readers' expectations of the swinging tennis lifestyle.[21] That's a pattern for a lot of his work, the springboarding from memory into invention, as with for example "On the Rainy River" and *Tomcat in Love*.

Erik Hansen's writing dream occupied a fair amount of O'Brien's attention. In addition to providing feedback, he convinced Lawrence to pay Hansen a little for the editorial help on O'Brien's books. He recommended magazines and journals and agents to Hansen, even sending in Hansen's stories for him when he was living overseas. O'Brien got Lawrence to look at Hansen's novel. He did everything he could from inside the *Ploughshares* editorial process to have the journal take a Hansen story, to no avail.

He was actively promoting *Northern Lights*. The last year he appears to have put in any serious work on the dissertation was 1975. The writing life could no longer be denied. On January 30, 1977, O'Brien called his Harvard adviser to withdraw from the process.[22]

In April, he and Ann took a trip with Bob and Kris Simpson to St. John in the Virgin Islands. They stayed at Gallows Point, a group of resort cottages run by the writer Richard Ellington. Ellington had fought at the Battle of the Bulge, and after the war was the main writer for the radio mystery drama *The Fat Man* as well as the author of the noir novels *Shoot the Works*, *It's a Crime*, *Stone Cold Dead*, *Exit for a Dame*, and *Just Killing Time*. He went by Duke. O'Brien always enjoyed a good mystery novel. Duke's office was in the resort bar, where he held court for whoever stopped by. The resort setting enthralled O'Brien, the "beat of the waves outside our cottage window, the sun, the island's unspoiled hills and water,"[23] as did Duke's storytelling, which perhaps reminded O'Brien of his father's and aunt's gifts at the kitchen table. Surely O'Brien remembered his father's heyday at the Royal Victoria Hotel in Nassau.

Going After Cacciato was all but finished when the O'Briens left for St. John. Three weeks later it was. Two and a half years from the first Paul Berlin story to the final manuscript.

20

OVER THE HILL

Going After Cacciato

At a weeklong symposium on the war in Việt Nam at Macalester in early March 1979, O'Brien admonished the audience, "Don't read war novels for the war part, read them for the art part."[1] Within two weeks, *Going After Cacciato* would be listed as one of the five fiction nominees for the National Book Award.

In the middle of the writing process, O'Brien wrote Erik Hansen about the supreme pleasure of the work, not the result:

> No, it's the doing, the creation, those rare moments when a guy knows he's immediately involved in approximating truth. Afterward, it may seem to have been an illusion, or the truths false, or the effect unsuccessful, but this is in no way to belittle, certainly not to deny, the wonderful fullness of the original act. I believe more than ever that fiction writing is important mainly as an artistic experience; that the experience is as important as the fiction that is written. I believe also, of course, that the better the fiction, the better the experience, the fuller the experience.[2]

Reading O'Brien's letters to Hansen and to Sam Lawrence is as close a thing as this biographer knows to stepping inside the writer's mind.

◊ ◊ ◊

O'Brien completed the first Paul Berlin story in November 1974. Titled "With Respect to the Catholic Church," this draft of more than thirty pages is lost. He'd wrestled with the idea for months and saw in it the basis of a novel, which scared and thrilled him. He told Hansen it was his best work yet.[3] When he finished the story either that day or the next, he wrote Hansen again:

> Spec Four Paul Berlin's solution is that he learns something in this awfully long story; which may emphasize, I hope successfully, what I was saying yesterday about the existence of suffering, the storyteller's obligation to record it accurately, and his greater obligation, if he is to be good, to propose imaginary answers and test them through invention.[4]

He enclosed a copy for Hansen's feedback and sent a copy off to *Playboy.*[5]

By the first week of January 1975, O'Brien had written two more Paul Berlin stories, "Night March" and "Speaking of Courage." A book was emerging.[6] The fourth story, "Going After Cacciato," was underway in February.[7] The real-world genesis was the AWOL episode of Shorty and Smitty, when Pfc. O'Brien mused about their humping all the way to Paris. "What are you going to do?" Baskir and Strauss's *Chance and Circumstance* documents a soldier's remarking about desertion: "Walk through Cambodia?" Actual desertion—*going over the hill*—only happened when a soldier was already out of the country on an R&R or other leave, or in the rare cases when a soldier switched sides or decided to live among the Vietnamese, either peacefully in the countryside or in underground street gangs[8]—as in the case of Nick Chevotarevich, the role played by Christopher Walken in *The Deer Hunter*, out the same year as *Cacciato*.

Redbook accepted "Night March" for its May issue but decided to rename it because the title, according to Anne Smith, "sounded too much in the 'war genre'"—to which O'Brien responded, "Holy Shit! War genre . . .

It is a war story, for Chrissake." After some contentious phone calls, all parties settled on "Where Have You Gone, Charming Billy?"⁹ A week later, having just finished proofreading *Northern Lights*' galleys, O'Brien was eager about a new novel tentatively called "A Man of My Age," to be set "in a warm and green climate" so that he could spend time in the Caribbean "to golf by day and write by night." He was "twenty pages or so" into the writing but was losing his grip on it. What was its import?[10]

For the next week and a half, O'Brien experimented with "The Observation Post," his first story with a first-person narrator. He also tried flipping conventional wisdom by telling more than showing, with the medic Doc Peret analyzing Paul Berlin. The experiment didn't pan out. But for the first time in a letter, O'Brien was thinking concretely about a Paul Berlin story collection, with "The Observation Post" as either "preface" or "epilogue." Fear was the stories' common ground. He wrote the letter with a black eye from a basketball game.[11]

O'Brien was on a roll. A few weeks later he completed three more stories, two "for the Paul Berlin book" and an unknown one done for the sake of not writing about the war.[12] One of the Paul Berlin stories was probably "The Tunnel," which he described as "pretty much straight action and talk and hinting at what happened to the mysterious Lieutenant Gleason." The other one was probably "The Way It Mostly Was."[13]

Tim and Ann spent about two weeks back in Worthington, beginning May 20, where Hansen joined him; his brother, Greg; and his dad for the annual spring golf tournament. O'Brien and Hansen talked for hours about *Northern Lights*, about Hansen's forever-in-progress novel, "The Inviolate House," about Hansen's stories and their publishing prospects, and about the Paul Berlin book, all wrapped up no doubt in more general conversation about the state of American letters and the purpose and possibilities of literature.[14]

By July 15, O'Brien had written two more Paul Berlin stories, "Getting Shot" and "War Stories." In the latter, O'Brien wove together tales from three different characters, "trying to show the repetitiveness of war stories, how the guts of each is similar to the guts of the next." It's probable that over the next several months he reworked some of the material from that lost story into his revisions of "Speaking of Courage." And he'd had his book's vision. The new vision shifted its focus from Paul Berlin to "the pursuit of Cacciato all the fucking way to Paris." The idea struck him in Worthington when Hansen had suggested making the story "Going After Cacciato" the lead chapter. The challenge daunted O'Brien: "Because it would be unrealistic. That word. That word I honor, and which I believe deserves honor. Realism."

He decided to rewrite "The Observation Post" from Paul Berlin's perspective, and he knew he wanted the book to pop seemingly erratically among the zany pursuit stories and the sharp-edged war stories of "what is being escaped." He was halfway through a new story, "Ringside Seats," featuring Cacciato before he hightails it for Paris. In the letter to Hansen, he retyped from the story a long description of Cacciato, most of which ends up in revised form in the published novel's first chapter—the round oafish face with its incomplete and indistinct look, the whistling, and the endless questions.[15] Cacciato's imbecility had a clear and smart novelistic purpose of genuinely posing the basic questions: *Who would get zapped next? What's on the other side of this here mountain? What does being blown into pieces feel like?* He would ask them like a child asking if he might get a puppy for Christmas. If Hansen didn't know yet, he would soon enough that O'Brien was visualizing Kline, the dullard who washed out of boot camp. (Neither friend remembers exactly when they phone-pranked him, O'Brien pretending to be Sgt. Guyton, their drill sergeant, chewing him out long-distance.)

Cacciato's flight was still a hypothesis to chase to ground. "It *could* have happened," he reiterated to Hansen. While such language saturates the final novel, O'Brien wasn't there yet. He didn't want the Cacciato plot to "betray the truth of war and Vietnam as I knew it." How could a crazy-ass fantasy of soldiers chasing a figment from Quảng Ngãi to Paris convey the experiential and moral truths? To check himself, O'Brien reread Hemingway's "The Undefeated" because it is "Real, true, meaningful, emotional, scary, punch [sic], shit-kicking."[16] He wrote Sam Lawrence about his excitement for a "new project," a "'leaving the war' novel that's been budding for many, many years." He reported 180 pages done, easily surpassing the anticipated midpoint.[17]

O'Brien's first time at the Bread Loaf Writers' Conference that August boosted his confidence. The book-in-progress received "lots of praise and some vehement antagonism." Its detractors wanted more "political rectitude," more explicit anti-war statements. They perhaps still suffered the highbrow lack of interest in the grunt experience. Workshops mulled over two of his chapters. John Gardner, the superstar of the day for the novels *Grendel* and *Nickel Mountain*, "parodied one of the chapters in his lecture. Wow."[18] O'Brien's assigned mentor, George Elliott, urged him to lose the fantasy pursuit, but Gardner and Seymour Epstein encouraged him to stay the course. Gardner took O'Brien under his wing, "holding forth for hours on subjects with which O'Brien was marginally familiar," and talking incomprehensibly into the early morning.[19]

Anne Smith called him at home with the news that "Where Have You Gone, Charming Billy?" would appear in *Prize Stories 1976: The O. Henry Awards*. O'Brien was even happier when the anthology used its original and proper title, "Night March."[20] Within a week the O'Briens moved to the Kirkland Street apartment (#4), and he flew to Minnesota for a week of *Northern Lights* promotion.[21]

Back home again, the new home, O'Brien struggled writing and rewriting (and rewriting) the flight-to-Paris sections because their style came unnaturally.[22] But he had faith it would work. On October 20, he mailed a partial draft to Lawrence and his agent, gunning for a two-book deal. To Hansen, he wrote:

> I've got them as far as Mandalay, with a brief prior stop in a Thai village named Rhabba Krone. But these two chapters are just tossed into all that war material, the war stories, and the form of the book, with its emphasis on and dominance by the trek to Paris, hasn't yet jelled very much. I'm just hoping that Sam Lawrence will see what the book will become.[23]

He would later ditch the Thai village bit, and he had not yet written the Alice in Wonderland hole-on-the-road-to-Paris chapters that get the squad to Mandalay.

Lawrence did see. "The great novel about the Vietnam war hasn't yet been written," two of his colleagues wrote in a joint memo. "O'Brien appears to be taking the risk, and it could pay off." They hesitated to offer an advance but thought much of the draft "brilliant." O'Brien is "the kind of writer who, properly nurtured, will pay off big. [. . .] He's going to be a winner."[24]

The writer Brendan Boyd praised the weaving of the fantasy and reality and the "chilling new way" the novel expressed "the wearying, pointless and destructive elements of war." He advised O'Brien to cut lengthy and unoriginal "descriptions of the horrors of war" so that the characters carry the story and its emotions. He faulted the disorienting chapter sequence, the "evocative set pieces" that worked as stories but not as elements of a novel, and the baldly "Hemingwayesque" style. O'Brien wasn't deliberately writing à la Hemingway, as he had in *Northern Lights*, although the two writers shared a fundamental being-there aesthetic. Boyd's memo to Lawrence concluded, "This book has a chance to be a truly major and original addition to the literature of human folly."[25] Terms for the contract for *Cacciato* plus an "untitled novel" were settled before Thanksgiving. O'Brien could finally afford the time to write what he wanted how he wanted.[26]

Part of the structural trouble was O'Brien's constant effort to place individual pieces. He wrote them to stand alone. "Landing Zone Bravo" appeared in the *Denver Quarterly*'s August 1975 issue, and in the new year he'd learn that another literary journal, *Shenandoah*, picked up two[27]—although only one, "The Way It Mostly Was," made it in (winter 1976)—and *The Massachusetts Review* would run another one ("Speaking of Courage," summer 1976).[28]

O'Brien agreed that the chapters did not work in concert. While the jumbled episodes replicated the experience, the book needed traditional novelistic development. He now recognized three strands: the war, the pursuit, and the "post-pursuit" of Paul Berlin's present. "So, I've been starting fresh. From the beginning." This was his practice in the typewriting years, to retype from page one. He considered the "gimmick" of giving Paul Berlin different ranks for the three time periods: Pfc., Spec. 4, and Sgt. He hadn't figured out that there would be no post-pursuit present because the pursuit *is* Paul Berlin's present, his act of imagining.[29]

A few days later, about the twenty-fifth of November, 1975, Cacciato was in India. O'Brien had figured out now about the present, using the seaside observation post "as the fulcrum" where Berlin's thoughts would move between the fantasy journey west and the recent war memories.[30]

Eventually, O'Brien tightened the integration by occasionally converging the narrative strands, with an imagined pursuit chapter briefly backing out to Paul Berlin at the OP reflecting on the imagined pursuit or remembering his combat experiences. The *he* who "could not imagine a happy ending" in chapter 10 is Paul Berlin's imagined self in pursuit of Cacciato *and* the Paul Berlin imagining the pursuit as his mind straddles both selves.[31] The imagined Paul Berlin is and is not the imagining Paul Berlin. Moreover, the imagining Paul Berlin in the observation post is and is not the imagining Tim O'Brien at his writing desk, wondering what will happen next, how it will all end, turning imagination's mirror on himself. *Going After Cacciato* anticipates the nested Tim O'Briens of *The Things They Carried*. While the later novel skirts the line of metafiction, *Going After Cacciato* cleaves strictly to realism.

O'Brien sent the first rewritten 148 pages to Lawrence just shy of Christmas, the prose more polished, the movement improved. Parts tickled him; parts scared him. In Lawrence's estimation, O'Brien had "never written more [b]rilliantly." He chiefly appreciated "the scenes of war, the *feel* of war," whereas the "speculative or philosophical sections" detracted from the "flow and force of the book."[32] It was the familiar O'Brien conundrum between head and heart.

O'Brien and Hansen met over Christmas in Minnesota for cross-country skiing and shoptalk.[33] A month later O'Brien delivered the squad to Delhi on their way to Tehran. His revisions focused on streamlining the "'thought-speculation' passages" and energizing the action. The real quest wasn't for the elusive Cacciato as much as for the elusive idea of "Civilization—the big C," of tranquility, peace, and beauty, represented by Paris. He felt as high on the story as he ever had.[34]

He and Ann had begun planning a May trip to Paris. O'Brien felt pulled to the city he had not seen since his college summer abroad, and then only fleetingly. Familiarizing himself with the place of his novel's to-be-written climax justified the expense:

I want it to be a crushing, deflating, exploding, destructive thing. Absolutely devastating. I want Paul Berlin to kill Cacciato. *Maybe!* I want him to chase the dumb fucker all over the city, track him down, stalk him, and blow his few brains out in the Metro or under the great Arc or among the pigeons in the Jardin des Tuileries. *Maybe.*[35]

The underlined *maybes* he wrote in the margin beside the typed sentences. The plot will go in a different direction, yet in its first chapter the book plants the idea of "murder" in Paul Berlin's and the reader's head, "Cacciato's skull exploding like a bag of helium: boom."[36]

Ten days later found the squad in "northwestern Afghanistan, on a train heading now for Tehran, hot after Cacciato." O'Brien had chosen an epigraph from Somerset Maugham's short story "Honolulu": "The wise traveller travels only in imagination. . . . Those are the best journeys, the journeys that you take at your own fireside, for then you lose none of your illusions."[37]

The plot stumped O'Brien in chapter 20. The "boys" needed "a few days rest" in Tehran, and the reader probably needed a respite from the plunging ahead. But not too much of a pause, and it must be a "meaningful" pause.[38]

Hansen's news that he'd finished "The Inviolate House" prompted O'Brien to reflect on the gratification in giving order to discrete events: "It's an explicit way of disciplining and fulfilling our human potentials, indeed our peculiarly human potentials for ordering, and it's this almost Aristotelian notion of fulfillment that seems to me to be at the heart of the artistic experience, the very wonder of it." By "ordering" he partly meant testing a supposition, something rarely done explicitly as he and Paul Berlin were doing, but "implicit in all art."[39] Paul Berlin's getting the chronology right matters. It's something to hold on to, it's where sense-making starts. It also doesn't matter: "The facts, even when beaded on a chain, still did not have real order [. . . ,] no sense of events unfolding from prior events."[40] It's the *story* and *plot* distinction, as E. M. Forster defined it in *Aspects of the Novel* (1927), story being the mere sequence and plot being the connective tissue. But Paul Berlin isn't talking about a novel. He's talking about his life. "Maybe always, but certainly now, for me," O'Brien would say in 1994, "the environment of war is the environment of life, magnified."[41]

When Paul Berlin distinguishes between the chained order and the real order, he believes he's landed on the proper chronology for the platoon's lost in action: Billy Boy Watkins, Rudy Chassler, Frenchie Tucker, Bernie

Lynn, Ready Mix, Buff, Sidney Martin, and finally Pederson.[42] It's not clear whether Paul Berlin has it right, whether O'Brien intended this order, intended Paul Berlin to have successfully sorted it out. A careful study of the novel as originally published and reprinted for decades reveals characters alive when they've already been killed or not appearing in a scene when they should.

The problem—if it was a problem—doubtless resulted from the several years of rewrites and revisions in the days of typewritten chapter drafts stacked on desk and floor. When presented with the issue in 2020, O'Brien took a few months to reconstruct his thinking. He consulted with Hansen. He knew he didn't care if Paul Berlin got the sequence right, but he decided he did care that the war storyline adhered to realism. In January 2021, he sent his publisher revisions for the next printing to fix the problem, along with minor style edits to reduce repetition (mostly in chapter 20) and some geographical tweaks—correcting the flow of the Trà Bồng River and adding "new ville names, some real, some fictitious."[43] Ever the tinkerer, ever the perfectionist.

◊   ◊   ◊

Ever the perfectionist, O'Brien in March 1976 planned another rewrite of the ongoing narrative after the *current* rewrite. So much to change. Entire episodes. More action, less talk. Keep things moving, return Cacciato to the spotlight. The story needed "a constant *feeling* of momentum, movement, pursuit" without devolving into "a straight go-and-get-em" chase novel.[44] This balance challenge was the one he had had with *Northern Lights*, between propelling action and developing character, between adventure and soul.

New characters climbed aboard only to be left behind later: a German missionary doctor with the unfortunate name Adolph Eichmann (after the Holocaust architect but O'Brien's spelling) and his wife; and Ducky McHugh, "a big redheaded reporter modeled after Gloria Emerson,"[45] the journalist whose book-length reportage on the war, *Winners & Losers: Battles, Retreats, Gains, Losses and Ruins from a Long War*, had been released in January. Emerson provided a fabulous blurb for the paperback edition of *If I Die in a Combat Zone*, which Dell rejected because they planned to market the memoir as a "powerful men's book."[46] Soon after O'Brien and Ann married, they invited Emerson to dinner at their D.C. apartment, where Emerson lectured Ann about O'Brien's postwar suffering. He resented the sanctimonious presumption that she knew more than anyone, including, it seemed, the men themselves. But O'Brien played nice, securing her endorsement that night or soon thereafter. In his fictional rendition, she's "a grunt groupie" who's "in love with soldiers and weapons and all that shit, a liberal too, always talking about how the boys, *her* boys, suffered over there, the corruption and anguish they saw and felt. She wants to put Berlin and Co, and Cacciato, in a book. Charming lady."[47]

Off to Europe in May, ten days in Paris followed by short stays in Nice, Metz, and Luxembourg. Paris was the main event. The O'Briens lodged in the first arrondissement, near Les Halles, where he had stayed on his way to Prague.

> We walked our tails off, visited all the tourist attractions, sought out Hemingway's apartments and cafés, Gertrude Stein's place on Rue de Fleurus. Maybe the best thing was the day spent in the impressionist museum, Jeu de Paume, where I really was stunned by what those guys, particularly Renoir and Manet, did with paint.[48]

Then Worthington in early June, where O'Brien and Hansen met up for more golfing and Cacciato talk. Bill and Ava drove with Tim and Ann back to Cambridge, flying home on June 29, leaving O'Brien both raring and skittish to resume writing.[49]

Within a week he started new material and finished several chapters: "How They Were Organized," "Who They Were, and Claimed to Be," "On Not Getting the Silver Star," "How Bernie Lynn Died, After Frenchie Tucker," and "Pick-Up Games." The first two anchored the narrative, the next three set up "The Tunnel," the chapter that hints at Lt. Sidney Martin's death by fragging and its role in spurring Cacciato's desertion. O'Brien completed "eight or nine chapters . . . in the last month," more than he had the entire time up to that point.[50]

On July 16, the planned war chapters done and a handful of inchoate ones biding their time, O'Brien went back to page one.[51] A week later he'd rewritten up to page 101—"the fucking novel's on fire!"—between half and two-thirds of it fresh material. The draft now ricocheted in "hard juxtaposition" between the imagined story and the war's reality. Which was more unfathomable, the absurdity of the war or of the trek to Paris? "Ah-ha!"

The road-to-Paris scenes included "Alice in Wonderland things," although thus far the draft resisted tumbling into the fantastic. A hole appeared in the road, and he'll "have his boys fall into that fucking hole, whatever it is." The problem was losing "the two aunties while keeping Sarkin Aung Wan."[52] Sarkin Aung Wan, the wistful Paul Berlin's love interest, parallels Cacciato. Indeterminacy defines both, of age, background, and motive. She's a refugee from Cholon, Sài Gòn's Chinatown, part ethnic Chinese, "part unknown." O'Brien knew Vietnamese names. He needed a name as confounding as the rest of her. The name is Paul Berlin's invention, perhaps from a dim memory of a *National Geographic* article on twentieth-century Burmese history. Paul Berlin can no more fully realize her than he can Cacciato. Her age, a "girl, not a woman, maybe twelve, maybe twenty-one,"[53] reflects that of the American boy-men forced into war, between innocence and experience.

Sarkin Aung Wan's companionship reified O'Brien's fantasy of Gayle Roby, a young woman more idea than person, improbably dropping everything to join him in Canada. "Perhaps we shall fall in love there," Sarkin Aung Wan supposes to Paul Berlin, having just met him and deciding to accompany him to Paris.[54] O'Brien set the novel a year before his time in Việt Nam, so Paul Berlin imagines leaving the war in late November 1968, precisely when O'Brien at advanced infantry training intended deserting to Canada. He'd hinted at his plans in that letter to Gayle that cited Heller's *Catch-22* and quoted in full Frost's "The Road Not Taken," two works that *Going After Cacciato* also quotes. "Miles to go and all that," says Lt. Corson.[55]

On Friday, August 6, Anne Smith called to say that *Redbook* wanted one of the four stories he'd sent in June.[56] "Misunderstandings" would be published as "Keeping Watch by Night" in December. There was a minor kerfuffle about the changed title, especially given its similarity to that of a new poetry volume, *Keeping Watch* (1976), by Robert Pack, O'Brien's friend and Bread Loaf's director. The story did not make the final novel. It gives Jim Pederson's background:

He was a missionary and a believer [in Jesus Christ], but the men did not hold this against him, partly because he was also a good soldier. He was strong, with lean hips and a very powerful grip and long legs, and his eyes had qualities of combined restraint and confidence. There was nothing self-righteous about him—he was no zealot—but he still had what Doc Peret called a "moral stance."[57]

Pederson shares a story from his missionary service in Kenya about helping save a desperately ill woman's life. He kept her company for hours talking about God and Christ's healing powers, testifying that might have led to her recovery even though he wasn't sure she understood English. Paul Berlin is dubious, yet he admires Pederson, and "there was still something to the moral stance business. Even Doc recognized it. The time Pederson stopped them from burning down Tri Nuoc 2, and the way he'd stopped them, so that nobody resented him afterward."[58]

The backstory matters for the published novel because when Oscar proposes the fragging of Lt. Sidney Martin in the interest of self-preservation, Pederson is the first to accede. His moral authority helps sway the others. The novel reduces the backstory to a single line at this critical moment: "Pederson nodded. He was a quiet kid, a former missionary to Kenya, but he nodded and looked away."[59] It's the novel's climax, if that term signifies when the subsequent becomes consequent. O'Brien excluded the chapter because it sidetracked the forward momentum for too long and because he couldn't find a good place to fit it in.

O'Brien returned to Bread Loaf for the second half of August, where Hansen joined him. Before then, he drafted the hole-in-the-road-to-Paris sequence that "violates the dictum" of keeping everything possible even if daring the reader's suspension of disbelief.[60] The Vietnamese major imprisoned underground represents another vision of desertion. At twenty-eight, the character is only one year younger than O'Brien was when writing him and "a brilliant student" before the draft notice appeared "in the mail." Unlike O'Brien, Li Van Hgoc has tried everything he can to legally dodge the draft. And fails. After basic training and receiving orders to deploy to combat in South Việt Nam, he hightails away, at first crashing with friends outside Hà Nội, then taking to the countryside. "Hiding, skulking," begging. Alone. Eventually captured.[61] O'Brien writes into this officer's fate his

fears about life on the run in Canada. Li Van Hgoc is the character who explains *xã*, the term for the sacred relationship of community, history, soul,
and soil, which O'Brien had learned from FitzGerald's *Fire in the Lake*. Li's
dereliction would seem more grievous than Paul Berlin's hypothetical one;
Vietnamese who die away from home become wandering ghosts.

Paul Berlin at the observation post insists he isn't dreaming, not even
imagining, not exactly, but a combination of pretending and plotting. Yet
the source for the Li Van Hgoc episode was in fact a recurring dream.
O'Brien had written about it in January 1973:

> Bad dreams are rare. When they come—the places around My Khe,
> the fear, the color of my rifle and its weight and feel—when those
> dreams come, they are interesting, not sweat filled and awful. I
> dreamed once about a VC tunnel, and as I went down into it, looked
> around, came across a kitchen-sized room, well-lighted, and I talked
> to some VC, and we had a chuckle together and made friends. I
> got their view of the fighting. We watched an infantry company go
> marching by, blind as bats, we chuckled and ate a can of mackerel. I
> learned more about the VC in my dreams than in a year of fighting
> against them.[62]

In some variants, torchlight; in others, steampunk fluorescent. The faces of
the Vietnamese changed. Sometimes buddies joined the scene. Its enact-
ment in the novel references Plato's allegory of the cave when Li Van Hgoc
has the American peer out through his periscope at themselves peering
into a VC tunnel. Imagination, rather than escaping the self, mirrors it.

O'Brien rekindled friendships at Bread Loaf and made new ones. This
time around, he was one of four associates, a teaching assistant. Toni Morrison gave a lecture titled "Clarity, Perception, and Language" and read
from her forthcoming *Song of Solomon*, like O'Brien's progressing novel
a flight of imagination, unlike O'Brien's an embrace of magical realism.
O'Brien read "How They Were Organized," billed as an excerpt from "a
very gory novel" (he probably didn't know which section he would read
until the very day).[63]

After Bread Loaf, O'Brien puttered his way back into writing. He worried he had shortchanged the war, so he thought up more to write, "a short

chapter called Small Talk, to give a feel for the conversations of war, or in war; a chapter called Mispronunciations, to dramatize the difficulties in communicating with the Vietnamese national—difficulties, shit; the impossibility of it"; and "Fire Fight," in which the soldiers rehash the action right after the first time Paul Berlin comes under fire. No one experienced the same thing.

Four hundred thirteen pages and growing. O'Brien planned to stuff it all in and cull it later. "Mispronunciations" turned into "The Things They Didn't Know." The gang has escaped from the Iranian jail and fled through Turkey and on to Greece, only now the pursuers are themselves pursued, propelled by fear. The theme was the old conflict between duty to self and duty to society. He kept trimming as he added "to make the story move faster."[64]

O'Brien got them to Paris on Monday, September 20, 1976. He immediately wrote Hansen—"Open the champagne"—and retyped the arrival in the letter. O'Brien credited "Berlin's fierce imagination" for "leaping obstacles in ways I couldn't." Significantly, Paul Berlin imagines the girl, Sarkin Aung Wan, imagining the squad's escape from the underground tunnel prison in a mystifying move that defies the male character's imagination. Arrived in Paris, but now what? O'Brien knew the thematic resolution:

In imagination, Cacciato won't be caught; he'll run forever, a fleer without hedging or afterthought or even pre—though in reality the victory goes to Stop: social law, tradition, duty, all that. But above both of these—imagination and reality—a higher truth wins out; namely, the Idea that it might have been done, and might still be. That, with courage, the Idea works.

Now for the dramatic resolution. What happens, and how? Was the murder plot off the table?

Shit. This is what it all boils down to, the next two weeks of writing. The whole scheme teeters on the dramatic effectiveness of the closing Paris scenes. Been building toward it for 469 pages now, and geez, it's got to be something special. All narrative, I think. All action, happenings, drive, drive. The story's got to take over completely;

the imagination has got to zoom out, crash and bang, and that's the whole of it. That's it.[65]

O'Brien finished the book verily with the speed of the train flying through the countryside to deliver the crew into Gare du Nord.

Perhaps too fast. The published Paris chapters violate O'Brien's it-could-have-happened dictum. Paul Berlin in the OP in late November 1968 is free to imagine pursuing Cacciato well into 1969. But he can't prognosticate the new year's historical events: Richard Nixon's inauguration, Dwight Eisenhower's death, the indictments of the Chicago Eight. Paul Berlin recalls missing the 1968 Democratic National Convention because "he was in basic training"—except he wasn't.[66] O'Brien was. Paul Berlin was in Quảng Ngãi, Việt Nam, where Rudy Chassler, Frenchie Tucker, and Bernie Lynn have been killed in the past two weeks.

Tim and Ann spent the first weekend in October at Erik Hansen's home in Randolph Valley, New Hampshire, where Hansen had moved from Minnesota in September. The three celebrated O'Brien's thirtieth birthday and O'Brien and Hansen enjoyed hours of constructive conversation. In Cambridge he settled into the final two weeks of trimming and some rewriting, reducing the overall length by fifty pages while adding material, including a chapter called "The Things They Carried, and How."

O'Brien wrapped up rewriting on October 21. The next afternoon he took the finished draft downtown to his publisher, where they made two copies before he and Lawrence celebrated over lunch and liquor.[67] Perhaps a pupu platter and some Navy Grogs at Trader Vic's.

◊ ◊ ◊

Lawrence recruited William Abrahams, the West Coast editor for Atlantic Monthly Press who edited the O. Henry prize anthology that "Night March" appeared in, for input.[68] O'Brien already wasn't sure about the unreality of the underground sequence. He also decided he needed a new title . . . *Going After Who?* His publishers agreed.[69] O'Brien taped instructions on his wall: "Cut 10 uses of the word imagination; cut 10 would have happened, might have happened, etc." Most of Hansen's feedback involved the imagined journey to Paris, verifying O'Brien's natural bent for realism. "I've got to improve my art, or my skills, or whatever the fuck you call it; I've got to learn to write, or manage, the world of imagination."[70]

Still no word from Abrahams. O'Brien shortened a jungle "monkey" scene that he would later deep-six. He kept Stink's shooting the water buffalo, a scene he had feared too gratuitously violent, but streamlined it. The novel needed it, perhaps to express Stink's frustration at not having caught Cacciato even as it "presages . . . the final outcome." O'Brien also kept it because he wanted to preserve the auntie's wailing as a refrain for that section of the novel since it had been a refrain in O'Brien's war. The hole-in-the-road underground sequence remained, but tightened, per Hansen's advice.[71] With it, he deliberately departed from the verisimilitude of Hemingway, Dos Passos, and Fitzgerald. He was tearing himself away from their influence and that allegiance. They weren't doing fabulism or magical realism. Then again, neither was he. The novel asserted the reality of daydreams. O'Brien's genius was his ability to combine the accustomed modernist and the edgy postmodernist sensibilities.

More good news. "Keeping Watch by Night" and "Going After Cacciato" were on magazine racks, in *Redbook*'s and *Gallery*'s December issues. Gene Lyons, a contributor to *The Nation*, had written a column about O'Brien and *Northern Lights* for its November 13 issue and planned to devote a column in December to *Going After Cacciato* based on published excerpts.[72] Lawrence was ecstatic. Who ever received a positive notice before a book was even finished?

The honing continued. O'Brien retyped over half the book. The final novel benefited from a new "willingness, even eagerness to see fault." Lawrence called to report that Abrahams's major criticism was the "time-place confusion." O'Brien rejected italicizing some sections. To disentangle them would give each part "a discrete quality it doesn't have in memory-imagination-longing." O'Brien sought "the *effect* of confusion" with an ordering structure.[73]

Within four days he'd retyped nearly three hundred pages. He'd cut almost twenty pages, "including one whole OP section."[74] O'Brien had his December meeting with Abrahams, whom he felt "only criticized" the novel for being "tedious" and "ridiculously long," with "no revelations at the end, too much war stuff, not enough fantasy, not letting myself go in the fantasy sections." O'Brien never wanted to surrender to the fantasy, because Paul Berlin's imagining the way to Paris wasn't fantasy. O'Brien reneged on plans to visit Hansen in New Hampshire because he wanted to get Abrahams a leaner version before leaving town for his in-laws' in Maryland for Christmas.[75]

In Worthington for the new year, O'Brien feared he'd lost the book's pulse. It was too long, but his "intuition" told him to write more. The Paris sections overrode the war's "pain and anguish." The initial Paul Berlin stories had coalesced around *fear*—where had it gone?—"not only of dying, but of the other-worldliness of war; he doesn't fit. Like I didn't." O'Brien worried his postwar "analytical" frame of mind obscured Paul Berlin's wartime terrors.[76] Perhaps for Abrahams, the wilder the fantasy, the more palpable the war's terrors that drove it. In a sense, Abrahams proposed what Francis Ford Coppola was at that moment creating in the Philippines with *Apocalypse Now*, filmed from March 1976 to May 1977: a plunge into the surreal to respect the war's reality. Yet containing the fantasy through rational consideration was Paul Berlin's natural emotional counter to the irrational horrors of his war.

O'Brien reconsidered Abrahams's complaint that nothing happened in Paris to produce "revelation." The solution, though, required him to write more—"to imagine or pretend peace and harmony, and to create a temporary fiction of fantasy-fulfilled; a real spiritual winger, happiness and bliss with Sarkin Aung Wan . . . some fleeting glimpse of how it truly might be if men did not make war."[77] He spent the next six weeks rewriting to emphasize the "jarring" sadness of returning to reality after a "poignant daydream," as he'd experienced in Việt Nam.[78]

The arrival in Paris now had the realistic lyricism of what it would have felt like. O'Brien had now imagined the negotiation table scene between Sarkin Aung Wan and Paul Berlin, although at this point Paul Berlin soliloquizes on "the pleasures of living, seeing things, eating and drinking," not on war, peace, or obligation. It's the language of O'Brien's *Mac Weekly* column arguing against the war. He worried about the "melodrama, allegory, intellectualizing, absurdism" of poor execution. Before then, the almost-lovers would look for an apartment.[79] Sarkin Aung Wan's desire to settle down explains her abandoning Paul Berlin at the end.[80]

The novel stages its thematic resolution as a negotiation between Sarkin Aung Wan and Paul Berlin at a circular conference table in the Salle des Fêtes of the Majestic Hotel. It's a mock version of the actual peace talks, complete with microphones, headsets, and formal case-making. Sarkin Aung Wan argues for the duty to oneself through desertion, self-preservation, and love. Paul Berlin's argument against deserting is Socrates's in *Crito* against fleeing lawful if unjust execution. More directly, it's Michael Walzer's in *Obligations: Essays on Disobedience, War, and Citizenship* (1970). Berlin's language of obligation, commitment, and consent comes straight from Walzer, a debt O'Brien has freely acknowledged.[81]

O'Brien the high school and college master debater inhabits the Majestic encounter. Indoor scenes always vexed O'Brien because people inside end up "sitting around talking," passively. "Good novelists understand that there should always be motion in a novel even during dialogue."[82] O'Brien had set an earlier debate scene in a Tehran dance club.

For the dramatic resolution, a foiled attempt to capture Cacciato in Paris replicates the foiled attempt to capture him in the mountains that concludes chapter 1 and ends the real-world pursuit, bringing the platoon back down to its seaside encampment and Paul Berlin's night in the OP. The three narrative threads gracefully, swiftly, and powerfully rejoin.

Roughly two weeks after meeting with O'Brien, Abrahams finally sent comments. He suggested compound chapter titles, "The War: ___" and "Interlude: ___" followed by their actual titles. O'Brien rejected the idea. Abrahams still experienced the chapters as too self-contained, and he still thought the war chapters bogged the book down.[83] O'Brien thought Abrahams would have preferred for the war chapters to progress in order, but that would have betrayed the subjective reality of the soldiers' jungle-meandering, aimless combat.[84] O'Brien's feelings were strengthened by a visit from another Alpha Company veteran. They hit a bar, "refought the war, lost it all over again." How much both men had already forgotten surprised him; their reconstruction of events must have invigorated O'Brien's writing of Paul Berlin's. They rehashed May 1969. "Something like a quarter of our company was wounded or killed that month. All in bits and pieces, a few each day, chipping away. That was what made it so dreadful, the way it never ended, or never seemed to end. The constant pressure, constant fatigue, waiting for the next mine or ambush."[85] It was a war novel, dammit.

The prose, Abrahams worried, "gets over-fancy, too 'poetic.'" O'Brien had already rewritten the final four chapters, trimming the Paris arrival passage by three to four pages. Abrahams preferred *The Road to Paris* as a title, which O'Brien thought silly, "like one of those old Bob Hope–Bing Crosby movies." Abrahams also liked *Freedom Trip*.[86]

Bill O'Brien had come up with *Freedom Trip* and *Freedom March* and *The Freedom Trail*.[87] O'Brien had pitched *Over the Hill*. Its reference to aging bothered him, so he provided alternatives: *Over the Last Hill, Over the Green Hill, Over the High Hill, Over the _____ Hill*, others he didn't send.[88] At one point he supplied Lawrence potential catalog and back cover copy for the novel that called it "Absent and Accounted For."[89] Probably on March 20, O'Brien called Lawrence to propose *The Blind Eye of the Moon*, from Louis Simpson's poem "Memories of a Lost War." He envisioned this stanza as the book's epigraph:

> *Hot lightnings stitch the blind eye of the moon,*
> *The thunder's blunt.*
> *We sleep. Our dreams pass in a faint platoon*
> *Toward the front.*

O'Brien loved the "dignity" and the "striking image." The novel likens round-faced Cacciato to the moon. "The title also seems to reflect the harsh, blind, unsparing, uncaring nature view that nature takes of man's pitiful war follies." He could see a moon on the cover.[90] Many great novels have odd titles, he wrote Hansen, naming novels by Faulkner, Hemingway, and Fitzgerald.[91]

Lawrence wasn't keen on it, and the New York "brass" nixed it for sounding "like the translation of some Japanese book of poetry that a lit'ry house like Farrar Strauss [*sic*] would publish and then sell 100 copies of." They'd be going with *Going After Cacciato* after all. O'Brien settled on the Siegfried Sassoon epigraph, "Soldiers are dreamers."[92] When Hansen read the epigraph, the novel's vision fully clicked for him.

In these final weeks, O'Brien and Abrahams were in frequent contact. O'Brien credited Abrahams with half the cuts. He dumped the Pederson backstory chapter along with "The Things They Carried and How," two OP chapters, "Still Tunneling," and "Touching Home." He aggressively slashed away. Abrahams helped O'Brien render Paul Berlin a more consistent character. He kept "How the Land Was" and "How They Were Organized," and he wouldn't hear of "labeling the chapters or of dividing the book into parts." As a final try, Abrahams suggested dates at the start of each war chapter—he still didn't grok what O'Brien was doing.[93]

O'Brien set the book aside for his early April trip with Ann and the Simpsons to the Virgin Islands. He received Abrahams's notes on the final version in mid-April, spent a few days with Hansen in New Hampshire, then returned for the final touches and the final submission to Lawrence on Tuesday, May 3.[94] He'd already been scratching for new material, and at times felt sick to death of *Going After Cacciato*, yet he couldn't help but miss it. "I still feel oddly committed to Paul Berlin and friends," he wrote Hansen, "and can't drop them or forget them. It's as if I'd gone along on that wretched trek, gone back to the war, and, as when I returned from Vietnam, I feel a groundlessness, wondering 'what next?' Having survived, what to do with life?"[95]

◊   ◊   ◊

After dropping out of community college, Paul Berlin, a twenty-year-old from Fort Dodge, Iowa, is drafted for duty in Việt Nam. He deplanes at Chu Lai on June 3, 1968, where he undergoes the American Division's six-day crash combat course. On June 9, Pfc. Berlin receives his orders for the 5th Battalion, 46th Light Infantry Regiment. A truck drops him at LZ Gator. On June 11, a resupply helicopter delivers him to First Platoon, Alpha Company. That afternoon, Billy Boy Watkins trips a mine, loses a foot, and dies of shock. That night a fit of frenzied giggles seizes Paul Berlin; a round-faced, childlike soldier named Cacciato calms him.

On the morning of August 13 and now back along the Sông Trà Bồng, Rudy Chassler steps on a mine on the path into Trinh Son 2. Not long after, Lt. Sidney Martin sends Frenchie Tucker into a tunnel. Everyone hears the shot. Bernie Lynn crawls in to recover Frenchie's body only to be shot himself before his feet even make it inside. Vaught gives morphine to a dying Bernie after they tug him out of the hole.

Ready Mix dies in the mountains.

After the sky rains bombs it rains rain for three days, the rain-filled corpse-bearing craters earning the area the nickname "World's Greatest

Lake Country." The platoon leader demands that the platoon search all tunnels thoroughly before blowing them.

The squad's remnants—Oscar Johnson, Stink Harris, Eddie Lazzutti, Harold Murphy, Vaught, Pederson, Ben Nystrom, Doc Peret, Buff, and Paul Berlin—agree to kill Martin, making their compact by touching a hand grenade from which Oscar has removed the pin. Cacciato, meanwhile, has rigged up a pole to fish the craters. Paul Berlin can't shake Cacciato out of his fishing reverie and can't convince him to touch the grenade. He pushes it into Cacciato's hand. Cacciato's paralysis in not pulling his hand away is the equivalent of Tim O'Brien's paralysis the summer he let himself be drafted. Paul Berlin enacts O'Brien's complicity and guilt.

Sidney Martin's murder, presumably by Oscar—it doesn't matter, they're all responsible—occurs off page. Soldiers called it fragging, in reference to fragmentation grenades. Grenades weren't the only weapon used, but they had their advantages. They could be rolled under cots or tossed into bunkers under the cover of darkness. They could be mistaken for enemy incoming or rigged explosives. For O'Brien, the grenade lent itself to the collective action.[96]

Pederson dies next, on a hot LZ, by friendly fire.

During a running battle by a village, Buff dies. In a roughly three-week period, from mid-August to early September, seven members of the platoon have been killed: Rudy, Frenchie, Bernie, Ready Mix, Sidney Martin, Pederson, and Buff. In early September, Vaught catches an infection and leaves the war. Then Ben Nystrom shoots himself in the foot.

In late October, Cacciato walks away from the war. The new platoon leader takes the squad after him. The weeklong pursuit into the mountains ends at the Laotian border, where Cacciato slips their grasp. The ill-with-dysentery lieutenant gives up the chase, just as the ill-in-Seattle private gave up his flight to Canada. The squad won't cross the river into Laos, just as the Tim O'Brien character of *The Things They Carried* won't cross the Rainy River into Canada.

In those final weeks of writing, O'Brien asked Hansen the question that had "plagued" him from the outset:

Do I perhaps underplay the importance of the murder (execution?) of Lt. Sidney Martin? Should more be made of it? In terms of Paul

Berlin's motivations for imagining flight? In terms of what makes Cacciato actually run? Please—let me have your thoughts on this. Berlin doesn't have guilt—at least not acknowledged guilt. He sees it as sad, but a necessary thing. But Cacciato may recognize what happened for what it was: outright murder.[97]

O'Brien clarified Cacciato's intelligence and motive *outside* the text.

On guard duty in late November, in an observation tower on the Batangan Peninsula overlooking the beach by the South China Sea, Paul Berlin passes the night by wondering. Could Cacciato have made it to Paris? "It was a way of asking questions."[98] It's April in Paris when the imagined Cacciato eludes them again and Paul Berlin loses Sarkin Aung Wan to Lt. Corson, who has quit the war as Paul Berlin could not bring himself to do, because "Imagination, like reality, has its limits."[99] That realization completes the novel's coming-of-age tale.

The ending picks up from where chapter 1 left off, the squad having lost Cacciato and left the mountains on their way to the sea. Paul Berlin and the lieutenant sit guard together, their terse conversation the prelude to the OP fantasy. The last line slant-echoes *Northern Lights'* final echo of *The Sun Also Rises*. Cacciato just might make it to Paris, Lt. Corson muses. Maybe, Spec. 4 Paul Berlin agrees.

"Yes," the lieutenant said. "Maybe so."[100]

O'Brien won over Billy Abrahams, who wrote Seymour Lawrence two days before O'Brien turned in the final manuscript.

[I]t is now a novel, rather than a collection of related stories, and brilliant it is too. I think it will make his reputation, and establish itself as one of the authentic war novels that are also authentic works of art. Those are few indeed. It's hard to find a comparison, because at heart it is a deeply original work. From THE ENORMOUS ROOM to GOING AFTER CACCIATO . . . There are, as you know, two built-in difficulties—one, that it is, and no disguising, a novel of the Vietnam War; and the other, that much of it is a fantasy. But the fantasy (the

possibilities) works: one believes in it as a story—it holds one. And
the writing is alive!

Abrahams urged Lawrence to send advance copies to William Styron,
Josiah Bunting, and other war novelists, but also to masters of peacetime
fiction, such as John Cheever, John Updike, and Walker Percy.[101]

Going After Cacciato owes much of its artistry to the fact that it was
O'Brien's second novel. It also owes much of its artistry to the fact that
O'Brien's war memoir freed him from the compulsion to write autobi-
ographically, the bane of most first war novels by veterans. His imagination could take flight. Now other veterans' could, too. Bruce Weigl, Larry
Heinemann, and Philip Caputo, three of the war's most important creative
writers, marveled at the new novel. It inspired their literary generation to
find the war by leaving it behind. Cacciato had led the way.

21

APPRENTICESHIP'S END

How rich. John Wayne, the hero of so many rah-rah war movies—including *The Green Berets* (1968)—handed the 1979 Academy Award for Best Picture to Michael Cimino for his disturbing 1978 treatment of the war in Việt Nam, *The Deer Hunter*. It and Hal Ashby's film *Coming Home*, starring anti-war activist Jane Fonda, dominated the awards that April night. Released in February 1978, *Going After Cacciato* hit the scene when U.S. audiences were ready to have the war turned into fiction, winning the National Book Award two weeks after the 1979 Oscars. Coppola's *Apocalypse Now* came out in August. Each in its own way, the films and the novel, departed from strict realism and dealt with the question of leaving the war behind.

Reviews of *Cacciato* split over two issues. First, the success of the Paris pursuit fantasy and its integration with the war stories. Second, the novel's apparent indebtedness to Joseph Heller's *Catch-22*. The pursuit daydream was deemed either a failure that broke its own spell and detracted from the war story, or a bold experiment that faltered at times but deserved celebration, or an astonishing and original accomplishment. The *Catch-22* comparison is more flummoxing.

O'Brien did not complain in any extant letters when Gene Lyons's preview in *The Nation*, based on the published excerpts, said that "O'Brien has chosen to write about Vietnam from the point at which Yossarian left off."[1] At the end of *Catch-22*, Yossarian has learned that his buddy Orr intentionally downed his plane and rafted to Sweden, out of the war. Yossarian plans to make a run for Sweden too, and barely escapes a stabbing on his way out the door, not unlike Cacciato's slipping through the squad's armed assault. "You'll never make it," Major Danby tells Yossarian. "It's almost a geographical impossibility." Cacciato physically resembles Orr, a "grinning lark" with a "deranged and galvanic giggle" who with his "raw bulgy face" was "one of the most homeliest freaks Yossarian had ever encountered."[2] O'Brien did not complain when his Bread Loaf friend Geoffrey Wolff or anyone else made the positive comparison.[3] He did complain, however, about a publisher's advertisement that began, in large type, GOING AFTER CACCIATO. PRONOUNCE IT "CATCH OTTO." AS IN CATCH-22.

One can imagine the angry phone call O'Brien placed to Lawrence over the liberty with his title. He liked the sound of Cacciato, borrowed from his LZ Gator boss; he liked learning that it means *hunted* or *caught* in Italian. As he wrote Lawrence, "my main concern is that it not appear that I'm an imitator of Heller's book. Much as I like it, and respect it, I certainly was not trying to write anything of the sort, and, in fact, I doubt that Cacciato even resembles 'Catch-22.'"[4] Heller's novel was knee-slapping, O'Brien's bluntly serious. For the rest of his life, O'Brien has insisted his novel did not intentionally take up where Heller's left off. Neither he nor Hansen remembers *Catch-22* entering their conversations about the novel in progress.

One could be forgiven for disagreeing. Paul Berlin "would look out to sea and imagine using it as a means of escape—stocking Oscar's raft with plenty of rations and foul-weather gear and drinking water."[5] The squad fishes in Oscar's raft; Orr fishes in his raft as he practices his escape, with "that goofy giggle of his and that crazy grin."[6] Goofy-smiling Cacciato fishes in bomb craters before his desertion. It's not as if O'Brien never mentioned Heller in letters to Hansen, and there's the Fort Lewis letter to Gayle Roby that used Orr to signal O'Brien's intention to desert. Sam Lawrence connected the two novels in a letter to Billy Abrahams.[7]

O'Brien has recognized the possibility of unconscious echoes of other works in one's own. His effort to distance his work from Heller's is understandable. All literature is derivative to some extent, but originality can still obtain. In quashing that advertisement, O'Brien wanted to preempt negative comparisons such as Christopher Lehmann-Haupt's in *The New York Times*:

[B]y repeatedly evoking "Catch-22" Mr. O'Brien reminds us that Mr. Heller caught the madness of war better, if only because the logic of

"Catch-22" is consistently surrealistic and doesn't try to mix in fantasies that depend on their believability to sustain. I can even imagine it being said that "Going After Cacciato" is the "Catch-22" of Vietnam. The trouble is, "Catch-22" is the "Catch-22" of Vietnam.[8]

Not to worry, as *The New York Times Book Review* lauded the novel on its front page and didn't cite Heller.[9] It did bring in Hemingway, as did John Updike's review in *The New Yorker*, which struck the opposite note as Lehmann-Haupt's: "As a fictional portrait of this war, 'Going After Cacciato' is hard to fault, and will be hard to better."[10]

Cacciato enjoyed plenty of glowing reviews, yet Updike's review had a huge impact on its success and helped convince the reading world to pay attention to the literature of O'Brien's war. As O'Brien's agent's office wrote to Lawrence, "The John Updike review in The New Yorker seemed to be the word that tipped the scales against resistance to a Viet Nam novel, and now all the scouts are asking for it."[11]

O'Brien wrote a few articles and book reviews in the wake of *Cacciato*. He liked the exposure and the money. It flattered him to be asked. For the moment, he had time. The reviews say as much about O'Brien as they do their subjects. He never wrote reviews again, because he learned that with literary friends and peers, even a good review might prove ticklish.

O'Brien trounced Vance Bourjaily's *A Game Men Play* for its moral pointlessness.[12] Craig Nova's *Incandescence* fared better but fell short in "psychological insight."[13] Nadine Gordimer's *July's People* achieved in both the moral and psychological fields, although its difficult prose sometimes irritated.[14] Lynne Sharon Schwartz's otherwise smart *Rough Strife* suffered from the first-person narrator's self-analysis eclipsing action and drive.[15] Raymond Carver's "splendid" collection *What We Talk About When We Talk About Love* actively engaged "moral aboutness," although the minimalism went too far.[16] There's nothing but praise for O'Brien's friend Geoffrey Wolff's *The Duke of Deception: Memories of My Father* and for Norman Mailer's *The Executioner's Song.*[17] Mailer's hefty book, about the life and relatively recent notorious trial and execution of the murderer

Gary Gilmore, amazed O'Brien, for whom the nonfiction or fiction label didn't "matter a whit: The book's *effect* is stunningly novelistic."[18]

Wouldn't you know it, with Barry Hannah's wild ride *Airships*, O'Brien judged its war stories the collection's best because "War *is* a mix of the absurd and the deadly real."[19] James Jones's posthumous *Whistle* could have used some imagination in trying for an original approach to a war story—the contrast with *Cacciato* is loud and clear. To O'Brien, *Whistle*'s four World War II veterans became indistinguishable; the novel contributed to the impression that all veterans struggle to readjust. The review flipped the received wisdom contrasting the untroubled generation of Jones's war with the troubled one of O'Brien's.[20]

In the late 1970s, the plight of Việt Nam veterans was once again topical, and not just because of Hollywood. In his first official act as president, Jimmy Carter appointed the first Việt Nam veteran to head the Veterans Administration. Max Cleland was thirty-four years old, an ex-infantry officer who had lost both legs and one arm to a grenade.[21] In his December 1979 *Esquire* essay "The Violent Vet," O'Brien interviewed Cleland as well as other major voices and critiqued the myths of their war's veterans as violent, incarcerated, drug-addicted, not honorably discharged, unemployed, and unwelcomed home. There was no hard data to support the stereotypes, O'Brien argued, and the available evidence suggested that the veterans of his war were no more likely to suffer these conditions than veterans of America's previous two wars. Because in the end, the experience is essentially the same. Rifles and mud and army BS. But the country *needed* "the image of a suffering and troubled veteran" of Việt Nam:

> Rather than face our own culpabilities, we shove them off onto ex-GIs and let them suffer for us. Rather than relive old tragedies, rather than confront our own frustrations and puzzlements about the war, we take comfort in the image of a bleary-eyed veteran carrying all that emotional baggage for us.[22]

Anne Mollegen Smith had left *Redbook* to lead *Your Place*, a new bimonthly for twenty-somethings, which ran O'Brien's "Vietnam: Now Playing at Your Local Theater" in August 1978 (and listed him as a contributing editor). That essay begins with O'Brien recollecting his Worthington boyhood: "With my buddies beside me, I stormed the D-Day beaches of Lake Okabena—splashing, stumbling, firing from the hip. [. . .] Lord, I was some fine soldier. I was a bloody hero." But he wasn't playing soldier. He was playing a movie star playing a soldier. And in Việt Nam, he watched real soldiers playing movie stars playing soldiers.[23] The first story that found its way into *The Things They Carried*, "The Ghost Soldiers," *Esquire* published not too long after the article, in 1981; it recycles the article's language about soldiers playing action heroes in war movies.[24] In 1986, O'Brien's second *Esquire* story for the eventual book—its title story—depicts soldiering as an act of imagination, of pretending.[25]

O'Brien's gushing review of Scott Spencer's *Endless Love* anticipated his future explorations of obsessive male romantic love. The things some men do. Spencer's novel opens after the young narrator has torched the home of his ex-girlfriend's family, an act that lands him in a mental ward. For O'Brien, "love, no matter how obsessive, is not merely destructive, and Spencer avoids such simplistic moralizing." O'Brien's takeaway was that "so-called 'normal life' with its 'normal' kinds of loving (affection, security, comfort, tenderness) seems dull and empty in contrast to the enormously heart-quickening, gut-thumping powers of true passion."[26]

O'Brien's first piece in *Your Place* appeared in its inaugural issue. The O'Briens had very nearly bought the condo they'd been renting—"Fear of Buying" is about that moment in a young marriage when the couple realizes it's time to give up the nomadic rental life and settle into a normal life of affection, security, comfort, and tenderness.[27] Ouch.

◊   ◊   ◊

O'Brien had begun casting about for ideas for his next novel while finishing *Going After Cacciato*. He was tired of writing about war, and he needed the advance.

The first idea merged his predilection for movement across landscapes with the autobiographical. As proposed to Lawrence in December 1976, "The Hunt" was to be about Ben Garrett, a sixty-year-old who joins a two-week hunt into the South Dakota Badlands for the wolves stealing his small town's sheep, only to find himself hunted by . . . someone. The man's searching his past for clues would have given O'Brien a vehicle for working with his father's past, as Ben Garrett and Bill O'Brien shared a Brooklyn Catholic boyhood, hotel work in the Bahamas, navy service during the war, moving to the Midwest for his new bride, then living a benumbed, normal life there as an insurance salesman for thirty years. O'Brien imagined a crisp, short, chapterless novel. Garrett will win the "brute" climactic battle but never learn the answers: Who was hunting him, and why? The novel would provide psychological insight without plot explanation or resolution[28]—a narrative idea not realized until *In the Lake of the Woods* (1994).

Six months later and *Cacciato* put to bed, O'Brien scrapped "The Hunt" for "The Sweetheart Mountains," a love story between two old people.[29] A month later the idea shifted. The same character, "around sixty-five, who fights the aging process by body-building and daily exercise," is married. The Sweetheart Mountains were to be a fictionalized version of the Black Hills, so that O'Brien could freely invent without fussing over maps and histories. He fancied a straightforward first-person story that didn't worry itself about themes or moral aboutness. The style was proving difficult— lyrical, future tense, direct address:

> Let me go to the Sweetheart Mountains. Let it be autumn. Let me wake early, before your dog, and let me curl against you as I do. Breathe softly. If I should kiss you, don't stir. Sleep with your wrist against your ear, listening to your blood as I have so often listened to your heart. Be silent. Through your dreams let me hear our house. Let me remember how we built it, board by board, squaring the rooms, our lives, you with a hammer and me with a saw.[30]

After a page and a half, he knew he couldn't sustain it. He taped a piece of paper on the wall behind his typewriter: "JUST TELL THE DAMN STORY."[31]

At Bread Loaf in August 1977, he didn't do a reading. By December, he'd chucked it all and started again.[32] Three months later he'd been reading about the eventual end of the universe in a second Big Bang and began thinking about dramatizing "the linkage between man's own mortality and the mortality of nature."[33] The story shifted again, its protagonist now "a seventy-year-old rancher out in the Dakotas whose land is bought up to put in Minuteman silos." Not wanting to live at ground zero for Soviet missiles, and failing to stop construction, "he finally rides out on his horse to blow the whole business up."[34]

In September 1978, after his third Bread Loaf conference, O'Brien headed to Rock, Kansas, and McConnell Air Force Base, outside Wichita; to Little Rock, Arkansas; and to New York City to investigate America's nuclear arsenal. He sought the physical "impressions of life at a missile site."[35] He wanted to touch a missile, literally "to touch the nuclear age."[36] The nuclear apocalypse terrified O'Brien, not just his own end but civilization's. The Kansas farmers flabbergasted him with their nonchalance. "Look, we've all got to die *somehow*," one of them harrumphed.[37] O'Brien never found the silo outside town. The storms rolling in across western Kansas, and the deserted streets of Rock, felt as apocalyptic as O'Brien's subject.

Gene Lyons, the Arkansas writer who had previewed *Going After Cacciato*, put O'Brien in touch with a former Titan II crew commander in Little Rock who hated his former job. That humanity had survived the early seventies struck the silo veteran as something of a miracle. "During my last night on duty, I climbed up to the highest part of that silo, aimed at the missile, and took myself a good, long piss."[38] Besides helping toward the potential novel, the fall's research resulted in an article, "Darkness on the Edge of Town," in *Feature* (January 1979).

In November 1978, O'Brien was back to the old man from "The Sweetheart Mountains." He had merged the two ideas of the old man fighting death and fighting silos into a single book.[39] In early October he had read a piece called "The Nuclear Age" at Middlebury College, which appears to have been a discrete story for an imagined collection about living in the Cold War inspired partly (if not wholly) by the trip for *Feature*.[40] Instead the story became the germ for another novel.

By March 1979, O'Brien had written what at the time was the new book's first chapter, "The Nuclear Age"—probably a developed version of what he'd read at Middlebury—and had placed it with *The Atlantic Monthly* (June 1979). He was working on both "The Sweetheart Mountains" and the new one, called *The Nuclear Age*.[41] He was 120 pages into "The Sweetheart Mountains," but the new idea excited him more. The writing was looser, more spontaneous. He predicted it would be his first blockbuster, and he was aiming for a film adaptation.[42]

O'Brien pitched *The Nuclear Age* as the novel of his generation, and also a "bizarre" novel:

> Sarah's swiping a nuclear warhead from the Air Force; William's subsequent caretakership of the warhead, traveling about the country in search of his two lost loves, the warhead covered up by a blanket in the back of his VW van. But these things, [though] bizarre, though funny, though a little absurd, are also fully compatible with the crazy times we live in: witness the SLA, witness terrorism, witness the nuclear mishap in Pennsylvania recently, witness the SALT talks, all that. Crazy, maybe, but not that crazy.

There's a touch of *Catch-22* in the sanity conundrum. Who's crazy, the guy building a fallout shelter or everyone else, putzing along as if all were normal, the apocalypse not a button-push away? O'Brien fills the final novel with national and global news, from the Cuban Missile Crisis and the St. Paul anti-war march to President Carter's pardon for draft dodgers. Several characters die in a scene very like the televised 1974 shootout between the Los Angeles Police Department and the Symbionese Liberation Army (SLA), a far-left revolutionary terrorist group.[43]

By May 1979, O'Brien had a two-book contract.[44] Two books about the Cold War. The nuclear threat mattered more than anything else of its era and seemed tailor-made for a writer concerned about characters confronting mortality, about people caught in history's currents, about art of moral consequence.

Life went on. After O'Brien submitted the final *Cacciato* manuscript in May 1977, he and Ann took a trip to Cape Cod followed by a trip with his parents to Vermont.[45] In late summer the entire family gathered at a Pequot Lakes resort in northern Minnesota[46]—O'Brien adored his family and spent as much time as he could with them. *Daniel Martin* confirmed John Fowles as O'Brien's model for making action and theme indivisible.[47] "The Fisherman," from *Cacciato*, appeared in *Esquire* in October 1977.

In early 1978, the O'Briens moved from the condo they almost bought on Kirkland Street to a nicer one at 49 Irving.[48] Through his connection with DeWitt Henry and *Ploughshares*, O'Brien taught a Great War Novels course at nearby Emerson College.

Going After Cacciato was hardly behind him. Interviews, interviews, interviews, for newspapers, magazines, radio, television. Random veterans wrote and called. "The letters meant a lot because I had wanted to touch on something that was common to us all. But I found myself involved in so many hour-long phone calls from shattered guys that it was like reliving the war all over again." It was a strange position for someone who hadn't come home shattered.[49] *The Deer Hunter*, though, "emotionally stunned" O'Brien, leaving him speechless. The Russian roulette scene was a perfect metaphor for the "raw confrontation with death." The film's deaths were as real as they could be: "That's how I felt when I saw friends die in Vietnam."[50]

Macalester joined the national moment of confronting Việt Nam with its "The Vietnam Experience and America Today" symposium during the first ten days of March 1979. It wasn't the first time the college recognized O'Brien—in August 1974, he had received a Charter Centennial Medallion for his journalism and writing career at the chapel convocation welcoming new students. The 1979 symposium's other headliners included Senator Eugene McCarthy, Father Daniel Berrigan, President Kennedy's adviser Theodore Sorensen, historian and Democratic adviser Arthur M. Schlesinger, Jr., anti-war activist Rev. Robert McAfee Brown, Special Forces veteran and historian Herbert Schandler, policy expert Richard J. Barnet, and journalists including Gloria Emerson and Peter Arnett. O'Brien felt out of place—he remembers Schlesinger stepping out of a limo, very debonair in his signature bow tie and accompanied by a "gorgeous taller woman," while O'Brien schlepped to campus alone in a cab.

Nevertheless, he was the main attraction, the young alumnus with his star on the rise. For his two days on campus, when not onstage he visited classes, gave interviews, joined group discussions, socialized with faculty, and did a television show, answering the same questions "over and over and over again."[51] One reporter thought he looked bored smoking alone in the foyer apart from the veterans testifying about how the system betrayed them. O'Brien told the reporter that talking about the war now felt "dishonest" because it happened ten years ago to someone he wasn't anymore. "And that's kind of why I don't want to write about it anymore. You're supposed to write about things you know, and I don't know it anymore"[52]— though he told a student reporter he would write about Việt Nam again "someday."[53]

After his Tuesday evening talk about craft and structure, O'Brien was joined onstage by three other novelists of the war: William Eastlake, author of *The Bamboo Bed*, James Webb, author of *Fields of Fire*, and Steven Phillip Smith, author of *American Boys*. O'Brien wanted to push against Webb's conservative, heroic vision of the war, but stayed quiet. Eastlake, a World War II veteran, spoke up. The *Mac Weekly* reported the exchange: "Webb said his novel was deliberately 'a-political.' And according to Eastlake, 'the biggest political statements I ever heard were the ones that were non-political.'"[54] Eastlake had visited Macalester when O'Brien was a student. At the time, O'Brien found him friendly if "freakish," like a strung-out "Buddhist monk." *The Bamboo Bed* was too zany to be taken seriously, the trap O'Brien had sought to avoid in *Going After Cacciato*.

Within two weeks, on his way to the University of North Carolina for his part in a ten-day Fine Arts Festival, his final stop on a college reading tour, O'Brien learned that *Going After Cacciato* had been nominated for the National Book Award.[55] Things moved fast—the judges met on April 23 and announced the winners that afternoon, two days before the Carnegie Hall ceremony.[56] No one expected *Cacciato* to win. O'Brien certainly didn't. The front-runners were John Irving's *The World According to Garp* and John Cheever's *The Stories of John Cheever*, with Irving the predicted winner since Cheever was vying for his second. The other contenders were Diane Johnson's *Lying Low* and David Plante's *The Family*.

O'Brien's upset win shocked everyone who paid attention. The judges, Alison Lurie, Mary Lee Settle, and Wallace Stegner, made their decision unanimously and easily, Settle defensively told the press.[57] She debunked the theory that O'Brien won as each judge's second choice when they couldn't agree on Irving or Cheever. They hadn't felt comfortable selecting a collection of stories dating back thirty years, so the choice narrowed to *Garp* and *Cacciato*, and it took five minutes to decide. Settle also dismissed the idea that they were "playing catchup on Vietnam" in the wake of the Oscars: "It's a novel that Wally Stegner and I both wished we had written.

That was the final judgment."[58] Some in the publishing industry carped that *Garp*'s commercial success doomed it for this panel of literary writers: 190,000 hardbacks and over a million paperbacks to *Cacciato*'s paltry 12,000 total.[59] But the choice only surprised, Settle said, because people hadn't read O'Brien's novel.[60] The award shouldn't be a popularity contest.

The award citation compared O'Brien's irony to Stendhal's, his landscapes to Tolstoy's, and his vision's "essential American wonder and innocence" to Stephen Crane's. "Tim O'Brien has added a new dimension to the literature of war by dealing fully for the first time with an essential part of the experience of soldiers—the dreams which preserve sanity at a time when reality has become insane." The experimental structure convinced the judges that "there was no other way to tell this story." It is about the U.S. war in Việt Nam, about all wars, and about "the lives and dreams of all men and women caught in the destructive routines of a world they never chose."[61]

Irving took O'Brien out to dinner to celebrate either the night of the announcement or the next night. He had expected he or Cheever would win and was disappointed when he didn't, but due to his "great affection for Tim and genuine admiration for *Going After Cacciato*, nobody else winning would have made me happier." They were great friends. The characters in their nominated novels practically grew up together at Bread Loaf and in Boston as the writers did readings and exchanged drafted material. O'Brien deeply appreciated the fact that Irving came to the ceremony, as not all non-winners bothered.

O'Brien's parents and his sister joined him and Ann in New York. Either the night before, or after the post-ceremony reception, the family went to a dinner hosted by Lawrence at Elaine's, the city's storied eatery and watering hole for actors and writers.

The television personality Dick Cavett hosted the ceremony. He appeared unprepared and bungling.[62] The speaker, Senator Patrick Moynihan, talked solely about Arthur Schlesinger, Jr., the biography winner for *Robert Kennedy and His Times*, to the neglect of the other writers but for an opening platitude about "inspiration and persistence."[63] O'Brien's remarks were gracious and confident. He celebrated the other nominees as well as other works from 1978: John Updike's *The Coup*, Richard Price's *Ladies' Man*, Barry Hannah's *Airships*, Richard Yates's *A Good School*.

O'Brien thought his book deserved to win, but so did Irving's. "I wish we might've shared this moment. In the sense of friendship, I know, we did."[64]

Anne Bernays and Joe Kaplan came to the ceremony and delighted in O'Brien's award. Anne Mollegen Smith also attended, pleased as punch for the writer whose first published story she had discovered. Either in the crowded Carnegie Hall lobby or at the reception, she caught his eye "for long enough to sign congratulations and maybe blow kisses. He looked so happy; he couldn't stop smiling and laughing, and tons of people were trying to talk to him and some were hugging him. He had a long streak of someone's lipstick along the side of his jaw." Her friend said he looked like "a boy on the biggest day of his life."

A boy seething beneath his joy at his father. Bill had spent those couple of days disappearing to visit his old Brooklyn haunts. Imagining the life that might have been proved too much. The night before the ceremony, after an argument with Ava over his drinking, he started driving back to Minnesota before turning back. She didn't tell her son about it until the next day. Then, at the Sherry-Netherland Hotel reception, Bill proceeded to get embarrassingly drunk. Jealousy over his son's writing success probably contributed. O'Brien was so distracted by his dad that he left the award trophy on the reception floor (someone found it and returned it later). At one point he put his hand on the back of his father's neck to lean in for a hushed scolding—not the affectionate touch that a photo of the moment conveyed.

A day or so later, O'Brien hopped in his car and drove down to northern Virginia to play golf and chill with his writer friend Richard Bausch. O'Brien recalls a dinner at the novelist Susan Shreve's house in D.C.—the reviewer Doris Grumbach was there, and Eugene McCarthy's ex-wife, Abigail, whose conversation absorbed him. One evening at Bausch's, O'Brien spent a couple of hours hogging the phone line with someone Bausch understood to be an old high school flame. It was Gayle Roby.

Ava Schultz and Bill O'Brien, 1944
(Permission by Tim O'Brien, HRC)

In 1947
(Permission by Tim O'Brien, HRC)

In Austin, Minnesota
(Permission by Tim O'Brien, HRC)

In Worthington, Minnesota
(Permission by Tim O'Brien, HRC)

In Worthington, Minnesota
(Permission by Tim O'Brien, HRC)

High school, senior year (1963–1964)
(Permission by Tim O'Brien, HRC)

Final semester at Macalester,
Mac Weekly, April 19, 1968, p. 1
(Permission by Tim O'Brien)

Pfc. O'Brien's basic training
photo, Fort Lewis, fall 1968
(Permission by Tim O'Brien, HRC)

On leave from training before Việt Nam, with Kathy and Greg,
Christmas 1968 *(Permission by Tim O'Brien, HRC)*

LZ Gator, c. 1969–1970
(Permission by Tim O'Brien)

View to the southeast from
LZ Gator, c. 1969–1970
(Permission by Tim O'Brien)

Alvin "Chip" Merricks,
spring 1969
(Permission by Tim O'Brien, HRC)

(Above) Pfc. O'Brien in Việt Nam
(Permission by Tim O'Brien, HRC)

"Trick or Treat" by Tim O'Brien,
The Professional, newsletter of the
5th Battalion, 46th Infantry, LZ
Gator, Việt Nam (Oct. 11, 1969)
(Permission by Tim O'Brien, HRC)

(Below) Sgt. O'Brien on LZ Gator,
late 1969 or early 1970
(Permission by Tim O'Brien, HRC)

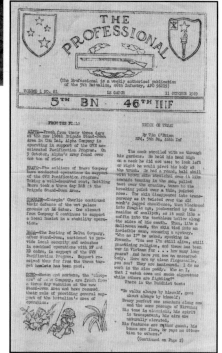

Tim and Kathy in Salem,
Massachusetts, c. 1970–1971
(Permission by Tim O'Brien, HRC)

Watergate Office Building
for June 17, 1972, recording
O'Brien's role in the top entry
*(National Archives; National
Archives Identifier: 304970)*

50

6.17.72 AT 4:47 Tim O'Brien- Reporter With
The Wash. Post ID #413 Walked In To Lobby
Door Breaking Glass. He Was Not Hurt.
Reported it To Maintenance. - (223-7438)
Mr. O'Brien Phone Number ———

6:20 Checked B2 Level Found Garage door Unlocked
Looked Around All Was Normal Locked door
And Continued My Rounds. Stairwell door on 13th
Floor Wont Lock We do Not Have A Key For it
Police Took door From 6th Floor Stair Way, Maintenance
Is Putting A Piece Of Ply wood Over It. Stair
door on 3rd Floor doesn't Catch Has been Reported
Several Times.

8:00 Building Secure- No Workers Allowed In DNC
On 6th Fl A member Of The Committe will be
Around Tomorrow morning Please Admit Him.

9:00 Checked Lower Three Levels All Secure With The
Exception Of B1 Stair Way door Wont Lock
No Key For It.

9:30 Made Check Of Entire bld Found door Open
On 5th Fl Checked The Area Nothing Unusal All
secure. Relocked The door.

10:15 Officer From Federal Reserve Came by To
Check- All Secure

11:05 Started My Rounds On B-3 Continued UP Found
Light On In Rm. 500 DNC door Was Locked
All Secure At This Time. 11:35

12:00 Relieved by Off Wills- All Secure

Photo upon publication of *If I Die in a Combat Zone, Box Me Up and Ship Me Home* (1973)
(Permission by Tim O'Brien, SL)

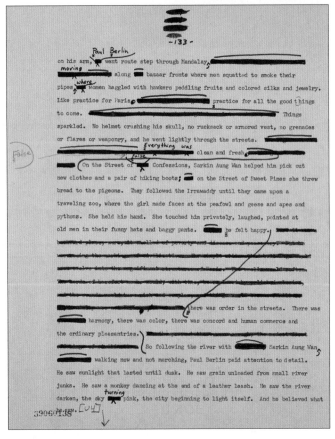

Page revisions to a typescript draft of *Going After Cacciato*
(Permission by Tim O'Brien, HRC)

PART III

22

DREAMS THAT SUPPOSE AWAKENINGS

The Nuclear Age

Tim O'Brien and Gayle Roby hadn't seen each other since the St. Paul anti-war march in May 1970. She and her husband returned from their Peace Corps stint in India in January 1972 and that summer moved to Providence, Rhode Island, for her graduate school. The following spring, they split. Around this time, as she recalls, O'Brien's publisher (Lawrence's office) sent her a notice about the publication of *If I Die in a Combat Zone, Lock Me Up and Ship Me Home*, doubtless on O'Brien's request.

After earning a teaching certificate, she moved to Bonn, Germany, where she taught English at the American School for three years, and where O'Brien sent her an inscribed copy of *Northern Lights*. A book dedicated to Ann. In his second letter, he told her he was married. She wrote back that she couldn't continue reconnecting, because she wouldn't wish such pain on another. For the second time, Roby waved O'Brien off by mail. She moved back to the United States in 1976, settling in Ann Arbor. This period of correspondence perhaps explains the cryptic note in a June 1976 letter to Lawrence: "One important thing—if you receive any personal mail in your care, please don't forward it to me. Hold on to it until the next time I see you. Dark secrets."[1]

Roby attended the 13th Annual Teachers of English to Speakers of Other Languages (TESOL) Convention at Boston's Sheraton Hotel from February 28 to March 4, 1979. She couldn't resist the proximity. She phoned him ("Remember me?"—as if he could have forgotten) and showed up to hear him read from *Going After Cacciato* at Emerson College. It blew her away. The two spent several hours together. "[T]hey took a walk across the campus and talked about their lives," O'Brien would write in "'The Things They Carried" about Lt. Jimmy Cross's 1979 reunion with Martha: "Nothing had changed. He still loved her."[2]

Roby flew home. O'Brien headed to the Macalester symposium on Việt Nam. Was that night at Richard Bausch's house the first time they had talked since news broke about his winning the National Book Award? When O'Brien traveled to Spokane to deliver his first commencement speech, at Eastern Washington University on June 8, Roby joined him. In their hotel room, he introduced her to a reporter as Bobbi Haymore, the name of the protagonist's love interest from his youth in the current vision for *The Nuclear Age*.[3] It was a gamble, or maybe a wink to the wise, to anyone who'd read "The Nuclear Age" in *The Atlantic Monthly*'s current issue. According to Roby, a friend told Ann O'Brien about the *Spokane Chronicle* article that mentioned her husband's "companion," and he returned to an understandably angry spouse. O'Brien says Ann never learned about the relationship.

O'Brien's and Roby's hazy memories agree on the essentials. At some point that summer, O'Brien visited Roby's parents' home in Decatur, Illinois. They liked him but did not know he was married. It also appears that O'Brien visited Roby in Ann Arbor that summer. Something about the visit surprised her, either *that* he was coming or *when* he was arriving. She had been at her boyfriend's place that morning. After she and O'Brien slept together, she admitted she'd been in bed with the other man a few hours earlier. Hurt and furious, he lost his temper. But their romance recovered its momentum due to the "enormously heart-quickening, gut-thumping powers of true passion," as he would soon describe the feeling—in contrast with marriage's dull affection—in his review of *Endless Love* that very October.[4]

Roby accompanied O'Brien to Bread Loaf in August as a poetry student and publicly as his other half (at least one person assumed she was his wife). Those were two "exciting" and "glorious" weeks for Roby. The conversation thrilled, the wine flowed. As the current National Book Award winner, O'Brien, not yet thirty-three, was the conference wunderkind. He gave a lecture called "Caring," he read from the *Nuclear Age* manuscript, he participated in a panel called "On Getting Started," and he led a fiction workshop.[5]

Roby recalls their agreeing to take a break, and then O'Brien's making a second trip to Ann Arbor after Bread Loaf. Or did they meet in Chicago? O'Brien talks about only one Ann Arbor visit, perhaps accurately, perhaps conflating two. While taking a walk with him in Ann Arbor, Roby realized "this guy really does love me" in a way she hadn't experienced before. A wide-open love with no need for pretense or petty dishonesties: "I felt it physically. I felt like my heart broke open from a cage." In the interest of this fresh unfiltered love, she disclosed that she had recently called another guy on his birthday to wish him well, news O'Brien didn't entirely trust. At the end of his stay, Roby drove O'Brien to the airport, watched him board, and on impulse bought a ticket with her father's credit card for the same plane to Boston. A flattered, puzzled O'Brien watched her beam her way down the aisle. He wondered about her emotional stability. On the flight, he made it clear that he would not leave Ann. Roby understood. Her compunction about being the other woman no longer stood in her way. It was September 1979.

They parted at the airport. Roby stayed with a friend in Arlington, a few miles northwest of Cambridge. Within a day or two, when Ann was at work, Roby rang the O'Briens' doorbell. He answered and told her where to meet the next morning at ten. By Thanksgiving, she'd loaded up a U-Haul and moved from Michigan. She rented an apartment in Arlington, and for the next nine and a half years Tim O'Brien led a double life.

They saw each other two or three times a week. Roby worked part-time jobs at different schools teaching English to adult learners. She taught in the mornings and evenings, leaving her afternoons free. O'Brien would go to see her after the day's writing. "Euphoria," Roby describes those first days, months, years. She believed him when he reminded her that he wouldn't leave Ann. He loved his wife, she didn't deserve it, and "he's an honorable person." Yet Roby hoped against hope: "I wanted every bit of what I got, and I wanted more."

Overwhelming romantic love versus everyday love, family, and allegiance. For all their difficulties, O'Brien's parents had stayed together. The word *divorce* must have threatened as much shame and embarrassment as the word *desertion* had in 1968 to this true son of Worthington. He couldn't bring himself to do either one. The old paralysis took over.

For a gift, O'Brien wrote out Auden's "This Loved One" by hand, inscribed "From G, summer of 1968." Roby added, "From Tim, Valentine's Day, 1985." Weeks after that Valentine's Day, he submitted the final manuscript of *The Nuclear Age*. It came out in the fall.

The Nuclear Age appears to have begun with the story "The Nuclear Age," read at Middlebury in October 1978 and intended for a story collection. In the spring of 1979, when asked about his next book, O'Brien talked about a cheerleader radicalized into a peacenik terrorist, the novel's Sarah Strouch. A month before the National Book Award, O'Brien submitted to Lawrence the partial outline and the first thirty-three draft pages of *The Nuclear Age*. One can only conjecture how much the Bobbi Haymore character changed after Gayle Roby reentered O'Brien's life.

In the outline, Sarah, Bobbi, and the male protagonist, William Cowling, know one another from their anti-war work in the late 1960s. After the 1968 Democratic convention, their crew breaks up. Sarah decides to practice law. William is drafted but absconds to Mexico. Bobbi earns a master's degree from Duke University in German language and poetry. "William, wallowing in Mexico, decides he loves Bobbi—he *does* love her, passionately. Always has, in fact. But he can't go chase her; he's in exile. Meanwhile, Bobbi gets married and goes to Bonn to teach the children of NATO officers."[6] Just as O'Brien, wallowing in Việt Nam, decided he loved Roby, who married and then taught in Bonn. In the drafted pages, Auden's poem becomes German poetry that Bobbi sends William and he struggles to translate:

Whenever I'd get stumped on a poem, I'd call her up and we'd go over it together, all the idioms and so on, and afterward I'd go crazy wondering what the poem *meant*, and what she meant. Naturally I didn't ask. Poems are supposed to soak through—meanings, I mean. She wouldn't say she loved me, and I didn't ask about that either. Nothing was soaking through. I was pretty dense.[7]

That passage was likely drafted before he and Roby met up again that spring. It's back to American poetry and Auden for the published novel, when at their first meeting Bobbi recites Auden, Frost, Dickinson, "and several of her own poems," and Cowling is a goner.[8]

As O'Brien failed to reach Roby from Australia, Cowling fails to reach Bobbi by phone. Then another letter arrives, the last from Bobbi, the one telling him about her new husband and Bonn. Also in the drafted pages, Bobbi no longer goes to Duke for graduate studies but the University of Michigan at Ann Arbor. In the published novel, William meets Bobbi on a plane—she's the flight attendant who comforts him during a minor panic attack. O'Brien translated the fateful flight he and Roby took from Ann Arbor to Boston into this fateful airborne encounter. "You're crazy, you know that?" Bobbi tells William on the plane when he professes his instant love and desire to run away with her, even have children;[9] O'Brien might very well have told the same thing to Roby on the plane when she professed her sudden commitment to their love. The unreliability O'Brien imagined in Roby informs the novel's characterization of Bobbi, whom William marries. "He shouldn't love her, but he does," O'Brien introduced his characters at his last Bread Loaf reading before the novel's publication: "She can't commit herself to anything, politics or William himself. In various stages in the novel she's left him and returned; her diaphragm has often left with her."[10]

Sarah Strouch, whom O'Brien considered "the best character [he'd] ever created," also began with someone he dated in college. The fall of his senior year after the summer in Europe, O'Brien dated two girls he met at the college president's welcoming reception for freshmen. One was the 1967 first runner-up national Miss Junior Miss. The other was altogether something else, another cute blonde but besides that the most compelling young woman he'd ever met. Vivian Vie had spent the last year and a half of high school in the Philippines, happy to be away from the St. Paul cold. Her father worked for the U.S. Agency for International Development (USAID) out of Sài Gòn's Tân Sơn Nhất International Airport, while the family joined the growing community of USAID and embassy wives and children in the Makati suburb of Manila. The older children attended the American school until midday, then relocated to the embassy/USAID compound pool for the afternoon.[11]

It was a heavenly existence made possible by the war. Vie had her own room for the first time in her life. The family had a Filipino maid. Her schoolmates and social circle came from around the world, from Turkey, from Germany, in many cases saddled with history. There were "refugees from Republican Spain, Bataan, and the Manila internment camp. Racists and Hitler lovers." Vie marveled at her new chums, teenagers openly ordering beer and seeming worldly beyond their years. American soldiers were around, too. Green Berets recounted graphic war stories with pleasure, stories Vie wasn't sure she should believe. The teenager wasn't yet aware of USAID and her father's collaboration with the military. Politically, Vie's turning point occurred on the plane back to the United States the summer before college. The graduate student seated beside her spent much of the flight inveighing against the war that Vie's dependent community had accepted as the given of their lives. The encounter left her with "the most upending feeling that I and the rest of America had been wrongly deceived."

At Macalester, the "very attractive" big man on campus Tim O'Brien spellbound Vie. He entered her life at a time when she felt "split down the middle" as she began dismantling the worldview nurtured by her upbringing. A shy seventeen-year-old, she opened up to him when she was struggling to "be genuine to anything." O'Brien returned the fascination. He sensed the split—he seemed to her the only person who did. She appeared to him a lonely, lost soul.

She questioned everything, she had an opinion about everything. O'Brien found their conversations "mind-blowing." Expression stumbled to catch up to her ideas, with O'Brien sometimes straining to follow the connections. Unlike most other smart young women that he had known, Vie owned her intelligence. She cared deeply about civil rights and the war, one of the few people who talked about the latter with O'Brien.

Twenty-some years later, Vie wrote a short story based on her freshman-year romance. "I see myself walking through the jungle and it makes me nuts," Kevin Matthews, the Tim O'Brien character, tells Belinda about imagining Việt Nam. "The Reading" was never published. In the story, Vie describes the first time her alter ego sees Kevin's dorm room:

> The student directory was open on his nightstand. Her face was one of those circled in black magic marker. She studied the copy of the painting above his headboard. The lion and the sleeping gypsy. The lion sniffing the body of the dreaming man, who because he dreams is fearless. This boy, she thinks, is a small hometown boy who believes in dreams. She knew things about him that were obvious because they were not hidden. He was someone who was talked about, someone who liked being talked about. He was a Phi Beta Kappa senior, a teaching assistant in the history department, and the star of the school's diving team, the only team besides chess that ever won. His diving medals hung over the mirror of his bureau along with a St. Christopher's medal. She looked at the titles in his bookcase: history mostly. She pulled one of them out. Notes in the margins in small precise writing. Loose leaf pages with outlines of chapters.[12]

In real life the books were a mixture of political science and history. O'Brien the Phi Beta Kappa senior was a student assistant in the politics department as well as a research fellow in sociology. He was taking a beginner's swimming course the semester they met.[13] (Vie doesn't think she ever knew he couldn't swim. "Hey Matthews," a lifeguard calls out after the O'Brien character botches a dive, "I thought I was going to have to go in after you that time.") O'Brien did not own a St. Christopher medal, but he did decorate his room with Henri Rousseau's *The Sleeping Gypsy,* one of the cheap, moody European late-nineteenth- or early-twentieth-century art posters, like Gustav Klimt's *The Kiss,* sold to students for their dorms. He worked on his never-published study-abroad novel "A Man of Melancholy Disposition" beneath that image. Vie was with him the night he dropped the manuscript off at the library for duplication, a hefty stack of pages in a cardboard box.

In the story as in life, per Vie's recollection, one night the young man declared himself a hedonist, perhaps an exaggeration to shock and entice her in the manner of those Green Berets' stories in Manila. The two of them went on fewer than a dozen dates. They saw *Barefoot in the Park* at the St. Clair Theater and the Czechoslovakian *Closely Watched Trains* at the Grandview.

Vie was veering to the left of O'Brien politically. She joined the Young Socialist Alliance, mostly because of its organized opposition to the war. One evening outside a movie theater on Hennepin Avenue in Minneapolis, near the YSA office, Vie explained the group's Trotskyite roots. The magnetism of her forthright, verbal personality, plus her new communist sympathies, overwhelmed O'Brien's small-town upbringing. She scared him. Early in Cowling's romance with Sarah, he realizes she's "volatile," if principled.[14] O'Brien started backing away from the budding relationship. Nevertheless, he invited Vie to visit Worthington over Christmas break. She went against her better judgment. O'Brien doesn't remember the visit. Vie recalled his mom mistaking her for another girl. "'Nice to meet you, Susan, I've heard so much about you.' Behind me, Tim and his sister giggled." Susan was the other person he had dated that fall. Vie wrote the visit into the story, after which "they made the long trip back to the college. He deposited her back at her dorm." O'Brien stopped calling. That was the January he met Roby. His senior year O'Brien also had a full plate with his studies, his uncertain future, and his Community Council presidency.

The YSA attracted Vie with its anti-war objectives and work ethic. That spring—depressed by the war, by homesickness for the Manila poolside life, by heartbreak, by "self-loathing"—she threw herself into building coalitions and managing protest legalities. Working with other Macites on the newsletter of the Minnesota New Mobilization Committee, the *Minnesota Mobilizer*, was a lifeline. "Time seemed to be able to move forward again."

According to Vie, she went with O'Brien to see *The Green Berets* the summer he was drafted. Its clichés and puff-chested righteousness riled her. At one point she cheered for the Việt Cộng, prompting O'Brien to turn and stare. This might have been the occasion she suggested he become a card-carrying socialist because the army didn't bring socialists into the ranks, even though she knew he wouldn't because of the dishonesty, "but one could always hope."

When he was at basic training, she traveled to the Democratic National Convention in Chicago, arriving the night the chaos commenced and tanks hit the streets. At Mac, she coordinated between the YSA and Macalester's Committee for Peace in Vietnam. The year O'Brien was in Việt Nam, she contributed three articles to the *Mac Weekly* drumming support for anti-war movement activities.[15] On the envelopes addressed to him overseas she shouted "BRING THE TROOPS HOME NOW!" until O'Brien implored her to stop. In April 1970, as he marched toward the capitol in St. Paul with tens of thousands of others, he didn't know that Vie was at the destination stage helping with coordination. Eventually she left the movement for the same reason O'Brien avoided organized causes, the rigid conformity of political and operational ideas and even personal behavior. You had to be clean-cut; you couldn't be openly gay or bi.

Sarah Strouch only began with Vivian Vie. She also merged with Ann O'Brien, as Sarah and Cowling have been a longtime couple before he chases after Bobbi. "Sarah is a tough lady and William should love Sarah, and doesn't," O'Brien introduced her to his August 1985 Bread Loaf audience. "She's lovable, I think. She thinks. Instead, our hero loves his wife," Bobbi, as O'Brien loved Roby. Sarah's refrain was Ann's: *I'm the committed one. I love you. Why don't you love and choose me?* In the end, Bobbi and Sarah are themselves, original inventions in O'Brien's continuing experiments with his usable past.

Like William Timothy O'Brien, William Cowling was born in a small town on October 1, 1946. Both Timmy and William converted their basement Ping-Pong tables into fallout shelters and crouched under their desks during school drills. O'Brien rewrote his opening to the "Going After Silos" article into the opening of *The Nuclear Age*'s second chapter, "Civil Defense," first published in August 1980 in *Esquire* and at times the front-runner for the first chapter. Like O'Brien, Cowling had a bicycle accident that resulted in a doctor's starting to stitch up his penis without anesthesia. When the doctor relented and "jammed the needle in," Cowling, like O'Brien, kicked him. "I don't remember it," Cowling says. "But my mother swears it happened."[16] O'Brien isn't sure if he truly remembers it or just knows it through Ava's routine retelling, laughing her head off.

Both found a safe space in a library overseen by a kindly woman. As teenagers, neither William fit in. O'Brien describes Cowling as "something of a loner," a "little arrogant, a little belligerent," a supreme "dork" who was a mite "creepy" to girls.[17] O'Brien and Cowling lived through the Cuban Missile Crisis, graduated from high school in 1964, and during college watched the war in Việt Nam escalate with only mild gestures of protest. In the 1979 outline that secured the book contract, Cowling is the leader of a group of anti-war radicals, "a toned-down Abbie Hoffman, perhaps," one of the Yippie leaders and member of the Chicago Seven. Hoffman's Yippie and Chicago Seven comrade Jerry Rubin is the better comparison. Rubin was the Yippie-turned-yuppie who, in an abrupt 1970s volte-face, left political activism to embrace capitalism, becoming a multimillionaire by the end of the decade. For his own 1970s volte-face, Cowling, who once considered nuclear weapons an abomination, successfully prospects for uranium and becomes rich off the sale of the deed. O'Brien aims the satire at his settling-down generation but also at himself, the writer profiting from the war he hated to his core.

Like O'Brien, Cowling graduates from college on May 27, 1968. The language O'Brien uses for Cowling's state of mind that summer, waiting to be drafted, matches the language he always used for his own:

> I couldn't decide. Like sleepwalking, except I couldn't move, the dynamic was paralyzing. [. . .] But no decisions. Vaguely, stupidly, I was hoping for a last-minute miracle. In Paris they were talking peace, and I wanted the miracle of a decision deferred into perpetuity. I wanted resolution without resolve. [. . .] But it was not my decision. The dynamic decided for me.[18]

Cowling receives his draft notice in August; O'Brien reported to the army in August. Sarah tells Cowling to run and he does, to her, already underground in Key West. He runs because there's a girl who loves him waiting. Cowling won't be alone, won't forgo love or his past.

Reimagining his imagined flight to Canada from the army and his fantasy of Gayle Roby, whom he hardly knew, going with him, O'Brien has Cowling meet Bobbi on his literal plane flight from the draft to Key West. He falls in love in a flash: "I told her I was caught up by current events. I couldn't separate right from wrong. I needed a hideout. Would she mind saving my life? Could we find an island somewhere?" That's when she recites Auden, Frost, and Dickinson before declining.[19]

In June 1979, the month Roby joined O'Brien in Spokane under the name Bobbi Haymore, Cowling graduates with a master's degree and begins his hunt for Bobbi Haymore. He becomes aware of Bobbi's record of infidelities. When he tracks her down in September, finding the final hard lead in Ann Arbor—the month and place O'Brien and Roby met up—Cowling confronts her with her betrayals and craziness yet declares his endless love for her anyway. "I swear to God—I swear it—I'll never let you go. Never. That means *never.*" O'Brien added the date details of June and September 1979 and the declaration *after* the first version of this section was published in *The Atlantic Monthly* in June 1979. He either knew something about Roby's romantic history or intuited it before the walk at Emerson at the beginning of March, having already written about Bobbi's fickle heart in the story *Esquire* initially planned to run in May.

Cowling and Bobbi marry. They have a daughter, Melinda.

Now it's 1995, when the published novel begins and ends. In the present, Cowling has locked his wife and daughter in a bedroom for the weeks it takes him to construct a bomb shelter. He carries their drugged bodies there and very nearly blows it up. Melinda wakes up enough to talk him out of it. (Spencer's *Endless Love* opens with its male protagonist setting fire to the home of the object of his obsessive love before a change of heart sends him into the burning house to save her and her family.) Cowling accepts living life in the moment and for the moment against the expected futures of his wife leaving him and the world ending:

> I will trust the seasons. I will keep Bobbi in my arms for as long as she will stay. I will obey my vows. I will stop smoking. I will have hobbies. I will firm up my golf game and invest wisely and adhere to the conventions of decency and good grace. I will find forgetfulness. Happily, without hesitation, I will take my place in the procession from church to grave, believing what cannot be believed, that all things are renewable, that the human spirit is undefeated and infinite always.[20]

The crosscurrents with O'Brien's personal life are striking. In April 1980, a year into the book and his relationship with Roby, O'Brien told hopefuls at Macalester that they need to be ready to sacrifice "everything for their craft," that "a real writer will go as far as giving up his wife and his children" for his art.[21] As Fowles's David Williams had not been able to do in *The Ebony Tower*. In length, pacing, and spirit, *The Nuclear Age*'s final paragraph resembles to an astonishing degree that of Don DeLillo's *White Noise*, published in January of the same year, 1985. O'Brien had written his ending a few years earlier. DeLillo's novel also highlights humanity's capacity to deny imminent demise at its own hands. O'Brien finished his novel on March 1, 1985.[22]

In the spring of 1979, O'Brien could hardly contain his enthusiasm for the potential novel. If *Going After Cacciato* proved his literary talent, *The Nuclear Age* would, he believed, establish his commercial power.[23] The initial manuscript due date of August 1980 for 1981 publication didn't last long. It was the hardest of his books to write and the one he's least fond of now. Greg Andrews, a Boston friend from Worthington a few years behind O'Brien and a regular golf partner during the early eighties, was aware of O'Brien's anguish and restarts. Sometimes O'Brien called him the night before tee time to cancel their game because of a pressing rewrite.

Although Erik Hansen advised O'Brien on *The Nuclear Age*, there is no correspondence trail of its composition. Either it has been lost or was never produced, those sessions having been conducted in person or over the phone. The best extant document is O'Brien's notes for his 1985 Bread Loaf lecture on the eve of publication.[24] An obvious issue was the competition with himself after the success of *Cacciato*, something that worried him from the outset. After two years, he started over. The problem was a minor character, a librarian, who had taken on a major role without developing into a person beyond stereotypes and plot device, and who steered the novel away from its foundational passion, the fear of nuclear annihilation. O'Brien's 1981 Bread Loaf reading featured the communist librarian he thereafter cut down to size. In her forties, Florence Jensen is engaged to Cowling his senior year of high school. At the end of the chapter, he has retreated post-prom to the library's basement reading room, where she succors him by taking his virginity in a Wild West buggy,[25] like the one in the basement of the Worthington library.

The reading mentions Florence's ample chest more than once, pays a fair amount of attention to Sarah Strouch's body, and makes homophobic jokes about "fag talk" and "fag wrestlers." To be sure, it's a first-person draft dramatizing the teenage Cowling's immaturity and gender insecurities, a draft O'Brien rejected, yet its effect is puerile. The wrestling jokes were perhaps an odd shout-out to his writer friends John Irving and Ron Hansen, both former wrestlers who sometimes wrestled at Bread Loaf, but more likely a dig at Mike Tracy, the Worthington bully O'Brien would later write into "The Lives of the Dead."

The next version suffered from a "*tonal*" problem. The jokes "were funny, often, but not literature. Too cute, at times. Too hip, other times. Straining, other times. Artificial quality to it all." He started over again.

Florence seems to have been the device for Sarah's conversion from wannabe Dallas Cowboys cheerleader to terrorist through traditional ideological suasion. But that process required speeches on the page, not dramatic or comedic action. Plus, O'Brien decided, such shifts often occur in more mundane ways. So he had Sarah develop a herpes sore that mars her beauty and relegates her to the second-string squad cheering for the archery team. That's when her life of protest begins. Her antics involve shaving her legs in a public fountain outside the football stadium to draw fans to follow her to the archery range.[26]

David Bain, a Bread Loaf regular and conference historian, thinks it might have been 1982 when, after reading from the draft, O'Brien "walked out of the theater without acknowledging the thunder of the applause of an audience that had been spellbound for an hour" and "stalked away into the night."[27] O'Brien doesn't remember it, saying he regularly left readings abruptly because he hated the obligatory chitchat where social niceties overrode honesty. Susan Thornton also believes O'Brien left the 1982 reading "visibly upset." (The verifiable 1982 reading consisted of a protracted draft of the "Chain Reactions" chapter, thankfully trimmed for the published novel.)[28]

Publication challenges started in 1982, when Delacorte, now owned by Doubleday, discontinued its relationship with Sam Lawrence. O'Brien wanted his contract to travel with Lawrence to his new house, E. P. Dutton. Delacorte fought hard to keep it, but in April 1983 a new contract took *The Nuclear Age* to Dutton.[29]

O'Brien didn't like the sound of his own voice during his 1983 Friday night Bread Loaf reading.[30] He had not discovered the novel's structure. He started over again. The 1983 reading, however, was the first at Bread Loaf to involve Cowling's daughter Melinda and his digging of the bomb shelter. The novel started coming together with the increased focus on the hole. It became the dramatic vehicle for Cowling's "craziness." It starts talking to him. The hole takes on the fulcrum function of the observation post in *Cacciato*, the still point of the present on the cusp of the future as it mines the past: "The structure took shape: alternating [between] a man digging for his life, escaping life, going mad in the backyard under Christmas lights, talking to his hole. With chapters of my character's life. It all seemed to come at once—a single conception."

"Quantum Jumps," a stitched-together version of the book's "Quantum Jumps" chapters, appeared in *Ploughshares'* last issue of 1983.[31] O'Brien finished the complete draft in early spring of 1984.[32] His new publisher didn't like it, offering a small print run with little marketing, but permitted O'Brien to seek a new publisher. Which he did, and in April 1984 Robert Gottlieb acquired *The Nuclear Age* for Knopf.[33] O'Brien and Gottlieb agreed it needed more revisions; Gottlieb provided several suggestions. A year and a rewrite later, O'Brien turned in the final manuscript. Seven and half years from start to finish, "9, 10, sometimes 12 hours a day. Weekends. Christmas Day." He worried the published book couldn't replicate the craft game he'd given himself of having every chapter end on a page of exactly fourteen lines. The book's final "Quantum Jumps" chapter appeared in *Granta*'s summer 1985 issue, the last excerpted teaser.[34] Wrapping up his August Bread Loaf lecture, O'Brien invited the audience to join him in dance and song to celebrate their artful yawping in the face of mortality and the end of the world.

O'Brien told a writer for *Esquire* that he "must have rewritten it thirty times."[35] Bain perceived O'Brien to be "wrestling with demons over the novel," as he and other Bread Loafers "worried at the toll it seemed to take from Tim's peace of mind."[36] O'Brien lost the original spark and forced the book to completion. Finances weren't an issue. The National Book Award had boosted sales of *Cacciato*; the publisher shuffling doesn't seem to have affected his up-front money; he won a 1981 Guggenheim Fellowship; he generated income publishing chapters; and Ann had her stable job at *Sail*. O'Brien spent a month after Bread Loaf in 1980 writing "The Ghost Soldiers,"[37] but otherwise doesn't seem to have been distracted from *The Nuclear Age* by writing more about the war. The change of publisher must have taken some toll in terms of time and energy. The more time that elapsed from his original excitement, the more difficult it must have been to sustain or recover it. O'Brien's double life, with its necessary lies and demands, not to mention the emotional anguish, must have taken its toll. The love triangle plot subsumes the novel's originating impulse in the fear of extinction. The overriding plot question becomes what the promise of love means to people and makes them do.

On the eve of publication, O'Brien described the process as a "horrible experience" that "made Vietnam look like a picnic." He was apathetic about the book's reception: "I don't care if anyone likes it or not. I know I'll get a few lovely reviews. I know I'll get some not-so-nice reviews. And I don't care anymore."[38]

◊   ◊   ◊

The Nuclear Age earned affirming notices upon publication in the fall of 1985. Stephen Schwandt of the *Minneapolis Star and Tribune* praised its "wonderfully realized scenes that recreate an entire generation's experience," its "dark humor" and "unblinking exploration of the Truth of modern life," making it "the best book [he's] read in a long time." Philip Gerard in *The Arizona Republic* saw in it the same "virtuosity of composition" as in *Going After Cacciato*, and appreciated its "main business," that of "salvaging the unsplittable atom of self, the irreducible core of human personality struggling for integrity in a world without reliable context, in which even the most mundane reassurances of civilization are not to be counted upon."[39]

The novel's detractors were more prominently placed and unsparing. *Kirkus Reviews* called it a "centerless, flogged-on, and jerry-built bomb of a book" that "just sits there and fizzles, on and on and on." Michiko Kakutani in *The New York Times* appreciated its ambition in tackling big questions but trashed its execution and its "sick adolescent humor."[40] Grace Paley, writing for the same paper's *Book Review*, criticized the novel for turning away from serious political questions to "mockery which usually means easy narrow characterization. In the case of the women this was particularly painful to me." O'Brien gets "William's love of Bobbi" right, but not the women themselves. Paley wanted the novel to be "either more surreal or less" rather than occupying "an untranscending middle which muffles the important cry of 'Doom, doom.'"[41]

Friends wrote to O'Brien of their high regard for the novel. Those who didn't like it, some said, weren't facing reality. One enclosed a copy of the letter he submitted to the *Book Review*, which blasted Paley for failing to locate it in the American male coming-of-age tradition of *Huckleberry Finn* and *The Catcher in the Rye*, as Paley overlooked "the unreliability of William Cowling's narration or the subtle interplay of history, nostalgia, nightmare and fantasy which the novel's structure makes explicit."[42]

Contra Paley, the novel's muddling of conventional realism and blatant surrealism was exactly O'Brien's point about the odd way people live in the nuclear age. It's supposed to be a cartoonish exaggeration. O'Brien and Paley had conflicted before. In the early eighties, the writer Frank Conroy, then the literary director at the National Endowment for the Arts, recruited O'Brien, Paley, the publisher David Godine, and one or two others for a panel to award NEA funding to small magazines. Paley supported *BOMB*, a new progressive publication out of New York that mixed visual art, film reviews, and contemporary writing. O'Brien championed the conventional *Antioch Review*. According to O'Brien, the panel did not recommend funding for *BOMB* and Paley was "livid" about the "conservative" result. O'Brien called Paley's damning review of *The Nuclear Age* a "feminist-rad response, not a literary response." If General Westmoreland, the commander of U.S. forces in Việt Nam until 1968, had reviewed *Cacciato*, O'Brien retorted, "I doubt it would've been judged by aesthetic standards."[43]

Paley's knee-jerk criticism wasn't exceptional in its conclusion. Others of O'Brien's writing circles, men and women, felt that he didn't write women characters as well as he wrote men. A fellow Bread Loafer recalled a reading from the novel-in-progress that "bombed," in her estimation partly because of its cluelessness about female psychology. No woman, however audacious, would shave her legs in a campus water fountain as Sarah Strouch did in that reading.[44] The person was also quick to praise O'Brien for taking risks with the drafts he publicly tested out and for heeding the responses. Yet Paley's criticism must have struck a nerve. Writing *Northern Lights*, O'Brien had worried about his and other male writers' "problems" writing women characters. "Why? They are objects of attention and concern in real life, not characters. They are related to, not developed. They are sought, not understood."[45]

As the publication timing of *Going After Cacciato* worked to that novel's advantage, the delayed completion and publication of *The Nuclear Age* hurt its reception. O'Brien had conceived of the novel as questioning the collective obliviousness to pending apocalypse: "No one is thinking or writing about it. Why isn't anyone scared. Am I crazy?" It was a valid cri de coeur in 1977 but an unoriginal refrain by the mid-1980s. President Carter's negotiations with the Soviet Union to reduce nuclear arsenals (SALT II), the rupture of the two superpowers' relationship over the Soviets' 1980 invasion of Afghanistan, and President Reagan's hawkish military budget and touted Strategic Defense Initiative—aka "Star Wars"—renewed Cold War anxieties, as reflected in the television films *First Strike* (1979) and *The Day After* (1983); books such as O'Brien's friend Corinne Browne and Robert Munroe's *Time Bomb* (1981), Jonathan Schell's *The Fate of the Earth*, Robert Jay Lifton and Richard A. Falk's *Indefensible Weapons*, Raymond Briggs's graphic novel *When the Wind Blows* (all 1982), and Edward Zuckerman's *The Day After World War III* (1984); and such feature films as *Mad Max* (1979), *The Atomic Cafe* (1982), and *Wargames* (1983).

O'Brien's peers jumped into the game. The 1983 International PEN Congress resolved to encourage members to "use their influence to promote nuclear disarmament and worldwide understanding, so that the education of the next generation, through literature, can be a language of peace."[46] Several anthologies appeared, including Jim Schley's *Writing in a Nuclear Age* in 1983—a special joint issue of the *New England Review* and *Bread Loaf Quarterly*, reprinted in book form the next year—and John Witte's *Warnings: An Anthology on the Nuclear Peril* (1984). Grace Paley contributed to the Schley book, and in 1983 interviewed the writer Christa Wolf for a PEN America program discussing "literature, politics, and activism in the age of the nuclear arms race."[47] In April 1984—the same month O'Brien signed his novel's final contract, with Knopf—the PEN America Center held a panel titled "Writers and the Nuclear Age" in advance of a fall weekend symposium on the subject. Moderated by Robert Jay Lifton, the April panel included fellow Sam Lawrence writer and O'Brien's new friend Jayne Anne Phillips, fellow Bread Loafer Galway Kinnell, and Paley.[48]

One wonders how Paley would have received *The Nuclear Age* on schedule in 1981, before she'd had years to develop a political agenda for literature's role on the subject and when the novel might have *led* the literary clamor. Or maybe *The Nuclear Age* is simply a mediocre novel with an angsty protagonist not nearly as appealing as Huck Finn and Holden Caulfield. The novel still has its admirers, but overall its reputation has not fared much better over the years.

◊ ◊ ◊

Whatever *The Nuclear Age*'s shortcomings, it bridges *Going After Cacciato* and *The Things They Carried*. "Our lives are shaped in some small measure by the scope of our daydreams," O'Brien ventriloquizes through Cowling. "If we can imagine happiness, we might find it. If we can imagine a peaceful, durable world, a civilized world, then we might someday achieve it. If not, we will not."[49] Reality and character constrain the possible. William Cowling could no more become a terrorist than Paul Berlin or Tim O'Brien could a deserter. Or a warrior.

Sarah Strouch prefigures Mary Anne Bell from "The Sweetheart of the Song Tra Bong," two athletic blondes in culottes who blow past their boyfriends in their "radical realignment."[50] Sarah becomes a domestic anti-war terrorist and Mary Anne hangs with Green Berets. Whereas Mary Anne leaves all men behind in merging with the land, however, Sarah pleads for Cowling to choose her. Cowling concludes that Sarah's exhibitionism is a way of "hiding herself, or from herself"—the opposite of Mary Anne's vanishing alone to "penetrate deeper into the mystery of herself."[51] But it's Bobbi who, like Mary Anne (and Martha), refuses to be solely possessed by anyone and preserves her mysteriousness. The male imagination can't contain them.

After Sarah dies, Cowling manages a state of mind where he talks with her. Being dead, Linda reports in *The Things They Carried*, is "like being inside a book that nobody's reading."[52] Both books contend with the paradox that although memory and books keep the dead around, in memory and books the dead just keep dying. Cowling's father plays Custer in the town's annual Custer Days celebration, "and he always died with dignity. Every summer he got scalped. Every summer Crazy Horse galloped away with my father's yellow wig."[53] When his dad does die (of unsaid cause), the fugitive Cowling watches the funeral through binoculars, remembering watching from the stand his father play Custer: "He always died so beautifully."[54]

Two months before submitting the final manuscript, at the Key West Literary Seminar, O'Brien said of Ernest Hemingway, "he writes the ultimate truth. And that is that there is only one fundamental challenge to life: Can we die well?"[55] Can we *write* well, and beautifully? For Hemingway and O'Brien, the questions are the same, often collapsed into the act of writing about dying. The O'Brien character in *The Things They Carried* longs to write well enough to redress the absolute indignity of (wartime) death. It's a fantasy, a mere trick, and he knows it, yet he chooses to linger in the spell for as long as he can.

For O'Brien, the terror of the end of civilization via nuclear annihilation was wrapped up in the burning of the pages and readers who keep writers around. One reviewer smartly observed that in Cowling's constructing the bomb shelter in which he'll deposit his family and possibly kill them, O'Brien challenges the reader to understand "whether Cowling is digging for their literal survival or for their survival-only-in-death."[56] Cowling's hole, his shelter, is O'Brien's book, the career he seemed to value above all else, the thing at which he labored, tirelessly and ambiguously, as a matter of living his full life or of achieving life-in-death. During the Bread Loaf lecture, O'Brien almost said as much. The hole "began to represent the hole in my writing, the hole in my art, [. . .] that which both was and would never be, the book I'd dreamed about but which was not, the unwritten masterpiece."[57]

Most covers depict Cowling's assiduous digging, which is to say O'Brien's assiduous writing, of the book in one's hand.

> Where on earth is the happy ending?
>> Kansas is burning. All things are finite.
>> "Love," I say feebly.
>> The hole finds this amusing.[58]

Cowling dug his hole, O'Brien wrote his books, desperate for everlasting love. It's hard not to read Roby as *that which both was and never would be.*

O'Brien did not want children. His art would be his legacy. Cowling inters wife and daughter in the bomb shelter he almost blows up, which would perversely save them and himself by sacrificing them (and revisit the war's logic of destroying a village to save it).[59] Cowling's daughter talks him out of it, talks him into giving up the hole—his ambition—to live his life in the moment, cherishing the days, the seasons, his family. When O'Brien finally did have children, starting in 2003, that's exactly what he would do.

23

HOW IT MOSTLY WAS

*G*oing *After Cacciato*'s surprise win was the proverbial straw that broke the camel's back with the National Book Award process. Mumblings about changes predated the win. Afterward, O'Brien and many other writers publicly objected to the proposed changes to no avail. In 1980, the National Book Awards became the American Book Awards, with more than double the categories and with the jury system replaced by a ballot system that opened voting to publishers, booksellers, and librarians. The PEN/Faulkner Award arose in response, replicating the NBA's trio-of-peers jury system as a rebuke to the ABA. O'Brien served as a judge for the inaugural PEN/Faulkner award in 1981. He initially advocated for Shirley Hazzard's *The Transit of Venus*, a book about love, power, and integrity, but William H. Gass persuaded him and Elizabeth Hardwick to select Walter Abish's *How German Is It*. O'Brien attended the April awards ceremony in the Rotunda at the University of Virginia.[1]

O'Brien had not only arrived but landed in the thick of the American literary scene and in high demand. A 1980 PEN New England panel "on the question of whether writers should have a social role, whether they should participate in politics or use their work to influence public opinion" was but one of many events with other writers, not necessarily about *Cacciato* or the literature of his war.[2] Anne Bernays, who ran PEN/New England, remembers a panel dialogue between O'Brien and James Carroll on the nature of truth in fiction. In April 1983, O'Brien spent three days as one of the writers leading the Sandhills Writing Conference.[3] And so on: campus visits, local readings, radio and television spots, newspaper and magazine articles promoting *Cacciato* and himself—he was on his way to becoming perhaps the most interviewed writer of his generation. Those efforts were a double-edged sword, because they kept him talking about the last novel and its success when he was trying to get out from under it to write the new one.

Other business took him away from writing *The Nuclear Age*. He found forty-two typos "quickly skimming" the paperback edition of *Going After Cacciato*. Dell's lackluster attention to the book, while he was contacting bookstores himself to get on their shelves, got his goat.[4] He slightly revised *Northern Lights* for its next paperback edition, mostly cutting. *Cacciato*'s success also led to a reprinting of *If I Die in a Combat Zone*.

O'Brien dedicated *The Nuclear Age* to his nuclear family—his parents, sister, and brother—plus Ann. On the copyright page opposite appears the standard disclaimer that the characters and events are entirely imagined. O'Brien adds that he "has tried to remain faithful to the flow of public events between the years 1945 and 1995"—ten years into the future!—"but on occasion it has seemed appropriate to amend history, most conspicuously by addition." Then there's this, which on the surface reads like a typical O'Brien remark about his aesthetic practice of imaginatively riffing on the real but beneath the surface reads like a coded dedication to Gayle Roby: "What is important, the author believes, is not what happened, but what could have happened, and, in some cases, should have happened."

Their end was in their beginning. Roby hoped for a family; O'Brien would not leave his wife. O'Brien never exorcised his feelings of Roby's unreliability and instability. Roby remembers him once telling or writing her, "the problem with you is that you can't want something, have it, and still want it." That line appears almost verbatim in the draft material of March 1979 through to the published novel. Roby remembers it directed at her, years into their relationship. Was she misremembering when he made the accusation? Did he make it in print in 1979 to Bobbi and years later repeat it to Roby? Did she remember it from the published writing? The line applied as much to O'Brien at the time as to Roby—probably more so.

In mid-1986, Tim and Ann moved north out of the city to Boxford, Massachusetts.[5] The new home at 17 Partridge Lane stood on a lot of over two wooded acres with a long private drive and a creek-fed knee-deep pond in the back. The O'Briens couldn't see their neighbors' homes through the trees. They had a stove-heated living room; when necessary, they turned on their central heat. As always, Ann did most of the cooking. O'Brien sometimes cut wood for the stove.

Roby believed O'Brien moved out of the city to put some distance between them and perhaps wean himself from her. For a while, he didn't call or come around and she didn't have his new number. The break (if that's what it was) didn't last, although the new house reduced the frequency of their times together. When she would drive up to Boxford, she only set foot in the O'Brien home once or twice in the next three years. Instead, the couple would drive around, or perhaps she'd accompany him on errands such as trips to the grocery store in the next town.

Spending less time together seems to have added fuel to O'Brien's distrust. Roby needed an actual social life. According to Roby, when an old high school boyfriend moved to Boston to teach at Brandeis and she hung out with him as friends, not lovers, O'Brien would confront her, telling her he'd been outside her apartment to see what he could see. But he really could only accuse her of dimming the lights. She did have a couple of innocent flirtations at her low-residency MFA program at Warren Wilson College in North Carolina, which O'Brien had suggested for her poetry, over which she says he was quite jealous. O'Brien remembers no such jealousy, only relief when she was away because it simplified his life.

Not that he always deserved her trust. Bread Loaf's reputation inspired the nickname Bed Loaf, and Tim O'Brien had an outsized reputation within that good-times milieu. "If you had a crush on someone of course you slept with him," the novelist Julia Alvarez once said.[6] Bread Loaf was far from a free-for-all, as most attendees shared a room, some participants brought family, and outdoor sex hardly appealed. The conference daily newsletter *The Crumb*'s cartoons, jokes, and innuendo suggest a collective pride in the conference's hookup culture—and sometimes fingered O'Brien. By 1981, O'Brien's reputation had wafted down the mountain into the world. The third paragraph of a *Washington Post* article on Bread Loaf that year reads, "Tim O'Brien, a smug reptilian grin spreading wide as the brim on his baseball cap, draws yet another awe-struck young woman into a private conclave."[7] Dan Wakefield said of him, "Tim must have screwed every good-looking girl there, and good for him!"

It wasn't true. Not to the extent that people gossiped and believed. He has acknowledged three transgressions at Bread Loaf, one in the seventies before reuniting with Roby, the other two in the eighties. But women were drawn to him "like groupies," another friend has said, and he enjoyed their company even as he never quite understood the magnetic effect. O'Brien was at his in-laws' home in Hagerstown when the *Post* article came out and managed to downplay it with Ann. By O'Brien's telling, the three times he strayed were a small portion of the opportunities to stray. He'll make this point with his comic cad of a narrator in *Tomcat in Love*: "Thus, over the course of a spotty career, I have enjoyed carnal relations with a paltry four women. (Or three. Depending.) On the other hand, I can boldly credit to my account one hundred twenty-eight near misses, two hundred twelve love letters, fifteen boxes of chocolates, well over five hundred significant flirtations and alliances and dalliances."[8]

In an environment ripe for literary snobbery, O'Brien put on no airs. "Tim was so disarming, modest, and slyly funny when I first met him at the Bread Loaf Writers' Conference in August 1979 that it would have been hard to not like him," recalls Ron Hansen. "There was no eminence or 'literary figure' quality to him. He even seemed blue collar, a guy in a base-ball cap whom you could hang with." Others have described him as down-to-earth, approachable, easygoing, and genuine, more interested in talking about the other person than about himself. The charm of those who don't try to charm. His social insecurities made him most comfortable in one-on-one conversations. Add to that demeanor and talent his fine features. "He was hot. He was the Bono of the literary scene," his second wife would say of him decades later, referring to the front man of the Irish rock band U2.

O'Brien helped get Roby into Bread Loaf as a poetry student for the 1979 conference, but after that year she only drove up for brief visits a cou-ple or three times. One time she went straight to his room, found it empty, sat down, and waited. He returned, with a woman, and said something about grabbing a manuscript. Roby never knew if she could believe him.

O'Brien ended the relationship in the spring of 1989 while finishing *The Things They Carried*. It had never been an affair, a word he slaps away because of its tawdry connotation. She was the first great love and passion of his adult life. But the relationship had gotten more difficult. He couldn't bear the inner turmoil any longer. He simply stopped. He stopped going to Arlington. He stopped calling. He stopped answering the phone when it might be Roby, or he answered "O'Brien residence" as he always had when Ann was home, to signal that he couldn't talk in case it was Roby, even though he was alone. It distressed her to no end. He was the love of her life, and, she knew, she was his. A few times she drove around Boxford to places he might be, watching him from a distance without ever making her presence known. In 1987 she'd started going to a Quaker meeting house, and after the breakup, her new faith community kept her going. Many years later, married and with a son, Roby developed sympathy for O'Brien's plight and forgave him his solution. It was what he needed to do, the only way he knew how.

O'Brien was an excellent Bread Loaf teacher and mentor. Susan Thornton chose him her first year there because they were close in age and he seemed accessible. She didn't know to be intimidated by the National Book Award:

> Our group had two meetings. At the first meeting, Tim praised one
> of the pieces of fiction I'd brought to show him and identified it as
> my work; at the next meeting he read a piece that didn't work and
> surprised the class by pointing out that I had written both pieces.
> His point, well taken, was that a good writer does not always produce
> good fiction.[9]

O'Brien took Thornton's work and her potential seriously. She and her classmates discovered what generations of future students would learn about him. O'Brien spent time studying student work, reading every piece twice or more. He carefully prepared for workshops and provided thorough feedback. After *Cacciato*, he drew veterans to Bread Loaf, including Larry Heinemann in 1979 and Bruce Weigl in 1981.

In workshops, O'Brien stressed his artistic credo that writing should dramatize the choice between conflicting goods, a credo very much the product of his experience when drafted and then ordered to Việt Nam. His friend Bob Reiss remembers one class when another Việt Nam veteran spoke up after O'Brien asked for a real story about such a choice. On the

way to the war, the veteran and a buddy each promised to put the other out
of his misery if he should become incapacitated. Not too long before Bread
Loaf that year, the vet had visited his buddy in the hospital, a quadriplegic now. *Just do it*, the buddy pleaded. O'Brien asked the class where they
would start that story. When the two were best friends as kids, someone
said. In Việt Nam, another said. How about boot camp? O'Brien rejected
them all. The story should begin, O'Brien said, when the vet walks into the
hospital room and is broadsided by the urgent need to choose.

That credo provided the gist of his early Bread Loaf lectures, in contrast
to John Gardner's principle of art as asserting certain values, a principle
premised on the knowledge of "*which* values to assert and which not to
assert."[10] O'Brien's credo was an epiphany for Reiss, and that was the value
of the conference—over those ten or twelve days one could count on one
such nugget worth years of lonely toil. O'Brien gave lectures and readings
at Bread Loaf every year but one from 1979 to 1992, to packed attendance.[11]
He presented his 1979 lecture on the very first day, at his request, as it
scared him and he wanted to get it over with. That lecture wondered about
the nature of care for fiction writers. "What *do* we care about? What *should*
we care about as writers? Why do the special (or, perhaps, unspecial) concerns of writers of fiction get translated into fictional form?" After all, caring "is what makes us writers."[12]

For Reiss, Bread Loaf's detractors in those years failed to understand
that the intellectual and the fun were indivisible. Both required and culti-
vated openness, vulnerability, friendship, and energy. Dances, sing-alongs
to David Bain's piano, poker, sports, meals, and alcohol fed the spirit.
O'Brien put his heart into it all.

Erik Hansen regularly popped down to Bread Loaf in August for an
evening or a day, to listen to a reading, stay up talking, or slip away with
O'Brien for a round of golf. Hansen lived in New Hampshire from September 1977 to September 1985, and after eight months in Norway bounced
around New England until setting down in Stowe, Vermont, in August
1987, where he lived for the next thirty-three years. Hansen remained
O'Brien's sounding board for both *The Nuclear Age* and *The Things They
Carried*, although their regional proximity meant they held their sessions
in person and over the phone, not in letters. Neither man remembers much
but the fun of staying up late talking and smoking. Several times Han-

sen spent Thanksgiving with the O'Briens. At Boxford, he helped cull the
deadwood and the trees, taking the extra wood to craft furniture and ban-
isters for his house.

O'Brien's Boston golf crew were mostly other writers: Theodore "Ted"
Vrettos (*The Elgin Affair*); Steve Bergman, a psychiatrist who published under the name Samuel Shem (*The House of God*); and—through Vrettos—
John Updike. They never talked writing. DeWitt Henry of *Ploughshares*
joined once or twice. O'Brien and Hansen golfed whenever they got together
and the weather allowed. In the early eighties, O'Brien's primary partner
was Greg Andrews, a fellow Worthington escapee a few years younger. (Andrews's cousins used to say that "Worthington is a town where everybody
thinks they are going to heaven.") O'Brien was intensely competitive and
always played for money, even if just a dollar a hole. Andrews recalls a 1982
dinner party at the Boxford house with the Updikes, the Vrettoses, and
Frank Conroy. The great jazz pianist Thelonious Monk had died the week
before; Conroy went to the O'Briens' piano and turned the dinner party
from literary shoptalk into an impromptu, dazzling concert of Monk
tunes.

With *The Nuclear Age* finished, *Esquire* sent O'Brien to do a story on
golfing at Pebble Beach. The California setting was spectacular, the golfing
glorious—but O'Brien had nothing else to say, no angle, so he returned the
travel money. A few years later he completed a similar assignment, checking out golf courses in the Caribbean by means of a chartered yacht with
his wife, his brother, Greg, and Greg's girlfriend, for Ann's editors at *Sail*
magazine.[13]

O'Brien holds his brother responsible for introducing him to casino
gambling in the eighties, at the Jackpot Junction in Redwood Falls, north
of Worthington (Greg isn't so sure). It became a lifetime pastime, around
Boston and Minnesota, Las Vegas, Atlantic City. Blackjack was his game.
He liked its mathematical simplicity, a kind of meditation and escapism
with stakes. He surrendered to probability and statistics in solidarity with
the other players at the table.[14] It was like writing in his losing himself to
the thing, in a clockless room for hours upon hours, even up to twenty-
four hours but for bathroom breaks, like writing without the work or pressure or aloneness. He seldom played for huge stakes, although he once won
sixty-five thousand dollars.

Harvard's basketball courts no longer a short walk away, O'Brien started weight training with a setup in the Boxford house and continued it for the next twenty-five years. The 1980s were bodybuilding's heyday in America, part of the "Let's Get Physical" revolution, with muscularity a defining attraction of action movies starring the likes of Sylvester Stallone, Arnold Schwarzenegger, and Linda Hamilton. Like writing, weight training meant a near-daily regimen. O'Brien hit the weights at the end of his writing day. Unlike writing, weight training gave a visible payoff, instantaneously so in terms of the immediate if temporary swelling. O'Brien became addicted to the endorphin rush. He preferred developing the upper-body mirror muscles—chest, shoulders, and biceps. He loved biceps curls. He hated leg work, which was hard to do anyway when he later lived in an upper-floor apartment. And O'Brien could pump iron with a cigarette in his mouth, as Phil Caputo remembered from a visit, or grab a smoke between sets.

A few years before, perhaps when O'Brien stayed at Caputo's house for the 1985 Key West Literary Seminar on Hemingway, if not earlier, Caputo told him about the time he was drinking with friends at a New York City bar waiting for a dinner table. They were talking about *Going After Cacciato*. A guy at the bar kept trying to get into the conversation. "What, what?" a drunk Caputo said. "You're going to tell me you're Cacciato, right?" He was, in fact, Richard Cacciato, there as the restaurant's liquor distributor. He confessed that the novel upset him. He had considered O'Brien a friend back in the S-1 shop on LZ Gator, but O'Brien demoted the character with his name from captain to private and turned him into a deserter.[15]

The context for how one remembered, reflected upon, and wrote about the war shifted over the decade as the nation's relationship with the war changed and new organizations and formal recognitions emerged.

The year-old Council of Vietnam Veterans reinvented itself as the Vietnam Veterans of America in 1979. In 1980, post-Vietnam syndrome officially became post-traumatic stress disorder in the American Psychological Association's *DSM-III*. O'Brien published "I Wish We Were More Troubled" in *The Washington Post* on May 25 of that year.[16] The Vietnam

Veterans Memorial Fund sent out its call for design proposals in November, recommending *If I Die in a Combat Zone, Box Me Up and Ship Me Home* and *Going After Cacciato* along with five other titles for aspiring entrants to read—one proposal included a quotation from *Cacciato* on its memorial.[17] The memorial, designed by Maya Lin, was dedicated on November 13, 1982. O'Brien went to the black granite V-shaped wall the next time he was in Washington, going straight to Alvin Merricks's name on panel 25W, line 30. The year 1982 also saw the early scholarly coming-to-terms with the literary coming-to-terms, with Philip Beidler's *American Literature and the Experience of Vietnam* and John Newman's *Vietnam War Literature*. PBS aired its most extensive and lauded documentary to date, the thirteen-part *Vietnam: A Television History*, at the end of 1983.

The war's literary witnesses enjoyed a related professionalization process. If in the 1970s most of the writers worked alone, with little sense of a cohort, in the 1980s they became personally acquainted. They became colleagues and in many cases friends.

Between the memorial's call for designs and its dedication, in 1981 the William Joiner Center for the Study of War and Social Consequences opened at the University of Massachusetts–Boston, the effort led by a committed group of Việt Nam veterans. In March 1982, O'Brien joined Frances FitzGerald, Robert Olen Butler, George Davis, and C. D. B. Bryan for a PEN America panel, "Vietnam Voices: The War in American Literature," followed in April by a panel with Robert Stone at the University of Cincinnati.[18] Stone's 1972 *Dog Soldiers*, an early fictional foray into the war era, won the National Book Award and was a lifelong favorite of O'Brien's. In the early eighties, revelations of the United States' interventions in El Salvador were very much on everyone's minds, and discussions about Việt Nam inevitably drew comparisons.

The Asia Society in New York organized what remains the largest gathering of writers about the war, "The Vietnam Experience in American Literature," in May 1985. Its seventy-some participants included a who's who of the war's writers, O'Brien among them.[19] O'Brien, Bill Ehrhart, and John Clark Pratt were guests on the Casper Citron radio show recorded at the Algonquin Hotel the evening before the conference began.[20] O'Brien participated on the "Fact and Fiction" panel, probably because he'd written both nonfiction and fiction about the war—he had yet to begin *The Things They Carried*, his book that would explicitly blur the line between the two modes.

Jim Webb's opening address prompted a protracted and heated challenge. Webb deliberately provoked his audience, accusing his fellow writers of being part of an "Academic-Intellectual Complex" that squashed views dissenting from anti-government "bravado."[21] Out of the conference came a proceedings volume, *"Reading the Wind": The Literature of the Vietnam War* (1986). It's a valuable document and resource even if, as Ehrhart charges, "it is poor journalism" and "terrible history" for leaving out much of the fiery debate and for rearranging events.[22] Ehrhart couldn't stay quiet those three days, relieving the burden from O'Brien to have to speak out. For Tim O'Brien from 1950s Minnesota, the exchanges were indecorous at best.

At its August 1987 national convention in Washington, the Vietnam Veterans of America honored thirteen veterans for excellence in the arts, O'Brien among them.[23] The success of Oliver Stone's 1986 film *Platoon* had persuaded VVA to give the awards. Before the Saturday dinner and ceremony but in the same venue, Stone held a press event of his own, in which he brought members of his infantry platoon onstage to recognize them with memberships in the VVA. All thirteen honorees spoke. Stone wrote in his diary a moving line from Steve Mason: "They taught me to hate with all my heart perfect strangers." Stone's speech bluntly condemned the war. In a hotel elevator with Stone and Larry Heinemann, O'Brien told Stone his speech took balls; a few days later, Stone wrote O'Brien to say that "your speech was not only funny, outrageous, but true. You said things I never thought you would get away with, and I loved it. You, too, have *Balls*."[24] Stone and Heinemann served in the Twenty-Fifth Infantry Division, and each based his major war work, Stone's *Platoon* and Heinemann's *Close Quarters*, on the New Year's Day Battle of 1968 (also known as the Battle of Suoi Cut and the Battle of Fire Support Base Burt).

Three months after the VVA event, Heinemann's second novel, *Paco's Story*, won the National Book Award over Toni Morrison's *Beloved*, a bigger upset than *Cacciato*'s and one that caused greater uproar. It was the year of the restored National Book Award, bookending the years of the

American Book Awards with controversial wins for novels about the war in Việt Nam.

The Joiner Center held its first writing workshop for veterans in early August 1988. O'Brien spent a few days on campus at the workshop during the first week. He did a reading event with two other veterans, Leo Cawley and John Balaban. Cawley read an essay in progress about a trip back to Việt Nam the year before. Balaban's 1974 poetry volume *After Our War* had been nominated for a National Book Award.

Balaban shared poems he was working on, then he and Thanh T. Nguyen presented poems found in the notebooks of killed North Vietnamese and NLF soldiers. She sang-read the Vietnamese originals followed by Balaban reading translations the pair had made in the past couple of days, one at six that morning. Balaban finished by reading Vietnamese folk poetry in Vietnamese and his English translations.[25] The well-muscled O'Brien anchored the lineup in jeans, a polo short, and his go-to Boston Red Sox cap, debuting "The Revival of the Short Story," an early draft of "The Lives of the Dead," which he had been revising that morning.[26] "We keep the dead alive with stories," the story concludes, Thanh and Balaban having just brought voices of the dead into that very room, Cawley to join their ranks in three years from cancer caused by Agent Orange exposure during the war.[27] Diagnosed in 1980, Cawley must have been feeling his mortality keenly. It was an extraordinary event.

The faculty for the full eleven days were Balaban, Bruce Weigl, and Larry Rottmann, and Lê Lựu and Ngụy Ngữ from Việt Nam. Under the leadership of Kevin Bowen, the workshop became the originating event for the historic collaboration between the Joiner Center and the Vietnamese Writers' Union that led to cultural exchange trips as well as translation projects. One can't overstate the significance of these veterans from both sides making Vietnamese literary voices available for the first time to Americans.[28] Lê Lựu's 1986 novel *Thời Xa Vắng*, translated in 1997 as *A Time Far Past* by the William Joiner Foundation, is a landmark of Vietnamese literature. Of that 1988 workshop, a speaker at Lựu's 2022 funeral remarked, "Lê Lựu's presence before American intellectuals and readers has changed the way the Americans looked at the country, the people, and the culture of Việt Nam. Lê Lựu had become Việt Nam's first ambassador of peace to arrive in America. Together with the American and Vietnamese veterans he had built the first span of friendship between the two peoples that would transform past hatred."[29]

Since the spring of 1986, O'Brien had been under contract for *In the Lake of the Woods*, back now with Sam Lawrence at E. P. Dutton. But that process stalled as the stories that would form *The Things They Carried* took hold. O'Brien returned to the Joiner Center for its 1989 summer workshop, this time for the full term. Ehrhart, Rottmann, and the poet Lamont Steptoe were the other instructors. From Việt Nam, Nguyễn Khải and Nguyễn Quang Sáng accompanied Lê Lựu.

O'Brien missed the most eventful evening, on July 26, when South Vietnamese displaced to the United States assaulted the visitors from communist Việt Nam outside the Boston Public Library. Expecting protests, the American hosts had kept close to their guests. The trouble was stirred during a panel with the three Vietnamese writers, three American war correspondents, and an American documentary filmmaker, believed to be the first panel on journalism and the war with both sides represented.[30] Audience members heckled the Vietnamese panelists as liars. At the reception afterward the heckles swelled into shouts of "Down with the communists!"

The Americans tried to slip their guests out a lower-level side entrance only to be waylaid by a throng of about fifty protesters brandishing placards and South Vietnamese flags. Khải took a blow to the head that drew a little blood; others were also whacked. The burly Joe Bangert, a former marine, snatched a flag and broke the staff while shouting in Vietnamese, so stunning the assailants that his friends broke away and got Lựu, Khải, and Sáng into Bruce Weigl's car. Weigl sped away.[31]

The following public events with the overseas guests were canceled, and they sheltered in Kevin Bowen's home as much as possible for the rest of the workshop. On the first of August, in lieu of a panel with O'Brien, Weigl, and Phil Caputo, they retreated with a dozen Americans for a videotaped three-hour conversation in Bowen's finished attic.[32] The conversation was very much each side explaining itself to the other. O'Brien emphasized the variety of American perspectives. He had never hated the Vietnamese—he pulled the trigger out of personal fear. To him, enemy soldiers were "ghostlike figures capable of flying, of sliding through barb wire." On guard at

night, "we'd say, 'The ghosts are out.'" He regarded his poorly equipped
enemy with "wonder and awe" for performing "military miracles." For him,
the "important issue" wasn't the possibility of a U.S. "victory," the issue was
"rectitude," and in his opinion "America didn't do what was right." He was
"very sad personally and for my country that we took the wrong side. We
should have been supporting the nationalistic efforts of Ho Chi Minh despite communism." Did the Vietnamese have racist language for Americans
equivalent to "dink" and "slope"?

The conversation's choicest moment was O'Brien's response to a war
story Nguyễn Khải told. War stories were very much on O'Brien's mind.
He had submitted *The Things They Carried*'s final manuscript to Lawrence
on July 7, less than three weeks earlier.[33] "You can tell a true war story
by the questions you ask," its fictional Tim O'Brien declares. "Somebody
tells a story, let's say, and afterward you ask, 'Is it true?' and if the answer
matters, you've got your answer." Not what the answer is, but whether the
answer matters. How you ask the question tells you whether a truth has
been communicated: "Absolute occurrence is irrelevant. A thing may happen and be a total lie; another thing may not happen and be truer than the
truth."[34]

In Khải's story, a Vietnamese soldier home from the French war hears
that his wife has taken a local official as a lover. One day he places a grenade under their bed and announces he has an errand to run. She calls her
lover to come over, and the grenade explodes while they are making love.
They are "fortunately" only injured. Khải said it was a common method of
revenge for cheated-upon soldiers.

The camera stays on Khải as O'Brien asks from beyond the frame, "Is
that a true story, or fiction?"*

---

* "It's a true story," Khải answered.

24

A WORK OF FICTION

The Things They Carried

No longer fresh-off-the-plane returnees, the war's writers in the 1980s increasingly moved away from the soldiering experience in Việt Nam to the veteran's experience in the United States. O'Brien's "The Ghost Soldiers," published in *Esquire* in March 1981 and then as the antepenultimate story of *The Things They Carried* in 1990, reflects this transition. The main character, Herbie—not yet the fictional Tim O'Brien—has left the field for a clerk job at his infantry battalion's base, where he finds himself in the war but also out of it, a comrade and a stranger to his former company mates, a betwixt and between emotional state. To take revenge on the medic whose shoddy novice treatment left him with a gangrenous wound, Herbie orchestrates a mock VC attack with noisemakers, flares, and ghostly silhouettes beyond the perimeter in front of the medic's nighttime position to scare the wits out of him, all controlled by ropes with Herbie feeling "Like a magician, a puppeteer." Afterward, the forgiven and forgiving medic tells Herbie he "should go into the movies or something."[1]

The brilliance of the story as a correlative for O'Brien's writing is how Herbie loses control as his creative reconstruction immerses him in those very debilitating memories he's playfully enacting. The story's original title, "How the War Was Won," gestures to O'Brien's tenuous personal victory over the war through writing.

The first documented reference to the story "The Things They Carried" appears in a letter to Erik Hansen from mid-October 1985. He'd already submitted it to Rust Hills at *Esquire*, who liked it a great deal except for a page's worth near the end he asked O'Brien to cut. O'Brien obliged. *Esquire* published the story in its August 1986 issue, the same month O'Brien read the finished story at Bread Loaf. The Bread Loafers gathered that evening saluted the story with thunderous applause—their awe is palpable in the audio recording.[2] The story won a National Magazine Award for Fiction and inclusion in *The Best American Short Stories 1987*, then in *The Best American Short Stories of the 1980s*, then in *The Best American Short Stories of the Century*, and in more general American fiction anthologies than any other story of its era.[3]

The story's emphasis on walking—plodding, humping—O'Brien's dedicated readers had seen before, in both *If I Die* and *Going After Cacciato*. In those books, the trudging made for descriptive passages; in the new story, it's an emotive thrust. One of the story's other emotive thrusts is Lt. Jimmy Cross's unrequited love for Martha. The backstory isn't just O'Brien's unrequited obsession for Gayle Roby in 1968 and 1969; it's also his requited passion for her in 1985. Auden's poem that O'Brien mouthed silently to himself while marching becomes the pebble Martha sends Cross that he "carried in his mouth, turning it with his tongue."[4]

Fast-forward to 1985, when Cross's "[d]ense, crushing love" for Martha expresses O'Brien's for Roby. Cross's love "was too much for him, he felt paralyzed, he wanted to sleep inside her lungs and breathe her blood and be smothered."[5] Cross (and O'Brien) doesn't desire an obliteration of self so much as an obliteration of the world beyond himself, the world that troubles his love. In the story, that moment of distraction leads to the death of one of Cross's soldiers, so the story's overarching emotion is guilt.

When the story was selected for *The Best American Short Stories'* annual edition, the series' editor, Shannon Ravenel, asked O'Brien for a biographical blurb and a short comment on the story. He provided both but did not want the latter published—he offered it only if required for his story to be included. Ravenel respected his wish and left it out. The comment, however, survives in the archives:

At the time this story was written, things were not going well for me. I was in some pain. As a writer, though, you have to expect disappointment and bad times; you can't complain in public; you have to carry the hurt inside you. So what you do is, you get up early in the morning and you work hard all day and sometimes all night and you try to build a story so beautiful that nothing else matters but the beauty. You dump that terrible weight into the story—all the rage and hurt—you pile it in and shape it into something else, you spend months fiddling with words and lines, you scan it like poetry, you make the rhythms keep step with the substance, you permit your sorrow to show itself in public, you try for perfection, you don't quit, you do your work, you finish the story and hold it in your hand and look up at god and say, Fuck you Fuck you. It's like with Vietnam: all that bad shit, but you're human, so you try to make it good.[6]

Part of the disappointment and pain belonged to his struggles with and the poor reception of *The Nuclear Age*—this would seem to be where the opening lines point. Part of the rage and hurt belonged to the war he couldn't get out of his system. Much of it belonged to his guilt-ridden anguish over Ann and Gayle. The comment testifies to how O'Brien discovered ways to sink his emotional life into stories whose plots never touched on their happening-truth source.

The need to end torment: In an unconscious allusion to Harry in Hemingway's "The Snows of Kilimanjaro," who as he dies imagines being flown by plane to safety the next morning, "high and away to the only thing left visible, as wide as all the world, great, high, and unbelievably white in the sun," Kilimanjaro, O'Brien's soldiers dream of refusing to budge, of shooting off a finger or toe, and of freedom birds, the jumbo jets that would carry them "purely borne" away from the war, "off the edge of the earth and beyond the sun and through the vast, silent vacuum where there were no burdens and where everything weighed exactly nothing."[7]

O'Brien's "fiddling" toward perfecting his prose was enhanced by his first computer. He typed "The Things They Carried" into the word processor as his "first practice," he wrote Hansen. The new technology very well may have enabled O'Brien's finest story to become O'Brien's finest story, his finest book to become his finest book. He submitted *The Things*

They Carried's final manuscript to his publisher Houghton Mifflin on two floppy disks.[8]

O'Brien presented the first version of "How to Tell a True War Story" in 1986 for his annual Bread Loaf lecture.[9] Although there's no extant recording to confirm the 1986 date or what exactly he read, the archives have two nearly identical versions of a lecture called "War Stories" with the headnote "Subject is: How to tell a true war story. Some tips on how to tell true ones from false ones."[10] The lecture offers three examples of how true war stories make the "stomach . . . believe." The first vignette, called "CUNT STORY," tells the story of a soldier named Scab who writes the sister of his best buddy, recently killed, but "The cunt never writes back." O'Brien worried about the nastiness of the word and considered *slut* or *cooze* instead. He read the vignette over the phone to Richard Bausch in advance. He remembers Bausch advising *cooze*; Bausch remembers telling him to hell with the niceties—the latter feels right to this biographer. Either way, the decision to go with the lesser obscenity resulted from the call. Even then, O'Brien's friend the poet Linda Pastan "gave me hell over 'cooze'" after the reading.

The vignette obviously has its basis in Chip Merricks's sister, who didn't write O'Brien back after Chip's death. It's one of the elements of the published "How to Tell a True War Story," with Scab changed to Rat Kiley. The second vignette O'Brien excerpted from *Going After Cacciato*, the passage about the first block of instruction at the Chu Lai Combat Training Center, when the corporal in charge has the newly arrived sit in silence for an hour, either preparing the new arrivals for the countless hours of boredom in their future or recognizing how little there was to say. (In real life, "There was actually a now-or-never lecture on the beach at Chu Lai—about stuff you could do that might keep you alive—and the corporal who gave the lecture didn't have much to say and stopped after five or ten minutes and sat in the bleachers with us." O'Brien "made up the rest.") The third vignette is a sketch version of what would become "On the Rainy River," the story about the Tim O'Brien character who flees to the Tip Top Lodge on the Canadian border only to decide to return home to be drafted.

O'Brien wrapped up the lecture by admitting his inventions, saying, "Most of this story is *not* true." O'Brien's admission rankled some audience members and pissed off others. They felt deceived. One or two let him know in no uncertain terms. It was his *lecture*, after all, not his reading of creative work—it was supposed to be nonfiction explication, not story-telling, not lying. In O'Brien's defense, his admission undid the potential deception, making his content a nonfiction lecture by preserving the actuality-invention distinction. The degree of people's negative reactions confirmed for O'Brien the emotional truths of the vignettes. *Esquire* published "How to Tell a True War Story" in October 1987; *Playboy* published "On the Rainy River" in January 1990 in advance of *The Things They Carried*.[11]

The earliest evidence of O'Brien imagining turning these stories into a book is a November 1987 letter he wrote to Robert Warde, a professor at Macalester he'd befriended during the 1979 symposium:

> I'm at work on a novel set up in Lake of the Woods—part love story, part ghost story, part mystery, part fantasy, part who-knows-what. Hard to explain: you'll have to read it, I'll have to write it. I've also done a few Nam stories (one of which you heard) and at some point soon I'd like to do a whole bunch more, twenty or thirty, just a nice fat collection with various characters appearing here and there, maybe connected by mini-essays about the act of writing, maybe with some commentary about the stories themselves and what they grew out of and how they came to be as they are, maybe throwing in some non-factual nonfiction—bald lies, in other words, the kind of lying that fiction writers always do. For now though, it's a matter of finishing up the novel within the next 12 months or so.[12]

O'Brien must have tabled *In the Lake of the Woods* soon thereafter. Even though Erik Hansen loved these latest stories, he advised against turning them into a book. *The war's over, Tim.* O'Brien pressed ahead. The book was going to be about more than the war.

By mid-December 1988, he had completed half the draft, with the working title of *War Stories*, and he had a final submission date of June 1989, with *In the Lake of the Woods* due the following spring.[13] It's safe to conclude, then, that he wrote all the other stories in the book with their destination as chapters in mind: "The Lives of the Dead" (*Esquire*, January 1989), "Sweetheart of the Song Tra Bong" (*Esquire*, July 1989), "In the

Field" (*GQ*, December 1989), and the rewrite of "Speaking of Courage" that was cut from *Cacciato*. The word processor sped up his process; he no longer had to retype a page for a small change. The story form for the chapters also expedited his process. He just missed his deadline, delivering the full draft to Lawrence on July 7, 1989, his most on-time manuscript since *If I Die in a Combat Zone*.[14]

"The Things They Carried" opens the book, followed by "Love," the story that introduces the book's fictional first-person narrator, also named Tim O'Brien. "Love" is the second and final Martha story, the story that rewrites O'Brien's reunion with Gayle Roby as Jimmy Cross's with Martha, although unlike Roby, the independent Martha shows no interest in conventional heterosexual romance. O'Brien modeled this aspect of Martha after a friend from Bread Loaf, a woman who didn't dress or act like most of the others, the sexually liberated souls of the 1970s.

With "Sweetheart of the Song Tra Bong," originally titled "Outpost," O'Brien riffed on the rumor he had heard about a soldier temporarily importing his girlfriend. O'Brien knew about the actual Special Forces compound on the Trà Bồng River. He doesn't remember knowing about Fire Support Base Mary Ann, in his division's area of operations during his tour of duty, which was overrun by the NVA in March 1971, the war's deadliest attack against an American base. The news broke two days after Lt. Calley's conviction; O'Brien probably read the Associated Press article in *The Boston Globe*. The story must have landed on television newscasts. The surprise after-midnight attack occurred west of Chu Lai against a sister Americal battalion. The AP reported, "Out of 178 Americans at Fire Base Mary Ann, 33 were dead and 76 wounded."[15] O'Brien definitely read about it in Corinne Browne's *Body Shop* in late 1973.[16] That the FSB is the story's heroine Mary Anne's near-exact namesake is amazingly coincidental or deeply unconscious (like the French before them, the Americans often used women's names for military locations and operations.)

The story's other sources are Conrad's novella *Heart of Darkness* and Coppola's cinematic reenvisioning, *Apocalypse Now*. All three stories are told within a frame story. Conrad's and Coppola's depict how civilized white men deployed to jungle life go natively savage in a racist vision of regressive devolution. O'Brien's dramatically proposes that innocent young women are just as susceptible to fierceness as innocent young men. That rosy-cheeked girl next door could just as easily have pulled the trigger standing over the ditch at Mỹ Lai 4.

In the end, the story limns the limits of imagination. The male story-tellers can't fathom what Mary Anne has become, which is to say what she always could have become. Eros colors their image of her. She relinquishes her weapon and disappears, alone, as neither the real nor the fictional Tim O'Brien had the courage to do when faced with going to war. Merging with the land, she becomes monstrously conventional in the age-old association of woman with nature. Her independence, an exaggeration of Martha's in "Love," betrays the traditional gender script. Becoming a ghostly part of the Vietnamese landscape, she becomes what the soldiers perceived as their enemy. Which in a sense she always has been—the nation embodied as a woman for whom the young men went to war to kill or be killed. In a story published during the American Civil War, a young man tells the marriage-aged young women pressuring him, in his role as a man, to en-list in the Union Army, "You're downright bloodthirsty!" And here's Mary Anne, "wearing her culottes, her pink sweater, and a necklace of human tongues. She was dangerous. And ready for the kill."[17]

One of O'Brien's inspirations was as far from someone *ready for the kill* as possible. Lady Borton, a Quaker who volunteered for Việt Nam with the American Friends Service Committee, served as a field director in Quảng Ngãi during O'Brien's time in Việt Nam. While O'Brien sat behind a clerk's desk on LZ Gator, Borton escorted the first journalist (from *News-week*) to Mỹ Lai after news of the massacre broke. Borton immersed herself in Vietnamese life, language, and culture. She was in Hà Nội in 1975 the spring the war ended; she lived for six months of 1980 in a Malaysian is-land camp for Vietnamese refugees; she visited Hồ Chí Minh City in 1983, and in December 1986 received permission to be the first American since the war to live in a Vietnamese village and participate fully as a commu-nity member.[18] This all happened long before the United States and Việt Nam restored official relations.

O'Brien had met Borton at Bread Loaf in the late 1970s.[19] According to O'Brien, she imagined she might turn her experiences into a novel. She lacked the chops for fiction, O'Brien recalls telling her, upsetting her, but he encouraged her to write creative nonfiction. She did, quite successfully. She published *Sensing the Enemy*, her book about her experiences in the war and with the refugees, in 1984, followed eleven years later by *After Sorrow*, her account of more contemporary Vietnamese life. In the foreword to *After Sorrow*, Grace Paley writes of Borton that "she had sworn herself in love and understanding to the Vietnamese people."[20] O'Brien's admiration for Borton's fierce dedication to Việt Nam and her unconventional, independent life fed into Mary Anne Bell.

O'Brien's physical model for the character was a young woman with the same first and last initials whom he met at Bread Loaf in 1988. Meredith Baker had just graduated from Middlebury. She'd written her senior thesis on Joyce's *Ulysses* and Twain's *Huckleberry Finn*, but theater was her passion. She and O'Brien talked easily in a group seated around the fireplace in the barn. Baker was athletic, a tennis and softball player and an ex-cheerleader. O'Brien took in her presence, her strapping build, long legs, and blue eyes. It was only two weeks after his first Joiner Center reading, where he'd read "The Revival of the Short Story," which he delivered now with the half-joking placeholder title "Death Sucks" and would present a few weeks later at Macalester as "Everybody Dies."[21] (O'Brien believes his *Esquire* editor, Rust Hills, asked for a new title, and the two of them arrived at "The Lives of the Dead.")

The month before, O'Brien received a letter from the brother of his former platoon leader, Lt. "Mad Mark" White. Thomas White had just read *If I Die in a Combat Zone*, made the connection, and wrote to inform O'Brien that Mark killed himself on April 30, 1975:

> He had done his tour and came home seemingly unscathed. After a semester in college, during which he made [the] dean's list, things began to go sour. Drug and alcohol abuse and violence began to change him. A marriage and a succession of jobs did nothing to help. After a series of stays in a mental hospital and visits to mental health clinics, he got a job as a cook in a small restaurant and appeared to be calming down. Then came his suicide.

Thomas bore his own trauma over his brother's death. He threw himself into books about the war in a quest to understand his brother's experiences.

O'Brien's memoir was one of several his wife had brought home from the library one day.[22]

Norman Bowker replaces Paul Berlin from the 1976 version of "Speaking of Courage." In the next story, "Notes," Bowker commits suicide after a succession of meaningless jobs and eight months at a community college. Three years earlier, in 1975, the fictional Bowker had read *If I Die* and written a letter to the Tim O'Brien character: "Norman's letter hit me hard. For years I'd felt a certain smugness about how easily I had made the shift from war to peace."[23] In addition to their survivor's guilt, both Tim O'Briens carry guilt over their portrayals of others in *If I Die*.

Bowker blames himself for Kiowa's death in the literal shit field beside a hamlet in "In the Field," the story inspired by the snafu death of Rodger McElhaney, shoved into the mud by a twelve-ton backward-churning armored personnel carrier. So much of his wartime happened-truth O'Brien transformed for the book—dead female bodies, kind old civilian men bullied by young GIs, water buffalo slaughtered by automatic fire, the uncertainty of whether the real or the fictional Tim O'Brien killed anyone but the certainty that their presence branded them complicit. In a book that proclaims that true war stories have no moral, the story sequence about Kiowa's death is intentionally didactic. Everyone's to blame, every soldier in the field, every politician, every citizen at a barbecue back home, yet as a result, individuals dodged blame: "It was a world without responsibility."[24]

Bowker's voice in O'Brien's head belonged to O'Brien's childhood, the voice of his chum Mike Bjerkesett. The summer of their fourth-grade year, Timmy and Mike regularly set up a lemonade stand at the seventeenth hole of the Worthington Country Club's golf course. "Most evenings, after dusk had fallen, Mike and I strapped on our helmets and played soldier out among the sand traps and water hazards." A car accident in 1967 left Bjerkesett a paraplegic, though he never lost his charm or ambition and lived a productive life until his death by suicide at age sixty-nine.[25]

Thomas White's letter did not specify his brother's method, so O'Brien didn't know he hanged himself in a hotel room when he imagined Bowker's hanging himself at the YMCA. It's possible he had in mind, consciously or not, the suicide by hanging of a Macalester English professor at the end of O'Brien's junior year. The local rumor mill blamed Ray Livingston's service in World War II, when he'd been a tank commander at the liberation of the concentration camps, but that was postmortem mythmaking about a man with a life's worth of troubles. As Eleanor Wade would say about her son John's life after Việt Nam in O'Brien's *In the Lake of the Woods*, "It wasn't just the war that made him what he was. That's too easy. It was everything."[26]

O'Brien named Elroy Berdahl in "On the Rainy River" after a boyhood friend who lived two blocks away from his first home in Austin and who once stole Timmy's pet turtle. O'Brien considers details from his life as acts of homage to the person and to memory. They can also be a means for him to see and hear what he's writing about even when the reader can't—to help make the stomach believe, his and then his reader's. The Tip Top Lodge, for example, was a real lodge on Whitefish Lake where the O'Briens vacationed after Ava's release from the state hospital, which O'Brien used as the fictional Elroy Berdahl's inn. Or the three-legged family dog Muggs in *The Nuclear Age*, named after the O'Brien family's three-legged dog. His turtle appears in fictional guise in *Tomcat in Love*, about which O'Brien's middle-aged narrator reflects, "The quick *t*'s on my tongue: *turtle*. Even after four decades I cannot encounter that word without a gate creaking open inside me. Turtle for the world—turtle for you—will never be turtle for me."[27] Never the same, yet ideally the emotional attachment attaches to O'Brien's readers.

The Things They Carried ends with its most direct evocation of O'Brien's childhood, the death from leukemia of Lorna Lou Moeller. The Linda in "The Lives of the Dead" is not exactly Lorna Lou, but she's very close. The same *The Man Who Never Was* war film outing followed by Dairy Queen, the same mean teasing by the real Mike Tracy, the story's Nick Veenhof. "The Lives of the Dead" equates Linda's death with the dead in Việt Nam, American and Vietnamese, none deserved, all before their time, making the war dead more relatable. It challenges the clichéd coming-of-age war story by having Timmy confront love and death as a kid. The book's final story, its final paragraph, portrays the present of the Tim O'Brien character as a forty-three-year-old veteran and writer inhabiting his childhood. He's a veteran reclaiming his prewar self, rebecoming Timmy in his Worthington basement, reading, writing, studying, escaping the world, playing alternative versions of himself in his imagination.

O'Brien had once praised Mailer's *The Executioner's Song* for its novelistic achievement of transporting the real Gary Gilmore into the company of enduring folk and literary characters—Ahab, Huck Finn, Joe Hill, Billy Budd—such that he "somehow survives his own death."[28] *The Things They Carried* goes much further in turning O'Brien's life into a work of fiction, and perhaps, in the process, accomplishes what the memoir couldn't, in allowing Tim O'Brien to somehow survive his own death.

◊   ◊   ◊

Much of the early material O'Brien generated for *The Things They Carried* is lost—he's grateful his crappy drafts vanished to "hyperspace" by the magic of the delete key[29]—but the correspondence documents his effort to interweave stories with commentary. There were to have been multiple chapters titled "Notes," perhaps one after each story. Lawrence pushed against this design even before the contract was signed. When he saw the drafted material in December 1988, he didn't care for the "Notes" chapter following "How to Tell a True War Story." It was "preachy." He also didn't like the inclusion of a letter (or a revised version of the letter) O'Brien had written in 1977 to a high school librarian from Saranac Lake, New York, who hoped he could offer a defense of the profanity in *If I Die* that she might use in her arguments with upset parents. Lawrence thought the letter too long, and he was right. It took O'Brien three pages to say, *Because that's how soldiers talked*.[30]

When O'Brien submitted the manuscript in early July 1989, he had reduced the number of "Notes" chapters to three, removing some and converting the rest to stories.[31] "Love," for example, replaced or significantly revised the "Notes" that originally followed "The Things They Carried." He had also chosen the title.[32] He'd been deciding between *War Stories* and *The Things They Carried* for months. *The Things They Carried* sounded too artsy. He preferred short, forceful titles. It was the title of his already-famous story, however, and thematically apt for the whole book. *War Stories* had two problems. Story collections don't sell, and the promise of a mere assemblage belied the book's unity. He also felt that a lot of potential readers wouldn't bother with a book of war stories because they didn't imagine it would be up their alley. Readers like to identify with a narrative, but women were excluded from the combat experience. Veterans didn't need O'Brien to tell them about their war: "The joy is not the joy of touching veterans or of touching people who have lived what you have lived. The joy is just the opposite."[33]

O'Brien and Lawrence both thought it was O'Brien's masterpiece.[34] It wasn't quite finished, however. His editor at Houghton Mifflin, Camille Hykes, loved the book except for its still-excessive commentary about itself. Hykes's letter of July 14 is a brilliant, graceful explanation for why O'Brien should eliminate the remaining three "Notes" plus a fourth chapter, effectively another "Notes," called "The Real Mary Anne." For Hykes, authorial interruptions explaining, for example, that the Tim O'Brien in the just-read story is not the Tim O'Brien who wrote it were unnecessary.

> Why do it if it's clear already? We perpetually weave fictions about ourselves—whether as individuals or as a given country (if I read you right). [. . .] Why should the magician pull up his sleeve & tell us— Look, this is where the birds come from—when really, deep down, we knew it anyway? These stories—those outside the Notes—are, too, not only about sunlight but about the crafting of art.

They tug apart the careful interweaving and, in their relative emotional weakness, they dilute the whole.[35] Had Hykes known about O'Brien's magician past?

Part of the problem involved dramatic integrity. As published, there's no difference between a fictional treatment of the historical Tim O'Brien or a fictional treatment of any historical person, of Marilyn Monroe, or John Brown, or King Henry IV. *The Things They Carried* is a fictional memoir that never breaks its fictional frame despite its real-world indices. With the "Notes," the otherwise unified text had two distinct yet not-so-distinct narrators operating inside—or was one outside?—the text. Future readers upset and angered upon realizing they hadn't just read real war stories are evidence that the published novel achieved its dramatic spell.

O'Brien sent Hykes a revised manuscript a week later. He agreed to remove the "Notes" that followed "On the Rainy River," where the narrator—or the author?—declares he isn't the Tim O'Brien character in the story, and to remove "The Real Mary Anne." He kept the "Notes" chapter after "The Man I Killed" but renamed it "Ambush," a story on the level of the rest. He kept the "Notes" chapter after "Speaking of Courage" as well as the title, now the only "Notes" in the book. "Notes" tells a story rather explicating and undoing the last one, plus it contributes vital plot information to the sequence of stories about Kiowa's death. O'Brien added a new third chapter, called "Remembering," eventually "Spin." This addition nudged "How to Tell a True War Story" closer to the center while still preceding "Sweetheart of the Song Tra Bong."[36]

A few days later he was off to the Joiner workshop and to Bread Loaf after that. His reading that year may have been the shortest of his Bread Loaf career. He introduced it as fragments he'd pieced together and was trying to decide whether to toss or "turn them into a story of some sort." All of it came from the book's draft. The piece began, "I remember . . ." and seamlessly brought together the text from "Style" (at the time called "The Dancer"), an almost final version of "Spin" ("Remembering"), and about two-thirds of the final "The Man I Killed."[37]

Back home, on Friday, the first of September, O'Brien sent Hykes the revised and final manuscript version of "The Man I Killed," which she received the same day he sent her the last new chapter, "Good Form," whose penciled edits were made by Hykes after phone conversations O'Brien had with her and then with another editor. The chief edit targeted, once again, a section of outright statements about fictionality: "the Tim who appears in this book, even at this instant, is not the Tim who sits here pecking away at a typewriter."[38] Those editing conversations happened the first part of the next week. On Wednesday, September 6, 1989, O'Brien handwrote Hykes a note with a single-line paragraph standing out between its ho-hum business matters:

"I'm *finished* with the manuscript."[39]

Before O'Brien had even submitted the final manuscript back in July, Lawrence gushed to him that *The Things They Carried* was "one of the most original and beautiful books I will ever publish."[40] The book's official publication date was March 28, 1990. It was an instant classic. Almost to a person, reviewers joined Lawrence in gushing, as readers can see for themselves in the eight front-matter pages of thirty-seven review excerpts O'Brien curated for paperback editions. The *New York Times* critic Michiko Kakutani, who had slammed *The Nuclear Age*, called *The Things They Carried* "a marvel of storytelling." *Entertainment Weekly* pronounced it "a brave new novel about peace." The *Detroit Free Press* hailed it for moving American literature "a step closer" to the unrealizable great American novel. *The Charlotte Observer* saw in it "something totally new in fiction," perhaps a "dramatic redefinition of fiction itself"; along the same lines, *The New Yorker* recognized it for achieving precisely what O'Brien wanted, a book with the "integrity of a novel and the immediacy of an autobiography."[41] It was a finalist for the Pulitzer Prize and the National Book Critics Circle Award, and the winner of the *Chicago Tribune*'s Heartland Prize, France's Prix du Meilleur Livre Étranger, and the Unitarian Universalist Association's Melcher Book Award, for, among other reasons, its power to "force a moral evaluation of personal implication in the consequences of international politics".[42]

> At a time when many Americans are congratulating themselves because our nation has fought a victorious war [the Persian Gulf War], *The Things They Carried* reminds us of the immorality of war, of the impossibility of victory in an enterprise which denies the interrelationship of all humankind. This book affirms the highest principle of Unitarian Universalism—the sanctity of life.[43]

The Melcher Book Award notwithstanding, part of the book's appeal stems from the understatement of its objections to the war's politics and conduct. No Americans die heroically, but it isn't a screed.

Most readers would struggle to place *The Things They Carried* in terms of the war's long history. It matters that the Tim O'Brien character was drafted in the spring of 1968 and that the war stories take place in 1969 and 1970, yet not to most readers, whose lack of such context helps the book transcend its historic specificity. O'Brien has always said he writes for the ages, not the moment or the prizes. The novel's title directs the reader's attention to the soldiers' experience without engaging in the pathos of victimization. The death of Ted Lavender in "The Things They Carried" does not absolve the platoon for destroying the village of Than Khe, even if they only shot dogs and chickens, not people. When Azar kills Lavender's puppy with a claymore mine, he exculpates himself by saying, "I'm just a *boy*," which O'Brien had originally written as "boys will be boys."[44] The soldiers' youth helps to explain their reactions and actions but does not morally excuse them. For O'Brien, playground bullying is evil, too. The book contains other minor acts of evil while avoiding actual atrocities such as the Mỹ Lai 4 massacre (which he was already writing about in *In the Lake of the Woods*), the kind of atrocities that would have more readily led readers to regard the book as anti-war, even to dismiss it as a typical liberal anti-war argument dressed up as fiction.

How many times would O'Brien hear from young men who signed up for the military *because* they read this book? It devastates him every time. A knife in the heart. "You poor dumb fucker," he tells himself over fancying that the book could only steer people away from war. Yet those young men are a testament to the book's refusal to commit the sin (per O'Brien) of moral absolutism.

Not everyone has loved the book. Some have found its metafictional strand—the reflecting Tim O'Brien narrator-character—too preciously highbrow and postmodern, divorced from the real war in its literariness. For O'Brien, however, the Tim O'Brien character helped solve the technical problems of at once delivering an emotional punch and securing moral gravitas. He found *If I Die in a Combat Zone* "inadequate" because it simply depicted and described.[45] Applying his imagination to his own experiences—now fifteen, twenty years in the past and written about several times—refreshed the experiences for him. It renewed those experiences; it created tensions and suspense and curiosities and challenges and immediacies; it restored his sense of mystery about himself, all of which his readers now have a chance to feel for themselves.

During the war and forever after, O'Brien expressed how unbelievable it seemed and continued to seem. Writing a Tim O'Brien narrator-character distinct from himself genuinely channeled his relationship with the soldier he once was. Pfc. Tim O'Brien was and was not Tim O'Brien; Tim O'Brien the author is and is not Tim O'Brien the narrator-character. Here's the fictional Tim O'Brien in the story "How to Tell a True War Story":

> In any war story, but especially a true one, it's difficult to separate what happened from what seemed to happen. [...] The pictures get jumbled; you tend to miss a lot. And then afterward, when you go to tell about it, there is always that surreal seemingness, which makes the story seem untrue, but which in fact represents the hard and exact truth as it *seemed*.[46]

The fictional Tim O'Brien narrator-character ideally approximates in the reader the confusions O'Brien underwent as a soldier and a writer: *Did that really happen? What really happened?*

Critics have also charged the book with sexism and racism, accusations O'Brien finds patently misguided and deeply painful. His legacy seemed to be in the hands of readers who forgot that to render ugly things, ugly things that historically happened—soldiers in his war did do and say sexist and racist things—does not entail endorsement or like-mindedness. O'Brien has acknowledged that "there's a simmering anger and resentment on the part of this Tim narrator toward women," a "rage . . . that was intentional but doesn't represent my own rage necessarily, but the rage that could be the consequence of men doing all the fighting and women being excluded from it [. . . and] a rage I saw exemplified on a lot of occasions."[47] Beyond merely depicting that rage, which might have only employed other characters, third-person characters, he wanted to *explore* it, which demanded that he use his namesake character-narrator. The system that did not require women to suffer combat arguably perpetuated sexist understandings of gender differences, a subject O'Brien addressed in "Sweetheart of the Song Tra Bong." Both the real and the fictional Tim O'Brien went to war to be loved, and romantic love has been a drumbeat driving men to battle since forever.

Besides, O'Brien argues, how could he write American women characters when they weren't there? How could he write perspectives that he didn't know? During the 1989 Joiner Center workshop, O'Brien asked Lê Lựu what he thought of the complaint about American writers who declined to present a Vietnamese perspective. "He gave me a funny look and he laughed. He said, 'Leave it to us. You don't know what we felt any more than you know what your wife feels at this moment.'"[48] Lựu's answer accorded with O'Brien's suspicion of the presumptuousness of such an act. Two years later, Robert Olen Butler published *A Good Scent from a Strange Mountain*, a collection that dared to include fictional voices of Vietnamese living in Louisiana. An intelligence officer and translator during the war, Butler had far more access to Vietnamese voices than most Americans. Precious few of the recently displaced had the language skills and the resources to write their stories for an English-speaking audience. Butler's book won the 1993 Pulitzer Prize; it also received a thumping for appropriating Vietnamese voices. Damned if you do, damned if you don't.

The Things They Carried dramatizes this issue in the story at its physical center. In "The Man I Killed," the Tim O'Brien narrator-character attempts to empathize with the Vietnamese soldier he just killed, to recognize their shared humanity and respect the man's individuality the only way he can, by imagining a person very much like himself, a bookish youth who did not belong in the infantry. The story respects the urge and moral duty to connect with others by seeing a little of ourselves in them and vice versa, even as it acknowledges the absolute limit of our imagination's ability to do so and the presumptuousness of the effort. In trying to peek into the other man's story and perspective, the narrator stares into the star-shaped hole that his hand grenade made of the dead man's eye, that perspective obliterated.

The story's draft underscored the racism of the war by having Kiowa, the platoon's Native American soldier, tell the narrator, "It's not cowboys and Indians, is it," more statement than question, in a war in which the American soldiers called everything beyond the perimeter wire of their firebases and landing zones *Indian Country*.[49]

Nguyễn Bá Chung, a Vietnamese American and longtime staff member at the Joiner Center, tells a story about O'Brien from one of the center's annual workshops. O'Brien was one of the writers at a session with Americans and Vietnamese. Each person was allotted five to ten minutes to speak. "When it came to Tim's turn, it took him only fifteen or twenty seconds. But what he said I would remember for the rest of my life." Looking at the Vietnamese writers, O'Brien spoke slowly to the audience, saying, "You don't know how happy I am to be able to sit next to these writers." And stopped. He added nothing else, leaving the entire class "stunned."

O'Brien has always held that *The Things They Carried* captures his year in Việt Nam better than the war memoir did. Its staying power bears his opinion out. By the end of the decade, *The Things They Carried* made *The New York Times'* list and many other lists of the twentieth century's best books. It and Herr's *Dispatches* became the standards against which future American war literature would inevitably be held.

O'Brien's friend from his days at *The Washington Post*, William Woods, sent his praise as soon as he got his hands on a copy and read it:

Do you remember that great line in Henry V—"Who hath measured the ground?" One of the French nobles says it the night before the

Battle of Agincourt. Some knight has crept up to the English lines in the dark and actually paced off the distance between the armies, and when he's identified, the other guy says, "A most expert and valiant gentleman." It seems to me that's what your new book does (as the others did as well)—measures the ground. And now you return to the actual ground and another kind of measuring—you of it, it of you, and so on—deep into your life, back into the book—[50]

25

WHEN PEACE IS HELL

With *The Things They Carried* submitted, in the fall of 1989 O'Brien and Hansen vacationed to Scotland for a week of golfing its storied courses. "A frivolous, blow-it-off, no-redeeming-social/cultural-value spree," Hansen wrote in his diary the night before departure. The planned trip almost didn't happen. Hansen had injured a tendon on a driving range a few days before and very nearly canceled, but he decided to play one-handed if necessary, so as not to disappoint O'Brien. At Boston Logan International Airport on September 23, he met Ann, not Tim, who couldn't find his passport that morning and had had to fly to D.C. for a new one and make it back in time for the overseas flight. At Prestwick on the twenty-seventh, they caught sight of Princess Diana entering the clubhouse as they were finishing up the course. Security wouldn't let them get closer, so per Hansen's diary they "stood around a half hour taking pictures of ourselves teeing off w/the big gallery lined up to watch but far enough away so one couldn't tell their backs were turned to us."

In late October 1989, O'Brien headed west for readings at Claremont McKenna College in California and the University of Hawaii at Mānoa.[1] That might very well have been the trip in which he island-hopped from Honolulu to Maui for a stay at Kipahulu on the east coast, where a woman collected him at dusk for a reading in a small hut overlooking a portion of the Haleakalā crater. Pitch-dark outside, a fire in the fireplace, maybe eight people could have squeezed into the hut. Nobody showed up.

The trip's fateful event had already happened, at Claremont McKenna.

A friend from O'Brien's early days at Bread Loaf, Liz Goodenough, arranged the visit. Wearing a baseball cap and sunglasses, he shared with her class of about fifteen undergraduates a story he said he'd never told anyone before—then proceeded to perform "On the Rainy River." As was his practice, he had thoroughly rehearsed it to create the effect of an impromptu telling. Afterward, he pointed out a student who had teared up as the reason he writes stories the way he does, to evoke truths the viscera know. He recommended an astonishing story he had just discovered, Delmore Schwartz's "In Dreams Begin Responsibilities." (A few years later he chose it for his friend Ron Hansen's anthology *You've Got to Read This*.)[2]

Goodenough also arranged for O'Brien to be interviewed by a friend's daughter who was thinking about a journalism or writing career. Kate Phillips had spent the year after graduating from Dartmouth in Beijing, teaching English at the Normal University and working for ABC News during the May 1989 pro-democracy protests and then the June 4 Tiananmen Square massacre of thousands of citizens by their own government.[3] O'Brien spoke on a Monday night in the Marian Miner Cook Athenaeum. Earlier in the day, Phillips and a *Claremont Courier* photographer had knocked on O'Brien's hotel room door. According to him, the mutual attraction with the petite blonde was as overwhelming as it was instantaneous, love at first sight. She hedged her answer when after the interview he asked her out for a drink. After his evening reading, she slipped him a note while shaking his hand outside the Athenaeum—she had a date with her. O'Brien now knew when to expect her later.[4]

Soon after O'Brien's trip to California and Hawaii, on November 9, the Berlin Wall opened its checkpoints for free and unrestricted passage. Berliners clambered to the top of the wall; they hacked pieces off. President Ronald Reagan's 1987 exhortation, "Mr. Gorbachev, tear down this wall!" was finally realized. The Cold War was over.

O'Brien didn't communicate with Phillips for some time after their meeting, although he sent her flowers once, and he next saw her at L.A.'s newish literary hotspot, Dutton's Brentwood Books, probably in March 1990 when on his book tour, hosted by Reagan's daughter, the writer and actor Patti Davis.[5] Davis, Phillips, O'Brien, and the art director and production designer Richard Holland went out afterward. O'Brien and Phillips were effectively a couple from that night on.

O'Brien's thirty-some-city book tour for *The Things They Carried* be-gan in Minneapolis–St. Paul the first week of March 1990 and ended in Phoenix two months later. Back in Boxford and fired up by the superlative reviews, he turned his attention to the paperback edition, making small edits, compiling review blurbs for the front pages, and pushing Penguin to produce it in a cheaper mass-market format instead of a trade edition, as he really wanted it "available to the common reader, not just to those who frequent book stores." He didn't want it to die a "'literary' death."[6] He hoped to finish *In the Lake of the Woods* by late 1991.[7] His new romance had reenergized the stalled novel. In August 1990, Phillips joined O'Brien at Bread Loaf and moved to Boston to start graduate school in American Studies at Harvard.[8]

On August 2, the Iraqi military under Saddam Hussein invaded and seized control of Kuwait and its oil fields. By the end of the month, the first U.S. military forces were on the ground in defense of Saudi Arabia, Iraq's and Kuwait's neighbor to the south. Seemingly overnight, the Middle East had become the new locus for America's global security concerns.

O'Brien watched that fall and winter with the rest of the world as the United States sent more troops and tanks and created a coalition of nations preparing for war to restore Kuwaiti sovereignty and stabilize the oil sup-ply. Television and print news issued grim warnings. Iraq had the fourth-largest army in the world, equipped with advanced Soviet weaponry as well as biological and chemical warfare capabilities. Its military had years of experience fighting Iran and a demonstrated willingness to use chemi-cal weapons. Hussein promised the mother of all battles.

In *The Boston Globe*, Mark Muro's "The Things They Carry" mimicked O'Brien's story in describing the soldiers and their gear headed to the Per-sian Gulf.[9] NO BLOOD FOR OIL became a standard protest slogan, and in January 1991, the air war against Iraq underway, protesters outside the White House chanted "Hey, hey, Uncle Sam, we remember Vietnam." Esti-mates of the demonstration ranged from 75,000 to 250,000.[10] All the while O'Brien had his head in crafting a novel forcing his fellow Americans to face how war can transform soldiers into murderers, as it had with Lt. Cal-ley's platoon at Mỹ Lai 4.

In September, the British filmmaker Christopher Sykes spent time with O'Brien. Sykes stayed a couple of nights at the O'Brien home in Boxford before accompanying O'Brien on a short trip of readings. The two met up with Phillips in Washington. The couple was obviously in love. O'Brien had told Sykes how they met. Sykes came back at the end of November for two weeks of filming.

Besides interview clips with friends and fellow writers Richard Bausch, Philip Caputo, and Carolyn Forché, plus some vintage footage from Việt Nam and Worthington, Sykes's film is all O'Brien—shots of him on a plane, at a reading, in the grocery store, driving around Worthington, at his writing desk, at home lifting weights (curls and bench presses), at a diner marking up pages. A lot of coffee-sipping. Hansen visiting for Thanksgiving. Sykes, knowing about Phillips, felt very uncomfortable shooting the domestic life-with-Ann scenes.

BBC never aired *How to Tell a True War Story*. Initially a film about Martha Gellhorn bumped it, then the *Omnibus* series editor decided not to run a second documentary about a war writer so soon after. The outbreak of Operation Desert Storm also contributed to setting the film aside.[11]

It must have been bizarre to watch on TV the war that launched CNN and the twenty-four-hour news cycle. The celerity and specious conclusiveness of the four-day ground war shocked and awed the world, O'Brien included. "It's a proud day for America," President George H. W. Bush blustered the day after the ceasefire. "And, by God, we've kicked the Vietnam syndrome once and for all." He doubled down the next day: "The specter of Vietnam has been buried forever in the desert sands of the Arabian Peninsula."[12] (Tell that, sir, to the war's veterans who took their own lives in the following decades, many in the wake of America's new wars.)

When later asked about the Gulf War, O'Brien spoke using the weight-training language that he knew: "'America came out of Vietnam feeling like a 92-pound weakling,' but, observed O'Brien, America has been 'pumping iron' ever since, up until the Gulf War [two] years ago. 'It makes me wonder why we pay our diplomats,' remarked O'Brien."[13] It was a very pithy, unaware update to the thesis of Susan Jeffords's 1989 *The Remasculinization of America: Gender and the Vietnam War*, a thesis his own new body coincidentally reified. He'd use the exact same language of the ninety-two-pound weakling a few years later, this time adding his contempt for America's Gulf War might-makes-right "bellicose pride," its old Lone Ranger, knight-in-shining-armor syndrome reborn.[14]

By August 1991, O'Brien moved out of the Boxford house to an apartment back in Cambridge.[15] Ann had confronted him in the car about his
emotional absence: *You're always distracted. If you don't want to be with
me, move out.* It was all he needed. That very day O'Brien drove to his old
neighborhood with a carload of essentials, found a building at the corner
of Massachusetts and Chauncy, and asked the super to call the landlord.
He signed the lease on the spot that night. He and Phillips never shared an
address, but they spent all their time together. After Roby, Phillips was the
second consuming love of his life.

◊   ◊   ◊

In addition to writing *In the Lake of the Woods*, O'Brien's work life proceeded apace. He revised *The Things They Carried* for the paperback
edition—one revision now has the Tim O'Brien character, on a trip back
to Việt Nam, slide a moccasin into the muck where Kiowa died instead of
a hunting hatchet, having realized he'd inadvertently enacted the cliché
burying the hatchet. "I don't want to leave behind something I know that
I'm less than capable of, or something that I know will put off a reader."[16]
When he could, he reprinted stories.

The most interesting placement was of "The Man I Killed" in *The Perimeter of Light: Short Fiction and Other Writing About the Vietnam War*
(1992), assembled by Vivian Vie Balfour, the Macalester girlfriend and
partial inspiration for Sarah Strouch in *The Nuclear Age*. Balfour's anthology is still considered one of the best on the subject for the quality and the
range of the writing and writers. O'Brien loves the title, reminiscent of
the concertina-wired perimeter of LZ Gator. He insists he did not attend the
book's Twin Cities launch party that fall, but a few months later he sent
Balfour feedback on a short story she'd shared with him, "The Reading," a
fictionalized version of their college relationship and of her listening to his
reading of "The Lives of the Dead" a few years earlier, changed in Balfour's
story to "The God of Death," no longer about Linda dying of cancer but
Becky "hit by a car on a summer evening in the alley behind her house."

Other than two slight margin notes—"good memory!!" and "familiar!!"—
O'Brien's feedback reads as impersonally as if she were any other student:
Avoid repetition. Don't break dialogue into separate paragraphs. Nice sen-

tence! The letter opens with a general compliment, offers its criticisms, and closes on an encouraging note one can imagine he'd written a hundred times before. He pushed back on the character based on him, not defensively, but because she'd drawn him flatly and hadn't done justice to the tension between the two characters, hadn't developed "the mystery beneath the surface."[17]

The achievement of *The Things They Carried* placed O'Brien in even higher demand for workshops, interviews, and appearances. Over the decades his mainstay readings were "On the Rainy River," "The Man I Killed," and a trio of short bits that he introduced by challenging the audience to discern the actual story from the invented ones. For the actual story, he would read from *If I Die in a Combat Zone* or an unpublished sketch, perhaps something about his childhood.

October 1990 found him at Pacific Lutheran University in Tacoma, Washington, at the invitation of Professor David Seal. Seal had been a part of the Hopkins High School debate squad, Worthington's main rivals for the Minnesota state championship. Seal and O'Brien became friends through competition. Seal was drafted into the infantry out of graduate school a year after O'Brien yet had the great fortune to be assigned to Germany. At Pacific Lutheran, the two drove by Fort Lewis, where O'Brien had undergone his initial training. Seal took a priceless snapshot of O'Brien, besweatered in his usual uniform of jeans, ball cap, sneakers, and cigarette, in front of the fort's north entrance sign, head cocked to the side, flipping the bird with both hands.

In May 1992 in New York, O'Brien was one of eight writers to receive an Arts and Letters Award in Literature from the American Academy and Institute of Arts and Letters. The 1990s also saw O'Brien transition from the Bread Loaf Writers' Conference to the Sewanee Writers' Conference. His last year at Bread Loaf was 1992, a few years before Robert Pack wound up his twenty-two-year conference directorship. Meanwhile Wyatt Prunty, a friend of O'Brien's from Bread Loaf, had taken the reins of the Sewanee conference at his undergraduate alma mater, the University of the South. Prunty likes to tell the story of his phone call to invite O'Brien to teach the summer of 1990. According to Prunty, O'Brien enthused about the prospect and graciously never asked about remuneration; according to O'Brien, he just didn't manage to break the money question into the conversation.

From that 1990 conference, O'Brien helped establish its convivial spirit under Prunty for the next nearly thirty years. He didn't teach every year, but was part of Prunty's regular rotation of faculty, nearly all of whom had won one of the majors, a National Book Award or a Pulitzer Prize.

O'Brien taught at the Joiner Center when he could from 1994 until the end of the decade. Those summer workshops were "incredibly meaningful" because of the camaraderie with literary-souled veterans and the Vietnamese writers in residence, who surprised him with their irreverence, kindness, and sense of fun.[18] Apparent to his Joiner peers, O'Brien in the early 1990s "was a very unhappy man," as Bill Ehrhart described him: "Certainly at that point I was thinking, for all of his literary success, I wouldn't trade my life for his."

These were O'Brien's darkest years. Would that one could give that period its deep-dive due. For all his passion for Phillips, more than once he tried to go back to Ann, but he couldn't see it through. The psycho-emotional forces that thrust him and Phillips together seem to have been the very forces that from time to time rent them yet kept them together. He refused to divorce despite his love for Phillips. He still struggled with his fears of betrayal and abandonment.[19]

O'Brien waffles on the subject of therapy. In his 1994 essay "The Vietnam in Me," he writes of years of therapy for depression; one interview quotes him saying he was "stuffed to the gills" on meds for clinical depression, another that he had punched holes in his apartment's plaster walls.[20] He's also said that he did see a professional a couple of times at Phillips's insistence but, judging it a waste of time, pretended to her that he continued going— a deceit he would write into *Tomcat in Love*. The language of "years," if true, suggests his therapy might have dated back to his decade with Gayle Roby. O'Brien's sessions revolved around his relationships with women and with his father, by some reckonings a source of his emotional anxieties: "I hate talking about it, really. The taunting. The silences at the dinner table. My own bafflement over why he would vanish from my life. He and I were never estranged, but the tension . . . For me, the feeling was just loss." The war figured into the depression, too, one of the "myriad of factors."[21]

Erik Hansen wasn't around to lend his best friend an ear. After their Scotland golf tour, the two drifted apart. Both traveled a great deal, O'Brien for readings and Hansen exploring northern Europe. While O'Brien spent

his days at home constructing the new novel, Hansen bought land and began building a house. They led full lives consumed by work and by matters
of the heart, Hansen even worrying that any conversation about their personal lives would be a case of "the blind leading the blind." Hansen had also
been upset by O'Brien's either not recognizing him or ignoring him when he
showed up for a Bread Loaf reading. Had he offended his friend in some way?
Was O'Brien too preoccupied with his adoring audience, or with some "major shit going down"? It would have been either 1990 or 1991. Archived photographs show Phillips at both Bread Loaf gatherings, so it's possible O'Brien
wasn't ready to face Hansen with his betrayal of Ann. Could he have simply
not seen Hansen? Was he high? Hansen avoided O'Brien partly out of envy
and shame over his own failed literary ambitions.[22]

In February 1993, O'Brien spent three days at Carthage College in Wisconsin by invitation of the associate dean. David Krause had met O'Brien
in the late 1980s at Trinity University in San Antonio through their mutual
friend the writer Lee Abbott. At a small group dinner, Krause and O'Brien
clicked. Krause found him shy, but his curiosity about other people opened
him up. Krause connected with O'Brien again in Cambridge, joining him
for a party of graduate students at Phillips's place. O'Brien escaped his
social discomfort by huddling in a corner giving his undivided attention
to Krause, his only peer in the room. Long after, Krause recalls, O'Brien
thanked him for being one of O'Brien's "better angels during those years."
At Carthage in 1993, O'Brien seemed more tickled than crowing about
the acclaim heaped on *The Things They Carried*. The students' enthusiasm
helped Krause bring him back the following year.

That April O'Brien wrote to the National Archives in Suitland, Maryland, for his battalion's after-action reports and casualty reports from his
time in the field with Alpha Company. He didn't receive a response until
June, and in August he refined his request, asking now for the price of reproductions of the battalion's daily journal for the first two weeks of May
1969.[23] He also began looking for military maps of the area. At some point
that fall he conducted research for himself at the Suitland archives. On
November 8 he wrote the Foreign Press Center in Hà Nội about a possible trip to Việt Nam for *The New York Times*, and by the end of the month
he signed an agreement with the *Times* to write a magazine feature on the
twenty-fifth anniversary of the Mỹ Lai massacre the next year.[24] Ironically,

love once again dispatched Tim O'Brien to Việt Nam against his instincts. In 1968, he couldn't endanger the love of family and home and girlfriends by not going into the army; in 1993, he agreed for the love of Phillips, under her strong encouragement. She wanted to go with him. He would not have gone otherwise.

The United States and the Socialist Republic of Việt Nam would not establish normal diplomatic relations until 1995. The Vietnam Veterans of America had arranged two trips in the early eighties, a politically controversial one in 1981 and a more benign one in 1983.[25] Then it was the writers' turn. In the winter of 1985–1986, Bruce Weigl, John Balaban, and Bill Ehrhart went as guests of Trần Kinh Chi, a retired North Vietnamese major general. In 1987, Kevin Bowen of the Joiner Center traveled to establish a rapport with the Writers' Union. The big Joiner Center writers' trip took place in summer 1990, the year after the Vietnamese writers visited Boston. Weigl, Ehrhart, Philip Caputo, Larry Heinemann, Yusef Komunyakaa, Larry Rottmann, and George Wilson joined Bowen and the center's codirector, David Hunt.[26] O'Brien initially said he would go, but later decided he wasn't emotionally ready.

Four days into 1994, Sam Lawrence died. The last several years felt in hindsight like a leave-taking. In 1990, O'Brien had been one of several of Lawrence's writers to speak at a Houghton Mifflin event celebrating Lawrence's twenty-fifth year in publishing. "He sees value in literature. He gives us space to write," O'Brien praised him.[27] In April 1993, much of the same group gathered in Oxford, Mississippi, to cut the ribbon on the Seymour Lawrence Room in the J. D. Williams Library at the University of Mississippi, where he'd agreed to donate much of his art collection and all his professional papers upon his death. Lawrence shared a home in Oxford with the writer Joan Williams. When his writers descended upon Oxford, his physical health was deteriorating. He later told Jayne Anne Phillips that he "danced too much that night" in the lead-up to losing a foot to diabetes. When O'Brien saw Lawrence a month before his death, he was in a wheelchair.[28] The immediate cause of his death was a heart attack.

O'Brien returned to Carthage College in the first week of February 1994. Krause gives this visit a mixed review. In their personal interactions, O'Brien was as gracious, inquiring, and self-deprecating as ever. O'Brien's public reading was excellent. Although mostly approachable, he was uncharacteristically snippy with students in Krause's class. "How's your daughter?" one of them asked, referring to the fictional Kathleen in *The Things They Carried*. "Look at the title page," he shot back. "'A Work of Fiction.' Do you know what fiction is?" Krause recalls O'Brien's muscularity coming into play as their classroom guest wore a muscle tee and may have even come extra-pumped from the gym. In February. In Wisconsin. O'Brien struck some of Krause's colleagues as unprofessionally gruff. This was not the Tim O'Brien of Bread Loaf in the eighties, described by his dear friend the poet Sue Ellen Thompson as having "a vulnerability about him that both drew people in and made them want to protect him." His more hardened persona surely contributed to impressions and rumors of a more aggressive posture toward women. To Krause, O'Brien second-guessed his upcoming trip to Việt Nam. He was extremely anxious.

O'Brien and other Lawrence writers spoke in tribute at a public memorial service at New York City's Harvard Club on Monday, February 14, days before O'Brien's departure for Việt Nam.[29] That last week before the trip, O'Brien shared his worries to his sister, Kathy, over the phone that he wouldn't return. It was the old fear, still a very real issue, of anti-personnel mines and unexploded munitions left from the war.

O'Brien had reached out for help arranging the trip to Lady Borton, who called upon her friend Lê Thị Hoài Phương. Phương had learned English during the war. In 1964, when she was twelve, she and her siblings were evacuated to one of the camps outside Hà Nội for workers' children— Phương's mother bicycled several hours on Saturday evenings to be with her two daughters and son. When she and other parents left twenty-four hours later, their kids ran crying after them. Phương shuttled about such camps for the next nine years, returning to Hà Nội after the Paris Accord of 1973, where she met Borton in 1975 and in 1990 began working for the American Friends Service Committee, called in Hà Nội the Quaker Service Vietnam (QSV).

The Vietnamese government strictly controlled visits by Americans who came through such offices as the Vietnam-American Association and the Foreign Press Center, neither of which would give O'Brien access to the people and places he sought. Borton wrote the visa application letter identifying O'Brien and Phillips as "specialists" visiting QSV projects in the north and exploring opportunities for future projects in Quảng Ngãi

Province. Phương understood the challenges of getting local authorities to accommodate any plans but the most regular and state-directed ones. With grit and savvy, dosed no doubt with cajolery, browbeating, and bribery, Phương made the Quảng Ngãi portion of the trip happen.

O'Brien and Phillips landed in Hà Nội the afternoon of February 19, 1994, two weeks after President Clinton lifted the trade embargo. On the aircraft's approach, O'Brien couldn't take his eyes off all the bomb craters. Borton and Phương met them at the airport. The couple stayed a couple of nights at the Metropole, the city's top luxury hotel. According to Phương, Princess Anne of England was expected any day at the Save the Children Fund's office next to QSV—people assumed Kate was Anne, and the rumor spread seemingly instantaneously among the many NGO offices that the princess wore her beauty without airs.

O'Brien met twice with a group of Vietnamese writers: "My main recollection is of fellowship—laughter, booze, toasts, storytelling, and the joyful feeling of brotherhood." Bảo Ninh, whose novel *The Sorrow of War* would become the most widely read Vietnamese novel abroad, joined one of the meetings. O'Brien spent most of one day touring Hà Nội on the back of the poet Nguyễn Quang Thiều's motorcycle: "Bizarre and wonderful. The evil enemy?"[30] At the hotel's Bamboo Bar, a cello, violin, and piano trio covered John Lennon's "Imagine," Frank Sinatra's "My Way," and Paul Anka's "Diana." O'Brien wrote in his trip notes, "These people fought for 50 years so they could play My Way."[31]

The *New York Times* photographer Edward Keating flew in from Cambodia and the Americans (sans Borton) traveled with Phương to Quảng Ngãi. Phillips's presence annoyed Keating because it robbed him of the ordinary one-on-one moments he counted on to get to know his subjects. He gave O'Brien the impression that he was preoccupied sampling the local marijuana in addition to the suitcase full he'd brought from Phnom Penh. For her part, Phương faced the interpretation challenge of what at times felt like working with three languages, as the dialect of Central Việt Nam could often be all but unintelligible to northerners and southerners. She constantly had to ask the Quảng Ngãi locals to repeat themselves. Phương described the area to O'Brien as "a different country. These people don't have much"; their lives were "very crude—very difficult. I think you had horrible bad luck to fight them."

Kathy, Bill, Ava, Tim, and Ann O'Brien celebrating the National Book Award, April 25, 1979 *(Permission by Tim O'Brien, HRC)*

With Erik Hansen, late 1970s/early 1980s *(Permission by Tim O'Brien, HRC)*

At Macalester College,
April 1980 *(Courtesy of
Macalester College Archives)*

(Below) At Bread Loaf
Writers' Conference, with
Hilma Wolitzer, Linda
Pastan, and Stanley Elkin,
August 1985 *(Photograph
by David Bain, courtesy of
Middlebury College Archives)*

(Bottom) At Bread Loaf
Writers' Conference,
August 1987 *(Photograph
by David Bain, courtesy of
Middlebury College Archives)*

Saluting the place where it all began, after the publication of *The Things They Carried*, October 1990 *(Permission by David Seal, HRC)*

Gish Jen, Tim O'Brien, Richard Bausch, Barry Hannah, Thomas McGuane, Jayne Anne Phillips, Jim Harrison, Seymour Lawrence, Frank Conroy, Susan Minot, Joseph Kanon, William Kotzwinkle, Tom Drury, and Dan Wakefield at the dedication of the Seymour Lawrence Room, University of Mississippi, April 17, 1993 *(Permission by Tim O'Brien, HRC)*

At the old LZ Gator site, February 1994 *(Permission by Tim O'Brien, HRC)*

The lagoon at CAP 142, February 1994 *(Permission by Tim O'Brien, HRC)*

The ditch at Mỹ Lai 4, February 1994
(Photograph by Edward Keating, permission by Carrie Boretz Keating, HRC)

Meredith Baker and Tim O'Brien, Christmas 1997 *(Permission by Julie Phillipps)*

(Below) In the Cambridge apartment, c. 1997 *(Permission by Meredith O'Brien)*

Tim O'Brien and Meredith Baker, c. 1999 *(Permission by Tim and Meredith O'Brien)*

Timmy, Meredith, Tad, and Tim O'Brien, Christmas 2005
(Permission by Tim and Meredith O'Brien)

Meredith, Tad, Timmy, and Tim O'Brien at the Dayton Literary Peace Prize
Foundation awards gala, November 11, 2012 (Veterans' Day)
(Permission by the Dayton Literary Peace Prize Foundation)

In a military cemetery in Belgium, summer 2013
(Permission by Tim and Meredith O'Brien)

"Masquerade Ball" magic show at the O'Brien Onion Creek home, Austin, Texas, August 2016
(Still from The War and Peace of Tim O'Brien *film, permission by Aaron Matthews)*

In 2019 *(Permission by Tim and Meredith O'Brien)*

(Below) Tad, Tim, Meredith, and Tim O'Brien, Rome, June 2024 *(Permission by Tim and Meredith O'Brien)*

The group arrived in Quảng Ngãi on February 22 and spent the next five days moving about the province, visiting LZ Gator and Nuoc Mau (the Ville) beside it, the Sơn Mỹ Memorial at Mỹ Lai 4, and the sites of O'Brien's injury and of McElhaney's absurd death that became Kiowa's absurd fictional death (to which he had returned in his imagination, accompanied by the fictional daughter, for the story "Field Trip"). O'Brien insisted they see the beach site of CAP 142, the lagoon, on the Batangan Peninsula, the most beautiful spot he had known that year in Việt Nam. He wanted Phillips to know it. O'Brien had brought with him the military maps he'd ordered and marked up from his research with Alpha Company's movements and casualties in May and July 1969. To his regret, they didn't have time to locate the hilltop pagoda where he'd chatted with a Buddhist monk about Graham Greene.

On Friday the twenty-fifth, the Americans joined Nuoc Mau's lunch commemorating the village's dead. Then to Da Nang on the twenty-seventh, and the next day on to Hồ Chí Minh City—formerly Sài Gòn—where O'Brien and Phillips played tourist until departing on March 4. Government loudspeakers cranked out Western music hours upon end: "Bridge Over Troubled Water," "Sacrifice," "Morning Has Broken," "Tell Me Why," "My Way," "As Tears Go By," "Do It to Me One More Time," and "I'm Gonna Be (500 Miles)."[32]

"Nothing here but ghosts and wind," he later wrote about LZ Gator, "utterly and forever erased from the earth."[33] Either preparing for the trip or preparing to write "The Vietnam in Me," O'Brien read "A Veteran Visits the Old Front—Wished He Had Stayed Away," Hemingway's essay about taking his wife Hadley to the area of his short ambulance duty and wounding during the Great War. Whereas the Italians took no interest in yet another white couple passing through, the villagers of Nuoc Mau were overjoyed to see the first Americans back since the battalion decamped and dismantled Gator in 1970, in the final weeks of O'Brien's tour. They gawked at Phillips's blond hair, the children especially. O'Brien's notebook, its writing sometimes in hands other than his, the Vietnamese names with their proper diacritics, is a vestige of the trip's open-hearted exchanges. "Dear God. We should've bombed these people with love."[34]

O'Brien talked with two women who had survived the massacre by hiding beneath bodies but whose families had not survived. Former enemy officers told him they mostly avoided the Americans because they were irrelevant to the civil war, and every time the Americans moved, they knew it. So loud, all geared up in their long columns. Someone made him pose awkwardly for a photograph with a Vietnamese man missing both legs from mid-thigh who was carried about in a chair, and a man who had lived most of the war underground. O'Brien had a secret meeting with a journalist.

In the evenings in the Quảng Ngãi City hotel room, O'Brien learned more about the area than he'd ever known by reading Jonathan Schell's 1968 *The Military Half.* He raged about the one-sidedness of the U.S. MIA teams conducting their searches with Vietnamese help:

> What if the Vietnamese were to ask us, or to require us, to locate and identify each of their own M.I.A.'s? Numbers alone make it impossible: 100,000 is a conservative estimate. Maybe double that. Maybe triple. [...]
>
> Even in the abstract, I get angry at the stunning, almost cartoon-ish narcissism of American policy on this issue. I get angrier yet at the narcissism of an American public that embraces and breathes life into the policy—so arrogant, so ignorant, so self-righteous, so wanting in the most fundamental qualities of sympathy and fairness and mutuality.[35]

The article doesn't mention his walking the ground where he was "hurt," as he captioned the back of the personal photograph.[36] O'Brien doesn't write about having to walk away from the Sơn Mỹ Memorial site to the actual ditch, or about Keating splashing into the ditch and holding his camera out of the water to get his shot. O'Brien doesn't write about the chintzy parts of the memorial, the concrete pig, cow, and chicken corpses, or the concrete paths indented with scurrying claw, hoof, and footprints, or the life-size plaster diorama of the terrorizing GIs inside the building. He doesn't write about meeting a thirty-eight-year-old man looking for his mother, whom the U.S. Army transported to the Chu Lai hospital in 1968 because of an illness and who was never seen again. She was thirty-seven.[37]

A local man fingered an LZ Gator barber as the informant who coor-dinated with the VC to kill Lt. Col. Barnes the May night of the sapper attack. O'Brien also learned that when sappers attacked a U.S. base, they presumed they would die. That Vietnamese opponents might share a meal and afterward go their separate ways, northerners and the VC to the mountains, southerners to their base. That news about Mỹ Lai hadn't made waves. Word of civilians killed by Americans was commonplace.

O'Brien was grateful to Phillips. She helped him see Việt Nam as Việt Nam, not his old war. With her there he could be a tourist, not a distraught veteran. In Cambridge that March, those military maps went up on the walls of the bedroom O'Brien used for his weight training. Having been to Mỹ Lai, he had revisions to make to the novel. He also had the *Times* article to write.

But in late April his sister called. She had a rare form of breast cancer. The prognosis was not good. A specialist agreed to treat Kathy with an aggressive protocol. Her first surgery was imminent. She started chemotherapy in May before moving on to radiation treatment for the rest of the year. It would have been May or June, then, when O'Brien flew to see her in a San Antonio hospital. He was funny and upbeat, good-naturedly joking about her condition, brightening her hospital stay. It took effort—when he first walked into her room, her pallor nearly floored him. She looked like a corpse. But the treatment worked, and she survived.

In mid- to late May, Phillips ended the relationship. The first week of June, he discovered she'd taken up with someone else. According to "The Vietnam in Me," O'Brien fought off suicide while drafting the essay, going back and forth between his writing desk and his upper-story window at four in the morning. Sleeping pills also beckoned. The newly prescribed oxazepam didn't impress him. Jettison the essay he was struggling with, or jettison his struggling self? Gayle Roby wasn't home when he called, seeking . . . what? Solace? Advice? Comfort? Evidence of love? He left a message on her answering machine that caused her to fear for him. She wanted to call him back, but that scared her, too. Would she end up repeating the bad old days of the 1980s? She was awfully messed up after O'Brien broke away. She might have called him back had her close friends not dissuaded her. *Gayle, get a life.*

What happened between O'Brien and Phillips that summer, indeed the ups and downs of their four years together, belongs to them and only them. Here is what he wrote in that essay, to which he says she did not object when he showed her a final draft:

I have done bad things for love, bad things to stay loved. Kate is one case. Vietnam is another. More than anything, it was this desperate love craving that propelled me into a war I considered mistaken, probably evil. [. . .] But in the end I could not bear the prospect of rejection: by my family, my country, my friends, my hometown. I would risk conscience and rectitude before risking the loss of love.[38]

O'Brien's treatment of Ann qualifies as a major one of those "bad things." Regarding Phillips, rumors have circulated about the things the two of them did to each other before and after the split. Not just the things men do, as Martha charged in *The Things They Carried*, but the things people do. O'Brien detests the person that he became for her.

Another vignette from *The Things They Carried* could provide a poetic explanation. An AWOL soldier hiding out with a Red Cross nurse giving him all the love he wants abruptly returns to his combat unit. His reason? "All that peace, man, it felt so good it *hurt*. I wanted to hurt it *back*."[39] Maybe O'Brien and Phillips's love felt so good it hurt. The force of the couple's initial attraction gave way to an equal and opposite reaction. In the summer of 1994, despair and tumult dominated. The essay acknowledges Phillips's pain and their shared if different responsibility for the hurt. Publicly they have remained steadfastly silent on the subject, a silence this biography respects. They have kept their distance, no love lost.

"The Vietnam in Me" appeared in *The New York Times Magazine* on Sunday, October 2, the day after *In the Lake of the Woods'* release and O'Brien's forty-eighth birthday. He never liked the assigned title. His notes suggest he considered "Homage to Quảng Ngãi." Some readers carped about the essay's likening of a literal slaughter of hundreds of innocents—not to mention the three million Vietnamese killed in the war—to a measly bourgeois broken heart. "You don't have to be in Nam to be in Nam," he'd written.[40]

O'Brien, however, couldn't untangle the experience of going back from his experience of Phillips. He was expressing a truth as he knew it, that both war and love can commandeer the soul to become the whole of one's universe. Both can result in a rejiggered moral compass and the unraveling of the world. "You go into those slow-motion droplets of now. You know, you look at your watch. It's four in the morning. You wait an hour. You look again. It's 4:02."[41] Without Phillips's presence, the essay would have been powerful but more predictable, less curious, and less memorable. Just another article decrying the atrocity at Mỹ Lai. Most readers seem to have received the essay's full impact. Friends and fans wrote O'Brien with their appreciation of its power and concern for his well-being.

The mixed reception was dizzying.[42] Having "The Vietnam in Me" published the weekend the novel launched, albeit a smart marketing tactic, did his mental health no favors. He spent the weekend doing events for the New England Booksellers Association at the World Trade Center in Boston and he spent the rest of the week doing interviews before flying out on Saturday to Chicago, the first stop of a two-month book tour. As he reflected to Charlie Rose for an interview taped and aired on October 19, he regretted the essay:

> You know, I did it to open up finally after years of holding inside the Tim O'Brien of about 25 years ago and the Tim O'Brien of a year ago. But you know, a heavy price was paid for that. [. . .] The price is pain to other human beings, people getting hurt by being open in a public forum.

Watching the show, Kathy worried when she saw her brother looking so dispirited. Where was his smile? The humor that had helped her through her cancer? "I'm tired of talking about personal things," O'Brien softspokenly rebelled against Rose's questions. "I've just got to stop. You know, I came to writing as a storyteller, and I moved away from it in that piece, and it sort of overshadowed my own desires as a storyteller. And what do you do afterward? You live it down."

The essay was not the main attraction he'd labored over for six years but a sideshow. He said to Rose what he often said: He writes to leave behind a small gift for the human species in the form of art. For him, that meant "pretty stories" that "entertain people" and "give their hearts a little squeeze." Stories and books, not articles. With *In the Lake of the Woods*, he strove to "salvage something beautiful from the wreckage of Nam and [. . .] everything since." That the novel is "extremely personal" is beside the point. What matters is that in one hundred years someone might happen upon it in a library, check it out, and "find pleasure" in its mysteries.[43]

26

DOUBLE CONSUMMATION AND CAUSAL TRANSPORTATION

In the Lake of the Woods

The origin of *In the Lake of the Woods* was an idea for a book Tim O'Brien and Erik Hansen would co-write, to be called *The Northwest Angle*, set in the same area as O'Brien's eventual novel.[1] The two would alternate writing chapters for what they imagined as a murder mystery potboiler. The friends saw it as a natural extension of their literary collaborations, and O'Brien hoped it would help Hansen realize, finally, a significant publication and the income that came with it. It must have been the late seventies or early eighties. Hansen believes they drafted three or four chapters, mailing them back and forth. Only a scattering of typescript pages from the first chapter, by Hansen, has turned up.

"Abe Martinsson cut back on the throttle and nosed the boat into the calmer waters of the cove on Amen Island," the story opens. "'Trouble ahead,' he had been thinking all the way out from the mainland, the bow of the runabout chopping into the whitecaps and spray of the big lake's wind churned surface. 'Trouble ahead.'" He's been drawn to the island by a shack set ablaze in order, he will come to suppose, to lure him away from the real crime to take place, back on the mainland. By chapter's end, he has discovered the body of Lennart Ecland, slumped at a table in Ecland's lakeside lodge where he wasn't supposed to be. A mystery.[2]

A more distant origin was O'Brien's childhood imagination. Timmy O'Brien never traveled north of Bemidji, Minnesota, yet he would "dream about it constantly, and think about it" while looking over maps: "There was something about the wild of Canada, and the possibility of choice—those things combined even as a child in my head. There was something about the wilderness and the lostness of it, the sort of sadness in my imagination as a kid that stuck with me and had something to do with my becoming a writer." So he told an audience in Northfield, Minnesota, in April 1994—after the trip to Việt Nam, before the heartbreak and the finished novel—but not in direct reference to the novel, which he said he'd just finished writing.[3]

The traceable origin is a précis O'Brien sent his agent, Lynn Nesbit, on the first of December 1985 to secure a contract and an advance. The main idea is there: John Wade, a rising star in Minnesota politics, loses a primary in a landslide. He and his wife, Kathy, escape to a cottage on the Lake of the Woods, where she disappears into thin air. O'Brien didn't know what the novel would reveal about her vanishing. The reader would ride the energy of O'Brien's curious quest. He looked forward to "pursuing the unknown" and held out the possibility that her fate would remain unknown. The campaign staffers accompanying the Wades to the cabin don't appear to have survived beyond the précis. The violence contained to one night in the published novel, of John Wade killing plants and possibly his wife with boiling water, pervades the original conception:

> Though a decent man, he feels overpowered at times by an inexplicable need to inflict pain, both emotional and physical. Example: one evening a playful bedtime kiss turns into something else. He's biting. He can't help himself. He laughs it off, but in the morning the marks are still here. Example: a quiet morning in the boathouse. He's filleting a string of walleyes, except it suddenly becomes a kind of random butchery. He just keeps hacking.[4]

The précis introduces "Hypothesis" chapters as "vignettes" of "John's own imaginative reconstruction of events," not yet the conjectures of the published novel's anonymous first-person investigative O'Brien avatar.

O'Brien would later cite Lieutenant Governor Sandy Keith's 1966 primary shellacking for the governorship as "sort of" his template, mixed with Richard Nixon's, Jimmy Carter's, and Walter Mondale's humiliations and subsequent temporary withdrawals.[5] Keith had been caught up in a financial scandal involving American Allied Insurance Company, and even if not criminally guilty, he was politically vulnerable through his work for a subsidiary.[6] The précis to Nesbit doesn't divulge the novel's dark heart, the fictional lieutenant governor's ambiguous participation in the Mỹ Lai massacre. O'Brien hadn't decided how to connect John Wade to it. While he wanted to explore the potential in anyone for violent acts of sheer inhumanity, he shied away from Mỹ Lai's sensationalism and yoking his book's import to a single episode from a particular war such that it wouldn't outlive it. He didn't want an unearned, unoriginal readymade, or knee-jerk rejection by reviewers for using the tired example anti-war types always trotted out. The British documentary *Four Hours in My Lai*, by Michael Bilton and Kevin Sim, aired in the United States as *Remember My Lai* on May 23, 1989, followed by a book (titled after the British film) in March 1992.[7]

The précis also doesn't mention the abortion that in the published novel Kathy undergoes at the outset of John Wade's political career, a source of guilt and shame overshadowed by the murdered Vietnamese children and babies.

Two months after writing Nesbit, O'Brien returned from a Hawaii vacation and reported to Hansen that contract negotiations had gotten "crazy" and "vicious." As for the story, O'Brien told Hansen he was "Drawing heavily on my own experiences over the past six months—which has not been a happy time."[8] He didn't elaborate. One personal source for John Wade's crushing defeat was the borderline hostile reception *The Nuclear Age* had received in important quarters. The other source was O'Brien's marriage and his double life with Gayle Roby, about which Hansen hadn't a clue. The novel is all about the secrets people keep.

O'Brien had his contract with Lawrence's new house, E. P. Dutton, on March 20, 1986, with a draft due in 1988.[9] How much progress did O'Brien make the rest of the decade? His November 1987 letter to Bob Warde at Macalester declined an invitation to visit because he needed time to wrap the novel up within a year but also mentioned the notion for a story collection, the notion that forthwith moved *Lake* to the back burner and became *The Things They Carried*.[10] Lawrence moved houses again, to Houghton Mifflin, in the spring of 1988, and O'Brien's novel went with him.[11] For a quick minute in 1989, O'Brien flirted with compiling what he might have thought of as a commercial sequel to the soon-to-be-published *Things*, "a collection of stories entitled SPEAKING OF COURAGE" as his agent's letter of representation referred to it. Perhaps published stories that hadn't appeared in book form, and pieces scrapped over the years, and new work (the undated scraps of story ideas in the archives may or may not have anything to do with this project).[12]

O'Brien had gone into the novel asking his tried-and-true questions. What could have happened? What might have been?

If he had gone into politics, for example.

His first year at Macalester, O'Brien lost the spring election for class vice president. During the Political Emphasis Week's model state legislature that April, the liberal faction stood O'Brien as its candidate for speaker of the house. The liberals touted with bemused gusto this bright-eyed freshman (the conservative candidate was bound to win). *Mac Weekly* reported that O'Brien's backers "warbled a lusty rendition of the now-famous 'Tim O'Brien Fight Song.' Old-timers in the audience agreed that a model assembly has seldom been moved to such a fever pitch of emotion."[13] College peers understood that he sought a political career, their evidence being his political science major, his student government leadership, his participation in YDFL, his political commentary in *Mac Weekly*, his relationship with Professor Mitau, and his silence on other possibilities. O'Brien said as much in interviews after the National Book Award.[14] After graduation, he wrote Roby saying he was headed to Harvard unless he got drafted, then "journalism followed by ventures into politics possibly" (he also typed out an E. E. Cummings poem for her).[15] In Việt Nam, as he started thinking about his postwar life, he wrote Macalester to have his transcript sent to Harvard Law School.[16] Law school has long been a stepping stone for political careers, and there's no evidence to suggest he ever considered practicing law.

The published novel uses John Wade the politician as a surrogate for

Tim O'Brien the writer. While in Việt Nam both men imagined the career benefits, war being a reliable political credential and, as Ernest Hemingway wrote to F. Scott Fitzgerald, "the best subject of all" for writers because it "groups the maximum of material and speeds up the action and brings out all sorts of stuff that normally you'd have to wait a lifetime to get."[17] Both jobs truck in rhetorical trickery and carefully crafted personae. Wade, too, chooses career over children. Wade has become caught up in his political ascent, losing sight of what public service positions him to do for others, a version of a predicament that possibly troubled O'Brien in the wake of *The Things They Carried*'s success. When O'Brien appeared not to recognize Hansen at Bread Loaf, Hansen worried his friend now valued attention and accolades over enduring art. The novel very much explores attention-seeking as a psychological motive for politicians. "Politics was just a love thermometer," Kathy Wade concludes. Her husband requires "the conspicuous display of human love—absolute, unconditional love."[18] The love and approval never felt from his dad.

If O'Brien's father had killed himself, as O'Brien believed he contemplated.

In the Lake of the Woods puts Bill O'Brien's personality on full display through Wade's father: the bullying of his son, the hospitalization for alcoholism. Like Timmy O'Brien, young John Wade retreats into magic. The scene with the "Guillotine of Death" at Kara's Studio of Magic in St. Paul rewrites a family trip to New York City for one of Bill's insurance conventions. Bill took his son to Lou Tannen's famous magic shop on Forty-Second Street, back when it was on the ground floor. It was one of the two or three such trips the family took to the city to spend time with Bill's mother, Mary, and sister Catherine. During these trips, Bill toured the family around Coney Island and other beloved spots of his childhood. Tannen, red-haired and spectacled, showed off a Hans Moretti sword box. In the version Tannen demonstrated that day, the magician's assistant places his or her head in the box, then the magician runs several swords through the box at various angles. When the box is opened, there's no head at all, only sword blades. Tannen suggested Bill stick his head in the box so his son could try it out.

Bill wouldn't do it. Timmy read fear in his eyes: *If anybody's gonna do it, you're gonna do it, Lou. Not my kid. My kid will kill me.* "And you know it was even half-funny then. Now, looking back at it, that was my real dad. Because he wasn't drunk, and he was fun, and maybe he was even acting about 'I don't want to put my head in that cage.' I don't know. But it was a moment that really vibrates for me."[19] The illusion was too expensive, yet the experience was the rare instance his father supported the hobby. Bill never outright disparaged it but took no active interest. O'Brien felt his dad watched his tricks and performances out of begrudging duty. In the novel, after Wade's father places his arm in the illusion for the Carrot Lady to operate, she steps back and lets John do it. "'Go on,' she said. 'Let him have it.'"[20]

Wade carries his hobby to Việt Nam where, nicknamed Sorcerer, he speaks cryptic words to the radio to make villages and people disappear. Wade can't always distinguish between himself and his performing self, and Sorcerer accompanies him home as prestidigitation figures into the novel's understanding of Wade's political life. It's another way for O'Brien to connect politics and writing.

O'Brien's 1990 Bread Loaf lecture "The Magic Show," his first after the publication of *The Things They Carried*, compared writing to magic. The endless practice and the artistic effect, the "sense of theater and drama and continuity and beauty and wholeness," the "abiding mystery at its heart." Like a shaman, a writer enters a trance for summoning the spirits to charm the audience.[21] Other than the occasional coin or card trick to amuse others or dawdle, O'Brien had left magic in Worthington. He'd written about it once, when in 1973 a *Boston Globe* editor asked him for an article on the city's magic scene. The semi-professional magicians O'Brien interviewed he could have quoted in the 1990s essay or novel: People enjoy a good bamboozling and a good mystery; magicians take pleasure in the psychology of it; there's "precision" and "daring," a "grace" and "glow" in doing it well. One practitioner might as well have been talking about John Wade: "Magicians are basically egomaniacs. That's the core of it. Magicians are people who crave a certain kind of power. It's hard to define but it's there. The power to control, to manipulate. To do the impossible, and to be nonchalant about it, as if it happens every day."[22]

"The Magic Show" offers a veritable blueprint for *In the Lake of the Woods*. The stories of our lives, much less others' lives, never resolve with clarity or certainty, a fact that frustrates and compels us. Nor will his novel—the reader never learns what happens to Kathy or to John Wade. A wrapped-up story—an *explained* story—like an explained magical act—no longer beguiles. It dies on the page. But the wonder ought to cling to the departing audience. Another blueprint of sorts, O'Brien's review of *The Executioner's Song*, cogently presents his conviction that explanation saps literature of its power:

> In less capable hands, Gilmore's life would be presented as a series of facts connected by motivational analysis or speculation. The heart of nonfiction, after all, is to dispel mystery. But the heart—and art— of fiction is both to generate and to celebrate human mystery, to allow ambiguities and contradictions to resonate, to explain little of a character's inner drives but rather to show those drives operating in a dramatic context. This is Mailer's strategy. After more than a thousand pages, after learning virtually all there is to learn about the "real" Gary Gilmore, we do not in the end fully understand the man. By not explaining him away, Mailer maintains the essential human mystery that keeps Gilmore alive in the reader's imagination.[23]

In the Lake of the Woods, with its Evidence and Hypothesis chapters and its investigating narrator, exploits the expectation of nonfiction's dispelling of mystery in order to novelistically celebrate mystery and keep its characters alive in the reader's imagination.

At Bread Loaf three days after the "Magic Show" lecture, O'Brien read an early version of "Loon Point," a story that wouldn't appear in a book until two novels later, in 2002's *July, July*. Originally a part of *In the Lake of the Woods*, the lost ur-chapter, probably written in the 1980s, explored Kathy Wade's affair with Harmon and "what happened at Loon Point."[24] By the Bread Loaf reading, O'Brien had extracted it from the novel. Kathy and John Wade are now Ellie and Jack Abbott. Harmon stays Harmon, the lover whom Ellie watches drown in the waters off Loon Point. She doesn't kill him, but her presence is guilt enough. Disappointed in love, post-affair Ellie imagines "wanting without object, pure wanting."

The huge difference between the Bread Loaf version and any later version is the character Billy Wing, Ellie's first extramarital lover.

Billy's "exotic genes" attract Ellie, "the Apache warrior entwined with the Chinese servant, equal measure brave and slave." The racist dimension of Ellie's desire played a part in O'Brien's dropping the character. After Ellie ends the relationship, Billy stalks her, sometimes breaking into her home. In her imagination, "which was not especially fertile," she pictures him entering the house "naked maybe except for a loin cloth and a feathered bonnet" while she sleeps, "his face painted crazy colors." In her daymare he slices her open with a lance and "squeezes her heart like a goatskin." Months after Harmon's death, Ellie meets Billy for coffee and learns that he was at Loon Point the day Harmon died. Billy "tidied up" the place after. Because he loves her. She has nothing to worry about; he's taken care of everything.[25] As part of the novel, the tall tale would have been one of John Wade's hypotheses, its strange violence circling the possibility that he murdered his sleeping wife.

Guilt pervades, Ellie's over her infidelity and over Harmon's death expressing Wade's (and O'Brien's) over so many things. Ellie wonders how "such gross evil could carry so few practical consequences. She expected more from the world, and in a way she wanted more." The war as the source of Wade's potentially murderous violence lurks in Billy Wing, half Apache and half Chinese—which is to say Asian or even Vietnamese if ethnically Chinese—plus the racist conflation of the Vietnamese wartime landscape with the American frontier. "Vietnam was where the Trail of Tears was headed all along," Michael Herr wrote in *Dispatches*.[26] (In the experience of O'Brien's friend from basic training, Blair GreyBull, Native American soldiers were often tasked to walk point because of some imagined affinity and sixth sense for the secrets of the woods and the native enemy.)[27]

The gross stereotype may have bubbled up from the depths of the Lake of the Woods in association with Mỹ Lai. The novel's setting reverberated with Wade's war experience beyond the bewildering terrain. The closest village to the Northwest Angle is Warroad, so named as "a terminus of a principal Indian war road, or warpath, of the Northwest." The French garrison suffering the winter of 1735–1736 at Fort St. Charles sent out a party to look for relief. The first night out the soldiers camped on an island, where "they were discovered and all 21 of them beheaded by a party of Sioux on the warpath." According to the *National Geographic* article O'Brien photocopied, it was now called Massacre Island.[28]

O'Brien's 1991 Bread Loaf reading was "The People We Marry," soon to be published in *The Atlantic Monthly* (January 1992) before becoming the novel's chapter 7, "The Nature of Marriage."[29] It's a key chapter that introduces the couple's college romance through their postwar wedding as well as John's boyhood magic and his return to it in Việt Nam. The chapter also first hints at his covered-up presence at Mỹ Lai. Students of the massacre can spot the published novel's clues: John Wade belongs to Charlie Company, a soldier named Weber is killed in Pinkville in February, and there's homicide near an irrigation ditch at Thuận Yến, the sub-hamlet's local name.

In the story's earlier form, O'Brien hadn't committed his book to Mỹ Lai, as John Wade's college and Việt Nam dates track to O'Brien's, so a year late for the historic massacre. In-country, he's with Bravo Company, not Charlie. Weber isn't yet the actual Spec. 4 Bill Weber from Calley's platoon but a made-up "Henderson" killed in the "foothills northwest of Chu Lai" in August. Mỹ Lai is to the south. There's no Calley, and O'Brien hasn't yet added the Thuận Yến legerdemain.

For his 1992 reading—his last time at Bread Loaf—he excerpted sections from the manuscript during the period he briefly considered renaming it *The People We Marry*.[30] To his audience, O'Brien distanced himself from his protagonist's violence and misogyny, calling Wade "mentally disturbed, a sick guy." The bits he read about John's childhood and about Kathy remain substantially the same in the final novel. The Việt Nam pieces reveal that O'Brien had not yet landed on Mỹ Lai for John's dark backstory. He's still with Bravo Company. Rather than a slaughter of innocents, he takes part in a pitched firefight. The American soldiers shoot *and receive* fire; Wade runs across Spec. 4 Davis "without chest or lungs." This version of Wade, unlike his published version, also shoots, also returns fire—blindly, perhaps, but nevertheless, "at burning trees, and burning hooches," at whatever moved or didn't move.

In the novel, he takes refuge among the Vietnamese bodies, "maybe a hundred," in an irrigation ditch, from where he shoots Pfc. Weatherby; in the 1992 reading, he takes refuge "behind a pile of white stones" from where he shoots the starting-to-smile Weatherby. In the novel, he's seen Weatherby murder little girls, kill "whatever he could kill," and shoot "twitching" bodies to stop the twitching. In the reading, there's no evidence Weatherby has shot anyone, civilian or combatant, such that Wade's action carried any poetic comeuppance. Whereas the novel presents the Mỹ Lai evil as unimaginable to him and therefore impossible, his presence there something he can feign away, initially he treats his murder of Weatherby that way:

> Sorcerer thought he could get away with murder. He believed it. After he shot PFC Weatherby—it was an accident, a reflex—he tricked himself into believing it hadn't happened the way it had happened. He pretended he wasn't responsible. He pretended he couldn't have done it and therefore hadn't. He pretended it didn't matter much. He pretended that the secret stayed with him, with other secrets. He could fool the world and himself too. He was convincing. He had tears in his eyes because it came from his heart. He loved PFC Weatherby like a brother.
>
> "Fucking VC," he said when the chopper took Weatherby away. "Fucking animals."

O'Brien when writing this passage was thinking about his ability as a writer and a performer of his writing fooling himself in the moment of fooling the world. To make the heart believe. He was also asking a genuine question. What if Pfc. Tim O'Brien, who had also shot without aiming, in the general direction of the enemy, pulling the trigger more by reflex than with deliberation, had killed another American? How complicit are we for what *could* have happened?

At the time of the reading, O'Brien was deep into "Ambush," the April 1993 *Boston Magazine* essay paralleling the battles of Lexington and Concord with an artificially truncated period of combat from his war, figuring the British as the professional occupying army committing atrocities against the colonists, guerrilla-style militiamen and civilians alike.[31] The "Evidence" chapters of *In the Lake of the Woods* draw on O'Brien's research for the essay and add readings from America's frontier wars and testimony about Mỹ Lai to remind readers that all peoples—all people—are as capable of cruel violence as they are of victimization.

The Mỹ Lai research included the Bolton and Sim book, the Peers Commission Report, Richard Hammer's *The Court-Martial of Lt. Calley* (1971), and O'Brien's inquiries into his unit's records. But it isn't clear when he made the monumental decision to rewrite the book to place John Wade at Mỹ Lai. The dates for Wade's college years the published novel adjusts to a year earlier to fit the story to Mỹ Lai. When in April 1993 he contacted the National Archives to request the battalion reports, his letter said he was writing a book about his experiences[32]—either that was more efficient (and less controversial) than saying a novel about Mỹ Lai, or, more likely, he had yet to decide.

He finished the draft the first week of February 1994 during his second visit to Carthage College, just prior to traveling to Việt Nam; he believed it his best novel yet. The publisher's "setting copy" with his final revisions and corrections is dated that May.[33] He must have undertaken the significant rewrite, from a fictional firefight perhaps loosely based on one of his own to a fictionalized version of the historic massacre he missed, in the second half of 1993 and into the new year. The only material unquestionably added post-trip is the reference to the narrator's visiting the Sơn Mỹ Memorial in the final note of chapter 16.

"It seemed worth the risk to drop Wade into the historical event itself," O'Brien has said. *Four Hours in Mỹ Lai* failed to ask the right questions about what had happened. He bemoaned the American response when it was fresh news and the ignorance of and attitude toward it twenty-five years later: "Evil has no place, it seems, in our national mythology. We erase it. We use ellipses. We salute ourselves and take pride in America the White Knight, America the Lone Ranger, America's sleek laser-guided weaponry beating up on Saddam and his legion of devils."[34] He needed his readers to wonder if, regarding the perpetrators, there but for the grace of God go they. He wanted them to understand that the seizing, unseizable human forces involved did not restrict themselves to those soldiers in this episode of that war. Maybe it was the sunlight, the narrator supposes, maybe that was the difference that led to the slaughter. O'Brien here nods to Camus's *The Stranger*, whose first-person narrator blames the sunlight for his murdering an Algerian. It's the novel O'Brien has reread more than any other.

The fictional narrator of *In the Lake of the Woods*—the voice in the footnotes, anyway—reflects on his effort to reconstruct what happened to the Wades and shares memories that are in fact O'Brien's: the trip to the Sơn Mỹ Memorial and the best friend Chip Merricks blown to bits. At Mỹ

Lai, John Wade shot an old Vietnamese man with a hoe, which he remembers (or tells the reader and himself he remembers) mistaking for a rifle in the heat of the moment. The narrator-character admits he has his "own old man with a hoe." For O'Brien the writer outside the text, that old man could be the farmer his lieutenant shot as target practice with O'Brien's sniper rifle, an act the private first class did not report. Or the prisoner he kicked a bit. Or any Vietnamese he might have killed firing into the trees, or whom someone else killed on his behalf. As for the narrator's "own PFC Weatherby," no, O'Brien did not shoot an American. But if in his haphazard shooting it *could have* happened, it *might as well have* happened. Tim O'Brien is not the first or last veteran to feel responsible for each and every death and casualty from their war.

Does Kathy Wade leave her sorry husband? Does he murder her? Do they orchestrate a joint flight from the world, what magicians call a *double consummation* topped by a *causal transportation*, fooling the audience by vanishing one object or person only to follow it up with an unexpected second, the magician's self-vanishing?[35] When the organizers of the 2016 Hemingway Society conference asked O'Brien which of his books to sell with special tickets to his presentation, he chose *In the Lake of the Woods*, the one novel that never quit perplexing him.

◊ ◊ ◊

The gamble paid off. Upon the book's publication in October 1994, the front page of *The New York Times Book Review*, harbinger and influencer, called *In the Lake of the Woods* O'Brien's "striking new novel" that plumbs a character's interiority as O'Brien "has never done before." The review concludes provocatively: "It is a novel about the moral effects of suppressing a true war story, of not even trying to make things present, a novel about the unforgivable uses of history, about what happens when you try to pretend that history no longer exists."[36] Frank Conroy, in a *Vanity Fair* piece celebrating Seymour Lawrence's loyalty and legacy, praised the novel for defying genre by pressing the reader into service as "O'Brien ponders the dynamics of guilt, denial, and loneliness with a kind of passionate meticulousness that refuses to simplify great problems merely in order to solve them. *In the Lake of the Woods* is a powerful, daring piece of work. It looks evil in the face and doesn't blink."[37] The Society of American Historians awarded the novel its James Fenimore Cooper Prize, and *Time* magazine named it the best novel of the year.

Some reviews objected to the lack of plot closure, for them an artistic and moral cop-out equivalent to creating a choose-your-own-adventure story when life always has endings that are known or knowable. But that's not true. *In the Lake of the Woods* anticipated the boom of true-crime television serials and podcast episodes of the early twenty-first century that, just as often as not, never solve the crime. Such criticisms overlooked the novel's citing of Ambrose Bierce, who wrote *Tales of Soldiers and Civilians* and in 1913 disappeared in Mexico; and of B. Traven, the pseudonym of the author of *The Treasure of the Sierra Madre* and *The Death Ship* about whom very little is known, and who managed to vanish into his pseudonym, also in Mexico. O'Brien was a fan of both Traven novels as well as the Karl S. Guthke biography of Traven, and it's fair to say that as Traven disappeared himself behind his pen name to elevate the books over their creator, O'Brien in some of his works took the opposite approach to accomplish the same thing, merging with his narrators to disappear the biographical self into the text.[38] Vladimir Nabokov's *Pale Fire*, another novel with a fictional voice supplying footnotes and an inconclusive story, was an O'Brien favorite.

The other primary criticism of the novel objected to the seeming interplay of fiction and nonfiction, which stretched beyond that of *The Things They Carried*. Michiko Kakutani, who had trashed *The Nuclear Age*, dismissed *Lake*'s narrator, writer, and creator as self-indulgent.[39] For O'Brien, the novel's plentiful mirror imagery—the Lake of the Woods' wilderness itself, its endless density of trees on island shores "a great curving mirror," as the first paragraph spells out—makes the book a mirror for the *reader's* introspection. Forms of the word *lost* appear seventy-three times in the novel, of *mirror* forty-three times. Seen that way, the book is a far cry from self-indulgence. In the *Detroit Free Press*, Linnea Lannon, who was sympathetic to the criticisms, nevertheless confessed in her review that *In the Lake of the Woods* "is the one book I've read this year that keeps nagging at me. Did John Wade kill his wife? Does it matter? Isn't it as important, or more important, that O'Brien got up close to deception and what it does to the soul, to a marriage? [. . .] It will never be a title I look at without pausing."[40] *Nagging* or *haunting*—one can imagine O'Brien using either, and smiling.

That fall, as O'Brien set out on the two-month book tour, his personal straits hijacked the interviews, profiles, and a fair number of book reviews. He announced the end of his writing career—there was nothing more to give, nothing else he wanted to do with his fiction. With *In the Lake of the Woods*, he said, he'd exhausted his well. The mystery of others. The accessibility of truth through fiction. The alternative realities he could imaginatively explore to their conclusion. War.

Imagine: two years from fifty, promoting what he believed to be his last novel, facing the end of the vocation to which he'd devoted nearly every day of his postwar life. He grieved for the loss of Phillips with all that comes with such grief—anger, disbelief, spite, self-pity, longing, incomprehension. O'Brien was alone with his success. Unloved, betrayed by the idea of love, and, he feared, unlovable. He had initiated divorce proceedings, partly for Ann's sake, partly as an act of defiance toward Phillips, for whom he hadn't gotten the divorce. During the tour he spent time on the phone with his lawyer and hunting down hotel fax machines. His father's lackluster affection and disappointment from childhood festered: "That's what I mean about evil not having a single source, like Vietnam or the death of buddies."[41] The war continued to occupy O'Brien's soul, yet history was leaving behind his *raison d'écrire*. "My own war does not belong to me," the narrator-character of *In the Lake of the Woods* concludes. "Maybe that's what this book is for. To remind me. To give me back my vanished life."[42]

One of his first tour stops was the original Borders bookstore in Ann Arbor on October 13. Phillips phoned O'Brien at the hotel shortly before his reading. Delayed, he had to run the eight blocks to the bookstore. During the reading, still rattled by her call, he stepped away to collect himself in the restroom before returning and resuming. The university newspaper reported O'Brien's having "delighted his audience at Borders with an emotional breakdown." Everyone assumed reading about the war had unraveled him.[43] Word of the episode spread, feeding belief in his work as an expression of his presumed PTSD.

After his Seattle reading on October 28, as he chatted and signed books, he noticed a young man hanging back, waiting for the line to clear, fidgeting.

O'Brien had seen it before—a veteran, soldier, or family member, compelled to connect with him. He'd experienced the ritual many times. This time, however, took him aback. The young man was Lt. Mark White's son. They did not talk long but soon entered a short correspondence in which O'Brien learned more about his platoon leader's postwar life and suicide, when the son was six months old. O'Brien had kind things to say about the father's combat acumen and skills, blunt things about his extremes. The son joined the marines expressly to look for Mad Mark, to learn even a sliver of what the military meant to the man he never knew.

O'Brien was back in Boston the second week of November. On Tuesday the eighth, Election Day, he played chess by himself and ate a frozen dinner. On the ninth, the night before divorce court, he called Phillips.[44] Gayle Roby finally called him back . . . in late summer? early fall? November? She'd been seeing someone she met at a Quaker meeting, only she didn't want to commit if she still had a chance with O'Brien. O'Brien said he couldn't talk because he was wrapped up in divorce business. They wouldn't speak again for nearly thirty years.

Next stop, Bill and Ava's fiftieth wedding anniversary over Thanksgiving at the Frontier Hotel and Casino in Las Vegas. Bill and sons gambled the days away. Kathy turned forty-seven while there, but the family didn't bother to celebrate. It pained her a great deal, especially after seven difficult months beating cancer. From there to Mississippi for readings at Square Books in Oxford, then Lemuria Books in Jackson. He'd made that drive before, with Sam Lawrence.

O'Brien was in uptown New Orleans at Tulane University for the first three days of December, for a conference cum reckoning called "Mỹ Lai: 25 Years After: Facing the Darkness," twenty-five years after the story broke. On the first day, a front-page photograph of entangled bodies waylaid readers of the *Times-Picayune*. Ironically, it had been at Tulane that President Gerald Ford, with an overrun South Việt Nam days away from demise, announced the end of the war and implored the students and the nation to stop "refighting a war that is finished as far as America is concerned," to forget "the battles and recriminations of the past."[45]

Fellow writers were there, plus Hugh Thompson, Jr., the army helicopter pilot who stopped the slaughter; Ron Ridenhour, the soldier who investigated it on his own, and upon return to the United States in 1969 wrote to the White House and two dozen congressmen; Seymour Hersh, the journalist who put the story in every living room and bar in America; and Aubrey Daniel, who prosecuted Lt. Calley. Other speakers included psychiatrists Robert Jay Lifton and Jonathan Shay; historians Stephen Ambrose, Marilyn Young, and George Herring; journalist David Halberstam; and displaced Vietnamese and career U.S. military officers. Even in such company, O'Brien had the last word, doing a reading on Saturday night, the final event of the conference.[46]

The usual politics modestly disrupted the proceedings. According to Randy Fertel, the conference organizer, local displaced Vietnamese interrupted a reading by Lê Minh Khuê and Wayne Karlin in the Tulane chapel, snatching and clinging onto the microphone for a heated rant. On the last afternoon, there were protesters at the lively meta-panel discussion with O'Brien and twelve others. The wife of one panelist, a former ARVN captain, called Fertel a communist dupe.

O'Brien's answers during a one-on-one with Fertel speak to the questions at the heart of *In the Lake of the Woods*. The "seeds of evil" are in everyone. The reasons Calley's platoon crossed the line are an "abiding mystery." Heroism is equally a mystery. "One wonders if, on another day, Thompson might not have landed. Or if, on another day, the guys in Charlie Company wouldn't have begun pulling those triggers." Because of the temperature. Because of who stood next to whom. "What would have happened to Ron Ridenhour if he had been sent to Charlie Company and been there that day?"[47] *Mystery* didn't mean some ineffable essence of deterministic selfhood but the unpredictability of a body's response to unique and urgent circumstances. *In the Lake of the Woods* eschews the reader's expectation whereby consequences circumscribe character. By declining plot resolution, it refuses to pigeonhole its characters.

O'Brien was distraught throughout the conference. Participants reported him hunkering in the bar drinking beer. O'Brien got in Fertel's face to scold him about the title: *There is no healing. We need to keep the wound open and look at it*—which was, to be fair, the point of the misnamed conference. And the novel. The fates of Kathy and John Wade must remain unresolved to keep the horror at Mỹ Lai unresolved. Wrapping up their story risks wrapping up the earlier one and the closure of the wound that humanity can't afford to close. For O'Brien, the Vietnam War and the Mỹ

Lai massacre will hardly emotionally register to future generations except, perhaps, through literature: "Stories are a way to somehow keep memory alive, to keep picking at the scab."[48] In the months ahead, he and Ridenhour talked a few times on the phone.

O'Brien had another personal connection to the weekend's subject. Since September, he'd been corresponding with Elizabeth Weber, an English professor at the University of Indianapolis. Weber's older brother Bill had been Lt. Calley's RTO—as O'Brien had been Lt. White's (and then the company commander's). Two platoon RTOs named William from Minnesota. According to some accounts Weber had read, her brother's combat death a month before Mỹ Lai fueled the rage that led to the massacre. One soldier reported thinking *You killed Weber* as he raped a Vietnamese woman.[49] Elizabeth's guilt was immense, her depression beyond the loss of the older brother she adored. "How could I go on living?"[50]

War's toll reaches wide and deep. Coincidentally, Weber had first written O'Brien about visiting her campus ten days before *In the Lake of the Woods*' publication, after a rereading of *If I Die in a Combat Zone* while on a June backpacking trip in Wyoming's Wind River Mountains had prompted dreams about Bill. It took time to accept how O'Brien had depicted and used Bill's death in the new novel—an acceptance process worked through partly in the correspondence with O'Brien. She acknowledged that in writing to him, she was truly writing to her dead brother.[51] Their letters were frank about their depression as they encouraged each other to hang on. They met briefly at his Wabash College tour stop, two weeks before the Tulane conference.[52]

O'Brien returned home to Cambridge on December 9. The judgment of divorce was entered on December 12. He spent Christmas and New Year's with his family in San Antonio, imagining that they would be his last.[53] "Suicide was on my mind almost daily from summer '94 through well into the following summer." That the novel was already in its fourth if not fifth printing did little for his mental health.[54]

He didn't remove himself to an island to golf away his days. The professional engagements continued. With poet Mark Strand, he coedited another *Ploughshares* issue and wrote an introduction for the prose section.[55] And he had a new book project after all. In a later book-tour interview, he clarified that although he had finished producing fiction, he was certain to keep writing. Despite his frustrations and regrets over the essay "The Vietnam in Me," he thought to write "a book based on that *Times* article, a series of personal essays [...] on various subjects, sort of linked by Vietnam."[56]

The last weekend of April 1995, O'Brien joined his friends Bruce Weigl, Larry Heinemann, and Lady Borton for "Vietnam Legacies," a weekend conference at UC Davis marking the twentieth anniversary of the fall of Sài Gòn. The war was hardly over for the forty Vietnamese Americans protesting the presence of North Vietnamese participants with shouts of "Communists go home!"[57] Nine writers, Vietnamese and American, took the stage Saturday night. One highlight was the Joiner Center's Nguyễn Bá Chung reading poems in Vietnamese from writers unable to leave the country, which were then read in English.

O'Brien began his turn at the lectern churlishly remarking that he was "tired of talking about Vietnam." He chided his audience by objecting to the *war writer* label: "We are human beings and we write about the human heart."[58] He picked up the pages of his work in progress:

July 1952, mid-century Minnesota, and on a silvery hot morning Herbie and I nailed two plywood boards together and called it an airplane. "What we need," said Herbie, "is an engine."[59]

There's a turtle named Toby, and a reenacted crucifixion with Herbie's sister Mary Jean nailed halfway through one palm to the abandoned airplane project's plywood crosspieces. Not a word about Việt Nam, not a word about war.

27

TOMCAT IN LOVE

Tomcat in Love

By the end of February 1995, when O'Brien had a letter of agreement with his agent for representation of "Untitled Non-Fiction,"[1] he'd scuttled the idea for a collection of linked personal essays circling the war. *Tomcat in Love* began as a childhood memoir.

Herbie Voorhees lived two doors down from Timmy O'Brien in Austin, Minnesota, in the largest house on the block. The elementary school across the street split the day, half the kids attending in the morning, half in the afternoon. Some days O'Brien watched Herbie crawl out a school window to meet him. Once the two hatched a plan to nail two boards in the shape of a cross to make an airplane, only Bill O'Brien gave his son a pet turtle instead of an engine. Herbie, a couple of years younger than Timmy, all of four or five, then suggested they nail his older sister Mary Joanne to it, like with Jesus. He went off to find her. End of story, except for the day another neighborhood boy, Elroy Berdahl, stole the turtle. Timmy found Elroy with Toby in the Berdahls' backyard; Elroy's dad told his son to give it back. "You don't have a turtle."

About fifteen pages into the memoir, when O'Brien found himself writing dialogue that didn't good-faith adhere to remembered events, and tempted to further exaggeration and invention "to strengthen the narrative" and make up for "a faulty memory," he called John Sterling—his editor from Houghton Mifflin for *In the Lake of the Woods* who was now at Broadway Books, which would publish *Tomcat* and republish most of O'Brien's titles, all in 1998—to ask how much he could depart from memory and still call it nonfiction. A few weeks later he succumbed. He was writing a novel after all.[2]

He'd treated the memory creatively before, in a poem written in college and published in Macalester's literary magazine. The last stanza of "Careful Not to Touch the Lilacs" reads:

Careful not to touch the lilacs
For they were young and delicate,
Summertime princes slayed dragons
Which barked and yipped out stinging flame.
Slayed with two crossed boards—blood red sword, now—
Which would someday, with Dad's new engine,
Soar from the backyard, lift to the sky,
With proud and laughing me aboard,
Overlooking purple and red,
Sweeping down to land, being
Careful not to touch the lilacs.[3]

The lilacs tether the youthful spirit of devil-may-care flight to order, security, and propriety; they suggest coddled and pretty innocence; they recall Whitman's elegy to Lincoln, "When Lilacs Last in the Dooryard Bloom'd," as O'Brien's poem seems an elegy to lost youth.

O'Brien finished the prose fiction version, imagined now as the new novel's first chapter and a standalone story for magazine publication, the first week of November 1995. In the cover letter introducing the chapter and proposed book to his agent, he described his intended tone as "partly funny, partly serious, finally weighted toward the tragic." The themes are the usual: "betrayal, pursuit, and revenge," maybe violent revenge. Maybe. He'd find out as he wrote, as he also tried to answer for himself why Mary Jean allowed her brother to nail her hand to the board, and why Herbie destroyed Mary Jean's marriage to Tom—eventually Thomas Chippering—the character who replaces Timmy O'Brien from the childhood memory.

"The relationships among the three chief characters are clearly weird to the point of warped. Incestuous, in a way, and sexually competitive, and driven by a mix of guilt and anger and a need for penitence." O'Brien knew the novel would play with the first-person narrator's relationship with language, although the letter doesn't say anything about Chippering's career as a linguistics professor.[4]

The letter also does not indicate whether O'Brien had yet imagined the character who would become Chippering's second and last wife, Donna, the former Mrs. Robert Kooshof, who wins Chippering over through her "essential goodness and tolerance and endurance and faith and forgiveness and rugged hope and never, never giving up," the woman for whom this middle-aged man finally (mostly) grows up. O'Brien had, after all, only just started dating the woman who would become his second wife and lasting partner.

◊   ◊   ◊

Meredith Hale Baker, twenty years O'Brien's junior, grew up bouncing around the Northeast, the middle daughter of a minister in the United Church of Christ (her dad) and a registered nurse (her mom). They lived in modest parsonages—Meredith recalls tacking up plastic to cover windows. Life revolved around the church. Choir, community meals, exactly what one might expect. In Maine, New York, the outgoing teen played tennis and softball, cheered, volunteered as a hospital candy striper, and did a lot of church-related service. "I was president of almost everything." She won election as the homecoming queen of Maine-Endwell High School not because she was in the right cliques, but because she got along with everyone, the farm kids and the townies. In Maine she also fell in love with community theater.

Looking back, she sees her busybody lifestyle as partly a mechanism for coping with her older sister Dale's mental decline. The family's first year in Maine, Dale fell in with a delinquent set. Their parents sent her to a boarding school. She came home from her senior year in Spain angry and totally detached. Her freshman year at New York University, she mentally collapsed. She was in and out of treatment facilities and halfway houses for the next few years before finally being committed as a ward of the state of Connecticut. Meredith and her slightly younger sister Susie grew into adulthood in fear of mental illness.

At Middlebury College, Meredith majored in English literature, minored in Latin American Studies, spent junior year abroad at the University of Exeter, and wrote plays. One was produced on campus. Her creative writing professor encouraged her to attend the Bread Loaf Writers' Conference the summer after her 1988 graduation. She'd never heard of Tim O'Brien. He had the aura of the conference golden child without at all being aloof. "If there was a party or a gathering at a fire, Tim was there." He made her feel like there "wasn't a chasm" between them. After the conference, she read everything he'd written.

She worked in Connecticut, spent nearly two years faking it as a tennis instructor for Club Med resorts, acted in a community theater back in Connecticut, trained in acting at Circle in the Square Professional Workshop in New York City, and was working the front desk of a temp agency when, in mid-September 1995, she saw a notice for a reading by O'Brien at the Barnes & Noble bookstore on Broadway and Eighty-Second. He'd just started touring for the paperback edition of *In the Lake of the Woods*.[5] She remembered "The Vietnam in Me"—she'd written him a quick hello right before it came out the year before,[6] and the magazine might have still been hanging out in her dreary apartment. Men her age tended to bore her. Why not go?

After he read, she clunked up to him in big heels, with shock-dyed blond hair over black clothes and black lipstick. She'd lost a sister to mental illness, then her mother to a heart attack in December 1992. She couldn't afford many clothes, and black-on-black always worked. The black nails were from a cheap manicure. The goth getup couldn't hide her tall, athletic frame. The effect on O'Brien was severe and off-putting. They went out afterward anyway. He flew out on his tour the next morning. They talked on the phone in the days following, and when she asked to see him again, he invited her to Minnesota for his brother Greg's wedding at the end of the month outside St. Paul. Ava looked her up and down and politely showed her to her own closet—which took fashion to the other extreme. Knowing no one, Meredith helped the men carry the kegs into the house. That impressed everyone. The morning after the wedding, on his forty-ninth birthday, O'Brien flew away to continue his tour and Baker flew back to New York.

The made-for-TV adaptation of *In the Lake of the Woods* began film-ing in Vancouver a couple of weeks later, starring Peter Strauss, Kathleen Quinlan, and Peter Boyle.[7] O'Brien hadn't known it was in the works (when it premiered the first Tuesday of March 1996 on Fox, O'Brien thought it a flat, lifeless production). At the University of Indianapolis on October 30, he was hosted by Elizabeth Weber, the professor whose brother's death pre-ceded the massacre at Mỹ Lai. Tired of reading from *Lake*, O'Brien read the drafted chapter of the new novel because he learned from reading his drafts to an audience. He could hear mistakes, he could judge the effect of the pace, the drama, the intended humor. During the Q&A, O'Brien named the first-person protagonist Timmy, a leftover from the memoir version, which created a more palpable and realistic connection to him for O'Brien that would translate to the reader's connection to the character (Timmy became Tom a few days after the event). To a question about cour-age, O'Brien the situational ethicist deflected from the war to the reading as he wondered if his protagonist's father acted cowardly in promising to get his kid an engine.[8]

For a year, Baker traveled to Cambridge on weekends by bus or a shuttle flight, back in time for work on Monday. O'Brien paid. With a doorman and double-door entryway, the apartment building on Massachusetts Avenue was nicer than any place she'd ever lived. His two-bedroom place was small, about seven hundred square feet. The bed was a mattress on the floor. In the living room, the printer sat on the box it came in. There was a futon.

With nothing to keep her in New York City, Baker moved to Boston in August 1996. She took a secretarial job at the Smithsonian Astrophysical Observatory. He didn't want to live with her, so she moved in with two roommates on Aberdeen Avenue in the Fresh Pond area of Cambridge. But she was at his place most of the time. They ate takeout or went to a nearby diner. When he wasn't writing or lifting weights, they watched television sitting on the rug. *Seinfeld* and *Cheers* were staple shows.

"Can we get a chair?" she once asked.

"We don't need one," he said. When she asked about the odd yellow color of the drapes, he explained, "That's the cigarettes. They used to be white."

◊ ◊ ◊

O'Brien originally intended *Tomcat in Love* to explore the effect on children of growing up in a religious family.[9] Christ's crucifixion as a springboard for the writerly imagination wasn't new for O'Brien. He had led a session at Bread Loaf in 1981 called "Rewriting of the Bible," which one attendee found "worked perfectly" as a point of instruction. As he wrote O'Brien days later, "I was most taken by the fact that given the 'conflict' scene—the 'crucifixion'—we could come up with many variations but given the resurrection—a static situation—there was not much to say."[10]

In the published novel, the children of the family in question are Herbie and Lorna Sue Zylstra, both curious if the driveway crucifixion would send Lorna Sue to heaven (a Christian lie to O'Brien). Afterward, Lorna Sue develops a serious complex about God, all in with her beliefs yet filled with resentment and spite. She commits relatively minor and quite major juvenile acts of desecration: graffiti on church steps, a cross-dressed statue of Christ, and church burnings. The arson persists into her adulthood. Herbie's Catholic guilt and need for penance result in a lifetime of taking the fall for her and protecting her. Chippering and the reader learn all of this in the novel's final pages, yet as plot revelation it's almost beside the point of Chippering's secular story of hubris, fall, and salvation in giving up his fantasies of Lorna Sue and his young women students and marrying Donna.

The Things They Carried borrows from Christianity in its own way, beginning with the title story's characters, Lt. Jimmy Cross (note the initials) and the young woman he pines for, a student at Mount Sebastian College, and ending with the acts of resurrection and immortality available through storytelling in "The Lives of the Dead." O'Brien's first novel, *Northern Lights*, had its roots in the cannibalism story titled "A Perfect Communion," considered the impact of a patrilineal religious upbringing on two generations of Perry sons, and told a once-was-lost-now-am-found tale, with Paul and Grace Perry the forbearers to Chippering and Donna.

Ava O'Brien had taken her children and very rarely her husband to her Methodist church. O'Brien describes himself as agnostic for as far back as he thought about such things. His early introduction to the havoc religion can cause a person came from his father. Ava was Bill's second wife. In July 1937, the twenty-three-year-old had married another Brooklynite.[11] The

marriage to a woman seven years older did not take—it's the biographical fact behind the rumor of Herbie and Lorna Sue's dad having a "previous, unacknowledged marriage."[12] According to the family, the couple
split within a few months and divorced as soon as possible.[13] In this tight
Irish Catholic community, the divorce would have brought embarrassment
and shame. Bill requested an annulment, appealing through his maternal grandmother to a cousin, the Most Rev. Raymond A. Kearney. Father
Kearney belonged to the same parish, the Church of the Nativity, and had
attended the same high school, Brooklyn Preparatory School, twelve years
earlier. Kearney served as the chancellor of the Diocese of Brooklyn from
1930 to 1934 before his appointment as its auxiliary bishop. A canon law
expert, Bishop Kearney was probably a hard-liner. The Church denied Bill's
suit. Remarriage without annulment constituted adultery and bigamy under the 1917 Code of Canon Law. As an adulterer and bigamist, Bill could
no longer receive the Eucharist and might have been excommunicated.[14]

The decision embittered Bill toward the Church from that day forward.
He loved Catholicism. He had attended Catholic elementary school;[15] he
had enjoyed being an altar boy, pranking the other altar boys, trying dis-
creetly to wake an older priest dozing during mass. He took the decision as
a betrayal based on zealotry about rules rather than on Christian love and
forgiveness. When his sister Mary became Sister Mary, he disapproved.
He worried about a life cloistered from the world, ruled by superstition,
and stunted in potential. Mary did not deserve the Church, nor did the
Church deserve Mary. Later in life he judged her harshly for her devotional
path, almost as if she had betrayed him personally. "How's married life?"
O'Brien remembers him heckling her. "Gettin' any from Jesus?"

Bill never lost his belief in God. It was the Church, not God, that had
forsaken him. His rancor, which extended in moderated form to all organized religion, habitually spewed out. For a long time, his children didn't
know its source. What little information they know about the brief marriage they learned from their mother when they were adults. In Bill's letters home from his second residency for alcoholism, God's existence was
a given. The relationship needed work: "I imagine it will be difficult to get
acquainted again with Someone you haven't talked to in a long time." Bill
chose to see Rev. Grimm rather than Father Garvey at Willmar "based
on the fact that I am not in truth a Catholic" and, moreover, because "the

issues at hand could be clouded if Garvey attempted the tedious effort of bringing back the lost sheep."[16]

The nonreligious O'Brien recognizes Catholicism's influence on him. He understands it as a fear of reverent solemnity, a far cry from the "Methodist hilarity at church basement potlucks" he grew up with. Timmy O'Brien feared his father's weekday rants and terrifying Sunday silences. O'Brien also ascribes his skepticism of institutions, authority figures, movements, and isms, in part to the legacy of his father's relationship with the Church. O'Brien's secular devotion to the word *mystery* sometimes partakes of its Catholic meaning, the meaning familiar to readers of Flannery O'Connor. Sister Mary became O'Brien's favorite of his parents' siblings, the only one he ever corresponded with or rang up to chat.

The published novel did not tilt to tragedy. Instead, it became O'Brien's seriocomic self-parody, a fun-house mirror and necessary purge that played with the gender politics of its day. Thomas Chippering, a habitual liar and professional student and manipulator of language, stands in for O'Brien, who has always described his trade as telling lies for a living. Chippering's childhood-rooted "insatiable appetite for affection" caricatures O'Brien's: "I would (and will) lie for love," Chippering confesses, "cheat for love, beg for love, steal for love, ghostwrite for love, seek revenge for love, swim oceans for love, perhaps even kill for love"[17]—as O'Brien might have done in Việt Nam, if his unaimed bullets ever killed. He'd gone to Việt Nam for love, after all.

The war haunts Chippering in the form of his semi-justified paranoia that former comrades-in-arms have been stalking him. It's part of O'Brien's self-parody. The novel pokes fun at "The Vietnam in Me"'s comparison of war's hell with love's grief—"I might someday author a monograph on the eerie similarities," Chippering muses[18]—and rewrites the essay's confession of O'Brien's almost killing himself by jumping out a window by having Chippering admit to nearly dropping himself over a balcony the day Lorna Sue left him for another man. The novel mimics the language of lostness, mirroring, and the mystery of others that riddled *In the Lake of the Woods*. Chippering's footnotes signal a snickering O'Brien doubling down on the narrator's footnotes in *Lake*, which the *New York Times* reviewer had critiqued as "gratuitous," "mannered," and "self-important."[19]

The politician's need for attention, approval, and love that O'Brien built into John Wade was corroborated when news broke, in January 1998, of President Bill Clinton's extramarital relations with a White House intern, around the time O'Brien submitted the novel's draft. Clinton's lies and language games were right up Chippering's alley. "It depends on what the meaning of the word 'is' is," Clinton famously testified on August 17. *Tomcat in Love* was officially released on September 16; two weeks later, O'Brien published a piece online addressed to Clinton in the sympathetic voice of the quasi-predatory Chippering.[20]

Lorna Sue combines O'Brien's adolescent fantasizing of a soulmate, his "eternal Magdalene," with his hurting and disbelief when Kate Phillips left him and soon took up with another man.[21] Phillips the young graduate student also informs the petite undergraduate student with whom Chippering flirts. Herbie's obsession with Lorna Sue and the whole Zylstra family, and his inflated self-regard, bears a large trace of Scott Spencer's *Endless Love*. Like Spencer's novel and John Barth's *The Floating Opera*, *Tomcat* has a male first-person protagonist less charming and self-aware than he imagines.

O'Brien scattered Easter eggs from his earlier books throughout *Tomcat*. The star-shaped hole from "The Man I Killed" in *The Things They Carried* becomes the star-shaped scar on Lorna Sue's palm from the botched crucifixion. Chippering catches acrimony for using the word *cooze*, as O'Brien had before him. With Chippering's reference to the scholarly journal *Critique*, O'Brien has a specific piece of feminist criticism in mind, "'The Things Men Do': The Gendered Subtext in Tim O'Brien's *Esquire* Stories," a 1994 article from the same journal.[22] Readers of *If I Die in a Combat Zone* will recognize boring, flat Owago, Minnesota, the Rock Cornish Hen Capital of the World, as a version of Worthington, the Turkey Capital of the World. Owago has also imported O'Brien's first childhood home, the small white stucco house, and Herbie, the airplane, and the turtle, from Austin.

Meanwhile, Phillips's novel *White Rabbit* came out in January 1996 from Houghton Mifflin. O'Brien's is the first name listed in the book's statement of gratitude for "support and encouragement."

Other women flitted in and out of O'Brien's life after Phillips, though by his account they hooked up with him, not the other way around. He wasn't looking for romance of any stripe. Many of the melodramatic and superficially farcical antics in Chippering's relationships have basis in

O'Brien's reality. The most significant parallel, however, is the one between lookalikes Donna (Mrs. Robert Kooshof) and Meredith Baker, both "part starlet, part mother figure."[23] The fictional and the real couple vacation at Club Med. The fictional and real protagonists finally let go the woman who left them, let go their boyish ways, and commit to the person with whom they'll spend the rest of their lives. *Tomcat in Love* fits the pattern established by *Northern Lights* and *The Nuclear Age*, O'Brien's first two non-war novels, of a redemptive story arc for the male protagonist who finally reconciles himself to domesticity and makes peace with his wife.

Assessing the new novel requires familiarity with O'Brien's oeuvre and its criticism. "We should have bombed these people with love," O'Brien had written in "The Vietnam in Me" about his return to Việt Nam; and in *Tomcat*, as a Special Forces team calls in a massive air strike, one of them shouts, "Love bombs! . . . Try a little tenderness!"[24] Chippering's and Thuy Ninh's over-the-top orgasm in sync with a B-52 strike sends up the sexualization of combat in a lot of war narratives, especially American works from O'Brien's war. Chippering's demands are O'Brien's, that everyone recognize their own Chippering tendencies: self-centeredness, self-justifications, Peter Pan–ism, unhealthy passions, sexual gazing. Barrack-room guy talk wasn't a foreign language to O'Brien. One hears stories of occasional unwelcome remarks.

Some of *Tomcat in Love*'s reviewers couldn't get past Chippering's insufferable voice or disentangle his piggishness from O'Brien's critique of it. Such criticisms understandably infuriated O'Brien. It was equivalent to accusing the 1970s sitcom *All in the Family* of misogyny and racism for calling out the buffoonish bigotry of Archie Bunker. Other reviewers cheered the art and comedy of Chippering's characterization as well as O'Brien's foray into the gender politics of the 1990s. The decade started with Anita Hill's 1991 Senate testimony about sexual harassment by Supreme Court nominee Clarence Thomas and with David Mamet's 1992 *Oleanna*, a play (and 1994 film) about the undoing of a professor based on an ambiguous exchange with a student and her accusations of sexual harassment. The good reviews and O'Brien's stature made it a bestseller. Jane Smiley, writing in *The New York Times Book Review*, admits to having "softened toward Chippering," and couldn't decide for herself whether O'Brien succeeded: "But like all comic novels, 'Tomcat in Love' is a complex affair that invites a complex response and offers a complex reward. Whatever O'Brien's motives in changing his style and direction, I, for one, hope he keeps it up."[25]

Tomcat in Love has never received the study and appreciation Smiley thought it deserved. O'Brien never stopped liking it and finding it funny. Twenty-first-century readers who bother to read the novel usually deplore it. Some of his writer friends consider it an embarrassment. *Tomcat* confirmed the emerging standard narrative: O'Brien's best books were those that grabbed the war by the horns, and they were behind him.

As a subject for literature, the American war in Việt Nam was changing hands. Vietnamese voices increasingly moved toward center stage, both translations of texts by Vietnamese writers—often with the support of the Joiner Center and done by its affiliated writers, both American and Vietnamese—and original works in English published by second-generation Vietnamese Americans, often born in Việt Nam but raised in America, in full command of the English language, and more than ready to tell their own and their families' stories. Wayne Karlin and Curbstone Press were responsible for several translated texts, particularly by Hồ Anh Thái and Lê Minh Khuê. Linh Dinh, a poet and prose writer, published a book of translated contemporary Vietnamese stories, *Night Again*, in 1996. Lan Cao, Andrew Lam, Andrew X. Pham, Kien Nguyen, Monique Truong, and Dao Strom constitute a woefully short list of accomplished Vietnamese American writers. Oliver Stone concluded his Việt Nam trilogy by following *Platoon* and *Born on the Fourth of July* with *Heaven and Earth* in 1993, based on Le Ly Hayslip's memoirs. GB Tran and Thi Bui produced graphic memoirs of their families' postwar emigration; plays by Qui Nguyen and Kimber Lee challenged the racism of *Miss Saigon*.

In 2016, Viet Thanh Nguyen's *The Sympathizer* won the Pulitzer Prize for fiction and Ocean Vuong published his acclaimed poetry volume *Night Sky with Exit Wounds*. O'Brien's last novel about the war, *In the Lake of the Woods*, was by then over twenty years old.

◊   ◊   ◊

When O'Brien brought Meredith Baker to the Joiner Center's summer 1997 writers' workshop and introduced her to his war writer buddies, he was beaming, according to Larry Heinemann: "Here came this tall, gorgeous blonde, and he was as happy as I'd ever seen him." O'Brien had read from the *In the Lake of the Woods* draft for a 1993 Veterans Day event at the center and taught in the June 1995 workshop[26]—just before and then at the tail end of his darkest days. His last Joiner workshop was in 1998. O'Brien stayed busy with campus visits and other appearances, including his periodic stints at the Sewanee Writers' Conference. Baker attended one, the two acting as if they weren't a couple.

In March 1998, he participated in a panel on the thirtieth anniversary of the Mỹ Lai massacre at the University of Indianapolis, along with Ron Ridenhour again; retired Col. William G. Eckhardt, the lead army prosecutor in the trial of Capt. Ernest Medina, Lt. Calley's superior officer; journalist Jonathan Schell, whose book on the war in Quảng Ngãi O'Brien had read on his 1994 return trip; and Hays Parks, a veteran from the time of the massacre and later a U.S. "law-of-war negotiator." David Anderson, the historian at the university responsible for the book about the Tulane conference that had just been published, *Facing My Lai*, moderated the event that Elizabeth Weber, Calley's RTO's sister, had organized.

Weber led with a powerful reflection. She sounded a lot like Tim O'Brien: "I have always wondered what would have happened had my brother lived and been with Calley at Mỹ Lai. I have no clear answer." She hoped he would have refused to participate, according to the values instilled by their parents. But she couldn't say for sure, just as she could no longer say for sure what she might have done. Her days of "clear righteous sorrow," of absolute certainty—the very attitudes that lead to war and massacres—were behind her. "Evil is never easy to spot, and it is full of good intentions," Weber said. For his part, O'Brien "let Charlie Company itself talk to you" by reading from soldiers' court-martial testimony of what they did.

Throughout the panel and the Q&A, O'Brien expressed outrage that only Calley paid the price. "If 105 Vietnamese were to come into this room and kill us all," kill twice as many people in the room, "more than one of those 105 people would be sentenced to do time." The event ended when an audience member, a Vietnamese American who fled his country at war's end in 1975, thanked the panelists and organizers because, he said, simply to talk of the dead is to honor them.[27]

(Ridenhour went back to Tulane for a solo talk nine days later, and less than two months later died after a heart attack while playing handball. He was fifty-two.)[28]

Baker moved into O'Brien's Massachusetts Avenue apartment probably that same March. It had been a life-changing few months. In the fall of 1997, she had started the MA program in Theater Education with a directing focus at Emerson. The couple broke up in December. Baker longed for a family. O'Brien resented her loving an idea more than she loved him, her choosing a fantasy over the reality of him. He worried he did not have it in him to be a parent. Too selfish of his time and set in his ways. He fretted that he would become a version of his father. Not an alcoholic, but otherwise absent and begrudging.

O'Brien's change of heart happened over the Christmas and New Year holidays with his family at Kathy's in San Antonio. As Kathy tells the story, she and her brother were talking about his anguish while walking along the river when she said, "Tim, you can afford a nanny," and he was on a plane back to Boston that night. Tim and Meredith opened up and hashed it out on "neutral ground"—she thinks it was the Harvest restaurant in Harvard Square. "In that Cambridge bar," O'Brien later wrote, "and in the weeks afterward, the realization began to stir in me that I too yearned for a happy, normal family life, even if I remained terrified of failing. There were no promises, exactly. But there was a prospect."[29]

Hollywood called again. Starting with *Northern Lights*, O'Brien had wanted films made from his novels. For the money, certainly. A film would bring more exposure to the written original. He recognized that films had replaced literature as the dominant storytelling medium—film adaptations would be another way to share his stories. *A Soldier's Sweetheart*, based on "Sweetheart of the Song Tra Bong," premiered at the Seattle International Film Festival in June 1998. Filmed in Auckland, New Zealand, it starred Kiefer Sutherland, Georgina Cates, and Skeet Ulrich. O'Brien had no part in making the film. Unable to land a theatrical distribution deal, the producers launched it on the cable channel Showtime on November 8, 1998. It's a decent production, far less stiff than the *In the Lake of the Woods* TV movie. O'Brien appreciated Sutherland's and Cates's performances as Rat Kiley and Mary Anne Bell. Some actors were unrealistically buff, a common war movie problem. In typical Hollywood fashion, the adaptation juiced up the ending. After Rat finishes telling the story, there's a three-minute firefight during which he spies Mary Anne in the jungle. She leads him down a trail. An explosion washes out the screen. The end.

A much more promising film project, for *Going After Cacciato*, was just then under development. The producer Butch Kaplan took the novel to Nick Cassavetes, the actor and director, most recently of 1997's *She's So Lovely*. Cassavetes had probably already begun work on the screenplay when *Sweetheart* aired.[30] Though the cameras never rolled, the three became friends. Kaplan and Cassavetes even attended O'Brien and Baker's wedding.

In the late 1990s, O'Brien contributed a chapter to the collaboratively written novel *The Putt at the End of the World*, a comic golf novel in the context of the end of the millennium with its inevitable apocalyptic mutterings.[31] When the writers gathered in Florida for a golf tournament to celebrate the book, O'Brien chaffed that only he and Lee Abbott took playing seriously. He was also writing the first stories that would form his next book of fiction, *July, July*.

The fall of 1998 promised to be busy, with O'Brien traveling for the *Tomcat in Love* tour and Baker directing Edward Albee's *Seascape* at Emerson, so they got out of Cambridge that summer. For the Fourth of July they retreated to an 1898 house on the Niantic River at Saunders Point that Meredith's family stayed in every summer because it was owned by friends of her grandmother—they called it Hoskins Cottage. Then they headed to Worthington. Baker videotaped O'Brien and his brother at the driving range at the Wilds Golf Club, southwest of Minneapolis. There's a priceless video she took a month later of O'Brien at a driving range, instructing her what to tell the camera about his body adjustments and the shot results, which she duly repeats for the camera, presumably for him to study later, his perfectionism on full display.[32]

In January 1999, the couple vacationed at Club Med Martinique.[33] Baker graduated in May. That fall, O'Brien began a one-year visiting writer gig at what was then Southwest Texas State University, later Texas State University, in San Marcos, outside Austin. It paid well; it would be an interesting change of pace. The O'Briens rented a home on Ballybunion Place, in the Onion Creek golf club community. At a faculty picnic O'Brien's boss of sorts, the writer Tom Grimes, convinced the university president to make the job permanent. No one was more surprised than the soon-to-be-newlyweds that they ended up raising their family in Texas.

28

WELCOME TO TEXAS

July, July

O'Brien and Baker bought a home on Pebble Beach Drive in the same Austin subdivision, with a backyard overlooking the Onion Creek golf course. Of the two houses they considered, they purchased his choice, an Italian-villa-style home, with four tall columns and rooftop urns over the cherubs decorating the cornice. O'Brien liked its European flair, the conspicuous opposite of his modest childhood homes. At least the single story was reminiscent. The tiered open floor plan struck him as ideal for staging magic shows, a thought he didn't share with his future bride and magician's assistant. The house had previously been owned by Jimmie Connolly, one of the founders of the golf club. His last day in the home, Connolly sat forlorn, looking out the back window at his course.

The house needed love and sweat, and money, and in future years underwent serious renovations. The carport in the back would be converted to O'Brien's study. When the pool needed to be stabilized, they had it reconfigured to a depth of four feet because of O'Brien's past near drownings. Bill and Ava, who had lived at a Worthington retirement facility since the mid-1990s, sold their home and moved to San Antonio, where they lived in the Village at Incarnate Word retirement community, near Kathy and her family. Dementia afflicted Bill, although its acute phase was behind him, his doctors having figured out the right medicine protocols. Most of the O'Brien clan now lived in Texas.

No longer able to jump in the car to go play blackjack at the Foxwoods Casino in Connecticut, Tim and Meredith started flying to Vegas, often purchasing the airline ticket an hour before heading to the airport. Meredith also accompanied O'Brien on more of his gigs. She fainted at a Houghton Mifflin event in Boston. She'd just had a physical exam in Austin, and the doctor called her in Boston to order her home. She fainted again at the airport.[1] She had developed type 1 diabetes and would be insulin-dependent the rest of her life. The university's health insurance was a major reason they stayed in Texas.

They became Tim and Meredith O'Brien on June 9, 2001, at six in the evening, on the back poolside patio of their new home. Her dad the minister presided, along with a Texas officiant. Beforehand, O'Brien, his best man, and her dad waited in O'Brien's original study. "I really love your daughter, and I will take great care of her," O'Brien told Don Baker. A man of few words, Baker only nodded in reply. On the heels of the ceremony, O'Brien hustled into the house to change into a tee, shorts, and ball cap. Singing and dancing broke out.

◊   ◊   ◊

One morning three months later, someone was sitting down with coffee to read "Too Skinny," O'Brien's new story in the latest *New Yorker*.[2] Someone else that morning was reading it on the subway headed into Manhattan. Other copies were on desks and waiting room tables in the Twin Towers that morning, September 11, 2001, when the planes struck.

The *July, July* manuscript's latest draft was with O'Brien's publisher. By the end of the month, O'Brien received two emails from Houghton Mifflin. His editor Janet Silver wrote,

> It's been really hard for me to read anything in the past two weeks, and of course everything has to be read in the context of September 11. But what astounded me about your novel is that it seems completely relevant, in all the most important ways—I mean, it speaks

so closely to idealism and optimism and patriotism at the same time that it shows the trajectory of personal and social and political events over the decades following such a traumatic time.

On the same day he heard from Wendy Strothman, an executive vice president:

> For the first time since September 11 I was pulled totally into a story outside the current horrors. I was completely entranced, by turns sad, rueful, laughing, nodding, recognizing real people. [. . .] As the train turned the corner toward the city and everyone got quiet looking at the naked skyline, I thought about all the novels that were probably finished last month that at this moment might seem off. This book will have touched people on September 10 and will certainly touch us all now.[3]

Preparation for the U.S. invasion of Afghanistan, the host country for al-Qaeda, the terrorist organization responsible for the 9/11 attack, was underway. Bombs began falling on October 7.

"There were no signs of the approaching storm" that, in the book's final chapter, brings down a plane with two characters aboard: "There was a shearing noise."[4] That's all O'Brien gives his reader. The rest, as with what happened in the four hijacked airplanes and in the doomed towers, is left to the imagination. Silver and Strothman must have winced when they read it. Readers wouldn't absorb one of the book's most prescient lines for another few years, as the wars in Afghanistan and Iraq dragged on and Americans re-became Americans. "The war went on," the character Jan Huebner reflects about Việt Nam: "People ate Raisin Bran."[5]

"Loon Point," the published novel's thirteenth chapter, is a rewritten version of the story that had appeared in *Esquire*'s January 1993 number, more than a year before *In the Lake of the Woods*, the novel from which it had sprung. Next up: "Class of '68," all of one page in the March 1998 *Esquire*, eventually the book's "Class of '69" chapter, where Dorothy Stier tells Billy McMann about her breast cancer. The story had its origins in O'Brien's sister's cancer. "The Streak" appeared a few months later, in the September 28, 1998, issue of *The New Yorker*, only two weeks after the release of *Tomcat in Love*. Its tale of two middle-aged newlyweds winning nearly $230,000 playing blackjack at a small casino had for its genesis an evening when O'Brien watched Meredith rake it in during a rare turn for her at the table.

"It was not a question of love," the narrator says of Amy Robinson's decision to marry Bobby—in the story, he's the one with the winning streak. "Amy was fifty-two years old, almost fifty-three," O'Brien's age when writing the story. Her new husband is "decent without flaw," full of "patience and humor and devotion and kindness" such that "she had run out of excuses." Her marriage of resignation, "no longer expecting a fairy-tale romance," does not in that way resemble Tim's commitment to Meredith, whom he cherished. Even so, he readily tapped into his former reluctance in characterizing Amy: "It struck her that this was a story he would be telling for the rest of his life, for years and years, which seemed an awfully long time."[6] O'Brien was retelling it as he wrote the story; the two of them would retell the real-life anecdote throughout the years to come, of how by 4:00 a.m. she'd turned twenty-five dollars into twenty-five *thousand* dollars.

The first time O'Brien performed this fictional trick of flipping the roles had been in a story he'd written as a young teenager, "Two Minutes," in which he'd imagined, through the character Nancy from Indiana, his mom Ava's fatal unhappiness if she'd moved from Minnesota to New York for Bill. In the stories that would become *July, July*, O'Brien strove to capture women's voices. Women weren't all that mysterious or different after all. Everyone laughs, cries, dreams, worries, suffers, loves. Silver's post-9/11 email addressed this very concern. For her, "the women's voices are exactly right. If you considered writing from the woman's point of view challenging, it doesn't show in the least."

As late as December 1998, O'Brien hadn't decided to make a book out of these stories. Maybe he would create a different book of stories, to be called *May '69* after the worst month of his war.[7] Meanwhile, he wrote "Nogales" in deliberate homage to Flannery O'Conner's "A Good Man Is Hard to Find" and loosely based on a bus adventure experienced by Bill and Ava. It came out in *The New Yorker* on March 8, 1999. In June, *Publishers Weekly* announced that O'Brien, acting as his own agent, had struck a two-book deal with Houghton Mifflin, for "a novel set in 1969, and a book of interrelated stories ('not unlike *The Things They Carried*') that will combine elements of fiction and nonfiction," neither of which describes *July, July*.[8]

The move to Texas and the beginning of his teaching life that fall crimped O'Brien's writing time. When he made it back to the desk, working toward some version of one of those two projects, his imagination returned to Việt Nam. The July 2000 *Esquire* story "July '69" parallels Apollo 11's trip to the moon with a soldier's struggle to survive his wounds along the Song Tra Ky. One passage near the end, from a hallucinated voice, expresses the despondent outrage:

> Amazing isn't it? [. . .] All that firepower, all that technology. They put those two peckerheads up there, let 'em jump around, but they can't do shit for the lost souls down here on planet Earth. Pathetic, isn't it? I mean, hell, they don't even know you and me exist. Back in the world, Davy, they're all doing somersaults, uncorking the California bubbly. This whole goddamn war's on hold.[9]

Yet it wasn't as if the soldiers didn't experience some awe and pride. Lt. David Todd in O'Brien's story embodies the emotional complexity of the moment. He feels buoyed by the lunar happenings. He hopes Aldrin, Armstrong, and Collins return home, and under their inspiration he chooses to survive and go home to face whatever pain home has in store.

David's debate about whether to survive and to face the hell of peace, or allow himself to die in Việt Nam, he conducts in conversation with Master Sergeant Johnny Ever, that hallucinated voice on a transistor radio. O'Brien's readers have heard this voice before, in *Northern Lights*' prophet-like Jud Harmor; in a radio voice offering deals on artillery in *Going After Cacciato*; in the A&W intercom in *The Things They Carried*; and in the bomb shelter hole in *The Nuclear Age*. Johnny Ever tells David Todd that his wife will betray him and leave him; William Cowling, the hole-digger, believes his wife has betrayed him and probably will again. Both opt to hold on to love, for as long as they can, anyway. Johnny Ever is Cowling's smirking hole.

The folks at *Esquire* loved "July '69." David Granger, the editor in chief, wrote to O'Brien, "It is truly one of the best pieces of short fiction I have ever read"; a staffer wrote him that the office was "going totally bonkers" over it.[10] The book's Marla is called Maria in the story, as O'Brien hadn't yet begun interweaving the stories into a whole.

O'Brien believes *The New Yorker* rejected "July '69" because its editors didn't understand there would be a follow-on story. "What Went Wrong" was the last story to appear prior to the novel's publication, in August 2002 (also in *Esquire*). Perhaps *The New Yorker* declined "July '69" because it was running another O'Brien story, "Winnipeg," in its August 14, 2000, issue. Written around the same time as "July '69," the two are companion stories, "Winnipeg," about Billy McMann, being an exercise in imagining the life of someone who had gone to Canada after graduation to avoid the war.

The final contract for *July, July* is dated July 10, 2001.[11] By this point, O'Brien knew his structure. The present is the Darton Hall College Class of 1969's reunion in July 2000, with chapters alternating between the reunion and short stories from revealing moments in the characters' lives, sometimes defining moments, sometimes such moments' results. The version at Houghton Mifflin in September 2001 was not the first submitted manuscript, and O'Brien's final revisions were completed by mid-January 2002.[12]

"Too Skinny," the *New Yorker* story on the newsstands on 9/11, was another story adapted from O'Brien's life. Ten years earlier, he'd received a letter from a woman in Winston-Salem, North Carolina, that began, "To the real Tim O'Brien . . ." In the story, to get and then keep a woman, Marv Bertel pretends that Thomas Pierce, the name of an actual successful literary author, is his pen name. Many of the story's details came straight from the deceived ex-fiancée's letter about the man who claimed *Tim O'Brien* was his pen name. The thick envelope the woman sent O'Brien included the man's letter of confession to her. The man had picked O'Brien because he didn't think anyone had ever heard of him. The pissed-off O'Brien chuckled as he reminded his story's readers otherwise, when Bertel's future wife tells Bertel, whom she thinks is a successful writer, "You're one of our great, great, great writers. [. . .] Everybody knows *about* you."[13]

The imaginative hopper for "Little People" (*Esquire*, October 2001), in which a plain young woman with "muddy brown" hair, "sunken" jaw, and "thin legs jury-rigged to the hips of a sumo wrestler" poses naked for private photo shoots, was the same one from which *Northern Lights'* Addie had originated, when she was Harvey Tillman's wife and the story ended in cannibalism. "Half Gone" (*The New Yorker*, July 8, 2002) picked up from "Winnipeg" with the story of Dorothy Stier, a Midwestern conservative blue blood who hadn't joined Billy McMann in Canada in 1969 and whose cancer survival story was inspired by O'Brien's sister, Kathy. Although other than the cancer the story had no resemblance to Kathy's life, O'Brien did not perform it at readings she and her husband attended. In the story, Dorothy defends the moneyed lifestyle like the one the O'Briens have just started living: "There's nothing wrong with a vacation in Nassau now and then," she says, "there's nothing wrong with sending your kids to good schools."[14] A few years down the road, the O'Briens would vacation in Nassau and their children would attend Austin's elite St. Andrew's Episcopal School.

Chapter 12's "Class of '69" story of a nude yoga session during a weekend retreat, everyone prancing about the meadow bared to the breeze, O'Brien got from Meredith. The summer after her mother's death, the very depressed Meredith Baker accompanied her father, at his invitation and expense, to his annual two weeks at the Shalom Mountain Retreat in the Catskills. Jerry Jud's Playground, her mom always called it, after its proprietor. Larry Tabor's Funny Farm, the character Paulette Haslo calls it in the book. The other attendees seemed intellectual enough to Meredith, talking about Carl Jung and chakras and the like. She did not expect the naked cavorting. Mortified at first, she went along with it, not knowing what else to do. Jud looked like a nutty, New Age Ichabod Crane. She never would have believed her undemonstrative father could be so unbuttoned.

Before the novel's final version, Johnny Ever helped hold the stories together. O'Brien drafted at least two chapters in Johnny Ever's trippy latesixties voice, chapter 15, "Everness," and chapter 23, "July, July," probably the final chapter. In "Everness," Johnny Ever tells us that he has flitted into all the major characters' lives, as the cop in "Loon Point," the midget in "Little People," the retired colonel in "Half Gone," the blackjack dealer in "The Streak," and in people's lives outside the book, including that of Sarah Good, burned at the stake during the Salem witch trials. O'Brien used Ever to directly address the reader more creatively than he'd done in the "Notes" chapters he'd cut from *The Things They Carried*:

Stuff like the witch trials, the Dark Ages, Vietnam, whatever—most folks figure that's what really counts. The big picture, the headlines.

Turns out, though, it's the tiny crap that sticks with you. Shit you barely even notice. Like when you pose for a few dirty pictures, or go on a diet, or miss a plane flight, or take yourself a little joy ride down to Mexico, or stop off at some miserable two-bit casino.

In "July, July," Johnny Ever blurts out the book's thesis, that every generation thinks it is special, and every generation loses its way. He addresses the characters as characters, a puppeteer telling his puppets what's up:

> I'm here to tell you that what you're goin' through is just part an' parcel of the overall story. It's *art*, follow me? High art. Art for art's sake. All them woes of yours, all that wee-hour melancholy, it's like the divine fuckin' comedy with some cool new twists. See my point? Art! What kind of a story is it, for God's sake, if there ain't a coffin in there someplace? Old age? Toe cancer? Somethin' to put the squeeze on? [. . .] I mean, when it comes to stories, who wants to hear about some goofy bastard who gets out of bed, goes to the sink, turns on the faucet, brushes his teeth, has fun all day . . . Seriously, you gotta break up the fuckin' happiness! Everybody's happy, *nobody's* happy. At some point, sooner or later, the story's gotta get weird.

"Busted hearts" and "busted balls" are everyone's lot in life, and the chapter in the draft ends with Johnny Ever's admiration:

> Breaks my heart, true enough, but like I say, Johnny loves y'all, every single lost soul, all you blind, brave, frisky little chimps down there, the weak and wounded, the marooned, the helpless, them poor blessed dipsticks in the class of '69, all the trippers and dippers and dead-end believers. Blows my mind, sort of. I mean, how you guys an' gals don't fuckin' quit. Not then, not now. Not ever. But, hey, that's the nifty thing about this job. Never ceases to amaze me.

With Johnny Ever, who introduces himself as an "information angel," not the top dog, O'Brien nevertheless takes up a godlike voice. Johnny Ever is above the fray, issuing fair warning in mysterious ways, the source of "them late-night goosey guilt-bumps," but he's also "in it," in life, has lived it, suffered it, and brought it and keeps bringing it about, involved beyond measure: "Fact is, I *am* it."[15]

O'Brien decided against including those chapters before sending along the draft that was on his editor's desk in September. For the version submitted around the end of the year, he strengthened Johnny Ever's presence in his various incarnations to compensate for removing the voice's solo chapters.

"A good story calls upon extraordinary means, extraordinary human behaviors and consequences, to illuminate the ordinary," O'Brien would tell a packed auditorium at the University of North Carolina in 2007. That doesn't mean good stories must involve "elements of the bizarre or the supernatural," even though "by temperament I'm disposed to what is called magical realism." He loves great realism, too. But "realism succeeds by reaching beyond mere verisimilitude."[16] Even the early devotee of realism from the *Northern Lights, Ploughshares,* and *Going After Cacciato* era sought the extraordinary in service to the ordinary, never strict realism for realism's sake but for the story's sake. Johnny Ever's solo chapters reached too far, in having the book explain itself, and in indulging the fantastic at the expense of story. *July, July* strikes the same balance as O'Brien's fiction always struck.

More than likely, the clock ticked to 3:11 in the morning when O'Brien first wrote the published novel's final passage, which ends at 3:11 a.m. On the plane seconds from crashing, a "pale old woman hissed at the void," but on the ground it was "July now, July always," as Jan Huebner and Amy Robinson head out to score some romance.[17] That's how O'Brien wrote, facing the void alone in the dark while fully inhabiting the moment, anticipating the book's future in some stranger's hands, an encounter fleeting, uncertain, shining.

July, July ends where *The Nuclear Age* ended, and it's a variation of what the Tim O'Brien character of "How to Tell a True War Story" imagined as Curt Lemon's final experience of the world, killed not by tripping a rigged artillery round but by stepping into the sunlight.

With the all-but-final manuscript submitted at the end of 2001, O'Brien treated himself to Las Vegas.[18]

◊ ◊ ◊

The two-month book tour in the fall of 2002 included October's National Book Festival in D.C., with an evening gala at the Library of Congress and a reading on the West Lawn of the Capitol the next day, a stop at Macalester, of course, and two days in November at the Texas State Capitol for the Texas Book Festival.[19] The National Book Festival took place in the middle of the Beltway Sniper shootings that in three weeks killed ten and wounded three people doing mundane things like putting gas in their cars. O'Brien doesn't remember that. He does remember the writer Sebastian Junger using his remarks at the Library of Congress gala to offer strategic advice to President Bush and Secretary of Defense Rumsfeld, who were in attendance. *Go whole-hog into Afghanistan or don't bother. The Afghans want us there, but in force and for the long term. Don't skimp. Don't abandon the country the way we did after helping them eject Russia, don't make this Charlie Wilson's second war. New York City requires forty thousand cops; the country of Afghanistan needs more than a couple thousand troops.* In a private aside that night, O'Brien complimented Junger on his courage, and Junger thanked O'Brien for the inspirational example of his art.

O'Brien began his session on the West Lawn the next day acknowledging the polarized reviews of *July, July* thus far. Among the haters was Michiko Kakutani, who savaged the book in *The New York Times* the day before. Kakutani charged that "the women in this book are all cartoonish parodies, depicted with the same sort of misogynistic energy that animated" *Tomcat in Love.* O'Brien read the first half of "Half Gone," about the psycho-emotional fallout of Dorothy Stier's double mastectomy. "Did that Dorothy Stier story sound misogynist to you?" O'Brien asked his audience. "I love her."[20] Commonality and relatability were the new book's guiding spirits.

For Michael Newton, writing in the *Times Literary Supplement,* the large character ensemble was fault as well as virtue: "The book's fragmented structure contains the limitations of a single life within the connections that bind the whole group; the things they carry are all borne separately, though for a moment it is as if they bore the burdens together." Newton, for one, concluded that the book successfully outmaneuvers the tired reunion plot device and transcends its Sixties-generation context.[21] In a cynical reading, the reunion serves to unconvincingly cobble a novel out of previously published stories. In one reviewer's admiring reading, the book shows off

O'Brien "the mad scientist in a laboratory of forms, reveling in new ways to tell a story, [who] reshapes himself with each novel, even if certain settings and themes are familiar." Another review declared the book "a small-scale tour de force by an American original."[22]

O'Brien wanted the moment of each character's story to represent the rest of their life. Such a tactic would seem to go against the grain of his devotion to the mystery and the enlargement of character, but it's of a piece with O'Brien's career-long exploration into the vexing relationship among character, history, circumstance, and imagination. And to some degree he took the criticisms to heart. Many years later, he and Meredith toyed with the idea of publishing the stories without the "Class of '69" connective tissue. Or at least include "Little People" in a future Tim O'Brien reader. That one is an O'Brien favorite.

The *Going After Cacciato* film project progressed in fits and starts, like most Hollywood projects. At some point in the process, Cassavetes and Kaplan showed the screenplay to Al Pacino in his New York apartment—he gave his usual noncommittal response. In May 1999, O'Brien attended a script reading in Los Angeles that included Leonardo DiCaprio (Paul Berlin), Tobey Maguire (Cacciato), Jon Voight (Lt. Corson), Owen Wilson (Doc Peret), and Keri Russell (woman in VW van). O'Brien read as the major at Berlin's promotion board.[23]

The script was faithful to the novel, with a Paul Berlin voice-over, except for two additions. In a flashback to Paul Berlin's send-off at Drake's Bar in Grand Marais, Minnesota, his drunk father takes him for a drive, gives him the truck and all the money he has (in cash), and tells him to drive north. "I can walk back from here. It's not that far. . . . Just drive and keep going. You'll find your way. There's no shame in it, son. No shame at all." Paul looks at the border crossing through the windshield before saying no, he's going to Việt Nam.

The script also added Paul Berlin's homegoing. Out-processing at Chu Lai, he shares in voice-over that "they said they found Cacciato's body in the mountains. They said he'd starved to death, but I really didn't believe them. No one ever saw the body and that's what the Army would say." In

Minnesota, he escapes from a welcome home party to his room, where he discovers blank postcards from Paris on his desk. The shot tracks *into* a postcard scene to a Paris café, where "at a corner table in the back, a slender oriental girl with winged eyes sits with an older man and a round faced boy with a beatific smile. They eat and drink and laugh. 'La Vie En Rose' plays over. And everything is fine." The end.[24] The whole moment, including the postcards on the desk, could be just another daydream.

The next March, O'Brien learned that the money had been pulled.[25] According to Kaplan, New Line Cinema "did not think a Vietnam war movie could earn its money back. The truth we will never know. We had already finished scouting in Vietnam and were back in Thailand on our way to Burma when we got the call."

The filmmakers persevered. In August 2000, *Variety* announced the film was to be shot in spring 2001.[26] Cassavetes was delayed finishing up *John Q*, and a few days after 9/11 emailed O'Brien that *Cacciato* would start filming in the spring. He had a few questions about the novel and promised to "make the most beautiful film on the face of the Earth."[27] The version history of Cassavetes's screenplay in the O'Brien archives bears out this history, with its printed OCTOBER 1999 date crossed out and changed to "2002" by hand.[28]

It must have been spring 2002 when the financing was killed again. One has to wonder if the decision was influenced by the fact that the United States was fighting a new war in Asia, the mountains of Afghanistan and the guerrilla enemy mixing with civilians too reminiscent of the mountains in *Cacciato* and that war's enemy. After 9/11, Miramax had shelved its adaptation of *The Quiet American*, Graham Greene's novel about the start of U.S. involvement in Việt Nam, because it "now could be seen as a searing critique of United States imperialism"[29] (the film ended up being released a year later). As a consolation prize—really because of the friendship with Kaplan and Cassavetes—the O'Briens were cast as Mr. and Mrs. Tuffington for an outdoor dining scene in Cassavetes's *The Notebook*.

In May 2002, O'Brien received an invitation to write a piece for *Harper's Bazaar*. The magazine was asking writers to contribute a brief response to an assigned visual artwork. The artwork and paired essays ran in consecutive issues of the magazine before becoming a 2003 calendar sold "to raise money for victims of terrorism."[30] O'Brien was given a 2001 Mariko

Mori lithograph, *Moonlight Mirror*, of a young Japanese woman with an ornament the size of her face atop her head, an upwardly tapering silver horseshoe, like Taurus's horns, cupping the moon, a textured golden orb. The girl looks askance; she's off-center in a circular frame cutting off everything below one shoulder. Her arms appear to be held out. A square yellow dress boxes her in. Her hair is a pasted magazine cutout.

O'Brien worries about her and the exhausting position she must maintain as an objectified woman. He marvels at her composure; he recognizes the strain. He imagines her aware of herself as part of the artwork. If she moves, the headpiece will topple, she will topple, it cannot hold forever: "For with each breath, we all choose to live. We choose the struggle, the treacherous daily balance. We choose to make art of our lives, knowing the end, knowing that apocalypse awaits, our eyes shifting in the wholly human hope of salvation, a reprieve, a miracle." Now she's all of us. At the end, O'Brien becomes self-reflexive. He senses he's encountered this "near-woman" before, in a dream, in a novel he has written or has yet to write. He worries he has "misrepresented her entirely," and imagines now not anxiousness but seething accusation, a "voice about to whisper, 'How dare you!'"[31]

Precariousness, resentment, and violent imposition of values were in the air that summer. The war on terror was in its first year. Fear gripped the country. Muslim and South Asian Americans experienced everyday vulnerability. Osama bin Laden, the al-Qaeda leader, had not been found. War with Iraq seemed the country's inescapable future.

For O'Brien, the October 2002 Authorization for Use of Military Force Against Iraq replayed the 1964 Gulf of Tonkin Resolution, passed weeks before he matriculated at Macalester. The evidence of Iraq's weapons of mass destruction seemed as spurious—or at the very least as uncertain—as that of North Việt Nam's attacks on U.S. naval ships that led to his war. People like John Negroponte and Donald Rumsfeld connected the wartime administrations. The spectacled, slick-haired Secretary of Defense Rumsfeld eerily resembled his Vietnam War predecessor, Robert McNamara, and in time would become even more reviled.

The United States invaded Iraq in March 2003. As he had with Afghanistan, O'Brien aired his concerns when asked. Going to war is easy; getting out is the hard part. Moral absolutism and demonizing are dangerous.

"The few times I've spoken since September 11, I've really pissed people off."[32] An all-volunteer military made the situation worse than with his war because leaders and citizen cheerleaders had no skin in the game. The new wars were easier to ignore. On May 1, President Bush landed on the USS *Abraham Lincoln* aircraft carrier to declare, tragically prematurely, the end of major combat operations and American victory.

In June, Meredith gave birth to the latest William Timothy O'Brien, called Timmy as a child like his dad before him. The next three months were torment, as the baby suffered from acid reflux, which was repeatedly misdiagnosed as colic. The O'Briens took turns with the shrieking child. About five weeks in, they drove through Albuquerque on the way to Las Vegas, Timmy crying the whole way. O'Brien gambled in both cities while Meredith struggled to placate their child. A friend from Paris flew to Austin to help, became exasperated, and flew back. Guilt racked Meredith. What if her diabetes or the early induction because of the diabetes contributed? What if Timmy had inherited whatever afflicted her two sisters? The one institutionalized, the other suicidal (she would kill herself a year later by crashing her car into a church, her third attempt). A desperate emergency room visit resulted in the right diagnosis and the medication to relieve Timmy's pain and his parents' troubled nerves.

Although in some interviews O'Brien said he enjoyed writing *July, July* as he hadn't the previous couple of books, by his son's birth he dreaded writing as a pleasureless chore. He'd proven himself long ago and took comfort knowing his best work would outlive him by many years. The compulsion to write abated. He was determined to be the father his father wasn't. "I would trade every syllable of my life's work for an extra five or ten years with you, whatever the going rate might be," he wrote in an epistolary essay to baby Timmy. "A father's chief duty is not to instruct or to discipline. A father's chief duty is to be present."[33]

29

FAMILY MAN AND ELDER STATESMAN

Dad's Maybe Book

It was another period of beginnings and endings. Bill O'Brien died in August 2004, two months after Meredith's sister's suicide and Timmy's first birthday. In March 2005, a friend from Bread Loaf, Norton Girault, a former navy captain, kindly arranged for Ava and Kathy to tour the naval base at Norfolk, where it had all begun during World War II. Trevor Hale O'Brien, called Tad after an oft-reproduced image of Abe Lincoln looking at a book with his son Tad, entered the world that June. With the children came all the glorious firsts: first smile, first step, first word, first playdate, first day of school. Ava O'Brien died in July 2009, while Tim, Meredith, and the boys were vacationing at a luxe resort in Saint-Jean-Cap-Ferrat, southeastern France. O'Brien missed both parents' deaths. He wrote their eulogies, delivered by his brother, Greg.

The O'Brien marriage followed more or less traditional gender roles. Neither Tim nor Meredith enjoyed cooking or had much aptitude for it, but it mostly fell to her, along with the grocery shopping. She coordinated Timmy's and Tad's activities and drove them to and from school. But she also taught acting at Texas State University beginning in 2000, and the meticulous O'Brien liked scrubbing floors and tidying the house (even though they had regular cleaners, who became family friends). Meredith combined her professional talent and her mothering by producing an annual Christmas show called "Onion Creek Children's Theatre," adapted from such classics as *A Christmas Carol*, "The Gift of the Magi," and *How the Grinch Stole Christmas*, cast with neighborhood kids and staged at the house. Christmas meant a lot to this minister's daughter. Neighborhood friends got involved, but Meredith wrote, directed, and produced the plays. Each year it was a pageant and a party, with over a hundred guests. The shows were "totally outside the box," her friend Kirsten Brunner says. "She never thought she couldn't pull something off."

The family's other holiday tradition came from O'Brien's childhood, lobster and seafood on Christmas Eve—a treat for his dad, who had grown up on the East Coast, had his heyday at the Queen Victoria in Nassau, and served in the navy. Sometimes they spent Christmas at the house, sometimes they traveled to San Antonio to celebrate with Kathy's family, and occasionally they went to the Bahamas. They first went to Club Med Saint Lucia in December 2004,[1] a reward for surviving baby Timmy's reflux, but then they discovered the Atlantis resort area in Nassau. They vacationed there about ten times over the next twenty-odd years and every two or three years traveled to Paris, where Meredith's friend Anne Dolan lived.

Two big trips a year. They took the kids to Switzerland once, and also did a home exchange to Belgium, where Regina, one of their nannies, was from. She joined them on the trip. Regina went on a handful of those quick Vegas trips to watch the kids. Meredith split her time watching her husband gamble and being with Timmy and Tad. There were infrequent trips back east to see Meredith's dad, who lived in Connecticut with his second wife. Tim took Meredith and the boys with him to enjoy the Tennessee mountain setting during his summer teaching stints at the Sewanee Writers' Conference (for the last time in 2019).

In 2014, the O'Briens very nearly moved to France. They thought to give it two years, after which they might stay or move back, perhaps to New England. They put their home on the market, enrolled the boys in a Paris school, obtained international driver's licenses, and had someone looking for housing. But they couldn't secure visas because of his self-employment, and they couldn't find repatriation insurance (for their corpses). Days before their scheduled departure, they scrapped the plan. Meredith was heartbroken. She cried when she and Tim went to the headmaster to get Timmy and Tad back into St. Andrew's Episcopal School.

O'Brien was the present, attentive, adoring father he hoped to be. But he could never be idle. Yard work and golf didn't suffice. Gambling was one way of checking out without doing nothing. He gave up weights because of an elbow he'd broken in middle school that had gradually calcified and hurt to move; if he didn't stop lifting, he might lose even more range of motion. As he always had, he scrutinized royalty statements for errors and he did the family's taxes by hand. He resumed magic after forty years away, often losing himself all day long, a kid again. Illusion apparatuses and magic books became the standard Christmas presents from Meredith.

O'Brien's creative writing class met once a week, on campus the first several years and then in the back house at the Katherine Anne Porter Literary Center, Porter's renovated home in Kyle, between San Marcos and Austin. Sam Lawrence had been Porter's publisher, another reason for O'Brien to join First Lady Laura Bush in making remarks for the center's dedication in June 2002. O'Brien's workshops were intense. He read student work several times to prepare. He let the students talk first, then offered his thoughts. He had little patience for grammatical gaffes and ignorance. Revision, revision, revision—he demanded his students care about how to craft sentences. In one-on-one conversations at post-workshop bar outings, O'Brien led students to the story they really wanted to write. Some students became good friends.

The writer's life didn't entirely cease. O'Brien wrote occasional essays, on being a father in "A Letter to My Son" (2004) and "The Best of Times" (2006); on veterans from the new wars rehabilitating at the Center for the Intrepid in "The War They Still Fight" (2008); on revisiting Worthington in "Fenced In" (2009); on well-imagined fiction in "Telling Tails" (2009); and sundry minor pieces.[2] He worked at a couple of ideas that eventually germinated *America Fantastica* in 2023. O'Brien traveled a lot for readings and lectures, often revising, recombining, and adapting set pieces to the occasion, sometimes writing new remarks. Different lectures included his fanciful story of taking toddler Timmy to the doctor for spontaneously uttering for his very first words Shakespeare's Macbeth's definition of life,

"'Tis a tale told by an idiot." His keynote for the "Thirty Years After" conference at the University of Hawaii was a compact aesthetic statement more
than an analysis of his war's literary and cinematic output.[3]

Meanwhile, the nation warred along. When news broke of potential
American-perpetrated atrocities in Haditha and Hamdania, Iraq, O'Brien
could only shake his head. No surprise there. Images from Abu Ghraib of
young American women soldiers as grinning abusers of Iraqi prisoners
he'd all but predicted in "The Sweetheart of the Song Tra Bong," a story
about how women are just as susceptible as men to war's powers of seduc-
tion. O'Brien would have given anything to have it otherwise, but America's
twenty-first-century wars only increased his stature. News outlets sought
him to comment on the unfolding wars, and war literature was relevant for
a new generation as it had not been for decades. At 9.3 ounces, *The Things
They Carried* was one of the things some U.S. soldiers and marines carried
in Afghanistan and Iraq.

College courses and scholarly panels, conferences, and publications
about war literature and film began to boom. Writing and literary programs for and about veterans and war emerged, an unprecedented pheno-
menon; among them were the National Endowment for the Arts' Operation
Homecoming, the Warrior Writers organization, the Missouri Humanities
Council's storytelling and writing workshops and annual anthology *Proud
to Be*, the Great Books Foundation's Talking Service project, and the National Endowment for the Humanities' Dialogues on the Experience of
War initiative.[4] *The Things They Carried* became a popular selection for
community-wide reading events, such as One Book, One Chicago in 2003.
Shared reading experiences were boosted starting in 2006 by the NEA's Big
Read grants, and after *The Things They Carried* joined the list of available titles for the 2009–2010 cycle, it would become the program's most requested
and funded novel. O'Brien's invitations to speak and participate at events
increased considerably. In 2009 he made his second National Book Festival
appearance even though he hadn't published a book in seven years.

O'Brien participated fully at academic conferences, not just as a headliner, but as a panel attendee and a regular guy at receptions and outings
and parties. As O'Brien walked into the venue at Brookdale Community
College in Lincroft, New Jersey, on March 8, 2009, a man about his age
approached. O'Brien stretched out his hand. "Hi, I'm Tim." The lack of

pretense or superiority struck the man. "To him, I was one more person . . . one of thousands over the years to attend one of his lectures and read his books. But he didn't talk down or ignore me. I found him to be a sincere man, a humble man who had not been altered or influenced by his popularity." The nervous man stumbled into his words: "Mr. O'Brien, what does a man have to do to get a rear job around this place?"

Oh, my God, it's BuddyWolf! The fellow soldier who'd been writing his wife when Spec. 4 Peterson killed himself fishing with grenades. Bob Wolf introduced her and three other Alpha soldiers there. Smiles, handshakes, and bear hugs all around. They talked for twenty minutes in the back of the auditorium while everyone waited for O'Brien to take the stage. Later they would learn of a fifth Alpha soldier in the audience. According to Wolf, O'Brien had to leave the room to regain his composure before mounting to the podium.

> It was an hour of total silence. You could hear a pin drop during the lecture. Everyone listened intently to the stories Tim told. But for the five of us who had lived those stories, they were more than tales spun by a master storyteller. The events and the people were real.
>
> Tim told of a blond-haired fellow by the name of Tom who threw a milk carton in the face of the blind Vietnamese man. The group was horrified. But I knew the man . . . from Baltimore. Tim almost cried as he recounted the deaths of Chip Merricks and Tom Markunas.

The person Wolf had known forty-one years earlier had not changed. Sixty-two years old and famous now but still low-key, genuine, modest, and kind.[5]

Several years earlier, Wolf had begun seeking out his Alpha Company comrades, compiling a roster to keep in touch, and amassing hundreds of digital copies of personal photographs. The email memory-sharing kicked into high gear starting in late 2007, when David Taylor, a former company commander in their battalion, started researching for his 2011 book *Our War: The History and Sacrifices of an Infantry Battalion in the Vietnam War, 1968–1971*.

O'Brien spent several weeks in the spring of 2010 on tour for a twentieth-anniversary edition of *The Things They Carried*—with more author edits,

naturally. Before the reprint, the book had sold just under 2.5 million copies in English. By the end of 2022, the number exceeded 6 million.[6] It's
unheard of for a book in its third decade to nearly double the sales of its
first two decades. The cultural cachet of *The Things They Carried* has been
astonishing. Articles, chapters, and exhibits frequently borrow its title
(at times to O'Brien's annoyance when not asked or credited). It has been
staged any number of times by amateur theaters. The director of the 2009
Iraq war film *The Messenger* ensured it appeared on a bookshelf and sent a
copy to his lead actor, Woody Harrelson.[7] The O'Brien Papers at the Harry
Ransom Center are replete with artwork inspired by his book sent to him
by the artists. Keiko Sato, a Japanese artist who was in New York City on
September 11, 2001, for an exhibit that was to open on the thirteenth, took
eight years to create a book mixing text, interviews, and original artwork,
How to Tell a Story of My Father (2009), that incorporated quotations from
The Things They Carried in its collages. Her father was a kamikaze pilot
who survived World War II.

The spring of the tour, O'Brien learned that he'd been selected to receive the Katherine Anne Porter Award for demonstrated literary achievement from the American Academy of Arts and Letters.[8] Other lifetime
achievement awards followed: In 2012, the Richard C. Holbrooke Distinguished Achievement Award by the Dayton Literary Peace Prize Foundation; in 2013, the Pritzker Military Library Literature Award for Lifetime
Achievement in Military Writing; in 2018, the Mark Twain Award for "distinguished contributions to Midwestern literature" by the Society for the
Study of Midwestern Literature.

Back home from the 2010 tour, Tim set to work practicing for and preparing a magic show. It would be the first of four shows he would put together and perform in the Onion Creek home. For the first two, in July
2010 and July 2011, he and Meredith performed most of the show, with
their friends Todd and Kirsten Brunner dressed as butler and French maid
playing hosts and assisting backstage—including rousing Timmy and Tad
for their parts—and doing intermission bits between the three acts. Everyone dressed up. The champagne flowed.

Unlike most magic shows, O'Brien told Kirsten Brunner in a videotaped interview for the first one, his had a storyline. "I wanted to do magic
for people who hate magic. It's not just the magic, it's the characters."

Trick-only shows preoccupy audience members with the *how-did-he-do it* question; they don't lose themselves in the moment. O'Brien wanted "to take the audience out of their ordinary lives," and one way of doing that was to have his guests "be a part of the show by dressing up," not just watch it "in Bermuda shorts." The result, one guest testified, was "bar none, the best party we have ever been to." The video ends with a quotation O'Brien wrote but attributed to a nonexistent *Magician's Handbook*: "Magic is not to be logically explained or 'figured out.' It is to amuse, delight, and transport. One must seek the inner child in oneself."[9]

The production kicked up for the third show, now with a title, "New Year's Eve at the Dead End's Casino and Lounge," a storyline with musical acts and a larger cast. They couldn't pull it off for New Year's, so it ran in August and September 2013. The party was even bigger.

O'Brien was a patient coach and an exacting taskmaster. The recruited friends and students had to practice, practice, practice. Work schedules and childcare could be a challenge. But all sensed they were a part of a once-in-a-lifetime joy, something extraordinarily unique. (Riding away from the first live screening of *The War and Peace of Tim O'Brien* with the filmmaker Aaron Matthews and O'Brien's family at the Austin Film Society Cinema, July 23, 2022, O'Brien from the minivan's middle row would remark that the only scenes that matched his impression of himself were the ones of him practicing and doing magic.)

Around the same time as the first magic shows, O'Brien had begun consulting on a couple of film projects. Gabe Polsky, at the beginning of his career as a director and producer, optioned *Going After Cacciato* in 2009.[10] For a minute Polsky had the interest of the legendary German filmmaker Werner Herzog. Polsky was one of the producers behind Herzog's just-released *Bad Lieutenant: Port of Call New Orleans*. O'Brien considered Herzog a genius whose "'take' on the world" and "artistic vision" were "very compatible" with his own.[11] He emailed Herzog to allay the concern that the war was a bust as a cinematic subject: "I can only offer my conviction that a beautiful movie will overcome the 'Vietnam problem,' in the same way that [your] AGUIRRE, THE WRATH OF GOD and FITZCARRALDO overcame their own historical distances. The epochs may be long gone, but madness and horror and man's relentless (if quixotic) quest for salvation remain with us." He believed Herzog to be "uniquely and eerily suited for this material—the journey motif, the darkness motif, the obsession motif, the tensions between the world as it is and the world as we imagine it." Who else to do justice to the "mad and sublime" act of soldiers humping it all the way to Paris?[12]

While in L.A. in mid-March 2010 on the anniversary tour, O'Brien had dinner with Herzog, just back from Europe, and a few others at Polsky's home.[13] He was in awe of Herzog in a way he'd never felt before. Herzog was working on *Cave of Forgotten Dreams*, a 3D film about the Paleolithic paintings and traces of animal and human life in the Chauvet Cave in France. He and three crew members had been granted access otherwise available to only a handful of scientists. He'd recently been inside for the first time and was preparing to go back to film. Herzog talked excitedly about these earliest-known examples of representational art. O'Brien found him "the most compelling guy I ever met," truly a "genius." It's easy to imagine Herzog, with the distinctive voice that narrates his documentaries, fishing aloud for language to use in the new film's voice-over, which will offer that cave art as "the beginnings of the modern human soul."

Herzog later declined to direct *Cacciato*. Though he admired the novel tremendously, some literature simply defies cinematic adaptation. Four years later, Polsky's team had a screenplay. O'Brien directed its writers to his friend the poet and veteran Bruce Weigl, who could be especially valuable making the dialogue sound "more soldierly" and "Vietnamesque," and "sharpen[ing] Berlin's internal struggle." O'Brien's most interesting feedback related to the ending:

> I think the conclusion needs to be more surreal and more spectacular and more dramatic in its imagery—the Eiffel Tower getting sucked up into the clouds—the streets of Paris rolling up and vanishing— the Jardin du Luxembourg beginning to bubble and darken and transform itself into a rice paddy—an old-man accordion player melting into a burning corpse—the Seine becoming the Song Tran Bong filled with 30 floating bodies—the sounds of traffic on the Place de la Concorde bleeding into the sounds of helicopters and artillery fire and men cursing and screaming and dying—the hills of Montmartre fading into foothills of Vietnam, where Cacciato has been encircled—the face of Paul Berlin, as a Paris tourist, transforming

into the face of Paul Berlin as a filthy, exhausted, scared-stiff soldier. And so on.[14]

O'Brien wanted an adaptation faithful to the novel's spirit yet artistically true to the new medium. No wonder he wanted Herzog, whose aesthetic of *ecstatic truth* contra strict vérité resembled O'Brien's story-truth.

Weigl rewrote the screenplay several times. Amazon Studios picked up the financial slack with the intent to release the film on its streaming service, but in late 2018 the company did not renew the option, citing (according to O'Brien) a strategic decision about the production company's direction.

The other consultation was a much surer project, Ken Burns and Lynn Novick's *The Vietnam War* for Florentine Films and PBS. O'Brien was the first person they talked to. Novick and producer Sarah Botstein met with him in Austin in the fall of 2009. His immediate response: *Don't do it. You can't get it right because nobody can, and if you can't get it right, why bother? You'll only upset a lot of people. The criticism will come from the left as well as the right.* He worried about the war porn problem—that no matter the intent, the film would excite bellicosity. Novick and Botstein had plenty of historians and military advisers; they wanted O'Brien because he was a great storyteller. He emailed in November to suggest that the filmmakers incorporate "pieces of potent prose and/or poetry" to "give the film a beautiful and distinctive *sound*"—and he rattled off a list of fifteen writers, most of whom were friends.[15] Novick and Botstein filmed their interview with O'Brien at his home in December 2011, and there was an advisers' meeting in October 2012. O'Brien told the filmmakers not to forget the mothers and the sisters, advice that led to some of the best contributions to the film.

The filmmakers screened their eighteen-hour rough cut to the advisers at Burns's barn in Walpole, New Hampshire, in June 2014. For O'Brien, the first two episodes played like a soporific middle school history lesson. The team reworked them and flew him back alone in January for feedback. There was a tense disagreement among advisers about playing "America the Beautiful" as POWs came home in closing episode 9. What rankled O'Brien as a dangerously sentimental banner for America's murderous exceptionalism, others—including the former Hanoi Hilton prisoner Hal Kushner—

found a stirring tribute. Editing efforts to ameliorate the trouble, chiefly by lowering the volume, fell short for O'Brien. He didn't think anyone would pick up on the subtlety of using the Black performer Ray Charles's version to call out the war's racism while also saluting the returnees. But overall, O'Brien thought the final film an amazing achievement.

In February 2015, O'Brien received two phone calls that would reinvigorate his literary life.

Erik Hansen had a dream that began with "typical Vietnam flashback stuff" before a big neon billboard appeared in the sky with the order "You must find Tim O'Brien." The best friends hadn't communicated in twenty years. He located Greg O'Brien in Eagan, Minnesota, who gave him O'Brien's phone number. Hansen called. He had a nephew in Denton, not far from Austin, so in March he traveled to Texas to see both, staying for a week with the O'Briens. Those twenty years fell away instantly. Erik and Tim spent their reunion week talking, golfing, drinking, golfing, talking. Hansen once again became one of O'Brien's trusted readers.

Only a few days later, the Ernest Hemingway Society invited O'Brien to speak at its 2016 international conference. O'Brien accepted, generously asked for a very low fee, and for the next seventeen months immersed himself in Hemingway and memory. The conference took place at Oak Park and River Forest, Illinois, Hemingway's birthplace and childhood stomping ground. O'Brien took the Lund Auditorium stage at Dominican University on Tuesday, July 19, 2016, two days before Hemingway's 117th birthday, to read "Timmy and Tad and Papa and I." The talk wove together O'Brien's reflections on Hemingway, on literary influence, on being his father's son and his sons' father, on old age, on war, on craft.[16] By all accounts, it was the most moving literary event its audience members had experienced—and with a roomful of professors, writers, and readers, that's no small feat.

At a dinner in the early evening prior to his reading, O'Brien told the two conference organizers who had invited him, "You saved my life. You made me a writer again." It was an undue kindness cradling a kernel of truth. "Timmy and Tad and Papa and I" was his most sustained significant literary effort since writing *July, July* over fifteen years earlier.

After the conference, O'Brien returned home to final preparations and rehearsals for the fourth magic show extravaganza, the Masquerade Ball, which ran in August 2016 with the biggest cast yet. O'Brien already had an idea for a hospital-themed show, but everyone needed a break. He returned to the Hemingway essay and yet another project of sorts. Aaron Matthews had interviewed O'Brien in December 2014 for the PBS documentary *The Draft* and found him so interesting that Matthews knew he wanted to make a film about O'Brien. It took time to convince him. Matthews didn't know what the story would be. He trusted his gut. He first interviewed O'Brien on May 22, 2016, sent a cameraman to film O'Brien at the Hemingway conference, filmed during the Masquerade Ball, and spent time with the O'Briens, periodically living with them and traveling with O'Brien, for the next three years.

The documentary's story turned out to be the writing of *Dad's Maybe Book*, O'Brien's memoir in the form of essays published in 2019. The book relates its origin: "My intent was to leave behind little word gifts for Timmy and his yet-to-be-born brother Tad, who had been conceived but was still waiting in the wings." Given his age, O'Brien knew his children would be lucky to know him as adults, but he could leave them "short messages in a bottle" they "might find tucked away in a dusty file long after my death." Snippets, not a book. Then, in late 2014, nine-year-old Tad suggested a *maybe book*—as in maybe someday a book.[17] O'Brien didn't make substantial progress until the Hemingway lecture assignment, however. Just shy of two months before the conference and hard at work on "Timmy and Tad and Papa and I," O'Brien suspected a new book was on the way, as he told Matthews in their first interview. He sure had a lot of pages.[18]

The practical catalyst—the circumstance that made the making possible—was the boys' growing up. Timmy turned thirteen that summer, Tad eleven. They required of their parents fewer hours of the day. The writing time O'Brien needed was back. He needed to catch their childhood on paper before it fled their bodies and his memory. Before the life of this chain-smoker of fifty years fled him. Given Bill O'Brien's last years, dementia was a possibility.

Six weeks before the Hemingway talk, O'Brien read from Robert Stone's

Dog Soldiers at a tribute for his friend at the Folger Shakespeare Library Theater in Washington, D.C.—Stone had died the year before.[19] Michael Herr, whose *Dispatches* may prove as enduring as *The Things They Carried*, died a month before the Hemingway talk. Hemingway's "great subject" wasn't war, O'Brien wrote, but death:

> Figuratively, but also literally, I'm quite certain that when Ernest Hemingway sat down to write in the early mornings, and as he slipped into the ballet of imagined events and imagined human beings, he was often engaged in something close to a dress rehearsal for his own coming extinction. He was practicing.[20]

So, too, was Tim O'Brien.

O'Brien nearly died writing the book in which this thought appears. The documentary took an unexpected turn when Matthews found himself filming O'Brien's rapidly declining health. O'Brien was talking about Hemingway's focus on death during his interview with Matthews on February 12, 2017. The day before, Matthews had filmed the visit to a medical clinic, already a bad sign considering O'Brien's stoic resistance to doctors. The diagnosis was a minor case of the flu, too far along for Tamiflu, but liquids, aspirin, and rest should do the trick.[21] That night Tim and Meredith had a spat about his "not having any pleasure in life." The writing had become miserable.

"Where does that leave me with a video camera in terms of the why bother?" Matthews asked. "Well, that leaves us with the Faulkner thing," O'Brien answered. He meant Hemingway:

> If you're going to give up, you commit suicide. Right. That's how you give up, you just say, Well, fuck this, I'm going to kill myself. And most people decide not to do it, and so you just sort of step forward knowing it's worthless. Knowing you're not going to convince anybody. Even yourself. Knowing your words will have no effect. Knowing that nobody will probably read them. You know all this in advance and yet you know you want to step forward. The problem with me is it's getting to where I don't want to step forward, and that's . . . there's a pain that is unbelievable.

The pain of writing. Yeah. The pain of uncertainty and that, the pain of the ugly sentence and you don't know why it's ugly, you just know it is.

But it was real and serious physical pain. "I'm sick. I want to go to bed. And never get up ever again. Until Aaron writes my book for me. Boy I, I am in bad shape again. [cough] Oh, god, it just pierces me when I do that."

On Monday the thirteenth, Matthews filmed O'Brien withered on the oversized den chair: "Welcome to my latest project called death." The next day O'Brien coughed his way through a radio interview in the studio with Dan Rather, and on Wednesday Meredith filmed Tim with her phone in the same chair talking gibberish.

On Saturday evening, he hallucinated hamburgers being delivered to the house from a body shop via a conveyor belt, and a golden-haired horn-helmeted Viking named Lars, the star player of the eighth-grade basketball team playing Timmy's team.[22] The next day Dr. Mark Malone, a family friend, told Meredith to take O'Brien to the hospital immediately. The hallucinations indicated that the nervous system couldn't "maintain homeostasis any longer." Malone believed that without treatment "within twenty-four hours, he could be dead." None of which he told Meredith. No cancer, but the hospital report identified "flu type a, streptococcal pneumonia, acute kidney failure, abnormal liver function, twenty-three-pound weight loss, acute gastritis, microscopic hematuria, microalbuminuria, and lipoprotein deficiency from impaired pancreas function." In other words, cascading organ failure.[23]

It took a long forty-eight hours for O'Brien to stabilize and begin to recover. He had checked in on the nineteenth, was emailing on the twenty-first, and checked out on the twenty-second. A month later he was on the road for a gig at Binghamton High School in New York. In *Dad's Maybe Book*, O'Brien compares the illness to "hitting buckets of balls in preparation for a final round of golf."[24]

He emailed a draft of the expanded Hemingway essay to select friends for feedback on April 9 and two months later finished the essay. It reached 106 double-spaced pages of 24,641 words.[25] The essay would end up being trimmed and spread across five reworked chapters for *Dad's Maybe Book*. One passage O'Brien cut involved an imagined conversation with Hemingway while doing dishes at three in the morning, with Papa Hemingway "gazing up at me from the soap bubbles in the kitchen sink."[26]

The Vietnam War's first episode premiered on PBS on September 17, 2017. The final episode, "The Weight of Memory," aired on September 28, when the filmmakers hosted a watch party in Washington for all the contributors. The last episode's title comes from *The Things They Carried*, and the film gives O'Brien its last words, reading from the title story. O'Brien did a few promotional events with Lynn Novick that fall, including one at Macalester in mid-October.[27] Novick routinely asked veterans from the war to stand up, and then asked anyone who had protested the war to stand and join the veterans for collective applause.

In early December, the O'Briens moved into a second house in Austin. Meredith and the boys spent too much of their lives driving back and forth to St. Andrew's. The new home, on Cobblestone Drive, was just a few minutes away from the school. The family would live there on weekdays, Onion Creek on weekends. They planned to sell the new one once Tad graduated.

On December 18, O'Brien emailed a friend that the manuscript that would become *Dad's Maybe Book* "has passed the 300-page mark, about halfway to what I hope will be the finish line." After wrapping up the Hemingway essay, he started with minor revisions to his 2004 essay "A Letter to My Son," the book's first chapter, then drafted "Row, Row" (chapter 3) and the prose poem "Skin" (chapter 4). Besides the Hemingway chapters, revised inclusions from earlier material, some rearrangement, and "later deletions and rewriting," he reported, "the book reads very roughly in the order in which it was written." He wrote "War Buddies"—maybe his favorite—much later than its final position as chapter 43 (of sixty) suggests.

He finished the draft in France the following July. The Hemingway Society's 2018 conference gave O'Brien an excuse to take his family back to Paris. He attended a few conference events—during the Q&A after one panel, O'Brien floated the provocation that Frederic Henry's emotionlessness during the murder of an Italian sergeant in *A Farewell to Arms* is the cold-bloodedness of the serial killer, necrophiliac, and cannibal Jeffrey Dahmer. Novick, at work on Florentine Films' *Hemingway* documentary, interviewed O'Brien for it in a hotel room. The O'Briens took a bike tour around Versailles, and they visited Ors, where Wilfred Owen was killed and buried at the very end of the Great War. In a British war cemetery,

O'Brien had Timmy read from Owen's for-the-ages anti-war poem "Dulce et Decorum Est." That vignette became chapter 41, titled after the poem, surely the very last essay he wrote, on the last day or two in Paris.

In *Dad's Maybe Book*, O'Brien says he began the book in 2004 as occasional musings, but this is somewhat misleading. The book includes modified versions of "Ambush" and "The Magic Show" from the early 1990s. "Trusting Story"—to the extent that we can trust it—dates to sometime after the July 2004 Sewanee conference, where O'Brien presented the tale of Timmy's first words being Shakespeare's line from *Macbeth* and was afterward confronted by an irate fellow offended that O'Brien reported an obvious fabrication in an ostensibly nonfictional lecture. The archives house two versions without the irate-fellow encounter, the first of which is titled "Sewanee lecture," presumably the 2004 lecture.[28] O'Brien did not mention the irate fellow in the version from Chapel Hill in 2007. Was he an invention? A sleight of hand? Don't dare ask, lest you align yourself with the man the book dismisses as a "literal-minded Philistine."[29]

O'Brien's July 2013 Sewanee craft lecture, a year before his late 2014 commitment to maybe write a book, contained elements that would appear in chapters throughout *Dad's Maybe Book*: His family watching *The Impossible* on television, a movie about a tsunami in the Indian Ocean whose takeaway for Tad was the message "Take your time peeing."[30] O'Brien's not hugging his father before his death. Tad's explaining his behavior by saying he had two heads telling him to do different things, followed by O'Brien's bedtime story of having had two heads about going to Việt Nam. Timmy's empathy for a homeless veteran. The lecture ended with a non sequitur— "If you support a war, go!"—which becomes the first discussion point in "Home School."[31]

Anecdote repurposing was O'Brien's modus operandi for lectures. The two-heads story appears in several lectures preserved in the archives; the language of having "two heads" about being drafted first appeared in the original iteration of the Rainy River story in O'Brien's 1986 "War Stories" Bread Loaf lecture. Had he remembered? Did his unconscious fetch it from the depths? In *The Things They Carried*, the two heads became "four arms and three heads."[32] A grandfather's invention of street-lane dividing stripes in a make-believe story from "Telling Tales (2)" began as Mrs. Robert Kooshof's grandfather inventing those white stripes in *Tomcat in Love*.[33]

In the fall of 2018, the book having undergone its first serious revision, O'Brien reconsidered the title. *Dad's Maybe Book* risked a certain unwieldiness. Meredith and others recommended *The Maybe Book*, or *A Maybe Book*, to preserve the nature of the book and the source of the title. And it would reflect the highly imaginative, suppositional character of so much of his work, the *What if a grievously wounded lieutenant near the Sông Trà Bồng has his radio talk to him?* quality. All of *In the Lake of the Woods* and most of *The Things They Carried* are maybe books. The last two words of *Going After Cacciato* are "Maybe so";[34] the note on the copyright page of *The Nuclear Age* states the author's belief in the truth of could-have- and should-have-beens. Furthermore, "every book is a maybe-book until it's a book-book, just as the next breath is always a maybe breath. Especially when you get old." He finally rejected *A Maybe Book* because of "its blurry, what-the-fuck-does-it-mean, and somewhat pretentious grandeur." He thought his original title less clunky and downright "musical." Plus, it honored the book's inspiration: the O'Brien boys.

That fall he also seriously considered scrapping the chapter numbers to emphasize the book's structure not of linearity but of recursive accretion, the way memory works, by resonance, not "causative and explanatory illusions." He decided to remove the fictional character Kiowa from the book's version of the 1994 essay "Ambush" (published chapter 34). He'd carried Kiowa into that essay from *The Things They Carried*. In "Ambush," he's a useful fiction for compacting the happened-truth. O'Brien gave him dialogue faithfully reconstructed from actual dialogue spoken by himself, by his best friend in the war, Chip Merricks, "who died not long after the night march described in the Lexington-Concord essay," and by a postwar friend. Is that any different from the war memoir's changing names and combining characters and scenes, often for the sake of privacy?

"One of the things that plagues me, and which has plagued me for years, is what I owe to the word *nonfiction* and what I owe to actual human beings. I want to be faithful to both," he says. Didn't the word *Kiowa*, the name of a people, not an actual person's name, signal the invention? Removing Kiowa may have had as much to do with the need to cut pages and improve the book's pace as it did a decision about what he owed its nonfiction status.

Most of the revision work involved cutting within chapters—the table of contents for the September 2018 version and the published book are basically identical.[35] He controlled structural rhythm and momentum by varying chapter length, tacking between the anecdotal and the meditative, and planting echoes. *Dad's Maybe Book* ranges widely, from his sons, Meredith, his parents, Worthington, writing, and death, to war. Political tirades target the leaders responsible for the new wars—George W. Bush, Dick Cheney, Donald Rumsfeld, Condoleezza Rice.

In "An Immodest and Altogether Earnest Proposal," O'Brien proposes replacing the word *war* and related terms wherever they appear with the words *killing people, including children*. Names of wars and monuments, the Department of Defense, the phrase *battle cry*, and the platitude *thank you for your service* will be accordingly revised.

> Who but the Hemingway Society would dare deny that *A Farewell to People-Killing, Including Children* comes melodiously—even bitingly—off the tongue? Can anyone of sound mind doubt that the United States People-Killing Academy will attract a more stalwart pool of applicants after its grand people-killing reopening? Hats will soar skyward; parents will beam; a golden age of people-killing candor will swiftly and surely dawn.[36]

O'Brien's second book of nonfiction is decidedly not an autobiography. Its ruminations preserve O'Brien's late-in-life voice and relate some significant, shaping elements, such as Bill O'Brien's alcoholism. They do not tell much of the full life story. As with Matthews's film, O'Brien saw the book as a way of sharing the experience of being human. Its exhortations matter less than the intimate connection with his readers. It's at its best in understated vignettes epitomizing, for example, the complexity of having both principles and emotions. Of having two heads. Yes, he considers himself a pacifist, he told Timmy, until the moment someone threatens his son.

> "What if he has a gun or something? Would you try to kill him?"
> "I guess so," I said.
> Timmy looked at me for a second. "What kind of pacifist is that?"
> "The father kind," I told him.[37]

Fittingly for a book written to pass to his children "the sound of your father's voice," O'Brien performed the reading for the audio version, a process he found "grueling, emotionally and otherwise."[38]

O'Brien joked that Houghton Mifflin Harcourt pushed the release date from Father's Day to October 2019 half anticipating his death, a solid marketing windfall—it's a refrain he used for the Matthews documentary and for this biography. On the book tour, O'Brien met up with old friends Phil Caputo, Carolyn Forché, and the poet Naomi Shihab Nye in Florida, and new friends Novick and Matthews, plus Iraq War writers Matt Gallagher and Elliot Ackerman, in New York. Gayle Roby came to a reading in Boston, where they shared a good last hug.

The reviews were kind, glowing even. But the book didn't receive enough attention by O'Brien's standard. Sales were underwhelming. O'Brien fumed. "Don't get him started," Meredith said, admitting to tiptoeing around the subject. O'Brien blamed the publisher. His book wasn't its nonfiction-list leader, and he thought the publicity budget paltry. He took his own ad out in *The New York Times Book Review*. Others thought the title and the cover, with a photo of Timmy and Tad in Batman and Robin costumes, hurt the book, promising at most "a literary turn on the how-to parenting manual," to borrow Gallagher's words in *Time*.[39] Nor was it the only epistolary memoir around, Ta-Nehisi Coates's 2015 *Between the World and Me* being the most prominent. O'Brien's couldn't claim originality of form. Two days after *Dad's Maybe Book*'s release date, the *Times* ran an essay by Parul Sehgal about this recent wave, an essay unfortunately written before Sehgal would have had a chance to see O'Brien's book.[40]

It was that much more meaningful, then, for O'Brien to receive notes of appreciation from writer friends. "I absolutely adored your new book, Tim," gushed the subject line of an email from Nye: "*Dad's Maybe Book* mesmerized me. It's the most powerful anti-war book I've ever read. A triumph. Thank you so much." In the fall of 2019, O'Brien couldn't spend all his energy stewing. He was a busy man.

30

THIS IS US

America Fantastica

Amerca started marking the fiftieth anniversary of its war in Việt Nam in 2017. In addition to the eighteen-hour Burns-Novick film, the year saw exhibitions at the New-York Historical Society and the National Archives, and *The New York Times* published its "Vietnam '67" series. O'Brien appeared on Rachel Maddow's 2018 MSNBC documentary special *Betrayal*, about then–presidential candidate Richard Nixon's unconscionable and illegal undermining of President Johnson's peace talks to boost his election prospects. In 2019, the Smithsonian American Art Museum opened *Artists Respond: American Art and the Vietnam War, 1965–1975*.

Coincidentally, the NBC dramatic series *This Is Us* decided it was time to bring in the war. Executive producer Dan Fogelman first read *The Things They Carried* as a required summer book for entering freshmen at the University of Pennsylvania. It became a lifelong "touchstone" text. He constantly referenced it during brainstorming sessions, sessions that mostly felt "silly" because no one on the team knew much at all about the war. A young co-showrunner suggested they consult O'Brien. Fogelman never would have imagined presuming to ask him.

O'Brien joined them in Los Angeles in mid-March 2018. O'Brien's demeanor surprised Fogelman. Down-to-earth in his cap and jeans. "Quiet.
Shy, until you get to know him." The room was filled with about a dozen
people, mostly thirtysomething L.A. screenwriters:

> He took like six smoke breaks outside before we really got started.
>
> And then we took him through our (very loose plan). And Tim
> started going. He would listen, process, think. Sometimes he'd come
> up with something immediately, sometimes he would get excited like
> a little boy and race into the room after lunch bursting at the seams
> ready to floor us with a story or idea. When Tim gets excited, you can
> see the little boy in him . . . the little boy who would become a man
> who loved telling stories. And he had great ones.
>
> Day after day he filled in all the details. Jack's experience of the
> draft. The location of our Vietnam village. Fishing in a boat, using
> grenades . . . and a terrible accident. He would call bullshit on our
> screenwriter-y notions. He would support young writers' pitches and
> you could watch their chest swell with pride.

Kevin Falls, a writer who'd been brought on for season 3, described O'Brien
as "channeling" his experiences very visually.

Before arriving, O'Brien had emailed photos from Việt Nam, a few of
his, a few from those BuddyWolf had gathered from Alpha Company. He'd
been reviewing the photos anyway as he continued to work on Matthews's
film and on *Dad's Maybe Book*. The book included one of them, of O'Brien
squatting next to a Vietnamese girl whom he described to Fogelman as
"the little girl in my head" initially imagined for the TV story, "dead in a
round boat on a sunny day in Quang Ngai Province" after the hand grenade accident. The character would become the boy, Lanh, in the aired
episode—in Lahn, one can detect the spirit of the actual girl killed in the
crossfire who has haunted O'Brien ever since.

The thirtysomethings were to O'Brien earnest babes in the woods who
didn't know thing one about soldiering. They didn't know the language;
they couldn't pull off the gruff dialogue. By the end of the month, O'Brien
agreed to help. The money was ridiculously good. He liked the people, and
he wanted them to get it right.

O'Brien worked on *This Is Us* from late March through August via email and telephone, and a week in September on set at Lake Piru in Ventura County. Although only receiving episode co-writing credit for "Vietnam" with Fogelman and "Songbird Road: Part One" with Falls, O'Brien contributed to the entire Việt Nam story. The show needed a wartime tragedy that would forever estrange Jack Pearson from his brother Nick. That event would be the accidental death of Lanh while Nick was fishing with grenades. Jack was on the beach, so couldn't know exactly what happened and blamed his malcontent little brother. O'Brien didn't receive credit for the "Six Thanksgivings" episode, for example, but Nick's speech about the death of his beloved commander from intel provided by the battalion's Vietnamese barber is all O'Brien, adapted from the death of Lt. Col. Barnes by sappers that sad night on LZ Gator.[1]

O'Brien wrote his not-fleeing-to-Canada experience into the story by having the drafted Nick head north only to turn back. Jack wakes up in their motel room the morning of the planned border crossing to find Nick gone, army-bound. The women wailing about the boy's death reprise the too-familiar lament from O'Brien's tour that he first wrote into *Going After Cacciato*. He'd told Falls about it on set at the Vietnamese village constructed on the shores of Lake Piru.

The lake was a backup plan after a San Diego beach fell through. O'Brien identified a village at the mouth of the Sông Trà Khúc in Quảng Ngãi that the filming location could reasonably represent (with the background mountains added by computer). He zeroed in on such details. Jack finds Nick at Alpha Company, LZ Gloria, in the Americal Division—it might as well have been Gator. O'Brien double-checked the uniforms. They weren't dirty enough. He wished the production could capture the soil's redness. The nighttime battle got it wrong by having a blaze of small-arms fire, when in reality the Vietnamese enemy fired one at a time as they popped out of holes to minimize exposure. But the scene couldn't drag out that long. O'Brien at least managed to ensure that the audience never sees the VC, as he never did. When a character loses his foot, O'Brien insisted he cry out to hold it, cradling it and carrying it with him for the dust-off. That shoot lasted until three in the morning.

O'Brien corrected an actor who had wanted to wear a military soft cap in the field. "Only weenies wore those," O'Brien said, meaning noncombatants. The guy pulled out a photo from his wallet of his father in Việt Nam: "Are you calling my dad a weenie?" O'Brien had already gone home and so couldn't protest when Jack Pearson (Milo Ventimiglia) wore a pristine white tee in the remote village. The crew "loved how much he cared," Fogelman says of O'Brien. They "loved his wit and intelligence." O'Brien became fast friends with Griffin Dunne, who played the older Nick Pearson.

One O'Brien suggestion didn't make the show. He wanted to complicate Jack's character in a way that the show didn't have the time or inclination to do. Jack's tendency to caretake his younger brother and his soldiers can be overbearing: "Beyond that," O'Brien wrote to the writing team, "Jack had a tendency to become nearly a tyrant at times, taking things into his own hands, almost trying to lead his brother's and his son's lives for them—as when Jack tries to 'remake' Nicky during the war and fails disastrously. Again—all out of love." O'Brien wanted Jack's black-and-white, take-charge hero complex to play out in the war by having him lead a couple of guys on a night mission to a little store on Highway 1, wrecking the place searching for a VC supply cache. The two women and old man who live there "scream and cry and beg." Jack's cobbled squad finds the makings for homemade mines. They set the place on fire, "payback for Robinson and their other comrades who were wounded or killed—"

> And MAYBE it turns out . . . that Jack had totally misread the situation. MAYBE these munitions were . . . intended for local defense **against** the VC. Or MAYBE—more likely—the VC had **compelled** the little store to become a munitions depot of sorts. MAYBE the poppa-san and mama-sans who owned and ran the store had no choice at all, yet had lost everything they had when Jack and his men burned the place down. AND JACK HAS TO CARRY THIS BURDEN FOR THE REST OF HIS LIFE.

O'Brien imagined Jack's platoon leader telling this story decades later to Jack's son, explaining it with the career-long refrain: "People can do bad things for love . . . People can lie for love, cheat for love, kill for love. And I should know—I was in Nam."[2]

◊   ◊   ◊

The first episode partly set in Việt Nam aired on October 16, 2018, as O'Brien was doing the final polishing and cutting to *Dad's Maybe Book*. The results impressed him. These young writers, toddlers if even alive during his war, had listened to him and got the "feel of the times" right. "It was fun to watch your own words come out of an actor's mouth," he told Aaron Matthews when the filmmaker was there in mid-November. "It's fun. It's almost a high." He looked forward to finishing the book and returning to normal life—playing more golf, eating in a restaurant, hanging out with the boys. He sometimes felt neglectful or distracted, but he also imagined it was good for Timmy and Tad to see their father be "productive and determined" and finish what he'd started so many years before. It was their first time living their dad's process.[3]

The War and Peace of Tim O'Brien offers a window on the O'Brien family's life. The boys are very direct about how their father's writing day dictates the house's mood. His bad days are everyone's as he withdraws into himself, his aggressive silence an oppressive pall that can be hard to live with. We see O'Brien scrubbing the kitchen floor while working on the book in his head. We also see him being a dad—playing Ping-Pong with Tad while talking about his schoolwork, playing basketball, watching their basketball games, overreacting to their smartphone and video game screen time. The intensity of O'Brien's adoration and pride is palpable.

Matthews's film offers only a sampling. "Hands up!" O'Brien shouts in the film at a son's basketball game, relatively tamely. More often his loud, coaching-from-the-bleachers encouragement carries the in-the-moment bite of disappointment from a father who knows in his heart that his kid can do better. You did not want to be an O'Brien son's high school teacher whose testing and grading struck O'Brien as wrongheaded or unfair. While he'd mellowed in the past few years, he hadn't entirely retired his trigger-happy anger. Most of it and the worst of it he reserved for only Meredith to hear:

> He and I have times where he's just beside himself over things. Like the photographs being placed in the wrong spot or the type size or somebody not writing him back. Or when he's just so overwhelmed by these pieces of the puzzle that are not in place. Especially with the magic, but probably with writing, too, he saves all his emotion for me.

With other people he puts on the face or whatever. But with me, he can show it all. And sometimes it's just really hard to be privy to all of it. Because Tim lets all his emotions out. When he's really mad and throws—well, not throwing things but slamming things down. And oftentimes it's toward technology. That technology. He and technology don't get along.[4]

One can see that rage for ease—is that what it is?—in their two homes' décor: not a piece of extra furniture, no clutter, in beiges and whites (but for the colorful mask collection on the guest half-bath wall). The family's one attempt to have a pet dog did not take.

For Meredith, O'Brien's fastidiousness and temper were no match for his kindness, sensitivity, good humor, attentive listening, and brilliance. The smartest, hardest-working person Meredith ever met. Every day with him delivered some surprise, some gem, some new delight. A story she hadn't heard. A truly interesting soul on the phone or visiting. A clever notion. A remarkable insight or turn of phrase. And she fascinated him, too. Beyond being his literary confidante, sounding board, and first reader, she was a creative artist in her own right. Her physical fitness always impressed him: "She can lift a couch, with me on it!"

Their sons academically excelled. Timmy had become a traveling Rubik's Cube competitor, a hobby that required a great deal of alone time, practicing, perfecting. In college, he would major in international relations and dabble in philosophy, while back home his brother, Tad, immersed himself in the mathematics of poker, studying the game for hours upon hours, and usually schooling his dad in games at the kitchen table. Neither son fell very far from the paternal tree. They got their patience from their mother.

Except when reading—he usually read two or three books a week, a mix of fiction and nonfiction, a fair amount of biography and military history—the spry O'Brien couldn't sit still. The film captures a little of this, with the magic shows, the cleaning, some back-deck plant tending. Well into his seventies, he did the yard work for both homes. He put up the substantial exterior Christmas decorations and clambered atop the Onion Creek home's flat roof to trim overhanging branches. His one home-life indulgence of mindlessness: true-crime and serial killer shows. He could watch them for several hours. Meredith compared it to gambling, something that occupies his mind without requiring much thought.[5] It's also familiar turf for O'Brien the writer, a way to revisit the mysteries of character, violence, and evil, without having to put in any work.

Matthews was ready to take *The War and Peace of Tim O'Brien* to spring and summer film festivals when COVID-19 hit, upheaving the globe. The World Health Organization declared the pandemic on March 11, 2020; by the end of the year, the Centers for Disease Control and Prevention calculated a U.S. death toll of 350,831.[6] On May 25, the murder by police of George Floyd in O'Brien's Minneapolis sparked a summer of protests for racial justice, with right-wing self-proclaimed militias mobilizing in response to those protests as well as to state governments' public health measures for controlling the pandemic. The civil schism that had wedged into America with the 2016 presidential campaign, in which Donald Trump defeated Hillary Clinton, widened considerably in 2020 and would only get worse. Not since the Việt Nam era had the United States experienced such a vicious, potentially explosive culture war.

The O'Brien family hunkered down during COVID. O'Brien's age, his medical history, and his smoking made him especially vulnerable; Meredith's diabetes was a preexisting condition. They were in the first group to receive the vaccine (which wrecked them both for a few days). Timmy and Tad completed the school year and attended classes the entire next year remotely. When Tad caught COVID, he and his mom stayed at Cobblestone while his dad and brother moved to Onion Creek, the family not reuniting for several weeks.

Even before COVID, O'Brien was a homebody. Partly because he traveled so much for talks and campus visits, when home he just wanted to be home; partly because he was still little Timmy O'Brien who relished alone time. Friends felt lucky when he joined Meredith for a social outing. At the beginning of the pandemic, playing Ping-Pong with Timmy outside, he slipped on a wet leaf while reaching for a shot "and ended up doing the splits at age seventy-three," pulling or tearing his hamstring and injuring his knee "even worse." He didn't seek professional care because of the virus. He planted himself on the couch. It took a couple of months to heal. He didn't venture into the world during the pre-vaccine era (before mid-December 2020), and only a little after.

In June 2020, O'Brien found himself drawn into a promising film adaptation of *The Things They Carried*. David Zander, who had optioned the rights, brought in Rupert Sanders as the director and Tom Hardy as a producer, working off a screenplay written by Scott Smith. Hardy, one of the most impressive actors of his generation, would play Lt. Jimmy Cross. O'Brien wasn't crazy about the idea of a film adaptation, but if one were to be made—and this one felt very likely, especially with Hardy's enthusiasm—he wanted it done as right as possible. Phone calls, conference calls, and long emails consumed his time. Zander and his team relished O'Brien's advice: "Tim is a genius." In November, various outlets announced the upcoming feature film, with production to begin in 2021. In addition to Hardy, the planned cast included Pete Davidson, Stephan James, Bill Skarsgård, and Tye Sheridan (slated to play the O'Brien character).

Financial and other setbacks stalled the project for the foreseeable future. For one thing, production and insurance costs skyrocketed because of the pandemic. Zander eventually purchased the rights outright. With his oldest son headed off to the pricey University of Chicago, O'Brien welcomed the lump sum from the sale.

The boys were starting to leave the nest, and Meredith resumed professional acting. Once life approached normal in the summer of 2021, she began a performance streak of seven plays in the next couple of years, including lead turns as Oscar Wilde in *Gross Indecency: The Three Trials of Oscar Wilde*, a homeless woman in the premiere of *rain falls special on me*, and Martha in *Who's Afraid of Virginia Woolf?* There was a Bollywood rendition of *Twelfth Night*, and parts in a staged reading of Agatha Christie's *The Hollow*, in Henrik Ibsen's *The Lady from the Sea*, and in Peter Rothstein's *All Is Calm*. O'Brien was thrilled for her. She adapted some of *July, July*'s stories into short scripts.

The world had begun to figure out how to carry on remotely. O'Brien did his gigs from home. Life sputtered slowly back to life. On March 2, 2021, *The War and Peace of Tim O'Brien* was released digitally and on cable video on demand, and O'Brien stepped up for interviews.[7] Florentine Films held a series of online conversations in advance of airing *Hemingway*. O'Brien participated in the first one, "Hemingway and Childhood." The ever-proud father wears a University of Chicago ball cap as he talks about one of the saddest sentences he's ever read, from a letter Hemingway wrote to his father, who had objected to the frank and modern content of his son's first major book, *In Our Time*, and returned the copies Ernest had sent him. He was all of twenty-five years old: "'If I write an ugly story that might be hateful to you or to Mother the next one might be one that you would like exceedingly.'" Hemingway, O'Brien says, "is essentially pleading with his father to like his work"; he's "talking to a father he partly idolized, almost worshipped in many ways, but also found wanting." O'Brien was talking about his own father. He knew that sadness all too well.[8]

Flying without Meredith to settle Timmy into the university in September 2021 was the first major trip outside the home for O'Brien since the pandemic began. By that point, he was working steadily on what would be billed as his last novel: *America Fantastica*.

At the end of *The War and Peace of Tim O'Brien*, Tim and Meredith are lounging on the back patio of the Cobblestone home. It's evening. He's wearing a white tee with a sketch of Timmy's face printed on it. *Dad's Maybe Book*, O'Brien tells Meredith, feels finished. He feels finished, as in no more books. She doesn't believe him—he has the same look in his eyes that he had fifteen years before, when he declared *July, July* the last one.

> "There is this character named Angie Bing. She's a bank teller. She's four feet nine inches tall. She's got this tinny voice."
> "You've already started to work on it."
> "I've written a few pages."

The film ends there, with this characteristic understatement. O'Brien had been kicking around a cluster of characters for over fifteen years. He has the same look in his eyes because he has the same characters in his head.

By December 2004, O'Brien had drafted two chapters in a computer file labeled "Jakarta." The unnamed first-person narrator, a thirty-seven-year-old man at the end of his journalism career, is on a flight home from Jakarta to California. Beside him sits Susan Booth, a twenty-six-year-old woman and a tycoon's daughter, whose story he had covered. She and her new husband, on their honeymoon in the Philippines, were kidnapped for a ransom. After a fruitless several-nation, months-long search, the father refused to pay the ransom. Her primitive captivity on an unknown island lasted thirteen months, the duration of O'Brien's tour in Việt Nam, such that he could draw on his experiences for her descriptions. Even her reasons for being there circled around O'Brien's, love and a certain willingness: "'We were dumbshit in love,' the girl said, 'and that made us dumber. Flashing cash. Tipping huge. Truth is, we were asking for it. Down on our knees, actually—begging. And we got it.'"

She's been free for all of two weeks. She reluctantly tells her story, a story of betrayal by the husband, which the skeptical narrator doesn't buy.

The second chapter opens with the narrator in his childhood home. "There are two Santa Monicas," this chapter begins, one "a fairy-tale of spangled gowns and improbable breasts and faces from the tabloids," the other "a neighborhood of tidy, more or less identical stucco houses separated by fourteen feet of cement and scorched grass." Much of this section would survive, with passages verbatim or near verbatim, in chapter 3 of *America Fantastica*. The narrator is now Junior, as Boyd Halverson would also be called in the published novel. Junior at home watches on television the United States go to war in 2003 driven by "the sanctimonious, slack-jawed bullyisms of a nitwit in cowboy boots," President George W. Bush. "Please note," the narrator adds: "I like Ike. I'm a devoted Republican. Thus the point I make is not political; the point is to place events in moral context. Oh, and this bit of context, too: A year or so earlier I had trod on a piece of human slush in the wreckage of a bombed-out nightclub in south Bali." Three weeks later, the news of Susan Booth's freedom breaks . . . and the draft ends.[9]

The story alludes to the October 12, 2002, terrorist bombings of a nightclub and the bar across the street in Bali, as well as the August 5, 2003, bombing of the Marriott hotel in Jakarta. O'Brien sought the moral urgency of the time through characters living through it if not necessarily of it. It's the familiar motive. But the war against terrorism, and the wars in Afghanistan and in Iraq, dragged on, confounding O'Brien's ability to write a narrative within the ongoing historical moment. The "Jakarta" draft also suggests that O'Brien is imagining a highly fictionalized version of himself had he pursued journalism. Sounding a lot like a young Tim

O'Brien leaving *The Washington Post* behind, Junior relishes his liberation from "the soul-sucking burden of moral disengagement. I could have an opinion. What pleasure—what release—to yell at my TV."

The idea of "Jakarta" lingered. In May 2007, O'Brien produced a list of eighty-nine "words and phrases for Jakarta" that included such gems as *hebetudinous, polyonymous, fogram, armillary, wamble,* and *calefacient.* Item 60, *zabernism,* defined in his notes as "the misuse of military power; aggression; bullying" (pasted from the internet), stays in the thematic orbit of the 2004 draft.[10] He imagined "Jakarta" as a long two-part story, then a novella, then a novel, but never achieved a solid vision even as he wished to hang on to the narrator's voice.

For two years he'd also been pursuing a separate narrative, which by the end of 2007 had reached sixty-six single-spaced pages over six chapters (or sections) in a file called "Odd Things, SUPERNEW." The first section begins with Boyd Halverson, a JCPenney manager in Fulda, California, an inveterate liar, robbing the local bank and leaving town with the bank teller, the diminutive, super chatty Angie Bing, in tow. The second begins, "There are two Santa Monicas." Plotwise, and with much of the language preserved, this draft takes the story into chapter 16 of *America Fantastica.*[11] Angie's boyfriend Randy Zapf is giving chase; the reader knows about Boyd's divorce from Evelyn and the death of their toddler son, in the draft named Tad. Tad O'Brien was a toddler when his dad wrote this material. The work stalled.

In late 2018, O'Brien was talking about a new Jakarta storyline, with the strangers meeting on the way to Jakarta followed by a plane crash on a remote island, their jungle survival tale, and then the main story, their struggle to survive the return to civilization. But he couldn't figure out the main story's happenings. The idea died. Matthews filmed O'Brien introducing Meredith to Angie Bing on April 9, 2019. O'Brien had proposed the scene to show him and Meredith just sitting together, doing nothing, a contrast to all the purposeful talking in the film's rough cut. At the time, O'Brien was wrapping up the revision and production of *Dad's Maybe Book,* turning toward its promotion, being a dad, and soon working practically full time on the film adaptation of *The Things They Carried.*

In January 2021—after the mob assault on the U.S. Capitol, on January 6, to prevent the routine transfer of power—he submitted the revisions to

Going After Cacciato that disentangled the chronology problem of soldiers' deaths. In February, the COVID booster knocked him and Meredith out for a few days, followed almost immediately by the winter storm that paralyzed much of Texas for eight days. As he emailed on the fifteenth: "I have my hands full here with the freezing weather, the pool water pipes, the pool pump, the on-and-off internet, the rolling power outages, the heat, the fireplace, two school projects due Wednesday, two manuscripts to read for my class, a half dozen stories to reread for the Hemingway [online panel], and a movie script that needs to be effing FINISHED."

During this same intense period, O'Brien's brother, Greg, received a diagnosis of type 2 high-grade bladder cancer with micropapillary variant. The long-term life expectancy was not good. What irony and guilt: O'Brien, not Kathy or Greg, had the lifelong smoking addiction, yet they were the ones cancer went after. The initial recommendation was an urgent removal of the bladder, prostate, and surrounding lymph nodes, because of the aggressiveness of the micropapillary variant. Greg researched and consulted on his own, opting against his brother's advice for another node removal, in April. Further testing revealed a fraction of the original micropapillary variant determination. Bacillus Calmette-Guerin (BCG) immunotherapy was now an option. Greg began that course of treatment in June, to immediate positive results.

The aborted film adaptation behind him, O'Brien returned to the dormant "Jakarta" and "Odd Things" material, by the end of April putting in three to four hours a day toward a novel. In mid-May, while cleaning dishes, he had his "eureka" moment for bringing the two stories together. Boyd and Angie's would be the backbone, with Evelyn the twenty-six-year-old daughter of a tycoon whom Boyd meets on a plane to Jakarta. From inception, the characters had trouble with the truth. It made ready sense to transport them from the early war-on-terror period with its lies to the last year of President Donald Trump's administration, the nation's new moral plight. A January article in O'Brien's old paper, *The Washington Post*, tallied "30,573 untruths" from Trump during his four years in office, "averaging about 21 erroneous claims a day," with 503 landing the day before the 2020 election.[12]

From the twenty-seven-thousand-word "Odd Things" draft of 2007, O'Brien hit seventy thousand words by Thanksgiving 2021 and ninety thousand by January 11, 2022. He usually wrote in the dark early-morning hours. He refused to suffer for this one—the instant a writing session stopped being fun, he left his desk. Were the book to become a chore, he had no qualms about letting it go. O'Brien finished the first version of *America Fantastica* (about 118,000 words) and emailed it to select friends and readers on March 3, the fastest and most fun novel he'd ever written.

Boyd's personal and professional lies catch up to him upon learning about his father-in-law's shipbuilding shortcuts and bribes that caused three ships to sink, killing a lot of sailors. To prevent Boyd from reporting the truth, Evelyn's father exposes Boyd's lifetime of fraudulence. His son dead, his wife remarried, and doomed to working at a small-town JCPenney, Boyd robs the bank before a foiled suicide attempt. End of part I. Part II tracks the comeuppance and potential redemption arc for all the characters. Only one gets away scot-free—Evelyn's dad, the heartless magnate, because his global business empire makes him all but untouchable. O'Brien slides COVID into the story without overplaying it. The pandemic provides a means to off one vile character. The story unfolds as a road trip, a flight, and a chase, returning O'Brien to his roots in *Northern Lights* and *Going After Cacciato*.

The pinnacle of Boyd's emotional journey is witnessing a veteran of Iraq and Afghanistan (three tours) kill himself by smashing a hole into a frozen Minnesota lake and plunging in. The hole freezes back over at night, and the next day Boyd gazes at the dead man's red parka "pressed up against the ice scab."[13] The two men had recently spent an evening exchanging confessions. The scene reverberates with O'Brien's impulse, from 1994 into 1995, to throw himself out his Cambridge apartment window, and with the final passage of *The Things They Carried*, of Tim imagining Timmy ice-skating with Linda, gripping onto that undying image for dear life, "riding the melt beneath the blades" and "trying to save Timmy's life with a story."[14] Boyd's reengagement with life reflects that of other O'Brien characters—William Cowling from *The Nuclear Age* and David Todd from "July '69," for instance—as the seventy-five-year-old O'Brien, writing in the spring of 2022, seems to have been taking stock.

From his readers, O'Brien wanted feedback on pace, momentum, and chronology. With *In the Lake of the Woods*, he had faced the big question of whether to dramatize the Mỹ Lai massacre directly. Would doing so limit the book's transcendence beyond the specific event? Would critics harp on its sensationalism? The gamble paid off. Now, he wondered whether to engage directly with the new era's trumped-up conspiracies and other public falsehoods, thereby risking confining the novel's received import to the moment and risking knee-jerk dismissal; or to absorb the body politic's affliction quietly into the novel's character study, risking his readers' overlooking the broader commentary. The draft sent to friends took this quiet approach. Then he changed his mind, even knowing half the country—the half who continued to support former President Trump and embrace misinformation, the MAGA (Make America Great Again) Republicans—would hate the book. O'Brien was never one to back down from a moral tussle. He'd get to be the narrator from "Jakarta" screaming at the television.

The result is the seven full and two partial "mythomania" chapters in the published novel. A narrator rhapsodically presents dozens upon dozens of symptoms of the lying contagion, some O'Brien took from the real world, some he giggled into being. The first chapter ends with a late-night radio talk show host claiming "that Lee Harvey Oswald '*war nicht so schlect*,'" a repurposing of his host's line that Hitler wasn't so bad when O'Brien was recuperating from his college Vespa accident in Hersbruck, Germany.[15] The novel's Truth Tellers organization is a less insidious and a leaderless version of QAnon, the far-right conspiracy network that emerged in 2017. Instead of having the mythomania voice-over float above and parallel to the characters' journeys, O'Brien involves Boyd before the novel's present. The former global news correspondent and consummate fibber was bored, voiceless, and exiled. He became a legendary fabricator of some of the most creative and viral lies infecting the nation. The novel implicates postmodern discourse in the right's weaponizing of epistemological uncertainty, dating perhaps to the White House official who, in the second year of the Iraq War, told a reporter that "we create our own reality."[16]

America Fantastica culminates a literary career obsessed with the lies people tell, to others, to themselves, exploiting ones, noble ones, ontological ones. O'Brien regards all his works as pieces of a whole, which the new novel affirms with echoes from earlier books. The most up-front is the epigraph from W. B. Yeats's "The Stare's Nest by My Window," the exact lines also the epigraph from *July, July* as well as a quotation in *The Nuclear Age*. It's most apt in the new novel given that the poem is about the Irish

Civil War: "no clear fact can be discerned," the second stanza says, and the last stanza bemoans that there's "More substance in our enmities / Than in our love." Culottes, unearned Silver Stars, and menacing hoes have appeared before; Boyd's desire to "crawl inside" Evelyn and "sleep there" has precedents in "The Things They Carried" and *In the Lake of the Woods*; his mendacity mantra that if something "sounds true" then "it is true" evokes the seductive message of "How to Tell a True War Story," where literal truth takes a back seat to something "truly told" that "makes the stomach believe."[17] As *The Wall Street Journal*'s review would note, "as a travesty of the American dream of reinvention, it has an essential point in common with his war novels. It, too, appreciates the addictive pleasure of spinning a story, of making things up."[18]

When at the end of the novel the polyonymous Boyd Halverson—aka Otis Birdsong, Junior, and Blackie—calls for a double date with Peggy Shaughnessy from Eau Claire, Wisconsin, and with her invented version of herself, Enni from Finland, O'Brien exaggerates a fundamental truth about the various selves we all possess, by circumstance, by creative choice. As he was writing the book, his son Timmy became Tim, a grown-up aspiring to an identity apart from his childhood, but he will always be both. And neither, not entirely. Like his father before him. The story we tell ourselves of who we are is, in the end, a story. A myth. A lie. So much of our life stories we've forgotten, after all, a point emphasized in *Dad's Maybe Book*:

> What we call memory is failed memory. What we call memory is forgetfulness. And if memory has failed—failed so colossally, failed so apocalyptically—how can we pretend to be faithful to it? How can we pretend to tell the truth? Is one small fraction of the truth the truth?[19]

Of all O'Brien's books, *America Fantastica* is the least skeptical in its agnosticism. Boyd mocks the idea of God, but while Angie's self-appointed mission to save troubled souls on God's behalf may be a self-delusional fantasy she needs to give her life purpose, well, it serves her and other characters well. The novel can't deny the possibility that Angie *is* God's agent. That God is.

In late April 2022, O'Brien was revising away. On May 18 in New York, he formally became an elected member of the American Academy of Arts and Letters. Erik Hansen visited Austin for a Memorial Day weekend of golfing and gabbing. O'Brien sent the finished manuscript to a couple of editors, and on June 28 he heard from Peter Hubbard at Mariner, an imprint of HarperCollins, who called it "the most enjoyable book he'd read in years," funny as hell: "Tell us what we can do to make you have faith in us." Within two months, the parties had a deal. The O'Brien family took the stage for a Q&A after a screening of Matthews's film at the Austin Film Society on July 23, his and Matthews's first in-person event together. A second joint appearance on August 13, at Fort Snelling on the banks of the Mississippi in St. Paul, gave O'Brien and Hansen more time together. Erik shared two chapters from his novel in progress. Tim "tore into them with his usual rigor and razor-sharp editor's scalpel."

O'Brien underwent cataract surgery on one eye on September 13, leaving him blind and panicked until his sight slowly began to return. It took a month to restore vision, in time for VonnegutFest in Indianapolis marking Kurt Vonnegut's one hundredth birthday, on Veterans Day.

In November, while working through his publisher's edits and queries, O'Brien briefly considered a new title, "American Stickup," to communicate both the storyline and "Trump et. al. sticking up our constitutional democracy." But *America Fantastica*'s elegance won out.

Hansen had an angiogram on December 1. The doctors halted an ablation two weeks later mid-procedure when they discovered the extent of the problem. On February 1, he received a triple bypass, mitral valve replacement, ablation, and an atrial clip (other complications protracted his recovery). COVID laid up Meredith in January 2023. Late February brought O'Brien his own cardiac scare, dangerously high blood pressure that took several weeks of intensive management to stabilize. On February 24, he learned that William Crawford Woods, his friend from his twenties in Washington, had a week to live, ambushed by cancer. A two-word email from O'Brien the next day: "William died." For Woods, there was some consolation knowing that his second book, a work of creative nonfiction and family history, a years-long labor of love, *Stand in the Fire: Three American Soldiers and Their Wars, 1900–1950*, would be published in May. O'Brien had been Woods's trusted reader on the project.

O'Brien finished reviewing his novel's page proofs on May 17. "DONE, NO MORE, NEVER AGAIN, FINI, THE END, OUT OF HERE!!" he shouted over email. The family took a vacation to Minnesota at the end of June, staying with Greg's family. On July 19, O'Brien with great relief saw in advance *Kirkus*'s starred review. Despite occasional stumbles, the review concludes, "it's one of those books where you can sense the author enjoying himself and it's fun to be along for the ride."[20] Other positive prepublication press followed, a good review in *Booklist* (August 1) and an admiring profile in *Publishers Weekly* (July 24). O'Brien beamed when the book received a late-breaking enthusiastic blurb from Haruki Murakami.

Meredith had hip replacement surgery on September 7, her hip having degenerated as the result of years of strenuous exercise. She was hobbling around her hospital room a few hours later, although the next two to three months were physically and emotionally trying. Timmy-now-Tim left home for a year's study at the London School of Economics. O'Brien turned seventy-seven on October 1. Twenty days later, he began a six-week book tour. A few days before, *The Boston Globe* praised the generosity and empathy accompanying the novel's angry sting: "*America Fantastica* holds a cracked mirror up to a poisoned zeitgeist and dares you not to laugh. Resistance is futile."[21]

The day of the *Globe* review, O'Brien braced himself for the "evil lurking down the pike." That evil pounced from the pages of *The New York Times Book Review*. It wasn't the only unamused review, but it was the meanest. Had O'Brien not added the mythomania sections, the reviewer, Noah Hawley, would have found the novel a successfully entertaining "comic misadventure." But the "veneer of topicality" ruined the book for Hawley, overburdening the characters with carrying the nation's blight—which the novel doesn't actually do. For Hawley, the novel fails to make a single person of the Boyd Halverson seeking death or redemption and the Boyd Halverson who mongers misinformation for the Truth Tellers: "O'Brien has created a novel that reads more like a cartoon."[22] Yet by definition satire partakes of the cartoon. *In the Lake of the Woods* had the advantage of exploring a national crisis twenty-five years in the past; *America Fantastica*'s standing might improve with the passage of time.

Hawley's review upset O'Brien, not for any wound to his ego but because of the stakes for his legacy and sales. In response, he paid for an ad that ran in the December 17 issue of the *Times Book Review* featuring blurbs from eleven other reviews, including three from publications listing *America Fantastica* as one of the best books of the year.

In interviews surrounding the novel's October 24 release, O'Brien declared it his last. As fun as *America Fantastica* was to write, the process still drained him. Severe carpal tunnel pain made the prospect physically daunting. He typed with one finger, and even that hurt. The tour did his body no favors. He turned down invitations to write, including one from *Harper's* to cover the Republican National Convention in July. *For the zillionth time, getting old sucks.* His hearing had declined enough that Meredith nearly always spoke with a raised voice around the house, and his hearing aids demanded frequent adjusting.

Into the new year he kept as busy as his pain and mobility allowed. Meredith started preparing the Cobblestone house to sell once Tad graduated in May. O'Brien went through his magic illusions, reteaching himself the contraptions to sell. They began planning an early summer European vacation to northern Italy, Switzerland, and Paris. Come September, Tad would join his brother at the University of Chicago. His sons' brilliance and sweet natures thrilled O'Brien to the core.

Before and during the book tour, O'Brien teased interviewers with an opening scene for a new novel, if he were to write one. He told me about it over the phone one afternoon that September. Meredith had shared a story with him on their back patio a few nights previously. A friend's elderly mother, who lived alone, walked into her bedroom from her shower to find a stranger asleep naked on her bed. "Now that would be a great story, wouldn't it? I'd start with her in the bedroom doorway seeing the man, right there in the first sentence—it's like with Gregor Samsa in Kafka. Of course then you have to write the middle and the end. Where would you go from there? Where would it take you? Too bad you can't just have a beginning. But wouldn't that be a terrific beginning?"

EPILOGUE

Peace Is a Shy Thing is the product of friendship and love, possessing all the advantages and faults thereof.

I met Tim O'Brien in the fall of 2003, when I brought him to visit classes and give a reading at Hendrix College, outside Little Rock, Arkansas, where I'd been teaching for two years. We were both new fathers, our eldest children born three months apart in the year our nation launched the second Iraq war. We spent some time together in November 2005 at the University of Hawaii at Mānoa's "Thirty Years After" conference. In 2007, during O'Brien's stint as the Morgan writer in residence at the University of North Carolina–Chapel Hill, I joined O'Brien and Loyd Little for a panel on telling war stories—I'm a combat veteran of the first Iraq war, in 1990–1991. The three of us and our host, the writer Bland Simpson, lunched beforehand at the posh Carolina Club. Before our food came, Little entertained us with a show-and-tell of artifacts from Việt Nam. From his bag he pulled out a punji stake from a pit trap. The second item I forget. He saved the shock for last, when he planted on O'Brien's white place mat a skull he said was Vietnamese. Some of the teeth, he said, he had affixed himself, souvenirs from his exes' dental procedures.

The years stuttered along. Whenever I traveled to Austin, Texas, to conduct research at the Harry Ransom Center, we'd get together for a meal and drinks. Our conversations centered around writing and war. After a lot of time together at the 2016 Hemingway conference, our interactions increased, and our friendship deepened.

In July 2018, we were in Paris for the next Hemingway conference, the one during which he finished drafting *Dad's Maybe Book*. At the Closerie des Lilas, at an outside corner table steps away from the Marshal Ney statue that figures prominently in *The Sun Also Rises*—we couldn't see even the tip of Ney's upraised sword through the bushes separating the brasserie from the sidewalk—O'Brien broached the subject of this biography. We continued the conversation over the next couple of days. For years he'd said he never wanted a biography written about him. He preferred his private life *his*. He worried about hurting others, whose privacy and right to their stories he respected: "People matter more than books."

What changed his mind? The near-fatal illness of February 2017 was a factor. He believed a biography inevitable; he wanted to be alive to be a resource. Letting Aaron Matthews into his home to film the documentary proved more fun than O'Brien had anticipated and helped relax his resistance.

Then, in March 2018, in the wake of Burns and Novick's *The Vietnam War*, the Vietnamese American novelist Lan Cao published a piece in *The New York Times* accusing *The Things They Carried* of being representative of American writing "uninterested in and indifferent to the Vietnamese."[1] An incensed O'Brien called a handful of friends to vent and to ask their advice on how—or whether—to respond. The Vietnamese writers he knew had always told him that that was *their* job, not his. On those calls he anguished over his legacy being determined by people who didn't know how to read. Cao's article was the proverbial straw that broke the camel's back after decades of charges of racism and sexism in his work, and by association in himself. He wisely decided against writing to the *Times* in his own defense. He let it go. Mortality decreed that he could never have the last word anyway.

Born twenty years apart, we are both middle-class Midwestern kids of the Cold War raised on the chest-thumping films of World War II, both bookish introverts ill-fitted for military service. I know the army intimately: the language, the relationships, the tools of its bloody trade, what it asks of one. He wouldn't have to explain any of it. We both know war's moral injury. We lean the same politically. We love our country but wince at chest-bumping patriotism. We both love making books. I suspect it tickled the former private first class that a former officer, a fuckin' butterbar second lieutenant, would be telling his story.

Deployed to the Persian Gulf when *The Things They Carried* was still first captivating critics and readers, I didn't read it until the late 1990s. I don't know that I'd ever been that moved by a book. I wept. Rat Kiley's shooting up the buffalo may have tapped into a body memory of Mom reading the deaths of the hunting dogs in *Where the Red Fern Grows* to my brothers and me on a long car trip. Or of seeing wild dogs feeding on Iraqi soldiers' corpses. Devastating. I've read, taught, and written about O'Brien's best-known novel too many times now, and with my war over thirty years gone by, to cry anymore.

But I cried researching this book. I teared up over discoveries in documents, recordings, and photographs, and after particularly generous, vulnerable interviews. I cried upon realizing that the 5th of the 46th didn't bother to report to higher command the civilian casualties it had logged; upon watching video of Thanh Nguyen and John Balaban reading poems found in the notebooks of dead Vietnamese soldiers; and upon hearing audio of the Vietnamese American thanking Mỹ Lai anniversary panelists for honoring the dead by publicly remembering them.

I cried when Larry Heinemann died.

I'd met him years before, at the Joiner Center. In July 2019, I drove to Bryan, Texas, to meet him, his partner, and his mobile oxygen tank for lunch. Carried away in our reconnection, we never got around to an interview about O'Brien. When we shook hands goodbye and he thanked me for coming, "for caring," his eyes told me what I would learn a few months later. He'd been diagnosed with stage 4 lung cancer. He expected it to kill him within six months. He asked me to stay mum. As for the novel-in-progress, "I ain't going to be able to finish the thing, not by a long shot, but I want to get to as much of it as I can. Just because I'm sick doesn't mean I should stop writing."

The news closed an afternoon email about the Battle of Suoi Cut. He believed the two infantry battalions and two artillery batteries had been sent for no objective but "to see if we could draw fire." Talk about moral outrage. Then the battle itself:

> It was one hell of a night, and I went through boxes of fifty[-cal] ammo. And the next morning when it got light enough to see, there was meat all over everything and the woodline looked like ruined drapes.

It was the worst night of my life, and the most obscene thing I have ever seen, and up until a couple years ago something I thought [about] just about every day. I don't know about anybody else who was there, American or Vietnamese, but I lost something precious that I have not been able to retrieve, not in more than 50 years. [. . .]

The bulldozer, sent out with the artillery to dig revetments for the 105s, dug a ditch, and we began burying the corpses, or what was left of them; that's when I picked up my AK. One of the first choppers sent out to us carried a load of quick lime (as well as reporters), and after we stripped the corpses we buried the bodies (etc.) like you make a lasagna—a layer of bodies, a layer of quick lime, etc. There was something like 500 corpses. That was the most obscene thing I have ever seen.

But the most obscene thing I have ever seen was the cameraman from one of the networks who asked me if he could stand on the deck of my track and film it. Yeah, sure, why not. So the guy climbed up, stood there, and filmed it for twenty minutes, half an hour; body count porn; fuck you, pal. None of that film was ever going to be broadcast or used in the Ken Burns (or any other) documentary, but somewhere in the film archive of one of the networks is twenty minutes of the most obscene thing I have ever seen. It is, in large part, undoubtedly among the large reasons I wrote 3 books about that fucking war.

This is the battle depicted onscreen in Oliver Stone's *Platoon*. Heinemann emailed a forgotten detail the same evening:

By the middle of the afternoon that corpse smell began to rise, and for the next three days we lived in a world of shit stink and bugs. I don't know what happened to the straight legs, or the artillery, but the 2/22nd moved around plenty and we were busy almost every day. Then on Tet when the war finally arrived in Saigon, we moved straight back to Dau Tieng. That shit stink became a body memory I've had to live with ever since; and imagery provoked by our sense of smell is the richest of all the senses. It is the one thing that film simply cannot handle.

That was November 4, our last contact. Larry died December 11. His story isn't O'Brien's story. Except that it is. Mine, too. And yours.

I cried when Daniel Ellsberg died. The older I get, the more I know my practice as a literary historian is to look into the eyes of those who came before the best I can. Scholarship as séance, keyboard as Ouija board.

The day before the O'Brien family flew out of Paris five and a half years ago, Tim emailed to caution me about accepting his invitation:

> No bull fights, no plane crashes, no submarine searches, no big game hunting. The substance and drama of my life has been the substance and drama of any ordinary human life. I like golf. I like reading books. I like being alone. I love my children. I have spent a good portion of my 71 years sitting at a desk, struggling to make decent sentences. This is to warn you, in other words, that you will find little biographical material (if any at all) that would interest anyone who is not already interested in the books I have written. Which leads to a third observation—also a warning of sorts: I believe in the artistic worth of my books, all but two of them, yet I'm fully aware that I am far from being a prince of the literary world. I am not complaining. I am being realistic.

Because of the "diminishment" of being labeled a "war writer" or a "Vietnam writer."

> But my point here is only that you would be taking on a project that will be viewed, by some if not by a great many others, as of minor importance. Again, I do believe in the value of my work, and I believe the best of it will endure, but that isn't the issue I'm raising with you. Rather, I worry that you may well encounter a "much ado about nothing" response to all your labor.[2]

Even knowing next to nothing of what I would learn, I obviously disagreed.

And I disagree with you now, Tim, today, whatever day it is when someone finishes this book. Shy peace is a worthy thing. Maybe the worthiest.

ACKNOWLEDGMENTS

The primary emotions in telling another person's life story—other people's stories—have been humility, gratitude, and joy. Thank you, Tim, for placing your trust and confidence in me, not to mention for the years of friendship and the legacy of your writing. You didn't read a single page of this biography before publication—thank you for respecting its integrity. Thank you to Meredith, Tim, and Tad O'Brien, for your openheartedness, and to Kathy O'Brien Adjemian and Greg O'Brien.

Beyond the family, several people went above and beyond in sharing and in moral support: Erik Hansen, Aaron Matthews, Bruce Weigl, Jane Reister Conard, and Gayle Roby.

David Krause has been a constant spirit and sounding board for this biography from before it got underway. He imagined it years before I did. His grace of being and his input have been gifts. Steve Paul's feedback on a sizable chunk of the first draft proved invaluable in helping me shape the final vision, as was Guy Choate's hosting me at the Argenta Reading Series around the same time. Thank you, Linda Wagner-Martin, Pat Hoy, Kristi McKim, and Steve Trout, for the many years of faith, advice, and love.

My agent, Tim Wojcik, and my editor, Michael Homler, are responsible for this book's being in readers' hands. Thank you, thank you, a thousand times thank you! And everyone else at Levine Greenberg Rostan Literary Agency and St. Martin's Press. I deeply appreciate the agents who passed on the book in its early forms. They were right to do so; their sound judgment steered the book toward what it needed to be.

My colleagues and students at Hendrix College, and my collaborators and friends in the Ernest Hemingway Society, you are all in this book, too. Two Hendrix student assistants helped with some of the in-the-trenches research—thank you, Ashton Leach and Portia Renee. The writing process was supported by a National Endowment for the Humanities Fellowship for the 2020–2021 academic year and by the M.E. and Ima Graves Peace Distinguished Professorship.

Christin, Anna Cay, and Quinn: Everything I am and do is because of, and for, you.

Through conversation and/or correspondence, the following shared memories, reflections, and material sources. Without their contributions and kindness, this biography would not have been possible.

Mary Ackerman	Patricia Bradford Cox	Harley Henry
Ben Anderson	Alvin Currier	Werner Herzog
David Anderson	Nicholas Delbanco	Leslie Hines
Greg Andrews	Evelyn Early	Richard Howorth
David Bain	W. D. Ehrhart	Ken Hruby
Vivian Vie Balfour	Kevin Falls	Amy Hu
Richard Bausch	Peter Fenn	Peter Hubbard
Charles Baxter	Randy Fertel	John Irving
Phil Beidler	Dan Fogelman	Tyrone Jaeger
Stephen Bergman	Ben Fountain	April Vance Johnson
Anne Bernays	Mike Fredrickson	Marilyn Johnson
Peter Bloch	James Galbraith	Steve Johnson
Lady Borton	Matt Gallagher	Sebastian Junger
Sarah Botstein	Steve Goff	Butch Kaplan
Kevin Bowen	Elizabeth	Wayne Karlin
Corinne Browne	Goodenough	Edward Keating
Kirsten Brunner	Tom Grimes	Tracy Kidder
Hedley Burrell	Erik Hansen	Robin Kleffman
Catherine Calloway	Ron Hansen	Mike Kleve
Philip Caputo	Mark Heberle	Fred Kramer
Michael Casey	Larry Heinemann	David Krause
Jane Reister Conard	DeWitt Henry	Wilson Lavender

Marc Leepson
Mark Linder
Ira Livingston
Paul Longgrear
Gene Lyons
Aaron Matthews
Gary Melom
Nguyễn Bá Chung
Lynn Novick
Naomi Shihab Nye
Linda Suby
  Pembroke
Dayne Peterson
Julie Phillipps
Jayne Anne Phillips

Lê Thị Hoài Phương
Samuel Popkin
Wyatt Prunty
Bob Reiss
Guy Reynolds
Gayle Roby
Constance Sayre
David Seal
Janet Silver
Robert Simpson
Anne Mollegen
  Smith
Joe Spieler
Oliver Stone
Christopher Sykes

David Taylor
Sue Ellen Thompson
Susan Thornton
Charles Underwood
Dan Wakefield
Robert Warde
Bruce Weber
Elizabeth Weber
Bruce Weigl
Robert Wolf
William Crawford
  Woods
Tim "Woody"
  Woodville
David Zander

The book would also not have been possible without the assistance of librarians, archivists, and other keepers of the historical record. A huge shout-out to John Shutt, Janice Weddle, Melissa Freiley, Sarah Bryan, and Britt Murphy, Hendrix College; Michael Gilmore, Hartlyn Haynes, et al., Harry Ransom Center, University of Texas–Austin; Jennifer Ford, University of Mississippi Special Collections; Rebecca Toov et al., University of Minnesota; Ellen Holt-Werle and John Esh, Archives and Special Collections, Macalester College; John Baky and Heather Willever-Farr, Rare Books and Manuscripts, Connelly Library, La Salle University; Danielle Rougeau, Joseph Watson, and Kaitlin Buerge, Middlebury College; Mitch Manning, William Joiner Institute for the Study of War and Social Consequences; Gwen Kirby and Plum Champlin, Sewanee Writers' Conference, University of the South; Michelle Romero and Jennifer Williams, Archives and Special Collections, Emerson College; Jenny McElroy et al., Minnesota Historical Society; Laurie Ebbers, Beth Rickers, et al., Nobles County Historical Society/Nobles County Library; Darci Fouste, U.S. Army Training Center; Erik Flint, Fort Lewis Museum, U.S. Army Center for Military History; Michael Lynch and Shane Reilly, U.S. Army Heritage and Education Center, Army War College; Sheon Montgomery, Vietnam Center and Archives, Texas Tech University; Sarah Mueller, Hedberg Library, Carthage College; Alyssa Pacy, Cambridge Public Library; Joshua Gonzalez, Cambridge District Court; Melissa Kunz et al., Special Collections and University Archives, McFarlin Library, University of Tulsa; Ashley Larson, Claremont Colleges Library; Reference Staff, Boston Public Library; Louis Round Wilson Special Collections Library, University of North Carolina–Chapel Hill; Lydia Brown, Georgia State University Library; Alice Kamps, Martin Gedra, et al., NARA; Reference Staff, Harvard University Archives, Pusey Library; Col. Mark Gagnon and Susan Lintelmann, U.S. Military Academy; Jonah Velasco and Eric Ewers, Florentine Films; Liz Pech, Alumni Engagement Office, Macalester College; Mark Seiderman, NOAA; Reference Staff, Library of Congress; Adam Crosby, Irvin Department of Rare Books and Special Collections, University of South Carolina; Hilary Justice and Stacey Chandler, John F. Kennedy Presidential Library; Julie Zhou and Joshua Feist, NEA Big Read/Arts Midwest; Tina Monaco, Augusta-Richmond County Public Library; Emily Pearson, Primrose Library, Whitman College; and Marc Jason Gilbert, Hue-Tam Ho Tai, Michael Resman, Jason Higgins, Bill Campbell, Kevin Tennal, Susan Foote, Dave McCauley, Christiane Citron, Sean Venables, David Cortright, Jenny Emery-Davidson, Gregory Daddis, Deb Stone, Charles Waugh, Mike High, Robert Short, Beth Hesler, and my classmates from the U.S. Military Academy class of 1989.

Other contributors have been acknowledged in the notes. My sincere regret and deep apology to anyone I have overlooked.

NOTES

Uncited quotations throughout are drawn from personal emails, interviews, conversations, and encounters. Unlocated items are either originals or copies in the author's collection. Unless otherwise indicated, all quotations from an O'Brien book come from its first edition, the edition closest to its biographical moment.

ABBREVIATIONS AND SHORT TITLES

America Fantastica	O'Brien, *America Fantastica* (New York: Mariner, 2023)
DMB	O'Brien, *Dad's Maybe Book* (New York: Mariner, 2019)
DSJ	5th Battalion, 46th Infantry Daily Staff Journal or Duty Officer's Log, NARA and David Taylor Collection, Vietnam Center and Sam Johnson Vietnam Archive, Texas Tech
GAC	O'Brien, *Going After Cacciato* (New York: Delacorte, 1978)
HRC	Tim O'Brien Papers, Harry Ransom Center, University of Texas–Austin
If I Die	O'Brien, *If I Die in a Combat Zone, Box Me Up and Ship Me Home* (New York: Delacorte, 1973)
July, July	O'Brien, *July, July* (Boston: Houghton Mifflin, 2002)
Lake	O'Brien, *In the Lake of the Woods* (Boston: Houghton Mifflin, 1994)
MHS	Minnesota Historical Society
Middlebury	Special Collections, Middlebury College
NARA	National Archives and Records Administration
NYT	*New York Times*
Northern Lights	O'Brien, *Northern Lights* (New York: Delacorte, 1975)
Nuclear Age	O'Brien, *The Nuclear Age* (New York: Alfred A. Knopf, 1985)

SL	Seymour Lawrence Collection, Department of Archives and Special Collections, University of Mississippi Libraries
Tomcat	O'Brien, *Tomcat in Love* (New York: Broadway Books, 1998)
TTTC	O'Brien, *The Things They Carried* (Boston: Houghton Mifflin, 1990)
VCSJVA	Vietnam Center and Sam Johnson Vietnam Archives, Texas Tech
WDG	*Worthington Daily Globe*
WP	*Washington Post*

PROLOGUE

1. *This Is Us*, season 3, episode 11, "Songbird Road: Part One" (aired Jan. 22, 2019).

2. S-2/3 DSJ, July 8, 1969, #20. See also DSJ, July 8, 1969, #27.

3. David Taylor writes that Peterson visited his fiancé and his parents, in *Our War: The History and Sacrifices of an Infantry Battalion in the Vietnam War, 1968–1971* (Medina, OH: War Journal Publishing, 2011), p. 293.

4. opensyllabus.org (accessed Apr. 20, 2020).

5. Kristi McKim, Professor of English and Film Studies, Hendrix College (Aug. 2018).

6. David Haward Bain, *Whose Woods These Are: A History of the Bread Loaf Writers' Conference 1926–1992*, ed. David Haward Bain and Mary Smyth Duffy (New York: Ecco Press, 1993), p. 128.

7. Susan Thornton, *On Broken Glass: Loving and Losing John Gardner* (New York: Carroll & Graf, 2000), p. 55.

8. Hilary Mills, "Publishing Notes: Going After Tim O'Brien," *Washington Star*, June 3, 1979.

9. In conversation with Anne Mollegen Smith at the Bread Loaf Writers' Conference (personal email from Smith, Apr. 27, 2021).

10. Interview with Aaron Matthews, unpublished transcript, May 24, 2016.

11. From Seymour Lawrence, Sept. 22, 1977 (HRC 3.4).

12. *If I Die*, p. 19.

13. Interview with Aaron Matthews, unpublished transcript, May 25, 2016.

14. Interview with Aaron Matthews, unpublished transcript, June 14, 2018.

1. COLLISION

1. Vietnam War U.S. Military Fatal Casualty Statistics, National Archives, archives.gov /research/military/vietnam-war/casualty-statistics.

2. *Tales of Suspense* 39 (Mar. 1963), p. 3.

3. On Oct. 19, 1964. SSS Form No. 1-A for William Timothy O'Brien, Jr.

4. The Classification Questionnaire was mailed to him on Nov. 9; he returned it on Nov. 16. The next day he received an I-A classification as available for military duty. On Dec. 15, he was reclassified II-S. SSS Form 102 for Local Board No. 77, Nobles County, National Guard Armory, Worthington, Minn., 56187 for Year of Birth 1946, S.S. Numbers from 151 to 180, Sheet No. 6.

5. National Archives, archives.gov/research/african-americans/vote/freedom-summer.

6. Evelyn Early personal interview, Nov. 2, 2020.

7. *Mac Weekly*, Mar. 26, 1965, p. 1.

8. John R. Thelin, *Going to College in the Sixties* (Baltimore: Johns Hopkins University Press, 2018), p. 86.

9. Dorothy Richards, Neveln Elementary, Austin, MN (second grade, 1953–1954); see the other end-of-year reports from Sumner Elementary and Neveln Elementary (HRC 55.4).

10. "Gets U.N. Scholarship," *WDG* clipping; and O'Brien postcard home (HRC 29.1).

11. "DCAS Vietnam Conflict Extract File record counts by INCIDENT OR DEATH DATE (Year) (as of April 29, 2008)," archives.gov/research/military/vietnam-war/casualty-statistics (accessed June 28, 2020); Selective Service System Induction Statistics, "Inductions by Year," sss.gov/history-and-records/induction-statistics/ (accessed June 28, 2020).

12. Interview with Aaron Matthews, unpublished transcript, May 25, 2016.

13. "Northfield [MN] Public Library Presents Tim O'Brien," Apr. 21, 1994, ntv.org/videos /authors/author-tim-obrien-at-the-northfield-public-library/.

14. *Mac Weekly*, Mar. 8, 1968, p. 7; *Mac Weekly*, Mar. 15, 1968, p. 3; *Mac Weekly*, Apr. 5, 1968, p. 2; *Mac Weekly*, Apr. 19, 1968, p. 4. On the orphanage fund, see *Mac Weekly*, Apr. 14, 1967. Other contributions from the Macalester community went to the Red Cross of Sài Gòn; see *Mac Weekly*, Apr. 5, 1968, p. 3. The failed resolution on the letter to President Johnson had been a response to a student survey in which 28 percent of the paltry 460 respondents sought immediate withdrawal and 39 percent wanted a gradual withdrawal (along with immediate cessation of bombing); low participation was one reason the resolution failed. See *Mac Weekly*, Dec. 8, 1967, p. 5.

15. *Mac Weekly*, Oct. 27, 1967, p. 4.

16. *Mac Weekly*, Nov. 3, 1967, pp. 1, 3; Charles Underwood personal email, July 12, 2020.

17. *Mac Weekly*, Nov. 10, 1967, pp. 1, 3.

18. *Mac Weekly*, Mar. 1, 1968, p. 4.

19. John Balaban, *Remembering Heaven's Face: A Story of Rescue in Wartime Vietnam* (Athens: University of Georgia Press, 2002), p. 58.

20. "Viet Cong Kill Vietnam Volunteer While Macalester Honors Him," *Minneapolis Tribune*, Feb. 5, 1968, p. 16.

21. *Mac Weekly*, Feb. 9, 1968, p. 4.

22. The U.S. government accused the National Liberation Front (Việt Cộng), the guerrilla militants in South Việt Nam fighting for the North. For IVSers the evidence pointed to soldiers or agents of South Việt Nam—possibly in cahoots with U.S. officials—due to Gitelson's continuing objection to the killing of nine civilians by a South Vietnamese air strike. See Balaban, *Remembering Heaven's Face*, pp. 78–89 (Balaban dedicates the memoir to Gitelson); Don Luce and John Sommer, *Viet Nam—Unheard Voices* (Ithaca, NY: Cornell University Press, 1969), pp. 175–176; Jerry Kliever oral history interview, Marc Gilbert Collection, VCSJVA, items 2679AU3059, 2679AU3060, 2679AU3061.

23. *Mac Weekly*, Feb. 23, 1968, p. 1.

24. To "Dad," dated Monday, Feb. 25, 1968—so actually either Sunday, Feb. 25, or Monday, Feb. 26 (HRC 29.4).

25. Details of Ava's schooling, employment history, and naval service are documented in her naval records (HRC 29.7).

26. Jerome L. Allen, Captain, U.S. Navy, Communication Officer, Eastern Sea Frontier, To Whom It May Concern, June 4, 1943 (HRC 29.7).

27. This date is listed in both Bill's naval records and the *Weeks*'s muster logs. U.S., World War II Navy Muster Records, 1938–1949, ancestry.com.

28. Promotion date of Oct. 1, 1944, recorded in his naval records (HRC 29.7) as well as the *Weeks*'s muster log for Oct. 16, 1944. U.S., World War II Navy Muster Records, 1938–1949, ancestry.com.

29. "O'Brien-Schultz," *Minneapolis Star Journal*, Nov. 27, 1944, p. 16.

30. O'Brien believes his father published several, although only two versions of one article are in the archives. The clipping "Tokoi Operaton" is the longer version of "Yeoman in NTS-Trained Crew Tells of Battle Action in Pacific Area," *Norfolk Seabag*, June 30, 1945 (HRC 29.7).

31. See *Reporting Vietnam: Part One: American Journalism 1959–1969* (New York: Library of America, 1998), pp. 581–582.

32. On Tuesday evening, March 5, in the Greeley Gas Building. O'Brien letter to Dad, dated Monday, Feb. 25, 1968—so actually either Sunday, Feb. 25, or Monday, Feb. 26 (HRC 29.4). Bill O'Brien also planned to go, and was considering supporting McCarthy. It is not clear whether O'Brien attended. He recalls meeting in the Nobles County Library's basement in Worthington, which would have been the countywide DFL convention on Saturday, March 30—but that memory isn't ironclad, either. It is likely he participated in both.

33. "Nobles County DFL Caucuses Give Support to President," *WDG*, Mar. 6, 1967, p. 1.

34. Undated Macalester reunion remarks, "It's great to be back . . ." [June 2, 2007], O'Brien private papers. The undated text references Steve Johnson, one of O'Brien's friends from the class of 1967, and it mentions the scheduled release of the Beatles' *Sgt. Pepper's Lonely Hearts Club Band* album on June 1, 1967—"forty years ago yesterday."

35. "Youth Who Ignited His Clothing Dies," *NYT*, Apr. 28, 1968, p. 73.

36. *Mac Weekly*, Mar. 15, 1968, p. 1.

37. *Mac Weekly* lists Superior, Wisconsin, where Reister and O'Brien went, as one of the cities for the March 23–24 weekend. It's possible they went a different weekend; the paper simply does not mention the destinations for the weekends of March 16–17 or 30–31 (possibly through April 2). *Mac Weekly*, Mar. 29, 1968, p. 1.

38. "McCarthy's Students to Invade Wisconsin," *Winona Daily News*, Mar. 21, 1968, p. 3A.

39. "County DFL Voted on Saturday Night: LBJ 51, McCarthy 12," *WDG*, Apr. 1, 1968, pp. 1, 4. O'Brien also remembers debating Jim Vance about Vance's support for Hubert Humphrey—except Vice President Humphrey was not yet in the race.

40. As reported in Max Frankel, "DMZ Is Exempted," *NYT*, Apr. 1, 1968, p. 1.

41. "Vietnam Veterans Against the War Statement by John Kerry to the Senate Committee on Foreign Relations," Apr. 22, 1971, as quoted in Geoffrey C. Ward and Ken Burns, *The Vietnam War: An Intimate History*, based on a documentary film series by Ken Burns and Lynn Novick (New York: Alfred A. Knopf, 2017), p. 480.

42. *Mac Weekly*, Apr. 26, 1968, p. 4.

43. "Worthington Reserves Called to Active Duty," *WDG*, Apr. 11, 1968, p. 1.

44. Lawrence M. Baskir and William A. Strauss, *Chance and Circumstance: The Draft, the War, and the Vietnam Generation* (New York: Alfred A. Knopf, 1978), pp. 50–51. This source revises the numbers upward to thirty-seven thousand activated and fifteen thousand deployed.

45. "Casualty Toll, 562, Is Worst 7 Days of War," *WDG*, May 16, 1968, p. 16.

46. historyisaweapon.com/defcon1/berrigancatonsvillenine.html.

47. Undated Macalester reunion remarks, "It's great to be back . . ." [June 2, 2007], O'Brien
     private papers.

2. BUSY TIMMY

1.   Twenty-three thousand in 1950 per "1950 Census of Population Advance Reports
     for Minnesota," www2.census.gov/library/publications/decennial/1950/pc-02/pc-2-37
     .pdf.

2.   Bill to Ava O'Brien, Oct. 17, 1962 (HRC 29.7).

3.   1920 United States Federal Census, New York, Kings, Brooklyn Assembly District 17,
     District 1064; 1925 New York U.S. State Census, ancestry.com.

4.   See *DMB*, pp. 158–159; and Dad's (William Timothy O'Brien) Eulogy, by Tim O'Brien, read
     by Greg O'Brien, Service of Remembrance and Love, Aug. 14, 2004, St. Joseph's Chapel,
     Incarnate Word Retirement Community, San Antonio, TX (HRC 50.4).

5.   Bill's naval records detail his schooling and employment history (HRC 29.7); his stenog-
     raphy certificate from the Packard School is dated Nov. 23, 1933 (HRC oversize 61).

6.   From Bill O'Brien, July 18, 1967 (HRC 29.6).

7.   In addition to Bill's naval records, see Printing Department documents (HRC 29.7).

8.   She'd previously trained at the Austin Teacher Training Department and St. Cloud State
     Teachers College. See her naval records (HRC 29.7).

9.   Baby book (HRC 28.1).

10. Kathleen Terese O'Brien, born Nov. 27, 1947.

11. City Directory for Austin, MN, 1950, p. 206, ancestry.com.

12. *DMB*, p. 108.

13. Records released to Tim O'Brien by email Dec. 9, 2019, and received by email the same
     day, Mayo Clinic, Health Information Management Services, Rochester, MN.

14. Human Services Division, State Operated Services, Aggregated Patient Cards; and Roch-
     ester State Hospital County Admission/Discharge Books, vol. C (Minnesota State Ar-
     chives, MHS).

15. Dr. Magnus Peterson, Rochester's superintendent, resisted the reforms, per Susan Bart-
     lett Foote, *The Crusade for Forgotten Souls: Reforming Minnesota's Mental Institutions,
     1946–1954* (Minneapolis: University of Minnesota Press, 2018), pp. 7–8, 58–64, 108–109;
     Annual-Biennial Reports, 1948–1954, Rochester State Hospital (114.B.11.4F), MHS.

16. Hospital Survey, 1954, Rochester State Hospital (117.A.4.5B), MHS.

17. Annual-Biennial Reports, 1948–1954, Rochester State Hospital (114.B.11.4F), MHS.

18. Hospital Survey, 1954, Rochester State Hospital (117.A.4.5B), MHS.

19. Michael Resman's novel *The Mailmen of Elmwood* (St. Cloud, MN: North Star Press,
     2013), set in the 1950s and based on Resman's work as an occupational therapist at Roch-
     ester through 1981 as well as on his research, describes insulin-induced comas as prepa-
     ratory to electroshock treatments.

20. Elaine Showalter, *The Female Malady: Women, Madness, and English Culture, 1830–1980*
     (New York: Pantheon, 1985), pp. 203–207. See also Jonathan Metzl, *The Protest Psychosis*
     (Boston, MA: Beacon Press, 2010); Joel Braslow, *Mental Ills and Bodily Cures* (Oakland,
     CA: University of California Press, 1997).

21. "Breakdown of Present Population by Diagnosis," Mar. 15, 1949, Population Statistics, Rochester State Hospital (117.1.4.3B), MHS.

22. Annual-Biennial Reports, 1948–1954, Rochester State Hospital (114.B.11.4F), MHS.

23. Rochester State Hospital County Admission/Discharge Books, vol. C (Minnesota State Archives, MHS).

24. Bill to Ava O'Brien, Oct. 17, 1962 (HRC 29.7).

25. At 2107 East Hope Street. *Polk's Austin City Directory 1953* (Omaha: R. L. Polk & Co.), p. 256, confirms Paul as householder and Nina as rooming there. The 1955 edition lists Paul Shultz, Nina Shultz, and Bill O'Brien at the Hope Street address (pp. 193, 228).

26. Elementary school report cards from Dorothy Richards (second grade, 1953–1954) and Dorothy Kosse (third grade, 1954–1955) (HRC 55.4). The 1953 (pp. 169, 241) and 1955 (pp. 241, 215) City Directories for Austin list both as Neveln Elementary teachers; the Austin Public Schools Human Resources office confirmed Richards taught second grade at Neveln for the 1953–1954 school year and Kosse taught third grade at Neveln for the 1954–1955 school year (by telephone, Jan. 25, 2021).

27. *GAC*, pp. 42–43.

28. "Census Determines: City Not 10,000," *WDG*, May 20, 1970, p. 1. Also 1960 Census of Population, Advanced Report Final Population Count, Nov. 18, 1960, PC(A1)-25, Minnesota, p. 14, Table 2, www2.census.gov/library/publications/decennial/1960/population -pc-a1/15611126ch3.pdf.

29. The City Directory for Austin, Minnesota, includes the O'Briens in 1955 (p. 193) but not in 1957 (p. 184) (1955: ancestry.com; 1957: ancestry.com). The last surviving elementary report card for Tim is from the 1954–1955 academic year (HRC 55.4). Gregory Paul O'Brien was born on July 19, 1956, in Worthington.

30. Wednesday, Oct. 17, 1962 (HRC 29.7).

31. Arthur P. Rose, *An Illustrated History of Nobles County, Minnesota* (Worthington, MN: Northern History Publishing Company, 1908), pp. 62–63.

32. "'Liquor' Store Seeks Place to Light Here," *WDG*, Apr. 2, 1947, p. 1; "City Property Site of New Liquor Store," *WDG*, Apr. 25, 1947, p. 1; *WDG*, "Start Remodeling for Liquor Store," Apr. 30, 1947, p. 5.

33. *WDG*, Nov. 26, 1969, p. 1.

34. O'Brien, "'The Crumbling of Sand Castles,'" *WP*, Nov. 18, 1973, pp. C1, C5.

35. Eulogy (HRC 50.4). Paragraph breaks added. See also *DMB*, pp. 42–43.

36. Marvis Moeller letter to O'Brien, Mar. 22, 1991 (HRC 29.3).

37. "Poise and great dignity" from *TTTC*, p. 258; *The Man Who Never Was* opened in Minneapolis's big theaters in March.

38. *TTTC*, p. 273.

39. Interview with Kathy (O'Brien) Adjemian, Greg O'Brien, Aaron Matthews, unpublished transcript, May 26, 2016.

40. *DMB*, p. 183; interview with Aaron Matthews, unpublished transcript, June 15, 2018.

41. Interview with Aaron Matthews, unpublished transcript, May 24, 2016.

42. Fred Lowry's Keep It Under Your Hat column, *WDG*, Mar. 24, 1960, p. 4.

43. Willmar State Hospital Patient Records, Patient Cards, Set 3 (Minnesota State Archives, MHS). When voluntary, the records indicate as much, and have an "admitted" date but

not a "committed" date. Bill was admitted and committed on the same date, with no in-dication of voluntary admission. The facility had opened its doors in 1912 as the Hospital Farm for the Inebriate, then became the Asylum for the Insane at Willmar (1917–1919) and Willmar State Asylum until 1937, when it took the name under which it received Bill.

44. Bill to Ava O'Brien, Oct. 17, 1962 (HRC 29.7).

45. O'Brien's junior high school activities included baseball (seventh to ninth grades), foot-ball (seventh to ninth grades), student council (seventh grade), newspaper (eighth and ninth grades), choir (ninth grade), and debate club (ninth grade) (HRC 55.4).

46. Vivian Vie Balfour, "The Reading," unpublished short story with O'Brien's marginalia and a feedback letter dated Jan. 11, 1993.

47. Bill to Ava O'Brien, Oct. 17, 1962 (HRC 29.7).

48. Voluntarily admitted Oct. 9, 1962, and discharged Dec. 14, 1962.

49. Bill O'Brien letters home dated Oct. 15, 1962, Oct. 17, 1962, Nov. 13, 1962, "Friday night," and "Sunday" (HRC 29.7).

50. Rhodes application (HRC 29.4).

51. Seven total self-immolations: Seth King, "U.N.'s Itinerary in Use in Saigon," *NYT*, Oct. 28, 1963, p. 12; "Two More Vietnamese Are Suicides by Fire," *NYT*, Dec. 4, 1963, p. 11; Malcolm Browne, *The New Face of War*, rev. ed. (Indianapolis: Bobbs-Merrill, 1968), p. 294.

52. O'Brien, "'The Crumbling of Sand Castles,'" *WP*, Nov. 18, 1973, pp. C1, C5.

53. O'Brien, "'The Crumbling of Sand Castles.'"

54. High school transcript (HRC 55.4).

55. *DMB*, pp. 117–118, 140.

56. Worthington High School yearbooks for 1963, 1964 (HRC 55.4).

3. SWEETHEART OF THE SÔNG KRÔNG NÔ

1. *TTTC*, p. 105.

4. SOAPBOX

1. Jack Raymond, "75,100 Report for Duty Today in Call-up of Military Reserves," *NYT*, Oct. 1, 1961, p. 20.

2. Sydney Gruson, "U.S. Tanks Face Soviet's at Berlin Crossing Point," *NYT*, Oct. 28, 1961, pp. 1, 3.

3. *WDG*, Aug. 16, 1961, p. 2.

4. *Mac Weekly*, Sept. 25, 1964, p. 1; *Mac Weekly*, Sept. 17, 1965, p. 1; *Mac Weekly*, Sept. 9, 1966, p. 1; *Mac Weekly*, Oct. 6, 1967, p. 1.

5. *Mac Weekly*, Sept. 25, 1964, p. 1; *Mac Weekly*, May 14, 1965, p. 3; *Mac Weekly*, Sept. 24, 1965, p. 1; *Mac Weekly*, Sept. 9, 1966, p. 1.

6. Jeanne Halgren Kilde, *Nature and Revelation: A History of Macalester College* (Minne-apolis: University of Minnesota Press, 2010), pp. 284–286.

7. Evelyn Early, personal email, July 19, 2020, quoting her response to a 2017 reunion prompt.

8. *Mac Weekly*, May 14, 1965, p. 4.

9. *Mac Weekly*, Nov. 12, 1965, p. 4.

10. *Mac Weekly* last mentions Tim's debate activity in October of his junior year. *Mac Weekly*, Oct. 28, 1966, p. 4.

11. *Mac Weekly*, Sept. 15, 1967, p. 3.

12. *Mac Weekly*, Oct. 27, 1967, p. 2; *Mac Weekly*, Dec. 8, 1967, p. 2.

13. *Mac Weekly*, Mar. 3, 1967, p. 4; *Mac Weekly*, Nov. 17, 1967, p. 2.

14. *Mac Weekly*, Mar. 8, 1968, p. 2.

15. To Dean Kramer, undated, received by the dean's office Mar. 24, 1969; to Kramer, [Aug.] 1969; to Kramer, [Aug.] 1969 ("Six months are gone now, six to go"); and from Dean Fred Kramer, Apr. 7, 1969. See *Mac Weekly*, Sept. 13, 1968, pp. 1–2.

16. "O'Brien on the Presidency," *Mac Weekly*, Apr. 19, 1968, p. 4.

17. *Mac Weekly*, Feb. 18, 1966, pp. 1, 4.

18. *Mac Weekly*, Sept. 9, 1966, p. 2.

19. *Mac Weekly*, Sept. 23, 1966, p. 3.

20. *Mac Weekly*, Oct. 7, 1966, p. 3.

21. *GAC*, p. 323.

22. *Mac Weekly*, Oct. 28, 1966, p. 2.

23. *Mac Weekly*, Dec. 9, 1966, p. 2.

24. "Transcript of the President's News Conference on Foreign and Domestic Affairs," *NYT*, July 29, 1965, p. 12.

25. "DCAS Vietnam Conflict Extract File record counts by INCIDENT OR DEATH DATE (Year) (as of April 29, 2008)," archives.gov/research/military/vietnam-war/casualty-statistics.

26. *Mac Weekly*, Mar. 9, 1979, p. 6.

27. *Mac Weekly*, Nov. 17, 1967, p. 6.

28. *Mac Weekly*, Sept. 23, 1966, p. 2.

29. *Mac Weekly*, Feb. 10, 1967, p. 1; *Mac Weekly*, Apr. 14, 1967, p. 4.

30. *Mac Weekly*, Nov. 17, 1967, p. 5; *Minneapolis Tribune*, Nov. 12, 1967, pp. 1A, 14A.

31. *Mac Weekly*, May 10, 1968, p. 4.

32. *Mac Weekly*, Feb. 24, 1967, pp. 1, 3; see also Neal Sheehan, "A Student Group Concedes It Took Funds from the CIA," *NYT*, Feb. 14, 1967, pp. 1, 7; Karen M. Paget, *Patriotic Betrayal: The Inside Story of the CIA's Secret Campaign to Enroll American Students in the Crusade Against Communism* (New Haven, CT: Yale University Press, 2015).

33. *Mac Weekly*, Sept. 29, 1967, p. 1.

34. *Mac Weekly*, Sept. 29, 1967, p. 3.

35. *Mac Weekly*, Jan. 19, 1968, p. 2.

5. Adventures in Amity and Melancholy

1. "SPANners Prepare for Summer Study," *Mac Weekly*, May 31, 1966, p. 3.

2. Send-off banquet program, Apr. 28, 1967 (HRC 29.6).

3. Two weeks and rain in undated postcard, O'Brien to Trisch Windschill (HRC 29.6).

4. Draft of article by Steven Van Drake (HRC 29.6). Published version not found.

5. O'Brien, "April, 1950: George Wheeler Gave Up U.S. for Czechoslovakia," *WDG*, July 19, 1968, p. 3.

6. To Hansen, Oct. 18, 1973 (HRC uncataloged).

7. O'Brien, "April, 1950: George Wheeler Gave Up U.S. for Czechoslovakia," p. 3.

8. From Harley Henry, June 7, 1968 (HRC 28.4).

9. From Barbara Newman, Ballantine Books, Aug. 6, 1968 (HRC 28.4).

10. Draft of article by Steven Van Drake (HRC 29.6). Published version not found.

11. Interview with Aaron Matthews, unpublished transcript, June 14, 2018.

12. On June 8, 1967. See Ryan McGaughey, "Former Worthington Resident Writes Book on How Brother Inspired Many Despite Handicap," *WDG* online, Feb. 19, 2020.

13. "Le Ledoc" interview notes (HRC 29.6).

14. "Le Ledoc" interview notes (HRC 29.6).

15. *If I Die*, p. 91. See also O'Brien, "Local Student in Prague Talks 'Politics' with North Vietnamese," *WDG*, July 16, 1968, p. 3.

16. From Vance to O'Brien c/o the American Embassy in Prague, June 5, 1967 (HRC 29.6).

17. E.g., Associated Press, "Detroit Is 'Ghost City' Away from Battle Scenes," *WDG*, July 25, 1967, p. 1; Associated Press, "Machine Guns Fire on Detroit Rioters," *WDG*, July 26, 1967, p. 1.

18. Draft of article by Steven Van Drake (HRC 29.6). Published version not found.

19. "I'm on the way," note from Steve Goff, July 21, 1967 (HRC 29.6).

20. *If I Die*, p. 90.

21. To Hansen, Jan. 19, 1977 (HRC uncataloged).

6. Greeting

1. SSS Form 102 for Local Board No. 77, Nobles County, NARA.

2. *If I Die*, p. 14.

3. The strategy worked up until the Tết Offensive. See Gary Melom, "Local GI in Saigon Tells of Ruthless Cong Tactics," *WDG*, May 9, 1968, p. 1. O'Brien might have read Melom's jingoistic thoughts. After the war, Melom recovered his prewar anti-war self with a vengeance.

4. Lawrence M. Baskir and William A. Strauss, *Chance and Circumstance: The Draft, the War, and the Vietnam Generation* (New York: Alfred A. Knopf, 1978), pp. 36–37.

5. Baskir and Strauss, *Chance and Circumstance*, pp. 24–26.

6. *DMB*, p. 169.

7. George Esper (Associated Press), "U.S. Casualties During Week Are Highest of War," *WDG*, June 6, 1968, p. 8.

8. *WDG*, May 21, 1968, p. 12; *WDG*, May 28, 1968, p. 1; *WDG*, June 1, 1968, p. 4.

9. "Dr. Spock, Yale Chaplain, Two Others Are Found Guilty," *WDG*, June 15, 1968, p. 4.

10. "U.S. Abandons Embattled Base at Khe Sanh," *WDG*, June 27, 1968, p. 1.

11. Leonard Neil, "'Hurricane' Sweeps over Region; Winds Are Clocked at 100 MPH," *WDG*, June 21, 1968, pp. 1, 4.

12. Norman Mailer, *Miami and the Siege of Chicago: An Informal History of the Republican and Democratic Conventions of 1968* (1968; repr. ed., New York: Random House, 1996), p. 4.

13. *TTTC*, pp. 46–47.

14. From Jane Reister, June 24, 1968 (HRC 28.4).

15. *TTTC*, p. 49.

16. Untitled, undated typescript lecture, "1. Last year, in my Bread Loaf lecture [. . .]" (HRC 27.1). A reference to the "late" John Gardner dates it after Sept. 1982, probably 1983—per *The Crumb*, Bread Loaf's newsletter, O'Brien's lecture title was "Everything I Know and Then Some," on the first day; the newsletter's last day jokes about making small talk with him by posing a moral choice challenge.

17. *If I Die*, p. 18.

18. *If I Die*, p. 17.

19. In a letter of June 28, 1968, Vance states his position about "stick[ing] by our guns in Vietnam and elsewhere," and closes with a nod to "differences of opinion on certain matters," a possible reference to O'Brien's temptation to expatriate to Canada (HRC 28.4).

20. 224 Vernon Street, per letter from Mrs. J. N. Hillgarth, Admissions Office, Harvard University, July 24, 1968 (HRC 28.4).

21. Letters from Jane Reister dated June 24 and 25, 1968, and sundry postcards (HRC 28.4).

22. From Jane Reister, July 3, 1968 (HRC 28.4).

23. Advertisement, *Minneapolis Tribune*, June 23, 1968, p. E2. He and his companion, Vivian Vie, did not see the movie the evening of July 5, as neither one recalls any protesters. See Lee Kottke, "Box Office Wins 'Battle' of Protestors," *Minneapolis Tribune*, July 6, 1968, p. 8.

24. Will Jones, "After Last Night," *Minneapolis Tribune*, June 28, 1968, p. 22.

25. The national "Calls for Inductees" number was 86,800; the Minnesota "Calls for Inductees" number was 1,773. The higher actual induction number includes draftees and volunteers, although the difference between the numbers does not equal the exact number of volunteers. Several states inducted fewer people than their calls, suggesting that for no state does the "Calls for Inductees" number necessarily equal the actual number of inducted draftees. See *Semi-Annual Report of the Director of Selective Service for the Period July 1 to December 31, 1968* (Washington, D.C.: U.S. Government Printing Office, Jan. 15, 1969), appendix 6, p. 39.

26. *Semi-Annual Report of the Director of Selective Service for the Period July 1 to December 31, 1968*, p. 8.

27. From Mrs. J. N. Hillgarth, Admissions Office, Harvard University, July 24, 1968 (HRC 28.4).

28. From Pfc. Rudolf A. Brynolfson (signed "Rudy"), July 26, 1968, to O'Brien at 224 Vernon Street, St. Paul (HRC 28.2).

29. From Jim Vance on *WDG* letterhead, June 28, 1968 (HRC 28.4).

30. O'Brien, "Local Student in Prague Talks 'Politics' with North Vietnamese," *WDG*, July 16, 1968, p. 3.

31. O'Brien, "April, 1950: George Wheeler Gave Up U.S. for Czechoslovakia," *WDG*, July 19, 1968, p. 3.

32. "Host of Loyal Cycle Friends Pay Tribute to Slain Mike Tracy," *WDG*, Aug. 1, 1968, p. 1; "Former City Man Slain by Shotgun in Park Attack," *WDG*, July 29, 1968, p. 1.

33. *If I Die*, pp. 18, 22.

34. *TTTC*, p. 63. See also *If I Die*, p. 65.

35. David E. Rosenbaum, "Draft Ratio Is Up for College Men," *NYT*, Nov. 21, 1968, p. 1.

36. Baskir and Strauss, *Chance and Circumstance*, p. 56.

7. In the Mill

1. HRC 27.6. Original: *WDG*, Aug. 14, 1968, p. 7.

2. *If I Die*, p. 21.

3. *If I Die*, p. 21. The processing station was at 320 South Second Avenue.

4. Graduation photograph, Third Platoon, Bravo Company, 5th Battalion, 1st Training Brigade (B-5-1), Cycle 11, Oct. 1968, Fort Lewis, Washington.

5. *If I Die*, pp. 31–32.

6. Erik S. Hansen, "Sisters," *TriQuarterly* 45 (Spring 1979), pp. 156, 161.

7. From "Dad," Sept. 25, 1968 (HRC 28.2).

8. To Hansen, [Jan. 16, 1970] (HRC uncataloged).

9. *If I Die*, p. 41.

10. *If I Die*, pp. 41–43. Italics added.

11. To Hansen, July 9, 1970 (HRC uncataloged).

12. For GreyBull's story, see his/her interview by Mason Funk, *Outwords*, Sept. 28, 2022: theoutwordsarchive.org/interview/blair-greybull/.

13. *If I Die*, pp. 38–39.

14. *If I Die*, pp. 39, 46. It's possible Kline was part of Project 100,000, known formally as the New Standard Men and informally as McNamara's Boys (after the secretary of defense who initiated it in 1966) and as the moron corps. These inductees "score[d] as low as the 10th percentile on the Armed Forces Qualifications Test," with their "deficiency in mental ability . . . made up for by concentrated and specialized attention during their training." *Semi-Annual Report of the Director of Selective Service for the Period July 1 to December 31, 1968* (Washington, D.C.: U.S. Government Printing Office, Jan. 15, 1969), p. 23. The same document's reported program success runs counter to fact—see Hamilton Gregory, "McNamara's Boys," *MHQ: The Quarterly Journal of Military History* 29, no. 3 (Spring 2017), and Hamilton Gregory, *McNamara's Folly: The Use of Low-IQ Troops in the Vietnam War plus the Induction of Unfit Men, Criminals, and Misfits* (West Conshohocken, PA: Infinity Publishing, 2015).

15. Conrad Crane et al., "Learning the Lessons of Lethality: The Army's Cycle of Basic Combat Training, 1918–2019," U.S. Army War College, Feb. 22, 2019, pp. 43–44, ahec.armywarcollege.edu/documents/Learning-the-Lessons.pdf.

16. See, e.g., "G.I. Underground: Antiwar Activity Spreads in Ranks," *Los Angeles Times*, Oct. 4, 1968, pp. 1, 10–11.

17. *If I Die*, p. 31.

18. From Kathy O'Brien, Sept. 12, 1968 (HRC 28.2).

19. From Kathy O'Brien, undated [c. Oct. 1, 1968] (HRC 28.2).

20. *If I Die*, p. 33.

21. *If I Die*, p. 33; *If I Die* final typescript, with revisions (HRC 4.1), p. 15.

22. *If I Die* final typescript, p. 16.

23. *If I Die* final typescript, pp. 16–17.

24. From "Dad," Sept. 25, 1968 (HRC 28.2), citing an editorial from the day before ("Some Reservists Are Acting Shamefully," *WDG*, Sept. 24, 1968, p. 3; see also "1,000 Iowa Guards Seek Legal Action," *WDG*, Sept. 24, 1968, p. 1). Other states that saw such suits include Maryland, Virginia, Iowa, Ohio, Hawaii, and California. On the Burbank unit, see *The Sacramento Bee*, Oct. 8, 1968, p. 3. Soldiers from Maryland filed a complaint that they had received insufficient training and that commanders covered up deficiencies (Peter Grosse, "Reservists Charge Army Falsified Records of Faulty Training," *NYT*, Oct. 11, 1968, p. 4).

25. *If I Die*, pp. 32–33.

26. *If I Die*, p. 34.

27. *If I Die*, pp. 32–33.

28. *If I Die*, p. 45.

29. *If I Die*, p. 34.

30. T. E. Lawrence, *The Mint: Lawrence After Arabia* (Tauris Parke, 2016), p. 165.

31. Lawrence, *The Mint*, p. 71.

32. E.g., Lawrence, *The Mint*, pp. 99, 131.

33. *If I Die*, p. 32.

34. Lawrence, *The Mint*, pp. 108, 110, 113.

35. From "Dad," Sept. 8, 1968 (HRC 28.2).

36. From "Dad," Sept. 20, 1968 (HRC 28.2).

37. From "Mom," Sept. 28, 1968 (HRC 28.2).

38. To Gayle Roby, Oct. 17, 1968 (HRC 27.6).

8. RUBICON DAYS

1. To Gayle Roby, Oct. 17, 1968.

2. Record of Assignments for Tim O'Brien, NARA.

3. *If I Die*, pp. 50–52.

4. *If I Die* final typescript, pp. 36–37. The document is called "Fire in the Hole" on the title page, although several chapters (including this one, "Escape") carry the book's first working title, "Pop Smoke."

5. From "Dad," Oct. 26, 1968 (HRC 28.2).

6. To Hansen, postmarked Dec. 8 or 9, 1968 (HRC uncataloged).

7. See Department of the Army, ATP 21–114, Male Military Personnel Without Prior Service, July 1966; and Department of the Army, Army Subject Schedule 7–11B10, MOS Technical and Refresher Training of Light Weapons Infantryman MOS 11B10, April 1966. By 1971, an AIT overhaul resulted in a new 168-hour Southeast Asia field exercise.

8. *If I Die*, pp. 60–61.

9. Graham Greene, *The Quiet American* (1955; repr. ed., New York: Vintage, 2002), p. 153.

10. To Hansen, postmarked Dec. 8 or 9, 1968.

11. Associated Press, "703 Deaths Now Blamed on Flu-Pneumonia Across U.S.," *WDG*, Dec. 20, 1968, p. 4.

12. From Jane Reister, Nov. 7 [1968] (HRC 28.2).

13. From Kathy O'Brien, undated [mid-Nov. 1968]; from Jane Reister, Nov. 14 [1968] (HRC 28.2).

14. *Mac Weekly*, no. 10 (Nov. 22, 1968), p. 1.

15. From Jane Reister, Dec. 3, 1968 (HRC 28.2).

16. From Ava O'Brien, Dec. 1 [1968]; Reister's letter of Dec. 3, 1968, confirms visit (HRC 28.2).

17. Maury Maverick quoted in Lawrence M. Baskir and William A. Strauss, *Chance and Circumstance: The Draft, the War, and the Vietnam Generation* (New York: Alfred A. Knopf, 1978), p. 141.

18. To Hansen, postmarked Dec. 8 or 9, 1968.

19. Bravo Company, 1st Battalion, 3rd Recruit Training Brigade. Record of Assignments for Tim O'Brien, NARA.

20. *If I Die*, p. 62.

21. Both downtown in *Seattle Times*, Dec. 13, 1968, p. 95; no *Finian's Rainbow* at all, and *The Graduate* at the John Danz Theater in Bellevue (not downtown), in *Seattle Times*, Jan. 25, 1969, p. 16, and *Seattle Times*, Feb. 1, 1969, p. 14.

22. Baskir and Strauss, *Chance and Circumstance*, p. 181.

23. Geoffrey C. Ward and Ken Burns, *The Vietnam War: An Intimate History*, based on a documentary film series by Ken Burns and Lynn Novick (New York: Alfred A. Knopf, 2017), p. 355.

24. David Cortright, *Soldiers in Revolt: GI Resistance During the Vietnam War* (Chicago: Haymarket Books, 2005), pp. 12–13, 16.

25. Jay Walz, "Canada to Admit Any U.S. Deserter," *NYT*, May 23, 1969, p. 5.

26. Cortright, *Soldiers in Revolt*, p. 53.

27. Underground GI resistance at Fort Lewis predated the Shelter Half. See "G.I. Underground: Antiwar Activity Spreads in Ranks," *Los Angeles Times*, Oct. 4, 1968, pp. 1, 10–11.

28. Cortright, *Soldiers in Revolt*, p. 58.

29. "The Great Invasion," *Counterpoint* 2, no. 14 (Aug. 7, 1969), pp. 4–5 (University of Washington, The Civil Rights & Labor History Consortium, Photos and Documents, Antiwar and Radical History Project, Antiwar GI Newspapers, depts.washington.edu/labpics /zenPhoto/antiwar/gipaper/Counterpoint-August-7-1969/p.-4.jpg/).

30. Lawrence B. Radine, *The Taming of the Troops: Social Control in the United States Army* (Westport, CT: Greenwood Press, 1977), p. 17; "in the fall, a second, stricter guideline was issued" (p. 32, note 33). There was a "Guidance on Dissent" dated June 23, 1969, as referenced by "Commanders' Orders versus Constitutional Rights," by Col. Bruce T. Coggins, Army Staff Judge Advocate (undated, Richard T. Knowles Collection, 2.4, VCSJVA, item #27180204010). The guidance mainly resulted from the highly publicized Fort Jackson Eight case in March 1969, which was not the only case making waves.

31. Cortright, *Soldiers in Revolt*, p. 62.

32. *Mac Weekly*, Nov. 22, 1968, p. 4; also *Mac Weekly*, Sept. 13, 1968, p. 2.

33. "Draft Information Center to Provide Counseling," *Mac Weekly*, Nov. 1, 1968, p. 1.

34. Baskir and Strauss, *Chance and Circumstance*, p. 38.

35. *This Is Us*, "Vietnam," season 3, episode 4 (aired Oct. 16, 2018), co-written by Dan Fogelman and Tim O'Brien. The two-minutes-to-midnight idea was Fogelman's.

36. Record of Assignments for Tim O'Brien, NARA.

37. Associated Press, "APOLLO IS OFF!," *WDG*, Dec. 21, 1968, p. 1.

38. "4 Vietnamese War Orphans Wish Globe Readers a 'Most Merry Christmas,'" *WDG*, Dec. 23, 1968, pp. 1, 3; "Orphans Fund Now $676.53," *WDG*, Jan. 8, 1969, p. 4; Roger Nystrom, "Area Man Is Fighting New Kind of Battle to Win Over Cong," *WDG*, Dec. 28, 1968, pp. 1–2; SP4 Bob Holden, "Local Reserves at Da Nang See Play Put On by Orphans," *Globe Town and Country* (insert), Dec. 27, 1968, pp. 2–3.

39. "Vietnam Wrote Two Chapters in Local History," *WDG*, Jan. 1, 1969, p. 12 (a continuation of "June 13 Brought Tornado Attack: Big News of 1968," p. 1).

40. Associated Press, "U.S. Marines Stream Ashore in Biggest Sea-Borne Invasion Since Korean War," *WDG*, Jan. 14, 1969, p. 1; Associated Press, "Marines Tighten Trap in Batangon [*sic*] Sweep," *WDG*, Jan. 15, 1969, p. 10.

41. Associated Press, "Long-Delayed Peace Talks Finally to Start Saturday," *WDG*, Jan. 16, 1969, p. 1.

42. DD214, Certificate of Release or Discharge from Active Duty for William Timothy O'Brien (HRC 27.6).

43. *DMB*, p. 210.

9. Into the Combat Zone

1. DD214 (HRC 27.6). See also O'Brien's letters about extending his tour "39 days," until March 16, to Mom, Dad, & Greg [Nov. 9, 1969] (HRC 27.6) and "41 days," until March 17, to Erik Hansen [Jan. 16, 1970] (HRC uncataloged). Flight attendant kiss: *If I Die*, p. 67.

2. *GAC*, p. 42.

3. Record of Assignments for Tim O'Brien, NARA; 1st Lt. Mike Wolfgang, "It All Begins Here: The Combat Center," *Americal: The Quarterly Magazine of the Americal Division, Vietnam* 2, no. 1 (Jan. 1969), pp. 23–24; O'Brien letter to Hansen [Feb. 17, 1969] (HRC uncataloged).

4. *If I Die*, p. 67.

5. O'Brien letter to Hansen [Feb. 17, 1969]. (HRC uncataloged).

6. According to both his personal Record of Assignments and the Feb. 18, 1969, Morning Report for Co A 5th Bn 46th Inf, 198th Inf Bd, NARA.

7. *If I Die*, p. 71.

8. Alpha reentered Gator at 1720 hours on Feb. 22 (DSJ, #31); it had departed by combat assault on Feb. 12 (DSJ, #13–14).

9. *If I Die*, pp. 71–72.

10. 5–46 Plans and Summaries, Feb. 23, 1969. *If I Die* says eight VC killed (p. 73).

11. *If I Die*, p. 73; DSJ, Feb. 23, 1969, #29, #34, #41, #49.

12. DSJ, Feb. 23, 1969, #67.

13. Both works first appeared in *The New Yorker* and thereafter as books. O'Brien's notes, written on a sheet bearing the title "Homage to Quang Ngai" (HRC 26.3), cite page numbers matching *The Real War* (New York: Pantheon, 1988). "Homage to Quang Ngai" appears to be a discarded title for the essay "The Vietnam in Me" (*NYT Magazine*, Oct. 2, 1994).

14. Jonathan Schell, *The Military Half* (New York: Alfred A. Knopf, 1968), pp. 8, 9, 10.

15. Film based on Daniel Lang, "Casualties of War," *The New Yorker*, Oct. 18, 1969.

16. Paul Longgrear quoted in email from Bob Wolf, Oct. 1, 2009 (HRC 51.2).

17. O'Brien letter to Hansen [Feb. 18–19, 1969].

18. David W. Taylor, *Our War: The History and Sacrifices of an Infantry Battalion in the Vietnam War, 1968–1971* (Medina, OH: War Journal Publishing, 2011), pp. 182, 205.

19. Taylor, *Our War*, p. 206.

20. O'Brien described the night mission in "Ambush" as occurring on a moonless, starless, pitch-black night (*If I Die*, p. 82); meteorological data for the area the night of Feb. 23 has a waxing moon and 42.8 percent illumination. The nearest moonless night doesn't occur until March 18, but the chapter references O'Brien as a "New Guy" (*If I Die*, p. 87) and suggests he is still a squad member and not the platoon RTO. The chapter mentions "Chip," whom O'Brien didn't befriend until April.

21. Interview with Aaron Matthews, unpublished transcript, May 22, 2016.

22. DSJ, Feb. 24, 1969, #54.

23. *If I Die*, pp. 75–76.

24. *If I Die*, pp. 24–25.

25. *If I Die*, pp. 95–97.

26. DSJ, Feb. 15, 1969, #29; DSJ, Feb. 17, 1969, #17.

27. DSJ, Feb. 17, 1969, #45; DSJ, Feb. 16, 1969, #28; DSJ, Feb. 19, 1969, #34.

28. Interview with Aaron Matthews, unpublished transcript [Dec. 12, 2014].

29. Frank Mankiewicz and Tom Braden, "More Civilians Are Killed than Soldiers in V-Nam," *WDG*, July 29, 1970, p. 3.

30. Kurt Vonnegut, *Slaughterhouse-Five* (1969; repr. ed., Dial Press, 2005), p. 19.

31. DSJ, Mar. 18, 1969, #14.

32. DSJ, Mar. 19, 1969, #16, #54.

33. DSJ, Mar. 20, 1969, #18, #22. First and Third Platoons plus the headquarters element reentered Gator, while First and Fourth went to Bình Sơn.

34. DSJ, Mar. 23, 1969, #20; DSJ, Mar. 28, 1969, #30; DSJ, Mar. 31, 1969, #14.

35. DSJ, Mar. 31, 1969, #34.

36. To Mom, Dad, Greg et al., Apr. 10 [1969] (HRC 27.6); DSJ, Mar. 31, 1969, #40.

37. DSJ, Apr. 1, 1969, #30, #37, #39.

38. *If I Die*, p. 35.

39. *If I Die*, p. 88.

40. In W. H. Auden, *Collected Poems*, ed. Edward Mendelson (New York: Modern Library, 2007), p. 36.

41. DSJ, Apr. 3, 1969, #36.

42. *If I Die*, pp. 79–80, which only mentions one dead Vietnamese.

43. DSJ, Apr. 4, 1969, #38. See also #34.

44. Taylor, *Our War*, p. 201.

45. *If I Die*, p. 79. Taylor's history takes great care to never name Mark White.

46. Associated Press, "U.S. Vietnam Casualties Now Exceed Losses in Korean War," *WDG*, Apr. 3, 1969, p. 6; Geoffrey C. Ward and Ken Burns, *The Vietnam War: An Intimate History*, based on a documentary film series by Ken Burns and Lynn Novick (New York: Alfred A. Knopf, 2017), p. 372.

47. DSJ, Apr. 5, 1969, #11; 5–46 Plans and Summaries, Apr. 5, 1969; DSJ, Apr. 6, 1969, #18.

48. Earl S. Martin, *Reaching the Other Side: The Journal of an American Who Stayed to Witness Vietnam's Postwar Transition* (New York: Crown, 1978), p. 131.

49. Gratitude to Bradley C. Davis and Edyta Roszko for their translation insights.

50. Taylor, *Our War*, p. 206.

51. To Mom, Dad, Greg et al., Apr. 10 [1969] (HRC 27.6). O'Brien probably became Anderson's RTO the day he wrote home.

52. *If I Die*, p. 101.

53. DSJ, Apr. 21, 1969, #44.

54. Minuteman: Spec. 4 William Crawford and Pfc. Dale Hartman, DSJ, Apr. 16, 1969, #46; S-1 DSJ, Apr. 16, 1969, #5; ambush: DSJ, Apr. 17, 1969, #16, #17.

55. DSJ, Apr. 17, 1969, #36, #48.

56. DSJ, Apr. 22, 1969, #17, #22.

57. *If I Die*, pp. 102–103.

58. *If I Die*, p. 100.

59. DSJ, Apr. 25, 1969, #43; DSJ, Apr. 26, 1969, #25.

60. *If I Die*, p. 100.

61. *If I Die*, pp. 109–111.

62. *TTTC*, pp. 153–154.

63. Interview with Aaron Matthews, unpublished transcript, May 22, 2016.

64. Interview with Aaron Matthews, unpublished transcript, May 22, 2016.

10. May Was the Cruelest Month

1. DSJ, Apr. 29, 1969, #19; DSJ, May 2, 1969, #7.

2. DSJ, May 3, 1969, #41, #47.

3. DSJ, May 3, 1969, #47; see also the next day's Plans and Summaries (May 4, 1969), which confirms the two captured-in-action ("CIA").

4. *If I Die*, p. 114.

5. Jerry Karr email to Tim O'Brien, Oct. 21, 2008 (HRC 51.2).

6. To Hansen, May 17, 1969 (HRC uncataloged).

7. Email from Robert "Bob" Mioducki to Robert "Bob" Wolf, Nov. 3, 2008 (HRC 51.2).

8. David W. Taylor, *Our War: The History and Sacrifices of an Infantry Battalion in the Vietnam War, 1968–1971* (Medina, OH: War Journal Publishing, 2011), p. 239.

9. *If I Die*, p. 114.

10. DSJ, May 3, 1969, #41.

11. *If I Die*, p. 114.

12. *If I Die*, chapter 11, "Assault," p. 107; and chapter 13, "My Lai in May," p. 114.

13. *DMB*, p. 216.

14. DSJ, May 3, 1969, #42, #53; Plans and Summaries, May 3, 1969; Taylor, *Our War*, p. 240.

15. DSJ, May 4, 1969, #15; DSJ, May 5, 1969, #5; Plans and Summaries, May 4, 1969. Although the battalion logs record a great deal of company-level coordination with ARVN units, usually the battalion, not the company, handled the coordination. The Americans and the Vietnamese on the ground were mostly unaware. Some of the coordination may have been on paper only—one former battalion officer called the logs "cover-your-ass political crap."

16. *If I Die*, p. 115. Although *If I Die* says the company crossed the Sông Diêm Điem, grid coordinates reported for the rest of the day do not place it on the other side, and the memoir even places them that night south of the river, "in a village of My Lai" (p. 116; see note 20 below). The bridge O'Brien describes is much smaller than the one over the Sông Diêm Điem.

17. O'Brien, "My Lai: 'They' Are Dinks and You Curse Their Lying Tongue," *WDG*, Jan. 21, 1970, p. 1.

18. DSJ, May 4, 1969, #36; S-1 DSJ, May 4, 1969, #3.

19. O'Brien, "Soldier Describes 1st Bloody Battle," *Minneapolis Star*, July 4, 1969, p. 7A. The time, place, and general nature of Kihl's injury matches O'Brien's article and present memory, but even at the time O'Brien did not know Kihl's name. It is possible that VC mortars wounded Kihl and the accident wounded someone else (and on a different day).

20. *If I Die*, pp. 115–116; DSJ, May 5, 1969, #5. *If I Die* calls it "a village of My Lai" (p. 116). The DSJ's grid coordinates suggest the neighboring sub-hamlet of Giêm Diên 1.

21. O'Brien, "Soldier Describes 1st Bloody Battle."

22. *If I Die*, p. 166.

23. Taylor, *Our War*, p. 241. Taylor's history concludes that an Alpha soldier must have fired the M79 because the recon platoon set up too far away, but he treats the incident as having happened the night of the fourth. This fits the DSJ's entry of one WIA that night to be dusted off in the morning (DSJ, May 5, 1969, #5), and the DSJ entry of Riley's being dusted off the next morning (DSJ, May 5, 1969, #18). The first entry does not name the WIA and ascribes the injury to enemy artillery. *If I Die* is more precise in describing Riley "crawl[ing] around on his hands and knees with everyone else" as the mortars fell that night and then documenting the fragging incident as happening in the morning, the morning of the logged dust-off (p. 166). The severity of the injury corroborates the memoir—the dust-off could not have waited until morning.

24. DSJ, May 5, 1969, #18.

25. DSJ, May 5, 1969, #37; *If I Die*, p. 167.

26. Interview with Aaron Matthews, unpublished transcript, May 22, 2016.

27. O'Brien, "Keynote Address: Thirty Years After," in Mark Heberle, ed., *Thirty Years After: New Essays on Vietnam War Literature, Film, and Art* (Newcastle upon Tyne, UK: Cambridge Scholars Publishing, 2009), p. 7. Address given at the University of Hawaii, Nov. 8–10, 2005.

28. DSJ, May 6, 1969, #19, #23.

29. Still in coordination with the ARVN company (Plans and Summaries, May 6, 1969; May 7, 1969; May 8, 1969).

30. *If I Die*, p. 8. This dating assumes the firefight occurred as described, a single event as opposed to a representative composite. The memoir places it "north and west of the Batangan Peninsula" (p. 3), although the company was south and west of the peninsula; and it includes Chip Merricks in the scene (p. 5). As described, the firefight must have occurred between April 29, the first day Anderson led the company in the field (west of Batangan), and May 9, the day Merricks was killed.

31. *If I Die*, p. 116.

32. *If I Die*, pp. 92–94.

33. *TTTC*, p. 203.

34. DSJ, May 9, 1969, #25, #35.

35. DSJ, May 9, 1969, #16.

36. *TTTC*, pp. 85–91.

37. O'Brien, "Soldier Describes 1st Bloody Battle."

38. *If I Die*, p. 116.

39. Email from Carl Foley to Bob Wolf, Oct. 18, 2008 (HRC 51.2).

40. *If I Die*, p. 116. See also DSJ, May 9, 1969, #25. The log wrongly records the incident as occurring inside a hooch.

41. Taylor, *Our War*, p. 242.

42. Email from Carl Foley to Bob Wolf, Oct. 18, 2008 (HRC 51.2).

43. *If I Die*, p. 121.

44. DSJ, May 10 and 11, 1969.

45. Joseph Conrad, *Heart of Darkness* (1899; repr. ed., London: Penguin, 1999), p. 22.

46. *If I Die*, pp. 116–117.

47. O'Brien's acknowledgment that he started the singing differs from the accounts in *If I Die* (pp. 107–108) and Taylor, *Our War* (p. 249).

48. DSJ, May 12, 1969, #28, #59; S-1 DSJ, May 12, 1969, #6.

49. Taylor, *Our War*, p. 250.

50. *If I Die*, pp. 133–134. *TTTC*, p. 85.

51. Pfc. Leo J. Adakai and Pfc. Joseph W. Barcus, DSJ, May 13, 1969, #21; S-1 DSJ, May 13, 1969, #3.

52. DSJ, May 13, 1969, #29, #30, #32, #41, #47. The KIA died after capture.

53. Pfc. Carl P. Jackson (chest), Spec. 4 Joseph Wickham (thigh), and Spec. 4 Herman M. McLendon (shoulder); DSJ, May 14, 1969, #24, #25; S-1 DSJ, May 14, 1969, #4. O'Brien remembers Capt. Anderson had been called back to the rear, perhaps to help manage the battalion after the attack on Gator. He might have stayed through the memorial service on the sixteenth. Lt. White commanded the company in his absence.

54. DSJ, May 14, 1969, #53.

55. DSJ, May 15, 1969, #31.

56. Pfc. Howard Rich (leg): DSJ, May 16, 1969, #28, #29, #35; S-1 DSJ, May 16, 1969, #5.

57. DSJ, May 16, 1969, #42 and Summary of Activities. *If I Die*, p. 117. The remaining platoon captured a VC village chief at Phú Nhiêu 1 (DSJ, May 17, 1969, #22, #25, #28).

58. At 4:20 p.m. (DSJ, May 17, 1969, #40).

59. To Hansen, May 17, 1969 (HRC uncataloged).

60. To Mom, Dad & Greg, May 18, 1969 (HRC 27.6).

61. DSJ, May 18, 1969, Summary of Activities & Plans and Summaries (for May 19).

62. DSJ, May 20, 1969, #13; DSJ, May 21, 1969, #38; DSJ, May 24, 1969, #28; DSJ, May 26, 1969, #37; DSJ, May 27, 1969, #24; DSJ, May 28, 1969, #27.

63. *GAC*, p. 7.

64. O'Brien, "Boredom Is Real Vietnam Enemy, State Soldier Says," *Minneapolis Tribune*, June 29, 1969, p. 10A. O'Brien's article gives no dates or locations besides the word *recently* for an article written in June. This article and his letter of June 1, 1969 must describe Hill 294. Both refer to the leeches. Whereas the article locates them on the mountain five nights, the battalion log has them there only two nights, ascending May 29 and descending May 31 (DSJ, May 29, 1969, #17; Plans and Summaries, May 31, 1969). O'Brien might have compressed several days in the southern Rocket Pocket and Hill 294 into one location for dramatic simplicity. An editor might have done this as well—a line from O'Brien included in the article's headnote but not in the article itself suggests editing was needed to shorten the piece.

65. To Mom, Dad, & Greg [June 1, 1969] (HRC 27.6). Internally, the letter dates itself June 1 at Gator—but Alpha did not return until June 2. It is possible that O'Brien and a few others returned a day early, as Alpha on the first was at Trì Bình 4, quite close to Gator; it is possible he simply confused the day; it is also possible that June 1 referred to the date in Worthington.

66. DSJ, May 29, 1969, #17; DSJ, May 31, 1969, Summary of Activities.

67. Tây Phước 1 matches the battalion log's coordinates for the company's night defensive position the day they came down from Hill 294 (May 31, 1969, Plans and Summaries), although the Tho An hamlet is a kilometer closer.

68. O'Brien, "Boredom Is Real Enemy." Nowhere does the battalion log mention three detained men. The company might not have reported it, or the battalion might have failed to record it.

69. *If I Die*, pp. 126–127. The memoir and the "Boredom" article differ. This version is a best-faith effort to reconcile the two.

70. To Mom, Dad, & Greg [June 1, 1969].

71. O'Brien, "Boredom Is Real Enemy."

72. *GAC*, p. 49.

73. Pfc. Joseph Mutnansky (DSJ, June 8, 1969, #41).

74. James Woodley (DSJ, June 22, 1969, #16).

75. From Alpha: Specialist Robert Bittle and Cpl. Gordon MacMillan, KIA; Pfc. Thomas Bahner, WIA (DSJ, June 21, 1969, #30; see also Taylor, *Our War*, p. 273).

76. "Macalester Crowd Boos at Graduation," *Minneapolis Tribune*, May 25, 1969, p. 15A. The Associated Press's reporting was picked up in papers around the nation.

77. Associated Press, "Vietnam Toll Now Exceeds WWI Toll," *WDG*, June 5, 1969, p. 1; Robert Cashel, "Families Jubilant; 452nd Coming Home!," *WDG*, June 18, 1969, p. 1.

11. THE SUMMER OF '69

1. David W. Taylor, *Our War: The History and Sacrifices of an Infantry Battalion in the Vietnam War, 1968–1971* (Medina, OH: War Journal Publishing, 2011), p. 302.

2. Forward TOC/LZ Stinson, DSJ, July 5, 1969, #16.

3. O'Brien, "Monsters of War Stir Quiet Lagoon," *Minneapolis Star Tribune*, July 27, 1969, p. 20A.

4. Taylor, *Our War*, p. 293.

5. To Hansen [July 17, 1969] (HRC uncataloged).

6. At 0715 hours: S-3 DSJ, July 13, 1969, #14, #15; S-1 DSJ, July 13, 1969, #2; O'Brien, "Monsters of War Stir Quiet Lagoon." The memoir includes Peterson's death and ends with the same language as the article, but dates Martin's death two days before Peterson's. Martin died five days *after* Peterson.

7. DSJ, July 14, 1969, #35, #49.

8. Taylor, *Our War*, pp. 297–298 (Alpha was the 5–46 company "under operational control of the ARVN").

9. DSJ, July 15, 1969.

10. Plans and Summaries, July 15, 1969; *If I Die*, p. 144.

11. DSJ, May 16, 1969, #18.

12. *If I Die*, p. 145.

13. O'Brien, "Prisoners of Peace," *Penthouse*, March 1974, p. 115. The article dates the episode on May 5, and furthermore describes it as occurring after jets destroyed a village, more reminiscent of the events of July 22 and a second elderly Vietnamese woman. See note 28.

14. DSJ, May 16, 1969, #21.

15. HRC 22.3.

16. To Hansen [July 17, 1969] (HRC uncataloged).

17. Morning Report for Co A 5th Bn 46th Inf, 198th Inf Bde, Feb. 18, 1969, NARA.

18. DSJ, July 16, 1969, #27, #36.

19. DSJ, July 15, 1969, #36; S-1 DSJ, July 15, 1969, #4, #6.

20. *If I Die*, pp. 148–149; Jerry Karr email to Tim O'Brien, Oct. 21, 2008 (HRC 51.2).

21. *TTTC*, p. 199.

22. *TTTC*, p. 197.

23. Associated Press, "814 GIs Wing Toward Homes, First of 25,000 in Vietnam Pullout," *WDG*, July 8, 1969, p. 1; Richard Pyle (AP), "Vietnam Lull Continues; Chief of U.S. Armed Forces Pays Visit," *WDG*, July 16, 1969, p. 2; Associated Press, "Vietnam War Lull Spreads; New Pullouts Weighed," *WDG*, July 17, 1969, p. 6; Robert Cashell, "Families Jubilant; 452nd Coming Home!," *WDG*, June 16, 1969, p. 1.

24. DSJ, July 16, 1969, #40; Plans and Summaries, July 17, 1969; Taylor, *Our War*, p. 306.

25. DSJ, July 18, 1969, #26; DSJ, July 19, 1969, #16.

26. Taylor, *Our War*, p. 309.

27. O'Brien, "Prisoners of Peace," p. 114.

28. *If I Die*, p. 153; O'Brien, "Prisoners of Peace," pp. 114–115; and Taylor, *Our War*, pp. 309–310. *If I Die* places the jets and the woman as part of the mission that took place a day later, the day Pfc. Myron Renne was killed, as O'Brien still remembers. According to Taylor, the

Vietnamese police discovered her. Taylor has his information from uncited interviews. "Veterans of War" conflates this woman and the woman from July 16, and dates the event on May 5—either an act of creative license or an honest confusion. The details of the memoir, the article, Taylor, and the battalion logs align to date the episode July 22. It's possible Taylor's sources confused the two women as well.

29. DSJ, July 22, 1969, #15, #27, #30, #42.

30. DSJ, July 22, 1969, #52.

31. Taylor, *Our War*, p. 313.

32. Plans and Summaries, July 22, 1969.

33. O'Brien, "Medal Mania," *WP*, Feb. 25, 1973, p. C1.

34. DSJ, July 23, 1969, #31. See *If I Die*, 152–153.

35. In later years O'Brien mistakenly remembered him as the brigade commander, the battalion commander's commander, misidentified as Col. Joseph Clemons. Yet Clemons did not take command of the brigade until November. Taylor takes O'Brien's later memory at face value (*Our War*, p. 312).

36. The article states, "The battalion commander won a Distinguished Flying Cross," in a single-sentence paragraph, slyly disassociating the medal from this episode while letting the implication stand. O'Brien, "Medal Mania," *WP*, Feb. 25, 1973, p. C1.

37. Other casualties that day: Pfc. Harold J. Rayborn, Sgt. John Franklin, Jr., 1st Lt. Henry Conklin, Pfc. Robert J. Olenzak, Pfc. Thomas Trabucco (S-1 DSJ, July 23, 1969, #4).

38. Jerry Karr quoted in email from Bob Wolf, Sept. 21, 2008 (HRC 51.2).

39. O'Brien, "Medal Mania"; and *If I Die*, p. 153.

40. DSJ, July 23, 1969, #31.

41. *If I Die*, p. 153.

42. O'Brien email to Bob Wolf, Sept. 5, 2007 (HRC 51.2).

43. DSJ, July 24, 1969, #24, #27.

44. S-1 DSJ, July 24, 1969, #5.

45. *If I Die*, p. 153.

46. O'Brien email to Bob Wolf, Sept. 5, 2007 (HRC 51.2). In both this email and a later one to Wolf, O'Brien retells the documented version of Brauburger's death—that detonation debris killed him. It is not clear why O'Brien would not have told BuddyWolf about the cooking accident (Oct. 18, 2008; HRC 51.2).

47. *If I Die*, p. 154. DSJ, July 25, 1969, #39. Coordinates 49PBS677859 (Sheet 6739 II, Series L7014, Edition 3-DMA, Quảng Ngãi).

48. O'Brien, "Trick or Treat," *The Professional* 1, no. 81 (Oct. 11, 1969, p. 2; revised for "'And you will leave tomorrow,' said the monk; 'I'll be happy,'" *WDG*, Jan. 31, 1970, p. 3).

49. DSJ, July 25, 1969, #59, #62.

50. DSJ, July 26, 1969, #18.

51. DSJ, July 26, 1969, Summary.

52. DSJ, July 29, 1969, #18.

53. Taylor, *Our War*, p. 319.

54. DSJ, July 29, 1969, Summary.

55. DSJ, July 30, 1969, #33, #43; S-1 DSJ, July 30, 1969, #4, #5.

56. DSJ, July 31, 1969, #12; DSJ, July 31, 1969, #44, Summary.

57. DSJ, Aug. 1, 1969, #23, #32, #40, #43, #53; DSJ, Aug. 2, 1969, #16, #17, #48, #50.

58. DSJ, Aug. 3, 1969, #16, #17, #23, #35, #40, #54.

59. DSJ, Aug. 4, 1969, #16, #35, #40, #42, #49. The casualties were Pfc. Robert E. Emerson (right foot) and Pfc. Eddie L. Thorton (high temp and racing pulse) (S-1 DSJ, Aug. 4, 1969, #7).

60. DSJ, Aug. 5, 1969, #25, #40; Casualty: Sgt. William W. Crowl (S-1 DSJ, Aug. 5, 1969, #5).

61. DSJ, Aug. 6, 1969, #13.

62. John Hollman email to Bob Wolf, Oct. 15, 2009 (HRC 51.2).

63. O'Brien radioed for the dust-off at 0853 (DSJ, Aug. 7, 1969, #16, #17, #18, Plans and Sum-maries; Taylor, *Our War*, p. 322). Wounded: Pfc. Ralph Greer, Pvt. Freddy Eason, Sgt. Ronny R. Dunn (S-1 DSJ, Aug. 7, 1969, #3); *If I Die*, p. 154. The August 7 episode might be referenced in "Step Lightly"—"three legs, ten minutes ago" (*If I Die*, p. 123). The letter to Hansen reveals he had a few minutes; the grid coordinate in the essay is in the very near vicinity; and the essay's frustrating dust-off request is suggestive of the radio call in Taylor. But the essay's three mines over three days, and seven legs and one arm, does not match with the days prior to August 7.

64. DSJ, Aug. 7, 1969, #48.

65. To Hansen, undated [Aug. 7, 1969] (HRC uncataloged).

66. *If I Die*, p. 118.

67. *TTTC*, pp. 5, 2–3.

68. Taylor's book presents uncited vignettes as facts that Taylor seems to have gleaned from one person's memory forty years later. It is quite possible his interview subject was re-membering the day Myron K. Renne died, when O'Brien argued with the battalion com-mander about picking up casualties.

69. To Hansen [Aug. 7, 1969].

70. Taylor, *Our War*, p. 323.

71. DSJ, Aug. 8, 1969, #23, #35, Frag Order 13–69; DSJ, Aug. 9, 1969, #24, #50, #53.

72. *If I Die*, p. 164.

73. Taylor, *Our War*, p. 327.

74. This account follows the battalion logs (DSJ, Aug. 10, 1969, #15, #24). *If I Die* says the tripped mine occurred an hour after Longgrear became commander (p. 164). O'Brien's timing is closer to the log's than Taylor's (*Our War*, p. 328), and the change-of-command time could have been logged an hour late. But O'Brien wasn't there. Casualties: Spec. Hector C. Mar-quez, Spec. James A. Rhode, Pfc. Luis L. Martinez, Sfc. Charles R. Gallagher, Sgt. Charles L. Barbo (DSJ, Aug. 10, 1969, #2).

75. Taylor, *Our War*, pp. 328–329; confirmed by Paul Longgrear.

76. *If I Die*, p. 151.

77. DSJ, Aug. 12, 1969, #16, #19, #25, #39.

78. DSJ, Aug. 17, 1969, #3, #38. The small-arms and M79 attack occurred late on the sixteenth. The unoccupied sub-hamlet, Phú Long 5, had evidence of a VC company's support base purportedly vacated an hour before the two Alpha platoons landed (Aug. 17, 1969, Plans and Summaries; DSJ, Aug. 18, 1969, #14, #17). Casualties: high temperature and rising (DSJ, Aug. 18, 1969, #45); convulsions (DSJ, Aug. 20, 1969, #41).

79. O'Brien mentions Shorty's going AWOL and then stepping on the mine in the memoir's chapter "Step Lightly" (*If I Die*, p. 120) as well as in the chapter's earlier incarnations.

80. DSJ, Aug. 21, 1969, #16, #21. Initial report was thirty VC; a late report finalized it at ten (DSJ, Aug. 21, 1969, #22). One hundred civilians were detained in Vân Tường 2 by a Popular Force unit (DSJ, Aug. 21, 1969, #16, #34).

81. *If I Die*, p. 168.

82. DSJ, Aug. 24, 1969, #15, #16, #18, #24. Casualty: Pfc. Teddy Delaney (S-1 DSJ, Aug. 24, 1969, #5; DSJ, Aug. 25, 1969, #3).

83. Paul Longgrear email to Bob Wolf, Aug. 31, 2009 (HRC 51.2); DSJ, Aug. 25, 1969, #48, #50, #51, #53; Aug. 26, 1969, Plans and Summaries.

84. *If I Die*, p. 169. DSJ, Aug. 27, 1969, #12, #15.

85. DSJ, Aug. 27, 1969, #17, #37, #48, #51.

86. DSJ, Aug. 29, 1969, #21; S-1 DSJ, Aug. 29, 1969, #5.

87. DSJ, Aug. 30, 1969, #21, #22, #28. The dog handler is identified only as "Weisfield." *If I Die* says the dog stepped on the mine; it does not mention the wounded woman. *If I Die* is the source for the under-construction refugee village (p. 170).

12. GATOR DAYS

1. DSJ, Sept. 1, 1969, #21.

2. Associated Press, "Ho Chi Minh Is Reported Near Death," *WDG*, Sept. 3, 1969, p. 1; Tillman Durdin, "Ho Chi Minh Dead at 79; North Vietnam Expected to Hold to War Policies," *NYT*, Sept. 4, 1969, p. 1.

3. *GAC*, p. 271.

4. DSJ, Sept. 6, 1969, #44.

5. DSJ, Sept. 8, 1969, #9. The language disseminated to battalions, emphasizing the need to keep American casualties "to an absolute minimum," suggests an additional motive of deflating the sails of the planned nationwide Moratorium to End the War in Vietnam.

6. DSJ, Sept. 24, 1969, #24. See James P. Harrison, *The Endless War: Vietnam's Struggle for Independence* (New York: Columbia University Press, 1989), p. 78. Less likely is the fighting against French reoccupation of Sài Gòn in September 1945.

7. *If I Die*, p. 172.

8. 198th Brigade, LZ Bayonet, *The Bayonet* 1, no. 17 (Oct. 13, 1969), pp. 1, 6. The description cribbed language from the award citation. It's possible O'Brien wrote the anonymous article for the battalion's newsletter. The ceremony took place at 11:15 a.m. on Oct. 5 (S-1 DSJ, Oct. 5, 1969, #4).

9. DSJ, Sept. 19, 1969, #28; DSJ, Sept. 20, 1969, #20, Summary; DSJ, Oct. 9, 1969, #15.

10. "Baby, the Rains Must Fall!," *The Professional* 1, no. 80 (Oct. 4, 1969), p. 2. Anonymous, but O'Brien's authorship is highly likely.

11. 198th Brigade, *The Bayonet* 1, no. 25 (Dec. 8, 1969), pp. 1, 4.

12. 198th Brigade, *The Bayonet* 1, no. 22 (Nov. 17, 1969), pp. 3, 5. The article includes an odd co-writer credit for *The Bayonet*'s editor, Pfc. Bill Eftink.

13. "A Reason for It All," *The Professional* 1, no. 80 (Oct. 4, 1969), pp. 1–2.

14. *The Professional* 1, no. 81 (Oct. 11, 1969), p. 6.

15. *The Professional* 1, no. 81 (Oct. 11, 1969), p. 8.

16. "Trick or Treat," *The Professional* 1, no. 81 (Oct. 11, 1969), pp. 1–2.

17. John Herbers, "Opponents React," *NYT*, Oct. 16, 1969, p. 1.

18. "Mondale Repudiates U.S. War Objectives," *Minneapolis Tribune*, Oct. 16, 1969, p. 1; Charles Hauck, "Mondale and Bond: Speaking Out Against the War," *Mac Weekly*, Oct. 24, 1969, pp. 1, 3.

19. He applied for October 25, per letter to Erik Hansen, undated [Aug. 7, 1969] (HRC uncataloged), and was back at Gator by Oct. 31 for his promotion to sergeant.

20. To Mom, Dad & Greg [Nov. 9, 1969] (HRC 27.6).

21. *If I Die*, p. 177.

22. To Mom, Dad & Greg [Nov. 9, 1969].

23. *TTTC*, pp. 1–2.

24. *TTTC*, 129–130.

25. *If I Die*, 161. The numbers vary. By 0340, seven hours after the initial reporting, the journal recorded twenty-four or twenty-nine evacuated wounded (second digit difficult to discern), seven non-evacuated wounded, and twenty killed (DSJ S-2/3, Nov. 9, 1969, #7); this closely matches O'Brien's letter written later that morning of twenty killed and thirty-five wounded (to Mom, Dad, & Greg, undated [Nov. 9, 1969] [HRC 27.6]). At 1320, the battalion revised the count—"11 initially KIA. 33 initially WIA and dusted off (2 died in hospital for a total of 13 [K]IA). 4 WIA and not d/o" (DSJ S-2/3, Nov. 9, 1969, #28)—the math matches the memoir for KIAs and nearly for WIAs. The entry concludes, "Prov[ince] chief told the people it was VC mortars so we did not apologize." The first round of solatium payments to next-of-kin was completed by Nov. 10, the same day an investigation began for additional payments (DSJ S-5, Nov. 10, 1969, #4, #6). Those would be the "twenty dollars for each wounded villager; thirty-three dollars and ninety cents for each death" delivered one "month later" noted in *If I Die* (p. 161).

26. 300–400 in Ben Cole, "Was 'Pinkville' Massacre Site?," *Indianapolis Star*, Nov. 14, 1969, p. 22; 460 per the Associated Press (e.g., "American Troops Blamed for Murder of 460 Viet Civilians," *Northwest Arkansas Times*, Nov. 17, 1969, p. 1); and 567 in Henry Kamm, "Vietnamese Say G.I.'s Slew 567 in Town," *NYT*, Nov. 17, 1969, p. 1.

27. Seymour Hersh, "GIs Call Viet Killings 'Point Blank Murder,'" *Plain Dealer* (Cleveland), Nov. 20, 1969, p. 5-B.

28. Seymour Hersh, *Cover-Up: The Army's Secret Investigation of the Massacre at My Lai 4* (New York: Random House, 1972), pp. 15–16.

29. To Hansen, Apr. 21, 1974, second entry of letter begun Apr. 20 (HRC uncataloged).

30. DSJ, Nov. 1, 1969, #11; DSJ, Nov. 9, 1969, #35, and Daily INTSUM [Intelligence Summary], Nov. 10, 1969, #84–69.

31. DSJ, Nov. 15, 1969, #33, #39.

32. Katy MacDonald and Dixie Clegg: "Playmate Visits LZs," *The Bayonet* 1, no. 22 (Nov. 17, 1969), pp. 3, 5; also "Playmate Visits Troops," American Division, *Southern Cross* 2, no. 39 (Dec. 26, 1969), p. 8.

33. O'Brien's memoir has Bob Hope on Christmas Day, although documents date it on Christmas Eve (S-5 DSJ, Dec. 24, 1969, #3; David W. Taylor, *Our War: The History and Sacrifices of an Infantry Battalion in the Vietnam War, 1968–1971* [Medina, OH: War

Journal Publishing, 2011], p. 380). It was a smaller affair than the prior year's Christmas Eve Chu Lai show, which had an audience of eighteen thousand ("Christmas '68 Brings Hope to 18,000 Troops," *Southern Cross* 2, no. 2 [Jan. 19, 1969], pp. 1, 4–5). The 1969 show was not mentioned in either of the division's publications, *Southern Cross* or *Americal*.

34. DSJ, Dec. 30, 1969, #62, #66; DSJ, Dec. 31, 1969, #23, #46. As recorded in the battalion log, this incident most closely matches O'Brien's memory of an event that happened in November or December of his time assigned to Gator.

35. *TTTC*, p. 271.

36. DSJ, Dec. 30, 1969, #17; OPLAN 11–69.

37. *If I Die*, p. 185.

38. My Lai 4 DSJ, Jan. 6, 1970, #31. An early visitor to the site, General John W. Donaldson, the Americal's assistant division commander, had, as a colonel, commanded the brigade to which Lt. Calley's unit belonged. Although he took over the unit seven months after the war crimes had been committed, his record as the 11th Brigade's commander would be stained by a 1971 accusation of his own war crimes for allegedly shooting Vietnamese civilians from his helicopter, killing six and wounding one, in seven distinct episodes. Donaldson made two visits before any outsiders arrived (My Lai DSJ, Dec. 30, 1969, #5; My Lai DSJ, Jan. 1, 1970, #22). See Douglas Robinson, "Army Drops Charges Against General Accused of Killing 6 South Vietnamese Civilians," *NYT*, Dec. 10, 1971, p. 18.

39. The Reuters reporter was Allen MacFlaid (My Lai DSJ, Jan. 8, 1970, #10).

40. To Mom, Dad, & Greg, Feb. 9, 1970 (HRC 27.6).

41. O'Brien, "My Lai: 'They' Are Dinks and You Curse Their Lying Tongues," *WDG*, Jan. 21, 1970, pp. 1, 4.

42. Congressional Record—Extension of Remarks, E735–E736.

43. From James Vance, Jan. 12, 1973 (HRC 4.5); handwritten note for "My Lai in May" chapter on *If I Die* final typescript, with revisions (HRC 4.2).

44. On the satchel charge, see Taylor, *Our War*, p. 389; on the long-term disabilities, see Paul Longgrear quoted in email from Bob Wolf, Nov. 28, 2011 (HRC 51.2).

45. DSJ, Jan. 4, 1970, #12; Plans and Summaries, Jan. 4, 1970.

46. To Hansen [c. Jan. 16, 1970] (HRC uncataloged).

47. *If I Die*, pp. 192–195. According the memoir, the XO grabbed a Delta Company soldier. But from before Operation Hammurabi ended on January 11 and well into March, Delta was based at AO Serene, west of Pinkville, far to the south of FSB Gator and Trì Bình. The Gator and Trì Bình mission belonged to Alpha until January 16, Charlie until January 29, and then Bravo until February 11, at which point Alpha resumed it. Presuming O'Brien would have remembered an Alpha soldier, the incident must have occurred between January 16 and February 11, the picked-up soldier either from Charlie or Bravo (see 5–46 Plans and Summaries for these dates). Michael Casey, from the 23rd Military Police Company at LZ Bayonet, was tasked to investigate the burned building. Casey confirms O'Brien's account.

48. E.g., DSJ, Jan. 26, 1970, #58; INTSUM #26–70, Jan. 26, 1970; DSJ, Feb. 1, 1970, #24; INTSUM #33–70, Feb. 2, 1970.

49. S-4 DSJ, Jan. 18, 1970, #3.

50. To Hansen [c. Jan. 16, 1970] and [c. Jan. 28, 1970] (HRC uncataloged).

51. This letter specifies the thirty-nine-day extension with a DEROS date of March 16 (O'Brien to Mom, Dad & Greg [Nov. 9, 1969] [HRC 27.6]). A later letter specifies a forty-one-day extension and a DEROS date of March 17 (to Erik Hansen [c. Jan. 16, 1970], HRC

uncataloged). One or both letters get the math wrong. No letters from O'Brien's time on Gator are dated or postmarked. With reasonable accuracy, their dates can be established from internal evidence, and then other events they mention—such as his leave to Manila—can be dated accordingly.

52. To Hansen [c. Jan. 16, 1970] (HRC uncataloged); to Fred Kramer, Dean of Students, Macalester College (received Sept. 25, 1969).

53. To Mom, Dad, Greg [Feb. 28, 1970] (HRC 27.6).

54. O'Brien, "From Vietnam: Some Thoughts on Mines, a War, and Bitterness," *WDG*, Mar. 23, 1970, p. 3. See *If I Die*, p. 123.

55. O'Brien, "'And You Will Leave Tomorrow,' Said the Monk; 'I'll Be Happy,'" *WDG*, Jan. 31, 1970, p. 3.

56. Plans and Summaries, Feb. 11, 1970; DSJ, Feb. 13, 1970, #7, #20. According to Taylor, a single door gunner kept firing after the other crews had ceased, wounding the two—Sgt. Wayne Cherrholmes and Pfc. Paul Curtis—and killing the third, Pfc. Michael Glenn (Taylor, *Our War*, p. 405).

57. DSJ, Mar. 3, 1970, #41.

58. Although letters home offer March 16 and then March 17 as his future departure date, O'Brien's official military records document his last day as March 15 (DD214, HRC 27.6). The fifteenth also more or less matches his last letter home, from Feb. 28: "In a week or less the battalion is being moved into Chu Lai, and in another week, I'll be flying home, out of the army" (to Mom, Dad, Greg, undated [HRC 27.6]). His reference to the first week of March must have referred to the first stage of the unit's departure, or to the initially planned first stage, as the battalion continued operating from Gator into the last week of the month.

13. RETURNEE

1. O'Brien, "Surviving in Vietnam and the U.S.A.," *Boston Phoenix*, Jan. 23, 1973, pp. 8, 26. O'Brien used a slightly revised version of the passage in "Prisoners of Peace," *Penthouse*, March 1974, pp. 46, 61.

2. Don McLeod, Associate Press, "Bibles, Flags, March in D.C.," *WDG*, Apr. 6, 1970, p. 8.

3. 1034 Summit Avenue, Carriage House, St. Paul: to Hansen, July 9, 1970 (HRC uncataloged); VA Benefits Card (HRC 27.6).

4. Associated Press, "Nixon: Peace Is Now in Sight," *WDG*, Apr. 21, 1970, p. 1.

5. Molly Ivins, "Rubin, Crowd Zero In on Honeywell," *Minneapolis Tribune*, Apr. 28, 1970, p. 20.

6. Richard M. Nixon, "Address to the Nation on the Situation in Southeast Asia," Apr. 30, 1970, millercenter.org/the-presidency/presidential-speeches/april-30–1970-address -nation-situation-southeast-asia.

7. Quoted in Geoffrey C. Ward and Ken Burns, *The Vietnam War: An Intimate History*, based on a documentary film series by Ken Burns and Lynn Novick (New York: Alfred A. Knopf, 2017), p. 454.

8. "Students Barricade Humphrey's Office," *Minneapolis Tribune*, May 5, 1970, p. 1.

9. Associated Press, "War Protests Swell on Campuses of Minnesota," *WDG*, May 7, 1970, p. 11.

10. Associated Press, "Bayonets Pierce 11 at N.M. War Protests," *WDG*, May 9, 1970, p. 1.

11. "State Anti-War Demonstration 'Largest Ever,'" *Winona Daily News*, May 11, 1970, p. 5.

12. Quoted in Ward and Burns, *The Vietnam War*, p. 451.

13. AP, "State Anti-War Demonstration Largest Ever." On claim of eighty-six thousand: United Press International, "Classes Resume After Massive State March," *St. Cloud Daily Times*, May 11, 1970, p. 14.

14. The President's Commission on Campus Unrest—the Scranton Report, published Sept. 26, 1970—cites Brandeis University's National Student Strike Information Center's evidence of 448 campuses. The number was surely higher, as the center popped up practically overnight, creating its network and methods on the fly.

15. President's Commission on Campus Unrest, p. 18.

16. Ted Smebakken, "Macalester Students Sober, Dedicated in Protesting War," *Minneapolis Star*, May 15, 1970, p. 15A. For a mostly accurate summary of those weeks at Macalester, see *Mac Weekly*, May 19, 1970, p. 2.

17. Molly Ivins, "Students Take Antiwar Messages to Churches, Classes, Homes," *Minneapolis Tribune*, May 19, 1970, p. 27. See also Smebakken, "Macalester Students Sober, Dedicated."

18. Juan de Onis, "Nixon Puts 'Bums' Label on Some College Radicals," *NYT*, May 2, 1970, pp. 1, 10.

19. *DMB*, pp. 296–297.

20. Associated Press, "Massachusetts Forbids GIs in Vietnam," *WDG*, Apr. 3, 1970, p. 4.

21. Associated Press, "Honor America Extravaganza: Politics Show?," *WDG*, July 3, 1970, p. 12.

22. To Hansen, July 9, 1970 (HRC uncataloged).

23. To Hansen, Jan. 17, 1973, and Jan. 23, 1973 (HRC uncataloged).

24. O'Brien, "Surviving in Vietnam and the U.S.A.," pp. 8, 26.

25. O'Brien, "Claudia Mae's Wedding Day," *Redbook*, Oct. 1973, p. 143.

26. O'Brien, "Claudia Mae's Wedding Day," p. 150.

27. William Pelfrey, "The Next Nick Adams," *NYT*, July 6, 1972, p. 37.

28. O'Brien, "Our Fathers' War," unpublished typescript, p. 6, "Misc Box 1," Wayne Karlin Papers, Connelly Library Special Collections, La Salle University.

29. O'Brien, "Our Fathers' War," p. 17.

30. O'Brien, "Our Fathers' War," p. 10.

31. See O'Brien, "The Violent Vet," *Esquire*, Dec. 1979, p. 99; *TTTC*, p. 179.

32. Sonya B. Norman and Shira Maguen, "Moral Injury," PTSD: National Center for PTSD, U.S. Department of Veterans Affairs, ptsd.va.gov/professional/treat/cooccurring/moral_injury.asp. See also Syracuse University's Moral Injury Project, moralinjuryproject.syr.edu/about-moral-injury/.

33. O'Brien in Patrick A. Smith, *Conversations with Tim O'Brien* (Jackson: University Press of Mississippi, 2012), pp. 113–114.

34. *DMB*, p. 266.

35. Robert Jay Lifton, *Home from the War: Vietnam Veterans, Neither Victims nor Executioners* (New York: Simon & Schuster, 1973), pp. 128, 283, 286–287.

36. Lifton, *Home from the War*, p. 128.

37. Lifton, *Home from the War*, pp. 191–192, 317.

38. Lifton, *Home from the War*, pp. 401–402.

39. Lifton, *Home from the War*, p. 402.

40. O'Brien, "Prisoners of Peace," p. 115.

14. LINES OF DEPARTURE (1)

1. To Hansen, Sept. 22, 1970 (HRC uncataloged). The letter mentions registration "tomorrow"; the Sept. 23 date is confirmed in the "Calendar," *Courses of Instruction for Harvard & Radcliffe, College of Arts and Sciences, 1970–1971*, p. v. Classes began on Monday, Sept. 28. iiif.lib.harvard.edu/manifests/view/drs:467339004$7i.

2. O'Brien, "Ambush," *Boston Magazine*, Apr. 1993, p. 66.

3. O'Brien, "Prisoners of Peace," *Penthouse*, March 1974, p. 115.

4. James Fallows, "What Did You Do in the Class War, Daddy?," *Washington Monthly*, Oct. 1975, p. 16.

5. *DMB*, pp. 85–86.

6. To Hansen, Oct. 21, 1970 (HRC uncataloged). Harvard University Transcript for William Timothy O'Brien issued Apr. 30, 2021; courses listed in *Courses of Instruction, 1970–1971*.

7. Taught, respectively, by Samuel Huntington and Samuel Popkin (government/political science), Stanley Hoffman (social science), and Alexander Woodside (history).

8. Andrew J. Gawthorpe, "'Mad Dog?' Samuel Huntington and the Vietnam War," *Journal of Strategic Studies* 41, no. 1–2 (2018), pp. 318–319.

9. Scott W. Jacobs, "Bomb Blasts CFIA Library; Damage Limited, None Hurt," *Harvard Crimson*, Oct. 14, 1970); Garrett Epps and Samuel Z. Goldhaber, "Police Seek Two Suspects in Explosion at the CFIA," *Harvard Crimson*, Oct. 15, 1970; "Letter," *Harvard Crimson*, Oct. 15, 1970; "CFIA Bombed," *Harvard Crimson*, June 17, 1971.

10. Michael E. Kinsley, "Enthusiastic Crowd Jams Teach-In," *Harvard Crimson*, Feb. 23, 1971; Thomas Oliphant, "'Rolling Thunder' Is Antiwar Theme at Harvard Rally," *Boston Globe*, Feb. 23, 1971, pp. A1, A4; Robert Healey, "Peace Students Changing Mood," *Boston Globe*, Feb. 24, 1971, p. 21. A second event featured a handful of local and student activists and drew an audience of about 150 (Jeffery L. Baker, "Teach-Ins Reveal U. S. Role in Indochina," *Harvard Crimson*, Mar. 13, 1971; see also Peter Shapiro, "A Spring of Rekindled Activism," *Harvard Crimson*, Sept. 1, 1972).

11. William Greider, "Calley Convicted of 22 Murders: 102 Total Reduced by Jury," *WP*, Mar. 30, 1971, pp. A1, A9.

12. William Greider, "Life at Hard Labor Ordered for Calley," *WP*, Apr. 1, 1971, pp. A1, A6; News Dispatch, "Officials, Veterans Groups Ask Clemency for Lt. Calley," *WP*, Apr. 1, 1971, p. A6.

13. William Greider, "Calley's Trial: The Moral Question and Battlefield Laws," *WP*, Apr. 5, 1971, p. A20.

14. To Hansen, Apr. 13, 1971 (HRC uncataloged).

15. To Hansen, Apr. 13, 1971 (HRC uncataloged).

16. In Patrick A. Smith, *Conversations with Tim O'Brien* (Jackson: University Press of Mississippi, 2012), p. 112.

17. Janny Scott, "Now It Can Be Told: How Neil Sheehan Got the Pentagon Papers," *NYT*, Jan. 7, 2021, updated Jan. 9, 2021, www.nytimes.com/2021/01/07/us/pentagon-papers-neil-sheehan.html.

18. Neil Sheehan, "Vietnam Archive: Pentagon Study Traces 3 Decades of Growing U. S. Involvement," *NYT*, June 13, 1971, pp. 1, 38–40.

19. Matt Schudel, "Ben H. Bagdikian, Journalist with Key Role in Pentagon Papers Case, Dies at 96," *WP*, Mar. 11, 2016.

20. New York Times Co. v. United States, 403 U.S. 713 (1971).

21. O'Brien, "Gravel: Public Is Final Judge," *WP*, July 5, 1975, p. A8.

22. *If I Die*, p. 18.

23. To Hansen, postmarked Aug. 11, 1971 (HRC uncataloged).

24. O'Brien, "Democrats Select Miami Beach," *WP*, June 30, 1971, p. A10.

25. O'Brien, "POW Kin Clash at Session Here," *WP*, July 23, 1971, p. A14.

26. O'Brien, "Relatives of War Prisoners Blast Madison Avenue Campaign," *WP*, Aug. 13, 1971, p. A6.

27. See Gerald Nicosia, *Home to War: A History of the Vietnam Veterans' Movement* (New York: Carroll & Graf, 2004), pp. 154–157; Michael J. Allen, *Until the Last Man Comes Home: POWs, MIAs, and the Unending Vietnam War* (Chapel Hill: University of North Carolina Press, 2009), pp. 52–53.

28. O'Brien, "Dec. 4 Is First in Lottery for 1972 Draft," *WP*, Aug. 6, 1971, pp. A1, A6; "Mitchell Rules Out U.S. Jury on Kent," *WP*, Aug. 14, 1971, p. A1, A7.

29. Stuart Auerbach, "Worden Walks in Far Space," *WP*, Aug. 6, 1971, pp. A1, A8.

30. O'Brien, "Business Poll Finds Legislators Don't Mirror Voters' Opinions," *WP*, Aug. 23, 1971, p. A2.

31. O'Brien, "GAO Hits Pentagon's PR Costs," *WP*, Aug. 22, 1971, p. A5. The program came to public light in the CBS documentary *The Selling of the Pentagon*, produced by Peter Davis (aired Feb. 23, 1971), and based on Senator J. William Fulbright's book *The Pentagon's Propaganda Machine* (New York: Liveright, 1970).

32. To Hansen [early Aug. 1971] (HRC uncataloged).

33. O'Brien, "Women Organize for More Power," *WP*, July 11, 1971, pp. A1, A10.

34. O'Brien, "Women Cry 'Sexist' at McCarthy, Spock," *WP*, July 12, 1971, pp. A1, A7.

35. O'Brien, "18-Year-Old Vote Officially Becomes the Law," *WP*, July 6, 1971, p. A4.

36. Papers were free to edit to fit their requirements and to supply a new title. The op-ed "American 'Real' Owners Hiding Behind Code Names" picked up by the *Capitol Journal* in Salem, Oregon (Aug. 11, 1971, p. 5) was incorrectly attributed to O'Brien. The original is Nicholas von Hoffman, "A Good Question: A Commentary," *WP*, Aug. 6, 1971, pp. B1, B4.

37. To Hansen, postmarked Aug. 11, 1971 (HRC uncataloged).

38. To Hansen [early Aug. 1971] (HRC uncataloged).

39. To Hansen, postmarked Aug. 11, 1971 (HRC uncataloged); to Aunt Mary [Oct. 1971].

40. To Hansen [early Aug. 1971] (HRC uncataloged).

41. To Aunt Mary [Oct. 1971].

42. Harvard Transcript; *Courses of Instruction, 1970–1971*, iiif.lib.harvard.edu/manifests /view/drs:467340222$1i); to Aunt Mary [Oct. 1971].

43. David Landau, "Popkin Re-Subpoenaed by Ellsberg Investigators," *Harvard Crimson*, Oct. 8, 1971; Richard J. Meislin, "Popkin: The Limits of Academic Privilege," *Harvard Crimson*, June 15, 1972; Meislin, "Popkin Released from Jail; Steiner's Action 'Significant,'" *Harvard*

Crimson, Nov. 29, 1972. See also Stanford J. Ungar, "FBI Calls on Ellsberg Friends," *WP*, July 25, 1971, p. A3; "Harvard's Specialist on Vietnam: Samuel Lewis Popkin," *NYT*, Nov. 22, 1972, p. 40; Bill Kovach, "Popkin Freed in a Surprise as U.S. Jury Is Dismissed," *NYT*, Nov. 29, 1972, pp. 1, 22.

44. To Lawrence, Jan. 12, 1972 (SL 54).

45. To Hansen, Jan. 14, 1972 (HRC uncataloged).

46. Jonathan Mirsky, "The War in Vietnam," *NYT*, Nov. 26, 1967, p. T10, review of *Vietnam* by Mary McCarthy and *Authors Take Sides on Vietnam*, ed. Cecil Woolf and John Bagguley.

47. Malcolm Browne, "Homage to Quang Ngai," *WP Book World*, May 27, 1973, p. BW3.

48. Fallows, "What Did You Do in the Class War, Daddy?," p. 17.

49. See Timothy J. Lomperis, *"Reading the Wind": The Literature of the Vietnam War; An Interpretative Critique*, with a bibliographic commentary by John Clark Pratt (Durham, NC: Duke University Press, 1987), pp. 43–44.

50. Three Caputo poems might be the earliest literary works from the war by a U.S veteran: "War Poem," *Midwestern University Quarterly* (1966), pp. 37–39; "The Veterans" and "The Walking Dead," *Midwestern University Quarterly* (1967), pp. 24–26.

51. Wayne Karlin, "Writing the War," *War, Literature & the Arts: An International Journal of the Humanities* 31 (2019), p. 8. See also W. D. Ehrhart, "Soldier-Poets of the Vietnam War," *Virginia Quarterly Review* (Spring 1987), vqronline.org/essay/soldier-poets-vietnam-war.

52. Sandra Wittman's *Writing About Vietnam: A Bibliography of the Literature of the Vietnam Conflict* (Boston: G. K. Hall, 1989), pp. 97–168, lists only four other titles that qualify as a combat soldier's memoir: David Bozek, *Artillery Medic in Vietnam* (1971); Charles Coe, *Young Man in Vietnam* (1968); Barry Sadler, *I'm the Lucky One* (1967); and Samuel Vance, *The Courageous and the Proud* (1970). It's extremely doubtful O'Brien knew about any of them. Donald Duncan's *The New Legions* (1967) was more screed than recollection. *Lieutenant Calley: His Own Story* (1971) hardly counted. There were a handful in the form of letters and diaries, David Parks's *G.I. Diary* (1968) the most important, plus a few first-person accounts by POWs, chaplains, and doctors.

53. Interoffice Memorandum, Seymour Lawrence to Ross Claiborne about POP SMOKE, Feb. 29, 1972 (SL 54).

54. From Lawrence, Feb. 29, 1972; also Jan. 16, 1972 (SL 54; also HRC 4.6). Optimism: to Hansen, Mar. 13, 1972 (HRC uncataloged). New chapters: to Lawrence, Mar. 3, 1972 (SL 54).

55. Delacorte Press/Seymour Lawrence contract information sheet, Apr. 24, 1971 (SL 54).

56. Ted Maas, Delacorte/Dial, to Seymour Lawrence, Aug. 4, 1972 (SL 54).

57. Richard Huett to Seymour Lawrence, Aug. 28, 1972 (SL 54).

58. From Lawrence, Oct. 12, 1972; C. Michael Curtis to Lawrence, Oct. 2, 1972 (SL 54).

59. Harvard Transcript.

60. To Aunt Mary, Jan. 18, 1973. Elsewhere he described it as about "war and rationality" (to Hansen, May 28, 1973 [HRC uncataloged]).

61. *If I Die*, p. 89.

62. To Hansen, Oct. 21, 1970 (HRC uncataloged).

63. O'Brien, "Multiple 1964–1968 Peace Efforts and Their Code Names," *WP*, June 27, 1972, p. A13.

64. Jack Fuller and Tim O'Brien, "Army Study Asks Use of Herbicides," *WP*, Aug. 13, 1972, pp. A1, A15.

65. O'Brien, "Signing Up Less-Educated Viet GIs for Benefits Poses Problems," *WP*, June 15, 1972, pp. H1, H2; O'Brien, "Improved Viet Vet Benefits Urged," *WP*, Sept. 14, 1973, p. A2. The Stuart F. Feldman Papers are kept by the Historical Society of Pennsylvania.

66. O'Brien, "Targets of Political Appeal," *WP*, July 20, 1972, pp. E1, E5.

67. *If I Die*, pp. 4–5.

68. O'Brien, "Targets of Political Appeal." O'Brien followed up in a second article: "Vietnam Veterans Start Nixon Drive," *WP*, July 29, 1972, p. A5.

69. O'Brien, "Poll Finds Student Turnout Heavy in Primary Elections," *WP*, June 5, 1972, p. A12; O'Brien, "FCC Allows Racist Ads of Candidate," *WP*, Aug. 4, 1972, pp. A1, A18.

70. O'Brien, "Postal Union Endorses McGovern," *WP*, Aug. 23, 1972, p. A12.

71. William Greider, "The Selection: Tripping from Crisis to Crisis," *WP*, Aug. 6, 1972, pp. A1, A14; O'Brien, "Shriver Loses Bid in South," *WP*, Aug. 24, 1972, p. A9; O'Brien, "Shriver Misses Dinner with Head of Ohio AFL-CIO," *WP*, Aug. 27, 1972, p. A2.

72. O'Brien, "Tennis Foreplay: New Sex-Courting Scene," *Gallery*, Sept. 1975, p. 93; O'Brien, "Shriver Misses Dinner with Head of Ohio AFL-CIO."

73. Alfred E. Lewis, "5 Held in Plot to Bug Democrats' Office Here," *WP*, June 18, 1972, pp. A1, A21. The other listed contributors were Bart Barnes, Kirk Scharfenberg, Martin Weil, Claudia Lery, and Abbott Combes.

74. Security Officer's Log of the Watergate Office Building Showing Entry for June 17, 1972 (National Archives Identifier: 304970), Collection RN-SMOF: White House Staff Member and Office Files (Nixon Administration), 01/20/1969–08/09/1974, Records of the Watergate Special Prosecution Force, 1971–1977, Record Group 460, NARA. See also "Author O'Brien's Watergate Role Revealed," *St. Paul Pioneer Press* clipping (HRC 18.4).

75. To Lawrence, July 21, 1972; Dell change memo, July 21, 1972 (SL 54).

76. From Hansen, Aug. 21 [1972] (HRC 4.6). Hansen's handwritten draft is attached to O'Brien's response, postmarked Oct. 1, 1972 (HRC uncataloged).

77. *If I Die*, p. 23.

78. To Lawrence, Sept. 11, 1972 (SL 54); to Hansen, postmarked Oct. 1, 1972; Office Memorandum, Lucy Hebard to Sam [Lawrence], Sept. 18, 1972 (SL 54).

79. To Hansen, postmarked Oct. 1, 1972 (HRC uncataloged).

80. Lawrence responded to the new title on July 23, 1972. He first expressed worry regarding FitzGerald's title on Oct. 2, 1972. See also his letter of Oct. 12, 1972 (HRC 4.6).

81. To Lawrence, Oct. 4, 1972 (SL 54).

82. Dell Change Memo, Oct. 19, 1972 (SL 54)

83. Kerry and Emerson in O'Brien to Lawrence, Sept. 28, 1972; Kerry, Baez, VVAW and other veteran organizations in "Author's Questionnaire"; Ellsberg in Lawrence to Daniel Ellsberg, Dec. 5, 1972; Mailer and Wolfe: to Lawrence, Sept. 28, 1972 (SL 54).

84. To Hansen [fall 1972], first line, "Arrival date in twin cities set . . . ," envelope addressed to Hansen at 2240 Hillside, St. Paul (HRC uncataloged).

85. To Lawrence, Feb. 18, 1972; Jan. 30, 1973; and Feb. 11, 1973 (SL 54).

86. From Lawrence, Nov. 5, 1973 (SL 54).

87. To Lawrence, July 5, 1973 (SL 54).

88. To Lawrence, Apr. 12, 1973 (SL 54).

89. To Lawrence, July 10, 1973; from Lawrence, July 15, 1973; to Lawrence [fall 1973] (SL 54).

90. To Lawrence, Apr. 12, 1973 (SL 54).

15. Combat Coda

1. To Hansen, postmarked Oct. 1, 1972 (HRC uncataloged).

2. Ernest Hemingway, *A Farewell to Arms* (1929; repr. ed., New York: Simon & Schuster, 1995), p. 3.

3. Joe Sharkey, "Count Cadence for Young Tim," *Philadelphia Inquirer*, June 15, 1973; "Tale of Battle," *Times Literary Supplement*, Oct. 10, 1973; Clancy Sigal, "Children of Violence," *Sunday Times*, Sept. 30, 1973.

4. To Hansen, postmarked Oct. 1, 1972 (HRC uncataloged).

5. *If I Die*, p. 110.

6. *If I Die*, p. 68.

7. To Hansen, Nov. 1, 1972 (HRC uncataloged).

8. To Hansen, May 28, 1973, and Apr. 5, 1973 (HRC uncataloged).

9. Bob Wolf email to O'Brien et al., Sept. 3, 2009 (HRC 51.2).

10. To Hansen, July 15, 1975 (HRC uncataloged).

11. SP5 James Brown, "Reflection of Battle," *Americal* 3, no. 1 (Jan. 1970), inside front cover, www.americal.org/wp-content/uploads/2024/01/AMCAL-Mags/AMMAG_7001_small .pdf.

12. Yusef Komunyakaa, "Combat Pay for Jody," in *Dien Cai Dau* (Middletown, CT: Wesleyan University Press, 1988), p. 49.

16. Lines of Departure (2)

1. To Hansen, Oct. 4, 1972 (HRC uncataloged).

2. "January 23, 1973: Address to the Nation Announcing an Agreement on Ending the War in Vietnam," Miller Center website, University of Virginia, millercenter.org/the-presidency /presidential-speeches/january-23-1973-address-nation-announcing-agreement-ending -war.

3. *If I Die*, p. 61.

4. Engagement: to Lawrence, Apr. 12, 1973 (SL 54); to Hansen, Apr. 26, 1973 (HRC uncataloged).

5. From Lawrence, Feb. 21, 1973; to Lawrence, Feb. 23, 1973 (SL 54).

6. O'Brien flew out of Boston on the fourteenth: to Lawrence, June 14, 1973 (SL 54). Advertisement for Friday, June 22, reading in *WDG*, June 19, 1973, p. B3 (SL 57).

7. Office Memorandum, Carol Duffy to Alan Wellikoff, June 20, 1973 (SL 57).

8. To Lawrence, July 5, 1983 (SL 54).

9. To Lawrence, July 25, 1973 (SL 54); to Hansen, July 28, 1973 (HRC uncataloged).

10. To Lawrence, July 25, 1973; to Eunice K. Boehl, Contracts & Copyrights Manager, Dell Publishing, July 25, 1973 (SL 54).

11. To Hansen, July 28, 1973 (HRC uncataloged). O'Brien gave out the *Post*'s address to friends beginning on Tuesday, Aug. 14, 1973 (to Eunice K. Boehl, Contracts & Copyrights Manager, Dell Publishing, July 25, 1973, SL 54).

12. "Vietnam War Book Author to Autograph Copies Here," *Daily Mail* (Hagerstown, MD), Aug. 16, 1973, p. 36; also ad on p. 44.

13. Ora Ann Ernst, "Vietnam War Book Author to Marry Paramount Girl," *Daily Mail* (Hagerstown, MD), Aug. 18, 1973, p. 8; reprinted as "Tim O'Brien: He 'Grew Out of One War into Another,'" *Morning Herald* (Hagerstown, MD), Aug. 20, 1973, p. 9. The second article preserves the future verb tense even though it ran the day after the wedding.

14. To Hansen, Apr. 26, 1973 (HRC uncataloged).

15. To Hansen, May 15, 1973 (HRC uncataloged).

16. O'Brien, "Claudia Mae's Wedding Day," *Redbook*, Oct. 1973, p. 150.

17. Kera Bolinik, "How Low Can They Go?," *Salon*, Dec. 11, 2001, salon.com/2001/12/10/women_s_mags/.

18. *Kirkus Reviews*, Mar. 1, 1973; "Tale of Battle," *Times Literary Supplement*, Oct. 10, 1973.

19. Clancy Sigal, "Children of Violence," *Sunday Times*, Sept. 30, 1973.

20. Malcolm Browne, "Homage to Quang Ngai," *WP Book World*, May 27, 1973, p. BW3.

21. Annie Gottlieb, "Two Sides of a Modern Disaster," a joint review with James Strahs's *Seed Journal*, *NYT Book Review*, July 1, 1973, p. 10.

22. To Hansen, May 28, 1973 (HRC uncataloged); Interoffice Memorandum from Lawrence, June 19, 1973 (SL 54).

23. From Lawrence, Feb. 4, 1974; from Eleanor K. Pourron, Chairman, Best Books for Young Adults Committee, Nov. 22, 1974 (HRC 4.6).

24. To Lawrence, Oct. 31, 1973 (SL 54).

25. To Lawrence, Aug. 22, 1973 (SL 54); Anthony Astrachan and Tim O'Brien, "Stiff N.Y. Law on Drug Use Takes Effect," *WP*, Sept. 1, 1973, p. A1.

26. To Hansen, Sept. 23, 1973 (HRC uncataloged).

27. O'Brien, "Revolt on the Turnpike," *Penthouse*, Sept. 1974, p. 64.

28. O'Brien and Peter Milius, "Truck Strike Continues as Talks Stall," *WP*, Feb. 7, 1974, pp. A1, A11.

29. O'Brien, "Revolt on the Turnpike," p. 132.

30. O'Brien, "Goldwater Lauds Nixon as Leader," *WP*, Jan. 14, 1974, p. A1; "Backstage with Esquire," *Esquire*, Oct. 1977, p. 91.

31. O'Brien, "Dr. King's Mother Is Slain," *WP*, July 1, 1974, pp. A1, A6.

32. O'Brien, "University Homosexual Group Stirs Furor in Maine," *WP*, May 7, 1974, p. A28.

33. Gerald Nicosia, *Home to War: A History of the Vietnam Veterans' Movement* (New York: Carroll & Graf, 2004), p. 309.

34. O'Brien, "Veterans Display Hope, Friendships, Ideals, Frictions," *WP*, July 4, 1974, p. B8.

35. Timothy Crouse, *The Boys on the Bus* (1973; repr. ed., New York: Random House, 2003), pp. 407–408.

36. To Hansen, postmarked Aug. 11, 1971 (HRC uncataloged).

37. O'Brien, "Simplistic Demagoguery," *WP*, Oct. 23, 1973, p. B6. Sack was the writer behind Calley's 1971 self-excusing memoir.

38. O'Brien, "On Post-WW II Intervention," *Boston Globe*, Aug. 19, 1973, p. 109 (review of Herbert Tillema, *Appeal to Force: American Military Intervention in the Era of Containment*). See also O'Brien, "All the New World Losers," *Boston Globe*, Aug. 5, 1973, p. 57 (review of John Keats, *Eminent Domain: The Louisiana Purchase and the Making of America*).

39. *Penthouse* joined *Playboy* in supporting veterans and questioning the war. The Feb. 1971 *Playboy* "contained a full-page ad for VVAW donated by Hugh Hefner." By the start of Dewey Canyon III in April 1971, VVAW membership had swelled to "about 12,000" veterans, most of whom "had joined the organization following the *Playboy* ad" (Nicosia, *Home to War*, pp. 91, 101). The two magazines embraced the *make love, not war* counterculture mantra.

40. Nina Fortuna, American Society of Magazine Editors, email to author, May 3, 2021. According to *Penthouse* office scuttlebutt, a feminist contingent of the deciding body doomed *Penthouse*'s chances.

41. To Hansen, Oct. 18, 1973 (HRC uncataloged); to Lawrence, Oct. 31, 1973 (SL 54). On the eighteenth, O'Brien wrote that it was due "tomorrow," but on the thirty-first that he'd been working on it "the past two weeks."

42. O'Brien, "Prisoners of Peace," *Penthouse*, March 1974, p. 116.

43. O'Brien, "Prisoners of Peace," p. 47.

44. O'Brien, "Prisoners of Peace," p. 64.

45. O'Brien, "Prisoners of Peace," p. 61.

46. O'Brien, "Prisoners of Peace," p. 113.

47. O'Brien, "Prisoners of Peace," p. 114.

48. "Penthouse Forum," *Penthouse*, June 1974, p. 6.

49. Letters to the Editor, *Penthouse*, July 1974, pp. 8, 10; Letters to the Editor, *Penthouse*, May 1974, p. 28.

50. "Static," *Penthouse*, Apr. 1974, pp. 59–60.

51. O'Brien, "The G.I. Bill: Less than Enough," *Penthouse*, Nov. 1974, p. 140.

52. William Crawford Woods, "The Vietnam Veteran Looking for a Job," *Penthouse*, June 1974; Corinne Browne, "The Vietnam Veteran in Prison," *Penthouse*, July 1974.

53. To Hansen, Feb. 15, 1974 (HRC uncataloged).

54. To Hansen, Nov. 22, 1973 (HRC uncataloged).

55. To Hansen, Feb. 15, 1974 (HRC uncataloged).

56. "Veterans' Protest Broken Up," *WP*, Mar. 29, 1974, p. A27. The *Post* article and photo caption (A1) names Kovic, Bill Unger, John Adams, and "Max Waddell," a confusion of Max Inglett and Bob Waddell: it's Inglett, not Waddell, in the front-page photo (Nicosia, *Home to War*, p. 335). Woods is probably the unnamed *Post* reporter mentioned in the article, as he phoned in his version of events to an editor. He thinks he might be the person behind the wheelchair in the photo. Woods remembers Jack McCloskey being there—the two of them would bring the number up to the "seven" reported by the *Post*.

57. William Greider, "Viet Vets: A Sad Reminder," *WP*, Mar. 30, 1974, pp. A1, A5.

58. To Hansen, Sept. 23, 1973 (HRC uncataloged).

59. Seymour Lawrence/Delacorte Press Author's Questionnaire for POP SMOKE (SL 57).

60. From Robie Macauley, Nov. 12, 1973 (SL 54).

61. To Hansen, Apr. 5, 1974 (HRC uncataloged).

62. To Hansen, Oct. 10, 1974 (HRC uncataloged).

17. Juvenilia

1. "In my sophomore year at college . . ." Possibly remarks made at the James Jones Symposium, Nov. 6, 2009.

2. See, e.g., *Mac Weekly*, Apr. 15, 1966, p. 2; *Mac Weekly*, Apr. 7, 1967, p. 1. After political science, the subjects in which he took the most courses were philosophy (four), French (four), and sociology (three) (transcript, HRC 29.4).

3. Frederickson became a lawyer and eventually published three crime novels: *Witness for the Dead*, *A Cinderella Affidavit*, and *A Defense of the Dead*. His Rhodes Scholar friend Karl Marlantes volunteered for the marines and much later published two books about the war: *Matterhorn: A Novel of the Vietnam War* and *What It Is Like to Go to War*.

4. Kathryn and Byron Jackson, illustrated by Eloise Wilkin, *Busy Timmy* (New York: Little Golden Books, 1948). O'Brien has sometimes mistitled it "Timmy Is a Big Boy Now" after the 1951 song based on the book; see Patrick A. Smith, *Conversations with Tim O'Brien* (Jackson: University Press of Mississippi, 2012), pp. 101–102; *DMB*, p. 141.

5. Dad's (William Timothy O'Brien) Eulogy (HRC 50.4).

6. Dave McCauley, *A Fair in Time: Adventures in the Turkey Capital of the World* (CreateSpace, 2018), p. 25. The wagon detail is from O'Brien.

7. "Northfield [MN] Public Library Presents Tim O'Brien," Apr. 21, 1994, ntv.org/videos /authors/author-tim-obrien-at-the-northfield-public-library/.

8. "Northfield Public Library Presents Tim O'Brien."

9. Bread Loaf interview, audio recording, Aug. 24, 1979, Middlebury.

10. *DMB*, pp. 141–142, 252.

11. Smith, *Conversations*, p. 102.

12. Smith, *Conversations*, p. 101.

13. "Story I read as a boy—started me dreaming about becoming a writer" (HRC 61).

14. Bread Loaf interview, audio recording, Aug. 24, 1979.

15. *DMB*, pp. 124, 183.

16. Mary Hemingway writes that they "headed west on U.S. Route 63" out of Rochester to Mitchell, SD (*How It Was*, p. 501). U.S. 63 ran north-south; the Hemingways' most probable route would have taken them south on 63 and then west on U.S. 16 through Worthington.

17. Bound editions of *The Gobbler*, 1958–1963 (Nobles County Historical Society). See O'Brien's articles of Oct. 28, 1960; Feb. 14, 1961; and Mar. 24, 1961, from his ninth-grade year (see HRC 55.4).

18. *TTTC*, p. 15.

19. *TTTC*, p. 273.

20. "Tim O'Brien Reading," University of Indianapolis, Oct. 30, 1995.

18. A Man of Mythic Realism

1. To Hansen, May 15, 1973 (HRC uncataloged).

2. "A Perfect Communion" typescript, enclosed in O'Brien letter to Seymour Lawrence, May 25, 1973 (SL 54).

3. United Press International, "Bush Pilot Tells of Cannibalism," *NYT*, Mar. 2, 1973, p. 5.

4. To Hansen, May 15, 1973.

5. Lawrence to James Dickey, Oct. 12, 1972; Interoffice Memorandum, June 19, 1970 (SL 54).

6. O'Brien in Patrick A. Smith, *Conversations with Tim O'Brien* (Jackson: University Press of Mississippi, 2012), p. 127.

7. "rising star": Interoffice Memorandum, June 19, 1970; grateful for the contract's terms: O'Brien letter to Lawrence, July 5, 1970 (SL 54).

8. Chapter I (untitled draft) and "A Man of Melancholy Disposition (Draft Outline)" enclosed in O'Brien letter to Lawrence, May 25, 1973 (SL 54).

9. To Hansen, Sept. 23, 1973 (HRC uncataloged).

10. To Lawrence, Sept. 25, 1973 (SL 54).

11. Skiing and cold: to Hansen, Oct. 8, 1973; "primitive and fertile": to Hansen, Apr. 5, 1974 (HRC uncataloged). What else Hansen contributed is lost. Hansen recognized some elements and details in the published novel he had helped brainstorm, wincing but not begrudging their use.

12. To Hansen, Oct. 18, 1973 (HRC uncataloged).

13. To Hansen, Oct. 18, 1973; Nov. 22, 1973 (HRC uncataloged).

14. To Hansen, Nov. 22, 1973 (HRC uncataloged).

15. To Hansen, Jan. 11, 1974 (HRC uncataloged).

16. To Hansen, Feb. 15, 1974 (HRC uncataloged).

17. To Hansen, Feb. 28, 1974 (HRC uncataloged).

18. To Hansen, Mar. 10, 1974 (HRC uncataloged).

19. To Hansen, Apr. 20, 1974 (HRC uncataloged); see also letter of Mar. 10, 1974; United Press International, "Guild Votes to End 17-Day Strike over Pay at Washington Post," *NYT*, Apr. 25, 1974, p. 50.

20. To Hansen, Oct. 10, 1974 (HRC uncataloged).

21. To Hansen, Nov. 13, 1974 (HRC uncataloged).

22. To Hansen, Nov. 13, 1974 (HRC uncataloged).

23. Ted Maas memo to Lawrence, Nov. 11, 1974 (SL 54).

24. To Hansen, Dec. 16, 1974 (HRC uncataloged).

25. To Lawrence, Jan. 26, 1974 (SL 53). See also to Hansen, Jan. 25, 1975 (HRC uncataloged).

26. Marilynn Meeker to Lawrence, Jan. 26, 1975 (SL 53).

27. To Hansen, Mar. 3, 1975 (HRC uncataloged). He had to shorten the UK edition before his English publisher, Calder & Boyars, would buy the rights—see O'Brien to Hansen, Mar. 11, 1975 (HRC uncataloged).

28. Smith, *Conversations*, p. 128.

29. To Hansen, Mar. 3, 1975 (HRC uncataloged).

30. *Northern Lights*, pp. 12–13.

31. *Northern Lights*, pp. 32–33.

32. "Notes" [on *Northern Lights*] (HRC 11.10).

33. *Northern Lights*, p. 360.

34. To Hansen, Apr. 20, 1974 (HRC uncataloged).

35. Ernest Hemingway, *The Sun Also Rises* (1926; repr. ed., New York: Scribner, 1995), p. 251. On O'Brien's career-long affection for this Hemingway sentence, see "One True Sentence #32 with Tim O'Brien," Nov. 16, 2023, hemingwaysociety.org/one-true-sentence-32-tim-obrien.

36. Hemingway, *The Sun Also Rises*, p. 188; *Northern Lights*, p. 148.

37. E.g., O'Brien in Smith, *Conversations*, pp. 43, 62. In the first cited interview, O'Brien names *The Sun Also Rises* and *A Farewell to Arms*, but he mistakes the latter title—the novel's evidence points to Robert Jordan in *For Whom the Bell Tolls*, and it's this view of Jordan that the Hansen correspondence discusses in reference to *Northern Lights* (e.g., Mar. 10 [1974] [HRC uncataloged]).

38. To Hansen, Dec. 8, 1974 (HRC uncataloged).

39. Nov. 28, 1966: *Mac Weekly*, Nov. 18, 1966, p. 1.

40. Jung quoted in Roy Arthur Swanson, *Heart of Reason: Introductory Essays in Modern-World Humanities* (Minneapolis: T. S. Denison & Co., 1963), p. 34.

41. *Mac Weekly*, Dec. 2, 1966, p. 1.

42. *Mac Weekly*, Nov. 18, 1966, p. 1; the student quotes Swanson from the same book (*Heart of Reason*, pp. 218–219).

43. To Hansen, Apr. 23, 1975 (HRC uncataloged).

44. To Hansen, Nov. 22, 1973 (HRC uncataloged).

45. W. F. Kirby, "Introduction," *Kalevala: Land of the Heroes*, Vol. 1 translated from the Finnish by W. F. Kirby (London: J. M. Dent & Sons, 1907), p. x, www.gutenberg.org/cache/epub/25953/pg25953-images.html.

46. *Northern Lights*, pp. 69–70.

47. "Notes" [on *Northern Lights*] (HRC 11.10).

48. *Northern Lights*, p. 89.

49. *Northern Lights*, pp. 70–71.

50. *Northern Lights*, pp. 59–60.

51. To Hansen, Oct. 22, 1975 (HRC uncataloged).

52. To Hansen, Sept. 14 "or so," 1975 (HRC uncataloged).

53. To Hansen, Sept. 14 "or so," 1975 (HRC uncataloged).

54. Robert Graves, *The White Goddess: A Historical Grammar of Poetic Myth*, amended and enlarged edition (New York: Farrar, Straus and Giroux, 1966), pp. 11–12.

55. To Hansen, Oct. 18, 1973 (HRC uncataloged).

56. *Kirkus Reviews*, Aug. 1, 1975, posted online Oct. 2, 2011, www.kirkusreviews.com/book-reviews/tim-obrien/northern-lights-7/.

57. To Hansen, Nov. 22, 1973 (HRC uncataloged).

58. To Hansen, June 11, 1975; see also his initial reaction in letter of June 4, 1975 (HRC uncataloged).

59. "Description: Realism Issue," pshares.org/product/fall-1974/.

60. Henry let Lawrence know he had accepted the story on Feb. 12, 1974 (SL 54).

61. The quoted review is John W. Aldridge, "Vision of Man Raging in a Vacuum," *Saturday Review*, Oct. 19, 1974, pp. 18–21.

62. To Hansen, Nov. 19, 1974; see also letter of Dec. 8, 1974 (HRC uncataloged), which includes a clipping of Shaun O'Connell, "The Chaos of Experimenters," *Boston Sunday Globe*, Dec. 8, 1974, p. A-18, a review of Alvin J. Seltzer's *Chaos in the Novel—the Novel in Chaos.*

63. Joseph Epstein's review defines the postmodern sensibility in terms strikingly similar to O'Brien's about absurdism (Joseph Epstein, "Joseph Heller's Milk Train: Nothing More to Express," *WP Book World*, Oct. 6, 1974, pp. 1, 3). O'Brien the *WP* reporter probably read Epstein's review.

64. "finest prose" to Lawrence, Apr. 7, 1974 (*WP* letterhead); "magnificent" and "classic" in undated letter (*WP* letterhead) in the archive folder between the letter of Apr. 7 and one of May 21, 1974 [spring 1974] (SL 54).

65. To Gary Melom, Jan. 30, 1975.

66. To Hansen, Jan. 11, 1974 (HRC uncataloged).

67. To Hansen, Sept. 14, 1975 (HRC uncataloged).

68. *Northern Lights*, pp. 341–342.

69. To Hansen, Jan. 25, 1975, and Mar. 28, 1975 (HRC uncataloged).

70. John Fowles, *The Ebony Tower* (Boston: Little, Brown, 1974), p. 53.

71. Fowles, *The Ebony Tower*, p. 99; O'Brien, *Northern Lights*, p. 313.

72. Fowles, *The Ebony Tower*, p. 38.

73. To Gary Melom, Jan. 30, 1975.

19. Endings and Beginnings

1. To Hansen, Dec. 16–19, 1974 (HRC uncataloged).

2. To Lawrence, Jan. 26, 1975 (SL 53).

3. To Gary Melom, Jan. 30, 1975.

4. To Hansen, Feb. 24, 1975 (HRC uncataloged).

5. To Hansen, Mar. 3, 1975 (HRC uncataloged).

6. Date of death: Department of Veterans Affairs BIRLS Death File, 1850–2010; and Pennsylvania Veterans Burial Cards, 1777–2012 (ancestry.com). Spruce Hotel in funeral notice, *The Scranton Tribune*, May 5, 1975, p. 5. Details of postwar troubles in Thomas White letter to Tim O'Brien, July 5, 1988 (HRC 23.8). An unnamed hotel as the site in Josh White letter to Tim O'Brien, Nov. 21 [1994] (HRC 4.5).

7. "MacLeish, His Poetry Launch Bicentennial," *Boston Globe*, Apr. 17, 1975, p. 8.

8. To Hansen, Apr. 23, 1975 (HRC uncataloged).

9. To Hansen, June 11, 1975 (HRC uncataloged).

10. D.C. research and Bread Loaf dates: O'Brien to Seymour Lawrence, Aug. 6, 1975 (SL 53). Bread Loaf nomination: to Lawrence, June 5, 1975 (SL 53).

11. To Lawrence, Aug. 26, 1975 (SL 53).

12. "F8 Bread Loaf Registrants" (Middlebury); this digital spreadsheet is not perfectly reliable.

13. To Hansen, Sept. 2, 1976 (HRC uncataloged).

14. Kirsten Michalski, Executive Secretary, American Center, to Lawrence, Sept. 15, 1975 (SL 53). Lawrence's cover letter submitting the novel is dated August 13, 1975.

15. Bread Loaf interview, audio recording, Aug. 24, 1979. His unrecorded lecture that year, "Caring," mentioned Stein along with Hemingway, Faulkner, Fowles, Dos Passos, Gass, O'Connor, Gardner, and O'Brien (to Bob Pack, Feb. 23, 1979). Both items: Middlebury.

16. To Hansen, May 8, 1977 (HRC uncataloged).

17. To Hansen, Mar. 28, 1975 (HRC uncataloged).

18. To Hansen, Feb. 24, 1976 (HRC uncataloged).

19. E.g., over the weekend of April 25–27, for the Book Affair at Boston University's George Sherman Union, cohosted by *Boston Phoenix* and organized by DeWitt Henry and *Ploughshares*. The affair featured Fanny Howe, Charles Simic, Alice Walker, and Robert Stow (*Boston Globe* Calendar section, Apr. 24, 1975, p. 15). See O'Brien to Hansen, Apr. 23, 1975 (HRC uncataloged).

20. Mark Feeney, "Justin Kaplan, Twain Biographer, Dies: Acclaimed Writer, Intellectual Was Pillar of Cambridge Literary Scene," *Boston Globe*, Mar. 4, 2014, p. B1.

21. O'Brien, "Tennis Foreplay: New Sex-Courting Scene," *Gallery*, Sept. 1975. Joe Speiler, the *Penthouse* editor who managed the veterans' series, had moved to *Gallery*.

22. To Hansen, Jan. 30, 1977 (HRC uncataloged).

23. To Hansen, Apr. 13, 1977 (HRC uncataloged).

20. OVER THE HILL

1. *Mac Weekly*, Mar. 9, 1979, p. 8.

2. To Hansen, Mar. 2, 1976 (HRC uncataloged).

3. To Hansen, Nov. 19, 1974 (HRC uncataloged).

4. To Hansen, Nov. 20, 1974 (HRC uncataloged).

5. To Hansen, Nov. 20, 1974 (HRC uncataloged).

6. To Hansen, Jan. 6, 197[5] (mistyped "1974"); the second page continues on Jan. 8. Postmarked Jan. 8, 1975 (HRC uncataloged).

7. To Hansen, Feb. 24, 1975 (HRC uncataloged).

8. Lawrence M. Baskir and William A. Strauss, *Chance and Circumstance: The Draft, the War, and the Vietnam Generation* (New York: Alfred A. Knopf, 1978), pp. 109–116; Jack Anderson, "GI Deserters Form Criminal Rat Packs in Vietnam Slums," *WDG*, Nov. 13, 1969, p. 3.

9. To Hansen, Feb. 24, 1975 (HRC uncataloged).

10. To Hansen, Mar. 3, 1975; Mar. 11, 1975; Mar. 28, 1975 (HRC uncataloged).

11. To Hansen, postmarked Apr. 11, 1975; see also O'Brien to Hansen, Apr. 23, 1975, and May 4, 1975 (HRC uncataloged).

12. To Hansen, May 4, 1975 (HRC uncataloged).

13. To Hansen, July 15, 1975 (HRC uncataloged). "The Way It Mostly Was" is the other story named here, not mentioned in an earlier letter but also not discussed as newly written.

14. See letters to Hansen dated June 4, 1975, and June 11, 1975 (HRC uncataloged).

15. *GAC*, p. 8. The photo album VUES OF VIETNAM was moved elsewhere (p. 119).

16. To Hansen, July 15, 1975 (HRC uncataloged).

17. To Lawrence, Aug. 6, 1975 (SL 53).

18. To Lawrence, Aug. 26, 1975. O'Brien was at Bread Loaf August 12–24 (letter to Lawrence, Aug. 6, 1975, SL 53).

19. David Haward Bain, *Whose Woods These Are: A History of the Bread Loaf Writers' Conference 1926–1992*, ed. David Haward Bain and Mary Smyth Duffy (New York: Ecco Press, 1993), p. 115.

20. To Lawrence, Aug. 27, 1975 (SL 53). "Night March," in William Abrahams, ed., *Prize Stories 1976: The O. Henry Awards* (New York: Doubleday, 1976), pp. 211–219. The story also appeared in Abrahams, ed., *Prize Stories of the Seventies from the O. Henry Awards* (New York: Doubleday, 1981).

21. To Lawrence, Aug. 6, 1975 (SL 53). On Aug. 26, a Thursday, O'Brien references leaving for Minnesota "Friday, after moving," so either Aug. 27 or more likely Sept. 3 (as he was writing letters and such on the twenty-seventh); to Lawrence, Aug. 26, 1975 (SL 53).

22. To Hansen, Oct. 14, 1975 (HRC uncataloged).

23. To Hansen, Oct. 22, 1975 (HRC uncataloged).

24. Bob Knight and Ernie Zobian, Office Memorandum to Lawrence, Nov. 12, 1975 (SL 53).

25. Lawrence's summary with the memos of Nov. 10 and 12, 1975; see Boyd's original (SL 53).

26. To Hansen, Nov. 17, 1975 (HRC uncataloged); contract for *GAC* and untitled novel with Delacorte Press/Seymour Lawrence, Dec. 11, 1975 (HRC 49.1).

27. To Hansen, Jan. 2, 1976 (HRC uncataloged).

28. To Hansen, Feb. 6, 1976 (HRC uncataloged).

29. To Hansen, Nov. 17, 1975 (HRC uncataloged).

30. To Hansen [Nov. 25, 1975] (HRC uncataloged).

31. *GAC*, pp. 74, 85.

32. To Lawrence, Dec. 1, 1975; Dec. 21, 1975; from Lawrence, Dec. 30, 1975 (SL 53).

33. To Hansen, Dec. 10, 1975, and Jan. 2, 1976 (HRC uncataloged).

34. To Lawrence, Feb. 6, 1976 (SL 53).

35. To Hansen, Feb. 6, 1976 (HRC uncataloged).

36. *GAC*, pp. 14–15.

37. To Hansen, Feb. 16, 1976 (HRC uncataloged).

38. To Hansen, Feb. 24, 1976 (HRC uncataloged). O'Brien didn't admit the stumping in letter to Lawrence, Mar. 3, 1976 (SL 53).

39. To Hansen, Mar. 2, 1976 (HRC uncataloged).

40. *GAC*, p. 206.

41. In Patrick A. Smith, *Conversations with Tim O'Brien* (Jackson: University Press of Mississippi, 2012), p. 97.

42. *GAC*, p. 206.

43. Email to author, Jan. 24, 2021. The twenty-eighth paperback printing in 2022 made all the corrections except one, which screwed up the chronology of Buff's death. To be fixed in the next printing.

44. To Hansen, Mar. 23, 1976 (HRC uncataloged).

45. To Hansen, Apr. 9, 1976 (HRC uncataloged).

46. Emerson handwritten note on Harvard University Kennedy School of Government letterhead. Undated, filed between documents dated Nov. 1 and Nov. 30, 1973 (SL 54); from Saul Cohen, Nov. 29, 1973 (SL 54).

47. To Hansen, Apr. 9, 1976 (HRC uncataloged).

48. To Hansen, May 27, 1976 (HRC uncataloged).

49. To Hansen, May 27, 1976; June 29, 1976 (HRC uncataloged); to Lawrence, May 24, 1976 (SL 53).

50. To Hansen, July 7, 1976 (HRC uncataloged).

51. To Hansen, July 15, 1976 (HRC uncataloged).

52. To Hansen, July 23, 1976 (HRC uncataloged).

53. *GAC*, p. 53.

54. *GAC*, p. 59.

55. *GAC*, p. 92.

56. To Hansen, July 7, 1976 (HRC uncataloged); to Lawrence, Aug. 9, 1976 (SL 53).

57. O'Brien, "Keeping Watch by Night," *Redbook*, Dec. 1976, p. 65.

58. O'Brien, "Keeping Watch by Night," p. 68.

59. *GAC*, p. 235.

60. To Hansen, Oct. 29, 1976 (HRC uncataloged).

61. *GAC*, pp. 95–96.

62. O'Brien, "Surviving in Vietnam and the U.S.A.," *Boston Phoenix*, Jan. 23, 1973, pp. 8, 26.

63. *The Crumb* 41, no. 9 (Aug. 1976; Middlebury); on reading "How They Were Organized": to Hansen, Mar. 28, 1977 (HRC uncataloged).

64. To Hansen, Sept. 11, 1976 (HRC uncataloged); to Lawrence, Sept. 12, 1976 (SL 53).

65. To Hansen, Sept. 20, 1976 (HRC uncataloged).

66. *GAC*, pp. 303–304.

67. To Hansen, Oct. 7, 18, and 22, 1976 (HRC uncataloged).

68. To Hansen, Oct. 22, 1976 (HRC uncataloged).

69. To Hansen, Oct. 29, 1976 (HRC uncataloged).

70. To Hansen, Nov. 10, 1976 (HRC uncataloged).

71. To Hansen, Nov. 20, 1976 (HRC uncataloged).

72. To Lawrence, Nov. 20, 1976 (SL 53); to Hansen, Nov. 20, 1976.

73. To Hansen, Nov. 26, 1976 (HRC uncataloged).

74. To Lawrence, Nov. 30, 1976 (SL 53).

75. To Hansen, Dec. 22, 1976; Nov. 30, 1976 (HRC uncataloged).

76. To Hansen, Jan. 3, 1977 (HRC uncataloged).

77. To Hansen, Jan. 3, 1977 (HRC uncataloged).

78. To Hansen, Jan. 19, 1977; see also Feb. 5, 1977 (HRC uncataloged).

79. To Hansen, postmarked Feb. 9, 1977 (HRC uncataloged).

80. To Hansen, Feb. 12, 1977 (HRC uncataloged).

81. O'Brien, "Author's Choice," *BOMC Magazine*, Oct. 1978, pp. 22–23; Bread Loaf interview, audio recording, Aug. 24, 1979 (Middlebury).

82. In Smith, *Conversations*, p. 19.

83. To Hansen, undated but with enclosed letter from Billy [William] Abrahams, Feb. 22, 1977 (HRC uncataloged).

84. To Hansen, undated but with enclosed letter from Billy Abrahams, Feb. 22, 1977; to Hansen, postmarked Mar. [10], 1977 (HRC uncataloged).

85. To Hansen, undated but with enclosed letter from Billy Abrahams, Feb. 22, 1977 (HRC uncataloged).

86. To Hansen, undated but with enclosed letter from Billy Abrahams, Feb. 22, 1977 (HRC uncataloged).

87. To Lawrence, Feb. 1, 1977 (SL 54).

88. To Lawrence, Mar. 1, 1977 (SL 54).

89. "ABSENT & ACCOUNTED FOR, a novel by Tim O'Brien," undated (SL 54).

90. To Lawrence, Mar. 21, 1977 (SL 54). See also O'Brien, "For Artist Designing Jacket," Mar. 26, 1977 (SL 54).

91. To Hansen, Mar. 21, 1977 (HRC uncataloged).

92. To Hansen, Mar. 28, 1977 (HRC uncataloged).

93. To Hansen, Mar. 28, 1977 (HRC uncataloged).

94. To Hansen, Apr. 13, 1977, and May 8, 1977 (HRC uncataloged).

95. To Hansen, Apr. 13, 1977 (HRC uncataloged).

96. On fragging estimates, see Haynes Johnson and George Wilson, *Army in Anguish* (1971), pp. 92, 110–111 [in Baskir and Strauss, *Chance and Circumstance*, p. 143]); David Cortright, *Soldiers in Revolt: GI Resistance During the Vietnam War* (Chicago: Haymarket Books, 2005), pp. 43–44.

97. To Hansen, [Mar. 10], 1977 (HRC uncataloged).

98. *GAC*, pp. 27–28, 30.

99. *GAC*, p. 323.

100. *GAC*, p. 338. This summary follows the order O'Brien established in Oct. 2021.

101. Billy Abrahams to Lawrence, May 1, 1977 (SL 54).

21. APPRENTICESHIP'S END

1. Gene Lyons, "Pieces of a Vietnam War Story," *The Nation*, Jan. 29, 1977, p. 121.

2. Joseph Heller, *Catch-22* (1961; repr. ed., Simon & Schuster, 2011), pp. 517, 262.

3. Geoffrey Wolff, "A Chronicle of War in a Vision of Peace," *New Times*, Feb. 20, 1978, pp. 68–69.

4. To Lawrence, undated (SL 54).

5. *GAC*, p. 48.

6. Heller, *Catch-22*, p. 354.

7. E.g., letter to Billy Abrahams, Mar. 6, 1977 (SL 54).

8. Christopher Lehmann-Haupt, "Books of the Times," *NYT*, Feb. 2, 1978.

9. Richard Freedman, "A Separate Peace," *NYT Book Review*, Feb. 12, 1978, p. 1.

10. John Updike, "Books," *The New Yorker*, Mar. 27, 1978, p. 130.

11. Maggie Curran at International Creative Management to Lawrence, Apr. 13, 1978 (SL 53).

12. O'Brien, "Honor Thy Commander," *Saturday Review*, Feb. 16, 1980, p. 50.

13. O'Brien, "Falling Star," *Saturday Review*, Feb. 17, 1979, pp. 53–54.

14. O'Brien, *New York*, June 22, 1981, pp. 64–65.

15. O'Brien, "The Many Ways of Growing Together, and Apart," *Newsday*, July 13, 1980.

16. O'Brien, *Chicago Tribune Book World*, Apr. 5, 1981, pp. 1–2.

17. O'Brien, "Tales His Father Told Him," *Saturday Review*, Sept. 29, 1979, pp. 46–48.

18. O'Brien, "The Ballad of Gary G.," *New York*, Oct. 15, 1979, pp. 67–68.

19. O'Brien, "Flying High," *Saturday Review*, June 10, 1978, pp. 37–38.

20. O'Brien, "Every Soldier, Coming Home," *Saturday Review*, Apr. 15, 1978, pp. 76–80.

21. See Gerald Nicosia, *Home to War: A History of the Vietnam Veterans' Movement* (New York: Carroll & Graf, 2004), pp. 362–394.

22. O'Brien, "The Violent Vet," *Esquire*, Dec. 1979, pp. 96–104. Tracy Kidder published a similar article in *The Atlantic*. Kidder recalls interviewing O'Brien for the piece and connecting their overlapping tours in the American Division's 2nd Brigade, but the article never mentions O'Brien: Tracy Kidder, "Soldiers of Misfortune," *The Atlantic*, Mar. 1978. See also Philip Caputo, "The Unreturning Army," *Playboy*, Jan. 1982.

23. O'Brien, "Vietnam: Now Playing at Your Local Theater," *Your Place*, Aug. 1978, pp. 61–65, 84–87. Digested as "The Old War Movie Becomes a Battle Casualty Itself," *Minneapolis Tribune*, Aug. 27, 1978, pp. 1D, 7D, 8D. See O'Brien, "All Quiet on the Western Front," *TV Guide*, Nov. 10, 1979, p. 19–20.

24. O'Brien, "The Ghost Soldiers," *Esquire*, Mar. 1981, pp. 90–100.

25. O'Brien, "The Things They Carried," *Esquire*, Aug. 1986, pp. 76–81.

26. O'Brien, "Burning Love," *Saturday Review*, Oct. 27, 1979, pp. 41–42.

27. O'Brien, "Fear of Buying," *Your Place*, Apr. 1978, pp. 6, 10, 111.

28. To Lawrence, Dec. 23, 1976 (SL 53). Bill O'Brien and the character also share an aborted early marriage resulting in excommunication.

29. To Hansen, June 19, 1977 (HRC uncataloged).

30. O'Brien, untitled, "Let me go to the Sweetheart Mountains . . ." (HRC 26.3).

31. To Hansen, July 6, 1977 (HRC uncataloged).

32. To Hansen, Dec. 9, 1977 (HRC uncataloged).

33. To Hansen, Mar. 14, 1978 (HRC uncataloged).

34. To Seymour Lawrence, June 13, 1978 (SL 53).

35. Seymour Lawrence, "To Whom It May Concern," undated (SL 53).

36. O'Brien, "Darkness at the Edge of Town," *Feature*, Jan. 1979, p. 42. *Feature* was formerly *Crawdaddy*, under which name O'Brien signed the contract to do the story. Reprinted in the *University of Washington Daily* (May 23, 1979). A shorter version appeared as "Going After Silos" in Peter Knobler and Greg Mitchell, eds., *Very Seventies: A Cultural History of the 1970s from the Pages of* Crawdaddy (New York: Fireside, 1995).

37. O'Brien, "Darkness at the Edge of Town," p. 48.

38. O'Brien, "Darkness at the Edge of Town," p. 49.

39. To Hansen, postmarked Nov. 28, 1978 (HRC uncataloged).

40. To Bob Pack he wrote that he was toying with ideas "for the next story" about Cold War life (Nov. 3, 1978, and Oct. 10, 1978, Middlebury).

41. Robert Armstrong, "Tim O'Brien: Writer Tied to Vietnam War but over His Protest," *Minneapolis Tribune*, Mar. 18, 1979, pp. 1G, 12G.

42. Armstrong, "Tim O'Brien: Writer Tied to Vietnam War But over His Protest." The article says the story was originally scheduled for the May issue of *The Atlantic*, the month also cited in "THE NUCLEAR AGE (Outline)," enclosed with a cover letter to Seymour Lawrence, Mar. 31, 1979 (SL 53). The page progress for "The Sweetheart Mountain" is reported in Kim McGuire, "Vietnam Experience Brings Author Fame," *Daily Tar Heel*, Mar. 26, 1979, p. 8.

43. O'Brien apparently wrote the scene unconscious of its historical inspiration, and when someone pointed it out to him, he revised the scene to mute the association (Bread Loaf interview, audio recording, Aug. 24, 1979, Middlebury). It's hard to imagine how the initial version could have been more blatant *and* its author unaware.

44. Julia Wallace to Lynn Nesbit, May 3, 1979 (SL 53).

45. To Hansen, July 6, 1977 (HRC uncataloged).

46. To Hansen, Jan. 3, 1977 (HRC uncataloged).

47. Bread Loaf interview, audio recording, Aug. 24, 1979 (Middlebury).

48. First letter to the new address (Apt. #3) is dated Feb. 27, 1978, to Lawrence (SL 53).

49. Maria Lenhart (Christian Science Monitor Service), "Vietnam, Internal Battles Led to Writing of Novels," *Flint Journal* [Michigan], Oct. 7, 1979.

50. Bread Loaf interview, audio recording, Aug. 24, 1979 (Middlebury).

51. Armstrong, "Tim O'Brien: Writer Tied to Vietnam War but over His Protest."

52. Christopher Evans, "'Vietnam's Not Me Anymore,'" *Minneapolis Star*, Mar. 10, 1979, pp. 4–5.

53. Adriane Markusen, "O'Brien Puts War into Writing," *Mac Weekly*, Mar. 9, 1979, p. 6.

54. Adriane Markusen, "Mac Grad-Writer-Vet Calls Novel A-political," *Mac Weekly*, Mar. 9, 1979, p. 8.

55. Kim McGuire, "Vietnam Experience Brings Author Fame," *Daily Tar Heel*, Mar. 26, 1979, p. 8.

56. Association of American Publishers, "Nominees Announced for the 30th Annual National Book Awards," press release, Mar. 19, 1979 (SL 53). O'Brien might have learned slightly earlier than the nineteenth, the announcement's official release date.

57. Michael Dirda, "The Fiction Upset," *WP*, Apr. 24, 1979, pp. B1, B4.

58. John Blades, "The NBAs: No Oscar in Wonderland," *Chicago Tribune Book World*, May 20, 1979, p. 2.

59. Sales numbers in Pattie Reilly, "Vietnam Grunt Tim O'Brien Gets Decorated on the Literary Front," *People*, May 14, 1979, p. 110.

60. John Blades, "The NBAs: No Oscar in Wonderland."

61. "30th National Book Awards Presented" (SL 56).

62. William K. Robertson, "Beyond Sham, Awards Matter," *Miami Herald*, Apr. 26, 1979, p. 7E.

63. "Remarks by Senator Daniel Patrick Moynihan (D. N.Y.) at the National Book Awards, April 25, 1979," Library of Congress, Daniel P. Moynihan, U.S. Senate Speeches and Writings File, Series II, Box 2869, Folder 12.

64. "Tim O'Brien Acceptance Speech" (SL 56).

22. DREAMS THAT SUPPOSE AWAKENINGS

1. To Lawrence, June 1, 1976 (SL 53).

2. *TTTC*, p. 30.

3. Hugh Davis, "Dreamer Tells Graduates Reality," *Spokane Chronicle*, June 15, 1979, p. 42. Roby remembered the alias as Martha, the name O'Brien used for the Roby-like girlfriend of Lt. Jimmy Cross in "The Things They Carried."

4. O'Brien, "Burning Love," *Saturday Review*, Oct. 27, 1979, pp. 41–42.

5. *The Crumb*, 1979 (Middlebury).

6. "THE NUCLEAR AGE (Outline)," enclosed with first chapter draft in letter to Lawrence dated Mar. 31, 1979 (SL 53).

7. "THE NUCLEAR AGE" first chapter draft, enclosed with Outline in letter to Lawrence dated Mar. 31, 1979 (SL 53).

8. *Nuclear Age*, p. 152.

9. *Nuclear Age*, p. 151.

10. Tim O'Brien reading, Bread Loaf Writers' Conference, Aug. 21, 1985, Middlebury.

11. Vie published two short stories drawing on her life in the Philippines, "Taxi" and "Belinda," in Madelon Sprengnether and C. W. Truesdale, eds., *The House on Via Gombito: Writing by North American Women Abroad* (Minneapolis, MN: New Rivers Press, 1991), pp. 427–443.

12. Vivian Vie Balfour, "The Reading," unpublished story.

13. Macalester transcript (HRC 29.4).

14. *Nuclear Age*, pp. 90, 93.

15. Vivian Vie in *Mac Weekly*: "Peace Group to Sponsor Talk on War, Plan March," *Mac Weekly*, Jan. 17, 1969, p. 1; "Student Asks Support for Anti-War Soldiers," *Mac Weekly*, Apr. 11, 1969, p. 6; "Mobilization Plans Tactics," *Mac Weekly*, May 9, 1969, p. 5. She wrote one additional piece: "Reaction to HHH Speech," *Mac Weekly*, Feb. 28, 1969, pp. 1, 3.

16. *Nuclear Age*, p. 18.

17. *Nuclear Age*, pp. 34–35; "dork" in Bread Loaf reading, 1982; "creepy" in Bread Loaf reading, 1981, Middlebury.

18. *Nuclear Age*, pp. 119–121.

19. *Nuclear Age*, pp. 151–152.

20. *Nuclear Age*, p. 312.

21. Paraphrased by Steve Smith, "Tim O'Brien, Veteran Writer, Returns to Mac," *Mac Weekly*, Apr. 25, 1980, p. 5. O'Brien spoke on Monday the twenty-first to kick off the Midwestern Writers' Festival.

22. "Lecture," typed with first line of "1. I hate lectures" [Aug. 19, 1985] (HRC 27.1).

23. "THE NUCLEAR AGE (Outline)." Enclosed with cover letter to Lawrence, Mar. 31, 1979 (SL 53).

24. "Lecture," typed with first line of "1. I hate lectures." The undated notes reference the Bread Loaf setting, his anxiousness for the reviews, and his upcoming Wednesday reading. This fits the 1985 Bread Loaf conference schedule of his Monday, Aug. 19, lecture and his Wednesday, Aug. 21, reading of the final chapter. A recording of the reading exists (Middlebury), but not of the lecture.

25. Audio recording, Tim O'Brien Bread Loaf reading, Aug. 11, 1981, Middlebury.

26. "O'Brien, Tim and Robert Stone: panel discussion; April 16th, 1982," The Elliston Project: Poetry Readings and Lectures at the University of Cincinnati, hdl.handle.net/2374.UC /697059.

27. David Haward Bain, *Whose Woods These Are: A History of the Bread Loaf Writers' Conference 1926–1992*, ed. David Haward Bain and Mary Smyth Duffy (New York: Ecco Press, 1993), p. 128.

28. Audio recording, Tim O'Brien Bread Loaf reading, Aug. 27, 1982, Middlebury. At the time of the reading, "Chain Reactions" was chapter 2, with "Civil Defense"—the Ping-Pong table chapter—still the planned first chapter.

29. Bruce Weber, "War and Peace," *Esquire*, Sept. 1985, p. 269.

30. The reading took place on Aug. 26, 1983, according to *The Crumb*, which matches the lecture notes description of "a couple of years ago" on a Friday night.

31. O'Brien, "Quantum Jumps," *Ploughshares* 9, no. 4 (1983), pp. 11–44. It then appeared as the lead story in Bill Henderson, ed., *The Pushcart Prize X: Best of the Small Presses 1985–1986* (New York: Penguin, 1985), pp. 3–31.

32. See Hansen to Lawrence, Mar. 10, 1984 (SL 53) and "Lecture," typed with first line of "1. I hate lectures."

33. Weber, "War and Peace."

34. "Quantum Jumps," *Granta* 16 (Summer 1985), pp. 147–161.

35. Weber, "War and Peace."

36. Bain, *Whose Woods These Are*, p. 128.

37. Letter to Marilyn Johnson, Sept. 16, 1980.

38. Mark Muro, "Believer in the Grand Theme," *Boston Globe*, Oct. 10, 1985, pp. 85–86.

39. Stephen Schwandt, "Author Makes Us Wonder Why There's No Nuclear War Panic," *Minneapolis Star and Tribune*, Nov. 24, 1985, p. 14G; Philip Gerard, "'Nuclear Age' Finds Power at Core of Human Soul," *Arizona Republic*, Nov. 10, 1985, p. F13.

40. Michiko Kakutani, "Prophet of Doom," *NYT*, Sept. 28, 1985, p. L12.

41. "Digging a Shelter and a Grave," *NYT Book Review*, Nov. 17, 1985, p. 7.

42. Steven Bauer, unpublished letter to the editor, *NYT Book Review*, Nov. 17, 1985 (HRC 15.3).

43. To Hansen, Dec. 19, 1985 (HRC uncataloged).

44. There's not a recording of the reading by which to date it.

45. To Hansen, Mar. 10, 1974 (HRC uncataloged).

46. PEN America Center Press Release, Mar. 29, 1984 (SL 61, Jayne Anne Phillips files).

47. "Christa Wolf, 1983 May 26," audio recording, PEN American Center Records, 1922–2008 (mostly 1930–1989), Princeton University Library Special Collections, findingaids .princeton.edu/catalog/C0760_c2232; recording online at PEN America Digital Archive, archive.pen.org/asset?id=373.

48. Plus Francine du Plessix Gray, Arthur Kopit, and Ted Solotaroff. "Writers and the Nuclear Age" Press Release, Mar. 29, 1984, PEN America Center (SL 61; Jayne Anne Phillips files). Audio recordings: "Panel on the Nuclear Threat, 1984 April 15," PEN American Center Records, 1922–2008 (mostly 1930–1989), Princeton University Library Special Collections, findingaids.princeton.edu/catalog/C0760_c2171; recording online at PEN America Digital Archive, archive.pen.org/asset?id=317.

49. *Nuclear Age*, p. 70.

50. *Nuclear Age*, p. 103.

51. *Nuclear Age*, p. 103; *TTTC*, p. 124.

52. *Nuclear Age*, p. 304; *TTTC*, p. 273.

53. *Nuclear Age*, p. 11.

54. *Nuclear Age*, pp. 246–247.

55. Ken Ringle, "Papa, You Old Softie," *Roanoke Times and World-News*, Jan. 20, 1985, p. E2. The "Hemingway: A Moveable Feast" seminar was held January 10–13, 1985. *The Nuclear Age*'s Key West gunrunning suggests Hemingway's *To Have and Have Not*.

56. Roger M. Haley, "Digging a Hole Deepens Man's Fear," *El Paso Times*, Dec. 22, 1985, p. 9E.

57. "Lecture," typed with first line of "1. I hate lectures."

58. *Nuclear Age*, p. 298.

59. O'Brien uses this language when he introduces his Bread Loaf reading, Aug. 21, 1985, Middlebury.

23. How It Mostly Was

1. Audio at "Faulkner Award Ceremony of The Rotunda, 1981 April 18," PEN American Center Collection, Princeton University, findingaids.princeton.edu/catalog/C0760_c1824; recording online at PEN America Digital Archives, archive.pen.org/asset?id=2.

2. "Panel Discussion PEN New England: The Writer, Private and Public," Jan. 31, 1980, with Daniel Aaron and Caryl River, moderated by Helen Vendler. PEN America Center Collection, Princeton University, findingaids.princeton.edu/catalog/C0760_c1963; recording online at PEN America Archives, archive.pen.org/asset?id=121.

3. "Sandhills Writing Conference Planned," *Augusta Chronicle*, Mar. 20, 1983, p. 59; "Writing Staff Announced," *Augusta Chronicle*, Mar. 27, 1983, p. 44; Marjorie Mayfield, "Novelist Advises Lying to Achieve Truth," *Augusta Chronicle*, Apr. 22, 1984, p. 71. He returned in May 1988: "Conference Gives Beginning Writers Chance to Learn from Professionals," *Augusta Chronicle*, May 8, 1988, pp. 41, 47; "Sandhills Writers' Conference to Start," *Augusta Chronicle*, May 12, 1988, p. 86.

4. To Lawrence, Jan. 15, 1978; undated typed "Typos in GOING AFTER CACCIATO (Paperback)" (SL 53).

5. O'Brien mentions looking for a home in a letter to Hansen, Mar. 10, 1986; his letter to Hansen of Sept. 15, 1986, uses the Boxford home return address (HRC uncataloged).

6. David Haward Bain, *Whose Woods These Are: A History of the Bread Loaf Writers' Conference 1926–1992*, ed. David Haward Bain and Mary Smyth Duffy (New York: Ecco Press, 1993), p. 285.

7. Curt Suplee, "Convening for the Literary Fix," *WP*, Aug. 31, 1981, pp. C1, C2, C3. See also Stephen Hunter, "Snobbishness, Drinking, Careerism . . . and Good Talk About Writing,"

Baltimore Sun, Aug. 30, 1981, pp. D1, D4; Rebecca Mead, "How to Be a Writer," *The New Yorker*, Oct. 15, 2001.

8. *Tomcat*, pp. 160–161. The pre-Roby episode may have happened in 1977. There's a reference in *The Crumb* about O'Brien "carrying roses into the Inn Friday afternoon," and after returning home he wrote Erik Hansen about "going through a lot of real shit." *The Crumb*, 1977 (Middlebury); letter to Hansen, Aug. 30, 1977 (HRC uncataloged).

9. Susan Thornton, *On Broken Glass: Loving and Losing John Gardner* (New York: Carroll & Graf, 2000), p. 10.

10. Untitled, undated typescript lecture, "1. Last year, in my Bread Loaf lecture [. . .]" (HRC 27.1). Probably 1983 (see chapter 6, note 16).

11. Except for 1984. He attended but was not on faculty that year.

12. To Bob Pack, Feb. 23, 1979, Middlebury. The lecture was titled "Caring" (*The Crumb*).

13. O'Brien, "Golf in the Leewards: Tee Off in the Trades," *Sail*, Aug. 1989, pp. 3–7.

14. Interview with Aaron Matthews, unpublished transcript, Aug. 15, 2017.

15. Caputo gave Cacciato's business card to Lawrence to pass to O'Brien in 1983: Lawrence to O'Brien, Mar. 1, 1983; Lawrence to Caputo, Mar. 3, 1983 (SL 53). See Caputo's introductory note to "The Things They Carried," *Esquire*, Aug. 1986, p. 76. Most of the anecdote's details are from Connie Sayre, who worked for Caputo's publisher and was in the dinner group that night.

16. O'Brien, "I Wish We Were More Troubled," *WP*, May 25, 1980, p. B3.

17. *Design Competition* (Washington, D.C.: Vietnam Veterans Memorial Fund, Nov. 24, 1980), p. 6. The other five titles: *After Vietnam: Voices of a Wounded Generation*, edited by A. D. Horne; *Many Reasons Why: The American Involvement in Vietnam*, by Michael Charlton and Anthony Moncrieff; *A Rumor of War*, by Philip Caputo; *Fields of Fire*, by James Webb; and *The Big Story: How the American Press and Television Reported the Crisis of Tet in 1968 in Vietnam and Washington*, by Peter Braestrup.

18. "Vietnam Voices: The War in American Literature," moderated by Harry Maurer, Mar. 30, 1982, PEN American Center Records, 1922–2008 (mostly 1930–1989), Princeton University Library Special Collections, findingaids.princeton.edu/catalog/C0760 _c2227; recording online at PEN America Digital Archive, archive.pen.org/asset?id =368. "O'Brien, Tim and Robert Stone: panel discussion; April 16th, 1982," The Elliston Project: Poetry Readings and Lectures at the University of Cincinnati, hdl.handle.net /2374.UC/697059.

19. Also Asa Baber, John Balaban, Philip Beidler, Lady Borton, William Broyles, C. D. B. Bryan, Robert Olen Butler, John Del Vecchio, Arthur Egendorf, Jack Fuller, Ron Kovic, William Pelfrey, Wallace Terry, Bruce Weigl, Stephen Wright, and others. See Timothy J. Lomperis, *"Reading the Wind": The Literature of the Vietnam War; An Interpretative Critique*, with a bibliographic commentary by John Clark Pratt (Durham, NC: Duke University Press, 1987), pp. 165–167. The conference was held May 7–9, 1985.

20. Aired on May 23, 1985.

21. Lomperis, *"Reading the Wind,"* pp. 18–19.

22. Ehrhart recalls challenging Webb's assertion that the United States is the greatest democracy on earth since Athens's golden age by reminding him of Athens's undemocratic practices of slavery and excluding women; and Al Santoli's lecturing the Vietnamese ambassador to the UN on Vietnamese history. O'Brien remembers Webb justifying the war

and America's ongoing interest in Việt Nam being the need for a deep-water port in the region and Ehrhart's attacking that idea, too.

23. On Aug. 1, 1987. The thirteen recipients: Tim O'Brien, Oliver Stone, Philip Caputo, Robert Olen Butler, Larry Heinemann, Lynda Van Devanter, Asa Baber, Tom Bird, Amlin Gray, Steve Mason, Blake Clark, Jeff Danziger, and Bruce Weigl (according to Marc Leepson, VVA co-coordinator of the event). See Leepson's discussion the afternoon before the award ceremony with O'Brien, Caputo, Butler, and Heinemann, "If I Write About a Combat Zone: Vietnam as a Novel Experience," *VVA Veteran*, Sept. 1987, pp. 29, 31.

24. From Oliver Stone, Aug. 11, 1987 (HRC 23.8).

25. See Thanh T. Nguyen and Bruce Weigl, translators, *Poems from Captured Documents* (Amherst: University of Massachusetts Press, 1994); and John Balaban, translator, *Cao Dao Việt Nam: Vietnamese Folk Poetry* (Washington: Copper Canyon Press, 2003).

26. "Center Hosts First Writing Workshop," *Joiner Center Newsletter* 2, no. 2 (Dec. 1988), pp. 1, 8. Video: "Lew Cawley, John Balaban, [Thanh] Nguyen, and Tim O'Brien Reading, 8–3–88."

27. "Leo Cawley, 47," *NYT* obit, Aug.3, 1991, p. 26L. Cawley's name isn't eligible to appear on the Vietnam War Memorial, although a plaque added in 2004 reads, "In memory of the men and women who served in the Vietnam War and later died as a result of their service. We honor and remember their sacrifice."

28. See George C. Wilson, "Vietnam Revisited," *WP*, Feb. 6, 1990.

29. Funeral remarks by Nguyễn Quang Thiều, President of the Vietnam Writers Association, in Nguyễn Bá Chung email of Nov. 19, 2022, to the Vietnam Studies Group listserv, "Re: [Vsg] passing of Lê Lựu last week."

30. The American panelists were H. D. S. Greenway, George Esper, Tom Condon, and Don North. "Workshop Highlights Summer," *Joiner Center Newsletter* 3, no. 2 (Feb. 1990), pp. 1, 4.

31. The scene was reconstructed with information from several of the Americans involved: Kevin Bowen, Nguyễn Bá Chung, Bruce Weigl, and Bill Ehrhart. See also Joseph Kirby, "Discussion on Vietnam Stirs Protest," *Boston Globe*, July 27, 1989, p. 27; "Vietnamese Authors' UMass Talk Canceled," *Boston Globe*, Aug. 1, 1989, p. 19; Fox Butterfield, "Though Unofficial, Change Is in the Air for U.S.-Hanoi Ties," *NYT*, Sept. 20, 1988, p. A1.

32. Planned panel: Robert Taylor, "Bookmaking," *Boston Globe*, Jul. 30, 1989, p. A14. The Americans in the room: Tim O'Brien, Bruce Weigl, Phil Caputo, Larry Rottmann, Lamont Steptoe, Joe Bangert, Kevin and Leslie Bowen, Robert Mason, David Hunt, one unidentified man, and one unidentified woman. "Vietnamese and U.S. Writers" video recording, Aug. 1, 1989.

33. July 24–Aug. 2: "Second Writers' Workshop Set for Summer," *Joiner Center Newsletter*, June 1989, p. 2; Seymour Lawrence to Douglas Gibson, July 11, 1989 (SL 53).

34. *TTTC*, p. 89.

24. A WORK OF FICTION

1. "The Ghost Soldiers," *Esquire*, Mar. 1981, pp. 96, 100. Reprinted in Tom Jenks, ed., *Soldiers and Civilians: America at War and at Home* (New York: Bantam, 1986), pp. 182–201.

2. Tim O'Brien reading, Aug. 15, 1986 (Middlebury), although according to *The Crumb* (Middlebury), O'Brien's reading occurred on Aug. 20, 1986. It does not title the reading.

3. Also in Robert Pack and Jay Parini, eds., *The Bread Loaf Anthology of Contemporary American Short Stories* (Lebanon, NH: University Press of New England, 1987), pp. 227–246.

4. *TTTC*, p. 9.

5. *TTTC*, p. 11.

6. To Shannon Ravenel, Mar. 23, 1987 (HRC 23.9).

7. "The Things They Carried," *Esquire*, Aug. 1986, p. 81.

8. John Blades, "Farewell to First Drafts," *San Francisco Examiner*, July 7, 1991, p. D-14.

9. On Aug. 18, 1986: *The Crumb.*

10. One version is titled "War Stories," the other "On the Rainy River (War Stories)" and has a few penciled revisions, notes, and questions (HRC 27.1). In his 1987 Bread Loaf lecture (see note 11), O'Brien says the lecture was improvised and afterward he asked for a tape so he could write it out from memory, but there was no tape. Not true. He invented the improvisation claim.

11. In a Bread Loaf lecture recording dated Aug. 15, 1988, O'Brien references the prior year's negative reaction to "How to Tell a True War Story"—as if it happened in 1987—and proceeds to read the final version. This dating is wrong. With a publication date of October 1987, there's simply no way he extensively rewrote the first version, submitted it, and had it published between August and October (and then read the final version a year later?). Furthermore, *The Crumb* dates his 1988 lecture to Aug. 20, not Aug. 15. The recording's Aug. 15 date matches the 1987 lecture date, according to *The Crumb*. Thus he presented the unrecorded version in 1986 and the recorded version in 1987, shortly before publication. "How to Tell a True War Story" later appeared in Robert Pack and Jay Parini, eds., *The Bread Loaf Anthology of Contemporary American Essays* (Lebanon, NH: University Press of New England, 1989), pp. 215–228. "On the Rainy River" also appeared in *Minnesota Monthly*, Mar. 1990.

12. To Robert Warde, Nov. 6, 1987 (HRC 25.9).

13. Lawrence memo to Joe Kanon, Dec. 15, 1988 (SL 53). Contract dated Jan. 31, 1989 (SL 102).

14. Seymour Lawrence/Houghton Mifflin to Doug Gibson at McClelland & Stewart, July 11, 1989 (SL 53).

15. Holger Jensen (Associated Press), "Fire Base Mary Ann—War's Costliest Attack," *Boston Globe*, Mar. 31, 1971, 14. Also Associated Press, "5 Top Army Officers Face Demotions Because of Losses," *WP*, Nov. 24, 1971, p. A3; United Press International, "General and Two Other Officers Reprimanded in Vietnam Incident," *WP*, Apr. 22, 1972, p. A13.

16. Corinne Browne, *Body Shop: Recuperating from Vietnam* (New York: Stein and Day, 1973), p. 85. O'Brien later interviewed the soldier, Tim "Woody" Woodville, for *Penthouse*.

17. Kate Sutherland, "The Laggard Recruit," *Arthur's Home Magazine*, Jan. 1862; *TTTC*, p. 125.

18. See George Black, *The Long Reckoning: A Story of War, Peace, and Redemption in Vietnam* (New York: Alfred A. Knopf, 2023), chapter 17.

19. Bread Loaf's not entirely reliable record of registrants lists a Lady "Bortner" with a rural Ohio address as attending in 1978, 1979, and 1981 ("F8 Bread Loaf Registrants," Middlebury). Borton moved to rural Ohio after the war.

20. Grace Paley, "Foreword," in Lady Borton, *After Sorrow: An American Among the Vietnamese* (New York: Viking, 1995), p. xv.

21. Audio recording of Tim O'Brien reading, Aug. 20, 1988 (Middlebury). The Mac read-

ing took place on Sept. 15, 1988: John Jester, "Symposium Features Mac Alumni," *Mac Weekly*, Sept. 16, 1988, p. 2.

22. From Thomas White, July 5, 1988 (HRC 23.8).

23. *TTTC*, p. 157.

24. *TTTC*, p. 178.

25. *DMB*, p. 167; Aimee Blanchette, "Mike Bjerkesett, a Pioneer of Handicap Accessible Housing, Dies at Age 69," *Star-Tribune* [Minneapolis], Feb. 2, 2017, startribune.com /obituary-mike-bjerkesett-a-pioneer-of-handicap-accessible-housing/412617083/.

26. *Lake*, p. 27.

27. *Tomcat*, p. 3.

28. O'Brien, "The Ballad of Gary G.," *New York*, Oct. 15, 1979, p. 67.

29. Blades, "Farewell to First Drafts."

30. On Lawrence's objections, see his memo to Joe Kanon, Dec. 15, 1988 (SL 53). On Saranac Lake banning, see letter to Lawrence, Feb. 12, 1977, and enclosed letter to Eunice Hunter, Feb. 7, 1977 (SL 55; HRC 4.5).

31. Lawrence to Doug Gibson, July 11, 1989 (SL 53); Camille Hykes to O'Brien, July 14, 1989 (HRC 18.3).

32. Lawrence to Doug Gibson, July 11, 1989 (SL 53).

33. In Patrick A. Smith, *Conversations with Tim O'Brien* (Jackson: University Press of Mississippi, 2012), pp. 98–99.

34. Lawrence to Doug Gibson, July 11, 1989 (SL 53).

35. Camille Hykes to O'Brien, July 14, 1989. Hykes wrote three undated memos to Seymour Lawrence that are clearly from this period of time (SL 53).

36. To Camille Hykes, July 22, 1989 (SL 53).

37. Tim O'Brien Bread Loaf reading, Aug. 24, 1989 (Middlebury). Joiner dates: July 24–Aug. 4, 1989. Bread Loaf dates: Aug. 16–27, 1989.

38. "The Man I Killed" "new version," dated Sept. 5, "received last Friday" (so Sept. 1, 1989]; to Camille Hykes, Sept. 1, 1989 (SL 53). The other editor was Larry Cooper.

39. To Camille Hykes, Sept. 6, 1989 (SL 53).

40. Lawrence to O'Brien, June 19, 1989 (SL 53).

41. Michiko Kakutani, "Slogging Surreally in the Vietnamese Jungle," *NYT*, Mar. 6, 1990, p. C21. *Entertainment Weekly* cover, Feb. 23, 1990. Linnea Lannon, review of *The Things They Carried*, Detroit Free Press, Mar. 11, 1990, p. 7L; Philip Gerard, "O'Brien's Fiction Carries Weight of Truth," *Charlotte Observer*, Apr. 1, 1990, p. 5D; "Briefly Noted," *The New Yorker*, June 4, 1990, p. 102.

42. The Ford Hall Forum, Unitarian Universalist Association of Congregations, News Release, Oct. 2, 1991 (SL 53).

43. 1991 Melcher Book Award citation (HRC 17.1).

44. *TTTC*, p. 37; audio recording, Tim O'Brien reading, Bread Loaf, Aug. 24, 1989 (Middlebury).

45. "Vietnam Voices: The War in American Literature," Mar. 30, 1982, PEN American Center Records, 1922–2008 (mostly 1930–1989), Princeton University Library Special Collections, findingaids.princeton.edu/catalog/C0760_c2227; recording online at PEN America Digital Archive, archive.pen.org/asset?id=368.

46. *TTTC*, p. 78.

47. In Smith, *Conversations*, p. 85.

48. In Smith, *Conversations*, p. 83.

49. Audio recording, Tim O'Brien reading, Bread Loaf, Aug. 24, 1989.

50. From W. C. Woods, Apr. 26, 1990 (HRC 18.2).

25. When Peace Is Hell

1. Vicki Viotti, "Teaching About Peace by Telling War Stories," *Honolulu Advertiser*, Oct. 25, 1989, pp. B1–B2.

2. Ron Hansen and Jim Shepard, eds., *You've Got to Read This: Contemporary American Writers Introduce Stories That Held Them in Awe* (New York: HarperPerennial, 1994), p. 472.

3. Kate Phillips, "Springtime in Tiananmen Square, 1989," *The Atlantic* online, May 29, 2014, www.theatlantic.com/international/archive/2014/05/springtime-in-tiananmen-square -1989/371542/.

4. O'Brien's reading was on Oct. 23, 1989; Kate Phillips, "One Writer's Odyssey from Vietnam to Storytelling," *Claremont Courier*, Oct. 28, 1989, pp. 6–7.

5. On Wednesday the twenty-eighth: *Los Angeles Times Book Review*, Mar. 25, 1990, p. 11. See also tour schedule as printed in *The Things They Carried* publicity packet (SL 54).

6. To Dawn Seferian, May 18, 1990 (SL 53).

7. Lawrence memo to Joe Kanon and Leslie Breed, May 17, 1990 (SL 53).

8. Phillips appears in photographs from Bread Loaf 1990 (Middlebury) and is listed in the 1990–1991 Harvard *Student Directory*.

9. Mark Muro, "The Things They Carry," *Boston Globe*, Aug. 23, 1990, pp. 81, 87.

10. Tom Bowman, "Anti-War Demonstration Draws 75,000 to Washington; Protests Take Place Across the Nation," *Baltimore Sun*, Jan. 27, 1991, p. 3A.

11. Sykes posted it online in 2012: youtube.com/watch?v=TXRSh6I1ECw.

12. "George H. W. Bush Proclaims a Cure for the Vietnam Syndrome," Mar. 1, 1991, *Voices & Visions: A Collaboratively Built Primary Source Reader for US Foreign Relations*, vand vreader.org/george-h-w-bush-proclaims-a-cure-for-the-vietnam-syndrome-01-march -1991/.

13. Monica Sowden, "O'Brien Speaks to Students," *The Arrow* [Carthage College student paper] 24, no. 16 (Mar. 3, 1993), pp. 1–2.

14. Q&A, "My Lai Symposium," University of Indianapolis, Mar. 15, 1998, audio recording.

15. Sarah Burnes memorandum to Eloise Waddell, "Subject: Tim O'Brien address change," Aug. 8, 1991 (SL 53).

16. David Streitfeld, "Book Report," *WP Book World*, May 19, 1991, p. 15.

17. Vivian Vie Balfour, "The Reading," unpublished story with marginal comments by O'Brien, cover letter dated Jan. 11, 1993.

18. The *Joiner Center Newsletter* has O'Brien at the workshop in 1988, 1989, 1994, 1995, 1997, and 1999.

19. Note on the back of O'BRIEN BIOGRAPHY on Viking Penguin letterhead [May 1994] (HRC 8.1).

20. "Heart of Darkness," *Spectrum*, July 23, 1995, p. 3; Joseph P. Kahn, "The Things He Carries," *Boston Globe*, Oct. 19, 1994, p. 69.

21. Kahn, "The Things He Carries," p. 72.

22. From Hansen, Mar. 25, 1995 (HRC uncataloged).

23. To Mr. Richard Boylan, National Archives, Suitland, Maryland, Apr. 22, 1993; from Boylan, June 3, 1993; to Boylan, Aug. 31, 1993; the reproductions for the requested May dates (May 2–15, 1969) are dated Dec. 13, 1993 (HRC 22.3).

24. To Mr. Do Cong Minh, Foreign Press Center in Hà Nội, "I have been asked by The New York Times . . . ," Nov. 8, 1993; agreement with the *Times* dated Nov. 29, 1993 (HRC 22.3).

25. On the 1981 trip, see Mary McGrory, "For a Moment at Christmas, Vietnam Evokes the Old Emotions," *WP*, Dec. 29, 1981; and "Delegation to Vietnam," *The MacNeil/Lehrer Report*, Dec. 28, 1981, American Archive of Public Broadcasting, americanarchive.org /catalog/cpb-aacip-507-kp7tm72t3k. On the 1983 trip, see Lynda Van Devanter, *Home Before Morning: The Story of an Army Nurse in Vietnam*, with a new afterword (Amherst: University of Massachusetts Press, 2001), pp. 304–315.

26. On the 1990 trip, see W. D. Ehrhart, "A Common Language," *Virginia Quarterly Review* (Summer 1991), vqronline.org/summer-1991/common-language; Philip Caputo, "Prisoner of Hill 52," *The New Age of Adventure: Ten Years of Great Writing* (Washington, D.C.: National Geographic, 2009), pp. 241–260 (reprint from *National Geographic Adventure*, winter 1999); Yusef Komunyakaa, "On Spike Lee's *Da 5 Bloods*—and My Own Return to Vietnam," *GQ*, July 13, 2020, gq.com/story/yusef-komunyakaa-on-spike-lee -and-vietnam. By one estimate, over 160 veterans returned between 1987 and 1990 by way of the VVA's Return Trip Committee (Alan C. Miller, "Column One: Veterans Find Peace in Vietnam," *Los Angeles Times* [July 5, 1990], www.latimes.com/archives/la-xpm -1990-07-05-mn-136-story.html).

27. Lawrence self-published a booklet with everyone's remarks: *Seymour Lawrence, Publisher: An Independent Imprint Dedicated to Excellence* (1990).

28. On Dec. 7: letter from Lawrence, Oct. 29, 1993 (SL 102). The Lawrence Room opening ceremony took place on Saturday, Apr. 17, 1993, although the party lasted all weekend.

29. Richard D. Lyons, "Seymour Lawrence, 67, Publisher for a Variety of Eminent Authors," *NYT*, Jan. 7, 1994, p. A22; "Lawrence Memorial," *NYT*, Feb. 10, 1994, p. B10.

30. Also: Phạm Tiến Duật, Tran Quang Qui, Thanh Thảo, and Thái Bá Lợ (O'Brien 1994 trip notes, HRC 22.3).

31. O'Brien 1994 trip notes (HRC 22.3).

32. Itinerary and song list in O'Brien 1994 trip notes (HRC 22.3); loudspeakers in "The Vietnam in Me," *New York Times Magazine*, Oct. 2, 1994, p. 57.

33. "The Vietnam in Me," p. 50.

34. "The Vietnam in Me," p. 50.

35. "The Vietnam in Me," p. 55.

36. HRC 22.5.

37. To the People's Committee of Binh Nguyen village and the association of senators of U.S. led by Mr. [Tom] Richard Carper, from Chu Nguyen Van, Aug. 24, 1992 (HRC 22.3).

38. "The Vietnam in Me," p. 52.

39. *TTTC*, p. 38.

40. "The Vietnam in Me," p. 55.

41. Charlie Rose interview, Oct. 19, 1994, charlierose.com/videos/8757.

42. Mark Leepson, "Tim O'Brien on Love," *VVA Veteran*, Dec. 1994, pp. 17–18.

43. Charlie Rose interview, Oct. 19, 1994.

26. DOUBLE CONSUMMATION AND CAUSAL TRANSPORTATION

1. Confirmed by letter to Hansen, Feb. 11, 1986 (HRC uncataloged).

2. Erik Hansen, untitled first chapter typescript, *The Northwest Angle*.

3. "Author, Tim O'Brien at the Northfield Public Library," Apr. 21, 1994, ntv.org/videos /authors/author-tim-obrien-at-the-northfield-public-library/.

4. To Lynn Nesbit, Dec. 1, 1985 (HRC 8.1).

5. Mary Ann Grossman, "Social Values Are Key to O'Brien's Work," *St. Paul Pioneer Press Dispatch*, Oct. 18, 1987, pp. 7E–8E.

6. Richard R. Edmonds, "How to Get Mangled in Minnesota Politics: Sandy Keith Succumbs to Sympathy Vote," *Harvard Crimson*, Nov. 1, 1966, www.thecrimson.com/article /1966/11/1/how-to-get-mangled-in-minnesota/.

7. *Remember My Lai*, May 23, 1989 (PBS *Frontline* Episode 14); Michael Bilton and Kevin Sim, *Four Hours in My Lai* (London: Penguin, 1992).

8. To Hansen, Feb. 11, 1986 (HRC uncataloged).

9. *In the Lake of the Woods* contract, Mar. 20, 1986 (HRC 49.2). The initially typed "June 15, 1988" was at some point changed by hand to Dec. 15.

10. To Robert Warde, Nov. 6, 1987 (HRC 23.9).

11. Lynn Nesbit (ICM) to Richard Marek (E. P. Dutton), Jan. 28, 1988; copy of advance return check of sixty thousand dollars dated Apr. 25, 1988; Marek to Houghton Mifflin, May 12, 1988; Lew Grimes (ICM) to O'Brien, May 24, 1988. Houghton Mifflin paid Dutton $10,133.33 in interest (HRC 49.2).

12. From Lynn Nesbit, Jan. 27, 1989 (HRC 48.6); "Story Ideas" and "Vietnam Stories" handwritten notes (HRC 26.3).

13. *Mac Weekly*, Apr. 9, 1965, p. 4.

14. *Mac Weekly*, Mar. 9, 1979, p. 6; "I Never Thought They'd Send Me to Fight," interview with Maralyn Lois Polak, *Philadelphia Inquirer Sunday Magazine*, Oct. 26, 1980, reprinted in Polak, *The Writer as Celebrity: Intimate Interviews* (M. Evans & Co., 1986), pp. 91–95. Politics or political science: Bread Loaf interview, audio recording, Aug. 24, 1979 (Middlebury).

15. Gayle Roby interview, May 2, 2020, reading from the letter.

16. To Dean Fred Kramer, received Sept. 25, 1969.

17. Hemingway to Fitzgerald, Dec. 15, 1925, in Sandra Spanier et al., eds., *The Letters of Ernest Hemingway: Volume 2, 1923-1925* (Cambridge, UK: Cambridge University Press, 2013), p. 446.

18. *Lake*, p. 55.

19. Interview with Aaron Matthews, unpublished transcript, May 25, 2016.

20. *Lake*, p. 71.

21. Audio recording, "The Magic Show" Bread Loaf lecture, Aug. 19, 1990; *The Crumb* (Middlebury) confirms the date. Quoted from Robert Pack and Jay Parini, eds., *Writers on*

Writing (Lebanon, NH: Middlebury College Press/University Press of New England, 1991), pp. 175–83.

22. O'Brien, "The Magicians of Boston," *Boston Globe*, June 10, 1973, pp. 28, 30, 32–33, 35–36.

23. O'Brien, "The Ballad of Gary G.," *New York*, Oct. 15, 1979, pp. 67–68.

24. *Lake*, p. 231.

25. Audio recording, "Loon Point" Bread Loaf reading, Aug. 19, 1990 (Middlebury).

26. Michael Herr, *Dispatches* (1977; repr., New York: Vintage, 1991), p. 51.

27. Blair GreyBull, interviewed by Mason Funk, Sept. 28, 2022, for *Outwords*, theoutwords archive.org/interview/blair-greybull/.

28. William H. Nichols, "Men, Moose, and Mink of Northwest Angle," *National Geographic* XCII, no. 3 (Sept. 1947), pp. 265–284 (HRC 7.1).

29. Audio recording, Tim O'Brien Bread Loaf reading, Aug. 16, 1991 (Middlebury). Date confirmed in *The Crumb*. The archives do not have a recording of his lecture on the nineteenth (per *The Crumb*). O'Brien, "The People We Marry," *Atlantic Monthly*, Jan. 1992, pp. 90–98.

30. Audio recording, Tim O'Brien Bread Loaf reading, Aug. 13, 1992 (Middlebury). Date confirmed in *The Crumb*. He presented the same material at Sewanee two weeks before.

31. O'Brien, "Ambush," *Boston Magazine*, Apr. 1993, pp. 62–67, 101–106.

32. To Richard Boylan, National Archives, Suitland, Maryland, Apr. 22, 1993 (HRC 22.3).

33. *In the Lake of the Woods* "setting copy," May 1994 (HRC 5.1). A handwritten "3" on the first page suggests this version could have been the third round of proofs.

34. O'Brien, "The Vietnam in Me," *New York Times Magazine*, Oct. 2, 1994, p. 52.

35. *Lake*, p. 192.

36. Verlyn Klinkenborg, "A Self-Made Man," *NYT Book Review*, Oct. 9, 1994, pp. 1, 33.

37. Frank Conroy, "Sam's Scribes," *Vanity Fair*, Oct. 1994, p. 184.

38. O'Brien might have been influenced by Donald Chankin's *Anonymity and Death: The Fiction of B. Traven* (1975), as Chankin had spoken at Bread Loaf in 1977 (*The Crumb*).

39. Michiko Kakutani, "A Novel with a Complex Strategy," *NYT*, Oct. 7, 1994, p. C31.

40. Linnea Lannon, "Looking Back at Books That Earned Bold Stars," *Detroit Free Press*, Dec. 18, 1994, p. 7G.

41. Joseph P. Kahn, "The Things He Carries," *Boston Globe*, Living Arts section, Oct. 19, 1994, pp. 69, 72–73.

42. *Lake*, p. 301.

43. "IN THE LAKE OF THE WOODS—Tim O'Brien, Tour Schedule" (HRC 7.2). His friends Nicholas Delbanco and Elizabeth Goodenough attended; Delbanco's wife Elena's daybook confirms the date (see also correspondence in HRC 7.3, 7.4). *The Michigan Daily* incorrectly includes the reading in its roundup of 1995 local book events, Jan. 18, 1996, p. 5B.

44. "IN THE LAKE OF THE WOODS—Tim O'Brien, Tour Schedule."

45. Gerald Ford, "Remarks of the President to the Tulane University Student Body," April 23, 1975, University Archives, Tulane University, library.search.tulane.edu/discovery /delivery/01TUL_INST:Tulane/12436745930006326.

46. Other veterans-become-writer participants: John Balaban, Robert Olen Butler, W. D. Ehrhart, Wayne Karlin, Basil Pasquet. See Marc Leepson, "Those Who Forget the Past:

Examining the My Lai Tragedy 25 Years After," *VVA Veteran*, Jan. 1995, pp. 15–16, 34–35; and David L. Anderson, ed., *Facing Mỹ Lai: Moving Beyond the Massacre* (Lawrence: University Press of Kansas, 1998).

47. "The Mystery of Mỹ Lai: Tim O'Brien," in Anderson, *Facing Mỹ Lai*, pp. 171–178.

48. "The Mystery of Mỹ Lai: Tim O'Brien," in Anderson, *Facing Mỹ Lai*, p. 177.

49. Elizabeth Weber, "Truth, Memory, Fiction and My Brother's Death," *Consequence* 5 (spring 2013), p. 167. See also S. L. Berry, "In Her Brother's Name," *Indianapolis Star*, Nov. 13, 1995, pp. C1–C2. Berry's claim that O'Brien was helping Weber write a book is just plain wrong.

50. Weber, "Truth, Memory, Fiction," p. 175.

51. From Elizabeth Weber, Nov. 2, 1994 (HRC 7.6).

52. On Tuesday, Nov. 15: "Author to Speak at Wabash College," *Indianapolis News*, Nov. 10, 1994, p. B8. The meeting is referenced in Weber's letter of Nov. 24, 1994, and his letter of Jan. 7, 1995 (HRC 7.6).

53. Divorce finalized on Mar. 13, 1995; letter to O'Brien from Jon Benson of Benjamin & Benson, Jan. 12, 1995. San Antonio in O'Brien to Elizabeth Weber, Jan. 7, 1995. He tells Weber he was on tour until Dec. 20, although the official itinerary has him back in Boston on Dec. 9 (HRC 7.2). Newspaper database searches yield no hits for readings after the twelfth. Suicide thoughts: *DMB*, p. 38.

54. Marc Leepson, "The Dark Side of the Heart: Tim O'Brien on Love," *VVA Veteran*, Dec. 1994, pp. 17–18.

55. The Winter 1995 issue. See Don Lee to O'Brien, Mar. 9, 1995; O'Brien to Don Lee, Mar. 17, 1995. O'Brien had agreed to the work as of Lee's invitation to Strand, July 6, 1994—weeks after the Phillips breakup (*Ploughshares* Papers, Emerson College Archives and Special Collections).

56. O'Brien in Leepson, "The Dark Side of the Heart," p. 18.

57. Laura K. Garrett, "Panel Addresses Impacts of Anti-War Activism, Protests," *California Aggie* 117, no. 70 (May 1, 1995), pp. 1, 7.

58. Kimberly A. Got, "Literary Readings by Vietnamese and American Writers Describe Life, Experiences During the War," *California Aggie* 117, no. 70 (May 1, 1995), pp. 1, 8.

59. First chapter attached to cover letter to Lynn Nesbit, Nov. 6, 1995 (HRC 21.3).

27. TOMCAT IN LOVE

1. Letter of agreement from Lynn Nesbit, Feb. 23, 1995 (HRC 21.3).

2. "Co-op Newsletter Questions for Tim O'Brien," ATTN: Debbie Stier [Aug. 1998, in response to Stier's questions faxed on Aug. 5, 1998] (HRC 21.5); see letter about the "proposed language concerning a mass-market edition of Tim O'Brien's new novel," John Sterling to Lynn Nesbit, May 25, 1995 (HRC 21.3). As a fun gesture, O'Brien used the name "Stier" and other names of publishing friends in *July, July*.

3. O'Brien, "Careful Not to Touch the Lilacs," *Chanter* 9, no. 1 (Spring 1966), p. 39.

4. To Lynn Nesbit, Nov. 6, 1995 (HRC 21.3).

5. On tour for *Lake* in O'Brien to Don Lee, Sept. 1, 1995 (*Ploughshares* Papers, Emerson College Archives and Special Collections); *Lake* tour to Aug. 30, 1995, at "Tim O'Brien Reading," University of Indianapolis, Oct. 30, 1995.

6. "Hey! Great to hear from you . . . ," O'Brien letter to Meredith Baker, Sept. 27 or 29, 1994 (HRC 28.3).

7. Fox News release, Oct. 16, 1995 (HRC 24.4).

8. "Tim O'Brien Reading," University of Indianapolis, Oct. 30, 1995. "Tom" in cover letter to Lynn Nesbit, Nov. 6, 1995 (HRC 21.3).

9. E.g., "Heart of Darkness," *Spectrum*, July 23, 1995, p. 3.

10. From Ede Don Dero, Aug. 29, 1981 (HRC 3.2).

11. Dorothy Wilber, "Marriage Licenses," *Brooklyn Daily Eagle*, July 2, 1937, p. 30. The license is dated July 1 (New York, New York, U.S., Marriage License Indexes, 1907–2018); they married July 10 (New York, New York, U.S., Extracted Marriage Index, 1866–1937), ancestry.com. Her last name is sometimes recorded Wilber, sometimes Wilbur; her middle initial sometimes F., sometimes E. for Estelle. Date of birth: Apr. 18, 1907.

12. *Tomcat*, p. 38.

13. The near impossibility of divorce in New York meant that they would have filed in another state, so dating the divorce would be a daunting task.

14. Canon 2356, *The 1917 or Pio-Benedictine Code of Canon Law in English Translation with Extensive Scholarly Apparatus*, foreword by Most Rev. John J. Myers, S.T.L., J.D., J.C.D., curated by Dr. Edward N. Peters, Curator (New York: P. J. Kenedy & Sons, 1918).

15. Graduation certificate, Nativity School of Brooklyn, dated June 19, 1927 (HRC oversize 61).

16. Bill to Ava O'Brien, Oct. 17, 1962 (HRC 29.7).

17. *Tomcat*, p. 160.

18. *Tomcat*, p. 206.

19. Michiko Kakutani, "A Novel with a Complex Strategy," *NYT*, Oct. 7, 1994, p. C31.

20. "My Dear Beleaguered Captain," ABCnews.com, Sept. 30, 1998 (HRC 21.6).

21. *Tomcat*, p. 290; used for Roby (not named) in *If I Die*, p. 88.

22. Lorrie Smith, "'The Things Men Do': The Gendered Subtext in Tim O'Brien's *Esquire* Stories," *Critique* 36, no. 1 (1994).

23. *Tomcat*, p. 100.

24. *Tomcat*, p. 164.

25. Jane Smiley, "Catting Around," *NYT Book Review*, Sept. 20, 1998, pp. 11–12.

26. *Joiner Center Newsletter*, Aug. 1994, Mar. 1995, Aug. 1995, Oct. 1997 issues.

27. "My Lai Symposium," University of Indianapolis, Mar. 16, 1998, audio recording. See Celeste Williams, "Massacre Still Raises Questions," *Indianapolis Star*, Mar. 17, 1998, pp. B1–B2; also in *Indianapolis News*, Mar. 17, 1998, A2.

28. "My Lai and Why It Matters," Ron Ridenhour at Tulane, Mar. 25, 1998, video recording. John H. Cushman, Jr., "Ronald Ridenhour, 52, Veteran Who Reported My Lai Massacre," *NYT*, May 11, 1998, p. A15.

29. *DMB*, pp. 15–16.

30. The third typescript draft is dated October 1999 (HRC 30.7).

31. Chapter 5, "Tight Lies," in Lee K. Abbott, Dave Barry, Richard Bausch, James Crumley, James W. Hall, Tami Hoag, Tim O'Brien, and Les Standiford, *The Putt at the End of the World* (New York: Warner Books, 2000).

32. The video date-stamps the Wilds on July 10; Worthington on July 16; driving range alone on Aug. 10.

33. O'Brien's old passport is stamped Martinique on Jan. 4, 1999.

28. WELCOME TO TEXAS

1. Possibly the first weekend of May 2002, when O'Brien attended a Houghton Mifflin event and gave a private reading (Wendy Strothman email to O'Brien, May 6, 2002 [HRC 11.3]).

2. O'Brien, "Too Skinny," *The New Yorker*, Sept. 10, 2001.

3. Both emails dated Sept. 28, 2001 (HRC 11.3).

4. *July, July*, pp. 301, 321.

5. *July, July*, p. 74.

6. O'Brien, "The Streak," *The New Yorker*, Sept. 28, 1998, p. 91.

7. James Lindbloom, "The Heart Under Street," *Gadfly*, May 1999, pp. 42–43, 54. The interview took place in Cambridge at the end of the *Tomcat in Love* book tour, so December 1998.

8. *Publishers Weekly*, June 14, 1999, p. 13. See also letter to O'Brien from Nader F. Darehshori at Houghton Mifflin, June 10, 1999 (HRC 11.3).

9. "July '69," *Esquire*, July 2000.

10. From David Granger, May 31, 2000; "bonkers" from Adrianna [Adrienne Miller?], June 9, 2000 (HRC 11.3).

11. *July, July* contract, July 10, 2001 (HRC 48.4).

12. Janet Silver email to O'Brien, Jan. 15, 2002 (HRC 11.3).

13. O'Brien, "Too Skinny."

14. *July, July*, p. 136.

15. *July, July* typescript chapter 15, "Everness," chapter 23, "July, July" (HRC 8.7).

16. Morgan Writer-in-Residence public lecture, Wilson Library, University of North Carolina–Chapel Hill, Feb. 28, 2007.

17. *July, July*, p. 322.

18. Janet Silver email to O'Brien, Jan. 9, 2002 (HRC 11.3).

19. National Book Festival, Oct. 11–12; Macalester, Oct. 29–30; Texas Book Festival, Nov. 16–17 (*July, July* author book tour, HRC 10.9).

20. Michiko Kakutani, "When the Magic of Youth Turns into Midlife Misery," *NYT*, Oct. 11, 2002, p. E45; Tim O'Brien at the National Book Festival, Oct. 12, 2002, loc.gov/item/webcast-3500/.

21. Michael Newton, "Those Old Babyboomer Blues," *Times Literary Supplement*, Nov. 1, 2002.

22. Brad Buchholz, "Summer Dreams," *Austin American-Statesman*, Sept. 27, 2002, pp. E1, E7; David Kirby, *Atlanta Journal-Constitution*, Oct. 13, 2002, p. 5H.

23. On dating the reading: "Tim O'Brien: An Interview by Anthony Tambakis," *Five Points* 4, no. 1 (Fall 1999), pp. 95–114. The interview took place in Cambridge on May 19, 1999, and O'Brien had just gotten back from Hollywood.

24. Nick Cassavetes, *Going After Cacciato* screenplay "THIRD DRAFT" (HRC 30.7).

25. Scott Peeples, "An Interview with Tim O'Brien," *Illuminations: An International Magazine of Contemporary Writing* 16 (July 2000), pp. 45–52.

26. Dana Harris, "Cassavetes to Helm 'Cacciato' Adaptation," *Variety*, Aug. 2, 2000, variety .com/2000/film/news/cassavetes-to-helm-cacciato-adaptation-1117784489/.

27. Nick Cassavetes email to O'Brien, Sept. 20, 2001 (HRC 44.5).

28. Nick Cassavetes, *Going After Cacciato* screenplay "THIRD DRAFT."

29. Anne Thompson, "Films with War Themes Are Victims of Bad Timing," *NYT*, Oct. 17, 2002, p. E1.

30. Untitled, "At first glance . . . ," Just Like a Woman series in *Harper's Bazaar*, Sept. 2002, p. 424.

31. Faxed versions between O'Brien and magazine dated June 3 and Aug. 5, 2002 (HRC 11.3).

32. In Christian Appy, *Patriots: The Vietnam War Remembered from All Sides* (London: Penguin, 2003), p. 545.

33. *DMB*, p. 3. The essay was originally published as "A Letter to My Son," *Life: America's Weekend Magazine*, Oct. 15, 2004, pp. 14–15.

29. FAMILY MAN AND ELDER STATESMAN

1. Meredith O'Brien's passport.

2. "A Letter to My Son"; "The Best of Times" (*Life*, June 16, 2006, pp. 18–19); "The War They Still Fight" (*Parade*, June 8, 2008, pp. 4–5); "Fenced In" (*Smithsonian*, Nov. 2009, pp. 14–18); "Telling Tails" (*The Atlantic.com*, Aug. 14, 2009). Sundry minor pieces, e.g., "A Letter from Home," with David Burnett, in Catherine Leroy, ed., *Under Fire: Great Photographers and Writers in Vietnam* (New York: Random House, 2005), pp. 124–125.

3. Keynote Address on Nov. 8, 2005, revised and published in Mark Heberle, ed., *Thirty Years After: New Essays on Vietnam War Literature, Film, and Art* (Newcastle upon Tyne, UK: Cambridge Scholars Publishing, 2009), pp. 3–9.

4. E.g., "Fellow Warriors: Iraq, Afghanistan, Vietnam," supplementary material to Ken Burns and Lynn Novick's documentary series *The Vietnam War* (2017). The segment was cut as the conclusion to the film in the interest of run time; pbs.org/kenburns/the -vietnam-war/veterans-resources. The Great Books Foundation includes "The Things They Carried" in Donald H. Winfield, ed., *Standing Down: From Warrior to Civilian* (Chicago: Great Books Foundation, 2013).

5. Dave Fallon, Mike Witkus, Jim Pene, and later Howard Koltus. Email from Bob Wolf to Marilyn Knapp Litt, Mar. 9, 2009 (HRC 51.2).

6. Per running sales totals kept by O'Brien.

7. Brad Buchholz, "Austin Writer, Veteran Recalls Forgotten My Lai," *Austin American Statesman*, May 30, 2010, pp. H1, H8.

8. Announced on Mar. 10, 2010, per Mar. 11, 2010, email from Michael Hennessy, English Department chair, Texas State University (HRC 44.6).

9. "An Evening of Magic and Champagne: The Making of a Magician and His Masterpiece," filmed July 2010.

10. Polsky Films LLC option for *Going After Cacciato*, Feb. 25, 2011; an extension to the original option dated Mar. 26, 2009 (HRC 49.3).

11. O'Brien email to Polsky, Jan. 21, 2010 (HRC 44.6).

12. O'Brien email to Herzog, Jan. 31, 2010 (44.6).

13. O'Brien had a tour event at the L.A. Public Library on Mar. 18, per Bridget Marmion (Houghton Mifflin Harcourt) email to O'Brien, Feb. 5, 2010 (HRC 44.6). Herzog spent most of February and the beginning of March in Europe (email to O'Brien, Jan. 30, 2010 [HRC 44.6]); it appears that he filmed in the cave in late March and early April; "Werner Herzog on the Birth of Art" interview, *Archaeology* 64, no. 2 (Mar./Apr. 2011), pp. 32–39.

14. "O'Brien Notes" in Bruce Weigl's Screenplay Notes folder.

15. Novick email to O'Brien, Nov. 9, 2009; O'Brien email to Novick, Nov. 9, 2009 (HRC 44.6). O'Brien's list: Graham Greene, Michael Herr, Philip Caputo, Larry Heinemann, Wayne Karlin, Lady Borton, Jonathan Schell, C. D. B. Bryan, Robert Mason, David Rabe, Bruce Weigl, John Balaban, Kevin Bowen, Yusef Komunyakaa, and Michael Casey.

16. hemingwaysociety.org/tim-obriens-2016-conference-keynote-video.

17. *DMB*, pp. 5–7.

18. Unpublished transcript, May 22, 2016.

19. "A Tribute to Robert Stone," May 2, 2016, PEN/Faulkner Podcast, episode 54, mixcloud .com/penfaulknerfoundation/episode-54-a-tribute-to-robert-stone/.

20. *DMB*, p. 344.

21. Filming dates provided by Aaron Matthews. Flu diagnosis: Matthews's interviews with Dr. Mark Malone, Nov. 18, 2018; and with O'Brien, Feb. 12, 2017, unpublished transcripts.

22. *DMB*, pp. 289–292.

23. Aaron Matthews interview with Dr. Mark Malone, unpublished transcript, Nov. 18, 2018.

24. *DMB*, p. 293.

25. Email to author, July 6, 2017. The attached essay file was last modified June 15, 2017.

26. "Timmy and Tad and Papa and I" draft dated June 15, 2017.

27. "Tim O'Brien & Lynn Novick on the Power of Storytelling," Twin Cities PBS, Oct. 18, 2017, mnvietnam.org/story/tim-obrien-lynn-novick-on-storytelling/.

28. Both in HRC 27.3.

29. *DMB*, p. 31.

30. *DMB*, p. 242.

31. Tim O'Brien craft lecture, Sewanee Writers' Conference, July 29, 2013.

32. *TTTC*, p. 54.

33. *Tomcat*, p. 249.

34. *GAC*, p. 338.

35. He split "Telling Tales" into two consecutive chapters, and he renamed "Wisdom" to "Hygiene."

36. *DMB*, p. 287. Likely a friendly dig at this biography's author, a Hemingway scholar and West Point graduate.

37. *DMB*, p. 180.

38. *DMB*, p. 3. The recording took place in the spring of 2019.

39. Matt Gallagher, "*The Things They Carried* Author Tim O'Brien Returns to Contemplate Fatherhood and America at War," *Time* online, Oct. 10, 2019; in print, Oct. 21, 2019, time .com/5696948/life-after-wartime/.

40. Parul Sehgal, "In Letters to the World, a New Wave of Memoirs Draws on the Intimate," *NYT* online, Oct. 16, 2019; in print as "For the Memoir, Age 1,600, a New Approach," Oct. 17, 2019, p. C2, www.nytimes.com/2019/10/16/books/memoirs-in-letters-breathe-imani -perry.html.

30. THIS IS US

1. Episode 4, "Vietnam," Oct. 16, 2018; episode 8, "Six Thanksgivings," Nov. 20, 2018; episode 11, "Songbird Road: Part One," Jan. 22, 2019. See also episode 7, "Sometimes," Nov. 13, 2018; and episode 9, "The Beginning Is the End Is the Beginning," Nov. 27, 2018.

2. O'Brien, MS Word document, "This is us, idea notes," July 9, 2018.

3. Interview with Aaron Matthews, unpublished transcript, Nov. 20, 2018.

4. Meredith O'Brien, interview with Aaron Matthews, unpublished transcript, Apr. 10, 2019.

5. Meredith O'Brien, interview with Aaron Matthews, unpublished transcript, Apr. 10, 2019.

6. "2020 Final Death Statistics: COVID-19 as an Underlying Cause of Death vs. Contributing Cause," Centers for Disease Control and Prevention, cdc.gov/nchs/pressroom /podcasts/2022/20220107/20220107.htm (accessed Jan. 7, 2022).

7. E.g., "Tim O'Brien on Late-In-Life Fatherhood and the Things He Carried from Vietnam," interview with Terry Gross, NPR, npr.org/2021/02/24/970880767/tim-obrien-on -late-in-life-fatherhood-and-the-things-he-carried-from-vietnam, Feb. 24, 2021.

8. "Conversations on Hemingway: Hemingway and Childhood," WTTW, aired online Feb. 21, 2021, pbs.org/kenburns/hemingway/filmmaker-q-a-hemingway-and-childhood. Hemingway to Clarence Hemingway, Mar. 20 [1925], in Sandra Spanier et al., eds., *The Letters of Ernest Hemingway: Volume 2, 1923–1925* (Cambridge, UK: Cambridge University Press, 2013), p. 284.

9. "Jakarta" MS Word file dated Dec. 25, 2004; see untitled printout (HRC 42.8).

10. "Words and phrases for Jakarta" MS Word file dated May 4, 2007; see untitled printout with attached sticky note, "words and phrases for Jakarta" (HRC 49.8).

11. Ending "Not too busy, I hope," p. 139. The file name, "Odd Things," is the first two words; the file continues with two pages of notes for chapter/section 7.

12. Glenn Kessler, Salvador Rizzo, and Meg Kelly, "Trump's False or Misleading Claims Total 30,573 over 4 years," *WP*, Jan. 24, 2021, washingtonpost.com/politics/2021/01/24/trumps -false-or-misleading-claims-total-30573-over-four-years/.

13. *America Fantastica*, p. 358.

14. *TTTC*, p. 273.

15. *America Fantastica*, p. 4.

16. Ron Suskind, "Faith, Certainty and the Presidency of George W. Bush," *NYT Magazine*, Oct. 17, 2004, www.nytimes.com/2004/10/17/magazine/faith-certainty-and-the -presidency-of-george-w-bush.html?searchResultPosition=3. O'Brien's other changes, such as the revisions and restructuring to (published) chapters 38 through 52, were standard craft improvements of less consequence.

17. *America Fantastica*, pp. 277, 185; *TTTC*, p. 84.

18. Sam Sacks, "True Deceivers," *Wall Street Journal*, Oct. 21, 2023, p. C10.

19. *DMB*, p. 186.

20. *Kirkus Reviews*, July 26, 2023, kirkusreviews.com/book-reviews/tim-obrien-1/america
     -fantastica/.

21. Chris Vognar, "Tim O'Brien's 'America Fantastica' Is a Dark Comedy About Our Poi-
     soned Zeitgeist," *Boston Globe*, Oct. 18, 2023, www.bostonglobe.com/2023/10/18/arts/tim
     -obriens-america-fantastica-is-dark-comedy-about-our-poisoned-zeitgeist/.

22. Noah Hawley, "Lying All the Way to the Bank in 'America Fantastica,'" *NYT* online, Oct.
     23, 2023, nytimes.com/2023/10/23/books/review/tim-obrien-america-fantastica.html;
     printed with the headline "Fabrication Nation" on Nov. 5, 2023, p. 21.

EPILOGUE

1. Lan Cao, "Vietnam Wasn't Just an American War," *NYT*, Mar. 22, 2018.

2. Email to author, Aug. 3, 2018.

INDEX

ABOUT THE AUTHOR

Melisa Pierce

From Prairie Village, Kansas, **Alex Vernon** graduated from the U.S. Military Academy at West Point (the only literature major in his class of over a thousand), served in combat as a tank platoon leader in the Persian Gulf War, and earned a PhD from the University of North Carolina–Chapel Hill. The recipient of an Army Historical Foundation Distinguished Writing Award and a National Endowment for the Humanities Fellowship, he is the M.E. and Ima Graves Peace Distinguished Professor of English at Hendrix College in Conway, Arkansas. This is his eleventh book.